D1035232

CULTURAL ASPECTS OF
THE ITALIAN RENAISSANCE
ESSAYS IN HONOUR OF Paul Oskar Kristeller

CULTURAL ASPECTS OF
THE ITALIAN RENAISSANCE

ESSAYS IN HONOUR OF
Paul Oskar Kristeller

EDITED BY
Cecil H. Clough

Manchester
University Press

Alfred F. Zambelli   NEW YORK, N.Y.

© 1976 CECIL H. CLOUGH

While copyright in the volume as a whole is vested in the editor, Cecil H. Clough, copyright in the individual papers belongs to their respective authors, and no paper may be reproduced whole or in part without the express permission in writing of the editor, the author and the publisher

Published by MANCHESTER UNIVERSITY PRESS
Oxford Road, Manchester M13 9PL
UK ISBN 0 7190 0617 1

USA   Alfred F. Zambelli
156 Fifth Avenue, New York, N.Y. 10010
US ISBN 0 9600860 1 3

Library of Congress Cataloging in Publication Data
Main entry under title:

Cultural aspects of the Italian Renaissance.

Includes bibliographical references and index.
1. Renaissance--Italy--Addresses, essays, lectures.
2. Italy--Civilization--Addresses, essays, lectures..
3. Libraries, Private--Italy--Addresses, essays, lectures. 4. Kristeller, Paul Oskar, 1905-
I. Clough, Cecil H. II. Kristeller, Paul Oskar, 1905-·
DG445.C87   945'.05   75-20150
ISBN 0-9600860-1-3

Printed in Great Britain
by Western Printing Services Ltd, Bristol

CONTENTS

LIST OF ILLUSTRATIONS

PREFACE

IT IS THE exceptional scholar who receives the tribute of an homage volume. Paul Oskar Kristeller will have three, all celebrating his seventieth birthday. Such a testimony of distinction appears unique. One volume associated with eight leading scholars in their field has already been presented under the title *Itinerarium Italicum: the Profile of the Italian Renaissance in the Mirror of its European Transformations*, and edited by Professor Heiko A. Oberman and Professor Thomas A. Brady, Jr. (E. J. Brill, Leiden, 1975). A second volume, jointly published by E. J. Brill and Columbia University Press, is very shortly to appear, with thirty-two essays contributed by Professor Kristeller's former colleagues, his former students, and fellow members of the Columbia University Seminar on the Renaissance. Its title is *Philosophy and Humanism: Renaissance Essays in Honor of Paul Oskar Kristeller*, and it has been edited by Professor Edward P. Mahoney; this volume contains the annotated bibliography of Professor Kristeller's publications. The volume here offered makes up the triple crown.

A work of this kind brings with it many debts. I am indebted to the staff of Manchester University Press, and to the printers, who have coped admirably with a very difficult script. The contributors have been very patient since the volume was first conceived in 1967, and they have been generously tolerant of my foibles.

Consistently and strongly I have been supported by Professor A. R. Myers and Professor D. B. Quinn, both of the School of History, the University of Liverpool; Mr Alfred Zambelli, a friend of my own Columbia days, most kindly undertook North American co-publication of this volume; I am sincerely grateful to all three. I wish to thank most warmly and publicly my wife, who has lived long with the volume, and who has acted as editor's assistant.

I am especially appreciative of the financial support to assist publication given by the following: the Marc Fitch Fund, the Twenty-Seven Foundation Awards, the British Academy (towards the provision of illustrations), Clare College, Cambridge (towards editorial expenses), the University of Liverpool (to promote the publication of the editor's own essay).

In conclusion it is worth stressing something that will appeal to the scholar to whom this volume is dedicated. There is a substantial index of manuscripts cited, and also a general index, which provides the approximate dates of many of the persons listed. Some of the Italian humanists indicated are not in Mario Cosenza's *Biographical and Bibliographical Dictionary of the Italian Humanists of the World of Classical Scholarship, 1300–1800*, Boston, Mass., six volumes, 1962–67, and hence the general index serves as a kind of supplement to Cosenza's work.

C.H.C.

DEDICATORY LETTER

DEAR PAUL

Your own publications will remain essential reading for future generations interested in the Italian Renaissance; indeed, your *Iter Italicum* is a research tool one cannot envisage ever being displaced. The present collection of studies in the field that will be associated with you has been made to please you for its content, and in affectionate tribute. Lorenzo de' Medici, consciously echoing Cicero's *Pro Archia Poeta*, wrote in a dedicatory letter that 'Honour is what gives nourishment to every art; nor are the minds of mortal men inflamed to noble works by anything so much as by glory'. Like Petrarch and other humanists, Lorenzo believed that the achievements of the ancients were motivated by desire for immortal fame, which was conferred above all by the praise of poets. In terms of humanistic thought, therefore, it might be argued that this collection in your praise is your most enduring monument— such a concept is at the very heart of the 'homage volume'.

Certainly the volume of studies here presented to you has been designed to have a permanent value for its illumination of what is really the core of the Italian Renaissance—the cult of Antiquity. Themes such as the funeral oration and anthologies of neo-Latin poetry are of key importance for an appreciation of this cult, yet have remained neglected. The detailed information concerning the libraries formed in the fifteenth century by Cardinal Domenico Capranica, by Francesco Sassetti and by Count Antonio Marsciano reliably reveal the extent to which humanistic texts were in circulation; details concerning Isabella d'Este's acquisition of antiques are equally significant for the light they throw on another facet of the cult. All in all, the studies are envisaged as a counterbalance to that excessive concentration on a particular city of Renaissance Italy which is now in vogue. This latter approach, in fact, appears to have resulted in the cult of Antiquity, which ought to be at the centre of Italian Renaissance studies, being rather obscured. Emphasis has shifted to questions that are concerned essentially with political, administrative and economic aspects of the city State, be it Florence, Venice or another. To redress this balance such essays as those concerned with the epistle and with attitudes to art theory and to music have been provided.

Accordingly the collection has been planned as a whole to illuminate the cult of Antiquity and as indispensable to anyone interested in the Renaissance in Italy. At the same time, by pointing out largely unexplored yet fertile fields, it is hoped that the collection will itself stimulate research in these areas. Finally the essays may modestly assist by illustrating methodology, reflecting as they do approaches by means of several techniques and skills: for instance, the use of aerial photography, of antiques and of archival documents.

Yours most cordially, as ever

CECIL

Gorsley, 23 August 1973

A. H. McDONALD   *Clare College, Cambridge*

I

STUDY OF THE RENAISSANCE MANUSCRIPTS OF CLASSICAL AUTHORS

IN A PAPER dedicated to the scholar whose learned journeys have taken him, for our benefit, into obscure places of bibliographical importance, one may appropriately treat the subject of textual research in practical terms and argue from direct experience, as if the newly discovered manuscripts still lay open on the table. No editor is likely to command all the skills that are requisite in his study. He may carry out the comparative examination of significant readings in the text but he has also to use the evidence of script, decoration, and external conditions. He needs the friendly advice of specialists and he will be in debt to a colleague who has interested himself in bringing scholars personally together. What follows here is written for Paul Kristeller in appreciation and gratitude.

My subject deals with humanistic MSS of the fourteenth and fifteenth centuries which contain the text of classical authors, and the evidence will be chosen in particular from work on Livy's Fourth Decade (books XXXI–XL). The period extends from Landolfo Colonna at Chartres and Petrarch in Avignon to the scribes of Florence and the early printed editions; some ninety MSS provide adequate material. The case is similar for other classical authors, where the text may be shorter but the number of MSS larger. First, then, to find the MSS, as many as possible. The task, after the initial stage of consulting familiar printed catalogues, is not a simple one, especially where MSS may be lying in small libraries. Hence the value of Kristeller's *Iter Italicum*, 'a finding list of uncatalogued or incompletely catalogued humanistic manuscripts of the Renaissance in Italian and other libraries', when this is added to the bountiful information held by the Institut de Recherche et d'Histoire des Textes et l'Étude des Manuscrits des Auteurs Classiques; and we may wish Professor Sweeny well in his preparation of a *Catalogus Codicum Classicorum Latinorum*.[1]

In approaching the collation and classification of manuscripts we may briefly recall Lachmann's basic work and the subsequent application and misapplication of his principles of study, which have influenced the course of editorial technique and continue to be the object of refined criticism.[2] There is no need for general discussion at this stage—it can wait until we are in closer touch with the MSS—but a few pointers may be set in place. For instance, how far is it valid to argue by inference from *recentiores* to the character of an 'archetype'? 'Stemmata quid faciunt?', and Housman warned editors not to assume that the streams of textual tradition might flow unmixed: 'The picture to be set before the mind's eye is rather the Egyptian Delta, a network of water courses and canals' (*Lucanus*, p. vii). Yet some 'stemmatic' argument may be worth attempting. In the humanistic MSS, where the scribes had increasing scope, e.g. at Florence, for comparison and 'contamination', any examination is largely concerned with a 'field of textual distribution'. Statistical analysis can help, though a 'calculus of variants' is too broad for detailed application, and a computer may play its part, but this requires that a text be first cleared of its 'insignificant' clerical errors.[3] On the evidence of common errors or agreement in particular 'emendation' one may identify subsidiary groupings, but where single MSS show signs of 'contamination' it is important to watch for intrusive readings from an alien line of tradition. Even where copying can be dated in successive stages, this does not mean that the revision of the text is necessarily progressive; for a scribe may find or cast back to a different exemplar: 'recentiores, non deteriores', as Pasquali showed.[4] So much as introduction—except to remind ourselves that the aim is not simply to find 'good' witnesses and surrender to them. Editing finally calls for 'rational criticism' as applied to the results of manuscript study, and J. F. Gronovius is not superseded by Lachmann.

For our purpose, then, we should welcome at least 100 *recentiores* as a basis of evidence on which to define the variations and 'contamination' of the humanistic tradition. But at what cost of time and effort? With a short text there is no problem. With a long text the burden of full collation will be intolerable, a threat to later progress in the work of editing; nor is it necessary. Keeping the total of MSS, the case is one for 'selective collation'. A list of 1,000 passages containing variants should be adequate, provided they are spread over the whole text. The selection must not be 'random' but positively designed to obtain the maximum of evidence, and special features can be noted in passing. The normal collation of earlier MSS for the *apparatus criticus* will give a lead, especially with reference to possible lines of descent. It is worth collating, say, four humanistic MSS written at different points between 1300 and 1450 for further guidance; some may be accessible locally, or microfilming will serve. Then previous editors are likely to have cited MSS, however occasionally, or marked passages of significant difficulty; in the end one must be familiar with those editors. On the basis of such evidence a list of 'test passages' can be drawn up.

The procedure is clearly illustrated in the textual study of Livy's Fourth Decade. There is no temptation for an editor to search hopefully for a single archetype. We know of three early lines of tradition.[5]

1 Frag. Placent. (F: Bibl. Pub. Bamb., Class. 35a, fifth century); from this exemplar Bambergensis. (B: Class. 35, eleventh century) was copied

and Spirensis (Sp: now lost) derived through another branch to be used by Gelenius (ed. Frob., 1535); and the *recentiores* (as below).

2 Cod. Mogunt. (now lost; ninth century?) was used by Carbach (ed. Mog., 1518) with collation notes.

3 Frag. Rom. (Vat. Lat. 10696, fourth to fifth century).

In preparing to edit the Oxford text in 1927 S. K. Johnson drew up a list of 180 'test passages' from books XXXIV–XXXVIII, where these MSS overlapped, in order to study their relations and gain a preliminary impression of the humanistic tradition; he also arranged for some full collation of books XXXI–XXXII.[6] On succeeding Johnson as editor in 1938 I used the evidence, along with Drakenborch's reference to eleven MSS in his notes and also Zingerle's *apparatus criticus*, to enlarge his list of passages with special attention to books XXXI–XXXII but covering the Decade (the *recentiores* and Spirensis lack book XXXIII); my list contained about 1,200 passages. Meanwhile the discovery of MSS was raising their number to ninety, and there remained the practical problem of handling so much text. What follows may be called 'time and motion' study.

It is one thing to plan 'selective collation', another to carry it out under the stress of travel, rapid change of libraries, and simple fatigue; even in using microfilm copies one has to make time and spare the eyes. Finding the passages in MSS can be irksome, copying the readings may slip into clerical error, and the work done on MSS in isolation will become tedious. There are two counter-measures. First, underline the passages in a plain text so as to facilitate the estimating of distance between them in the manuscript; note, too, in selecting the list, that one may often find clusters of significant readings. Secondly, tabulate the known variants for each passage, leaving space to add new ones; then give the MSS short *sigla* chosen solely (with a key) for this purpose, and enter the *siglum* opposite the relevant variant. For example:

XXXI. 1.5. velut qui <u>proximis litori</u> vadis inducti.

proximi litori: B, b, ...   proximis litoris: g, Ed. vet., ...
proximi litoris: V1, V2, ...   proximis litori: Carb., ...

This method not only saves time and effort; it also focuses concentration, briefly and sharply, where that is most necessary, viz. at the point of placing the *siglum*. The grouping of *sigla* will suggest possible association of MSS, preliminary to the arrangements for classification, and one has the interest of following the fortune of each new MS; it encourages young, well qualified scholars to lend their assistance.[7]

In applying our collation notes to the task of classification we have to recall Housman's warning and restrain our hopes, especially where popular works have been widely copied and interpolated from early times, long before the humanistic scholars took their text in hand. Since the loss of simple faith in a *textus receptus* one tends to look for a 'stemma' that will reveal the stages of its growth and to establish a text by critical argument. Yet the discovery of MSS is subject to the law of chance. The evidence, even when it indicates group-ings, will not necessarily prove their place in a line or lines of descent. We must not press 'probability' to a definitive 'stemmatic' conclusion: to seek is not always to find.[8]

Nonetheless this procedure opens the way to textual analysis, and we may start from the principles laid down by Paul Maas. In tracing the relationships of MSS with reference to line of descent or group association only 'errors' are significant, for an 'authentic' reading could be transmitted down any line or appear in any group. The significant errors are of two kinds: 'separative' and 'conjunctive'. In other words, if one MS shows an 'error' where another MS preserves an 'authentic' reading, the latter has descended independently of the former; again, if two or more MSS share an idiosyncratic 'error', viz. an 'error' not attributable to simple coincidence in misreading or omission, this reading derives from a single exemplar and the MSS may be brought together as a group. But how does one establish what is 'authentic' in copying that has been subject to 'emendation'? A scribe might well correct plausibly in a small context. Again, how far can one go in grouping if a text has been 'contaminated' by borrowing from other MSS? Idiosyncratic 'errors' or, indeed, 'emendations' may then derive from different exemplars. Maas would not apply his method under such conditions, and he certainly excluded the humanistic MSS.[9] Yet general criticism does not close the question. For instance, the charge of risking 'argument in a circle' is met by proposing not necessarily to draw up a 'stemma' but to construct a 'working hypothesis'. With regard to 'authentic' readings early MSS may help; in the *recentiores*, as personal work on their text shows, the degree and style of 'emendation' and 'contamination' may vary, and there will be cases of corruption where the 'authentic' reading is still recognisable.

The worst problem in analysing 'contaminated' MSS is a practical one. How do we plot the relevant evidence so that it can be comprehended in its complex associations? Sometimes a grouping, at least in its chief MSS, is clearly indicated: more often the course of humanistic scholarship has led to a tangle of mixed readings. The immediate answer lies in a 'distribution chart'. Using graph paper one can readily co-ordinate 'significant variants' with the MSS in which they appear. Thus:

Variants	MSS (*sigla*)			
	V1	V2	b	g etc
(1)	√	√	–	√
(2)	√	√	√	–
(3)	√	–	–	√
etc.				

This procedure is designed not as repetition but as a 'breakdown' of our collation notes, with as many 'charts' as the notes suggest there may be groups. That is, where a number of MSS are associated in a series of passages they should have a 'chart' to themselves; so enter the relevant variants, then the *sigla* of the relevant MSS as they emerge, and mark the co-ordination. It is a matter of judgement to distinguish consistent representatives, marginal associates, and casual borrowers. The same process should be repeated for other possible groupings, and MSS may appear in more than one 'chart', depending upon their degree of 'contamination'. In the end there will remain a number of thoroughly mixed up MSS, which need special examination by reference to the collation notes. The method is practicable in treating, say, 100 *recentiores*, and more if the editor has an aptitude for this kind of work.

Not every scholar, however, has confidence in his ability to scan a large and complex 'distribution field' and control the data. At this point the computer offers its assistance, not to save time but to assure reliability. The preparation of evidence for the 'charts' will serve as a basis for programming, and the operation is relatively simple: on cards (but note the developments in 'optical scanning'). The editor will still need to exercise his judgement after as before having recourse to the computer.[10]

Textual examination of the MSS provides the basic evidence on which to establish a classical edition, but it should be reinforced by study of the script, decoration and external conditions. *Überlieferungsgeschichte*, since Traube, is no longer disreputable, and one can follow the exemplary method of Billanovich and his circle.[11] This work in detail requires specialised knowledge of the Renaissance period: the classical editor will usually have to solicit friendly co-operation; yet there is mutual benefit, for what the humanistic scholar helps to place in its setting may also prove useful with reference to classical influences. For instance, the preface and *apparatus criticus* of an edition could be designed, within limits, to serve both parties. An annotated survey of commentaries, too, like that which owes so much to Paul Kristeller, contributes seriously to the history of scholarship.[12]

By good fortune the *recentiores* of Livy's Fourth Decade allow us to illustrate the case (Oxford text's *sigla*). Fig. 1.1 shows the position of the *recentiores* in

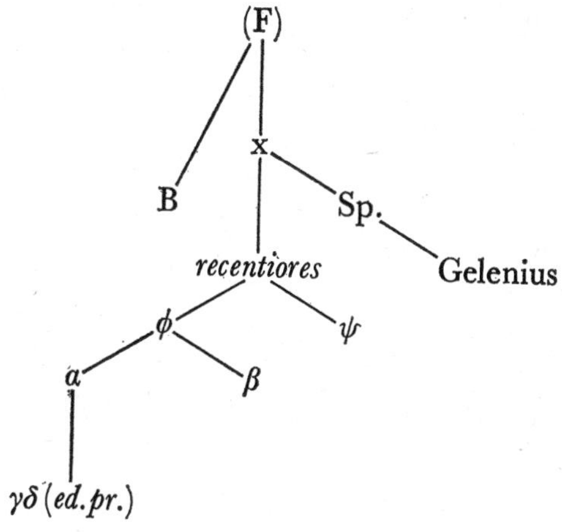

FIG. 1.1

their line of tradition, with B and Sp (as reported by Gelenius) helping to check 'authentic' readings. The MSS do not betray any alien intrusion but are variously 'emended' and 'contaminated' among themselves. After classification

I found evidence for six groups (with marginal associates). The script dated three in the fourteenth century, respectively early (φ), mid-century (α), late (β), and the text indicated that α and β derived separately from φ, the former roughly emended, the latter elaborately edited. The other three could be dated in the fifteenth-century period of 'humanistic' script; γ and δ cast back to the φα line, the latter emending stylishly to establish the *editio princeps* (1469), but ψ emerged (to Pasquali's delight) as a better witness for the tradition than even φ.

Here the matter stood in 1949, when Eduard Fraenkel introduced me to Billanovich. We compared notes, and he brought my bare results to life. The effect now needs only brief reference.[13] The exemplar of φ was a Chartres MS (Vetus Carnotensis). Landolfo Colonna took a copy (lightly corrected) to Avignon, where he had it rewritten, as did Petrarch: Landolfo's is Paris., B.N. Lat. 5690 (P); Petrarch's is B.M., Harl. 2493 (A: Agennensis): their date was 1328–9. The mid-century α group is based on the Agennensis (with Petrarch's early emendations); the text is probably that which Bersuire translated.[14] Meanwhile, it would seem, Petrarch continued his study of the Fourth Decade and edited the text more fully in β; this group is best represented in B.M., Burn. 198 (fourteenth to fifteenth century). The work of Petrarch and his circle was prolific in emendations, which entered anonymously into the increasing 'contamination' of the *recentiores*; his name lost its place in Latin editing as the professional copyists enlarged their activity.[15] The line descending from φα, e.g. in γ and δ, re-emerged for fashionable use.

The situation at Florence after 1400 presents new problems for the editor. B. L. Ullman's study of the 'humanistic' script established the method of analysis,[16] but one needs equal knowledge and flair to apply it in detail to other Livian MSS; and the enigma of the ψ group also remained when I published my edition of Livy, books XXXI–XXXV, in 1965. It was afterwards that I enjoyed the benefit of Albinia de la Mare's interest in my fifteenth-century MSS. Her study is readily accessible, and I mention only its chief points for the present purpose.[17] From the script and decoration she has dated MSS more precisely and accurately, identifying scribes and discussing the relevant external conditions. Once again a bare textual classification has come to life, with reference to an important period of classical scholarship. In particular we have a new approach to group ψ as represented by two MSS: Oxford, New College 279 (N: *c.* 1430–40) and Vat. Lat. 3331 (V: 1453–4). Both MSS are Florentine, and the New College MS may have been associated with the library of Santo Spirito, to which Boccaccio bequeathed his books. Did the ψ exemplar belong to Boccaccio? We shall have to begin discussion by examining the text of his translation.

This paper opened with manuscripts on the table: it has closed by returning to them. The Livian examples are instructive both for method and for the light they throw on 'humanistic' scholarship, where the MSS of other classical authors have less to show in positive terms. Is it necessary for a classical editor to go beyond his textual evidence, treated strictly in its own right? Perhaps not, though he should be careful about correctors' hands. More generally, if external study supports and amplifies his results the pattern of his 'working hypothesis' will appear firmer. But the case for co-operation is more extensive. In perspective our classical scholarship should not only reconstruct the ancient texts but, in its technical activity, also assist the appreciation of their later influence, above all, in the Renaissance.

NOTES

[1] P. O. Kristeller, (i) *Latin Manuscript Books before 1600*, New York, third edition, 1965; (ii) *Iter Italicum*, I, 1963; II, 1967. *Classical Influences on European Culture, A.D. 500–1500*, ed. R. R. Bolgar, Cambridge, 1971, chapter I (R. D. Sweeney on Latin MSS and their catalogues), 2 (M.-Th. d'Alverny and M.-C. Garand on the Institut de Recherche et d'Histoire des Textes); note Bolgar's Introduction.

[2] S. Timpanaro, *La genesi del metodo del Lachmann*, Florence, 1963.

[3] B. M. Metzger, *The Text of the New Testament: its Transmission, Corruption, and Restoration*, Oxford, 1964, II, 6 ('Modern methods of textual criticism').

[4] G. Pasquali, *Storia della tradizione e critica del testo*, Florence, second edition, revised, 1952, 4.

[5] L. Traube, 'Bamberger Frag. der IV Dekade des Livius', *K. Bayer. Akad. Wiss., III Kl.*, XXIV, 1, 1904; ibid., *Sitzungsb.*, 1907, p. 108; Vattasso, *Frammenti d'un Livio del V secolo*, Vatican City, 1906; G. Billanovich, 'Petrarch and the textual tradition of Livy', *Journ. of Warburg and Courtauld Instit.* XIV, 1951, pp. 180–5, 199 ff; O.C.T.: *Titi Livi ab urbe condita*, ed. A. H. McDonald, V, Lib. XXXI–XXXV, 1965, 'Praefatio'.

[6] S. K. Johnson, *Class. Quart.* XXI, 1927, pp. 67 ff; Nan Holley applied the list, adding descriptive notes, to eighteen MSS in the Vatican; E. Gardner Crewe collated books XXXI–XXXII in four MSS in Paris and Florence.

[7] Alison Duke applied my list to some thirty MSS at Holkham Hall (*Loveliani*) and in Oxford, Paris and the Escurial, and J. Carnegie to eight MSS in the British Museum. For the rest I write from my own experience, mostly by direct collation, sometimes in microfilm (after 'sighting' the MSS).

[8] For further discussion, arising from personal study of MSS, consult R. D. Dawe, *The Collation and Investigation of Manuscripts of Aeschylus*, Cambridge, 1964, followed by O.C.T.: *Aeschyli Tragoediae*, ed. Denys Page, 1972, with his exemplary *apparatus criticus*; then J. M. Moore, *The Manuscript Tradition of Polybius*, 1965, adapting the 'stemmatic' method; finally *Claudian: De raptu Proserpinae*, ed. J. B. Hall, 1969, introduction and *app. crit.*, handling intractable evidence.

[9] P. Maas, *Textual Criticism*, Oxford, 1958; *Oxford Classical Dictionary*, s.v. 'Textual criticism': first edition, 1949, P. Maas; second edition, 1970, A. H. McDonald (with bibliography).

[10] In general note *The Computer and Literary Studies*, ed. A. J. Aitken, R. W. Bailey and N. Hamilton-Smith, Edinburgh, 1973, p. 199 (W. Ott on 'Computer applications in textual criticism'), p. 283 (B. R. Schneider, jr., on 'Optical scanning'). I first raised this matter at the fourth International Congress of Classical Studies, Philadelphia, 1964, Concurrent session C, 'Problems in text tradition', II (A. H. McDonald), tape-recorded.

[11] G. Billanovich in Bolgar (ed.), *op. cit.*, 5 ('I primi umanisti e l'antichità classica'), with reference to *Italia medioevale e umanistica* I, 1958, ff.

[12] *Catalogus Translationum et Commentariorum: Mediaeval and Renaissance Latin Translations and Commentaries*, ed. P. O. Kristeller, Washington, D.C., I, 1960, II (with F. E. Cranz), 1971; n. 11, p. 331: 'Livius, Titus' (A. H. McDonald).

[13] See Billanovich on 'Petrarch and the textual tradition of Livy' and MacDonald's 'Praefatio' in the Oxford Text of Livy, books XXXI–XXXV, as cited above, n. 5.

[14] K. V. Sinclair, *The Melbourne Livy*, Melbourne, 1961, a study of Bersuire's *Tite-Live* based on Nat. Gallery of Victoria MS Felton 3; reviewed, with reference to the

probable Livian text, in *Class. Review*, new series, XIII, 1963, p. 75 (A. H. McDonald).

[15] Note E. J. Kenney on 'The character of humanist philology' in Bolgar (ed.), *op. cit.*, p. 122.

[16] B. L. Ullman, *The Origin and Development of Humanistic Script*, Rome, 1960.

[17] T. A. Dorey (ed.), *Livy*, London, 1971, VIII (Albinia de la Mare, 'Florentine manuscripts of Livy in the fifteenth century'), with full references; note especially pp. 177–9.

ANTHONY LUTTRELL   *Royal University of Malta*

2

CAPRANICA BEFORE 1337:
PETRARCH AS TOPOGRAPHER

LATE IN 1336 Francesco Petrarch set out from Provence on his first journey to Rome, where he was to join Bishop Giacomo Colonna, the brother of his protector, Cardinal Giovanni Colonna. He sailed to Civitavecchia and then made his way across country to Capranica, near Sutri, to be welcomed in the castle of Orso dell'Anguillara, whose wife, Agnese Colonna, was the sister of Giacomo and Giovanni (plates 2.1–2). Petrarch reached Capranica some time before 26 January 1337 and, having received news that it was dangerous to move, since the opponents of the Colonna were in control of the roads, he stayed there three weeks or more. On 26 January Giacomo Colonna and his brother Stefano had journeyed from Rome to fetch their guest with an escort of more than a hundred horse, but this force was insufficient to ensure a safe journey to Rome, and Petrarch was apparently still at Capranica on 13 February, when he dated a sonnet there. Well content at Capranica, he was not altogether anxious to move on, and he gratefully extolled the virtues and hospitality of his hosts in both prose and verse.[1] Before travelling down the ancient Via Cassia to Rome some days later he addressed to Giovanni Colonna a letter which later became the twelfth in the second book of his *Familiares*:[2]

To Cardinal Giovanni Colonna: a description of another journey[3]

I find myself in the province of Rome at a place which would be ideally suited to my studies, were my heart not eager to be off elsewhere. In the past it was called the Hill of Goats, the reason being, in my opinion, that owing to its dense cover of wild thickets it was populated more by goats than by humans. The situation of the place and its obvious fertility were, as they became known, responsible for attracting, little by little, a fair number of inhabitants, who constructed a citadel for themselves on a mound of sufficient eminence together with such dwellings as the cramped confines of the hill permitted; but it did not lose its old name of the Hill of Goats. Humble Capranica is surrounded by illustrious names; on one side Monte Soracte, famous as the residence of Silvester, but whose praises were sung even before him by poets; next the lake and mountain of Cimino, both mentioned by Virgil; then Sutri, barely two miles away, a place most pleasing to Ceres and said to have been an ancient colony of Saturn. Close to the walls can be seen the plain where it is said that a king from a foreign land planted the very first corn seed to be sown in Italy, and harvested the first crop with his pruning knife. He won the devotion of the local inhabitants by this miraculous benefit; the people in their gratitude made him their king during his life, and on his death they regarded him as a god, whom they represented as an aged king holding a pruning knife. The air here, so far as a brief sojourn allows one to judge, is most healthy. On all sides there are numerous hills, easy to get at and to climb, and affording unimpeded views; then, in the valleys between these hills, there are shady hollows with dark caves around them. Everywhere grow leafy groves which provide shelter from the sun, except to the north, where a lower hill opens up a sunny flank, a flowery haunt for honey-making bees. Deep in the valleys sweet springs gurgle; stags, bucks and wild goats, and all the wild woodland animals wander on uncovered hills; birds of every type raise their murmuring voices on the waters or in the branches. I pass over not only the herds of cows and other domestic animals, and the fruits of human labour, the sweetness of Bacchus and the fruitfulness of Ceres, but also those other gifts of nature, the nearby lakes and rivers, and the sea itself at no great distance. The one thing which I cannot claim to be present is Peace, though I know not by what human crimes, by what heavenly law, by what fate or force of the stars, it is an exile from these lands. For—would you believe it?—the shepherd, with arms at his side, keeps watch among the woods, fearing not so much wolves as robbers. The ploughman in his cuirass uses his spear in place of the usual rustic rod to prod the reluctant ox. The fowler protects his nets with a shield. The fisherman suspends his bait on deceptive hooks from a rigid swordpoint. And, something you would call ridiculous, the man preparing to draw water from the well ties a rusty helmet to the sordid rope. In short, no one here does anything without carrying arms. What of the mournful wail of the sentries on the walls through the night, the voices issuing the call to arms? These are the sounds which have replaced the ones I used to play on my soothing strings. Among the inhabitants of this region you would see nothing that was safe and secure, hear nothing peaceful, feel nothing human; you would find nothing but war, hatreds and all manner of devil's work. I have been here sixteen days now, illustrious Father, uncertain whether I want to stay or not; and such is the force of habit in all human activity that, while all the rest rush to the citadel amid the din of soldiers and the blare of trumpets, you would often see me wandering among these hills, assiduously meditating on something which might win me the favour of posterity. I am gazed on with admiration by all, a man of leisure, without fear, quite unarmed; on the other hand, I marvel at all of them, anxious, afraid, armed. Such is the variety of human action. But if by chance I were asked whether I would prefer to leave here, I could not easily answer. It would be to my advantage to leave; staying would fill me with delight. I am more inclined to the former. It is not that I am suffering any harm here, but my original reason for leaving home was to see Rome. Yet it is a matter of human nature that the mind does not rest until its appointed aims are accomplished. It was for this reason in particular that I was attracted to the theory that the souls of the dead will only be free to enjoy the Beatific Vision, that vision in which human happiness achieves its consummation, when they have rejoined their bodies, which is in itself something that they cannot, in the very nature of things, cease desiring. Though this theory has been rejected by the better judgement of many men, and was buried together with its author long since,[4] give pardon, I pray you, since I know you had a strong love for him, if not for his errors. Farewell.[5]

This letter, originally composed at an early stage in Petrarch's career, may have been polished considerably before reaching its final published state. The description of Capranica revealed the poet in several interesting lights. It reflected that sensitivity to nature and landscape, to the woods, streams, lakes and caves of the area, which was also expressed in Petrarch's remarkable account of his ascent of Mont Ventoux. In the Capranica letter he displayed his feeling for local topography, informed as it was by a reading of the classical authors, by his concern for the ancient past, his intuitions concerning the early medieval origins of the village, and his appreciation of contemporary conditions. Within the limits of a few hundred Latin words he managed to give a surprisingly comprehensive picture of Capranica and the countryside around it. He ended his letter, somewhat awkwardly, with an allusion to the controversy which had been raging at Avignon on the subject of the Beatific Vision, a doctrine in which Petrarch had shown some interest and which had been formally defined by Pope Benedict XII in 1336. Petrarch maintained the view, 'buried together with its author', Pope John XXII, who died in 1334, that the souls of innocents and of the purged do not enjoy the Vision of God before the Universal Resurrection.[6]

Although Petrarch must have known something of the Etruscans through the Roman authors, who had a good deal to say about them,[7] his letter made no reference to the Etruscan people as such; indeed, contemporaries were scarcely conscious of their identity. At Orvieto in the twelfth century Goffredo de Viterbo and other anti-Roman Ghibelline writers had connected legendary theories that the town had non-Roman origins with the names of Saturn and of *Turno*, a *rex Thuscorum* who was presumably the *Turnus* of the *Aeneid*; while at San Giovenale, not far from Capranica, there had been a continuous inhabitation of the site from pre-Roman times at least down to the late thirteenth century.[8] Capranica, by contrast, was scarcely occupied until the central medieval period, and Petrarch, who would surely have mentioned any significant remains or inscriptions found in the immediate vicinity, was probably correct in supposing that it was neither a pre-Roman settlement nor a Roman town; in fact it was not on the original Roman Via Cassia.[9] Petrarch considered, again more or less correctly, that in ancient times the whole area, with the Monti Cimini to the north and the Monti Sabatini to the south, was still forest. The Romans did do much to cut the woodlands along the Via Cassia and around Sutri,[10] and there was some scattered settlement in the area around Capranica, but these Roman sites fell into ruin and the forest partly returned, so that Petrarch may have remained unaware of the existence of ancient farms and villas.[11] In describing Capranica as an obscure or humble place—*locus ignobilis*—surrounded by famous ancient sites, the poet was expressing, at least implicitly, the typically humanist attitude of a man who could write, 'What else, then, is history, if not the praise of Rome?'; he was consigning Capranica to a 'Dark Age'—elsewhere he actually used the word *tenebrae*—which followed the disintegration of the Roman empire.[12]

The places around Capranica mentioned in the letter were Sutri, the Monti Cimini, the Lake of Vico, and Caere, which lay towards the south (fig. 2.1). On Monte Soracte, which was visible in the distance, Petrarch cited Virgil and, by implication, Horace; and as a midwinter visitor he may particularly have appreciated Horace's lines:

> Vides ut alta stet nive candidum
> Soracte nec iam sustineant onus
>   silvae laborantes geluque
>   flumina constiterint acuto.[13]

The commentaries which Petrarch found in manuscripts of Virgil and Horace provided no extra topographical information concerning the places he mentioned, and in his own copies of these works he added no marginalia

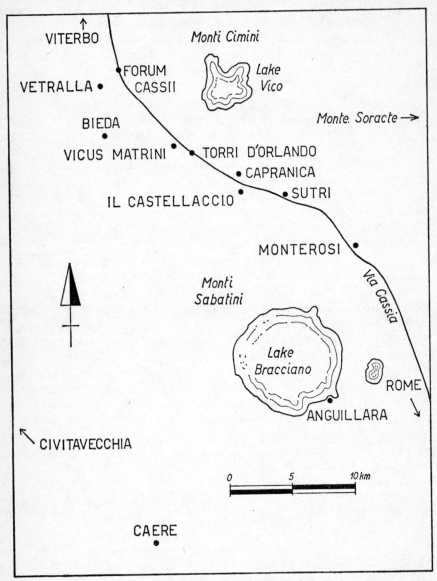

FIG. 2.1   The area round Capranica

of topographical significance to the passages involved. The gloss on the passage in the Horace which he purchased in 1347 was a version of the so-called 'pseudo-Acro' commentary,[14] while in Petrarch's Virgil the comments on the lines to which he was referring were those of Servius.[15] Petrarch did not refer in his letter either to Pliny on Monte Soracte[16] or to Livy, whose description of the Ciminian forest as trackless and terrifying he certainly knew: *Silua erat Ciminia magis tum inuia atque horrenda . . .*[17] He did, however, refer to the long-established myth, transmitted, for example, in the *Liber Pontificalis*, according to which Pope Silvester had been exiled on Monte Soracte.[18] Petrarch moved in a literary circle, balanced between Avignon and Rome, in which this particular medieval source was well known,[19] while the legend had been perpetuated by the foundation on Monte Soracte of a monastery dedicated to Silvester.[20]

Petrarch correctly remarked that Sutri was a Roman colony, as he may have known from Pliny or other ancient authors.[21] He also reported less reliable stories according to which the *colonia* was connected with Saturn and beloved of Ceres, while he recorded a legend concerning the king with the pruning knife who planted the first grain in Italy near Sutri. Some of these myths apparently derived from false etymological connections between *Sutrium* and *Saturnia*, which Petrarch or one of his contemporaries may have derived from the classical texts or from the available commentaries on them.[22] Virgil himself mentioned that Saturn settled a race in *Latium*, but where Virgil spoke of Sabinus with his pruning knife,[23] Servius' commentary misread him as referring to Saturn rather than Sabinus.[24] Petrarch may also have been influenced by Festus, who spoke of Saturn as *agrorum cultor* and also described him as holding a pruning knife: *nominatus a satu, tenensque falcem effingitur.*[25]

Petrarch had no real information about the origins of the *castrum* at Capranica, and he lived in an age of economic contraction when the processes of expansion which had once stimulated new settlements and foundations were no longer part of men's immediate experience; yet he did speculate intelligently as to what might have occurred. He thought that Capranica's name derived from the goats or *capre* which had fed in its ancient woodlands,[26] and that subsequently its healthiness and fertility had attracted settlers who built a castle and covered the top of the narrow rocky promontory with as many houses as the space would hold. This was just one variation on a range of theories which have considered the foundation of early medieval hilltop and promontory villages as part of a movement away from the settled surroundings of Roman roads and cultivable valleys to more defensible sites, perhaps because of barbarian invasions, because of malaria or some other catastrophe.[27] This movement probably reached a peak in the ninth and tenth centuries, but it had been under way at least since the fourth.[28] It could have been that at some point the inhabitants of *Vicus Matrini*, the old Roman station well beyond Sutri along the Cassia, had deserted that site and moved on to the Capranica promontory, much in the way that a little farther north along the Cassia the old station at *Forum Cassii* was abandoned for the hill site of Vetralla.[29] By about the eleventh century there was a church with a Romanesque campanile, but not apparently any considerable settlement, standing next to a Roman mausoleum right on the old Via Cassia at a position some five kilometres north of Capranica.[30] There was also a strongly fortified area across the Via Cassia about 1,500 metres south of Capranica, and that site, though apparently pre-medieval in construction, may well have

been occupied at some point in the post-classical period.[31] Sutri was captured
by the Lombards in about 727[32] and Saracen bands were later active in the
area; around 915, for example, there was a battle against them on the
Cassia south of Sutri.[33]

Petrarch's letter made no attempt to date the occupation of the promontory,
which may have occurred at any time in the early medieval period before
the eleventh century. Since Capranica had a *castellum vetulum* by 1050,[34] the
outer *borgo* had possibly been developing for some time, so that the original
site was known as the 'old' castle.[35] In 1177 there was a reference to a
Gualfredus de Papa who was *habitans in castello Caprallica prope Sutrium*.[36]
There were several Romanesque churches within the inner *borgo*, which was
separated from the promontory by a deeply cut ditch; there was probably a
castle immediately inside this ditch guarding the entrance across it. Outside
the ditch was another comparatively small *borgo* or suburb which by the
thirteenth century contained the church of San Francesco and a hospice
with a fine Romanesque portal.[37] As in the case of many villages built along a
spur, there was a long main street along the ridge with narrow passages
leading off it. When the outer *borgo* grew up, perhaps around a market
originally held outside the first wall and ditch, this street was naturally
extended along the ridge until it issued from the new outer wall.[38] Capranica
was attacked in 1215 by the men of Viterbo, who captured its *signore*, a
certain Giordano, and in 1243 it was taken by the Romans;[39] there must
have been many such incidents but, together with the identity of those who
normally controlled the place, they may already have been forgotten in the
time of Petrarch who would, however, have known the castle and churches,
the streets and walls.

The Anguillara had probably held Capranica only since about 1330, and
the family archive perhaps contained no reference to the town earlier than
1331, when Orso and Francesco dell'Anguillara dated a document there on
30 November.[40] The original lords of Capranica left no record of their rule.
Possibly it passed to Orso dell'Anguillara as a result of his marriage to
Agnese Colonna about 1329; in any event, Orso was seeking to extend
Anguillara power in the area, and in 1331 the family made a determined,
though unsuccessful, attempt to capture Sutri. The Anguillara's position at
this period was therefore somewhat ambiguous, and Petrarch perhaps judged
it tactful to avoid all reference to this recent history.[41] Capranica often
received no mention in contemporary documents. For example, there was no
reference to it in the report on the state of the Patrimony sent to the Pope in
1319–20;[42] nor in lists of places represented in assemblies of the Papal
States;[43] nor in the accounts of collectors of the papal taxes.[44] Yet by 1363
it had a *sindicus* and some form of community or *comune*,[45] while its population
was then perhaps as high as 750.[46] Even so, it was still not, apparently, on the
Via Cassia, which probably changed its route so as to pass right by Capranica
only after Petrarch's time.[47] Petrarch himself was there not because it was
an important station on a main road but on account of his connections with
the Anguillara family.

Petrarch wrote of Capranica as if it were a mere castle surrounded by peasants. The poet himself probably lived in the *rocca* which was inhabited by the Count of Anguillara or, in his absence, by his *vicecomes*; it was there that they held their *curia*. The place, always known as *castrum capralice*, was divided into the *castrum vetullum* and the *castrum novum*. There was a small professional class of churchmen, connected especially with San Lorenzo, Santa Maria, San Pietro and San Giovanni, a surgeon, and various notaries whose registers recorded wills and dowries, a good deal of money lending, and the buying and selling of vines, chestnut woods, sheep, goats and pigs. Particularly important was a partnership known as the *soccita a frategodente* through which one party bound itself to farm the other's animals *ad bonam consuetudinem et bonum usum castri capralice*, dividing the flock after three years. One such contract was for sixty-nine goats, another for 208 sheep. In 1345 Agnese Colonna, Countess of Anguillara, herself entered into an arrangement to farm 324 sheep.[48] The ranching and cattle raising which became a feature of the countryside north of Rome was already well established around Capranica; and, in this case at least, the local nobility, in the person of that Agnese whom Petrarch compared to seventeen Roman matrons and virtues,[49] participated in it.

Petrarch's letter made an exaggerated, literary contrast between the peace and beauty of the countryside seen in the heart of winter, and the prevailing atmosphere of war and insecurity, in which the peasants toiled with their weapons at hand, the sentries shouted from the battlements at night and soldiers were continually called to battle. The thirteenth century had been a period of prosperity, and in 1300 the great papal jubilee brought enormous crowds of pilgrims down the Via Cassia to Rome; Sutri and its area must have flourished. Then the papacy moved to Provence; Rome and its hinterland declined, and the nobility reasserted its factious predominance. The 1330s saw a spell of bad harvests, but the worst disasters still lay ahead; it was only after 1337 that the major Florentine banks went bankrupt, that the great plague came, that the campaigns of the Vico family, of Cardinal Albornoz and of the mercenary companies thoroughly devastated the countryside and helped to produce the abandonment of so many inhabited sites.[50] Capranica itself was to survive, thanks perhaps to its proximity to the Via Cassia, but by 1337 the situation was already serious and the rivalries of the local nobility, and notably the poet's own Colonna and Anguillara patrons, produced that state of disorder and insecurity which he so vividly described.[51]

Petrarch probably retouched his Capranica letter some time after 1337. Presumably he did write to Giovanni Colonna during his stay at Capranica, and there is a reasonable chance that he kept a copy of the letter until about 1351, when he elaborated or even invented much of the material in the early books of his *Familiares*.[52] He had special reason to remember Orso dell' Anguillara as the man who had crowned him during his celebrated coronation at Rome in 1341. Petrarch was a reactionary in his attitude to many developments which were of great importance for the progress of the physical sciences, but he was markedly ahead of his times as an enthusiastic antiquarian, a numismatist and epigraphist, and a student of ancient texts; in fact he often erred through too heavy a reliance on literary, and especially on classical, sources.[53] His letter from Capranica had a particular interest: written at the very time when Cola di Rienzo was reading *li antichi pitaffij* on the stones of Rome,[54] it showed Petrarch relying not only on the ancient authors but also on his own sensible instincts concerning the topography and development of the Italian countryside. His notions of the ancient and medieval history of the area around Capranica were surprisingly sound.[55]

APPENDIX 2.1

Eodem anno et mense decembris die xij°

Actum in Rocca capralice presentibus Jannucio macellario de capralica et petrono pecudario de Sutrio [etc] Massucius de Sutrio confessus est habuisse in soccitam a magnifica muliere Agnete comitissa Anguillari, ccc^{tas}, xxiiij^{or} pecudes inquibus ipse massucius misit tertiam partem Quas promisit tenere hinc ad tres annos proximos futuros incipiendo in festo omnium sanctorum preterito, ad usum bone soccite, quibus finitis dictus massucius faciet duas partes de ipsis re[ddere] et promisit contra predictam non uenire ad penam xxv. libr. [etc].[56]

APPENDIX 2.2

Ad Iohannem de Columna cardinalem, alterius peregrinationis descriptio.

Peroportunum curis meis locum, si non alio properaret animus, nactus sum in regione romana. Caprarum mons dictus est olim, credo quod, silvestribus virgultis obsessus, capris quam hominibus frequentior haberetur. Paulatim cognitus loci situs et spectata fertilitas habitatores aliquot sponte contraxit, a quibus arx eminenti satis tumulo fundata; et domorum quantum collis angustus patitur, adhuc vetus caprarum vocabulum non amisit. Locus ignobilis, fama nobilioribus cingitur locis. Est hinc Soracte mons, Silvestro clarus incola, sed et ante Silvestrum poetarum carminibus illustris; hinc Cimini cum monte lacus, quorum meminit Virgilius; hinc Sutrium, quod nonnisi duobus passuum milibus abest, sedes Cereri gratissima et vetus, ut perhibent, Saturni colonia. Campus ostenditur non longe a muris, ubi primum in Italia frumenti semen ab advena rege iactum dicunt, primam messem falce desectam; quo beneficio miraculoque delinitis animis, in partem regni vivens, in opinionem divinitatis vita functus, favore hominum exceptus senex rex et falcifer deus est. Aer hic, quantum breve tempus ostendit, saluberrimus. Hinc illinc colles innumeri, altitudine nec accessu difficili et expedita prospectui; inter quos et umbrosa laterum convexa et opaca circum antra subsidunt. Undique submovendis solibus frondosum nemus erigitur, nisi quod ad aquilonem collis humilior apricum aperit sinum, mellificis apibus floream stationem. Fontes aquarum dulcium imis vallibus obstrepunt; cervi damme capreoli et feri nemorum greges apertis vagantur collibus; omne volucrum genus vel undis vel ramis immurmurat; nam boum et omnis mansueti pecoris armenta, et humani laboris fructus, Bachi dulcedinem et Cereris ubertatem, ad hec et illa nature dona, vicinos lacus ac flumina et non longinquum mare, pretereo. Pax una, quonam gentis crimine, quibus celi legibus, quo fato seu qua siderum vi ab his terris exulet, ignoro. Quid enim putas? Pastor armatus silvis invigilat, non tam lupos metuens quam raptores; loricatus arator, hastam ad usum rustici pugionis invertens, recusantis bovis terga solicitat; auceps retia clipeo tegit et piscator hamis fallacibus herentem escam rigido mucrone suspendit; quodque ridiculum dixeris, aquam e puteo petiturus rubiginosam galeam sordido fune connectit. Denique, nichil sine armis hic agitur. Quis ille pernox ululatus vigilum in menibus, que voces ad arma conclamantium, que michi in sonorum locum quos blandis e fidibus exprimere consueveram, successere? Nichil incolis harum regionum inter se aut tutum videas, aut pacatum audias, aut humanum sentias; sed bellum et odia et operibus demonum cunta simillima. His in locis, pater inclite, inter volentem ac nolentem dubius, iam sextumdecimum diem ago; et—quantum potest in rebus omnibus consuetudo!—fragore militum et stridore lituum ceteris in arcem concurrentibus, me sepe per hos colles vagum videas atque aliquid quod posteritatem michi conciliet, assidue meditantem. Omnes me cum admiratione respiciunt, otiosum, intrepidum et inermem; contra, ego omnes admiror pavidos, solicitos et armatos. Hec est humanarum varietas actionum. Quodsi forsan interroger an hinc migrare malim, non facile dixerim; et ire iuvat, et manere delectat. Ad primum pronior sum; non quod hic molesti quicquam patiar, sed Romam visurus domo moveram. Est autem secundum naturam, ut usque in finem votorum animus non quiescat. Ex quo maxime colorem michi videtur habuisse opinio illa, que beatifica visione Dei, in qua consummata felicitas hominis consistit, defunctorum animas tandiu carituras astruebat, donec corpora resumpsissent, quod naturaliter non optare non possunt; quamvis illa sententia multorum saniori iudicio victa et cum auctore suo—da veniam, queso, qui valde eum, sed non errores eius dilexisti—sepulta iampridem sit. Vale.[57]

NOTES

[1] Undated letters in Francesco Petrarca, *Le familiari*, ed. V. Rossi, I, Florence, 1933, 99–102 (Lib. II, Nos. 12–13); see also Francesco Petrarca, *Le 'Rime sparse' e i Trionfi*, ed. E. Chiòrboli, Bari, 1930, Nos. 38, 49, 98. Discussion and dating in A. Pakscher, *Die Chronologie der Gedichte Petrarcas*, Berlin, 1887, pp. 14–17; A. Foresti, *Aneddoti della vita di Francesco Petrarca*, Brescia, 1928, pp. 33–4, 43–4; E. Wilkins, *Petrarch's Correspondence*, Padua, 1960, p. 52. In Biblioteca Vaticana, Vat. Lat. 3196, f. 9r, canzone 49 was dated: *13 feb. 1337 cap*[ra]r. [the infra-red lamp suggests that the '7' was written over some other number or letter]. On the various feuds of the Anguillara and Colonna see I. Vinogradoff, 'Miscellanea Romana', *English Historical Review*, XLV, 1930, pp. 613–15.

[2] Petrarch's description of Capranica has received surprisingly little detailed discussion. Professors Giuseppe Billanovich, Denys Hay and Norman Zacour most generously provided advice on various Petrarchan points.

[3] The reference in the title is to another journey described in an earlier letter in the *Familiares* (I, 4) sent to Giovanni Colonna and headed . . . *peregrinationis propie descriptio* (Rossi, I, 24–7).

[4] *sepulta iampridem*: John XXII died in December 1334, little more than two years before the letter was written; the *iampridem* possibly constitutes evidence for a later revision of the letter.

[5] This translation, based on the text in Rossi, I, 99–101 (reproduced in appendix 2.2), was kindly made by Mr Lawrence Keppie.

[6] Petrarch's interest in the subject, concerning which he had intervened with Benedict XII in 1335, is documented in M. Dykmans, *Robert d'Anjou Roi de Jérusalem et de Sicile: La Vision Bienheureuse—Traité envoyé au pape Jean XXII*, Rome, 1970, p. 88*.

[7] E.g. W. Harris, *Rome in Etruria and Umbria*, Oxford, 1971, pp. 4–31 *et passim*.

[8] A. Lazzarini, 'Coscienza etrusca in Orvieto medievale', and A. Boëthius, 'La continuità dello habitat etrusco nella zona di S. Giovenale di Bieda', both in *Sopravvivenza e memorie etrusche nella Tuscia medievale. Colonna di Quaderni d'Archeologia e Storia: Fondazione per il Museo Claudio Faina*, I, Orvieto, 1964. For a later, fifteenth-century 'Virgilian' interest in Etruscan archaeology and bogus etymologies concerning nearby town origins see P. Supino Martino, 'Un carme di Lorenzo Vitelli sulle origini troiane di Corneto', *Italia Medioevale e Umanistica*, XV, 1972.

[9] G. Duncan, 'Sutri (Sutrium)', *Papers of the British School at Rome*, XXVI, 1958, figs. 1, 3.

[10] See J. Ward-Perkins, 'Monterosi in the Etruscan and Roman periods', and other papers in G. Hutchison *et al.*, *Ianula: an Account of the History and Development of the Lago Monterosi, Latium, Italy. Transactions of the American Philosophical Society*, LX, part 4, Philadelphia, 1970; these studies use pollen analysis and other scientific techniques as well as traditional historical–archaeological data. For a clear general pattern see also J. Ward-Perkins, 'Etruscan towns, Roman roads and medieval villages: the historical geography of south Etruria', *Geographical Journal*, CXXVIII, 1962, pp. 391–3.

[11] Duncan, pp. 91–6, figs. 5–7 *et passim*, plotting archaeological remains and Roman pottery finds, but there is more to add to his maps. Note the Roman villa near the modern station of Capranica; R. Paribeni, 'Capranica di Sutri: Scavi in contrada Pecugliaro', *Notizie degli Scavi*, 1913, pp. 379–81; the Roman cistern some 600 metres north-west of Capranica: the fort at *Il Castellaccio* (*cf.* Duncan, p. 130, plate XXIVa), which does have Roman pottery strewn close by; and the thirty Roman coins found in the area of *Vicus Matrini*. *Annali dell'Istituto Italiano de Numismatica*, VII–VIII, 1960–61, p. 328. Signorina Maddalena Andreussi will document these and other sites in her forthcoming volume in the *Forma Italiae* series.

[12] T. E. Mommsen, 'Petrarch's conception of the "Dark Ages"', *Speculum*, XVII, 1942 (reprinted in *id.*, *Medieval and Renaissance Studies*, Ithaca, N.Y., 1959).

[13] Horace, *Opera*, ed. F. Klingner, Leipzig, 1959, 11 (*Carm.* I, ix); Virgil, *Opera*, ed. R. Mynors, Oxford, 1969, pp. 278, 387 (*Aen.* VII, 696–7; XI, 785).

[14] Photo-reproduction in *L'Orazio laurenziano già di Francesco Petrarca*, ed. E. Rostagno, Rome, 1933, f. 5v; *cf. Pseudacronis Scholia in Horatium Vetustiora*, ed. O. Keller, I, Leipzig, 1902, p. 48. The young Petrarch did, however, own another Horace (not here studied): G. Billanovich, 'Tra Dante e Petrarca', *Italia Medioevale e Umanistica*, VIII, 1965, p. 22.

[15] Photo-reproduction in *Francisci Petrarcae Vergilianus Codex*, ed. G. Galbiati, Milan, 1930, f. 160r, 217r and v; *cf. Servii Grammatici qui feruntur in Vergilii Carmina Commentarii*, ed. G. Thilo and H. Hagen, Leipzig, three vols., 1923, II, pp. 184, 564.

[16] Pliny, *Natural History*, II, ed. H. Rackham, London, 1947, 518 (VII, 2, 19).

[17] Livy, *Ab urbe condita*, II, ed. C. Walters and R. Conway, Oxford, 1919, IX, 36, i; *cf.* G. Billanovich, 'Petrarch and the textual tradition of Livy', *Journal of the Warburg and Courtauld Institutes*, XIV, 1951.

[18] L. Duchesne, *Liber Pontificalis*, revised by C. Vogel, I, Paris, 1955, pp. cxix, 170.

[19] G. Billanovich, 'Gli umanisti e le cronache medioevali: il "Liber Pontificalis", le "Decadi" di Tito Livio ed il primo umanesimo a Roma', *Italia Medioevale e Umanistica*, I, 1958; see also G. Billanovich, 'Il Petrarca e gli storici latini', *Tra Latino e Volgare: Per C. Dionisotti*, ed. Gabrietia Bernardoni Trezzini and others, Padua, two vols., 1974, I, pp. 67–145.

[20] M. Mastrocola, 'Il monachesimo nelle diocesi di Civita Castellana, Orte e Gallese fino al sec. XII', *Miscellanea di Studi Viterbesi*, Viterbo, 1962, pp. 352–68.

[21] Pliny, II, 40 (III, 5, 51–2); *cf.* Duncan, pp. 67–9.

[22] Nothing is known of such a cult; see L. Taylor, *Local Cults in Etruria*. Rome, 1923, 106–11, and, with more detail, G. Duncan, 'The Etruscan and Roman town of Sutrium (Sutri)', Ph.D. thesis, Cambridge, 1959, pp. 118–25, listing the known cults of Sutri.

[23] Virgil, 261 (*Aen.* VII, 178–80).

[24] *Servii Grammatici*, I, p. 372.

[25] Festus, *De Verborum Significatu*, ed. W. Lindsay, Leipzig, 1913, p. 202. These last references were kindly provided by Dr Nicholas Horsfall.

[26] Petrarch's other letter written *apud Capranicam* (*Fam.* II, 13) began: *In hoc ecce caprarum, imo vero leonum et tigridum monte*, . . . (Rossi, I, pp. 101–2).

[27] Such theories largely hold the field, e.g. Duncan, p. 125; Ward-Perkins, 1962, pp. 400–2; M. Mallett, 'Medieval and later history of Monterosi', in Hutchinson *et al.*, p. 13; see also the general treatment in A. Kahane, L. Murray Threipland and J. Ward-Perkins, 'The Ager Veientanus north and east of [Veii]', *Papers of the British*

School at Rome, XXXVI, 1968, pp. 161–79. These authors tend, with reservations, to place the shift to about the tenth century, on the admittedly somewhat unsatisfactory grounds that this is the date of the earliest surviving documents which mentioned the villages involved.

[28] References in P. Jones, 'L'Italia agraria nell'alto medioevo: problemi di cronologia e continuità', *Agricoltura e mondo rurale in Occidente nell'alto medioevo*, Spoleto, 1966, pp. 70–2. P. Toubert, *Les Structures du Latium médiéval : le Latium méridional et la Sabine du IXe siècle à la fin du XIIe siècle*, Paris, two vols., 1973, places in the tenth century a major, expansive process of *incastellamento*, which he sees as a movement of growth and colonisation rather than of defensive retreats; he does note the existence of some hilltop *castelli* before 900. Despite certain technical uncertainties, the pottery evidence also points to eighth- or ninth-century occupation of a number of similar sites; see D. Whitehouse, 'Sedi medievali nella campagna romana: la *domusculta* e il villaggio fortificato', *Archeologia e geografia del popolamento. Quaderni storici*, XXIV, 1973, and further observations in A. Luttrell, 'La campagna a nord di Roma: archeologia e storia medievale', *Colloquio Internazionale di Archeologia Medievale: Palermo 1974*, Palermo (forthcoming).

[29] E. Martinori, *La Via Cassia (antica e moderna) e sue deviazioni* . . ., Rome, 1930, pp. 37, n. 2, 39; this author connects the origins of Capranica with an alleged but completely undocumented destruction of *Vicus Matrini* (never securely identified) in the eighth century.

[30] O. Mazzucato, 'Capranica: Relazione sui saggi di scavo presso le *Torri d'Orlando*', *Notizie degli Scavi*, eighth series, XXIV, 1970; unfortunately the early medieval pottery does little to date the site.

[31] The site, known as *Il Castellaccio*, cannot really be dated (but see above, n. 11): there is no evidence that it is medieval, but it may well have been the ruined castle of Donazzano, somewhere between Capranica and Bassano di Sutri, mentioned in 1451: V. Sora, 'I Conti dell'Anguillara dalla loro origine al 1465', *Archivio della Reale Società Romana di Storia Patria (A.R.S.P.)*, XXX, 1907, p. 108.

[32] *Liber Pontificalis*, I, p. 407.

[33] Benedetto monaco di S. Andrea del Soratte, *Chronicon*, ed. G. Zucchetti, Rome, 1920, p. 157.

[34] In February 1050 a certain Pietro and his daughters sold a *petium de casalino* . . . *positum intus castello vetulo qui appellatur Capralica*: text in P. Fedele, 'Carte del Monastero dei Ss. Cosma e Damiano in Mica Aurea', *A.R.S.P.* XXII, 1899, pp. 92–3.

[35] In a diploma of 996 the emperor Otto III confirmed the Roman monastery of SS. Bonifacio and Alessio on the Aventine in all its possessions, which included the properties of a certain Pietro and his brother Stefano: *hoc est cortem quae dicitur Petrozano et castellum quod dicitur Sorbo et Anzano et Capraricam cum molendinis suis, una et cum omnibus quae iam dicto Petro vesterario et Stephano fratri eius pertinere visa sunt*: text in *Monumenta Germaniae Historica: Diplomatum regum et imperatorum Germaniae*, II, part 2: *Ottonis III. Diplomata*, Hanover, 1893, pp. 620–1 (No. 209); Miss Hannah French kindly checked the reading from the original in the library of Wellesley College, Mass. *Cf.* E. Moffett, 'A *Bulla* of Otto III in America', *Speculum*, IX, 1934, and *id.*, 'A lost diploma of Otto III', in *Persecution and Liberty*, ed. G. Burr, New York, 1931. The early history of Capranica has to be written on the assumption that it had no other name, while it is confused by the existence of other places with the same name or a similar one, e.g. near-by Caprarola. G. Sercia, *La pretesa feudalità di Capranica e le concessioni di Paolo II sul territorio di Vico* . . ., Ronciglione, 1933, p. 3, presumed that the 996 diploma concerned Capranica. It seems possible that it referred to Sorbo, Mazzano and Capracorum, all of them lying farther south and apparently belonging to the estates of the former *domusculta* of Capracorum; see Kahane *et al.*, pp. 161–5, and P. Partner, 'Notes on the lands of the Roman Church in the early Middle Ages', *Papers of the British School at Rome*, XXXIV, 1966, pp. 74–6. The *castellum* of Mazzano was granted to S. Gregorio on the Caelian in 945, and Partner, p. 71, n. 17, states that it remained with

S. Gregorio until the fourteenth century; this is probable but not certain, since the documents he cites date to 1299 and 1327, and there may have been temporary alienations or conflicting claims. There was a *curtis Petrocciana* somewhere on or near the Tiber: G. Tomassetti, *La Campagna Romana antica, medioevale e moderna*, III, Rome, 1913, p. 272, with other references. Apart from the Sorbo near Formello, there was another near Tivoli and a *Vallis de Sorbo*—marked on the modern map at the south-west corner of the Lago di Vico—near Sutri, according to G. Tomassetti, 'Della Campagna Romana', *A.R.S.P.* xxx, 1907, pp. 359–61, but without references. There is now a Poggio Anzano 10 km due east of Montefiascone. Sercia, p. 3, maintains that a document of 992 of S. Maria in Via Lata mentioned *Capranica–Castellum* as a station of the Cassia, but there seems to be no trace of any such document; *cf.* L. Hartmann, *Ecclesiae S. Mariae in Via Latina tabularium*, Vienna, three vols., 1895–1913.

[36] Text in *Annales Camaldulenses*, ed. J. Mittarelli and A. Costadoni, IV, Venice, 1759, p. 75.

[37] B. Apollonj Ghetti, *Architettura della Tuscia*, Vatican, 1960, pp. 59, 79, 188; figs. 27, 122–3, 188; plate XLIII; J. Raspi Serra, *La Tuscia romana*, Milan, 1973, p. 140, n. 1; fig. 395; *et passim*. See also 'Capranica di Sutri', in *Quaderni di Ricerca urbanologica e tecnica della pianificazione: Facoltà de Architettura, Università di Roma*, IV, 1969, pp. 107–10, with aerial photograph, plans of the village and other photos. The *fototeca* of the Biblioteca Hertziana at Rome contains an excellent set of photographs of Capranica. None of the sculpture shown there can be dated earlier than the eleventh century. For an early thirteenth-century painting, a Christ, at Capranica: W. Volbach, 'Il Cristo di Sutri e la venerazione del SS. Salvatore nel Lazio', *Atti della Pontificia Accademia Romana di Archeologia* (third series): *Rendiconti*, XVII, 1940–41, p. 112; fig. 8; [I. Faldi and L. Mortari], *La pittura viterbese dal XIV al XVI secolo*. Viterbo, 1954, p. 20; plate 5.

[38] These features, and especially the ditch, are clearly visible on the aerial photograph (plate 2.1); *cf.* M. Zocca, 'Aspetti dell'urbanistica medioevale nel Lazio', *Palladio*, VI, 1942, with a series of village plans.

[39] Niccola Della Tuccia, in *Cronache e statuti della Città di Viterbo*, ed. I. Ciampi, Florence, 1872, pp. 14, 24; one version gives the *signore* as *Giordano Soprano*, the other as *Giordano loro soprano*.

[40] Sora, pp. 102–3. The 1331 document is in the Orsini dell'Anguillara family papers now in Rome, Archivio Storico Capitolino; that archive was also searched for earlier documents, in vain, by Sercia, who in addition used the *consiglio* and other later records in the Archivio Storico Comunale di Capranica (publishing the *Catasto rustico* of 1434, which contains a wealth of local topographical detail) for the later history of Capranica. The earliest material now at Capanica is apparently a notarial register of 1373–81 (MS index No. 1049; *cf.* Nos. 1037–8).

[41] L. Gatto, in *Dizionario Biografico degli Italiani*, iii, Rome, 1961, pp. 304, 312–13, with references. Sercia argues that Capranica was not a true feudal possession of the Anguillara, who had secured it by force and were merely tolerated there.

[42] M. Antonelli, 'Una relazione del vicario del Patrimonio a Giovanni XXII in Avignone', *A.R.S.P.* XVIII, 1895.

[43] P. Fabre, 'Une registre caméral du Cardinal Albornoz en 1364', *Mélanges d'archéologie et d'histoire*, VII, 1887.

[44] *Rationes Decimarum Italiae nei secoli XIII e XIV: Latium*, ed. G. Battelli, Vatican, 1946; for a reference of 1297 to an archpriest of S. Lorenzo *de Crapalica* (Sutri), *ibid.*, p. 416.

[45] ... *scindicus comunis et hominum ipsius castri*: Sora, p. 103.

[46] Assuming that the twenty-five *rubra salis* it consumed implied such a figure: text in G. Tomassetti, 'Sale e focatico del Comune di Roma nel Medio Evo', *A.R.S.P.*, xx, 1897, p. 352; the date is debatable.

[47] Duncan, p. 126, guesses that the change came 'probably after the end of the fourteenth century'.

[48] All this information is derived from the earliest surviving registers, for *c.* 1345–6 and *e.* 1354–9 in the Archivio Notarile di Capranica (now in Viterbo, Archivio de Stato, where the Director, Dott. A. Porretti, kindly facilitated their consultation); these registers are unnumbered, mostly unpaginated, in pieces, and in parts totally illegible. *Cf.* C. Gennaro, 'Mercanti e bovattieri nella Roma della seconda metà del Trecento: da una ricerca su registri notarili', *Bullettino dell'Istituto Storico Italiano per il medio evo*, LXXVIII, 1967. The text of December 1345 is given in appendix 2.1. A. Cretoni, *Il Petrarca a Roma*, Rome, 1962, plate III, is a photograph of the house in Capranica where Petrarch is traditionally supposed to have stayed.

[49] *Fam.* II, 15 (ed. Rossi, I, 103–4).

[50] For a preliminary survey see C. Klapisch-Zuber and J. Day, 'Villages désertés en Italie: esquisse', in *Villages désertés et histoire économique: XI–XVIII siècles*, Paris, 1965. M. Mallett and D. Whitehouse, 'Castel Porciano: an abandoned medieval village of the Roman Campagna', *Papers of the British School at Rome*, XXXV, 1967, pp. 114–15, report traces of over seventy-five abandoned settlements 'between Rome and Viterbo'.

[51] On the whole area in the later medieval period see P. Partner, *The Lands of St Peter: the Papal State in the Middle Ages and the Early Renaissance*, London, 1972, cap. XIII *et passim.*

[52] G. Billanovich, *Petrarca letterato*, I, Rome, 1947, pp. 3–55, and E. Wilkins, *The Making of the 'Canzoniere' and other Petrarchan Studies*, Rome, 1951, pp. 311–17, both provide general discussions and accept *Fam.* II, 12, as basically genuine; see also H. Baron, 'The evolution of Petrarch's thought: reflections on the state of Petrarch studies', in his *From Petrarch to Leonardo Bruni*, Chicago, 1968, and *id.*, 'Petrarch: his inner struggles and the humanistic discovery of man's nature', in *Florilegium Historiale: Essays presented to Wallace K. Ferguson*, ed. J. Rowe and W. Stockdale, Toronto, 1971. Billanovich (*op. cit.*, I, p. 49) notes that Petrarch did not make wide use of Horace before 1350–1, but in any case the Servius commentary in Petrarch's Virgil (f. 160r) actually cited the Horace passage (*Vides ut alta . . .*) to which Petrarch was presumably alluding in *Fam.* II, 12. The letter does not survive in the original missive form, and there was no significant variation between the intermediate stage and the definite form (Rossi, I, pp. cv, 99–101).

[53] For a general picture and references, R. Weiss, *The Renaissance Discovery of Classical Antiquity*, Oxford, 1969, pp. 30–8 *et passim.*

[54] Anonimo Romano, *La vita di Cola di Rienzo*, ed. A. Frugoni, Florence, 1957, p. 33.

[55] Pollen analyses, radio-carbon dating and other modern techniques have yet to be exploited fully to make good the absence of early documents in such cases, while a well laid trench within a church or elsewhere inside the walls might produce stratified and datable pottery which would help to fix the date of Capranica's origins. T. Potter, 'Excavations in the medieval centre of Mazzano Romano', *Papers of the British School at Rome*, XL, 1972, pp. 135–45, has produced pottery evidence suggesting a possible eighth-century foundation for Mazzano, though the technicalities remain debatable. At Capranica modern research has so far scarcely progressed beyond Petrarch's intuitions.

[56] Register for 1345–6 (modern foliation: f. 23v) in Archivio Notarile di Capranica, in Viterbo, Archivio di Stato; the date is 12 December 1345, since previous documents are for that year and the next entry is dated 2 January 1346.

[57] Text reproduced unchanged from Rossi, I, 99–101.

JOHN LARNER *University of Glasgow*

3

BOCCACCIO AND LOVATO LOVATI

IT HAD ORIGINALLY been my intention to call this essay 'Did Lovato Lovati write a poem on Yseult?' Such a title, however, might have suggested a theme of merely antiquarian interest, when the question is related to an important issue in the interpretation of fourteenth-century culture. Again, it might have lured the reader on in the hope that the following pages would provide some definite answer, when all that will be offered are a series of reflections and *suasiones*. None the less it is this query which is central to our discussion.

Though the importance of his work is generally recognised, comparatively little is known about the Paduan pre-humanist Lovato Lovati.[1] That he wrote a poem on Yseult, however, is suggested by two pieces of evidence. The first appears in codex XXXIII, 31, of the Biblioteca Medici-Laurenziana, a compilation of Latin writings in the handwriting of Boccaccio.[2] Here, at f. 46r there appear the words 'Versus domini lovatti de padua' and six lines of poetry:

> Turris in amplexu laticum fabricata virentem
> despicit agrorum faciem, procul exulat arbos
> sponte sua; tristi ridens patet area bello.
> Huc studio formata dei, cantata britano,
> Hyseis ardenti totiens querenda marito
> venerat insanos frustans Palamedis amores.[3]

Gardner's tentative translation of these lines runs as follows:

The tower, reared, within the embrace of waters, looks down upon a verdant stretch of country; the boat, of its own accord, glides far off; the smiling plain lies exposed to dismal war. Hither Iseult, made by divine and sung by Britannic art, so oft to be sought by her ardent spouse, had come, frustrating the mad love of Palamede.

This interpretation, he pointed out, might be associated with the incident of the 'nef de joie' and 'Isle de la Fontaine' in one of the thirteenth-century French prose romances of Tristan.[4] Against this Dr D. Branca[5] has proposed the meaning 'moat' (around the tower) for 'amplexus laticum', and 'tree' for 'arbos'. In this case the passage might be put in another context where

Palamede hung his shield upon a tree when Yseult fled from him to a tower.[6] Obviously, however, six lines by themselves provide little scope for any precise determination of context.

Lovato's authorship of these verses appears to be confirmed by a passage in an eclogue addressed to Mussato Mussati by Giovanni del Virgilio.[7] Here Giovanni declares that one Lycidas has bequeathed Mussato his pipe:

> ipse quibus Lycidas cantaverat Ysidis ignes.
> Ysidis ibat enim flavis fugibundula tricis
> non minus eluso quam sit zelata marito
> per silvas totiens per pascua sola reperta
> qua simul heroes decertavere Britanni
> Lanciloth et Lamiroth et nescio quis Palamedes.

whereon Lycidas himself had sung Isotta's flames—for Isotta strayed wandering with yellow tresses, her husband eluded in measure as herself was longed for, time and again found all alone amongst the glades and pastures whereon the while Britannic heroes fought, Lancelot and Lamoracke and who hight Palamede.[8]

A marginal annotation explains that 'Lycidas' is Lovato: 'Lycidas, idest dominus Lovactus.' The manuscript tradition of this epistle derives from another compilation in Boccaccio's autograph, the celebrated 'Laurentian Zibaldone Boccaccesca' (Medici-Laurenziana, xxix, 8), which is a 'twin' to codex xxxiii, 31. (The two codices had been formed by dividing into two an ancient Beneventan liturgical work, from which the original text was erased.)[9]

So far we seem to be on firm ground. Thanks to Boccaccio we know that Lovato had written a poem on Yseult with which Giovanni del Virgilio was acquainted. It is perhaps strange, certainly more than coincidental, that in each of the two six-line passages there should appear the words 'totiens', 'Britannus', and 'Palamedes' and that both should preserve the ideas that Yseult is 'sung', and that she is pursued by her 'marito'. But might not del Virgilio's passage have been inspired directly by Lovato's lines, and might indeed Boccaccio not have copied out those in xxxiii, 31, precisely because he was struck by their correspondence? Yseult, it is true, takes two forms in the two manuscripts ('Hyseis' and 'Ysidis'). Yet Latin forms of *volgare* names were very flexible; it has been seen already how Boccaccio has written both 'Lovattus' and 'Lovactus' for Lovato. This suggestion at least would explain, what is perhaps rather curious, that this indefatigable copyist should have taken down only six lines of the original poem. (Why else? Because they struck him as particularly felicitous? On the surface it seems improbable, though it would be risky categorically to deny it.)

What prevents us from leaving the question there is the particular character of codex xxix, 8, which is a key source for the understanding both of Dante and Boccaccio and of the literary culture of their generations. In this compilation we find, among many other matters, at ff. 45v–48r our 'Egloga magistri Johannis de Virgilio de Cesena'. At ff. 54v–57r there is Boccaccio's first version of his own eclogue, the 'Egloga magistri Joh[annis] cui nomen Faunus incipit'. At ff. 60v–61r there are the copies of three letters apparently written by Dante. The first of these, headed 'Cardinalibus ytalicis D de Flor', seems, both from its style and by references to it at an early date, to be genuine.[10] The second, though strange in content, has quite high claims to authenticity. It begins: 'Exultanti Pistoriensis Florentinus exul immeritus'.[11] The third, beginning 'In litteris vestris reuerentia debita', is generally accepted as authentic, though stylistically it is wholly different in character from any other epistle from Dante's hand.[12] This last letter was used by Boccaccio as the basis for a passage in both the Toledo and Chigiana manuscripts of the *Vita di Dante*.[13] None of these epistles exists in any other manuscript.

Coming to f. 65*r* we find one of the most interesting parts of the *Zibaldone*: the letter of one Frate Ilario to Uguccione della Faggiuola. This relates how the good friar, wandering one day in the Lunigiana, came to the monastery of Corvo, and there met and talked to Dante. During the conversation the poet explained to him that he had begun to write the *Divine Comedy* in Latin— we are given the first three lines of the original work—but, on realising that the liberal arts were in decline, had decided to compose in Italian instead. Finally he had asked the friar to send the *Inferno* to Uguccione, to whom it was to be dedicated, and announced his intention of dedicating the *Purgatorio* and *Paradiso* to Moruello Malaspina and King Federigo of Sicily respectively. It is unnecessary to elaborate on the manifest improbability of all this, nor on the fact that here we are face to face with a Boccaccian *novella*.[14] One thing should be underlined, however, that Boccaccio meant his readers to take this letter as being an authentic document, for repeatedly, up to the end of his life, he was reiterating points made in it. In the first version of the *Vita di Dante*, written around 1348,[15] he repeated the story of the triple dedication and gave again the first three lines of the Latin *Comedia*. In the later, first and second *Compendio* these tales reappeared unchanged. In the *Genealogia deorum* of the early 1370s he wrote of Federigo's friendship with Dante, and towards the end of his life in the *Comento* produced once again the lines 'Ultima regna canam . . .'[16]

It is not clear why Boccaccio should have stressed so strongly the dedications to the three men mentioned, particularly in the case of King Federigo, which, given Dante's uniformly hostile references,[17] seems positively peverse. But his attachment to propagating the idea that Dante had begun to write the *Comedy* in Latin can be seen as a response to the humanist climate of the 1340s, as an attempt to preserve his beloved *prima fax* from the harsh imputation, levelled by such as Petrarch, that Dante was in some way second-rate because he had written in the *volgare* rather than in Latin.[18] More than this, to turn Dante into a man of the highest Latin culture who also wrote in Italian was a justification too of Boccaccio himself and his own uncomfortable fascination with the vernacular. This is what people of the highest culture could do, and it was unnecessary to turn on one's own writings in Italian, as Petrarch had affected to do, and declare them to be necessarily of no moment.

How strongly in fact did Boccaccio feel on this point? His feelings were strong enough, certainly, to concoct the fictitious letter of Fra Ilario. But, more than this, did he feel so strongly that he was prepared actually to forge works in Dante's own name? This is the question that engages us at ff. 65v–70v, containing four verse epistles between Dante and Giovanni del Virgilio. These letters reveal Dante as a master of Latin verse and as one who, like Petrarch, had been offered the laurel crown. In recent years Aldo Rossi, in a series of closely argued studies, has suggested that these poems (together with the 'Versus Magistri Johannis de Virgilio' at f. 73r) are in fact the work of Boccaccio, and that they were forged for the same purpose as the Fra Ilario epistle.[19] This thesis has not yet, by any means, come to be generally accepted in the worlds of Dante and Boccaccio scholarship, but to speak, as Dr Padoan has done, of 'l'unaninime scetticismo che ha accolto la sua "scoperta"' seems premature.[20] There is an immensely strong case to be considered here.

Having seen something of the general context in which the Virgilio–Mussato epistle, with its reference to the Lovati poem, appears, we may ask whether this letter itself is authentic. One thing is certain: the question of its authenticity is bound up with the authenticity of the Virgilio–Dante letters. Within the setting of the codex it seems, indeed, almost strategically placed to whet the reader's appetite and prepare his mind for what is to follow. On f. 54v he reads lines 1–13 of the epistle to Mussato, in which Giovanni asks him to receive his eclogue 'as once did Tityrus who though a Lydian now sleeps on the Adriatic shore'. In the margin appear the words 'Tityrus, idest Dantes qui sibi bis buccolico rescripsit carmine. Lydius, idest Tuscus. in litore, apud Ravennam'. Later, at f. 60, he is reminded of Dante's abilities as a writer in the Latin prose of the *cursus*. At f. 65r he learns that Dante had begun the *Comedy* in Latin verse. Accordingly, when he turns the page to 65v he is delighted and not too surprised to find the actual correspondence about which he has been informed earlier. From a stylistic point of view it is impossible that the Virgilio–Dante letters might have been forged on the basis of this passage in an authentic Virgilio–Mussato letter: all the verse letters stand or fall together. Accordingly, were it to be shown that the Yseult passages were the work not of Giovanni del Virgilio and Lovato Lovati, but of Giovanni Boccaccio, there would be very strong cause to follow Rossi in seeing all of the Dante–del Virgilio correspondence as the work of Boccaccio. Furthermore we would examine again, and with keener suspicions, the authenticity of the three Dante letters (in particular of 'In litteris vestris . . .') preserved in the codex.

In these circumstances it seems worth enquiring whether Lovato would have been likely to have written a poem in Latin on the *matière de Bretagne*. Courtly and chivalric literature, it is true, whether in Provençal, French, Franco-Italian or Italian, enjoyed an immense vogue in Italy during and after Lovato's lifetime. The *matière de France*, the *matière de Bretagne* and the no less courtly *matière de Rome* were favourite reading matter among the upper classes. The researches of Dr Hyde into Lovato's own city have recently drawn scholarly attention to the milieu of Zambone d'Andrea and Giovanni da Nono, with their enthusiasm for Carolingian genealogies and the joustings of King Dardanus,[21] while around the early 1320s the author of the epic on Roland called the *Entrée d'Espagne* proudly wrote:

> Mon nom vos non dirai, mai sui Patavian
> De la citez qe fist Antenor le Troian
> En la joiose Marche del cortois Trivixan.[22]

Yet apart from Zambone these men seem to have had very little contact indeed with the circle of Lovato and Mussato, and one wonders in fact how far among these pioneers any fusion of chivalric and humanistic rhetoric would have been possible, for both schools of literature tended to mould their material in very strong conformity with the conventions they followed. Certainly Guido delle Colonne, at Messina, translated Benoît de Sainte Maure's *Roman de Troie* into Latin,[23] but his claim to be a humanist (on the strength of his supposed corrections of his matter against Dictys!) is slim indeed. Again, despite Benoît's portrayal of Romans and Trojans as twelfth-century knights, the very classical character of the story made its casting into Latin more acceptable.

It is difficult to think of other examples in this period. And when one examines, for instance, the different ways in which Ezzelino da Romano appears in courtly and early humanist rhetoric, one's doubts about the possibility of cross-fertilisation between the two manners grow. On the one hand we have the voice of the classical world in Mussato's Nuntius solemnly recounting the tyrant's death to the chorus:

> —acerque moritur fronte crudeli minax
> et patris umbras sponte Tartareas subit.[24]

On the other there is the Franco-Italian story of the *Chevalier Ogier* telling of his tyranny and death under the guise of:

> un Sarasin, pesimo tiran
> Qe mantenait Marmore, una cité valan
> Le Masimo Cudé sil 'apela la Jan.[25]

Again, in the Arthurian world of the *Prophecies de Merlin*, composed by a Venetian between 1274 and 1279, the tyrant of Marmore (Verona) appears as 'li mauvaise dragonel' and then as 'roi de Patarie'.[26] Thinking of these contrasts, was it really possible, one wonders, for the circle of Lovato to look upon contemporary courtly authors in a spirit of friendly tolerance and interchange, or was it more likely that their attitude should have been as aggressively hostile to other literary genres as was that of so many of their successors?

In itself this hardly seems a valid line of thought, for in many ways Lovato was less of a true humanist than his pupil, the author of the *Ecerinide*. Of Lovato the late Professor Weiss wrote, with great justice, 'non sente come un umanista ma come un rimatore politico-moraleggiante del primo Trecento'.[27] Indeed, in one of his poems he does utilise Tristan material. Speaking of how in his sorrow he can only weep and sing as did Ovid, Arion and Orpheus, he continues:

Vulneris autorem subiit Tristanus Yseldam,
Dum streperet vario concita corda sono.[28]

Here is a clear mingling of classical and modern themes. Yet to mention Tristan and Yseult in an aside is clearly a very different matter from actually writing a full-length work on them. (It will be noticed, incidentally, that Yseult's name appears in a different form here from that found in the Boccaccio manuscripts.)[29] Could he in fact have done this? Another poem from his hand, which discusses what is permissible in a work of literature, suggests—at least on the surface—that this is improbable. Unfortunately its meaning is obscure, so obscure that two wholly different interpretations have been given to it. Foligno suggested that Lovato was arguing here that it was legitimate to draw epic material from the deeds of French heroes.[30] Given Sabbadini's criticism,[31] this seems untenable, and it is much more probable that the poem is arguing against the use of *volgare*, as opposed to classical language and themes. For the principal arguments the reader should refer to Sabbadini's own discussion. In addition one may consider the first ten lines of the work, which at least have the merit of being clear and textually uncontroversial:

Fontibus irriguam spatiabar forte per urbem
Quae tribus a vicis nomen tenet, ocia passu
Castigans modico, cum celsa in sede theatri
Karoleas acies et gallica gesta boantem
Cantorem aspitio; pendet plebecula circum
Auribus arrectis; illam suus allicit Orpheus.
Ausculto tacitus: Francorum dedita lingue
Carmina barbarico passim deformat hiatu
Tramite nulla suo, nulli innitentia penso
Ad libitum volvens; Vulgo tamen illa placebant.[32]

I was walking by chance through the town watered by fountains which takes its name from its three *vici* (i.e. Treviso), passing my leisure at an easy pace, when I see on a high theatre bench a singer who declaims the French *gestes* and the Carolingian ranks. The little people hang around, their ears cocked; their Orpheus charms them. In silence I listen. With a barbaric accent he deforms here and there the song composed in the French tongue, mixing it up at will, aimlessly and without art. However, the mob liked it.

Does this passage indicate a scorn for current French literary productions as such? Could not its theme be a contempt for its plebeian deformation rather than for the original material? After all, the Carolingian stories were not the exclusive preserve of the *cantastorie* and the people in the market place. The thirteenth-century Franco-Italian texts in the Marciana which preserve them are *manuscrits de luxe* which indeed came from the library of the Gonzaga lords of Mantua. Could not Lovato be accepting the *matière de France* as a literary genre while despising its popular manifestation? It does not seem possible to argue along these lines. For the extant texts themselves, however popular in court circles, preserved still the deformed French which Lovato emphasises. The Franco-Italian or Franco-Venetian dialect, in fact, was precisely the French tongue, adapted by minstrels to the ear of Italians, and it seems certain that the substance and manner of what was sung to the

plebecula and *vulgo* were broadly the same as those found in the surviving
manuscripts. [33]

However, was it possible perhaps to enjoy the *matière de Bretagne*, the tales of
Arthur and Tristan, while at the same time scorning the *matière de France*, the
gallica gesta? At first sight this seems to be so. Francesco da Barberino, in his
Documenti d'Amore, advised the reading of Tristan but not of the stories of
Guillaume d'Orange: 'Tristanum propterea non obmictes. De paladinis
autem loqui hodie videtur exosum nec multum cara lectura gestuum
Guillilmi de Auringia et similium quorum fabule tam aperta fingunt
mendacia.' This despite the fact, he continued, that 'novitates tamen palatii
dicti Guillelmi adhuc indicant ipsa magna fecisse'. [34] If enthusiasts for Tristan
could decry the epics of the paladins on the grounds of their untruth, so too
did the spokesmen of the *matière de France* sneer at 'Arthurian fables' for the
very same reason. The author of the *Entrée d'Espagne* recommends his work
in precisely these terms:

> Segnors car escoltez, ne soit ne cri ne hu
> gloriose cançons, c'onques sa pier ne fu;
> ne vos samblerount mie de les flabes d' Artu. [35]

Writers of chivalric epic, indeed, seem to have adopted a topos on the
theme of the truth of their material as opposed to the falsehood of Arthurian
themes. So, around 1350, Niccolò da Casola, in his *Attila*, wrote:

> Or intendes im pais, seignur, cest çhançon
> Et tout ceus que delite a oir nove tençon,
> Estormes et batailles et grant campleson.
> Nen croy vous çhanter des fables de Berton
> De Ysaut, ne de Tristan, ne de Breuz li Felon,
> Ne e la royne Zanevre, que amor mist au baron,
> Quelle dame dou Lac nori iusque infançon,
> Ne delle rois Artu, ne de Hector li bron;
> Mes d'une ystoire verables, que n'i est se voire non,
> Si cum ie ai atrue in croniche por raison. [36]

Enthusiasts for chivalric and Arthurian literature respectively, that is to say,
often distinguished their work from each other, and saw their themes as
rival rather than complementary. At first sight, then, even if Lovato's
description of the *cantastoria* of Treviso were thought of as revealing a hostility
to chivalric literature, it would not necessarily follow that he might not be an
avid reader of the tales of Yseult.

Yet at this point one begins to have doubts. By the beginning of the fourteenth century the chivalric genre was becoming rapidly assimilated to the
courtly mode. [37] To take one characteristic example: the *Entrée d'Espagne*,
already mentioned. Here Roland, insulted by Charlemagne in Spain, sets off
as a knight errant for the exotic East, disguised as a pagan, and, momentarily
forgetful of Alde la bel, jousts in defence of the honour of a fair saracen maid.
True, he returns in the end to Spain, hears from a hermit a prophecy of his
death, and takes up arms again with his uncle; but we are a long way here
from the thought world of the eleventh century, though very close to the
sentiments of Arthurian literature. Significant too in the poem is the develop-

ment of Estout, who fulfils an anti-heroic, mocking and cowardly role, similar in some ways to that of Kay in the Arthurian legend.[38] Again, although some modern critics have discerned a strong Christian feeling in the poem,[39] its values are profoundly ambiguous. There is an emphasis on the virtues of *largece*, and a taste for elegance and sumptuousness, which recall at once the world of Chrétien de Troyes. The author informs us that he had been commanded in a vision at night to write his story down by no less a figure than Archbishop Turpin. But if the Turpin of the Chanson de Roland could have read the *Entrée d'Espagne*, would he have not repeated these words, put into his mouth in the eleventh-century epic?

Deus tut mal te tramette!
Tel as ocis dunt al coer me regrette.[40]

To sum up, whatever the claims of its authors, the chivalric poems were by now deeply interfused in sentiment and manner with the Arthurian tales. In these circumstances if Lovato's taste were so uncatholic as to reject the chivalric genre, so similar now to the courtly material, is it likely that he could at the same time reconcile the wholly alien styles of the *matière de Bretagne* and of early humanism?

By this stage, however, the reader will have his own questions to ask, as for instance, 'Even if Boccaccio had some motive for falsely asserting that Dante wrote Latin verse, what possible reason could he have for claiming that Lovato wrote a poem which he did not in fact write?' Yet to answer this does not seem difficult. The Fra Ilario letter suggests clearly that Boccaccio was abnormally sensitive to the literary opinions of his humanist contemporaries and particularly of Petrarch. And Petrarch made abundantly clear the strong contempt he affected to feel both for the writings of others in the Italian *volgare*—one thinks of the letter upon Dante to Boccaccio and his own frigid review of the Decameron[41]—and for the courtly tales of French literature,[42] for all those who 'semper in angulis inter mulierculas ac fullones vulgaria eructuare problemata'.[43] Given this, how was Boccaccio to see his own early writings? His first works at Naples in the 1330s had all been based on French courtly romance. *Floire et Blanchefleur*, the *Roman de Troie*, the *Roman de Thèbes*—these had been the inspiration for the *Filostrato*, the *Filocolo* and the *Teseida*. On his return to Tuscany in the '40s his mind was filled with that vision of transfiguring and courtly love found in the Arthurian stories. In the *Amorosa visione* he brooded on 'Tristano e quella di cui elli fu più che d'altra mai innamorato'.[44] Like Madonna Fiammetta, he read 'li francheschi romanzi, a quali se fede alcuna si puote attribuire, Tristano e Isotta, oltre ad ogni altro amante essersi amati'.[45] His supreme masterpiece he was to call after 'li sires des Lontaines Illes', the Arthurian knight moved by love: *Il libro chiamato Decameron cognominato Principe Galeotto*.[46]

In the interests of a classical purism was all this beauty to be thrown overboard and this past to be repudiated? It was not Boccaccio's interests alone which were at stake here. He was concerned with a judgement upon a whole body of literature, on all those who had written or enjoyed the 'Arturi regis ambages pulcherrime'.[47] In the Fra Ilario letter it has been seen how Boccaccio had reacted when invited by Petrarch to throw over his love for Dante: not by meeting his friend's objections through reasoned argument but by what came more naturally to the author of the *Decameron*, the construction of a fable. It may not be impossible, given this temperament, that he should have reacted in a similar way to contemporary humanist scorn for the themes of French literature. In this case the fable would be that a leading Latin writer had already acknowledged that these were worthy and excellent subjects for the literary imagination. Lovato himself had written a poem on that material, that 'Lovatus patavinus' who, in Petrarch's opinion, 'fuit nuper poetarum omnium quos nostra vel patrum nostrorum vidit etas facillime princeps'.[48]

Let us summarise our reflections on the question 'Did Lovato write a poem on Yseult?'

1 Boccaccio had a motive for forgery, and, as the Ilario epistle shows, forgery was not alien to him.
2 There are similarities between the six lines of the Virgilio—Mussato eclogue, and the six lines of the Lovato–Yseult extract. These cannot arise purely from chance, though they can be explained in a way favourable to their authenticity.
3 There is no other reference to Lovato's poem. This is hardly an important argument. There is, for instance, only one reference to Lovato's lost poem *De conditionibus urbis Padue et peste Guelfi et Gibolengi nominis*.[49]
4 On the other hand there is no reason to think that the subject of the *De conditionibus* was repugnant to Lovato. There is some reason to doubt whether he admired the themes of *volgare* literature in a courtly vein.

By themselves these considerations seem inconclusive. None the less, what induces me to bring in the Scottish legal verdict of 'not proven' rather than 'not guilty' against Boccaccio is the studies of Dr Rossi, referred to previously. (The reader will understand, of course, how truly inapplicable, given a sense of historical relativity, such words as 'guilty' really are here.)

Reflecting on the issues raised by Rossi, one wonders, in our context, what importance should be given to that letter, dated around or after 1367,[50] in which Boccaccio introduced the collection of his own eclogues to Fra Martino da Signa. Here, after mentioning Theocritus and then Virgil as authors of bucolic poetry, he lets fall the words 'Post hunc autem scripserunt et alii, sed ignobiles, de quibus nil curandum est, excepto inclito preceptore meo Francisco Petrarca . . .'[51] When he penned those lines what was at work in Boccaccio's mind? Had he momentarily forgotten the eclogues of Giovanni del Virgilio and of Dante, 'qui sibi bis buccolico rescripsit carmine', those verses which he had laboriously transcribed some twenty to thirty years before? Or had he now decided perhaps that these were to be classified among the 'ignobiles de quibus nil curandum est'? Or could it be, last of all, that what is to be discerned in this passage is a sudden spontaneous expression of a modest self-depreciation?

NOTES

[1] On whom R. Weiss, 'Lovato Lovati', *Italian Studies*, VI, 1951, pp. 3–28.

[2] Described in A. M. Bandinius, *Catalogus Codicum Latinorum Bibliothecae Mediceae Laurentianae*, II, Florence, 1775, cols. 124–8.

[3] I adopt the punctuation of E. G. Gardner, *The Arthurian Legend in Italian Literature*, London, 1930, pp. 217–18. With a slightly different reading it had been published previously by L. Padrin, *Lupati de Lupatis, Boretini de Bovetinis, Albertini Mussati, nec non Iamboni Andreae de Favafuschis carmina quaedam*, Padua, 1887 (Nozze Giusti-Giustiniani), p. 42.

[4] Gardner referred to E. Löseth, *Le Roman en prose de Tristan, le roman de Palamède et la compilation de Rusticien de Pise* (Bibliothèque de l'École des Hautes Études, fasc. 82), Paris, 1891, pp. 304–7.

[5] D. Branca, *I romanzi italiani di Tristiano e la Tavola ritonda*, Florence, 1968, p. 15, n. 8.

[6] Referring to Löseth, *Le Roman en prose de Tristan, cit.*, pp. 43–4.

[7] On whom see P. O. Kristeller, 'Un "ars dictaminis" di Giovanni del Virgilio', *Italia medioevale e umanistica*, IV, 1961, pp. 181–3.

[8] P. Wickstead and E. G. Gardner, *Dante and Giovanni del Virgilio*, London, 1902, p. 190 (carmen VI, lines 210–6). For another edition, see A. Albini, 'L'egloga di Giovanni del Virgilio ad Albertino Mussato', *Atti e memorie della R. Deputazione di storia patria per le provincie di Romagna*, third series, XXIII, 1905, pp. 260–1.

[9] In facsimile, ed. G. Biagi, *Lo Zibaldone Boccaccesco mediceo-laurenziano, Plut. XXIX, 8*, Florence, 1915. See H. Hauvette, 'Notes sur des manuscrits autographes de Boccace à la Bibliothèque Laurentienne', *Mélanges d'Archéologie et d' Histoire*, XIV, 1894, pp. 87–145 (reprinted with same pagination in H. Hauvette, *Études sur Boccace, 1894–1916*, ed. C. Pellegrini, Turin, 1968), particularly pp. 135–7; F. di Benedetto, 'Lo Zibaldone Laurenziano del Boccaccio e restauro testuale della prima redazione del "Faunus" ', *Italia medioevale e umanistica*, XIV, 1971, pp. 91–129. For a full bibliography relating to Laurentian MSS XXIX, 8 and XXX, 31, see Evi Lauri, 'Elenco dei manoscritti autografi di G. Boccaccio', *Modern Language Notes (Italian issue)*, LXXVI, 1971, pp. 103–4.

[10] *Dantis Alagherii Epistolae*, ed. P. Toynbee, second edition, Oxford, 1966, pp. 122–124.

[11] *Ibid.*, p. 20.

[12] *Ibid.*, p. 151.

[13] Giovanni Boccaccio, *Il comento alla Divina Comedia e gli altri scritti intorno a Dante*, ed. D. Guerri, Bari, 1918, I, pp. 45–6; 94.

[14] P. Rajna, 'Testo della lettera di Frate Ilario e osservazioni sul suo valore storico' in *Dante e la Lunigiana*, Milan, 1909, pp. 234–85.

[15] M. Barbi, 'Qual è la seconda redazione della "Vita di Dante" del Boccaccio?' in his *Problemi di critica dantesca*, Florence, 1934–41, I, p. 423.

[16] *Il comento alla Divina Comedia e gli altri scritti, cit.*, I, pp. 53–4; 99–100; 126; *Genealogie deorum gentilium libri*, ed. V. Romano, Bari, 1951, II, 712 (book XIV, chapter 11).

[17] *De Vulgari eloquentia*, ed. P. V. Mengaldo, Padua, 1968, I, 20–1 (I, XII, 4–5); *Il Convivio*, ed. G. Busnelli and G. Vandelli, Florence, 1954, II, pp. 69–70 (IV, VI, 20); *Purgatorio*, VII, 119–20; *Paradiso*, XIX, 130–4; XX, 63. I assume that *Purgatorio*, III, 116, refers to Alfonso III rather than to his brother.

[18] As in F. Petrarca, *Le familiari*, ed. V. Rossi, 1933–42, IV, pp. 94–100 (XXI, 15).

[19] See A. Rossi, 'Dante, Boccaccio, e la laurea poetica', *Paragone*, 150, 1962, pp. 3–41; 'Il carme di Giovanni del Virgilio', *Studi danteschi* XL, 1963, pp. 133–278; 'Boccaccio autore della corrispondenza Dante–Giovanni del Virgilio', in *Scritti su Giovanni Boccaccio*, Florence, 1964, pp. 20–6. Rossi sums up to date in 'Dossier di un'attribuzione. Dieci anni dopo.', *Paragone*, 216, 1968, pp. 61–125.

[20] See the reviews of G[iorgio] P[adoan] in *Studi sul Boccaccio*, I, 1963, pp. 517–40; II, 1964, pp. 475–507; V, 1968, pp. 365–8; and E. Cecchini, 'Giovanni del Virgilio,

Dante, Boccaccio. Appunti su un' attribuzione controversa', *Italia medioevale e umanistica*, XIV, 1971, pp. 25–56.

²¹ J. K. Hyde, 'Medieval descriptions of cities', *Bulletin of the John Rylands Library*, XLVIII, 1966, pp. 330–2; and 'Italian social chronicles in the Middle Ages', *ibid.*, XLIX, 1966, pp. 107–13. See too P. Rajna, 'Le origini delle famiglie padovane e gli eroi dei romanzi cavallereschi', *Romania*, IV, 1875, pp. 161–83.

²² *L'Entrée d' Espagne*, ed. A. Thomas, Paris, 1913, II, p. 108 (lines 10974–6).

²³ Guido delle Colonne, *Historia destructionis Troiae*, ed. N. H. Griffin, Cambridge Mass., 1936; see H. Buchtal, *Historia troiana: studies in the history of medieval secular illustration*, London, 1971, pp. 5–8.

²⁴ Albertino Mussato, *Tragoedia Ecerinis*, ed. L. Padrin, Bologna, 1900, p. 58.

²⁵ H. Krauss, 'Ezzelino da Romano—Maximo Çudé. Historische Realität und epischer Strukturzwang in der frankoitalienischen Chevalerie Ogier', *Cultura neolatina*, XXX, 1970, pp. 233–49. The text has been edited by B. Cerf, 'The Franco-Italian Chevalerie Ogier', *Modern Philology*, VIII, 1910–11, pp. 187–216; 355–61; 511–25. For the Maximo incident, pp. 189–216.

²⁶ *Les Prophecies de Merlin*, ed. L. A. Paton, London, 1926–27, I, pp. 94, 141.

²⁷ Weiss, 'Lovato Lovati', *cit.*, p. 20.

²⁸ C. Foligno, 'Epistole inedite di Lovato de' Lovati e d'altri a lui', *Studi medievali*, II, 1906–07, p. 42.

²⁹ See above, p. 23.

³⁰ Foligno, 'Epistole inedite', *cit.*, p. 42.

³¹ R. Sabbadini, 'Postille alle Epistole inedite di Lovato', *Studi medievali*, II, *cit.*, pp. 257–8.

³² Foligno, 'Epistole inedite', *cit.*, p. 49.

³³ S. Roncaglia, 'La letteratura franco-veneta', in *Storia della letteratura italiana*, ed. E. Cecchi and N. Sapegno, II, 732–44.

³⁴ Francesco da Barberino, *I documenti d' amore*, ed. F. Egidi, Rome, 1905, I, p. 101. So in thirteenth-century France a rudimentary historical consciousness had persuaded Alberic des Trois Fontaines that poems such as *Macaire* were composed of 'fabule … ex magna parte falsissime'; see Jessie Crosland, *The Old French Epic*, Oxford, 1951, p. 110.

³⁵ *L'Entrée d'Espagne*, *cit.*, I, p. 2 (lines 22–4).

³⁶ Niccolò da Casola, *La guerra d'Attila*, ed. G. Stendardo, Modena, 1941, I, pp. 3–4. So too Boccaccio, *Comento alla Divina Comedia*, *cit.*, II, p. 1444, deemed the stories of Lancelot 'per qual ch' io creda, più composte a beneplacito che seconda la verità'.

³⁷ *Poemi cavallereschi del Trecento*, ed. G. G. Ferrero, Turin, 1965, p. 10.

³⁸ *Ibid.*, pp. 17–20.

³⁹ *Ibid.*, pp. 14–16; Anna Finoli, 'Personalità e cultura dell' autore dell' Entrée d'Espagne', *Culture neolatina*, XXI, 1961, pp. 175–81.

⁴⁰ *La Chanson de Roland*, lines 1608–9.

⁴¹ See n. 18; also *Epistolae Seniles*, XVII, 3, in *Francisci Petrarchae Epistolae selectae*, Oxford, 1932, pp. 211 ff.

⁴² F. Petrarca, *Poëmata omnia*, Basle, 1541, pp. 575–6 (*Ep. Met.*, III, 30).

⁴³ F. Petrarca, *Prose*, ed. G. Martelloti, Milan and Naples, 1955, p. 1066 (*Ep. Sen.*, II, 1).

⁴⁴ *Amorosa visione*, ed. V. Branca, Florence, 1944, pp. 131, 307.

⁴⁵ *L'Elegia di Madonna Fiammetta*, ed. V. Pernicone, Bari, 1939, p. 155.

⁴⁶ On this title see Gardner, *Arthurian Literature*, *cit.*, pp. 237–8.

⁴⁷ Dante, *De vulgari eloquentia*, *cit.*, I, pp. 20–1 (I, x, 2).

⁴⁸ F. Petrarca, *Rerum memorandum libri*, ed. G. Billanovich, Florence, 1943, p. 84 (II, 61).

⁴⁹ Weiss, 'Lovato Lovati', *cit.*, p. 12.

⁵⁰ G. Boccaccio, *Opere latine minori*, ed. A. F. Massera, Bari, 1928, pp. 261–2.

⁵¹ *Ibid.*, p. 216.

Cecil H. Clough *University of Liverpool*

4

THE CULT OF ANTIQUITY: LETTERS AND LETTER COLLECTIONS

In a letter of 29 March 1528 to Henry Botteus, Erasmus (1466–1536) wrote that he devoted half his day to the reading and writing of letters.[1] Today some 1,600 of his letters are known, which can be only a representative sample of his entire epistolary production, even if one accepts with reservation his claim that on some days he wrote sixty or ninety letters.[2] That the letter form was coming to the fore as a literary genre in the early sixteenth century is suggested by two letter collections. These were very influential in stimulating a climate of opinion in Germany hostile to the authority of the Church in the years immediately prior to Luther's famous stand at Wittemberg in 1519. Johann Reuchlin (1455–1522), a scholar of Hebrew, was put on trial by monastics of Cologne for unorthodoxy, and after his acquittal he had printed the letters of sympathy that he had received. This collection, entitled *Clarorum virorum epistolae* . . . (Tübingen, Thomas Anshelm Badensis, 1514), was followed by a parallel one, entirely imaginary, supposedly addressed to Ortuin Gratius, one of Reuchlin's principal antagonists, which was published as *Epistolae obscurorum virorum ad Ortuinum Gratium: cum multis alijs epistolis,* and its printer falsely given as Aldo Manuzio of Venice. Probably its authors were Orotus Rubianus and Ulrich von Hutten, and the earliest printer (there were three printings within a year or so) was Friedrich Peypus of Nuremberg. What seems the earliest reference to the work is found in a letter from Wolfgang Augst to Erasmus which accompanied the gift of a copy of the *Epistolae* in print; this letter has the date 19 October, and appears to be of 1515.[3]

By the turn of the fifteenth century the letter was replacing the oration as the prime means by which scholars, and particularly those devoted to the cult of Antiquity, disseminated their ideas and made their case in scholarly controversy. Erasmus wrote his letters exclusively in Latin, and only in this was he exceptional in comparison with some contemporary Italian humanists of his stature, who wrote both in Latin and in the vernacular. After his sojourn in Italy Erasmus should have been acquainted with Italian, but possibly he rejected it as being merely Latin that had been corrupted by the barbarians. Pietro Bembo (1470–1547), on the other hand, who was given place of honour as the doyen of living scholars in the famous gallery of portraits of illustrious men that was formed by Paolo Giovio at his villa in Como, spent his energies in the 1530s preparing his letters, both Latin and Italian, for publication.[4] Indeed, by the mid-sixteenth century, when Bembo's personal letters in Latin were printed, the controversy in Italy over the merits of Latin as against Italian had largely been settled in favour of the latter.[5] Bembo's Italian letter collection was reprinted some six times in the half-century prior to 1600, whereas his Latin collection achieved only the single issue.[6] In Italy few were the letter collections or anthologies in Latin published in the fifty years after 1550, as against well over a hundred in Italian, each of which was often in several volumes. Montaigne, for instance, writing in 1580, stated that he had a hundred or more volumes of printed Italian letter collections on his shelves.[7] Erasmus's letter collection suffered from this shift to the vernacular; after the first sizable printing of 1519 there were numerous reprintings until the middle of the century, but none in the following fifty years.[8] Contrary to what may be thought, Erasmus's pre-occupation with the letter form in Latin was towards the end of the main stream of humanistic tradition, not a source from which a river flowed. His collection was typical of its period, when humanists laboured to compose their letters in Ciceronian Latin; when these letters were transcribed for dispatch in humanistic script;[9] when a letter writer himself edited his letters into a collection in emulation of the classical models.

Perhaps because it is so familiar to us, the place of the letter, and the letter collection, in the Renaissance has been overlooked, save for a few remarks by Jacob Burckhardt, perceptive as always.[10] The purpose of this study is to establish the main outlines of the development of the letter collection in the Renaissance, and, since it is Italy that dictated the nature of the whole Renaissance movement, the examples will focus on the Italian Renaissance. First and foremost some definition of terms is required. The Italian Renaissance can be summed up as the cultural consequence of an idea, the search for Antiquity—classical Greece and Rome—in all its aspects. The cult of Antiquity grew (and changed as it did so) from the idea of one man, Petrarch (1304–78), spreading by way of disciples, notably Boccaccio, to Florence and thence to the courts of Italy. Its chronological phases in broad terms are: 1350 to 1400, when Petrarch and his disciples had the idea almost exclusively; 1400 to 1450, when the citizens of Florence absorbed it; 1450 to 1550, when the cult was centred on the courts of Italy. The scholars who subscribed to the cult of Antiquity can be called humanists, and what they practised 'humanism'.[11]

During the Italian Renaissance letters were written and dispatched by means of messengers. The humanists wrote not only for their correspondents but with a view to the publication of some, at least, of their correspondence during their own lifetime. In his prefatory letter to Beatus Rhenanus, which appears in front of the collection of his letters published in 1521, Erasmus said that when he was a young man[12]

I hardly wrote any [letters] for publication. I practised my style . . . not expecting that my friends would copy out and preserve such trifles. For when I was in Siena the most courteous [Jacopo] Piso, then the king's ambassador to Pope Julius II, found for sale a volume of Erasmus's letters, at a bookseller's, written in manuscript, which he bought and sent me. Although there was much in it which might have seemed worthy of preservation, yet I was so annoyed by such an unlooked-for incident that I burned the whole volume.

Awareness that one's letters might be collected and published caused the writer to elaborate every letter into a conscious literary creation. Secondly, it sometimes meant that the writer himself wanted to edit his own letters for a collection, the justification being of the kind that Erasmus hints at in the letter quoted above: the preservation only of that which was meritorious.

Editing, be it by the writer himself, or another person, brought with it changes of all kinds. These, particularly in the case of the writer's editing his own letters, could go far beyond the omission of passages and stylistic perfecting of the chosen letters; in the case of Petrarch, for instance, a series was filled out with fake correspondence, while Bembo so reordered a series to give a dramatic narrative in one of his collections that the resulting picture was the very antithesis of the truth.[13] In general terms a humanist's letter collection has its dangers as a source of historical documents, and this complication has not usually been sufficiently appreciated by modern editors, who intersperse authentic letters actually dispatched with those extrapolated from the writer's own self-edited collection. A letter collection was seen by the humanist of the Renaissance as a literary work in its own right.

Closely associated are the prefatory letters and those of dedication or presentation. These were written by humanists in quest of patronage, and they were not necessarily dispatched or even written at the time suggested by the date given. The epistle was itself a literary form, and much favoured by humanists for debate; as such it was adopted by Erasmus for his *Enchiridion Militis Christiani*, his *De Virtute Amplectanda* and his *De Ratione Studii*. Symptomatic of the interest in the letter as a literary form was the production of works whose theme was the perfection of the epistolary style. Erasmus, once again, was in the main stream with his *Opus de Conscribendis Epistolis*, which drew on examples from Cicero and Pliny among the Ancients, and from Poliziano (*c.* 1454–94) among the Renaissance humanists; his letters to Beatus Rhenanus commended as admirable also the letters of Aeneas Silvius Piccolomini.[14]

How and when was it that letters came to play an important part in Renaissance culture? Part of the classical legacy that did not perish in Italy with the barbarian invasions was the Roman epistolary form, which continued to be employed for legal documents. With the growth of towns in the twelfth century and the associated requirements of their administrations there developed the *Artes dictandi*, which were compilations of rulers, with examples, based on the Roman epistolary form, to teach notaries in particular how to write letters and frame legal documents. There were medieval elements, but it was believed that from the Ancients came the divisions, which were in essence ancient rhetoric adapted to the written *dictamen*. The basis for this rhetoric was inferred from Quintilian's work, from Cicero's *De inventione rhetorica*, and from the *Auctor ad Herennium*, which was wrongly attributed to Cicero.[15] Another branch of medieval rhetoric was oratory, which likewise had its roots in Antiquity, as the memory rules of the Middle Ages testify.[16] The humanists inherited both forms of rhetoric, but at first placed greater emphasis on oratory. Indeed, Petrarch, the initiator of the cult of Antiquity, adopted both forms to spread his idea. Petrarch had a considerable correspondence for a private individual in his day, and now some 574 of his letters are known; of these all save seventy-seven derive from his own letter collections, for he arranged three separate ones.[17] Originally Petrarch planned epistles in verse, but in 1345 his discovery of Cicero's *Epistolae ad Atticum* caused him to create a prose collection. As his prefatory letter to his first collection states, he believed himself to be in the tradition of Epicurus, Cicero and Seneca. His aim in this collection was to portray for posterity his morality and wisdom as an *exemplum*.[18] He believed, as Erasmus himself was to echo, that one could hope for fame from one's writing.[19]

As a result particularly of the researches of Remigio Sabbadini the details of the recovery of the letter collections of Antiquity from the time of Petrarch onwards are now familiar. For instance, Petrarch knew the work of Sidonius Apollinaris, while Cicero's *Epistolae ad familiares* were discovered shortly after Petrarch's death.[20] There was naturally a time lapse between the first discovery and a particular scholar's knowledge of a work until such a work was widely circulated. Leonardo Bruni (*c*. 1369–*c*. 1444), was not able to read Cicero's *Epistolae ad Atticum* until the first decade of the fifteenth century; Cicero's *Epistolae ad familiares*, seemingly known to Bruni in 1400, became one of the basic texts in the school of Guarino (*c*. 1370–*c*. 1460), and in April 1419 Guarino inaugurated in Verona a course of instruction focused on this work.[21] What remains still to be done is to provide information for every significant humanist regarding his knowledge and ownership of texts of letters of classical Antiquity, for only thus can the full extent of interest in such texts be established—here Sabbadini's *Storia e critica di testi latini* signposts the way forward.[22] As the fifteenth century advanced there was increasing knowledge of Greek texts in general, and these were often disseminated by being translated into Latin. The letters of Phalaris and of Diogenes the Cynic were translated from Greek into Latin by Francesco Griffolini (b. 1420), and the Greek letters of Brutus and Hippocrates were translated by Alamanno Rinuccini (*c*. 1426–1504). Interestingly enough, Griffolini's translation of the letters of Diogenes was dedicated to Aeneas Silvius Piccolomini (1405–64) when he was Pope Pius II, and Rinuccini's was dedicated to Pope Nicholas V.[23] The various manuscript copies of such translations need to be listed and their owners identified, for these translations also indicate interest in letters of Antiquity, and so far this aspect has been overlooked.

What of the letter collections of the humanists which were essentially inspired by the classical models? Here a considerable amount of work remains to be done, for the quantity of autograph drafts and original letters sent by the humanists, and copies of them, is considerable, while the number of manuscript copies of selections from the *epistolario* of a humanist, of individual letter collections and of anthologies is very extensive. In the case of Lorenzo Valla (*c.* 1407–*c.* 1457), who apparently never undertook to arrange his correspondence into a collection, forty manuscripts have been found which provide the eighty-five letters of his known today.[24] Guarino similarly did not arrange his own letter collection, but in his case some 550 manuscripts provide the thousand or so letters he is known to have written.[25]

It is by no means easy to know what a humanist's self-edited letter collection was intended to be, since copyists tended to transcribe only those letters that interested them, thereby making a selection, or, alternatively, they expanded a collection by adding additional material they had found from sources other than the self-edited collection. A manuscript of a selection from the correspondence of Pier Paolo Vergerio il vecchio (1370–1444), who seemingly did not edit his own collection, provides an interesting case study of the considerations involved. This manuscript was transcribed early in the 1420s by Agostino Santucci (1393; d. before 1468) during his student days at Padua University. Vergerio had been a teacher at Padua and had taken service in 1410 with the emperor Sigismund, who had crowned him poet laureate and so placed him squarely in Petrarch's line. In Santucci's miscellany the letters of Vergerio had a place with those of Gasperino Barzizza (*c.* 1359–1431), rector of the University of Padua, of Guarino, and of other distinguished humanists; there were also orations of Barzizza, Guarino and Poggio Bracciolini (*c.* 1380–1459). The miscellany reflects the way in which students at Padua were taught, in other words it shows that both the letter form and oratory were part of the curriculum. It also suggests that by the 1420s letters were being formed into anthologies for the purpose of instruction in the epistolary style. In the case of the letters of Vergerio and of Barzizza that Santucci copied into his miscellany one can make the further speculation that these came from a collection of letters written by the two scholars and formed in Padua, probably, prior to the end of 1418, and not at the wish of either writer.[26] This puts into perspective and strengthens Bertalot's case that a collection of Barzizza's letters covering the period 1407–21 was prepared in Padua in 1424, and that a copy of it exists in Damiano da Pola's manuscript now in Balliol College Library, Oxford.[27] One can speculate, too, that it was interest in his letters that inspired Barzizza to create the fictitious collection as a formulary.[28]

The publishing of a humanist's letters as a *corpus*, as was done recently in the case of Vergerio, while useful, is not enough.[29] Rather, the letters of the humanist in question need to be studied in the various contemporary manuscript miscellanies in which they appear. The nature of the selected letters of a particular humanist and their relationship to those of other writers in the miscellany will throw light upon the creators of these miscellanies by revealing their motives in making their compilations. Certainly one will see the kinds of letters that aroused most interest. I suspect one will find that letters such as those of Barzizza and of Vergerio were transcribed into miscellanies mainly to serve as models in composition. Perhaps pupils, who were instructed by such epistolary models and themselves came to write authentic letters echoing the style of these models, were inspired eventually to create a collection of their own letters. Scholars like these, too, would have been eager to read the letter collections of their fellow humanists. If these speculations concerning epistolary models prove correct one will have uncovered a factor which was not simply the desire to imitate classical Antiquity.

Meanwhile an exploratory survey suggests that, prior to the mid-fifteenth century at least, the self-edited letter collections of humanists were less influential than might be thought the case: in fact the preponderance of transcriptions appear to be of selections of letters made like the miscellany of Santucci considered above. Petrarch's own letter collections appear to be no exception. The first public library since classical times, that of San Marco in Florence, founded with the residue of Niccolò Niccoli's manuscripts and opened in 1444, did not, on the evidence of its first inventory, have any of Petrarch's letter collections. A miscellany did include 'Multae epistolae Francisci Petrarcae' but this was a selection made independently of Petrarch's wishes.[30] It seems that many, if not most, of the manuscripts containing Petrarch's letters that were transcribed prior to about 1450 were merely excerpts from Petrarch's own collections, or independent selections like that in the library of San Marco.[31] There is no evidence, for example, that Coluccio Salutati (1331–1406) owned a manuscript of Petrarch's letter collections.[32] Moreover the first printed edition of Petrarch's letters did not appear until 1492, which further underlines the insignificant part his actual letter collections played in stimulating those of the humanists.[33] This, of course, is not to deny that his idea of editing his own letters was widely known and seen by the humanists as confirming the rightness of their editing their own letters.

The transcription of an entire letter collection such as any one of Petrarch's was a long and laborious task, and the humanist-scholar had not the means to afford a scribe. Another explanation of the lack of interest in Petrarch's epistles throughout the fifteenth century is that they were somewhat premature, and in large measure anticipated the discovery of the letter collections of Antiquity which the humanists claimed as the source of inspiration for their own. By and large, also, during the infancy of the movement, prior to about 1450, scholars were more eager to devote their energies to discovering and studying the classical texts, and to their own creative writings about these texts, than to the adulation of a fellow humanist even of Petrarch's stature. As the fifteenth century progressed it became increasingly the case that the humanists were attached to a university, or to a school, with a stipend dependent upon their giving satisfaction as teachers. Emphasis in the university courses in Italy was on Rhetoric in the form of oratory, though writing, including the letter form, was taught. Teachers like Guarino carried these tenets into the instruction given to the children of the court circle, so there likewise Rhetoric came to predominate. For example, at Ferrara the *Ad Herennium* was the starting point, supplemented with Cicero's *De Oratore*, with his *Orator*, and with the range of his speeches, and likewise with his *De Officiis* and his *Tusculanae Disputationes*.[34] Francesco Filelfo (1398–1481), the tutor of Ludovico, son of Francesco Sforza of Milan, wrote a commentary on the *Ad Herennium* for his pupil, who as a youthful exercise transcribed it in a fine hand for presentation to his mother on Christmas Day, 1467.[35] When children thus taught came to authority in the court, oratory received a new impetus with the introduction of a formal oration to mark occasions of state: the marriage or funeral of a prince or of some member of the prince's family, the arrival of an envoy from another State, the consecration of a bishop. Not surprisingly, the humanists were commonly called 'orators'.[36]

Petrarch's friend and disciple Giovanni Boccaccio (1313–75) merely collected together seven of his youthful Latin letters, seemingly in imitation of Petrarch, and hence his collection is, like Petrarch's, outside the main stream. Barbato da Sulmona, one of Boccaccio's correspondents, gathered together the letters he had received from Boccaccio and inserted copies of his own replies, but this collection did not circulate and today is known only in a fragment.[37] Coluccio Salutati was a professional letter writer, being chancellor of the republic of Florence from 1373 until his death. A contemporary said of him that he was the best letter writer of his day, and he was judged to surpass even Cassiodorus of Antiquity. Salutati stressed the importance of the written word in the form of the epistle, and he sent various selections of his correspondence, which consisted of both the letters written in his capacity as Florentine chancellor and those sent privately to various friends. Despite his claim that he was going to leave it to his disciples to make a definitive selection of his public and private correspondence for general circulation, from the evidence skilfully marshalled by the late B. L. Ullman it appears probable that he had not only prepared a letter file but had also made from it a selection for posterity. It may have been Petrarch who influenced him in this, as in so much else, and since his collection did not circulate its influence seems to have been just as limited as Petrarch's.[38]

During the first half of the fifteenth century there flourished in Florence humanists of a circle that was particularly interested in the epistolary collection. Of this circle Leonardo Bruni and Poggio Bracciolini edited their own letters into a letter collection, and these two collections circulated in manuscript copies in their entirety, not merely in excerpts. Both men, be it noted, were Salutati's successors as chancellor of Florence. Bruni recalled his letters from correspondents and arranged them into a collection in eight books about 1440. Some early manuscripts of the collection have a ninth book, which was formed of Bruni's letters of the years 1441–42, and it is probable that from 1440 Bruni himself had retained copies of his letters for a book supplementary to the main collection.[39] Poggio arranged his collection differently from Bruni, for his collection grouped the letters principally by individual addressees.[40] It was probably the Florentine circle that inspired two associates to edit their letters—Ambrogio Traversari (*c.* 1386–1439) and Francesco Barbaro il vecchio (1390–1454). If the number of existing manuscript copies of their collections is any guide, neither collection appears to have enjoyed much popularity, and certainly less than those of Bruni and Poggio.[41] Bruni's collection was the most sought after and one suspects that it was his that considerably moulded taste for such collections. This point is given emphasis by the fact that Bartolomeo Facio (b. before 1410) in the last years before his death in 1457 likewise edited his own letter collection, but the few contemporary transcripts suggest it was without influence.[42]

The fictitious letter collection of Gasperino Barzizza has already been mentioned, and this was in circulation some twenty years before Bruni's. However, it must be stressed that the purpose of his collection was different from that of Bruni's, being essentially a formulary to teach style. Barzizza's model appears to have been the thirteenth-century *dictatores*, and although his collection achieved wide circulation in manuscript, and subsequently in print, it does not seem to have had Italian imitators.[43] Guiniforte (1406–63), Barzizza's son, took service with the Visconti in Milan, and then with the Sforza. He chose to follow Bruni's model, rather than his own father's, when he edited his collection, and perhaps was directly inspired by Pier Candido Decembrio (1392–1477).[44] Decembrio was the secretary of Filippo Maria Visconti and a correspondent of Bruni. He appears to have made three collections of his own letters, the first of which, consisting of fifty-nine letters and orations covering the years 1419–33, with the title 'Epistolarum iuvenilium ad B. Capram libri octo', he published about 1433. His second collection had 290 letters of the decade from 1433, and was circulating about 1445; his third collection included 270 letters covering the years from 1440 to 1468. In the years before his death Decembrio was engaged in ordering his collection into thirty-four books, where the letters were to be in chronological order.[45] Decembrio certainly formed his first collection before that of Bruni, but as the project developed over the years it seems to have been influenced by Bruni's collection. Moreover its grandiose scale meant that it did not circulate widely. Decembrio, however, probably did influence his associates such as Guiniforte by his enthusiasm for the letter collection as a vehicle for self-expression. Decembrio dedicated his second collection to Tranchedini, who, as will be considered in due course, likewise edited his own letter collection.[46] Giorgio Valagussa (whose dates of birth and death are unknown) for a time was a tutor in Francesco Sforza's household, and he edited his own letter collection, which apparently exists in a unique manuscript copy; once again Decembrio was probably the source of inspiration.[47]

Antonio Beccadelli, known as Panormita (1394–1471), who had close contact with the Florentine circle and with the court of the Visconti where Decembrio was, so extensively elaborated his letters in his collection that it is thought to be largely fictitious.[48] This, of course, brings forward another problem, since it is only in exceptional instances, where the autograph or draft of a letter actually sent exists, that a comparison may be made with the edited version in a writer's own collection.[49] It is likely that all the editors made modifications in the texts of the letters they included, and the precise extent of such changes can never be known.

It has been suggested that the influence of Petrarch's letter collections was less than might be assumed, and that Bruni and Decembrio, who moulded the taste for the humanistic letter collection, looked essentially to Antiquity for their model. Yet it must be said that the inheritance of the Middle Ages with regard to the epistle was not entirely sloughed off, as one sees most strikingly in the case of the *Epistolae* of Dante (1265–1321). There is the evidence of Dante's contemporaries that he wrote letters, and Villani in his *Cronica* specifically mentions three letters of his. Some of these letters written by Dante were personal and some in the nature of political tracts. There is no certainty that Petrarch knew his letters, but given his general interest in Dante's writings it is likely that he did, and a case can be made for supposing that Giovanni del Virgilio's correspondence in verse with Dante was the source of inspiration for Petrarch's original plan of a letter collection in the verse form. Boccaccio in his 'Vita di Dante' (written *c.* 1357–62) mentions Dante's letters, and portions of some of them were incorporated into Boccaccio's found in his own self-edited collection. Bruni also wrote a life of Dante and stated that he had seen several autograph letters of his; he mentioned two that can be identified, and quoted passages (in Italian translation) from others now lost. Francesco Filelfo was a student of Dante, and thus it is perhaps not surprising that his son, Giovanni Mario (1426–80), wrote another biography of the poet. There it is said that Dante wrote a considerable number of letters—a detail which, if erroneous, at least indicates the degree of interest in correspondence among humanists in the second half of the fifteenth century. It also tends to suggest that Giovanni Mario had come to assume that Dante had had the same interests as he had himself.[50]

The broad shift of interest in humanist circles to letter collections occurred in the last three decades of the fifteenth century, and the heyday was in the 1470s. Gasperino Barzizza's collection had the distinction of being among the first books printed in Paris, and there were at least a further eleven printings before 1501, all elsewhere. In Paris, yet again, in 1471, while Bessarion (*c.* 1403–72), its author, lived, was published an untitled work which by the end of the century appeared again in print as *Epistolae et orationes*. This title is misleading, since although the work includes two short letters addressed to Bessarion and one of his own its core is Bessarion's oration urging the rulers of Italy to unite against the Turk: indeed, Ludovico Carbone's Italian translation makes it clear, with its title *Oratione a tutti gli signori d'Italia confortandogli a pigliar guerra contra il Turcho* ([Venice, Conrad Valdarfer], 1471), that it is not the first humanistic collection of genuine letters in print. Here its interest is that it does help emphasise the close link between the letter form and oratory. The editor of the first printing, Guillaume Fichet, sent presentation copies of the work to various influential people, and among several existing copies, each with its individual covering letter, is one to King Edward IV of England.[51]

The significant date is 1472, when the collection of Leonardo Bruni's letters was printed in Venice. This was Bruni's own selection, despite the suggestion of 'editing' by the two humanists who, presumably, prepared the text for the Venetian printing house that published it. Moreover Francesco

Filelfo's self-edited letter collection appeared in print either in 1472 or in the following year, again in Venice; the collection of Aeneas Silvius Piccolomini's letters known as *Epistolae in Pontificatu editae* first appeared in print in Milan in 1473, and a second collection, *Epistolae in Cardinalatu editae*, was printed in Rome two years later. Bruni's collection was reprinted five times prior to 1501; Filelfo's, in one form or another, was reprinted eighteen times over the same period. In comparison there were twenty printings of the two collections of Piccolomini's, his *Epistolae in Cardinalatu editae* accounting for seventeen of these. Subsequently were printed the letter collections of the most distinguished humanists of the day: those of Giovanni Antonio Campano (*c.* 1427–77), Giovanni Mario Filelfo, Marsilio Ficino (1433–99), Giovanni Pico della Mirandola (1463–94), Poliziano and Robert Gaguin (*c.* 1440–*c.* 1502) all appeared prior to 1500. All save the latter, a Frenchman, were Italian, be it noted. With the exception of Pico's, each of these collections, probably in part, if not entirely, was edited by the individual humanist whose name graced it; Pico's was edited by his nephew, Gianfrancesco, and done in haste, presumably on the basis of drafts of letters that the writer had preserved. It is worth remarking that within seven years of Ficino's death reports circulated in his native Florence that his letter collection was spurious and actually the work of Bastiano Salvini, his nephew. Despite the claim having the authority of Giovanni Corsi, who made it in a dedication letter dated 18 April 1505 prefacing his biography of Ficino, it appears to be an erroneous conjecture deriving from the first identification of the script as Salvini's. This, however, can be simply explained as a natural consequence of Salvini's having been Ficino's secretary. Ficino's collection as he first assembled it consisted of forty-five letters, and was probably compiled in the mid-1470s; it was this collection that Ficino expanded over some twenty years until its publication in 1495.[52] Campano's collection was formed by the writer himself in the 1470s too, in all probability, though not printed until after his death. Michele Ferni of Milan, the editor of the nine books for the press, in a dedication letter which he addressed to Cardinal Todeschini Piccolomini (to whom Campano had previously dedicated his translation of the letters of Phalaris), stressed that the collection was in the epistolary tradition shaped by Aeneas Silvius Piccolomini, Francesco Filelfo, Petrarch, Pliny and Cicero.

Of course, not all the letter collections assembled after the advent of printing found their way into print. A selection of letters addressed to Nicodemo Tranchedini (*c.* 1411–*c.* 1485) of Pontremoli appears to have been prepared with a view to publication, possibly by Tranchedini himself in the 1470s; correspondents included the titillating names of Francesco Filelfo, Piccolomini, Bessarion and Agostino Dati (1420–78). Girolamo Alioffi (1412–80) formed a collection of his own letters, and this apparently exists in a unique manuscript (Bibl. della Fraternità dei Laici, Arezzo, MS 400). A collection of letters of the Florentine humanist Bartolomeo della Fonte, also known as Fonzio (1445–1513), likewise remained unprinted, as did that of Federigo da Montefeltro (1422–82). Federigo, Duke of Urbino, was the most distinguished patron of the arts in the 1470s, and had contact with many of the outstanding humanists in Italy, as well as having been a protégé of Aeneas Silvius Piccolomini when the latter was Pope. The collection of letters written in Federigo's name over the decade from 1470 was probably made shortly after his death with a view to its being printed. The selection, no doubt from letter books in the ducal chancery archives, consisted essentially of letters to heads of state, and its main purpose, one can suppose, was to eulogise the Duke of Urbino. As already mentioned, the influence of such letter collections as these that remained in manuscript, and hence had a very limited circulation, was minimal.[53]

What can be termed anthologies of letters written in Latin by humanists and other notable figures of the fifteenth century were included in Aeneas Silvius Piccolomini's *Epistolae in Cardinalatu editae*, starting with the edition dated to about 1476. Prior to 1500 there were ten printings of Piccolomini's collection that included such an anthology, and eight of these were different editions. From 1499 to 1520 there were at least six anthologies of similar Latin letters published as independent collections. These anthologies never matched the extraordinary popularity the genre in Italian was to attain in the second half of the sixteenth century, when Italian letter collections of individuals were equally successful. In this connection it is worth mentioning that there were printed a few early letter collections in Italian, the fictitious one of Luca Pulci, *Pistole al Magnifico Lorenzo de' Medici*, being the first, followed by the *Epistole* of St Catherine of Siena. The main spate of these collections, however, did not occur until after the appearance of Aretino's first volume, printed in 1537.[54]

What of the printing of the letter collections of Antiquity, principally those of Cicero, Seneca and Pliny? Here, as in the case of humanist letter collections, Italy was first in the field and retained pride of place in Christendom. Cicero's *Epistolae ad familiares* was one of the earliest books printed in Italy, there being two Rome printings before 1470, of which one was in 1467 and the other in 1469, as well as two Venetian printings, both of 1469. Marino Sanudo recorded the event under 1469 where (but not elsewhere) he thought that Cicero's *Epistolae* was the first work printed in Venice, though since Sanudo was writing years later he may have erred in this: 'A dì 18 septembrio fo scomenzà a Veniesia a stampar libri: inventor uno maistro Zuane de Spira todescho et stampò le Epistolle di Tullio et Plinio et morite; in locho suo successe Nicolò Janson qual vadagnò col stampar assai danar'. The first printing of Cicero's letters was limited to 100 copies, but in consequence of rapid sales a second edition with two issues each of 300 copies followed; seemingly within some seven months 700 copies in all were printed.[55] By 1501 there had appeared at least fifty-two printings, and one can estimate 300 copies on average for each, which produces the staggering figure of some 5,000 copies a year; remarkably, too, all but one of the printings was in Italy. Cicero's *Epistolae ad Brutum* ... was read considerably less widely, and though first printed in 1470 in both Rome and Venice had only three or so reprints before the end of the century. Seneca's letters first appeared in print either in 1470 or in 1471, Pliny's were printed in 1471; both collections enjoyed moderate popularity, each with ten printings prior to 1501. There were some thirty-two printings in Latin translation of the Greek letters attributed to Phalaris, and two independent Italian translations in print by 1475. The letters of Phalaris were first printed in Rome in 1468, and the collection was only a little less popular than Cicero's *Epistolae ad familiares*, a fact that has hitherto been little appreciated. The Greek text was first printed in Venice in 1498, edited by Bartholomaeus Justinopolitanus, and reprinted in the following year, again in Venice, in a collection of allied material that was edited by Marcus Musurus for Aldo Manuzio. This latter collection was published in two parts under the Latin title *Epistolae Diversorum Philosophorum Graecorum* (Venice, March and April 1499). Its impressive list of writers, real or supposed, included Synesius, Demosthenes, Plato, Aristotle, Philippus, Alexander, Hippocrates, Democritus, Heraclitus, Diogenes the Cynic, Crates, Anacharis, Euripides, Alciphron, Philostratus, Aelian, Aeneas, Procopius, Dionysius, Lysis, St Basil the Great, Libanius, Apollonius of Tyana and Julian the Apostate. The letters of Diogenes the Cynic had been available in print in Latin translation since about 1475, and had been reprinted twice at least, supplemented with the letters of Hippocrates and those of Brutus originally written in Greek, likewise in Latin translation. The translation of Diogenes was the work of Francesco Griffolino of Arezzo, who had supplied the frequently printed translation of Phalaris' letters; the translation of Hippocrates and Brutus, however, was the work of another Aretine, Alessandro Rinuccini. The supposed letters of Plato had been translated into Latin by yet another Aretine, Leonardo Bruni, in the early fifteenth century, and it was his version that was printed in Paris in 1472. Some eighteen years later Marsilio Ficino's translation was printed.[56]

It seems as though the key factor in stimulating the interest in letter collections was the advent of printing (see fig. 4.1).[57] Where previously letters had been considered as destined for a limited audience, their publication by the printing press bestowed upon them a much increased circulation. It should be stressed that oratory did not cease in consequence in any dramatic way. The printing presses published orations and treatises on the art of oratory, as well as the classical texts on the subject, in greater numbers than publications connected with the letter during the last decades of the fifteenth century. It was probably the Italian wars that began in 1494 which tilted the scales in favour of printed letter collections. This because in the course of the wars many of the numerous courts were liquidated, while those surviving had not the means to pay for the ceremony associated with the oration. By the time Erasmus was publishing his collection the printed word, in Europe in general, had replaced the spoken for disseminating not only the cult of Antiquity but ideas of all kinds, including those connected with religious thought.

Aeneas Silvius Piccolomini was another influential force in the rising fortunes of the letter form in the last three decades of the fifteenth century (see plate 4.1). His two letter collections were probably edited by him in the first instance, though possibly elaborated by his nephew, Cardinal Francesco Todeschini Piccolomini, assisted by Campano, some ten years after Piccolomini's death, with a view to printing.[58] The appearance in print of the two collections in the first half of the 1470s was fortunate. The letters had a broader appeal than those of humanists like Bruni and Francesco Filelfo.

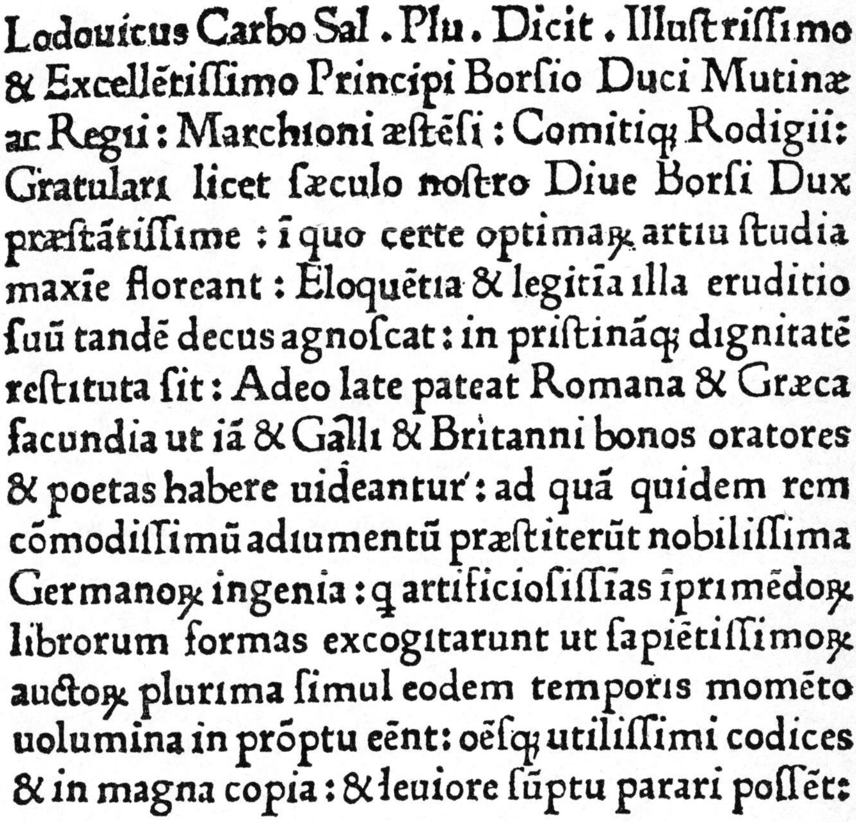

Lodouicus Carbo Sal . Plu . Dicit . Illuſtriſſimo & Excellētiſſimo Principi Borſio Duci Mutinæ ac Regii : Marchioni æſtēſi : Comitiq; Rodigii: Gratulari licet ſæculo noſtro Diue Borſi Dux præſtātiſſime : ī quo certe optima℞ artiu ſtudia maxīe floreant : Eloquētia & legitia illa eruditio ſuū tandē decus agnoſcat : in priſtināq; dignitatē reſtituta ſit : Adeo late pateat Romana & Græca facundia ut iā & Galli & Britanni bonos oratores & poetas habere uideantur' : ad quā quidem rem cōmodiſſimū adiumentū præſtiterūt nobiliſſima Germano℞ ingenia : q̄ artificioſiſſias īprimēdo℞ librorum formas excogitarunt ut ſapiētiſſimo℞ aucto℞ plurima ſimul eodem temporis momēto uolumina in prōptu eēnt : oēſq; utiliſſimi codices & in magna copia : & leuiore ſūptu parari poſſēt:

FIG. 4.1 Ludovico Carbone's praise of the invention of printing in the dedicatory letter prefacing his edition of Pliny, *Epistolae*, [Venice, Christopher Valdarfer], 1471, f. a iir (copy in the Library of Congress, Washington, D.C., Vollbehr collection, H 13110).

They related to affairs of the immediate past that were the concern of Christendom, and were deemed to be in the category of history. The fact that they were written in a racy style, with wholesale condemnation of international figures, made them all the more attractive. It seems safe to say that though Francesco Filelfo's came a close second, Piccolomini's letters were the most popular humanistic ones of the Renaissance. Piccolomini had also written in about 1444 his *De duobus amantibus historia*, the first epistolary novel of modern times. It was first published in 1473 and reprinted about twenty times prior to 1500; by then, too, there were translations in German, Italian, French and Spanish.[59] Piccolomini also wrote a tract in the letter form: *Epistola de Curialium miseriis,* likewise first printed in 1473. It was Piccolomini's writings in the letter form that were the taste-makers, though it is fair to say, too, that the advent of printing created the opportunity.

Scholars are often known for their sharpness rather than for their humility and kindness. Even so, the second half of the fifteenth century witnessed excessive acrimony and vituperation among scholars. There had been an over-production of humanists in the first half of the century, and, as it progressed, patrons increasingly turned from the scholarly pursuits of the cult of Antiquity to its more practical manifestations: building and the acquisition of works of art. Progressively, therefore, humanists found it more difficult to find a post, and any they did obtain tended to be poorly re-munerated.[60] A consequence of this was that frustrated and bitter scholars zealously criticised one another as rivals. Scholars were quick to appreciate the value of the press as a means of bringing their work and their criticisms to notice. This affected the use of the letter form in two ways. From the 1480s, if not in the decade before, there developed the use of the tract, written in the form of an *epistola,* for scholarly altercation. Thus in Venice, where printing was well established by 1480, Cornelio Vitelli (*c.* 1450–*c.* 1502), who was teaching privately and was embroiled with Giorgio Merula (1431–1494), Professor of Eloquence at the Studio there, printed one such *epistola* in reply to others directed by Merula against Francesco Filelfo. A now lost collection of letters written by Niccolò Perotti (*c.* 1430–80), assembled by Annio da Viterbo (1432–1502), was really an attack in letter form on Domizio Calderini (*c.* 1446–78), a fellow scholar.[61] Such was the background to the letter form selected for the celebrated 'De imitatione' dispute between Gianfrancesco Pico della Mirandola and Pietro Bembo, first printed in 1518, and to Baldassare Castiglione's biography of Duke Guidobaldo of Urbino, likewise printed for the first time in that same year.[62] These tracts and slender treatises written in the form of a letter were often of ephemeral interest and are known today in a few printed examples only, while being sometimes better represented in manuscript. It is, in consequence, impossible to hazard a guess as to their quantity in the last two decades of the fifteenth century. The second development in the use of the letter form concerned prefatory, dedication and presentation letters. These, of course, had been employed by humanists from the time of Petrarch, but their number increased rapidly in the second half of the fifteenth century.[63] The reason was that in their thrusting for patronage humanists wrote more creative works than had been the case in the first hundred years of the Italian Renaissance from 1350. Wealthy patrons received, presentation gifts of the humanists' work; between about 1468 and his death in 1482 Federigo da Montefeltro, for instance, was donated at least thirty such.[64] Often the work was furnished with a dedicatory or presentation letter. Scholars gave their works to their colleagues much as they distribute offprints today, and often each copy had a presentation letter inside, which was carefully preserved with the work donated; Bernardo Bembo (1433–1519), the father of Pietro, had several such items in his library. A printed volume with a dedication letter to a potential patron might be accompanied by a presentation letter in manuscript which was addressed to another person.[65]

Interest in letter collections and the letter form resulted in manuals in Latin and eventually in Italian dealing with the niceties of letter writing.[66] One of the most influential, perhaps in some measure because it was the first to be printed and also since it covered orations, was Agostino Dati's *Elegantiolae* [Cologne, 1470?], of which there were some fifty-six printings at least by 1500. The *Epistolares formulae* of Charles Menniken (in Latin: Carolus Viruli) (b. *c.* 1410), a teacher in the Arts Faculty of the University of Louvain from 1435 until his death in 1493, was published first in 1476. This work was rather more regional than Dati's in its influence, as is suggested by the fact that almost all the twenty-seven printings that appeared by 1500 were in the Low Countries and Germany. Menniken's book was probably the one used most commonly in the schools of the Brethren of the Common Life, and was possibly the textbook prescribed for Erasmus in his youth. The works of Dati and of Menniken represent what can be seen as two opposed methods of instruction, the one preferred in Italy, the other in the north. Dati's approach was scholarly and directed to the intelligent and advanced student and, as what may be called its subtitle implies (*Libellus pro conficiendis epistolis et orationibus*), was essentially concerned with the language and expression of a Latin letter or oration; it provided examples of grammatical usage culled from classical sources. The work contained no definition of the nature of a letter or any model letters. Menniken's work, on the other hand, as its title made clear, was a formulary and in the tradition of Barzizza's fictitious collection. It consisted of 337 letters which could be used to provide a model letter for every occasion. His manual was directed to the young and to the less capable pupils. While it could be said that Menniken's Latin was not a faithful Ciceronian model in its idioms, the author had consciously sought to imitate in the letters he provided both those of Antiquity and such of the humanist tradition as were available to him, and in particular those of the printed collections of Bruni and of Piccolomini.

Erasmus appears not to have left a record of his views of Dati, but he deemed Menniken a mediocre scholar.[67] Moreover Erasmus's *Opus de conscribendis epistolis* opposed Menniken's theory of how to teach, and can be considered as an attack on the medieval *formulae* for letter writing. In the tradition of the *ars dictaminis* going back to Alberis of Monte Cassino in the eleventh century, every letter was divided into five: *salutatio, captatio benevolentiae, narratio, petitio, conclusio*. These divisions had been vested with the authority of Cicero by Alberis, and were so accepted by many of the fifteenth-century scholars. Erasmus, however, was opposed to such division, which he believed to be artificial and not supported by the letters of the ancient world. Not surprisingly, therefore, Erasmus had little favourable to say of the letter-writing manuals that preceded his own. In a letter of November 1499 to Lord Mountjoy he poured scorn on the *Modus epistolandi*, of Francesco Nigri (1452–d. after 1523), which had first appeared in print in Venice in 1488.[68] This work appears like a revision of Menniken's formulary, and indeed it came to supersede Menniken's in the schools of the Low Countries and neighbouring Germany—there were twenty-six printings in the first twelve years of its existence.

Giovanni Mario Filelfo published his manual on letter writing in 1484 in Milan, and it was only twice reprinted, one of these occasions being 1486 in Louvain. Erasmus was familiar with this work, and condemned it to Lord Mountjoy as confused and unsatisfactory. He also mentioned, somewhat more kindly, the chapter that Niccolò Perotti had written ('De componendis epistolis') in his grammar, first published in 1473, and frequently reprinted, and Giovanni Sulpizio's *De componendis et ornandis epistolis*, first published in Rome about 1490 and only once reprinted.[69] Sulpizio wanted the best of both worlds, for he published also a treatise on the art of oratory.[70] There were two other letter manuals that enjoyed only a moderate success; first a *Modus epistolandi* published twice in Rome by Bartholomaeus Guldinbeck, about 1475 and again about 1485, which was a work fathered on Poggio Bracciolini to give it humanistic authority but whose real author remains unknown; secondly a treatise with the same title printed in Cologne about 1480 which was the work of Frater Guillermus Saphonensis and had four further printings.

A miscellany consisting of short treatises on letter writing, together with some letters written by Giovanni de Veris and other allied material, exists in a unique manuscript that was copied from a now lost original within a few years of the latter's compilation.[71] Evidence suggests that the collection, which includes some humanistic orations and poems as well as the epistolary material, was formed by De Veris about 1467–69, when he was a teacher in the Arts Faculty at Louvain; possibly the compilation was made in part, at least, to assist him in his teaching. A treatise included bears the title 'Magistri Anthonii Han[e]ron dictandi epistolandique precepta incipiunt ornatissima', and Haneron had been a teacher in the same faculty at Louvain as De Veris from 1430 to 1441; at least one fifteenth-century printing of his *Ars epistolandi* was printed, but with no place of printing, no printer's name and no date, though it is usually assigned to the mid-1470s.[72] There are also 109 fictitious letters from the formulary of Menneken (likewise of Louvain, be it remembered), which are different from those published in the formulary of 1476. There is also a very brief manual, 'De arte dicendi precepta', copied twice, which at the time of its inclusion was attributed independently to Guarino and to Lorenzo Valla, though actually could not be the work of either, and its author is unknown: it is not Valla's 'De conficendis epistolis libellus'.[73] De Veris's correspondents in the miscellany were all Flemings, and among them was an illegitimate son of Duke Philip of Burgundy, Raffaele Marcatelli, Abbot of St Peter's, Oudenburg, near Bruges. Material transcribed, however, which includes letters from the fictitious collection of Barzizza and from Poggio Bracciolini, as well as the treatises ascribed to Guarino and Valla, indicates that De Veris looked to Italy. Thus the miscellany is a fascinating example of the process of cross-fertilisation of the northern Renaissance with the Italian.

The part that notaries played in transmitting the Roman epistolary form has been mentioned, and among early printed books were manuals for the notary. Examples of these are now very rare, presumably since they disintegrated in consequence of frequent use; *Ars Notariatus* is the title commonly found at the head of editions of these manuals. All the copies of the various fifteenth-century printings that I have examined cover the same ground—contracts, wills, codicils and suchlike—and none mentions the art of writing letters or provides a formulary.[74] Accordingly, contrary to what might be expected, the *Ars Notariatus* had no influence on the growth of interest in the letter and letter collections of the fifteenth century.

Let Erasmus have the last word: to Beatus Rhenanus he wrote that the word 'letter' should not be applied to those letters that were really conceived as books. That he was thinking of Ovid's *Heroides*, of Apollinaris Sidonius, Jerome, Cyprian and Augustine is confirmed by his *Opus de conscribendis epistolis*, where such works are scarcely mentioned.[75] These writings appear to have played no significant part in stimulating the letter collections of the humanists. One may perhaps conclude that Erasmus's view, probably not unrepresentative, explains the lack of popularity and influence of Petrarch's letter collections.

THE METHOD USED FOR THE COMPILATION OF APPENDICES 4.1–5 INCLUSIVE

The lists given in appendices 4.1–5 are probably not complete, in that some printings, particularly of the manuals of letter writing, which were used as school books, are likely to have disappeared entirely. On the other hand, since many early printings are undated and without the name of the printer or even the place of origin, efforts have been made to ensure that a list has not been falsely inflated by including more than once what is in fact a single printing or edition that has been attributed differently as to place, printer and date by several authorities. The copies are to be found in: F. R. Goff, *Incunabula in American Libraries: a Third Census*, New York, revised edition, 1973; *British Museum: General Catalogue of Printed Books to 1955*, London, 1964–65, with the revisions incorporated in *Short-title Catalogue of Books Printed in Italy . . .*, London, 1958, *Short-title Catalogue of Books Printed in the Netherlands and Belgium . . .*, London, 1965; M.-F. and A.-C. Campbell, *Annales de la typographie neerlandais au XVe siècle*, The Hague, 1874; 'Indice generale degli incunaboli delle Biblioteche d'Italia', *Ministero della Pubblica Istruzione. Indice e Cataloghi*, new series, I, Rome, 1943–73, I–V. The defects in both Campbell and the 'Indice generale . . .' have meant that these have been used with caution.

R. Bertieri, *Editori e stampatori italiani del Quattrocento. Note bio-bibliografiche*, Milan, 1929, is still useful for details of many of the Italian printers.

APPENDIX 4.1

THE LETTER COLLECTIONS OF THE HUMANISTS PRINTED PRIOR TO 1501

BARZIZZA, Gasperino da; also known simply as GASPARINUS

1470   *Liber epistolarum* (Paris, [Ulrich Gering, Martin Crantz, and Michael Friburger, 1470]).

1472?   — (Basel, Michael Wenszler and Friedrich Biel, [not after 1 December 1472?]).

1472?   — ([Basel, Martin Flach, 1472?]).

1480?   — ([Basel, Ulrich Gering, 1480?]).
1483?   — ([Reutlingen, Johann Otmar, 1483?]).
1485?   — ([Deventer, Richard Pafraet, 1485?]).
1485?   — ([Louvain, Johann de Westfalia, 1485?]).
1486   — ([Strassburg], Johann Prüss, 24 December 1486).
1487   — ([Deventer], Jacob de Breda, 1487).
1492?   — (Deventer, Jacob de Breda, [1492?]).
1498-9   — (Paris, Guy Marchant, 16 February 1498-9).
1499?   — ([Basel, Michael Furter, not after 1499]).

BESSARION

1471   [*Epistolae et orationes de arcendis Turcis a Christianorum finibus*]. Ed. Guillaume
           Fichet ([Paris, Ulrich Gering, Martin Crantz and Michael Friburger,
           April 1471]).
1500   — ([Paris], Guy Marchant, 21 October 1500).

BRUNI, Leonardo

1472   *Epistolarum familiarum liber primus (–octavus)*. Ed. Antonio Moreto and
           Girolamo Squarciafico ([Venice, A. Moreto?], 1472).
1483?   — ([Louvain, R. Loeffs, 1483?]).
1495   — Ed. A. Moreto and G. Squarciafico ([Venice, begun Damiano da
           Gorganzola; finished Pietro de Quarenghi], 15 June 1495).[76]
1495   — ([Basel, Johann Amerbach, 1495]).
1499   — nonus. Ed. J. Honorius (Leipzig, Jacob Thanner [after 27 October],
           1499).

FILELFO, Francesco

1472-3?   *Epistolarum liber primus (–decimussextus)* ([Venice, Vindelinus de Spira, 1472
           or 1473]).
1481?   — ([Basel, Johann Amerbach, 1481?, and certainly not after 1488]).
1485   — (Brescia, Jacopo de' Britannici, 1485).
1487   — (Venice, Studio of Giovanni Rosso [Joannes Rubens], January 1487).
1488-90?   — ([Deventer, Richard Pafraet, 1488-90?]).
1489   — (Venice, Studio of Bernardino de' Cori, 1489).
1492   *Epistolae* (Venice, Filippo Pinzi, 1492).
1493?   — ([Paris], Félix Balligault, 1493).
1493-4   — (Venice, [Bernardino Benali], 1493-4).
1495   *Epistolae familiares* (Venice, Matteo Codecá, at the expense of Ottaviano
           Scoto, 1495).
1495?   — ([Deventer, Richard Pafraet, 1495?]).
1495?   — ([Basel, Johann Amerbach, 1495?]).
1496?   — ([Basel, Johann Amerbach, 1496?]).
1498   *Epistolae*. Ed. Jean Petit ([Paris], Félix Balligault, 30 April 1498).
1498   — (Venice, Giovanni Tacuino, 20 September 1498).
1499   *Epistolae breviores* (Deventer, Richard Pafraet, 1499).
1500   *Epistolae* (Basel, Nikolaus Kessler, 1500).
1500   — (Venice, Joannes and Gregorius de' Gregoriis, 1500).

PICCOLOMINI, Aeneas Silvius

1473   [*Epistolae in Pontificatu editae*; also known as *Epistolae de Conventu Mantuano*]
           (Milan, Antonio Zaroto, 25 May 1473).
1475   [*Epistolae in Cardinalatu editae*; also known as *Epistolae familiares*] (Rome,
           Johann Schurener, 14 July 1475).

1475? — Ed. Nikolas von Wyle ([Esslingen?, 1475?]).

1476 — (Paris, [Louis Simonel, Richard Blandin, Jean Simon and Co.], 'in Vico Sancti Jacobi ad intersignium virisis follis', 3 January 1476).

1476? —, *orationes et tractatus*, ed. Nikolas von Wyle ([Strassburg, Adolph Rusch, before 1478, 1476?]). Includes a collection of other letters, for which see appendix 4.2.

1476? — ([Cologne, Arnold der Hoernen, 1476?]). Includes a collection of other letters, for which see appendix 4.2.

1477 — ([Louvain, Jan Veldener], 1477). Includes a collection of other letters, for which see appendix 4.2.

1477? — ([Rome, Bartholomaeus Guldinbeck, 1477?]).

1478 —, *orationes et tractatus* ([Cologne], Johann Koelhoff, dated 1458 for 1478). Includes a collection of other letters, for which see appendix 4.2.

1478–80? — ([Rome, Johann Bulle, 1478–80?]).

1481 [*Epistolae in Pontificatu editae*]. Ed. P. A. Filelfo (Milan, Antonio Zaroto, 'impendio' Giovanni da Legnano, 31 May 1481).

1481 [*Epistolae in Cardinalatu editae*] *orationes et tractatus* (Nürnberg, Anton Koberger, 16 September 1481). Includes a collection of other letters, for which see appendix 4.2.

1483 — (Louvain, Johann de Westfalia, 1483). Includes a collection of other letters, for which see appendix 4.2.

1486 — (Nürnberg, Anton Koberger, 17 July 1486). Includes a collection of other letters, for which see appendix 4.2.

1487 [*Epistolae in Pontificatu editae*] ([Milan], Antonio Zaroto, 'impendio' Giovanni Pietro da Novara, October 1487).

1490? [*Epistolae in Cardinalatu editae*] ([Rome, Stephan Plannck, 1490?]).

1490? — ([Rome, Eucharius Silber, 1490?]).

1496 —, *et varii tractatus* (Nürnberg, Anton Koberger, 17 May 1496). Includes a collection of other letters, for which see appendix 4.2.

1496 —— Ed. A. Archintus and rev. J. Vinzalius (Milan, Ulrich Scinzenzeler, 10 December 1496). Includes a collection of other letters, for which see appendix 4.2.

1497 —— (Lyons, Jean de Vingle, 1497). Includes a collection of other letters, for which see appendix 4.2.

BECCADELLI, Antonio (PANORMITA)

1475? *Epistolae familiares*, I, II ([Naples, Sixtus Riessinger, 1475?]).

FILELFO, Giovanni Maria

1489 *Epistolae* (Bologna, Bertochus Bacileriis, 1489).

1492 — (Venice, Giovanni [Tacuino] de Tridino, 1492).

1498? — (Venice, Giovanni Tacuino, 1492 for 1498?).

PETRARCA, Francesco

1492 *Epistolae familiares*. Ed. S. Manilio (Venice, Joannes and Gregorius de Gregoriis, 13 September 1492).

1496 [*Opera latina*] Ed. Sebastian Brant? (Basel, Johann Amerbach, 1496).

FICINO, Marsilio

1495 *Epistolae* (Venice, Matteo Capcasa of Codecá, for Girolamo Blondo, 11 March 1495).

1497 — ([Nürnberg], Anton Koberger, 24 February 1497).

CAMPANO, Giovanni Antonio

1495 [*Opera*]. Ed. Michele Ferni of Milan (Rome, Eucharius Silber, 31 October 1495).

PICO DELLA MIRANDOLA, Giovanni

1495/6   [*Opera*]. Ed. Giovanni Francesco Pico della Mirandola (Bologna, Benedetto Faelli, 2 vols., 1495, 1496).

1498   *Opera omnia* (Venice, Bernardino [dei Vitali], 2 parts, 9 October and 14 August 1498). This contains also the letters of Giovanni Francesco Pico della Mirandola.

AMBROGINI, Angelo (POLIZIANO)

1498   *Omnia opera*. Ed. A. Sarzio (Venice, Aldo Manuzio, July 1498).

1499   — Ed. Leonardo degli Arrighi, Florence ([Brescia, Bernardino Misinta], 1499).

PICO DELLA MIRANDOLA, Giovanni Francesco

1498   See above under PICO DELLA MIRANDOLA, Giovanni.

GAGUIN, Robert

1498   *Epistolae et orationes* ([Paris, D. Gerlerus, 1498]).

1498?   — (Paris, Félix Balligault, [1498]).

BOSSO, Matteo[77]

1498   *Epistolae familiares et secundae* (Mantua, Vincenzo Bertocco, 9 November 1498).

1502   *Epistolarum, tertia pars* (Venice, Bernardo de' Vitali, 13 August 1502).

APPENDIX 4.2

ANTHOLOGIES AND SELECTIONS OF LETTERS OF HUMANISTS
AND OTHERS PRINTED PRIOR TO 1520

1476?   A. S. Piccolomini [*Epistolae in Cardinalatu editae*], *orationes et tractatus*. Ed. Nikolas von Wyle ([Strassburg, Adolph Rusch, before 1478, 1476?]). Added to the collection of Piccolomini's letters as originally printed were N. de Wyle's 'Epistola omnibus et singulis humanitatis studio deditis', with letters that in many cases were not addressed to Piccolomini (though some may have derived from his archives), being from 'Ferdinandus Rex Aragoniae, Franciscus Foscari, Fridericus III Imperator, Gaspar Novariensis, Julianus Cesarinus Card. S. Angeli, Hannibal Dux Numidiae, Venceslaus Scriba'.

1476?   — ([Cologne, Arnold der Hoernen, 1476?]). Added letters are from 'Alphonsus Rex Aragonum, Nicolaus Amidanus, Bartholomaeus Ep. Cornetanus, Stephanus Cacia, Johannes Campegius, Antonius Fortunius, Fridericus IV Imperator, Michael Fullenderphius, Gaspar Novariensis, Johannes [de Torrecremata] Card. S. Sixti, Johannes Custos Varadiensis Ecclesiae, Julianus [Cesarius] Card. S. Angeli, Gregorius Lollius, Adam de Mulin, Nicolaus PP V, Petrus Noxetanus, Franciscus de Picciolpassis, Franciscus Ptolomaeus, Franciscus Quadratus, Richardus Valentinus, Sbigneus Card. S. Priscae et Ep. Cracoviensis, Gaspar Schlick, Sigismundus Dux Austriae, Marianus Soccinus, Venceslaus Bohemus, Venceslaus Scriba'.

1477   — ([Louvain, Jan Veldener], 1477). Added letters are from 'Nicolaus Amidanus, Jacobus Arcimboldus, Bartholomaeus Ep. Cornetanus, Johannes Campegius, Andreas Contarius, David Imperator Trapassundarum, Andreas Donatus, Borsius De Este, Bartholomaeus Fatius, Antonius Fortunius, Fridericus III Imperator, Gaspar Novariensis, Georgius Rex

Persarum, Gorgora Dux Georgianae, Johannes De Turrecremata Card. S. Sixti, Julianus [Cesarinus] Card. S. Angeli, Nicolaus Liscius, Georgius Lollius, Gregorius Lollius, Ludovicus XI Rex Francorum, Adam de Mulin, Petrus Noxetanus, Johannes Peregallus, Franciscus de Picciolpassis, Poggius Florentinus, Franciscus Pychonius, Franciscus Quadratus, Richardus Valentinus, Gaspar Schlick, Franciscus Sfortia, Marianus Soccinus, Ambrosius Traversarius, Venceslaus Bohemus, Venceslaus Scriba'.

1478   —, *orationes et tractatus* ([Cologne], Johann Koelhoff, dated 1458 for 1478). Added to the letters from correspondents listed under ([Louvain], 1477) above are those from 'Calixtus PP III, Carolus VII Rex Francorum, Lodrisius Crebellus, S. Johannes de Capistranis, Johannes Chrysostomus Ep. Constantinopolitanus'; omitted from the correspondents is 'Antonius Fortunius'.

1481   —, *orationes et tractatus* (Nürnberg, Anton Koberger, 16 September 1481). Added to the letters from correspondents, listed under the ([Cologne] 1478) above are those from 'Leonardus Brunus, Cristernus Rex Daciae, Hannibal Dux Numidiae'; omitted from the correspondents is 'Antonius Fortunius'.

1483   — (Louvain, Johann de Westfalia, 1483). The supplementary collection is precisely that of ([Cologne], 1478) above.

1486   — (Nürnberg, Anton Koberger, 17 July 1486). The supplementary collection is that of (Nürnberg, 1481) with 'Franciscus Foscari' added.

1496   —, *et varii tractatus* (Nürnberg, Anton Koberger, 17 May 1496). The supplementary collection is precisely that of (Nürnberg, 1486).

1496   ——. Ed. A. Archintus and J. Vinzalius (Milan, Ulrich Scinzenzeler, 10 December 1496). Added to the letters from correspondents listed under (Nürnberg, 1481) are those from 'Stephanus Cacia, Antonius Fortunius, Franciscus Foscari, Michael Fullendorphius, Johannes [de Carvajal] Card. S. Angeli, Sbigneus Card. S. Priscae et Ep. Cracoviensis'. Omitted, however, is 'Hannibal Dux Numidiae'.

1497   —— (Lyons, Jean de Vingle, 1497). There is an introduction by A. Archintus. The supplementary collection is precisely that of (Nürnberg, 1486).

1499   *Epistolae illustrium virorum.* Ed. Anton Koberger ([Lyons], Nikolaus Wolff, 13 February 1499). The letters included are from 'Tydeus Acciarinus, Michael Acciarinus, Jacobus Antiquarius, Hermolaus Barbarus, Johannes Franciscus Benedictus, Philippus Beroaldus, Matthaeus Bossus, Filippo Bonaccorsi, Caesar Carmentus, Bartholomaeus Chalcus, Paulus Cortesius, Petrus Crinitus, Hieronymus Donatus, Lucius Fazini, Marsilius Ficinus, Scipione Fortiguerra, Maffeo Fosforo, Baptista Guarinus, Innocentius PP VIII, Johannes II, Pomponius Laetus, Nicolaus Leonicenus, Augustinus Maffeus, Aldus Manutius, Lorenzo de' Medici, Georgius Merula, Macarius Mutius, Ludovicus Odaxius, Pius PP III, Jacopo Piccolomini, Johannes Picus, Angelo Poliziano, Franciscus Puccius, Antonius Sabellicus, Bartholomaeus Scala, Lodovico Maria Sforza, Baccius Ugolinus, Antonius Urceus Codrus'.

1500   F. Filelfo, *Brevioresel egantioresque Epistolae . . . ex eiusdem toto epistolarum volumine . . . collectae*; with fifteen letters of A. Poliziano (Deventer, Jacob de Breda, 1500).

1508   The above collection of letters of Filelfo and Poliziano, to which was added Giovanni Pico della Mirandola's *Auree epistole* (Antwerp, 1508).

1513   The collection of letters of Filelfo and Poliziano, as under 1500 above (Strassburg, 1513).

1516   The collection of letters of Filelfo and Poliziano, as under 1500 above (Tübingen, Thomas Anshelm Badensis, 1516).

1519   The collection of letters of Filelfo and Poliziano, as under 1500 above,
         with a selection of the letters of Seneca added (Augsburg, Silvan Otmar,
         1519).

APPENDIX 4.3

THE LETTER COLLECTIONS OF CLASSICAL ROME
PRINTED PRIOR TO 1501

CICERO, Marcus Tullius

1 *Epistolae ad familiares*

1467   *Epistolae ad familiares* (Rome, Conrad Sweynheym and Arnold Pannartz,
         1467).
1469   — ([Venice, Joannes de Spira], 1469).
1469   Another printing ([Venice], Joannes [de Spira], 1469).
1469   —. Ed. J. Andreae (Rome, Conrad Sweynheym and Arnold Pannartz,
         4 November 1469).
1470   — ([Venice, Vindelinus de Spira], 1471).
1470?   — (Foligno, Emiliano [Orfini] and Johann Numeister [1470?]).
1471   —([Venice, Vindelinus de Spira], 1471).
1471   — ([Venice, Adam de Ambergau], 1471).
1471   — ([Venice], Nicolas Jenson, 1471).
1472?   —. Ed. Giuliano de' Merli (Milan, [Panfilo Castaldi, before April 1472]).
1472   — ([Mondovì, Antonio di Mattia and Baldassare Corderio], 1472).
1472   —([Milan], Filippo da Lavagna, 25 March 1472).
1472   — (Rome, Conrad Sweynheym and Arnold Pannartz, 5 September 1472).
1474   — (Naples, Arnald de Bruxelles, 7 August 1474).
1475   — ([Venice], Nicolas Jenson, 1475).
1475   — (Venice, Filippo di Pietro], 1475).
1475   —(Milan, Antonio Zaroto, 20 September 1475).
1476   — ([Venice, Thomasius de Blavis], 1476).
1476   — (Milan, Antonio Zaroto, 24 November 1476).
1476?   — (Milano, Filippo da Lavagna, [1476?]).
1477   — (Venice, Jacopo da Fivizzano, 1477).
1477   — (Milan, Filippo da Lavagna, 19 March 1477).
1478   — (Milan, Filippo da Lavagna, 1478).
1479   — (Milan, Leonhard [Pachel] and Ulrich [Scinzenzeler], 18 March 1479).
1480   — (Milan, Giovanni Antonio and Benigno d'Onate, 8 February 1480).
1480   — (Milan, Leonhard Pachel and Ulrich Scinzenzeler, 22 April 1480).
1480   —. Commentary of Hubertinus Clericus [Crescintinas] (Venice, 1 July
         1480).
1480   — (Venice, Filippo di Pietro, 5 August 1480).
1481   — (Venice, [Baptista de Tortis], 1481).
1482   —. Ed. Giovanni da Legnano (Milan, Antonio Zaroto, 12 February 1482).
1482   — (Parma, Andreas Portilia, 24 April 1482).
1482   —. Commentary of Hubertinus Clericus (Venice, Baptista de Tortis, 24
         May 1482).
1483   —. Commentary of Hubertinus Clericus (Venice, Andrea Torresano and
         Bartholomaeuse de Blavis, 31 January 1483).
1483   —. Commentary of Hubertinus Clericus (Milan, Leonhard Pachel and
         Ulrich Scinzenzeler, 1 February 1483).
1485   — (Venice, Baptista de Tortis, 24 May 1485).
1485   —. Commentary of Hubertinus Clericus (Milan, Leonhard Pachel and
         Ulrich Scinzenzeler, 26 August 1485).
1487   —. Commentary of Hubertinus Clericus (Venice, Andrea [Paltasichi],
         18 June 1487).

1488   —. Commentary of Hubertinus Clericus (Venice, Andrea Paltasichi, 14 May 1488).

1488   —. Commentary of Hubertinus Clericus (Venice, Bernardinus de Choris, 5 December 1488).

1489   —. Commentary of Hubertinus Clericus (Milan, Ulrich Scinzenzeler, 1489).

1491   —, *cum tribus commentis* (Venice, [Bernardinus de Choris], 1491).

1491   —. Commentary of Clericus and three others (Venice, [Filippo Pinzi], 20 September 1491).

1492   —. Has four commentaries (Venice, Bartolomeo Zani, 19 October 1492).

1493   — —, (Milan, Ulrich Scinzenzeler, 26 April 1493).

1493   — — (Venice, Bernardino Benali, 21 May 1493).

1494   — —. Ed. Ottaviano Scoto (Venice, Boneto Locatello and Cristoforo de' Persi, 22 September 1494).

1495   — — (Venice, Simone Bevilacqua, 26 June 1495).

1496   — — (Milan, Leonhard Pachel, 17 August 1496).

1496   — ([Lyons], Jean de Vingle, 1496).

1497   — — (Venice, Simone Bevilacqua, 1497).

1499   — — (Milan, Leonhard Pachel, 15 January 1499).

1500   — — (Venice, Bartolomeo Zani, 16 December 1500).

2 *Epistolae ad Brutum, ad Quintum fratrem, ad Atticum*

1470   *Ad M. Brutum & ceteros epistolae.* Ed. J. Andreae (Rome, Conrad Sweynheym and Arnold Pannartz, 1470).

1470   *Epistolae ad Atticum, Brutum et Quintum fratrem cum Attici vita* ([Venice], Nicolas Jenson, 1470).

1490   *Epistolae ad Brutum, et alios.* Ed. B. Salicetus and L. Regius (Rome, Eucharius Silber, 17 July 1490).

1495?   — ([Venice, Filippo Pinzi, 1495?]).

1499   — (Venice, [Filippo Pinzi], 12 June 1499).

3 *Selections*

(a) *General in Latin*

1477?   *Epistolae selectae* (Rome, Bartholomaeus Guldinbeck, [1477?]).

1480?   — (Naples, Francesco di Dino, [not after 1480]).

1485?   — (Rome, Bartholomaeus Guldinbeck, [1485?]).

1485?   —. Ed. Martino Filetico ([Rome, Eucharius Silber, 1485?]).

1488?   —. Ed. Martino Filetico ([Naples, Francesco del Tuppo, 1488?]).

1492   — (Rome, Stephan Plannck. 9 January 1492).

(b) *General in Latin and in Italian*

1480?   *In flosculis epistolarum Ciceronis Vernacula interpretatio*, ed. G. Valagussa (Milan, Antonio Zaroto, 1480?).

1498   — (Venice, Manfredus de Monteferrato, April 1498).

(c) *Ad Familiares in Latin*

1485?   *Epistolae ... ex libro Epist. Familiarium excerptae* (Rome, Eucharius Silber, [1485?]).

1489   — ([Siena, Henricus de Colonia], 7 October 1489).

4 *Collected works*

1498–9   *Opera.* Ed. Alessandro Minuziano. Four vols. (Milan, Guillaume Le Seignerre fratres, 1498–9).

SENECA, Lucius Annaeus

1 *Epistolae*

1470?   *Epistolae* ([Strassburg, A. Rusch, 1470?]).
1475   — (Rome, Arnold Pannartz, 1475).
1475   — (Paris, [Louis Simonel, Richard Blandin, Jean Simon and Co.], 147[5]).
1493   — (Leipzig, Arnold de Cologne, 1493).
1495   — (Leipzig, Arnold de Cologne, 1495).

2 *Collected works*

1475   *Liber de moribus* [and other works]. (*Liber epistolarum*). Ed. B. Romerus, two parts (Naples, Mathias Moravus, 1475).
1478   — — (Treviso, Bernardinus de Colonia, 1478).
1490   *Seneca moralis.* [*Epistolae*]. Two parts (Venice, Bernardinus [de Choris] and S. de Luere, 1490).
1492   *Omnia opera.* Another edition (Venice, Bernardinus de Choris, 31 October 1492).
1495?   *Opera.* Another edition ([Venice, Joannes and Gregorius de Gregoriis, 1495?]).

PLINIUS DAECILIUS SECUNDUS, Caius

1 *Epistolae*

1471   *Epistolarum liber primus(-octavus).* Ed. Lodovico Carbone ([Venice, Christopher Valdarfer], 1471).
1474–5? — ([Rome, Johann Schurener, 1474–5?]).
1476   —. Ed. J. Maius (Naples, Mathias Moravus, July 1476).
1478   — (Milan, Filippo da Lavagna, 26 February 1478).
1483   — (Treviso, Joannes Rubeus, i.e. G. Rosso, 1483).
1490   —. Ed. P. Laetus (Rome, Eucharius Silber, [after 19 March] 1490).
1498   —. Ed. Filippo Beroaldo (Bologna, Benedetto Faelli, 19 October 1498).

2 *Collected works*

1492   *Opera.* With other works ([Venice, Joannes Roscius, 1492?]).
1500   —. Ed. Filippo Beroaldo (Venice, Albertinus Vercellensis, 20 April 1500).
1500?   — — ([Venice, Joannes Rubeus, 1500?]).

APPENDIX 4.4

THE ANCIENT GREEK LETTER COLLECTIONS
PRINTED PRIOR TO 1501

PHALARIS

Latin translation

1468–9? *Epistolae*, Latin translation by Francesco Griffolino of Arezzo (dedicated to Malatesta Novello) ([Rome, Ulrich Han (Udalricus Gallus), 1468–9?]).
1470–1? —. Ed. G. A. Campano ([Rome, Ulrich Han, 1470–1?]).
1471   — ([Milan, Filippo da Lavagna], 1471).
1471   — (Treviso, Geraert [van de Leyden], 1471).
1471–2? — ([Bologna, Balthasar Azoguidus, 1471–72?]).
1471–2? — ([Paris, Ulrich Gering, Martin Crantz and Michael Friburger, 1471–1472?]).
1472?   — ([Venice, Printer of Duns, *Quaestiones*, 1472?]).
1472?   — ([Naples]?, Sixtus Riessinger?, 1472?]).
1473?   — (Brescia, Thoma Ferrando, 1 September [1473?]).

1474?   — ([Naples, Printer of Silvaticus, 1474?]).

1474–5?   — ([Rome, Johannes Gensberg, 1474?]).

1475   — (Santorso, province of Vicenza, Johannes de Reno, 1475).

1475   — ([Rome, Johannes Reynard], 1475).

1475?   — (Cologne, Johannes Koelhoff, [1475?]).

1475?   — ([Albi, province of Catanzaro, Printer of Pius II, 1475?]).

1475?   — ([Rome?, 1475?]).

1475?   — ([Valencia, Lambert Palmart, 1475?]).

1476   — ([Italy, Printer of Cornazzano], 18 July 1476).

1478–80?   — (Messina, Henricus Alding, [1478–80?]).

1479   — (Pavia, Francesco da San Pietro, 21 August 1479).

1479–80?   — ([Rome, Stephan Plannck, 1479–80?]).

1481   — (Venice, [Antonio di Alessandria della Paglia et Socii], 10 March 1481).

1481–7?   — ([Rome, Stephan Plannck, 1481–87?]).

1484   — (Milan, Antonio Zaroto, 29 April 1484).

1485   —, with other works (Oxford, Theodore Rood and Thomas Hunte, [1485]).

1487–8?   — (Florence, Antonio de Francesco, Venetus, [1487–88?]).

1490?   — ([?], [1490?]).

1490–1?   — ([Venice, Maximus de Butricis, 1490–91?]).

1493   — (Paris, Guy Marchant, 3 September 1493).

1495?   — ([Venice, Filippo Pinzi, 1495?]).

1496   — (Valencia, Nicolaus Spindeler, 2 November 1496).

1498   —. Ed. J. H. Crispus (Leipzig, Jacob Thanner, 31 May 1498).

Greek text

1498   Ἐπιστολαί, and other letters. Ed. Bartholomaeus Justinopolitanus ([Venice], Bartholomaeus Pelusius, Gabriel Bracius, Johann Bissolus and Benedictus Mangius, 18 June 1498).

1499   *Epistolae Diuersorum Philosophorum Graecorum*. Ed. M. Musurus (Venice, Aldo Manuzio, two parts, March, April, 1499); the supposed letters of Phalaris are in part II.

Italian translation from the Latin

1471   *Le epistole di Phalari*, trans. Bartolomeo della Fonte (Fonzio), from the Latin of Francesco Griffolino ([Padua, Laurentius Canozius], 1471), also attributed ([Florence?, Printer of Mesue, *Opera*], 1471).[79]

1474–5?   —, trans. Giovanni Andrea Ferabò ([Naples, Printer of Silvaticus, 1474–1475?]).

PLATO

Latin translation

1472   *Epistolae*. Latin translation by Leonardo Bruni[79] ([Paris, Ulrich Gering, Martin Crantz and Michael Friburger, 1472]).

1490?   —. Latin translation by Marsilio Ficino; edited by Paulus Niavis ([Leipzig, Conrad Kachelofen, 1490?]).

Greek text

1499   *Epistolae Diuersorum Philosophorum Graecorum* (Venice, Aldo Manuzio, two parts, March, April, 1499); see also under 'Phalaris', above.

DIOGENES THE CYNIC, BRUTUS, HIPPOCRATES

Latin translation of Diogenes

1475?　　*Epistolae.* Latin translation by Francesco Griffolino of Arezzo (Nürnberg, Friedrich Creussner, [1475?]).

Latin translation of Diogenes, Brutus and Hippocrates

1487　　*Epistolae.* Latin translation of Diogenes by Griffolino, as under 1475? above; Latin translation of Brutus and Hippocrates by A. Rinuccini (Florence, Antonio de Francesco, 'Veneto', 22 June 1487).

1492　　— (Florence, Antonio de Francesco, 'Veneto', 22 June 1487, [but really Venice, Tommaso di Piasi?, 1492]). A variant reprint has the year date altered to 1492.

Greek text of Diogenes, Brutus and Hippocrates

1499　　See under 'Phalaris', above.

SYNESIUS, DEMOSTHENES, ARISTOTLE, PHILIPPUS, ALEXANDER, DEMOCRITUS, HERA-CLITUS, CRATES, ANACHARIS, EURIPIDES, ALCIPHRON, PHILOSTRATUS, AELIAN, AENEAS, PROCOPIUS, DIONYSIUS, LYSIS, ST BASIL THE GREAT, LIBANIUS, APOLLONIUS OF TYANA, JULIAN THE APOSTATE

Greek text

1499　　*Epistolae Diuersorum Philosophorum Graecorum* (Venice, Aldo Manuzio, two parts, March, April, 1499); see also under 'Phalaris', above.

APPENDIX 4.5

MANUALS ON THE ART OF LETTER WRITING
PRINTED PRIOR TO 1501

DATI, Agostino

1470?　　*Elegantiolae* ([Cologne, Ulrich Zel, 1470?]).
1471　　— (Ferrara, [André Belfort], 12 March 1471).
1471　　— (Ferrara, André Belfort, 19 October 1471).
1472　　— (Naples, Arnald de Bruxelles, 4 June 1472).
1472?　　— ([Mantua, Johann Vurster, 1472?]).
1472?　　— ([Venice], Adam [de Ambergau, 1472?]).
1472?　　— ([Venice, Florentius de Argentina, 1472?]).
1472?　　— ([Venice, printer of Duns, *Quaestiones*, 1472?]).
1472?　　— ([Venice?, 1472?]).
1474　　— (Naples, Arnald de Bruxelles, 9 March 1474).
1475　　— (Milan, Filippo da Lavagna, 18 March 1475).
1475　　— (Ferrara, [André Belfort], 20 September 1475).
1475?　　— ([Rome, Johann (Reinhard) Grüninger, 1475?]).
1476　　— ([Milan], Filippo da Lavagna, 5 March 1476).
1476–7?　　— ([Venice, Vindelinus de Spira?, 1476–7?]).
1477　　— ([Low Countries?], 1477).
1478　　—. Ed. B. Accursius (Milan, Leonhard [Pachel] and Ulrich [Scinzenzeler], 1478).
1478?　　— ([Naples, Giovanni Adamo di Polonia and Niccolò Luciferi, 1478?]).
1478–9?　　— (Parma, Andreas Portilia, [1478–9?]).
1478–9?　　— ([Rome, Johann Bulle, 1478–9?]).
1480　　—. Ed. Giovanni da Legnano (Milan, [Antonio Zaroto], 1480).
1480?　　— (Valencia, L. Palmart, [1480?]).

1480–3? — ([Venice, Antonio de Strata, 1480–3?]).
1481   —. Ed. Giovanni da Legnano (Milan, Antonio Zaroto, 29 November 1481).
1481?   — (Perugia, [Stephanus Arndes, 1481?]).
1483   — (Parma, Deifobo Olivieri, 8 April 1483).
1483   — (Verona, 29 July 1483).
1485?   — ([Rome, Stephan Plannck, 1485?]).
1486   —. Ed. Giovanni da Legnano (Milan, Antonio Zaroto, 23 December 1486).
1487?   — (Siena, Henricus de Colonia, [1487?]).
1488?   — ([Venice, Joannes Rubeus, i.e. G. Rosso, before 28 April 1488]).
1488   — ([Lérida, Heinrich Botel], 8 July 1488).
1488   —. Ed. Giovanni da Legnano (Milan, Antonio Zaroto, 31 July 1488).
1488?   — (Basel, Johann Amerbach, [1488?]).
1490?   — ([Venice, Bernardino Rizzo, 1490?]).
1490?   — ([Antwerp]), Mathias Goes, [1490?]). In DATI, A., *Elegantiolae.*
1490–5? — ([Venice, Joannes Rubeus, 1490–5?]).
1491   — (Rome, Eucharius Silber, 28 March 1491).
1491   — (Venice, Giovanni Battista Sessa, April 1491).
1492   — (Milan, Ulrich Scinzenzeler, 9 April 1492).
1492   — (Venice, Giovanni Tacuino, 22 December 1492).
1492   — (Deventer, [Richard Pafraet], 1492).
1492   — (Ferrara, André Belfort, 20 September 1492).
1493?   — ([Venice, Andrea Calabrese, before 19 January 1493]).
1494?   — ([Reggio Emilia, Francesco Mazzali?, 1494?]).
1495   — (Venice, Giovanni Tacuino, 22 August 1495).
1495?   — Ed. Piero Pacini (Florence, [Lorenzo de' Morgiani and Johannes Petri, 1495?]).
1495?   — ([Vienna, Johann Winterburg, 1495?]).
1496   — ([Brescia], Bernardinus de Misintis, 10 February 1496).
1497   — (Venice, Pietro de Quarenghi, 29 July 1497).
1498   — (Venice, Giovanni Tacuino, 26 April 1498).
1498   —, with other works; commentary by J. Clichtoveus (Paris, G. Mercatoris, 'pour J[ean] Petit', 11 December 1498).
1499   — (Venice, Giovanni Battista Sessa, 25 October 1499).
1499   — (Vienna, Johann Winterburg, 1499).
1499   — ([Spires, Conrad Hist], 1499).
1500   —, and other works. Commentary of J. Clichtoveus and J. Badius (Paris, Thielman Kerver for Jean Petit, 1500).

HANERON, Anthony

1475?   *De epistolis brevibus edendis* ([1475?]).
1490?   — (In DATI, A., *Elegantiolae* ([Antwerp], Mathias Goes [1490?]).

ANON. (falsely attributed to BRACCIOLINI, Poggio)

1475?   *Modus epistolandi* ([Rome, Bartholomaeus Guldinbeck, not after 1475?]).
1485?   — ([Rome, Bartholomaeus Guldinbeck, 1485?]).

MENNIKEN (or MANCKEN), Charles (known as Carolus Virulus)

1476   *Epistolares formulae* (Louvain, Johann Veldener, [14]76).
1476   — (Louvain, Conrad de Westfalia, 1 December 1476).
1478   — (Paris, P. Caesari, 1478).
1480?   — ([Cologne, Conrad Winters de Homborch, 1480?]).

1480? — (Zwolle, Peter de Breda, [1480?]).
1482 — (Rütlingen, Johann Otmar, 1482).
1483 — (Deventer, Richard Pafraet, 8 April 1483).
1480's? — ([Louvain], Johann de Westfalia, [1480's?]).
1483–91? — ([Antwerp], Mathias Goes, [1483–91?]).
1485 — ([Strassburg, Johann (Reinhard) Grüninger], 1485).
1486 — ([?], 1486).
1486 —. Another ed. ([Strassburg, Johann (Reinhard) Grüninger], 1486).
1486 — ([Spires, Peter Drach], 24 October 1486).
1486 — ([Cologne, Heinrich Quentell], 5 December 1486).
1487 — ([Strassburg, Martin Schott], 28 June 1487).
1488 — (Lyons, Janon Cercain, 1488).
1488 — ([Heidelburg, Friedrich Misch], 1488).
1490 — (Deventer, 1490).
1491 — (Deventer, Johann de Breda, 1491).
1493 — (Cologne, Heinrich Quentell, 17 September 1493).
1493 — ([Strassburg, printer of the *Casus Breves Decretalium*], 1493).
1495 — (Lyons, [Gaspard Ortuin], 1495).
1496 — (Deventer, Jacob de Breda, 16 June 1496).
1498 — (Deventer, Jacob de Breda, 1498).
1498 — (Cologne, Heinrich Quenttell, 24 November 1498).
1499 — (Paris, J. Petit, 1499).
1500 — (Paris, Antoine Denidel for Robert Gourmont, 1500).

GUILLERMUS (or GULIELMUS), Saphonensis, frater

1480? *Modus epistolandi* ([Cologne, Bartholomaeus de Unkel, 1480?]).
1485 — (with the title *Epistolarum conficiendarum. Ars perutilis*) ([Lyons, Guillaume Le Roy, 1485?]).
1487? — ([Paris], Antoine Caillaut, [1497?]).
1498 — (Paris, Guy Marchant, Denis Rose, 24 September 1498).
1499 — ([Leipzig?], 1499).

FILELFO, Giovanni Maria

1484 *Octaginta epistolarum scribendarum genera* (Milan, Leonhard Pachel and Ulrich Scinzenzeler, 1484).
1486 *Novum epistolarium.* Ed. L. Mondellus (Louvain, Egidius van der Heerotraten, 1486).
1487 —. Ed. L. Mondellus (Milan, Ulrich Scinzenzeler, 1487).

NIGRI (or NIGER), Francesco

1488 *Modus epistolandi* (Venice, Hermanus Liechtenstein, 5 February 1488).
1489 — (Antwerp, Gerard Leeu, 5 December 1489).
1490 — (Modena, Domenico Rocociolo, 1490).
1490 — (Paris, Georg Mittelhus, 14 August 1490).
1490 — (Venice, Boneto Locatello, 9 September 1490).
1490? — ([Leipzig, Conrad Kachelofen, 1490?]).
1492 — (Venice, Matteo Codecá, 3 August 1492).
1493? — ([Paris], Félix Balligault, [1493?]).
1493? — ([Paris], Michel Le Noir, [1493?]).
1494 — (Deventer, Jacob de Breda, 1494).
1494 — (Venice, Jacopo Ragazzoni, 10 April 1494).
1494 — (Burgos, Friedrich Biel, 12 April 1494).
1494 — (Barcelona, Pedro Posa, 26 April 1494).
1494 — (Rome, Eucharius Silber, 13 June 1494).

1495   — (Barcelona, Johann Rosenbach and Johann Luschner, 27 July 1495).
1495   — (Deventer, Jacob de Breda, 4 September 1495).
1495?   — (Venice, Simone Bevilacqua, [1495?]).
1495?   — (Deventer, [Richard Pafraet, 1495?]).
1496   — ([Spires, Conrad Hist], 1496).
1497   — ([Leipzig, Conrad Kachelofen], 1497).
1498?   — (Paris, Antoine Denidel, [1498?]).
1499   — (Leipzig, Melchior Lotter, 1499).
1499   —([Freiburg im Breisgau], Friedrich Riedrer, 1499).
1499   — ([Augsburg, Johann Schönsperger], 1499).
1499   — (Deventer, Richard Pafraet, 29 June 1499).
1500   — (Venice, Giovanni Tacuino, 21 July 1500).

SULPIZIO, Giovanni, da Veroli (SULPICIUS VERULANUS, J.)

1490?   *De componendis et ornandis epistolis* ([Rome, Eucharius Silber, 1490?]).
1491   — (Rome, Stephan Plannck, 3 June 1491).

NOTES

[1] Information regarding the humanists mentioned in this paper is to be found in *Dizionario biografico degli italiani*, I–XVI (CAL), all published to date, and in M. E Cosenza, *Biographical and Bibliographical Dictionary of the Italian Humanists of the World of Classical Scholarship in Italy, 1300–1800*, Boston, Mass., six vols., 1962–67.

D. Erasmus, *Opus epistolarum*, ed. P. S. Allen, Oxford, twelve vols., 1906–58, VII, letter No. 1985, p. 376; quoted by J. W. Binns, 'The letters of Erasmus', in *Erasmus*, ed. T. A. Dorey, London, 1970, p. 56.

[2] Erasmus, *Opus epistolarum*, IX, Nos. 2451 and 2466, pp. 186, 230; quoted by Binns, p. 56.

[3] F. G. Stokes, 'Introduction' to *Epistolae obscurorum virorum . . .* , ed. and trans. F. G. Stokes, London, 1909, pp. lvi–lxviii; A. A. Renouard, *Annales de l'imprimerie des Alde*, Paris, third edition, 1834, p. 319, Nos. 13–15; Erasmus, *Opus epistolarum*, II, No. 363, pp. 152–3.

[4] *Cf.* E. Müntz, 'Le musée de portraits de Paul Jove', *Mémoires de l'Institut National de France: Académie des Inscriptions et Belles-lettres*, XXXVI, Paris, 1901, p. 276; P. Giovio, *Elogia veris clarorum virorum imaginibus apposita quae in Museo Ioviano Comi spectantur*, Venice, 1546, f. 77*v*. The portrait of Erasmus was included in Giovio's collection. E. Travi, 'Pietro Bembo e il suo epistolario', *Lettere Italiane*, XXIV, 1972, pp. 279–80.

[5] C. Grayson, *A Renaissance Controversy: Latin or Italian?* Oxford, 1960.

[6] P. Bembo, *Lettere*, I, Rome, 1548; Venice, 1552; Venice, 1560; Venice, 1562; Venice, 1564; Venice, 1575; Venice, 1587; II, Venice, 1550–1, then from 1552 to 1587 as I above; III and IV, 1552 to 1587, as I above. P. Bembo, *Epistolarum familiarum libri VI*, Venice, 1552.

[7] M. E. de Montaigne, *Essays*, trans. Charles Cotton, 1585 edition, book I, 39, but in more recent French editions, book I, 40. *Cf.* K[atherine] T. Butler, 'Introduction' in *The Gentlest Art in Renaissance Italy*, compiled by K. T. Butler, Cambridge, 1954, p. 1.

[8] See 'The principal editions of Erasmus' *Epistolae*', appendix VII, in Erasmus, *Opus epistolarum*, I, pp. 593–602.

[9] The authority for humanistic script is B. L. Ullman, *The Origin and Development of Humanistic Script*, Rome, 1960; now see also *The Handwriting of Italian Humanists*, I, fasc. i, ed. A[lbinia] C. de la Mare, London, 1973.

[10] J. Burckhardt, *The Civilization of the Renaissance in Italy*, trans. S. G. C. Middlemore, introduction by B. Nelson and C. Trinkaus, New York, 1958, I, p. 239. The two best introductions to the subject of the letters of the humanists are: R. Sabbadini, 'Commento' to his edition of Guarino Veronese, *Epistolario*, III, in *Miscellanea di*

Storia Veneta, third series, XIV, 1919, pp. iii–vii (the edition, in three volumes, is in *Miscellanea* . . ., third series, VIII, XI, XIV, 1914–19); A. Perosa, 'Sulla pubblicazione degli epistolari degli umanisti', in *La Pubblicazione delle Fonti del Medioevo Europeo negli ultimi settante anni (1883–1953)*. *Relazioni al convegno di studi delle fonti del Medioevo Europeo in occasione del 70º della fondazione dell'Istituto Storico Italiano* (Rome, 14–18 April 1953), Rome, 1954, pp. 327–38. There is a short consideration of the letters of the humanists in: P. van Tieghem, *La Littérature latine de la Renaissance*, Paris, 1944, pp. 220–2; Jean Robertson, *The Art of Letter-writing: an Essay on the Handbooks published in England during the Sixteenth and Seventeenth Centuries*, London, 1942, pp. 9–10; A. Gerlo, 'The *Opus de conscribendis epistolis*', in *Classical Influences on European Culture: Proceedings of an International Conference held at King's College, Cambridge, April 1969*, ed. R. R. Bolgar, Cambridge, 1972, pp. 103–14. There is little concerning the letters of humanists in C. I. Kany, *The Beginnings of the Epistolary Novel in France, Italy and Spain*, Berkeley, Cal., 1937, p. 47, or in Miss Butler's 'Introduction', cited in n. 7, p. 11, or in G. G. Ferrero's 'Introduzione', *Lettere del Cinquecento*, ed. G. G. Ferrero, Turin, 1948, pp. 10–12. The brief study by A. Greco, 'Tradizione e vita negli epistolari del Rinascimento', in *Civiltà dell'umanesimo. Atti del VI, VII, VIII Convegno Internazionale del Centro di Studi Umanistici Montepulciano, 1969, 1970, 1971*, ed. Giovannangiola Tarugi, Florence, 1972, pp. 105–16, is discursive and in no way analytical.

[11] D. Hay, *The Italian Renaissance in its Historical Background*, Cambridge, 1962; *cf.* C. H. Clough, 'The cultural identity of the Italian Renaissance', *Polychronicon*, No. 5, Liverpool, 1972, pp. 4–14; A. Campana, 'The origin of the word "Humanist"', *Journal of the Warburg and Courtauld Institutes*, IX, 1946, pp. 60–73.

[12] Erasmus, *Opus epistolarum*, IV, No. 1206, p. 499; quoted by Binns, pp. 57–8.

[13] For Petrarch see G. Billanovich, 'Dall *'Epystolarum mearum ad diversos liber* ai *Rerum Familiarum libri XXIV'*, in his *Petrarca letterato*, I, *Lo scrittorio del Petrarca*, Rome, 1947, pp. 3–55, also E. H. Wilkins, *Petrarch's Later Years*, Cambridge, Mass., 1959, pp. 303–14, and E. Casamassima, 'Un autografo petrarchesco. La seconda epistola al Pontefice Urbano V . . .', in *Miscellanea in memoria di Giorgio Cencetti*, Turin, 1973, pp. 235–55. U. Dotti, 'I primi sei libri delle "Familiari" del Petrarca, *Giornale storico della letteratura italiana*, CL, 1973, pp. 1–20. For Bembo see P. Bembo and Maria Savorgnan, *Carteggio d'amore*, ed. C. Dionisotti, Florence, 1950, p. xxxvi.

[14] Erasmus, 'De conscribendis epistolis', in his *Opera omnia*, ed. J. Le Clerc, Leyden, ten vols., 1703–06, I, cols. 341–484, makes frequent reference to letters of these writers; and see also Gerlo, 'The *Opus* . . .', cited in n. 10. For Erasmus's letter to Rhenanus see *Opus epistolarum*, IV, No. 1206, p. 501; quoted by Binns, pp. 59–60.

[15] A brief history of the *ars dictaminis* and its relationship with the medieval art of epistolography is given by James J. Murphy, 'Rhetoric in fourteenth-century Oxford', *Medium Aevum*, XXXIV, 1965, pp. 7–8, and succinctly by Gerlo, cited in n. 10, p. 104. For more detail see the first five of the studies reprinted in the section entitled 'Italian culture in the age of Dante' of Helene Wieruszowski's *Politics and Culture in Medieval Spain and Italy*, Rome, 1971, pp. 331–474, and particularly pp. 331–45, 363–4, as well as P. O. Kristeller, 'Matteo de' Libri, Bolognese notary of the thirteenth century, and his *Artes Dictaminis*', in 'Miscellanea G. Galbiati', three vols., II, *Fontes Ambrosiani*, XXVI, Milan, 1951, pp. 283–320. See also addenda, p. 67.

[16] Frances Yates, *The Art of Memory*, London, 1966, pp. 50–104.

[17] E. H. Wilkins, *Petrarch's Correspondence*, Padua, 1960, pp. 5–6.

[18] E. H. Wilkins, *The 'Epistolae Metricae' of Petrarch* . . ., Rome, 1956; U. Dotti, 'Saggio introduttivo' to F. Petrarch, *Le familiari, libri I–IV*, trans. U. Dotti, Urbino, 1970, p. 62.

[19] *Cf.* F. Petrarch, *Four Dialogues for Scholars*, ed. and trans. C. H. R[awski], from Petrarch's *De remediis utriusque*, Cleveland, 1967, 'On the fame of writers', pp. 54–5; for Erasmus see his *Opus epistolarum*, II, No. 564, pp. 524–5; quoted by Binns, p. 76.

[20] R. Sabbadini, *Le scoperte dei codici latini e greci ne' secoli XIV e XV. Nuove ricerche*, Florence, 1914, p. 252, for Petrarch's knowledge of Apollinaris Sidonius; R. Sabba-

dini, *Le scoperte dei codici latini e greci ne' secoli XIV e XV*, Florence, 1905, p. 34, and B. L. Ullman, *The Humanism of C. Salutati*, Padua, 1963, p. 222, for the discovery of Cicero's *Epistolae ad familiares.*

[21] R. Sabbadini, *Storia e critica di testi latini*, Padua, second edition, 1971, pp. 53–62, and *cf.* H. Baron, *Humanistic and Political Literature in Florence and Venice at the Beginning of the Quattrocento*, Cambridge, Mass., 1955, p. 121 and n. 20, for Bruni's knowledge of Cicero's *Ad Atticum*; Sabbadini, pp. 45–53, for Guarino and the *Ad Familiares*, and *cf.* W. H. Woodward, *Studies in Education during the Age of the Renaissance, 1400–1600*, Cambridge, 1906, pp. 40, 42–3.

[22] Cited in n. 21 above.

[23] *Cf.* a manuscript of each of these translations existed in the library of Major Abbey; see J. J. G. Alexander and A[lbinia] C. de la Mare, *The Italian Manuscripts in the Library of Major J. R. Abbey*, London, 1969, pp. 73–6, where the manuscript of the letters of Phalaris is shown to be a special dedication or presentation copy for King Alfonso I of Naples, having four extra letters 'quas nuper in alio libro inventas'; for the sale of the letters of Diogenes and others see *The Celebrated Library of the late Major J. R. Abbey, Eighth Portion: Hornby Manuscripts*, I (auction catalogue, Sotheby & Co., London, sale, 4 June 1974, pp. 93–5. See also addenda, p. 67.

[24] C. Andreucci, 'Il carteggio di Lorenzo Valla, II, Le Fonti', *Italia Medioevale e Umanistica*, xv, 1972, pp. 180–213, particularly at 186–204; *cf.* also F. Pontarin, 'Il carteggio . . . I, Dagli autografi alle edizioni', *ibid.*, pp. 171–9.

[25] Sabbadini, 'Commento' to his edition of Guarino, *Epistolario*, III, cited in n. 10, pp. xxiii–xxvii.

[26] M. Zicàri, 'Il più antico codice di lettere di P. Paolo Vergerio il vecchio', in *Studia Oliveriana*, II, Pesaro, 1954, pp. 33–59.

[27] L. Bertalot, 'Die älteste Briefsammlung des Gasparinus Barzizza', *Beiträge zur Forschung (Studien aus dem Antiquariat Jacques Rosenthal)*, new series, II, 1929, pp. 39–84, and *cf.* also R. Sabbadini, 'Lettere e orazioni edite e inedite di Casparino Barzizza', *Archivio storico lombardo*, XIII, 1886, pp. 363–78, 563–83, 825–36; R. Sabbadini, 'Dalle nuove lettere di Gasparino Barzizza', *Rendiconti dell'Istituto Lombardo di Scienze e Lettere*, second series, LXII, 1929, pp. 881–90. G. Martellotti, 'Gasperino Barzizza', in *Dizionario biografico degli italiani*, VII, pp. 34–9.

[28] See above at p. 40.

[29] P. P. Vergerio, *Epistolario*, ed. Leonard Smith (*Fonti per la storia d'Italia*, LXXIV), Rome, 1934, and *cf.* the review of this edition by V. Rossi, *Giornale storico della letteratura italiana*, CVIII, 1936, pp. 313–17.

[30] B. L. Ullman and P. A. Stadter, *The Public Library of Renaissance Florence*, Padua, 1972, p. 229, No. 888; B. L. Ullman, 'The comparison of Petrarch's *De vita solitaria* . . .', in *Miscellanea G. Mercati*, Vatican City, four vols., 1946, IV, pp. 112, 116, reprinted with revisions in B. L. Ullman, *Studies in the Italian Renaissance*, Rome, second edition, 1973, pp. 170, 174.

[31] This is the conclusion reached after considering the manuscripts indicated in *Censimento dei codici petrarcheschi*, I–IV (all published to date), Padua, 1964–72, and P. O. Kristeller, *Iter Italicum*, I–II (all published to date), London and Leyden, 1963–7.

[32] Ullman, *The Humanism of C. Salutati*, does not list any such manuscript as existing in Salutati's library.

[33] See the printings listed under 'Petrarch' in appendix 4.1.

[34] R. R. Bolgar, *The Classical Heritage . . .*, New York. 1964, pp. 330–1. Woodward, *Studies in Education . . .*, p. 45.

[35] L. Firpo, introduction to his edition of F. Filelfo, *Il Codice Sforza*, in the series *Strenna UTET, 1967*, Turin, 1967, pp. 7–15.

[36] *Cf.* Burkhardt, I, pp. 239–46; E. Santini, *Firenze e i suoi 'oratori' nel quattrocento*, Milan and Palermo, 1922; M. Baxandall, *Giotto and the Orators*, Oxford, 1971, pp. 1–4.

[37] G. Boccaccio, *Le lettere autografe del cod. Laur. XXIX. 8*, ed. G. Traversari, Castelfiorentino, 1905; A. F. Massèra, 'Nota' to his edition of G. Boccaccio, *Opere latine*

minori, Bari, 1928, pp. 306–59; R. Weiss, 'Barbato da Sulmona . . .', *Studi petrarcheschi*, III, 1950, pp. 13–22; V. Branca, *Tradizione delle opere di G. Boccaccio*, Rome, 1958, pp. 104–8; R. Abbondanza, 'Una lettera autografa del Boccaccio nell'Archivio di Stato di Perugia', *Studi sul Boccaccio*, I, 1963, pp. 5–13; G. Auzzas, 'Studi sulle "Epistole" ', *Studi sul Boccaccio*, VI, 1971, pp. 38–45.

³⁸ Ullman, *The Humanism of C. Salutati*, pp. 19–23, 271–80; *cf.* C. Salutati, *Epistolae* . . ., ed. G. Rigaccio, Florence, two vols., 1741–42, and *Epistolario*, ed. F. Novati (*Fonti per la Storia d'Italia*, xv–xviii), Rome, 1891–1911.

³⁹ E. Garin, 'I cancellieri unmanisti della Repubblica Fiorentina da Coluccio Salutati a Bartolomeo Scala', in Garin, *La cultura filosofica del Rinascimento italiano*, Florence, 1961, pp. 3–37; Ullman, *The Humanism of C. Salutati*, pp. 112–14; F. P. Luiso, *Mezzo secolo di umanesimo fiorentino*, I, Studi sull'*Epistolario di L. Bruni* (set in proof but not published, 1904); H. Baron, 'L. Bruni Aretino . . .', in *Quellen zur Geistesgeschichte des Mittelalters und der Renaissance*, I, 1928, pp. 187–228; L. Bruni, *Epistolae*, ed. L. Mehus, Florence, two vols., 1741, which includes the ninth book, and also a tenth, added by Mehus, wherein he added supplementary letters; Luiso collected further letters for an eleventh book, see the list in Baron, pp. 222–8; see also E. Garin, 'L. Bruni', *Giornale critico della filosofia italiana*, XXXI, 1952, pp. 385–6.

⁴⁰ P. Bracciolini, *Epistolae editas collegit* . . ., ed. T. Tonelli, Florence, 1832; E. Walser, 'Poggius Florentinus. Leben und werke', *Beiträge zue Kulturgeschichte des Mittelalters*, XIV, Leipzig and Berlin, 1914; P. Bracciolini, . . . *Letters to N. de Niccolis*, ed. and trans. Phyllis W. G. Gordon, New York, 1974.

⁴¹ A. Traversari, *Latinae epistolae a domino Petro Canneto . . . in libros xxv tributae* . . ., ed. L. Mehus, Florence, two vols., 1759; F. P. Luiso, *Riordinamento dell'epistolario di A. Traversari* . . ., Florence, two vols., 1898–1903; A. Dini Traversari, *Ambrogio Traversari e i suoi tempi*, Florence, 1912; P. G. Ricci, 'Ambrogio Traversari', *Rinascita*, II, 1939, pp. 578–612. For Francesco Barbaro see G. Gualdo, 'F. Barbaro', in *Dizionario biografico degli italiani*, VI, pp. 101–3. R. Sabbadini, *Centotrenta lettere di F. Barbaro*, *predecedute dall'ordinamento critico cronologico dell'intero suo epistolario*, Saleno, 1884; A. Luzio, 'Cinque lettere . . .', *Archivio veneto*, XXXVI, 1886, pp. 337–41. For the manuscripts see also Kristeller, *Iter Italicum*. Lapo da Castiglionchio the younger (*c.* 1405–38) was also of the circle: see F. P. Luiso, 'Studi sull' Epistolario e le Traduzioni di Lapo . . .', in *Studi italiani di filologica classica*, VII, 1899, pp. 205–99.

⁴² P. O. Kristeller, 'Bartolomeo Facio and his unknown correspondence', in *From Renaissance to the Counter-reformation: Essays in Honor of G. Mattingly*, ed. C. H. Carter, New York, 1965, pp. 57–9; the partial collection (sixty-six letters) in a MS in Valladolid University library is headed 'Bartolomei Faccii Genuensis ad amicos eius ac familiares epistolae incipiunt'. The full collection apparently edited by Facio himself contained 150 letters.

⁴³ Gasperino Barzizza and Guiniforte Barzizza, *Opera* . . ., ed. J. A. Furietto, Rome, two vols., 1723; see also n. 27; Bolgar, *The Classical Heritage* . . . , p. 330; P. O. Kristeller, 'The European diffusion of Italian humanism', *Italica*, XXXIX, 1962, p. 11. For the printings of Barzizza's collection see appendix 4.1.

⁴⁴ For his letters see those in the collection cited in n. 43 above; G. Martellotti, 'Guiniforte Barzizza', in *Dizionario biografico degli italiani*, VII, pp. 34–9.

⁴⁵ V. Zaccaria, 'L'Epistolario di P. C. Decembrio', *Rinascimento*, III, 1952, pp. 85–118; V. Zaccaria, 'Sulle opere di P. C. Decembrio', *Rinascimento*, VII, 1956, pp. 13–74.

⁴⁶ For Tranchedini see above at p. 42.

⁴⁷ The unique MS is in the Laurenziana Library, Florence, Acquisti 227; see Sabbadini, 'Commento' to his edition of Guarino, cited in n. 10, p. iii, n. 6. Apparently a promised edition, seemingly Sabbadini's own, has never appeared; *cf.* R. Sabbadini, 'G. Valagussa', in 'Briciole umanistiche', *Giornale storico della letteratura italiana*, L, 1907, pp. 56–7; none is given in E. and Myriam Billanovich, 'Bibliografia di R. Sabbadini', in R. Sabbadini, *Storia e critica* . . . , pp. xi–xli; *cf.* also an edition of Valagussa's selection of Cicero's letters indicated, in appendix 4.3 under 'Cicero, 3, Selections (b)'.

⁴⁸ *Cf.* Sabbadini, 'Commento' to his edition of Guarino, cited in n. 10, p. iv; for Antonio Beccadelli see the study by A. F. C. Ryder in this volume, esp. p. 137 n. 2.

⁴⁹ One such autograph letter that was sent, which can be compared with the author's self-edited version for his letter collection, is that to Pope Urban V indicated in the study by Casamassima cited in n. 13.

⁵⁰ P. Toynbee's introduction to Dante, *Epistolae*, ed. P. Toynbee, Oxford, second edition, 1966, particularly pp. xiii–xxxi. P. H. Wicksteed and E. G. Gardner, *Dante and Giovanni del Virgilio*, London, 1902, where at pp. 287–304 the text of the correspondence in verse is provided; *cf.* also Rosetta Migliorini Fissi, 'La lettera pseudo-dantesca a Guido da Polenta. Edizione critica e ricerche attributive', *Studi danteschi*, XLVI, 1969, pp. 101–272. Lovato Lovati (1241–1309) also wrote correspondence in verse; see L. D. Reynolds and N. G. Wilson, *Scribes and Scholars*, Oxford, second edition, 1964, p. 110.

⁵¹ For the printings of the humanists' letter collections see appendix 4.1. L. Frati, 'Di L. Carbone e delle sue opere', in *Atti e Memorie della Deputazione Ferrarese di Storia Patria*, XX, 1910, pp. 58–80, and E. Garin, 'Motivi della cultura ferrarese . . .', in E. Garin, *La cultura filosofica* . . ., cited in n. 39, pp. 402–31. For the various dedication copies of Fichet's edition see A. Claudin, *The First Paris Press*, London, 1898, pp. 52–3, and for Bessarion's relations with Fichet see E. Legrand, 'Cent-dix lettres de F. Filelfe', *Publications de l'École des langues orientales vivantes*, third series, XII, Paris, 1892, pp. 221–89; I am much indebted to Dr Lotte Labowsky for these references.

⁵² For Bruni see Baron, cited in n. 28; Francesco Filelfo also wrote a consolatory espistle: *Ad I. A. Marcellum . . . consolatio*, Rome (really Milan, F. da Lavagnia), 1475–6, for which see V. Scholderer, 'Printing at Milan in the fifteenth century', in his *Fifty Essays*, ed. D. E. Rhodes, Amsterdam, 1966, p. 100; *cf.* also A. Calderini, 'I codici milanese delle opere di F. Filelfo', *Archivio storico lombardo*, fifth series, XLII, 1915, pp. 335–411. For Campano see G. Lesca, *G. A. Campano, detto l'Episcopus Apretinus*, Pontedera, 1892. For Ficino see A. della Torre, *Storia dell'Accademia Platonica di Firenze*, Florence, 1902, pp. 42–104, and P. O. Kristeller, *Supplementum Ficinianum*, Florence, two vols., 1937, I, pp. lxxxvii–cxi, and see also lxvii–lxviii and 25–72. For Pico see E. Garin, 'Richerche su G. Pico della Mirandola: L'Epistolario', in Garin, *La cultura filosofica del Rinascimento italiano*, pp. 254–79. For Poliziano see Biblioteca Riccardiana, Florence, MS 974, indicated in *Mostra del Poliziano . . . (Firenze, 23 settembre–30 novembre 1954). Catalogo*, Florence, 1954, pp. 110–11, item No. 132, and see A. Campana, 'Per il carteggio del Poliziano', *Rinascita*, VI, 1943, pp. 437–72. R. Gaguin, *Epistolae . . .*, ed. L. Thuasne, Paris, two vols., 1903.

⁵³ Tranchedini's letter book is Biblioteca Riccardiana, Florence, MS 834; see Kristeller, *Iter Italicum*, I, pp. 206–6; I am greatly indebted to Dr Labowsky for this reference. Della Fonte's collection is MS Palat. Capp. 77, Biblioteca Nazionale, Florence, indicated in *Mostra del Poliziano . . .*, pp. 161–2, item No. 233. For Federigo, Duke of Urbino, see C. H. Clough, 'Federigo da Montefeltro's patronage of the arts', *Journal of the Warburg and Courtauld Institutes*, XXXVI, 1973, pp. 129–44; for the collection of his letters see F. da Montefeltro, *Lettere di Stato e d'Arte, 1470–80*, ed. P. Alatri, Rome, 1949.

⁵⁴ For the printed letter anthologies see appendix 4.2. Luca Pulci, *Pistolae . . .*, Florence, A. Miscomini, 1481–2; Butler, *The Gentlest Art . . .*, p. 1.

⁵⁵ For the first printing in Venice see Horatio F. Brown, *The Venetian Printing Press . . .*, London, 1891, pp. 5, 10.

⁵⁶ For the printings of the letter collections of Antiquity see appendices 4.3 and 4.4, and for the nature of the letters themselves see W. Roberts, *History of Letter-writing from the Earliest Period to the Fifth Century*, London, 1843. For the average of 300 copies produced for each printing *cf.* V. Scholderer, 'Printers and readers in Italy in the fifteenth century', in his *Fifty Essays*, p. 204, and see also p. 211 for a printing of 1490 of 800 copies. For the Aldine printing of 1499 see Renouard, *Annales . . .*, pp. 18–19.

⁵⁷ Something of this aspect of printing is indicated in the essay of Scholderer cited in n. 35 above, pp. 202–15; it is unfortunate that the useful analysis of Venetian

editions before 1481 provided by Scholderer, *Fifty Essays*, p. 88, does not have a sub-heading for letter collections. *Cf.* also Elizabeth L. Eisenstein, 'The advent of printing . . .', *Past and Present*, No. 45, 1969, pp. 29, 50. For a contemporary view of the advantages of printing see Angelo Cato's dedicatory epistle, printed in C. A. J. Armstrong, *The Usurpation of Richard III*, Oxford, second edition, 1969, p. 31.

[58] For the nature of the collections see C. H. Clough, 'The Chancery letter files of A. S. Piccolomini', in *E. S. Piccolomini—Papa Pio II. Atti del convegno per il V centenario della morte*, ed. D. Maffei, Siena, 1968, pp. 117–32.

[59] E. S. Piccolomini, *Storia di due amanti*, ed. and trans. Maria Luisa Doglio, in the series *Strenna UTET, 1973*, Turin, 1972, pp. 24–123; Kany, *The Beginnings of the Epistolary Novel . . .*, pp. 37–40; the printings are indicated in the catalogues cited in 'The method used for the compilation of appendices 4.1–5 inclusive'.

[60] *Cf.* Clough, 'Federigo da Montefeltro's patronage of the arts', p. 142.

[61] C. Vitelli, *In defensionem Plinii et D. Calderini contra G. Merula . . . ad H. Barbarum . . . Epistola* [Venice, B. de Tortis, 1481?], *cf.* also C. H. Clough, 'Thomas Linacre, Cornelio Vitelli and humanistic studies at Oxford', in *Linacre Studies*, ed. F. Maddison, Oxford, 1975, p. 15; G. Merula, [*Epistolae adversus Franciscum Philelphum*]; [Venice, N. Girardengno, 1480?]. Two lost volumes of epistolary abuse written by N. Perotti are mentioned by R. P. Oliver in his 'Introduction' to N. Perotti, *The Enchiridion of Epictetus*, ed. R. P. Oliver, Urbana, Ill., 1954, p. 10, and *cf.* G. Mercati, *Per la cronologia della vita . . . di N. Perotti*, Rome, 1925, pp. 101–3; for Annio da Viterbo see R. Weiss, 'Traccia per una biografia di Annio da Viterbo', *Italia Medioevale e Umanistica*, v, 1962, pp. 425–41. Erasmus concluded his treatise *Opus de conscribendis epistolis* with a section devoted to the dialectical epistle, or 'disputatoriae genus'; see Gerlo, p. 108.

[62] *Io. Francisci Pici . . ., libri duo . . ., Petri Bembi, . . . de Imitatione liber unus*, Basel, J. Froben, 1518, and see G. Santangelo, 'Introduzione' to G. F. Pico and P. Bembo, *Le epistole 'De Imitatione'*, ed. G. Santangelo, Florence, 1954, p. 20. B. Castiglione, *Epistola de vita et gestis Guidobaldi Urbini ducis*, Fossombrone, O. Petrucci, 1513; the title of Castiglione's work, however, was probably the printer's invention rather than the author's intention; see C. H. Clough, 'Baldassare Castiglione's *Ad Henricum Angliae Regem Epistola . . .*', *Studi Urbinati*, XLVII, new series, 1973, pp. 227–36.

[63] *Cf.* the dedicatory letter addressed by Giovanni Boccaccio to Andrea Acciaiuoli, in his *De claris mulieribus*; G. Boccaccio, *Concerning Famous Women*, trans. G. A. Guarino, London, 1964, pp. xxxiii–xxxv. B. Botfield, 'Some remarks on prefaces to the first editions of the classics', *Bibliographical and Historical Miscellanies: Philobiblon Society*, I, 1854, pp. 1–24, provides a useful list of prefaces, where many dedicatory letters are to be found, and the material thus listed and further supplemented is printed in full in B. Botfield, *Praefationes et epistolae editionibus principibus auctorum veterum praepositae* [*Prefaces to the first editions of the Greek and Roman Classics . . .*], London, 1861.

[64] Some of these are indicated in the study by Clough, 'Federigo da Montefeltro's patronage of the arts', cited in n. 53. pp. 129–44.

[65] Three presentation copies with letters to B. Bembo are indicated in P. de Nohlac, *La Bibliothèque de F. Orsini*, Paris, 1887, pp. 193, 240–1; examples of a different nature are provided by P. O. Kristeller. 'Some original letters and autograph manuscripts of M. Ficino', in *Studi di bibliografia e di storia in onore di T. de Marinis*, Verona, four vols., 1964, III, pp. 14–17, and by C. A. Miller, 'P. Zambeccari and a musical friend', *Renaissance Quarterly*, XXV, 1972, pp. 426–7.

[66] For the printing of the various manuals see appendix 4.5. There were manuals in Italian at least from [C. Landino], *Formulario de epistole . . .*, Bologna, Ugo di Rugerio, 28 June 1485, and see also C. Landino, *Scritti critici . . .*, ed. R. Cardini, Rome, two vols., 1974, I, p. 180. This manual is also found under the name of B. Miniatore, though was actually Landino's.

[67] Erasmus, 'De conscribendis epistolis', cited in n. 14, I, cols. 352 C, 364 B; quoted by Gerlo, p. 110.

[68] Erasmus. *Opus epistolarum*, I, No. 117, pp. 271–2; quoted by Gerlo, p. 109.

[69] *Ibid.*

[70] G. Sulpizio, *De octo partibus orationis* ... [Venice, C. da Pensis, 1490?].

[71] See G. G. Meersseman, 'La raccolta dell'umanista fiammingo Giovanni de Veris: "De arte epistolandi" ', *Italia Medioevale e Umanistica*, xv, 1972, pp. 215–81; *cf.* also G. G. Meersseman, 'L'épistolaire de Jean van der Veren et le début de l'humanisme en Flandre', *Humanistica Lovaniensia*, xix, 1970, pp. 119–200.

A manuscript of a treatise 'Ars nova epistolarum' of Giovanni Serra is in the State Library, Munich, MS Lat. 4393, ff. 125r–146r; see Andreucci, 'Il carteggio di Lorenzo Valla . . .', cited in n. 24, p. 181, n. 5. I have not been able to consult this manuscript and cannot identify Serra, but I suspect that the work was originally compiled for teaching in the Low Countries or Germany.

[72] W. A. Copinger, *Supplement to Hain's Repertorium Bibliographicum*, London, 1898, II, part I, p. 290, No. 2891; I have been unable to locate a copy.

[73] A printed edition of this is in A. Dati, *Elegantiolae* . . . *Addito insuper opusculo de conficiendis epistolis clarissimi oratoris Laurentij Vallensis*, Venice, L. Spineda, 16⟨25?⟩ (the date is rubbed), ff. 52v–63v; there is a copy in Cambridge University library, shelf number Aa* 12 21 F. The earliest printing of this supposed work of L. Valla known to me is in A. Dati, *Elegantiolae* ... *addito insuper libello clarissimi oratoris L. Vallensis*, Venice, F. Bindoni and M. Pasini, 1538, *cf. The National Union Catalog pre-1956 Imprints*, CXXXIII, p. 501, but I have been unable to see it.

[74] Eight fifteenth-century printings are listed under *Ars Notariatus* in *General Catalogue of Printed Books. British Museum*, VII, 1965, col. 498; thirteen such printings under the same heading are in F. R. Goff, *Incunabula in American Libraries: a Third Census*. . . Millwood, N.Y., revised edition, 1973, p. 60.

[75] Erasmus, *Opus epistolarum*, IV, No. 1206, p. 499; quoted by Binns, p. 59.

[76] See E. H. Wilkins, 'The *Epistolae Familiares* of L. Bruni ...,' *The Papers of the Bibliographical Society of America*, XXXVII, 1943, pp. 157–8.

[77] For Matteo Bosso of Verona (1427–1502) see G. Soranzo, *L'umanista canonico regolare lateranense Matteo Bosso* ..., Padua, 1965, and for the printing of his letters see also L. Pescascio, *L'arte della stampa a Mantova nei secoli XV–XVI–XVII*, Mantua, 1971, pp. 79–83, and G. C. Schizzerotto, *Libri stampati a Mantova nel Quattrocento. Catalogo della Mostra, 1–20 ottobre 1972*, Mantua, 1972, pp. 62–6.

[78] For this see D. E. Rhodes, 'Ancora per lo stampatore del Mesue', in *Studi offerti a Roberto Ridolfi*, ed. Berta Maracchi Biagiarelli and D. E. Rhodes, Florence, 1973, pp. 408–12.

[79] For this see Baron, cited note 39, pp. 135–8.

Addenda

Page 62, n. 15 end. See also J. R. Banker, 'The *Ars Dictaminis* and Rhetorical textbooks at the Bolognese University in the fourteenth century', *Medievalia et Humanistica*, new series, v, 1974, pp. 153–68.

Page 63, n. 23 end. The Phalaris MS has now been auctioned; see *The Celebrated Library of the late Major J. R. Abbey, Ninth Portion: Hornby Manuscripts*, II (auction catalogue, Sotheby & Co., London, sale, 25 March 1975), pp. 68–9.

Page 65, n. 52. For Ficino see also M. Ficino, *Letters [Book I]*, trans., London, 1975, I.

D. S. Chambers *Warburg Institute*

5

STUDIUM URBIS
AND *GABELLA STUDII*:
THE UNIVERSITY OF ROME IN
THE FIFTEENTH CENTURY

Hastings Rashdall devoted just over one page of *The Universities of Europe in the Middle Ages* to the University or Studium of the city of Rome.[1] This rather neglected institution was founded by Pope Boniface VIII in 1303. Unlike the migratory Studium of the Roman Curia or the Palace,[2] the Studium Urbis, which was conceived as a *studium generale* for all comers, with teaching in all faculties, was to have civic associations in the manner of other Italian universities which took Bologna as their model. The foundation statute of 20 April 1303, reissued at Anagni on 6 June, even suggests that the new Studium was to promote the *renovatio* of Rome: 'the same city which gave laws to mankind ought also to become fertile in learning and produce men conspicuous for the maturity of their counsel'. To this 'fountain of learning' were expected to resort 'not only the inhabitants of the city and the surrounding region but others who flock to Rome almost continually from various parts of the world'.[3] It was a function of papal benevolence to establish universities for learning or to raise existing schools to that status. But a civic university in Rome, the capital city of the Church, more subject than anywhere else to papal interference, was bound to present special problems of administration. This essay will investigate some of them.

The Studium Urbis survived the nemesis of its founder, the subsequent exile of the papacy from Rome, and the Great Schism; the traces of its first century and a quarter of existence have been recorded elsewhere[4] and need only be summarised quickly. Boniface VIII created a notary of the Studium,[5] and may have made more constitutional provisions than appear in the short foundation statutes, but he cannot have seen the university develop far before his death. Its civic character seems to have been limited. Although the Capitoline Court had jurisdiction over members of the Studium, the latter were in some way supervised by the *fraternitas clerum*, a body of Roman clergy,[6] and the bull of 3 June 1303 was addressed to three prelates who were perhaps special protectors. These were the abbot of San Lorenzo fuori le mura, the prior of the basilica of San Giovanni in Laterano (whose cathedral school may have been a forerunner of the new Studium) and the archpriest of

Sant' Eustachio. This connection with Sant' Eustachio, very centrally placed near the Pantheon, was to endure. It has been suggested that the sacristy of Sant 'Eustachio contained the original archive of the Studium; in 1317 the archpriest of Sant' Eustachio wrote to a canon of Arezzo as a doctor 'in Romano Studio'.[7] The Studium Urbis was not permitted to grant degrees until 1318, when Pope John XXII, in a provision which refers to the teaching of canon and civil law, permitted this: it has been suggested that Boniface VIII had withheld the privilege, wanting to protect the Studium of the Curia.[8]

Scattered documents throw more light upon the early administration. By a deed of October 1319 'Nos rectores et Senydici Romanae fraternitatis', assembled in the church of San Salvatore in Pensilis, 'ubi moris est Nos congregari ad tractandum negotia iam dicti Studii', nominated a lecturer in canon law who should receive an annual salary of 100 florins from the tribute paid by the feudatories of Tivoli and Rispampano (a fortress in wooded country near Corneto).[9] The clerical fraternity were, however, joined by some lay officials—the conservators of the Camera Urbis—in a supplication about the declining Studium sent to John XXII in 1331,[10] and the secular authority seems to be predominant in university affairs in the revised statutes of the city in 1363.[11] Here it was laid down that the conservators and four councillors, together with thirteen worthy men chosen by them to represent the *rioni* (districts of the city) and four legal scholars, should elect three doctors to teach civil and canon law who must reside in Trastevere: these three would each be paid an annual salary of 200 florins from the customs duties of the Ripa, paid on goods brought to Rome by river. The same committee was obliged to appoint masters to teach medicine and grammar, who were to receive the rather lower salaries of 150 and sixty florins respectively. Teaching evidently continued, and one may infer that the troubles of the papacy temporarily aided the civic character of the Studium to develop. Later, in 1406, Innocent VII, Pope of the Roman obedience, announced plans to restore as a centre of learning the city in which 'the whole range of wisdom and learning first began or else was conveyed from the Greeks', proposing to set up Chairs of Greek and Latin literature, medicine, philosophy, logic and rhetoric.[12] Had these provisions, drafted by Leonardo Bruni, been carried out the Studium Urbis would have been an early follower of Florence, where the Chair of Greek studies had been founded for Chrysoloras in 1396. There is evidence at least that Latin rhetoric was taught during the following years by Giovanni Ponzio and Francesco da Fiano, who had Cencio de' Rustici among his successful pupils.[13]

The election of Martin V—the first Roman baron to become Pope since Boniface VIII—and the return of a united papal court to Rome in 1420 might seem to have augured well for the Studium Urbis. However, not much evidence has come to light of Martin's patronage,[14] whereas his successor, Eugenius IV, seems to have taken a greater interest in it. At the same time, however, the autonomy of the city's—and therefore the university's—administration was being curtailed. By the early 1430s the cardinal chamberlain (*camerlengo*), head of the Apostolic Chamber or principal office in the papacy's financial administration, had extensive control over the city: his deputy, the *vice-camerlengo*, was ex-officio governor, while the relics of civic independence, the office of senator and the Camera Urbis, the city's financial department run by the elected conservators, were in practice closely supervised by papal authority.[15]

On 10 October 1431, within a few months of his accession, Eugenius IV reissued the foundation statute of Boniface VIII.[16] This appears to have been in response to a petition, for the bull was addressed to various clergy (was the *fraternitas* still in existence?)—the archpriests of Sant' Eustachio and San Celso e Giuliano and the abbot of San Lorenzo fuori le mura—as well as to the conservators of the Camera Urbis and the thirteen *caporioni*, all of whom are named. What appears to be entirely new is a financial provision for the Studium in the form of a surcharge on the tax paid on imported wine (*gabella vini forensis*)[17] sold in Roman taverns. According to the bull, this had been agreed both in private discussions with the Pope and in public council, though a later fifteenth-century writer states there had been controversy.[18] The tax was to be levied at the rate of three and a half soldi in addition to the six denari in the lira already paid by the tavern keepers. It was to be collected and held according to the orders of the rector of the Studium—who seems to have been a papal nominee, Jean Le Jeune, Bishop of Amiens—and four Roman citizens named as reformers (*civium Romanorum Reformatorum*). A rector and elective body called reformers were officers familiar to Bologna and other Italian universities; what is not clear is whether these Roman reformers were already *reformatores studii* or the *reformatores Urbis* instituted in 1416.[19] They were to spend the money collected from this tax 'pro salario doctorum per eos ad legendum in dicto Studio conductorum, et omnium expensarum in Studio hujusmodi occurentium'. A clause followed enacting that the money should not be put to any other use: 'Volentes insuper, ac eadem auctoritate statuentes, ut pecuniae praedictae in alium usum minime exponi possunt, nec additio et gravamen hujusmodi duret ac persistat, nisi dicto Studio durante, et permanente.'

Another bull was issued on 7 February 1433 in reply to a supplication from the conservators of the Camera Urbis and the thirteen *caporioni*.[20] It confirmed the privileges of the university and the grant of wine tax, and introduced provisions for the election of the reformers, now specifically described as *reformatores studii*. Every December the conservators and the *caporioni* were to elect twelve among the more notable citizens of Rome, including doctors of civil or canon law and three public notaries, who should present themselves to the cardinal chamberlain. He or the *vice-camerlengo* would then select four from the twelve, including one doctor of law, to act as reformers and one of the notaries to act as *studii notarius*, though in practice it appears that, like other appointments, these could be subjected to even more direct papal control.[21] At the end of their year in office the reformers had to give an account of their administration before a committee consisting of the cardinal chamberlain, the conservators, three of the *caporioni* elected from the thirteen by themselves and a trustworthy nominee of the cardinal chamberlain.

Afterwards this annual committee, together with the reformers newly elected for the following year, were to sell the collectorship of the tax on imported wine to a reputable merchant in business at Rome and the reformers should pay the salaries of the teaching staff. Any of the money left over should, with the consent of the annual committee, be used for the building of a house or college for poor students and the acquisition of property to assist that end—an interesting reference to the problem of student accomodation, which will be considered later.

Raising university funds from local taxation was common in other cities, and of course it was not new to Rome, though the old charges upon Rispampano, Tivoli and the customs duty of the Ripa had probably been discontinued. Nevertheless Eugenius' initiative seems remarkable, and may have been inspired by his memory of the University of Padua, where he had studied. There a citizen body of four *reformatores studii* had administrative responsibility to the ruler: first to the Carrara *signoria* and since 1406 to the doge and senate of Venice. Francesco Novello da Carrara had reserved for the university the proceeds of the ox tax, waggon tax and tax upon prostitutes, and the Venetian government made an additional grant of 1,500 ducats in 1406, raising this to an annual sum of 4,000 ducats in 1407 with the proceeds of the wine tax in addition.[22] This example of munificence was being followed in Rome on a rather more modest scale.

There are no figures available to illustrate the first benefits which the Studium gained from its new funds, but there are indications that the yield on the *gabella vini forensis* or *gabella studii*, as it soon came to be called, was high: perhaps higher than was first anticipated. A safe conduct issued on 10 October 1432 for a doctor called Yvo de Copulis to come from Perugia and take up a teaching post in Rome may be significant.[23] Issued by the papal treasurer, as *locumtenens* of the cardinal chamberlain, it presumes a high salary, for Yvo was to bring, besides his books, a retinue of up to twenty-four persons.

Papal authority could, however, take away as easily as give. The clause prohibiting the use of the *gabella studii* for non-academic purposes was soon set aside. As early as 12 July 1433 the cardinal chamberlain, Francesco Condulmer, acting on the Pope's verbal instructions, ordered the reformers (described as *provisori*) to lend 1,000 florins for two weeks to the conservators of the Camera Urbis and the caporioni: 'exponendos per eos in quibusdam negotiis opportunis pro statu dicte Urbis . . . Non obstantibus literis apostolicis quibus cavetur quod dicte pecunie non convertantur in alium usum quam pro Studio predicto.'[24] A mandate of 31 July from the chamberlain to two Roman citizens, *emptores* or purchasers of the right to collect the *gabella*, forbade them to pay to the reformers their takings for the last two months, amounting to 1,900 curial or cameral florins; they were instructed to hold this sum on deposit.[25] In spite of the threatened fine for disobedience, it appears that this sum was nevertheless paid over, for on 5 August another mandate to the reformers (this time described as *anteposti*) ordered its transference to the treasurer of the Camera Urbis.[26] A bull of 29 September (below, appendix 5.1) addressed to the reformers makes clear the purpose of this appropriation. It explained that the doctors of the university would not suffer, but the surplus was needed for more urgent expenditure; the less important cause (presumably the foundation of a college) had to give way to the more urgent. Payment was also promised to the notary and beadles (*bidelli*) of the Studium, and to the friars of Aracoeli for bell ringing. But the defence of the city against the disorders (which would cause Eugenius IV himself to flee to Florence in June 1434) came first. The bull was addressed from the church of San Lorenzo in Damaso, where Eugenius was already in refuge during the attack on the city by Niccolò di Fortebraccio, urged on by Duke Filippo Visconti of Milan, and it specifies payments to be made for an offensive against the 'castra Noni' (the Torre di Nona?) for the hire of a *condottiere* and the expulsion of the 'son of iniquity' Niccolò della Stella.[27]

Another problem was the dishonesty of the merchants who collected the *gabella*. From the evidence above it appears that the *emptores* were expected to pay in the monies they collected at two-monthly intervals, the sum they had bid for the right of collection being paid back presumably at the end of the year or in instalments by the *depositarius*. On 15 December 1433 the cardinal chamberlain ordered the senator to imprison the buyers of the *gabella* on account of certain irregularities: not all the tax had been collected on unsold wine.[28] After the removal of the papal court to Florence the irregularities seem to have grown worse: a mandate issued from there in March 1436 ordered the arrest and confiscation of the goods of the partners, who had absconded, of Stefano Vasti *de Urbe*.[29] Perhaps it was because of these troubles that a bull was issued on 25 May 1438 in response to a petition from the conservators and the caporioni, removing from them the administration of the *gabella* and the responsibility for paying salaries and conferring it upon the guardians of the Compagnia di SSmo Salvatore al Laterano.[30] However, the reformers appear to have regained power in spite of this measure, perhaps soon after the return of Eugenius IV to Rome in 1443.

Little has come to light about any co-ordinated policy towards the university shown by the Popes of the mid-fifteenth century. It has been alleged that Nicholas V bestowed on the Studium the revenues of a church, San Biagio in Cantu Secuta (San Biagio della Pagnotta), but if so this can have been only a short-term benefit, for he conferred the revenues upon Cardinal Isidore of Kiev in 1451.[31] While Calixtus III in 1456 suspended all concessionary payments from the city's revenues in the interest of his crusading fund,[32] it seems unlikely that this extended to cutting off all money from the Studium: at all events, in November 1457 he conceded that the four reformers should themselves each receive an annual salary of twenty-five cameral florins.[33] Paul II has been acclaimed as a restorer of the university,[34] but it does not appear that he made any new provisions beyond confirming its existence in his general confirmation of the city's statutes in 1469. The medal issued that year with the devices A. BO. and LAETITIA SCHOLASTICA probably refers not to the Studium Urbis and (as was formerly believed)

the signature as artist of Aristotele of Bologna but to the University of
Bologna ('Academia Bononiensis'), the privileges of which Paul II had
enlarged in 1465.[35]

For the later fifteenth century, and in particular the pontificate of Sixtus
IV (1471–84), there is rather more documentation for an administrative
history of the Studium Urbis. The rest of this outline study, drawing upon
some of the unpublished material, will concentrate upon three main problems:
first, the masters teaching in the university, their subjects and salaries;
second, the provision of buildings and accomodation; third, the students.
Various administrative problems will be apparent in the course of what
follows: particularly that of the papal–civic dichotomy and the operation in
practice of the *gabella studii*.

Eugenius IV had promised that masters of the Studium would not suffer
as the result of his appropriating funds from the *gabella* in 1433. Mandates of
the Apostolic Chamber from that period show that some ample payments
were authorised: for instance, on 23 February 1434 the rector and reformers
were to pay 100 cameral florins to Gaspare de Battarellis of Perugia for
teaching civil law, even allowing for absence on papal business; a canon
lawyer, Antonio de' Roselli, was treated similarly.[36] There seems to be no
way of knowing whether these were exceptional cases, for until the time of
Sixtus IV the names and salaries of teachers are traceable only through such
scattered entries in the archives, or other stray references. The knowledge
that Gaspare of Verona was teaching in the Studium Urbis *c.* 1445–49
depends, for instance, on an autobiographical comment in his *Regulae
grammaticales*,[37] and that Lorenzo Valla first taught privately and then from
1450 held a Chair of Rhetoric (for one year running a rival course against
George of Trebizond) depends on two of his letters to Giovanni Tortelli.[38]
Writing in the autumn of 1451, he told Tortelli that he was in danger of
losing his job on account of an interesting if narrow-minded attempt of
Nicholas V to restrict appointments to those of Roman birth—a move which
may have reflected civic pressure but also the strong influence of Bologna as a
model university.[39] Valla launched into a passionate defence of his own
Romanitas (in fact he retained the post until his death in 1457):

Velim certiorem me facias, si quid scis, an ego sim in numero eorum qui a legendo
revocati sunt. Res autem ita se habet. Cum quidam et apud dominum nostrum anno
superiore et cum reformatoribus nuper egissent, ut legerem oratoriam artem, ut
satisfacerem eis legi et anno superiore concurrens cum Trapezuntio et isto sine
concurrente. Proximis autem diebus, ne multa repetam, domino nostro placuit
imminuere numerum doctorum et, ut dicebatur, relinquere cives, abrogare externos.
Iussit itaque afferri, ut appellant, rotulum in quo descripti cives essent, quem suo
chirographo confirmaret. Allatus est sed sine meo nomine, quasi ego Romanus non
sim . . .

There are grounds for supposing that the salaries of the Studium Urbis
were lower than in some other universities. In Florence, for example, in 1431
Carlo Marsuppini was given a starting salary of 140 florins for teaching
rhetoric, and in 1451 was offered 350 florins.[40] On the other hand Giovanni
Ponzio, who had been teaching grammar, poetry and rhetoric in Rome for

forty-eight years and was also rector of the university, protested in 1458 to Pope Calixtus III that he was still paid only seventy florins *de camera* annually, on which he had to keep a family. Calixtus III did heed his supplication, and the new Pope Pius II confirmed on 3 September 1458 that Ponzio's salary should be raised to 100 florins: his letter[41] to this effect is addressed to the Bishop of Spoleto and the abbots of San Gregorio and Sant' Anastasia in Rome, which may suggest that the *fraternitas clerum* were, as well as the reformers, still playing a vague part in the running of the Studium. Another humanist teacher whose financial position was improved thanks to the patronage of the most literary of Popes was Pietro Odo da Montopoli. On 24 October 1458 his three-year contract *ad lecturam Oratorie Poesis et Humanitatis* was renewed (he had already been teaching in the Studium Urbis for about eight years), and because he needed money not only for living expenses but also to buy books his salary was raised to 100 *ducatos auri ex pecuniis gabelle Studii*.[42] These increments, however, depended on initiatives coming from below, and were far from lavish; meanwhile the trend under Pius II would seem rather to have been towards stringency. On 1 February 1460 in a letter to the Bishop of Mantua higher salaries were promised for those who lectured most usefully and seemed most necessary but no money was to be available for superfluous lecturers; the Pope referred to a letter in which the conservators of the Camera Urbis had informed him that lecturers in the Studium were unwilling to go on teaching because of a reduction in salaries.[43] This tightening of administration may also be reflected in the order by the *vice-camerlengo* in 1461 that an annual roll of the Studium should be drawn up:[44] ten years earlier Valla's letter (quoted above) shows that this normal practice was being followed in Rome, but perhaps the university notary had been growing lax. Under Paul II the picture seems to have been much the same. His biographer, Gaspare of Verona, wrote that Paul raised salaries,[45] but as under Pius this was probably on a selective basis (perhaps including Gaspare); Pomponio Leto, the university's most celebrated teacher of rhetoric, left a memorandum among his papers that he went away from Rome in 1467 because he had not been paid.[46] What was happening to the funds of the university will be illustrated later.

The fullest evidence about who taught in the Studium and what they were paid in the later fifteenth century lies in certain surviving registers of the *depositarius gabellae studii* among the archives of the Camera Urbis in the Archivio di Stato, Rome. Some of this incomplete series of registers are those recording incoming payments: as such they are particularly valuable to historians of Roman civic society and the wine trade.[47] But the six surviving registers of outgoings,[48] payments made in accordance with mandates either from the conservators of the Camera Urbis and the reformers, or sometimes the cardinal chamberlain himself, are of much greater general interest, although relatively few historians have used them.[49] They not only provide a substitute for the university's annual *rotuli*, of which (though some payments were made for drawing them up)[50] no examples appear to have survived before the well known one of 1514.[51] For they are more than a mere roll of names and salaries promised under contract: they record some of the realities of financial administration in the Studium Urbis.

The following information is based mainly upon the registers of 1473–74 and 1482–84, taken as samples. Unfortunately the latter (see appendix 5.2) in part fails to specify the subjects taught by the individual masters receiving payment, an omission which recurs throughout the two surviving registers of the 1490s. Certain other registers, in the archives of both the Camera Urbis and the Camera Apostolica, can be used in addition to trace mandates for payments of salaries and other disbursements from the *gabella studii*: particularly valuable is a register for 1473–76 of the cardinal chamberlain Latino Orsini.[52]

A count of the masters paid during these years shows that the total number was high, even allowing that the periods covered by the registers do not correspond neatly with academic years, nor even clearly defined financial years, since payments were so often in arrears. In any one year the total may not have been much different from the eighty-eight recorded in the well known roll of 1514. The geographical distribution of places of origin is not always easy to trace, but there seem to have been a distinctly high number coming from Rome and its region (including the 'Cioceria' of the mountainous south-east hinterland)[53] even if Nicholas V's ordinance was not being strictly enforced. Most clearly the analysis shows that Law was by far the largest faculty; even if the various descriptions for 'humanist' masters are all combined, only with the inclusion of the grammar masters of the *rioni* do they beat the doctors of medicine to second place.

Table 5.1

	1473–74 (Reg. 118)	1482–84 (Reg. 124)
Civil law	23	19
Canon law	18	12
Grammar (in the *rioni*)	22	14
Rhetoric	9	8
Latin and/or Greek	2	2
Tre lingue (Latin, Greek, Hebrew)	–	1
Theoretical medicine	10	9
Practical medicine (*pratiche*)	8	5
Surgery	4	3
Theology	2	3
Metaphysics	2	–
Philosophy or moral philosophy	2	2
Natural philosophy	1	–
Logic	2	2
Teachers of unidentified subjects	2	62
Total	107	142

Note Neither of the above registers lists a lecturer in astronomy, but *cf.* Reg. 123, f. 42v, where on 3 October 1481 'Giovanni da Padova lettore in strologia' received for his first *terzaria* 66 *fior. rom.* 24 b. 8 d. (32 *fior. de cam.* 46).

Salaries were normally payable by termly instalment (Pius II's contract to Pietro Odo specifies that he was to be paid at Christmas, Easter and presumably at the end of the academic year),[54] though the registers show that the payments for each term (*terzaria*), were sometimes irregular, with only half or another fraction of the salary being paid, or even not paid at all. In any case, a long interval might elapse before the mandate for payment due was issued by the conservators of the Camera Urbis and the reformers, and another long delay before the *depositarius* of the *gabella* acted upon the mandate. The payments below (table 5.2), which were made to a sample of individual masters in the different faculties, illustrate these abuses; a closer study of a particular register (e.g. the last part especially of register 124 in appendix 5.2 below) shows their prevalence almost to the point of chaos in accountancy. The examples also illustrate how widely salaries might vary between masters in different or even the same faculties. Jurists, particularly canon lawyers, appear generally to have done well;[55] so do doctors of medicine,[56] but individual reputation and length of service were presumably taken into account first of all in the issue of a contract (compare, for instance, how little Stefano Infessura received compared with some of the other law teachers) and also the number of teaching hours, daily or only on *feste*. Of the humanists, it is interesting that Pomponio Leto was paid less than Porcelio or Paolo Marsi, but his salary rose over the years, and in 1496 he was paid a total of 300 Roman florins.[57] He and certain other masters sometimes had their salaries collected by a named proxy (perhaps a servant or a pupil?).[58] Grammar masters in the *rioni*—whose continued employment is in itself an interesting fact—seem in some cases to have received as much as did certain masters teaching in the central Studium: on the other hand there are a few cases of their being paid much less.[59] Another point which will have been noticed already is that two different coinages are quoted. The most usual of these, the so-called *fiorini romani*, was originally the senatorial or civic gold currency of Rome which since the time of Eugenius IV, with his extended control over the city's administration, was also known as *fiorini papali*.[60] It was subdivided into a silver coinage of *bolognini* (about thirty-five to the florin) and *denari* (about sixteen to the *bolognino*). The other coinage, *fiorini de camera*, was the gold florins of the Apostolic Chamber, which were worth about twice as much as the *fiorini romani*, and properly subdivided into silver *carleni* (ten to the florin), but in practice the units of *bolognini* and *denari* were usually given. The register for 1473–74 quotes payments in the equivalents of both coinages (in table 5.2 *fiorini de camera* are shown in brackets) so that it is not quite clear which was being used simply for accounting purposes and which for cash outlay. In the later registers, however, the payments are almost always given in Roman florins alone, except for the extra-mural expenses and sometimes the payments to the university's non-academic staff (reformers, notary, beadles, etc):[61] possibly a source of ignomiy and grievance to the masters.

The *gabella studii* clearly was a major business undertaking, and it may be assumed that the yield rose fairly steadily with the growth of Rome's population, both seasonal and permanent.[62] Another study would be needed to explain its administration, which would throw new light upon the activities of merchant syndicates in Rome both as *emptores* and *depositarii*. The sale of the *gabella* was announced by public proclamation;[63] by the end of the century the usual purchase price was stated to be 14,000 Roman florins. A document dated 5 December 1499[64] records the sale then held in the Palace of the Conservators, in the presence of the Treasurer General of the Church, Francesco Borgia, three of the conservators, the prior of the *caporioni*, one Gaspar Bonadies, who was one of the reformers, and three witnesses. On that occasion, since the sale was for the year 1500, the usual price was raised: 'cum augumento in anno Jubillei dumtaxat 2,000 ducatos'. Roughly noted figures of total sums handled which appear at the beginning or end of some registers suggest a considerable turnover: in 1497, for instance, the income of the *gabella* recorded by the *depositarius* was 13,050 Roman florins, and the outgoings were 7,901 only.[65]

It is not surprising that such a lucrative fund should have been tapped to serve some of the other heavy demands upon papal revenues, and that the clause prohibiting this, first set aside by Eugenius IV in 1433, was never restored. A deputation of Romans to the cardinals during the papal *sede vacante* in July 1471 appealed that the income destined for the Roman University should no longer be diverted to other objects, but the plea seems to have fallen upon deaf ears.[66] Under Sixtus IV the diversions were enormous. It could be argued that when there were good civic purposes in mind—defence, as during the time of Eugenius IV, or environmental improvements—some diversion of what was in any case a civic tax on wine drinking was quite justifiable. Sixtus IV seems, in fact, to have financed much of his programme of rebuilding and refurbishing the city out of the *gabella studii*. The construction of the Ponte Sisto, the repair and maintenance of the city walls and the aqueduct of the Trevi fountain, even the restoration of the equestrian statue of Marcus Aurelius ('Constantine'), were paid for in prompt assignments of cameral florins by the *depositarius gabelle*.[67] Charges on the *gabella* for road works were recurrent items in the registers; the *maestri stratarum* received standing payments, also in cameral florins.[68]

Injustice occurred, however, when the appropriations were such that they deprived the Studium of its funds for the current expenditure on salaries; it was a lesser injustice that they deprived it also of funds for capital outlay. Real hardship must have been suffered by some of the enrolled teachers during these years. The arrears and gaps in the register for 1473–74 are themselves suggestive; in January 1475 the cardinal chamberlain even ordered an all-round reduction in the salaries of doctors of the Studium,[69] to be implemented by Meliaduse Cigala, the Genoese financier acting as *depositarius* of both the Camera Urbis and the *gabella*.[70]

Some record survives of the indignation these proceedings aroused. The best known of the protesters, an old and professional hand at invective, was Francesco Filelfo. After much effort Filelfo had at last obtained a Chair of rhetoric in Rome in 1474. On 17 September of the previous year he had

Table 5.2 Payments to a sample of masters in the Studium Urbis.

	1473 First term	Second term	Third term	1474 First term
Rhetoric				
Pomponio Leto			50	
Gaspare Veronese	40 (19.42)		50	
Porcelio Pandoni			133⅓ (64.20)	83⅓
Martino Filetico (Greek)	23⅓ (11.30.3)	33⅓		33⅓
Domenico Calderini da Verona (Greek)	33⅓ (16.23)	33⅓	33⅓	66⅔
Andrea Brenzi				
Paolo Marsi				
Grammar (in *rioni*)				
Gaspare Scantiglie (r. Sant' Angelo)	33⅓	33⅓		33⅓
Civil law				
Domenico de Bonis Auguriis	26⅔ (13.4)	26⅔		33⅓
Stefano Infessura	26⅔			13⅓ (6.38)
Andrea de Bonciis	83⅓ (40.57.3)			
Tito Veltri, Bishop of Acquapendente				
Canon law				
Francesco Pellati da Padova	(50)	60 (29.27)		133⅓
Richo da Siena				
Coronato de Planchetis	50 (24.34.3)	50		50
Giovanni de Rossi, Bishop of Alatri (1478)	10 (4.64.3)	10		8⅓ (4.5.3)
Theology				
Francesco Sansoni	66⅔ (32.46)	66⅔		100 (48.68)
Antonio da Pinerolo				
Logic				
Rolando da Pavia	16⅔ (8.11.3)	16⅔		
Alessandro da Gennazano				
Medicine				
Antonio da Anguillara (theoretical)	33⅓ (16.2.3)	66⅔		66⅔
Filippo della Valle (theoretical)	50	50		66⅔
Giulielmo di Campo (practical)	33⅓	33⅓	33⅓	66⅔
Giovanni Agnolo de Vettoris (practical)				10 (surgery)
Surgery				
Lorenzo Cerrini	10	10		
Horlandino				

For the nature of the currency given in this table see p. 76.

1482 Second term	1482 Third term	1483 First term	Register 118 references	Register 124 references
94.33.36	66.23.8	126.22.24	xxxvir xxiv xxxxvir xxiiv	xiiv xiiiv xivr xvv xvir 22v
50	50		xviiir xxiiiv xxxii xxiiiv xxivr xxxviir	xiiir, xviiiv, xxv
82.46.24	83.11.12	100		xiv xivv xviiiv
116.22.24	102.46.16	116.23.8		xiv xvir xviir xviiir xxiir
16.23.8 (half owing)	33.11.12	70	xxiiir 32v 35v	xiiv xviiiir 21v 28r
116.23.8	116.23.8	100	xviiv 31v xxxviiir	xiiir xivv 27v
45	40	85	xxiiv xxxviv xviir	xir xvir xviiiiv 28r 22r
56.13.24	66.23.8			xiiir xivv 27r
	133.11.12	166.23.8	xviir 32v xxxviv	xvr xxv 25r
100	100	100		xiv xviiir xxv 21v
25	50	56.23.8	xviiir 33r xxxxv	xiiiv xviiiir 22v
20	20	33.11.12	xxiv 28r xxxviir	xir xvir xviir 22r
66.22.24			xxr xxxviir xxxviiir	xir xxr
33.11.12		30	xxir 29v	xvr 24v
100		100	xviir xxvr 34r xviiir xxxviiiv 34v xxvir 30r 34r xxxviir	xviiiv 24v
	33.11.12	50	xxxviiiir	xviiiiv 24v
20.23.8	26.23.8	33.11.12	xxvv 29v	xiiiv xvv 23r
	16.23.8	46.22.24		xvr xviiiir 26r

written to Lorenzo de' Medici that his appointment was being prevented because Sixtus IV had been told that he (Filelfo) was unwilling to give lectures and was too old in any case.[71] However, thanks to Cardinal Pietro Riario and his brother Girolamo, Filelfo was now expecting to be summoned to Rome, and intended to leave his pregnant wife with his family in Milan until Easter. Over a year later, on 26 October 1474, he wrote again[72] from Milan, telling Lorenzo that he had been appointed with an annual salary of 600 Roman florins [sic] and the promise of a scriptorship in the papal chancery; he had learnt by a letter of 15 October from Cardinal Gonzaga that the roll of the Studium had already been published and included his name. His arrival seems to have been delayed, but he wrote from Rome on 14 January 1475 that he was in high favour with Sixtus IV.[73] On 20 June he wrote to Duke Galeazzo Maria Sforza to announce that he was returning to Milan to collect his family, with the Pope's permission and goodwill.[74] Again he delayed about half a year before coming back to Rome (he explained that this was because his wife was ill and two of his children had died) but trouble arose after he had applied in April 1476 for an advance payment to travel again to Milan. Cardinal Latino Orsini, the chamberlain, had sent a special mandate to Cigala on 10 May 1476 ordering payment of 100 cameral florins to Filelfo,[75] but it appears this was disregarded, for on 25 July 1476 Filelfo wrote[76] in fury to Sixtus IV that Cigala was an inept humbug and an infamous monster, dropped insinuations about licentious parties for adolescent boys held at his house, and proposed that he should be hanged and left on the scaffold for crows to eat. On 3 January 1477 he wrote again, complaining that Cigala had cheated him.[77] In the absence of Cigala's full records of accounting it is difficult to be sure what had been going on. In fairness to the *depositarius* it must be recalled that he had general orders to withhold payments to teachers, and there was no good reason why Filelfo should not have had to suffer with the rest, or even more than the rest, since he had often been absent, and in any case his salary, at 600 Roman florins, was greatly in excess of the normal rates in the Studium Urbis. However, it may be that Filelfo had succeeded in bringing some pressure to bear upon the Pope and chamberlain to have second thoughts about the wisdom of their punitive financial policy—at least so far as it affected some one so prominent and vociferous as himself. On 31 July 1477 a mandate to Cigala acknowledged that recently many extraordinary expenses had prevented ordinary payments from being made: 'multi: tam Doctores ad legendum in Studio dicte urbis conducti: quam alie persone' had not received the money owed to them. Cigala was ordered to put sufficient money from the *gabella* on interest in order to meet these obligations.[78]

Another who expressed his discontent was the scurrilous diarist Stefano Infessura. Infessura not only taught civil law in the Studium but later held the office of *scribasenato* (equivalent to a notary of the Camera Urbis),[79] so in these matters at least he was in a good position to know his facts. He recounts that when Giovanni Marcellini, one of the reformers, petitioned Sixtus IV that contracted payments ought to be honoured the Pope replied that he had told him previously that salaries would not be paid, then corrected himself, recalling disingenuously that he had said this to another of the reformers.[80] According to Infessura the appropriations continued (as indeed the registers for the early 1480s confirm), and the teachers of the Studium were deprived on account of military expenditure (presumably the papal war with Venice over Ferrara).[81] Again, the *depositarius* may have been caught in a difficult position: in the register for 1481–82 he accounted a higher sum on outgoings than on income;[82] in January 1484 the *vice-depositarius* Niccolò Calcaneo was paid his salary of twenty-five ducats and complimented for managing so well in a time of war, even at the risk of not being repaid what he spent.[83] There are rumbles, however, which suggest that a head-on collision between papal authority and civic autonomy was looming over the university's administration. In January 1484 the chamberlain, Cardinal Rafaelle Riario, was trying to find a compromise over the anomalous situation in which both the conservators and the *caporioni* had appointed two notaries, who were Roman citizens, to serve the reformers, and the Pope had appointed another.[84] Then, in the *sede vacante* of August 1484, renewed pressure was brought to bear upon the cardinals by the citizens of Rome. Infessura claims to have seen for himself at the Palace of the Conservators a document which he describes as the 'bullam studii'. But the new Pope, Innocent VIII, violated his promise to ensure that only Romans should be elected to civic offices, appointing his son-in-law Gherardo Usodimare, another Genoese, as *depositarius pecuniarum gabelle studii*, shabbily saving his face by creating Usodimare a Roman citizen.[85] There is evidence that Usodimare even paid Innocent VIII's doctor's bill of 100 florins out of the *gabella studii* in April 1485,[86] and Infessura commented that the Pope's offer in 1486 to provide 1,000 florins for the masters of the Studium out of the 26,000 florins he had raised from selling offices was not out of any spirit of generosity but because they had recently been deprived again. (The defence of Rome against the Duke of Calabria's army was presumably at their expense.)[87] In 1489 Infessura complained of more appropriations,[88] but there is other evidence that Innocent VIII was by then trying to give them a better deal.[89]

That long-established teacher of canon law Francesco Pellati of Padua also complained of the injustice, but less vituperatively, by means of petition. In 1482 he complained to the Pope, the cardinal chamberlain and vice-chamberlain that he had not been paid the third instalment of his salary; eventually, on 16 August 1482, Cardinal Riario sent a special mandate to Simone da Lucca 'conductori Gabelle vini' to pay Francesco 133⅓ Roman florins.[90]

The Studium Urbis had a central location, close to the church of Sant' Eustachio, but evidence suggests that until the end of the fifteenth century the teaching premises were scarcely adequate, which places the papal raiding of the funds in a further unfavourable light. There seem to have been several adjacent houses, though the fourteenth-century *domus studii* may have passed into private ownership.[91] One source suggests that the civic authorities bought a house for the Studium *c.* 1431;[92] certainly Eugenius IV obtained possession of a house in 1433 from the abbot of San Paolo Fuori le Mura (the tenant was ordered to vacate and hand over the keys within a week), and arrangements for its purchase were made by an assignment on the Monte of Florence.[93] In 1448 the Compagnia of the SSmo Salvatore al Laterano granted a lease on a house called the 'Domus Studii' for an annual rent of three gold florins to Francesco da Padova, lector in the Studium.[94] This lease raises several problems. Does it illustrate a continuation of the managerial interest in the Studium which Eugenius IV had granted to the Compagnia ten years earlier? Was it issued to Francesco da Padova in his official or his private capacity? Meanwhile there is a letter of Lorenzo Valla in June 1449 which refers to accomodation in a house belonging to the Studium.[95] Valla wrote to Giovanni Tortelli of his difficulty in trying to obtain rooms in it. One room he wanted was occupied (he thought only for drinking and fornication) by a certain Stephanus, *familiaris* of Juan de Mella, Bishop of Zamora (later a cardinal). Valla had lost fifteen days' work in going first to the reformers, then to the *vice-camerlengo* and others. One of the reformers, Pietro Melini, had told him only the Pope could settle the matter, which Valla thought absurd, but he asked for Tortelli's intercession. There was also a kitchen next door, the noise and smells from which disturbed study; moreover the university beadle had a bed in it. Valla thought this had no academic usefulness; could he obtain the kitchen he would have access also to a small garden, to which he promised he would invite Tortelli for pleasant supper parties in summer. There were other rooms he mentions, including three which 'd. Franciscus' held, although he had more than he needed in his own house. This was presumably the same Francesco da Padova whom Valla describes as auditor of the *vice-camerlengo* and therefore difficult to evict.

Most of the teachers presumably held their classes in these buildings, apart from the grammar masters of the *rioni*. Payments were made for the ringing of the church bells of Sant' Eustachio.[96] Repairs to the Domus Studii were made in 1473 and 1476;[97] payments for running repairs (particularly the repair of benches) were made either to the reformers[98] or to the beadles; the latter were paid for various jobs, including their services at the *festa* of St Luke, probably the opening day of the academic year.[99] A payment on 2 October 1482 also records that 'Piero Fiorentino' had made a marble shield of arms placed on a wall of the Studium.[100]

That these premises were inadequate is recorded later by Paolo Cortesi, a former student. He wrote that Pomponio Leto 'often cursed the civic governors of all nations and people (i.e. the government of Rome) with vehemence, that they seemed to want a narrow and sordid auditorium to be in the theatre of the civilised world, whereby should be symbolised the broken virtue and loss of power of Rome'.[101] On the other hand until late in the fifteenth century teaching accomodation may not have been much better in other Italian universities: it was only then that large-scale building was under way.[102] According to one of the humanist teachers in the Studium, Giovanni Sulpizio, Innocent VIII had ambitious plans,[103] but it was his successor Alexander VI who authorised a start on building to be made in 1497.

Why did the Borgia Pope take this step? He may have been receiving petitions for several years from the reformers or the teaching body, and took action in his mood of expiatory zeal after his son, the Duke of Gandia, had been murdered. He may also have been influenced by his family lawyer[104] and eulogist,[105] Camillo Beneimbene, who had himself held various civic posts and offices relating to the university's administration (including that of *peciarius*)[106] and had among his other clients Cardinal Nardini[107] and Pomponio Leto.[108] Whatever the motive, on 17 December 1497 a papal mandate *motu proprio* to the cardinal chamberlain and treasurer ordered that the *depositarius* should pay 1,000 ducats to the rector and reformers for the repair and enlargement of the buildings.[109] On 16 November 1498 another papal mandate ordered a further 1,000 ducats to be sent according to the orders of a special building committee consisting of the rector of the university, Orlando Orsini, Pedro Isvalies, governor of Rome (later cardinal), and the papal secretary, Ludovico Podocatharo.[110] The money was to go to two Florentines, Sante and Andrea, 'architectis et muratoribus'. Three similar payments, one of 500 and two of 300 ducats, are recorded in 1499,[111] and more were to come. Alexander VI himself went to visit the site on 5 May 1499.[112] Unfortunately there seems to be no drawing in existence of these Borgia buildings; they must have been demolished before Giacomo della Porta began building the Sapienza in 1575.[113] There is a literary description, however, by Andrea Fulvio, praising the Pope for his munificence in the erection of such buildings, reminiscent of the academies of Antiquity with their porticoes, galleries, courts, halls and central apartments.[114]

If teaching accomodation had been meagre, so was residential accomodation for students. One of the few specific clauses in Boniface VIII's foundation statute, repeated in 1431, provided for the inspection of houses let as lodgings for masters and students and for the fixing of rents—a system copied directly from Bologna. How well this worked is not clear: the demand and price of lodgings in Rome must usually have been high and the need obvious for specially endowed hostels and colleges. Though the intention to found such a college for poor students had been announced in 1433,[115] other demands upon the *gabella* had priority. Although there were hundreds of charitable foundations in Rome, the city compared badly with other places in this respect: Padua, for instance, had nine small colleges before 1500.[116] Paolo Cortesi suggested that it was the duty of the cardinals to endow colleges and provide for students from their home towns or countries,[117] but few founded them in Rome. In 1427 Cardinal Branda da Castiglione had obtained permission from Martin V to found a residential college in all the arts at the palace where he lived by Sant' Apollinare,[118] but nothing seems to have come of this. There were two exceptions. First was the college founded by Cardinal

Domenico Capranica for students of theology and canon law.[119] Its seat was
his palace after his death in 1458, until 1478, when it moved next door.
Capranica's foundation was close in spirit (as well as physically) to the
Studium Urbis. Its revenues came from property held in trust for the founder
by the Compagnia del SSmo Salvatore al Laterano, whose *guardiani*, together
with the conservators of the Camera Urbis and the *caporioni*, had visitatorial
functions. It gave preference to students of Roman birth: eighteen places for
Romans were in the presentation of the *caporioni*. Second of the colleges was
the small theological seminary founded by Stefano Nardini under the terms
of his will of 1480 (four years before his death): it too was entrusted to the
Compagnia del SSmo Salvatore.[120] Apart from these two institutions it is
possible that some non-Roman students lodged in the respective hospice for
pilgrims of their nation. In January 1497 Henry VII wrote to the confraternity
of the English hospice of St Thomas, expressing the wish that it should follow
the example of similar institutions, and accomodate some scholars of its
nation.[121]

Who and how many were the students of the Studium Urbis and how content
were they? There are no records of matriculation, and little survives about
the granting of degrees. This side of university life connects with another
difficult problem: the relationship, not fully explained by an argument of
separate development, between the Studium Urbis and the Studium of the
Roman Curia. The latter may have been losing some of its *raison d'être* after
the permanent resettlement of the papacy in Rome,[122] but it continued to
exist, and the cardinal chamberlain was described as the chancellor of both
institutions.[123] As 'Cancellarius Universitatis Studii Romanae Curiae' it was
in his name that in November 1425, for instance, a candidate was to be
examined and, if successful, granted a doctorate of medicine *Studii Curiae*, and
this was apparently to take place in the church of Sant' Eustachio, seat of
the Studium Urbis.[124] In 1424 a candidate for the doctorate of theology was
to be examined by professors 'in Romana Curia et almae Urbis studio'.[125]
Perhaps, since theology was the special concern of the Studium Curiae, the
biggest overlap occurred in this faculty.[126]

There is no evidence that students in Rome were organised into national
communities as at Bologna and other universities. But Cardinal Capranica's
college gave preference to students of Roman birth, and the Studium also
considered their needs in providing the grammarians of the *rioni*; it would
seem that in keeping with the policy of having the roll of doctors as Roman
as possible the students—despite Boniface VIII's original wish—were drawn
mostly from the urban patriciate and baronage of Rome and its region.
Numbers may have been swollen by hangers-on of the papal court when
anyone famous was giving lectures—particularly the humanists. Gaspare
of Verona wrote *c.* 1451 that there were about a hundred listeners, mostly
wearing beards, at his lectures on Terence and Virgil and Aristotle's *Ethics*;[127]
the notebooks survive of two students, Piero Pacino da Pescia and one
Marianus of Palestrina, who heard Martino Filetico's lectures on Juvenal

and Persius *c.* 1470; Marianus described himself as one of an innumerable crowd of students;[128] Martino Filetico himself declared that vast audiences came regularly to hear him expound Cicero's letters;[129] Filelfo also drew large numbers.[130]

A student of law called Pierangelo, who came from Sicily, is also known from the letter he wrote to a friend about 1471.[131] Pierangelo sounds rather disillusioned with the Studium Urbis and the loutishness of young Romans:

> Here if the crowd of jostling youths should catch sight of someone in a ragged worn-out cloak, either hastening towards the market or to the school for his classes, they challenge him with loud laughs and immediately shove him in the mud, push him forward with blows, throw stones at him from behind (a very clear sign of their being blockheads) and call him a glutton, a humbug, a buffoon.

Pierangelo was also shocked by the student custom of writing scurrilous or obscene verses in bad Latin, worthy (he curiously observes) of a priest of Babel, and recited with great vanity and impudence. Such verses were even inscribed on the back of the chair used by one of the professors of eloquence, Giovanni Porcelio, though from what some other sources have to say about Porcelio this mockery may not have been undeserved.[132] Worse than this, some of the students painted indecent pictures upon the walls or urinated upon them. Pierangelo's conclusion was that Rome was a barbaric city and he advised his friend, 'If at last you have made up your mind to join me, which I strongly urge you to do, let us not remain here, where all virtue is exhausted, but let us go to Bologna, that city most rich in everything [quasi *bona omnia*], including virtue . . .'

Pierangelo evidently suffered in Rome from his outraged earnestness and sense of being an outsider. Perhaps he would have been less miserable had there been an organised *nazione* and college for Sicilians. One of the merits of Bologna, he went on to say, was that there was a good Sicilian professor of law there. On the other hand rough horseplay (the frequent repairs to the benches in the *Domus Studii* may also be evidence of this) was certainly not peculiar to Rome among the Italian universities. Besides the *festa* of St Luke the carnival was probably a special occasion for it; participation was even encouraged, and in February 1473 a student called Antonio de' Cancellieri was paid twenty-six Roman florins to organise festivities.[133] Moreover the teaching methods of the humanist professors, if not the jurists too, positively stimulated animosity and ridicule. The students of rival professors, such as Angelo Sabino and Domizio Calderini, revelled in the controversy they heard;[134] and it is hardly surprising if they tried to relate to contemporary life the lectures they heard, for instance, on Juvenal's *Satires*. The writing of topical verses and epigrams was a part of their education: it became the special feature of the new *festa* of Pasquino,[135] who may himself have been a Roman grammar master. A decrepit antique statue near his house came to be named after him; at the *festa* in April it was decorated and surrounded with such writings. In the early years of the sixteenth century one of the teachers of rhetoric, Donato Poli, collected selections, which were printed at the expense of Cardinal Caraffa and his successors who lived in the adjacent palace.

There was, however, a more dangerous element in Roman student life, which Pierangelo does not mention, but which could have prejudiced the Pope and cardinals against the Studium Urbis: namely, political involvement in movements supporting baronial power and civic liberty in Rome. The republican conspiracy of Stefano Porcaro in 1453 may have made the papal court wary of an institution which, by its nature, caused crowds of young Romans and members of the patrician families to collect together in the city. During the violent disturbances of 1459–60, while Pius II was absent at Mantua and elsewhere, it seems likely that students were among the gang of several hundred who followed Tiburzio, Stefano Porcaro's nephew, and terrorized the city.[136] In 1468 Paul II acted swiftly when informed of an alleged conspiracy against his life, supported by armed force;[137] immorality and religious backsliding were not the only pretexts for his persecution of the *sodalitas amicorum antiquitatis*, which included the notable professor Pomponio Leto. It is strange, however, that Porcelio, who back in 1434 had supported the Colonna in the civic rising against Eugenius IV and been imprisoned,[138] and Gaspare of Verona, an old associate of the Porcaro family, should have escaped censure; in Gaspare's case the austere moral tone of his lectures, his servility towards Paul II and the fact he was from the Veneto rather than a Roman may help to account for the fact.[139]

The events of the Tiburzio rising, described in Pius II's *Commentaries*,[140] even suggest that beneath the cause of the Roman republic and vengeance for Porcaro there may have been particular motivations of student discontent. Tiburzio's gang occupied the Pantheon, very close to Sant' Eustachio and the Domus Studii, and then, having been driven out, took possession of the nearby palace of the late Cardinal Domenico Capranica, where the new college was to be established. Maybe an issue was the enforced resignation from the rectorship of the Studium of Niccolò Capranica, who had just succeeded his dead uncle as Bishop of Fermo, and his replacement, on Pius II's nomination, by a doctor of theology, Giovanni Stefano de' Butigellis.[141] Even if they could take no part in the appointment of a rector, Roman students might have had strong feelings in support of a local patrician figure with patriotic Roman attitudes, rather than a pedantic theologian. It is interesting that Niccolò Capranica is again heard of as rector from 1466 to 1473.[142] Subsequently the Orsini, whose stronghold at Montegiordano was not far away, seem to have been in control. From 1473 to 1495 Orso Orsini, nephew of the cardinal chamberlain Latino Orsini, was rector,[143] and his brother, Battista Orsini, is recorded as vice-rector in 1475–76.[144] In 1495 Orlando Orsini, Bishop of Nola, became rector.[145]

The conclusion seems clear that in spite of some particular encouragement from Eugenius IV, with the introduction of the *gabella studii* and the donation of a house, and from Alexander VI, with the eventual building of new premises, and in spite of the considerable number of teachers and the high attendance at some of the lectures given by celebrities, the Studium Urbis of the fifteenth century fell short of Boniface VIII's original hopes. It was more Roman (which, paradoxically, meant more provincial) than a *studium generale* should have been; it suffered from the papacy's financial appropriations of the *gabella*, from uncompetitive and often suspended salaries, poor accomodation, and administrative interference which curtailed the civic prestige enjoyed by other Italian universities. Perhaps it also suffered from the workings of what may be called Rashdall's law, according to which Italian universities flourished most in the fifteenth century not in the largest and wealthiest cities, where the cost of living and the distractions were too great, but in smaller cities nearby, as Milan, Venice and Florence respectively were served by Pavia, Padua and to some extent Pisa.[146]

It may seem surprising that in a period when Popes and cardinals were apparently so much in favour of learning they took, on the whole, such limited or spasmodic interest in supporting the University of Rome. The fear of subversion, both intellectual and political, on their own doorstep may provide one explanation. Moreover in addition to the amorphous Studium of the Curia there were other universities to which they had responsibilities or personal attachments: in the Papal State alone there were Perugia and Bologna, which was particularly favoured by Martin V, Eugenius IV, Nicholas V and Paul II.[147] Furthermore the Popes and cardinals—like the Florentine *ottimati*, for instance[148]—probably preferred to conceive their patronage of learning as a non-institutional matter of household academies and the provision of jobs, benefices and favours for individual scholars, prestigious book collecting and the commissioning of translations, editions and orations. In these ways fame for liberality and studious gravity were more safely acquired.

Further study of the Studium Urbis (and an investigation is needed of the developments under Julius II and Leo X, its acclaimed reformer) may confirm or modify some of these conclusions; but in general it seems fair to say that during the fifteenth century the Studium was facing the problem familiar to many universities today, of being launched with ambitious plans and then denied the money to see them through.

APPENDIX 5.1

PAPAL LETTER OF EUGENIUS IV TO THE REFORMERS OF THE STUDIUM URBIS, 29 SEPTEMBER 1433
(Vatican archives, Reg. Vat. 372, ff. 229r–230r)

Eugenius etc. dilectis filiis Andree de Santacruce legum doctori consistorii nostri advocato, Laurentio Petri Omnisancti, Paulo Petri Paulutii et Petro Cecchi Pauli, reformatoribus studii almae Urbis salutem etc. Licet ex litterarum nostrarum tenore pecunie studio Urbis deputatis in alium usum converti non debuissent, considerantes tamen pro rerum exigentia minorem necessitatem oportere cedere maiori, maxime cum eidem studio nulla incommoditas sequeretur, sed pro doctoribus qui conducti erant et aliis oportunis pecunie ad suficientiam superessent propter expugnationem Castri Novi ipsi Urbi adversarii, vobis ac dilectis filiis conservatoribus capitibusque regionum mandavimus, ut ex pecuniis huiusmodi studio deputatis solverentur dilectis filiis Jacobello Antonii Laurentii Guidolini, uni ex conservatoribus predictis, et Laurentio Benedicti Uguitionis, priori capitum regionum, florenos mille auri de Camera, quos florenos mille eisdem in nostri presentia prout mandaveramus manualiter persolvistis; et postea pro solutione Riccii, quem de partibus Campanie conduci fecimus cum certis gentibus, ne ex dictis gentibus periculum inesset Urbi, quod verisimiliter imminebat, simili mandato nostro venerabili fratri Angelo Episcopo Parentino florenos mille, et otto similes ac bononinos triginta duos et dimidium dedistis et assignastis in quarum partium recompensatione, silicet pro pretio, florenorum mille de Camera domum quandam quam emimus a priore, capitulo et conventu monasterii Sancti Pauli prope Urbem ordinis Sancti Benedicti, que posita est in regione Sancti Eustachii, cui ab uno dilecti filii Petri de Casatiis domus, ab alio venerabilis fratris Archiepiscopi Neapolitani orti et ab alio via publica lateribus coherent, dedimus et consignavimus ac presentis tenore damus et consignamus ex nostra plenitudine potestatis, supplentes omnes defectus ex certa scientia, pro qua domo eidem monasterio de annuo redditu sexaginta florenos auri de Florentia super Monte communis Florentie integre et sine aliquo onere percipiendorum ex certis pecuniis ipsius Montis ad nos et Cameram Apostolicam spectantibus providimus; et pro doctoribus per vestros huiusmodi officio predecessores ad legendum conductis pro duabus pagis, et fratribus de Araceli pro pulsatione campanarum, florenos similes noningentos et quadraginta duos et bononi⟨no⟩s quinquaginta sex; et pro bulla officii vestri, et notarii ac bidellorum sallariis, et aliis expensis necessariis, florenos nonaginta duos; et demum alios florenos mille et quadringentos similes dilecti filio Francischo de Bosculis depositario nostro quos expendi oportuit pro expulsione filii iniquitatis Nicolaii de la Stella, qui insultum fecerat cum certis gentibus contra Urbem prefatam, similiter de speciali mandato nostro consignastis et persolvistis. Idcirco ne de prefatis pecuniarum summis, que in totum capiunt florenos de Camera quatuor milia quadringentos et quadraginta tres et bononinos viginti sex, per vos ut prefertur persolutis ullo possitis tempore molestari, ex eo maxime quia fuerunt aliis maioribus necessitatibus quam studii, etiam sine ipsius studii incomodo applicate [ms. applicatis] cum omnes dictas quantitates, vos ex nostro mandato persolvisse ac easdem in prefatis causis pervenisse nobis appareat et liquidissime constet, tenore presentium vos ab omnibus et singulis predictis summis absolutos esse voluimus, et totaliter liberatos, prout vos et vestrum quemlibet absolvimus, tenore presentium liberamus privilegiis et litteris nostris illis, presertim per quas continetur quod pecunie studii in alios usus applicari non debeant, consuetudinibus et aliis in contrarium facientibus non obstantibus quibuscunque [etc.]

Datum Rome apud Sanctum Laurentium in Damaso anno incarnationis Domini millesimo quadringentesimo tricesimo tertio kalendas Ottobris pontificatus nostri anno tertio.

APPENDIX 5.2

REGISTER OF PAYMENTS BY NICCOLÒ CALCANEO,
DEPOSITARIUS OF THE GABELLA STUDII, 1482–84
(A.S.R., Arch. Cam. Urbis, Busta 43, reg. 124)

The following tabulation aims to reproduce the essential information in the original (see text above, particularly nn. 48–9). The spelling of names of persons and places has not been standardised (e.g. Foligno appears as Fulcineo on f. xi*r* and Fuligno on f. 28*r* and there are many minor variants of surnames). When a payment was received by a proxy his name is shown in brackets after the master's. Payments are given in Roman florins, except where it is stated they were in cameral florins. The alteration of numerals from a Roman to an arabic sequence after f. xx has been kept as in the original.

Folio and year	Date (and date of mandate)	Name	Subjects	Term	Payment		
xi*r*							
1482	30 May						
	(25 April)	Stefano Infessura	Civil law (eves.)	Half second	20		
	,,	Tomaso delle Vetere	Medicine (eves.)	,,	25		
	,,	Luca de Fulcineo	Moral philosophy	,,	10		
	(15 April)	Giovanni Agniolo de Vettoris	Pratiche	,,	16	23	8
	(25 April)	Antonio de Pinerolo	Theology and metaphysics	,, ,,	33	11	12
	,,	Bartolomeo de Ballioniibus	Papal decretals	,,	16	23	8
	,,	Bartolomeo Artes	Theology and physics	,,	11	23	8
	,,	Giovanni di Cipro	Medicine (morns.)	,,	16	32	8
	,,	Giovanni de' Rossi Bishop of Alatri	Decretum (fest.)	,,	10		
	,,	Antonio Mazano	[Grammar] rione Pinea	,,	13	11	12
xi*v*							
	(15 May)	Nicholo de Grassi	Medicine (eves.)	,,	33	11	12
	(25 April)	Giovanni Sichulo	Rhetoric (fest.)	,,	20		
	,,	Bernardo de Tedallenis	Medicine	,,	33	2	12
	,,	Andrea Benzi	Latin and Greek	,,	41	23	12
	,,	Buonohomo de Buonihuomini	Clementines (fest.)	,,	16	23	8
	,,	Richo da Siena	Canon law (morns.)	,,	50		
	25 April	Bernabo Azio	[Grammar] rione S. Eustachio	,,	10		
	,,	Choluccio de Lucca	[Grammar] rione Campitelli	,,	8	11	12
	,	Jachopo di Batista	[Grammar] rione Ripa	,,	10		
xii*r*							
	,,	Stefano de Varis	Medicine (eves.)	,,	11	23	8
	,,	Giovanbattista de Varis	Pratiche	,,	10		
	,,	Cristofano da Fano	Civil law (eves.)	,,	20	23	8
	,,	Pietro Marso	Rhetoric	,,	25		
	,,	Petro	[Grammar] rione Ponte	,,	10		
	,,	Orlandino	Surgery (eves.)	Second	16	23	8
	,,	Tito [Veltri] Bishop of Acquapendente	Codex	Half second	33	2	12
	,,	Pagholo de Bondi	Institutes (fest.)	,,	8	11	12
	,,	Ludovico de Vassiano	[Grammar] rione Arenula	,,	10		
	,,	Ludovicho da Siena	Metaphysics	,,	11	23	8
xii*v*							
	,,	Guasparre de Schandriglie	[Grammar] rione S. Angelo	,,	16	23	8
	,,	Antonio da Lucca	Medicine	,,	41	23	12
	30 May						
	(25 April)	Pomponio (Juliano suo)	Rhetoric	Half second	33	11	12
	,	Suplizio	Rhetoric	,,	25		

Folio and year	Date (and date of mandate)	Name	Subjects	Term	Payment
1482	(25 April)	Giovanni Collino	[Grammar] rione Trastevere	„	8 11 12
	„	Paolo Emilio de Albertonibus		„	13 11 12
	„	Agniolo Jachobini	Canon law (eves.)	„	50
	„	Giovanni Corrini	Surgery [?]	„	51 23 12
	„	Paolo Marzo	Rhetoric	„	33 11 12
	(31 March)	Giovanni Antonio di Parma	Canon law	Second	66 23 8
xiiir	(22 May)	Simone da Lucha 'conduttore della detta chabella per la sesta parte in dedu-zione di 300 simili fiorini in prezo della detta chabella rimissoli'			50
	(25 April)	Guido Antonio da Siena	Civil law	Second	66 23 8
	„	Lucha Casali		„	100
	„	Domenico de Boni aughuri ('suo charzone')	Civil law	„	116 23 8
	„	Lodovicho da Viterbo	Theology	„	16 23 8
	(31 May)	Ciriarcho Canponi (notaro)	Per cera et charta		3
1 June	(25 April)	Martino Fileticho	Latin and Greek	Half second	25
4 June	(25 April)	Giovanni de Japoccis		Second	8
	(14 May)	Antonio Ambrosii	[Grammar] rione Parione	Half second	10
	(15 May)	Antonio Bernardino da San Gemignano	Institutes	„	10
	(25 April)	Ghuglielmo Ramondo	'Tre linchue' [Latin, Greek, Hebrew]	„	16 23 8
xiiiv	„	Tomaso da laquila	Philosophy	Second	26 23 8
7 June	(25 April)	Ponpilio	Rhetoric	Half second	18 11 12
8 June	(30 April)	Chorenato de Planche ('il suo gharzone')	Canon law	„	25
	(15 April)	Lorenzo Cerrini	Surgery		20 23 8
	(18 March)	Nicholo Buttaglino	[Grammar] rione Trevi	Second	20
	„	Pietro di Giuliano	Institutes (fest.)	„	10
9 June	(10 April)	Antonio Flores	Papal decretals	Half second	13 11 12
10 June	(15 April)	Heronimo de Chavellanis	Civil law	„	50

Folio and year	Date (and date of mandate)	Name	Subjects	Term	Payment
	11 June				
	(25 April)	Giovanni Deondi da Padova		,,	50
	(9 May)	Antonio Volsci	Rhetoric	,,	25
	13 June				
	(20 April)	Quintilio	Rhetoric	,,	11 23 8
xivr					
	18 June				
	(15 April)	Sigismondo de Gigantibus	[Grammar] rione Monte	Half second	10
	22 June				
	(22 June)	Francesco Tascha, notario delle maestri delle vie			40
	(19 June)	Antonio Muciano, scrittore de conservadori e notario delle provisioni sopra le dette reparazione de mure		Three months' salary	8 6 = 4 cam. flor. 22 b.
	,,	Egidio dandrea di Toccho	Maestro di murare e di legniamie	Three months' salary	15 11 4 = 7½ cam. flor. (at 72 per flor).
	30 June				
	(1 June)	Pagholo de Albertonibus	Institutes	Half second	11 23 8
	(25 April)	Ponponio (Juliano suo)	Rhetoric	Rest of second	33 11 12
	12 July				
	(9 May)	Antonio Volscho	Rhetoric	,,	25
xivv					
	(25 May)	Luca de Chosarii	Canon law (fest.)	Half second	11 23 8
	27 July				
	(1 July)	Domenicho de boni auguri	Civil law (mat.)	Third	116 23 8
	19 August				
	(25 April)	Andrea Benzi	Latin and Greek	Rest of second	41 23 12
	20 August				
	(5 August)	Giovanni Francesco Franciotti conto a mino da ciecho	Del credito che anno della detta gabella		1149 17 10
	,,	Simone da Lucca conperatoro di detta gabella	Per la sesteria inde de zugno e trecento simili fiorini chella chamerlengo li rimette del prezo di detta gabella		50
	19 September				
	(16 September)	Antonio Musciano	Notario dell-proveditori delle mure di Roma	Three months	3 8 6
	(1 July)	Francescho de Chastello (Giovanni da Trevigi)	Institutes	Third	10
	25 September				
	(25 April)	Bernardo de Tedallini		Rest of second	13 11 12

Folio and year	Date (and date of mandate)	Name	Subjects	Term	Payment		
xv*r*							
1482	(25 May)	Horlandino	Surgery	Third	16	23	8
	(15 April)	Alessandro de Gennazano (Alessandro dantonio Turchi)	Logic	Second	33	11	12
	,,	Giovanni Shalves		Third	46	23	8
	,,	Mario Salamone	[Civil law?]	Second and third	26	23	8
	(15 June)	Luca Chasali	Canon law	Third			
	2 October						
	(15 June)	Francesco [Pellati?] da Padova 'per noi da Simone da Lucha e fattoli buoni nella sua sesteria'	[Canon law?]	Third	133	11	12
	(1 October)	Ciriarcho de canponi	Notario in detto studio		3		
	(3 October)	Paholo de Bondii	(fest.)	Third	16	23	8
	(6 June)	Piero Fiorentino	Per uno arme de marmo missa in studio a M. Aricho Bruno		10 = 45 *carleni*		
xv*v*							
	5 October						
	(2 October)	Pomponio	Rhetoric	Third	66	23	8
	(16 September)	Egidio de Toccho	[Maestro di murare e legniamie]	Three months	15 11 4 = 7½ cam. flor.		
	10 October						
	(15 April)	Santo de Caprarola		Second	23	11	12
	15 October						
	(1 July)	Guido antonio Boninsegni	Civil law	Third	66	23	8
	,,	Pietro di Gugliano	'Fatura' (fest.)	,,	10		
	25 October						
	(15 April)	Antonio de Leoni da Tivoli (Giovanni da Treviso)		Second	30		
	2 November						
	(1 October)	Lauro Cerrini	Surgery	Third	26	23	8
	1 October						
	,,	Agniolo Jachobini	Canon law	,,	100		
xvi*r*							
	2 November						
	(1 October)	Giovanni [?de Rossi] Bishop of Alatri		Rest of second	10		
	,,	Agniolo Jachobini		,,	50		
	,,	Pietro Marso		,,	25		
	,,	Stefano Infesura		,,	20		
	,,	Lucha de Fulgnio		,,	10		
	,,	Giovanbattista de Taris		,,	10		
	,,	Tomaso de Vetere		,,	25		
	,,	Stefano de Variis		,,	11	23	8
	,,	Pietro Fanelli		,,	25		
	,,	Ponpilio		,,	10		
	,,	Bernaba		,,	8	11	12
	,,	Giovanni Cellini		,,	8	11	12
	,	Jachopo Batista		,,	10		
	,,	Nichlaso de Grasse		,,	33	11	12

Folio and year	Date (and date of mandate)	Name	Subjects	Term	Payment		
xvi*v*							
	15 November						
	(1 October)	Bartolomeo da Pavia		,,	16	23	8
	,,	Ludovicho Sanreno		,,	11	23	8
	,,	Giovanni Sichulus		,,	20		
	,,	Bonomo de Buono-mini		,,	16	23	8
	,,	Ghulielmo Ramondi		,,	16	23	3
	·,	Filippo de Pontechorvo		,,	25		
	,,	Lodovicho		,,	10		
	,,	Antonio de Gennazano		,,	13	11	12
	,,	Antonio Tomaso		,,	10		
	,,	Giovanni Cerini		,,	41	23	8
	,,	Bartolomeo Artes		,,	11	23	9
	,,	Cristofano da Fano		,,	21	23	8
	,,	Teverino and Valerio de Pallis		,	10		
	,,	Jeronimo di ——?		,,	50		
xvii*r*							
	25 November						
	(1 October)						
	,,	Pagholo di Bondi		,,	8	11	12
	,,	Choluccio di Lucca		,,	8	11	12
	,,	Antonio Flores		,,	13	11	12
	,	Tito [Veltri] Bishop Acquapendente (Pietro Amadei)		,,	23	11	12
		Pagholo Marzo (Fedele Subileo)		,,	33	11	12
	,	Lucrezio de Chosciari		,	11	23	8
	,,	Bernardino da San Gemignano (Ludovicho)			13	11	8
	,,	Sigismondo de Gigi-antibus		Rest of second	10		
	,,	Antonio de Lucha		,,	41	23	8
	28 November						
	(7 October)	Santo de Restituti	Civil law	Third	23	11	12
	(12 October)	Nicholino Foliotto and Simonetto Balistari bidelli	Per hornamento e cera alla messa in Sancto Eustachio		6	4	8
	(8 October)	Christofano da Fano	Civil law	Third	43	11	12
	1 December						
	(2 October)	Giovanni de Rossi, Bishop Alatri	Decretals		20		
xvii*v*							
	(20 November)	Simone de Lucha conperatore di detta gabella	Per la terza paga di fl. 300 se le re-lassano del prezo di detta gabella		50		
	11 December						
	(15 November)	Antonio Musciano notario		Three months	8	6	
		Paolo de Albertoni-bus		Rest of third	11	11	12

Folio and year	Date (and date of mandate)	Name	Subjects	Term	Payment
1482	(8 December)	Nicholo Battaglino	[Grammar] rione Trevi		20
	,,	Francesco Maffo		Two months	148 8 2 = 70 flor. de cam. 75
	(24 December)	Jacopo de Giuliano uno dei reformatori	Per piu spese fatte per reparazione delle stanze dello dello studio		63 9 4 = 30 flor. de cam. 5
	(2 October)	Guglielmo Ramondo	'Tre linchue' [Latin, Greek, Hebrew]	Third	33 11 12
xviiir	15 December				
	(12 December)	Egidio di Tocho	Soprastante e rimendatore delle mure	Three months	15 11 4 = 7½ fl. de cam.
	23 December				
	(22 December)	Antonio da Chastro	Medicine and logic	First	50
	24 December				
	(22 December)	Lodovicho Marzano	Maestro delle strade di Roma	Six months	50
	(18 December)	Priore di Santa Croce di Roma	Per la pigione della chasa della zecha per uno anno (frate Giovanni de Santo)		81 24 12 = 40 de cam.
	(2 October)	Francesco de Chapello (Giovanni de Trevigi)	[Grammar] rione Ripa	Third	16 23 8
	,,	Richo da Siena		Rest of second	50
xviiiv	,,	Giovanni Batista de Tari	Pratiche	Third	20
1483	28 January				
	(2 December)	Antonio de Leoni	Institutes	Third	20
	(26 November)	Filippo della Valle	Medicine	Second	100
	(22 December)	Santi da Caprarola	Civil law	First	33 11 12
	(2 October)	Guisano da Velletri	Civil law	Third	26 23 8
	(22 December)	Girolamo Castellani	Civil Law	Third	100
	(15 June)	Andrea Brenzio	Latin and Greek	Third	83 2 12
1483	28 January				
	(10 June)	Bernabo Azio		Third	20
	(25 April)	Martino Fileticho (Valentino dantonio da fiorentino)	Latin and Greek	Rest of second	25
xviiiir	(2 October)	Bartolomeo de Baglioni	Decretum	Third	33 11 12
	,,	Giovanni Sichulo	Rhetoric	,,	40
	,,	Pagholo Marso	Rhetoric	,,	66 23 8
	,,	Patricio Perleone		,,	20
	(22 December)	Horlandino	Surgery	First part of first	23 11 12
	(1 October)	Antonio de Veteranis	Hordinandum lettere		50
	(2 June)	Guasparre Schiandriole		Third	33 11 12

Folio and year	Date (and date of mandate)	Name	Subjects	Term	Payment		
	(3 October)	Antonio Troyolo de Marchia	Medicine	,,	66	23	8
	(1 July)	Choronato de Planchetis	Decretals	,,	50		
xviiii*v*							
	14 March						
	(3 October)	Tito Veltri Bishop of Acquapendente	Codex	,,	66	23	8
	(2 October)	Antonio Volscho	Rhetoric	,,	50		
	(1 July)	Stefano Infesura	Civil law	,,	40		
	,,	Giovanni Agniolo de Vettoris	Pratiche	,,	33	11	12
	(2 October)	Pagholo Emilio	Institutes	,,	23	11	12
	,,	Ponpilio	Rhetoric	,,	36	23	8
	(1 July)	Jachopo de Battista	[Grammar] rione Ripa	,,	36	23	8
	(15 June)	Suplizio	Rhetoric	,,	40		
	(2 October)	Lucha de Fulcineo	Philosophy	,,	20		
	(3 May)	Jachopo di Gottifredi (Chola Antonio suo figliuolo)	Pratiche (mat.)	Second	100		
xx*r*							
	15 March						
	(3 October)	Bartolomeo Artes	Theology	Third	23	11	12
	(10 June)	Giovanni Collino	[Grammar] Trastevere	,,	16	23	8
	(6 July)	Bernardo de Tedaldenis	Medicine	,,	26	23	8
	(20 July)	Antonio Sancto Ambruose	[Grammar] rione Arenula	,,	20		
	(15 July)	Lodovicho da Bassano	[Grammar] rione Arenula	,,	20		
	(2 October)	Antonio Flores	Sext (fest.)	,,	26	23	8
		Antonio da Pinerolo (Pietro Brettona suo chameriere)		Rest of second	33	11	12
	(23 December)	Fabiano de Giochi	Civil law	,,	50		
	1 July	Giovanni Cierini	Surgery	Third	83	11	12
	13 January	Antonio Musciano notario de proveditori delle mure		Three months	8 6 = 4 fl. de cam.		
xx*v*							
	29 March						
	(20 December)	Gabriello da Fano		First	33	11	12
	(2 October)	Martino Fileticho		Third	50		
	9 April						
	(2 July)	Richo da Siena		,,	100		
	10 April						
	(12 March)	Gilio de Tocho, rimeditore delle mure di Roma		Three months	16	11	4
	(22 December)	Francesco da Padova		First	66	23	8
	(9 March)	maistri delle strade (Simone de Lucha)	Per spendere in reparazione alle strade e chase de Roma		171	20	

Folio and year	Date (and date of mandate)	Name	Subjects	Term	Payment		
1483	15 March						
	(2 October)	Coluzo di Lucha	[Grammar] rione Campitelii	Third	16	23	8
	(22 June)	Pietro Marso	Rhetoric	,,	50		
21r							
	22 April						
	(2 October)	Antonio da Genazano	[Grammar] rione Pinea	.,	26	23	8
	(2 October)	Lodovicho da Siena		,,	20	11	12
	3 May						
	(2 October)	Bernardino da Sangimignano		,,	26	23	8
	(2 October)	Lucrezio de Cosarii		,,	23	11	12
	(22 December)	Giovanni Cierrini		First	83	11	12
	2 June						
	(22 April)	Paolo Emilio		,,	33	11	12
	(22 December)	Nicholo Battaglino		,,	20		
		Jacopo de Gottifre-dis (Cola Antonio suo figliuolo)		Third	100		
	(22 December)	Pietro demigliano		First	16	23	8
21v							
	20 June						
	(22 December)	Pietro Marso	(eves.)	,,	66	23	8
	,,	Marcho Antonio di Santo Ambrogio		,,	20		
	,,	Gasparre Schantiglia		,,	50		
	,,	Sulpizio		,,	50		
	,,	Giovanni Antonio		,,	20		
	,,	Domenicho da Tivoli	(eves.)	,,	150		
	,,	Julio famano		,,	10		
	,,	Antonio de Leoni		,,	36	11	12
	,,	Lucrezio de Choserii		,,	23	11	12
	,,	Richo da Siena		,,	100		
22r							
	28 June						
	(22 December)	Tomaso delle Vettere		,,	83	11	12
	,,	[Giovanni de Rossi] Bishop of Alatri		,,	33	11	12
	,,	Bernardino de Tedallini		,,	33	11	12
	(3 May)	Cholino Foliott	[Bidello]	Year	20		
	(6 June)	Tranquillo da Narni		First	23	11	12
	(22 December)	Paolo Marso		,,	66	23	8
	,,	Agniolo Jachobini		,,	100		
	,,	Stefano Infesura		,,	50		
	,,	Lodovicho delli Albertoni		,,	50		
	,,	Giovanni Cellino		,,	20		
22v							
	?30 June						
	(22 December)	Coluzio da Stabia		First	20		
	,,	Ludovicho da Vassano		,,	20		
	,,	Pietro da Imola		,,	16	23	8
	,,	Girolamo de Velletri		,,	16	23	8

Folio and year	Date (and date of mandate)	Name	Subjects	Term	Payment		
	(22 December)	Franchesco da Chastello		,,	16	23	8
	,,	Antonio Coronato de Planche		,,	56	23	8
	,,	Petreio?		,,	20		
	,,	Andrea Vines		,,	20		
	,,	Lucha da Fulignio		,,	20		
	,,	Ponponio		,,	83	11	12
	,,	Giovanni Antonio da Parma			33	11	12
23r	10 July						
	(22 December)	Giovanni da Chapranicha		First	26	23	8
	(15 April)	Simonetto Balistrari		Half a year	20		
	(22 December)	Paolo		First	20		
	,,	Lodovicho da Siena		,,	33	11	12
	,,	Lorenzo Cerini		,,	33	11	12
	,,	Vincenzo da Narni		,,	20		
	,,	Pietro da Capo-maestri		,	50		
	,,	Pietro Grazie		,,	33	11	12
	,,	Lionardo		,,	20		
	,,	Bartolomeo Artes		,,	23	11	12
	,,	Giovanbatista de Tari		,,	33	11	12
23v	12 July						
	(24 December)	Batista Arcione	Maestri delle strade				
		Lodovicho Muzano	Per spendere in li edifizi sui fanno per Roma e detti denari ebono dalli spinelli piu		1000		
	(22 December)	Maestro Bernabo		,,	20		
	,,	Bartolomeo de Astalli		,,	33	11	12
	,,	Antonio da Lucha		,,	83	11	12
	,,	Jacopo Marcelli		,,	33	11	12
	(23 December)	Nicolo Vestino		,,	23	11	12
	(22 December)	Stefano Vari		,	33	11	12
	,,	Bartolomeo da Stabia		,,	40		
	(30 April)	Andrea Brenzio		,,	100		
	(22 December)	Giusano da Velletri		,,	66	23	8
24r	15 July						
	(22 December)	Troilo dela Marcha		First	83	11	12
	,,	Maestro Lippo		,,	50		
	,,	Maestro Ponpilio		,,	43	11	12
	,,	Mario Salamone		,,	16	23	8
	,,	Jacopo de Batista		,,	23	11	12
	,,	Paolo de Bondi		,,	16	23	8
	,,	Scipione Lancilotti		,,	20		
	,,	Giovanni Sichulo		,,	50		
	,,	Bernardino de Amici		,,	16	23	8
	,,	Giovanni Galbes		,,	23	11	12
	,,	Antonio da Bologna		,,	20		

Folio and year	Date (and date of mandate)	Name	Subjects	Term	Payment		
24v							
1483	16 July						
	(22 December)	Giovaniglio de Vettori		,,	50		
	,,	Lucha Chasali		,,	100		
	(25 March)	Filippo della Valle		Second	100		
	(1 March)	Agniolo da Tiboli		First	16	23	8
	(22 December)	Antonio Lippola		,,	16	23	8
	,,	Antonio da Gianazano		,,	30		
	,,	Giovanni Japoccis		,,	8		
	,,	Tito Veltri Bishop of Chastro		,,	66	23	8
	,,	Luigi da Vinegia		,,	16	23	8
	,,	Antonio Volscho		,,	50		
	,,	Antonio Flores		,,	43	11	12
25r							
	20 July						
	(22 December)	Domenicho Jachobacci	[Canon law?]		33	11	12
	(14 June)	Antonio Musciano, notario de proveditori		Three months	8	6 (4. cam)	
		Egidio di Tocho, soprastante delle mure		,,	15 11 4 = 7½ cam.		
	11 August						
	(13 April)	Batista arcione e Lodovicho Marzano, maestri dell strade		Salary till December	200		
	,,	Massimo e Jacopo Palone, notario di detti maestri		One year	40		
	(10 March)	4 riformatori dello studio e loro notario		One year	304 15 = 127 doro in oro		
	18 August						
	(23 June)	Francesco da Padova (per mano dalto del nero)		Second	166	23	8
	,,	Fabiano de Giochi		First	50		
	4 June	Giovanni Francesco Franciotti olim depositario di detta gabella per tante chelvi nerosco chreditore per saldo fatto cholla chamera apostolica per mano di maestro Antonio da Forli			525 20 12 = 258 23 de cam.		
25v							
	25 August						
	(1 March)	Nicholozo Battaglino	Grammar	Second	20		
	(26 March)	Antonio da Lucha	Medicine	Second	83	11	12
	(25 March)	Troyolo de Marchie	Medicine	Second	83	11	12

Folio and year	Date (and date of mandate)	Name	Subjects	Term	Payment
	(2 October 1482)	Giovanni Antonio	Canon law	Third (1482)	66 23 8
	30 September (16 September)	Musciano notario de proveditori delle mure		Three months	8 6 = 4 de cam.
	8 October (sottoschritto di mano di NS)	Rdo p. Marco Antonio, Bishop of Fano, a Maestro Bartolomeo de Manfredi		Third	66 23 8
	15 October (1 June)	Troyolo delle Marche		Third	83 11 12
	(22 December)	Cristofano da Fano (Gabriello suo procurator)		First	50
26r	20 October (30 September)	Ciriacho Canponi, notario dello studio per schrittura del ruotolo de lanno presente			6 13 8 = 3 fior. cam.
	(25 March)	horlandino		Second	23 11 12
	(10 October)	Simonetto Balistari, bidello dello studio per spese fate per la festa di santo Lucha e a chonciare di finestre e banche			6 75
	(2 October 1482)	Jacopo Marcelli		Third	23 11 12
	(23 June)	Maestro horlandino		Third	23 11 12
	„	Nicholo Battaglino		Third	20
	(16 September)	Gilio de Tocho		Three months	15 11 4 = 7½ cam.
1484	16 February (2 February)	Berardo de Richarti		One year	120 11 = 58 65 22 de camera
26v	5 March (21 February)	Simone da Lucha per la integra recompensa in detta ghabella			500
	(24 February)	Maestri delle strade di Roma: Giuliano Gallo loro depositario			500
	(23 December)	Fabiano de Giochi (per lui a m. Catalano protenotario da chasale)		First	100
	15 March (23 June)	Giusano da Velletri		Second	66 23 8
	(26 March)	m. Justino		Third	66 23 8

Folio and year	Date (and date of mandate)	Name	Subjects	Term	Payment
1484	15 March				
	(9 March)	Bishop of Chiavigo[?]	Per fare fare banche in detto studio e altre spese necessarie		65 29 4
	(23 December)	Guglielmo Bodvit(?)		Part of first	20
	,,	Tranquillo da Narni		,,	15
	,,	Bernardino da Narni		,,	10
27r					
	15 March				
	(23 December)	Giovanni Cellino		Part of first	15
	,,	Bernaba Azio		,,	15
	,,	Agniolo Jachobini		,,	60
	,,	Giovanni Batista Tari		,,	50
	,,	Tomaso delle Vetere		,,	50
	,,	Stefano de Vari		,,	12
	,,	Jacopo Batista		,,	15
	,,	Giovanni Batista		,,	15
	,,	Lucha Chasali		,,	60
	,,	al detto m. Lucha		Part of second	70
27v					
	18 March				
	(23 December)	Domenicho de Boniaugurii		Part of First	100
	,,	Sulpizio		,,	35
	,,	Francesco da Padova		,,	100
	(25 March)	Bartolomeo de Astalli		Part of second	20
	,,	Santi da Chaparola		,,	20
	(23 December)	Pietro Sabino		Part of first	10
	,,	Giovanni di Chrapanicha		,,	15
	,,	Lodovicho da Bassano		,,	15
	,,	Tomaso delle Vetura		Part of second	50
	(26 March)	Bernardino de Amici		,,	10
	(23 December)	Bartolomeo de Chasalli		Part of first	18
28r					
	28 March				
	(23 December)	Chasparre Schantiglia		Part of first	20
	,,	Stefano Infesura		,,	35
	,,	Girolamo Vallati		Part of second	10
	,,	horlandino		First	23 11 12
	(25 March)	Chasparre Schantriglia		Part of second	30
	(23 December)	Pietro Grazia		Part of first	15
	(26 March)	Domenicho de Boni Auguri		Part of second	100
	,,	Leonardo ?Tirunde		,,	15

Folio and year	Date (and date of mandate)	Name	Subjects	Term	Payment			
	(26 March)	Domenicho Jacho-baccio		,,	30			
	(23 December)	detto m. Domenicho		Part of	25			
	,,	Lucha da Fuligini		,,	15			
28v								
	20 March							
	(23 December)	Bartolomeo Artes		Part of first	15			
	26 March							
	(26 March)	Coronato de Planche		Part of second	50			
	,,	Stefano Infesura		,,	35			
	,,	Antonio Flores		,,	43	11	12	
	(23 December)	Jeronimo de Vellatri		Part of first	8			
	(25 March)	Antonio da Gen-nazano		Part of second	15			
	,,	Stefano de Vari		,,	20			
	(23 December)	Lionardo		Part of first	10			
	(25 March)	m. Ponpilio		Part of second	15			
	(23 December)	Ponpilio		Part of first	15			
	(26 March)	Agniolo Jachobini		Part of second	70			
	(23 December)	Coronato di Planche		Part of first	30			
29r								
	20 March							
	(23 December)	Domenicho da Stimigliano		Part of first	10			
	,,	Mario Salamone		,,	8			
	,,	Lodovicho da Viterbo		,,	10			
	,,	Lorenzo Pagholini		,,	10			
	(26 March)	Mario Salamone		Part of second	10			
	(23 December)	Nicholo Battaglino		First	20			
	,,	Pietro Marso		,,	66	23	8	
	,,	Chabriello Zerbo	[Medecine]	,,	66	23	8	
	,,	Jacopo de Marcelli		Part of first	12			
	,,	Girolamo Chastellani		,,	60			
	,,	Sulpizio		,,	20			
	,,	Calisto de Johanini		,,	8			
29v								
	,,	Nicholo de Grassi		,,	40			
	,,	Lucrezio de Chosciari		,,	10			
	,,	Lucrezio de Chosciari		Part of second	15			
	,,	Girolamo da Siena		Part of First	15			
	,,	Coluzo		,,	15			
	,,	Mariano da Monte Janaro		,,	10			
	,,	Girolamo Chapel-lani		Part of second	70			

Folio and year	Date (and date of mandate)	Name	Subjects	Term	Payment
1484	(23 December)	Agniolo da Tivoli		Part of first	10
	,,	Lodovicho delli Albertoni		,,	30
	(26 March)	Lodovicho delli Albertoni		Part of second	35
29v	20 March				
	(26 March)	Giovanni Bishop of Alatri		Part of second	20
	(23 December)	Antonio de Leoni		Part of first	15
	,,	Giovanni [Rossi] Bishop of Alatri		,,	20
30r	22 March				
	(26 March)	Jacopo Batista		Part of second	15
	(23 December)	Giovanniglio de Vettori		Part of first	30
	,,	Vincenzo da Narni		,,	10
	(2 October 1482)	Stefano de Vari		Third	23 11 12
	(23 December)	Cristofano delli Albertoni		Part of first	10
	(26 March)	Giovanni Agniolo de Vittori		Part of second	35
	(23 December)	Nicholo Bonello		Part of first	30
	,,	Antonio Flores		First	33 11 12
	(23 June)	Antonio Flores		Third	43 11 12
	(25 March)	Pietro de Chapomaestri		Part of second	35
	,,	Jacopo Marcelli		,,	20
	(23 December)	Pietro da Imola		First	16 12 8
	(23 June)	Filippo della Valle		Third	100
30v	(23 December)	Filippo della Valle		First	33 11 11
	,,	Paolo Marso		Part of first	30
	,,	Pietro da Chapomaestri		,,	20
	,,	Pietro Paolo de Bochatti		,,	8
	,,	Giovanni Batista de Santo Severino		First	33 11 12
	,,	Triolo de Propositi		First	83 11 12
	29 March				
	(25 March)	Bernardo de Tedallini		Part of second	20
	(23 December)	Bernardo de Tedallini		Part of first	20
	(15 March)	Antonio Musciano		Three months	8 6 = 4 de camera
	(26 March)	Richo da Siena		Second	100

Anno domini 1484 die v Aprilis 1484 dominus Nicholaus Calcaneus depositarius pecuniarum gabelle studii almae urbis exhibuit coram dominis camere in plena Camera in fidem ubi presentem librum computorum dicte gabelle in Quo iuramus esse notata vera computa dicte gabelle et. Reverendus dominus dominicus [?] vice camerarius commisit ea veduta Reverendis presentibus

d. An. de Vite ⎱
d. F. de Noxeto ⎰ clericis et commissariis

NOTES

[1] Ed. F. M. Powicke and A. B. Emden, second edition, Oxford, 1936, II, pp. 38–9. Basic documented studies remain J. Carafa, *De Gymnasio Romano et de eius professoribus*, Rome, two vols., 1751; G. Marini, *Lettera . . . al chiarissimo Monsignore Giuseppe Muti Papazurri*, Rome, 1797; above all, F. M. Renazzi, *Storia dell'Università degli studi di Roma, detta communemente La Sapienza*, I, II, Rome, 1803–04. H. Denifle, *Die Entstehung der Universitäten des Mittelalters bis 1400*, Berlin, 1885, pp. 310–17 gives a more useful summary than N. Spano, *L'Università di Roma*, Rome, 1935. F. M. Ponzetti, 'L'archivio antico dell'Università di Roma', *Archivio della Reale Società Romana di Storia Patria* (hereafter cited as *A.R.S.P.*), LIX, 1936, pp. 245–302, indicates the lack of the university's own records before the sixteenth century.

[2] Rashdall, II, pp. 28–31; R. Valentini, 'Lo "Studium Urbis" durante il secolo XIV', *A.R.S.P.* LXVII, 1944, pp. 372–4. See also R. Creytens, O.P., 'Le Studium Romanae Curiae et le Maître du Sacré Palais', *Archivum Fratrum Praedicatorum*, XII, 1942, pp. 5–83, and below, nn. 122–6.

[3] G. Digard, *Registres de Boniface VIII*, Bibliothèque des Écoles françaises d'Athènes et de Rome, second series, IV, fasc. 7, Paris, 1921, pp. 737–8, 779–82. Renazzi, I, pp. 59–60, discusses the bulls and includes the first, doc. XXI, pp. 258–9.

[4] Besides Renazzi, I, *passim*, and Valentini, *A.R.S.P.* LXVII, 1944, pp. 371–89, see also R. Valentini, 'Gli istituti Romani di alta cultura e la presunta crisi dello Studium Urbis 1370–1420', *A.R.S.P.* LIX, 1936, pp. 179–202.

[5] Renazzi, I, p. 61.

[6] Valentini, *A.R.S.P.* LXVII, 1944, pp. 372–3; G. Ferri, 'La Romana fraternitas', *A.R.S.P.* XXVI, 1903, pp. 453–66.

[7] Renazzi, I, p. 62.

[8] *Ibid.*, I, p. 61; doc. XXVIII, pp. 266–8.

[9] *Ibid.*, I, pp. 68–9, doc. XXV, pp. 261–3; discussed by Denifle, p. 313, and Valentini, *A.R.S.P.* LXVII, 1944, p. 378.

[10] Valentini, *A.R.S.P.* LXVII, 1944, p. 383; *cf.* R. Cessi, 'Roma ed il Patrimonio di S. Pietro in Tuscia dopo la prima spedizione del Bavaro', *A.R.S.P.* XXXVII, 1914, p. 84.

[11] C. De Re, *Statuti della Città di Roma*, Rome, 1883, pp. 244–6.

[12] Valentini, *A.R.S.P.* LIX, 1936, p. 199, pointed out Bruni's signature (Vatican Archives, Reg. Vat. 334, f. 181*v*) overlooked by Renazzi, I, doc. I, pp. 273–4. *Cf.* also G. Griffiths, 'L. Bruni and the restoration of the University of Rome (1406)', *Renaissance Quarterly*, XXVI, 1973, pp. 1–10.

[13] Valentini, *A.R.S.P.* LIX, 1936, pp. 195–202, 217–22.

[14] Valentini (*loc. cit.*, 207–17) seems to claim more for Martin than his evidence justifies.

[15] P. Partner, *The Papal State under Martin V*, London, 1958, pp. 161–9; M. L. Lombardo, *'La "Camera Urbis". Premesse per uno studio sulla organizzazione amministrativa della città*, Rome, 1970, pp. 27–56. Detailed documentation about civic office holders (for March–June 1457) is in O. Tommasini, 'Il Registro degli Officiali del comune di Roma esemplato dallo scribasenato Marco Guidi', *Atti della R. Accademia dei Lincei*, fourth series, *Memorie Scienze Morali, Storiche e Filologiche*, III, 1887, pp. 169–222.

[16] Vatican Archives, Reg. Vat. 381, ff. lxviir–lxviiiir. Renazzi, I, doc. II, pp. 274–6, gives the text from a transcript in the Archivio Capitolino which omits, or reads differently, the words italicised below in the first sentence of the last paragraph: '. . . et consuetudinibus *dictarum ecclesiarum* juramento, confirmatione Sedis Apostolicae, vel quacumque firmitate alia roboratis, etiamsi de illis servandis per se, vel Procuratores, suos *praestassent* forsitan juramentum'.

[17] On the regulation of the retail wine trade in Rome and the *gabella vini ad minutum* see the text of the statutes of Boniface IX in S. Malatesta, *Statuti delle gabelle di Roma*, Rome, 1885, especially pp. 96–9.

[18] B. Platina, 'Vita G. B. Mellini' in A. Ciaconius, *Historiae Pontificum Romanorum et S.R.E. Cardinalium*, Rome, 1677, III, p. 59.

[19] Partner, p. 39. On *reformatores* generally see Rashdall, I, p. 212.

[20] Vatican Archives, Reg. Vat. 372, ff. 138*r*–139*v*; reissued in the same form on 1 November 1433, Reg. Vat. 372, ff. 251*v*–253*v*. The text in Carafa, *De Gymnasio Romano*, pp. 576–9, is careless; the names of several *caporioni* are misread and one, Silvestro de Temperiis (Parione), is omitted.

[21] A mandate dated 26 May 1434 (i.e. in mid-term) of the cardinal chamberlain instructing the conservators to admit four new reformers and a notary (Renazzi, I, doc. IV, p. 277) points to this.

[22] Rashdall, II, p. 216; G. de Sandre, 'Dottori, Università, Comune a Padova del Quattrocento', *Quaderni per la storia dell'Università di Padova*, I, Padua, 1968, pp. 17–18; *cf.* p. 28, n. 3.

[23] Renazzi, I, doc. V, p. 277.

[24] Valentini, *A.R.S.P.* LIX, 1936, doc. VII, A, p. 238.

[25] *Ibid.*, B, pp. 238–9.

[26] *Ibid.*, C, p. 239.

[27] M. Creighton, *A History of the Papacy*, London, 1897, II, p. 232. On 25 August 1433 Niccolò della Stella, called Fortebraccio, had captured the Ponte Molle, see P. Partner, *The Lands of St Peter*, London, 1972, pp. 406–7.

[28] Valentini, *A.R.S.P.* LIX, 1936, doc. VII, E, pp. 240–1.

[29] *Ibid.*, I, p. 243.

[30] Vatican Archives, Reg. Vat. 374, ff. cclxxiiv–cclxxiiiiv.

[31] Renazzi, I, pp. 159 ff; *cf.* note by P. Paschini, *Roma*, IX, 1931, p. 387.

[32] A. Theiner, *Codex diplomaticus temporalis S. Sedis*, III, Rome, 1862, p. 395–6.

[33] G. Marini, *Lettera . . .*, 1797, doc. IV, pp. 91–2; Renazzi, I, p. 207.

[34] R. Weiss, *Un umanista veneziano: Papa Paolo II*, Venice and Rome, 1958, p. 18. The encomium by Gaspare of Verona is vague: 'gymnasiorum publicorum auctor, emendator et benefactor'. In A. Andrews, 'The "lost" fifth book of the Life of Paul II by Gaspar of Verona', *Studies in the Renaissance*, XVII, 1970, 40–1.

[35] R. Weiss, 'Una medaglia di Papa Paolo II (1464–71) per l'Università di Bologna', *Italia Numismatica*, IX, 1962, *estratto*, pp. 3–4; *cf.* G. Hill, *A Corpus of Italian Medals of the Renaissance*, London, two vols., 1930, n. 778.

[36] Renazzi, I, doc. III, p. 276; Marini, *Lettera*, docs. II–III, pp. 90–1.

[37] 'Et annos quattuor legi Romae in gymnasio publico tempore Eugenii Quarti et Nicolai Quinti . . .'. E. M. Sanford, 'Gaspare Veronese, humanist and teacher', *Transactions and Proceedings of the American Philological Association*, LXXXIV, 1953, 197.

[38] L. Barozzi and R. Sabbadini, *Studi sul Panormita e sul Valla*, Florence, 1891, doc. 80, pp. 132–3; G. Mancini, *Vita di Lorenzo Valla*, Florence, 1891, pp. 248–9; M. Fois, *Il pensiero cristiano di Lorenzo Valla*, Rome, 1969, pp. 394–8.

[39] *Cf.* Rashdall, I, pp. 213–15.

[40] L. Martines, *The Social World of the Florentine Humanists, 1390–1460*, London, 1963, p. 130.

[41] Marini, *Lettera*, doc. V, pp. 92–4; Renazzi, I, doc. VII, pp. 278–9; Valentini, *A.R.S.P.* LIX, 1936, p. 201; doc. II, pp. 229–31.

[42] Marini, *Lettera*, doc. VI, pp. 94–5; Valentini, *A.R.S.P.* LIX, doc. III, pp. 231–3. On Pietro Odo see R. Avesani, 'Epaeneticorum ad Pium II Pont. Max. libri V', in *Enea Silvio Piccolomini Papa Pio II*, Atti del Convegno per il Quinto Centenario della Morte, ed. D. Maffei, Siena, 1968, pp. 19, 25–7 and *passim*; also A. della Torre, *Paolo Marsi da Pescina*, Rocca San Casciano, 1903, pp. 67–72.

[43] Renazzi, I, doc. IX, p. 280. 'Scribunt ad nos dilecti filii Conservatores Camere alme Urbis nostre super Salariis Legentium in Universitate Romana, asserentes

propter extenuationem Salarii nolle illos ulterius legere . . . Ad salaria igiture Legentium placet, ut habeatur delectus eorum, qui utilius legunt; et necessarii magis apparent, illisque ita salarium augeatur, ut in legationibus perseverent, nec tamen propterea taxa pecuniarum hoc anno deputata excrescat, qua in parte volumus superfluos Legentes recusari.'

[44] Renazzi, I, doc. XVI, p. 285.

[45] Gaspare da Verona and Michele Canesi, *Le vite di Paolo II*, ed. G. Zippel, in *Rerum Italicarum Scriptores*, new series, III, part 16, Città di Castello, 1904–11, p. 54.

[46] V. Zabughin, *Giulio Pomponio Leto*, Rome, 1919–20, I, p. 26.

[47] Archivio di Stato, Rome (hereafter referred to as A.S.R.), Arch. Cam. Urbis I, Busta 39, reg. 108, 109 (1442–43, 1445–60); Busta 40, reg. 110–14 (1457, 1466–69); Busta 41, reg. 115–17, 119–20 (1469–72, 1475); Busta 42, reg. 121, 122 (1479–81). These registers of receipts were used, though not at all fully, by U. Gnoli, *Alberghi ed osterie di Roma nella Rinascenza*, Spoleto, 1935, pp. 31 ff.

[48] A.S.R., Arch. Cam. Urbis I, Busta 41, reg. 118 (1473–74); Busta 42, reg. 123 (1481–82); Busta 43, reg. 124, 125, 126 (1482–84, 1494–96, 1496). Reg. 124 is given in appendix 5.2.

[49] They eluded Renazzi but were noted *alla sfuggita* by A. Bertolotti, 'Professori allo Studio di Roma nel secolo XV', *Il Bibliofilo*, IV, Bologna, 1883, pp. 89–90, and used by O. Tomassini, 'Stefano Infessura. Studio preparatorio alla nuova edizione di esso', *A.R.S.P.* XI, 1888, pp. 494–5. Editors of texts in the new edition of Muratori's Rerum Italicarum Scriptores have referred to specific entries, so have B. Pecci, *L'Umanesimo e la 'Cioceria'*, Trani, 1912, pp. 21, 118, 162–3, and V. Zabughin, *Giulio Pomponio Leto*, I, pp. 280–1, 350–1. Dott. Maria Luisa Lombardo of the A.S.R. informs me that their publication (or publication of the names they contain) is intended.

[50] E.g. reg. 124, f. 26r (appendix 5.2); or 'Andrea Jacovaccio notaio dello studio per lo rotolo 13 fl. 4' in reg. 125, f. 17; similarly five florins *de camera, ibid.*, f. 20v; see also reg. 126, f. XV.

[51] Marini, *Lettera*, pp. 12–16; Renazzi, II, doc. II, pp. 235–9. A. Maganelli, 'I manoscritti di Costantino Corvisieri nella Biblioteca della R. Società Romana di Storia Patria', *A.R.S.P.* XXXI, 1908, pp. 410–30, lists (p. 422) Busta XIV, (*m*) i. Ruolo dello Studio di Roma, 1481; ii. *ibid.*, 1496; (*n*) Libro della Gabella dello Studio, 1482; (*o*) Rotulo dello Studio, 1504. I have not been able to check these, but with the possible exception of the latter (which may, however, be a misprint for 1514) they would appear to be transcripts from some of the registers in n. 48 above.

[52] Vatican Archives, Arm. XXIX (Div. Cam.), 38, f. 6; and e.g. payments of 100 florins to Francesco da Padova and Martino Filetico on ff. 5, 13. Marini, *Lettera*, doc. VII, pp. 95–6, gives the mandates for payment to Porcelio of 12 January 1473 and 10 May 1476.

[53] See B. Pecci (above, n. 49): this is a revised version of his article 'Contributo per la storia degli Umanisti nel Lazio . . .', *A.R.S.P.* XIII, 1890, pp. 451–526.

[54] Above, n. 42.

[55] *Cf.* remarks on the high salaries and prestige of jurists in Italian universities by M. Gilmore, *Humanists and Jurists: Six Studies in the Renaissance*, London, 1963, pp. 64–6.

[56] R. Valentini, 'L'insegnamento medico nello Studium Urbis dal XV al XIX secolo', *Annali di Medicina Navale e Coloniale*, II, 1946, *estratto*, pp. 3–4, deals only briefly with the period before 1514 and does not discuss payments. He mentions Paolo and Filippo della Valle, Gabriele de Zerbi the anatomist, Giovanni Filippo de Legnano and Pietro Leoni, who was an exponent of Galen.

[57] A.S.R., Arch. Cam. Urbis I, Busta 43, reg. 126, ff. viiiiv, xiiv, xiiiv, quoted in Zabughin, I, pp. 350–1.

[58] For Pomponio's 'Giuliano' and others' *charzoni* and factors see reg. 124 in appendix 5.2. e.g. ff. xiiir, xiiiv, xivr, xviiiv, xiiiiv, xxr, xxir, 25r, etc.

[59] E.g. Giovanni Forlano (rione Monti) was paid only 10 *fior. rom.* in March 1474 (reg. 118, f. xxxiiiiv).

[60] On these Roman coinages see V. Capobianchi, 'Appunti per servire all'ordinamento delle monete coniate del Senato Romano dal 1184 al 1439 e degli stemmi primitivi del comune di Roma', *A.R.S.P.* XVIII, 1895, and more particularly *ibid.*, XIX, 1896, pp. 103 ff.

[61] E.g. in March 1474 the reformers were paid collectively 100 cameral florins (reg. 118, f. xxxviiii*v*); to Mariano de Astallis, 'notario Studii', two florins were paid the previous October (*ibid.*, f. 30*v*); in 1483 reformers and notary were paid 127 cameral florins *doro in oro* (reg. 124, f. 25*r*: see appendix 5.2, *passim*).

[62] The receipts reflect rising consumption of wine, particularly during the summer months, owing to the heat but also the presence of tourists, pilgrims, etc., e.g. during the jubilee year of 1475 they vary from 6,486 lire in May to 1416 lire in December (reg. 119, f. 94*v*, or reg. 120, f. 106*r*); the year's total is given as 21,820 lire, 27 soldi.

[63] Payment was made on 8 February 1482 of two florins *de camera* 'a banditori e trombetti di campitolio per bandier la chabella dello studio per detto del vice chamerlencho' (reg. 123, f. 33*v*).

[64] Vatican Archives, Arm. XXXIV, vol. II (Instrumenta Cameralia), ff. 75*r*–77*r*; vol. 15, f. 5*v*. A mandate of 12 June 1503 refers to the sale on 15 November 1501 at 1,400 ducats; see A.S.R., Arch. Cam. Urbis I (Mandati), Busta 857, f. 74*r*, printed in P. De Roo, *Materials for a History of Pope Alexander VI, his Relatives and his time*, Bruges, 1924, IV, doc. 182, p. 564.

[65] Reg. 126, ff. 4, xvi*v*, 21*r*.

[66] L. von Pastor, *History of the Popes*, English edition, 1894, IV, p. 198, quoting Milanese and Mantuan dispatches of 28–9 July.

[67] Many relevant extracts from reg. 118 are in Zabughin, I, pp. 280–1; *cf.* O. Tommasini, 'Stefano Infessura . . .', *A.R.S.P.* XI, 1888, pp. 559–60, using additional evidence (up to 1476) from Vatican Archives Arm. XXIX (Div. Cam.), vol. 59 (*sic* for vol. 38?). There is also much material in A.S.R., Arch. Cam. Urbis I (Mandati), 846, 856.

[68] See appendix 5.2, *passim*. On the revival of this magistracy see E. Re, 'Maestri di strada,' *A.R.S.P.* XLIII, 1920, pp. 5–102; C. Scaccia Scarafoni, 'L'antico statuto dei magistri stratarum e altri documenti relativi a quella magistratura', *ibid.*, L, 1927, pp. 239 ff.

[69] Vatican Archives, Arm. XXIX (Div. Cam.), 38, f. 150*v* (20 January 1475): 'volumus postmodum retinere de salariis omnium doctorum in dicto studio legentium in hic anno videlicet de unoquoque floreno Romano dicti salarii 2 solidos monete Romane'. A mandate of 8 February gives the proceeds of this deduction as 125 florins *de camera*: Tommasini, *A.R.S.P.* XI, 1888, p. 559, no. 2.

[70] Dr A. V. Antonovics intends to publish a study of this interesting personality. Many of the mandates in the above register are addressed to Cigala, named as Depositarius Urbis together with Clemente de Vivaldis; others up to 1480 are in the *mandati camerali* in A.S.R.

[71] G. Benaducci, 'Prose e poesie volgari di F. Filelfo', *Atti e Memorie della R. deputazione di Storia Patria per le provincie delle Marche*, V, Ancona, 1901, pp. 198–9.

[72] *Ibid.*, p. 203; *cf.* his letters to Cardinal Gonzaga and the Pope in C. de Rosmini, *Vita di F. Filelfo. Monumenti inediti*, Milan, 1808, pp. 370–6.

[73] Benaducci, p. 206.

[74] *Ibid.*, pp. 209–10.

[75] Vatican Archives, Arm. XXIX, 38, f. 223*r* (marginal note 'pro solutione domino Francesco Filelfo': 'ut de pecuniis gabelle studii solvatis et ricercatis S^mo d.n. pape florenos auri de camera in auro 100 per totidem quos eius Sanctitas ex certibus rationibus causis solvit de sua capsa in utilitate pro dicte gabelle studii').

[76] Rosmini, pp. 415–17.

[77] Rosmini, p. 414: '. . . Et pateris tu Pater Innocentissime eiusmodi esse quaestorem tuum, qui de pecuniis bonorum virorum ac tuis publice foeneretur? . . . iusserat tua clementia, ut mihi Milliadus quaestor dinumeraret aureos ducenos qui reliqui erant ex annuo mihi abs te praemio constituto. At bonus vir Milliadus Cicada

cum animadverteret diutius me praestolari non posse, vix centum dinumeravit . . .
ut cum venissem Mediolanum, ii centum aurei vix quattuor et octoginta com-
plerint.'

[78] Vatican Archives, Arm. xxix (Div. Cam.), 39, f. 137.

[79] Tommasini, *A.R.S.P.* xi, 1888, pp. 496-8.

[80] Tommasini, *Diario della Città di Roma di Stefano Infessura*, Rome, 1890, p. 159.
This appears to be the year 1484, but *cf.* footnote recording Marcellini as a reformer
in 1476.

[81] *Ibid.*, p. 158; *A.R.S.P.* xi, 1888, p. 559.

[82] Statement of 3 June 1482 of Leonardus de Claritis, factor for the Franciotti as
depositarii: 'summa tuta uscita f. 5556 d. 20' (reg. 123, ff. 47*v*-48*r*); *cf.* 'summa tutta
entrata f. 4789 d. 22' (*ibid.*, f. 1*v*). These accounting notes are very rough, however,
and raise problems which further analysis needs to elucidate.

[83] Vatican Archives, Arm. xxix (Div. Cam.), 41, ff. 242*r*-243*r*; *cf.* Tommasini,
A.R.S.P. xi, 1888, p. 560 n.

[84] Renazzi, i, doc. xviii, pp. 286-7.

[85] *Diario*, pp. 168, 176-7.

[86] Mandate of 6 April 1485 to Jacopo di S. Ginesio, A.S.R., Arch. Cam. Urbis i,
(Mandati Camerali), 848 (labelled 846), f. 121*v*.

[87] *Diario*, p. 203.

[88] *Ibid.*, p. 252.

[89] *Ibid.*, n. 1 (mandate dated 11 November 1488 to Pietro de' Ricasoli for payment
to the doctors 'pro complemento eorum salario'); *cf.* mandates of 14 May 1489 to
Jacopo Sinibaldi and Ciriaco de Ciamponibus (the Pope's man as notary in 1484,
now an *emptor*), 'de primis pecuniis . . . quamquid summam solverint doctoribus et
lectoribus in dicto studio', also mandates to Gerardo Usodimare as *depositarius* of
3 June 1489 to pay 'Francisco Appellato de Padua Advocato Consistoriali . . . 100
ducatos *auri papales*' and 31 August 1489 'Johanni Episcopo Castrensis 100 florenos
in dicta Urbe currentes pro ultima tertiaria anni 1488 ratione sue lecture in theologia
. . .'. A.S.R., Arch. Cam. Urbis i, Mandati, 1237, ff. 63*r*-63*v*.

[90] Marini, *Lettera*, n. x, pp. 101-3 (the letter to the *Camerlengo* is signed 'Franciscus
Pellatus Patavinus, Advocatus Consistorialis et Pauper'). *Cf.* his reappointment to
teach canon law for a year, 25 September 1484, in Renazzi, i, n. xxi, p. 290, Marini,
Lettera, n. xii, p. 104. *Cf.* above, n. 89.

[91] Renazzi, i, p. 104.

[92] As above, n. 18.

[93] Valentini, *A.R.S.P.* lix, 1936, doc. vii D, pp. 239-40; see also appendix 5.1 and J.
Kirschner, 'Papa Eugenio IV e il Monte Comune', *Archivio Storico Italiano*, cxxvii,
1969, pp. 339-82.

[94] A.S.R., Ospedali, SS^mo. Salvatore, (Istromenti)No. 24, ff. xxxiii, xlvii. I am
grateful to Dr A. V. Antonovics for this reference.

[95] L. Barozzi and R. Sabbadini, *Studi sul Panormita e sul Valla*, Florence, 1891, doc.
69, pp. 120-1. *Cf.* Mancini, *Vita di Lorenzo Valla*, pp. 248-9.

[96] E.g. 14 June 1473 (mandate of 21 March), payment to 'Sancti Dominici Lappi
pulsatori campanie Sancti Eustachii 8⅓ *fior. rom.* = 4 .5. 2. *de cam.*'; similarly to
'Andrea Lionardi pulsatori' (reg. 118, f. xxxxir); 4 September 1481, 'a m. Andrea
canonico e camerario di Santo Eustachio campanaro 4 *flor.* 6. 12'; similarly on 8
February 1482, 'a m. Andrea di Nardo canonico di Santo houstachio sonatore della
campana di detta chiesa' (reg. 123, ff. 33*v*, 42*v*); in 1495 'Capitolo Sancto Eustachio
per la campana 25 *flor. rom.*' (reg. 125, f. 21*r*).

[97] (October 1473) 'Salviato quondam Andrea di Tocho muratori . . . pro reparatione del studio e altre cosse . . . necessarie: 30 flor. *de cam.*' (reg. 118, f. 30*r*); mandate
of the *camerlengo* to Cigala, 2 March 1476, 'Magistro Marsilio Johannis de Florentia
muratori florenos papales 10 pro residuo et complemento solutionis operis per eum
facti in reparatione Domus Studii prefatae Urbis' (from Vatican Archives, Arm.
xxix, 38, f. 204*v*, in Renazzi, i, n. xvii, pp. 285-6).

[98] E.g. 8 February 1481 to 'Valeriano Frayapane reformatore dello studio per reparatione de banchi di detto studio 35 flor. 15' (reg. 123, f. 32v). *Cf.* reg. 124, ff. xviiv, xxviv in appendix 5.2.

[99] E.g. 8 February 1481, 'Simonetto Baliestieri e Colino Foliot per la festa di San Lucha 7 fl. *de cam.* 3'; 20 February 1481, 'Colino Foliot e Simonetto Balestrieri cursori per nettare lo studio 5 fl. *de cam.*'; 4 September 1481, 'Simonetto Balistari per terreno chavato 5 fl. *de cam.* 15'; 20 October 1481, 'Colino Foliot bidello dello studio per reperationi 12 fl. 36'; 24 December 1481, 'Colino Foliot cursori per reperatione delle banche 1 fl. 51. 12' (reg. 123, ff. 32v, 33r, 42v, 43r); *cf.* reg. 124, ff. xviir, 26r in appendix 5.2; 27 February 1495, 'Nofrio e Bosco bidelli per spese facte in lo studio 7 fl. *papali* [*sic*] = 18 fl. *rom.*'; 13 October 1495, 'Nofrio e Bosco bidelli per la festa di Sancto Lucha 5 *fl. de cam.* = 13 *flor. rom.* 4. 4.'; 5 November 1495, 'Nofrio e Bosco bidelli per reperatione allo studio 4 *flor. de cam.* = 8 flor. *rom.* 18' (reg. 125, ff. 17r, 20v); 14 January 1496, 'Nofrio e Bosco bidelli per reperationi allo studio fl. 8 *rom.*' (reg. 126, f. xv).

[100] Reg. 124, f. xvr (appendix 5.2).

[101] P. Cortesi, *De Cardinalatu Libri Tres*, Casa Cortese, 1510, 'De erogatione pecuniarum', f. ciiiiv; quoted also by Zabughin, i, 249–50.

[102] E.g. Bologna (Rashdall, i, pp. 217–18), or Pisa: G. B. Picotti, 'Lo Studio di Pisa dalle origini a Cosimo Duca', *Bolletino Storico Pisano*, xii, 1943, pp. 38–9.

[103] Sulpizio's dedication (*c.* 1487–88) of an edition of Vitruvius to the Cardinal Chamberlain Rafaelle Riario: 'De gymnasio nostra evertendo et magnifice construendo (quod utinam praeccupasses, ibi enim quotidiana omnium disciplinarum eduntur spectacula) prudentissimi reformatores jam iniere consilium et eurythmiam et symmetriam disposuere'. B. Pecci, *L'Umanesimo e la 'Cioceria'*, Trani, 1912, pp. 53–6.

[104] Beneimbene's notorial register (A.S.R., Archivio del Collegio dei Notari Capitolini, 175) contains many Borgia transactions. See F. Gregorovius, 'Das Archiv der Notare des Capitols in Rom und das Protocollbuch des Notars Camillus de Beneimbene von 1476 bis 1505', *Sitzungsberichte der philosophische- philologischen- und historischen-Classes des k.b. Akademie der Wissenschaften zu München*, iv, 1872, pp. 491–518.

[105] The unedited eulogy is in the Vatican Library, Cod. Lat. Ottoboniensis 2280. A few extracts are given by De Roo, *Materials for a History of Pope Alexander VI*, ii, doc. 92, pp. 469–70.

[106] On *peciarii*, who controlled the academic book trade, see Rashdall, i, p. 189. Beneimbene is described as 'pecerius' or 'pacierus' in 1481–83 (A.S.R., Arch. Cam. Urbis i, Mandati, 846 = 848, ff. 95v, 100r, together with Coronato de Planca); he was a *maestro stratarum* in 1495, 1497 and 1499 (Mandati, 856, ff. 110v–112r; C. Scaccia Scarafoni, *A.R.S.P.* L, 1927, docs. viii, ix, pp. 288–90; he may have been a reformer in December 1484, according to Ceccarelli's additions in *Il Diario di Antonio de Vascho*, ed. G. Chiesa (*R.I.S.*, new series, xxiii, 3, p. 467).

[107] See below, n. 120.

[108] Zabughin, i, ii, 269–70.

[109] Vatican Archives, Arm. xxix (Div. Cam.), 52, f. 45v; Renazzi, i, doc. xi, p. 281; De Roo, iv, doc. 181a, pp. 562–3.

[110] *Ibid.*, 52, f. 138r; Renazzi, i, doc. xii, p. 281; De Roo, iv, doc. 181b, p. 563.

[111] A. de Zahn, 'Notizie artistiche tratte dall'Archivio Segreto Vaticano', *Archivio Storico Italiano*, third series, vi, part 1, 1867, p. 178; De Roo, pp. 451–2 and doc. 181c, p. 564.

[112] J. Burckhard, *Liber Notarum*, ed. E. Celani, *R.I.S.*, new series, xxxii, Città di Castello, 1907, ii, 140.

[113] L. Callari, *I Palazzi di Roma*, Rome, 1944, p. 244.

[114] Renazzi, i, p. 198; De Roo, iv, p. 452. See R. Weiss, 'Andrea Fulvio—antiquario Romano (*c.* 1470–1527)', *Annali della Scuola Normale Superiore di Pisa, Lettere, storia e filosofia*, second series, xxviii, 1959, pp. 19–22.

[115] Above, n. 20.

[116] Rashdall, II, p. 19.

[117] *De Cardinalatu*, f. ciiii. This subject will be discussed more fully in a book about the College of Cardinals, 1417–1517, planned by A. V. Antonovics and myself.

[118] Valentini, *A.R.S.P.* LIX, 1936, pp. 213–15; appendix VI, pp. 235–7.

[119] M. Mopurgo-Castelnovo, 'Il Cardinale Domenico Capranica', *A.R.S.P.* LII, 1929, pp. 89–97.

[120] G. Zippel, 'Il palazzo del Governo Vecchio', *Capitolium*, VI, ii, 1930, pp. 366–8, 376.

[121] Archives of the Venerable English College, Rome, Lib. 17, f. 20r, B. Newns, 'The Hospice of St Thomas and the English Crown, 1474–1538', *The Venerabile*, XXI, sexcentenary issue, 1962, pp. 178–9.

[122] R. Creytens (above, n. 2), pp. 82–3 points out that there is no firm evidence about its disbandment, formerly thought to have taken place under Leo X. As late as 1501 he notes a Dominican friar appointed 'in sacro palatio ad legendum sententias'.

[123] E.g. in September 1483 Cardinal Riario was referred to as 'qui Universitatis studii Curiae et Urbis earumdem Cancellarius existit' (Carafa, pp. 579–81). *Cf.*, on the rectorship, below, n. 142.

[124] Renazzi, I, doc. XVIII, pp. 255–7.

[125] Valentini, *A.R.S.P.* LIX, 1936, doc. IV, pp. 233–4.

[126] Creytens, pp. 80–1, suggests that, for teaching theology and controlling doctrine in the Curia, the Studium had even been rising in importance; Torquemada himself had been its academic head as Master of the Sacred Palace. A papal mandate of 7 July 1474 (Marini, *Lettera*, n. viii, pp. 97–100) to pay 'Johanni de la Brixa' [*sic*] 100 florins for teaching logic, philosophy and theology significantly mentions that he had for a long time been a teacher 'sacrarum aliarumque lectionibus litterarum in Studio almae Urbis et Romanae Curiae . . .'. Since it also mentions that he had lectured at San Marco, he may have been the friend of Gaspare Veronese whom A. Andrews (above, n. 34, *op. cit.*, pp. 41–2) could not clearly identify.

[127] E. M. Sanford, 'Gaspare Veronese, humanist and teacher' (above, n. 37), p. 198; Zippel, *Le vite di Paolo II*, p. xxviii.

[128] E. M. Sanford, 'Renaissance commentaries on Juvenal', *Trans. American Philol. Assoc.* LXXIX, 1948, pp. 101–2; G. Mercati, 'Tre dettati universitari dell'umanista Martino Filetico sopra Persio, Giovenale ed Orazio', *Classical and Mediaeval Studies in Honor of Edward Kennard Rand*, New York, 1938, p. 222.

[129] Mercati, p. 223, n. 12: 'concursio frequens erat innumerabilium et variae nationes et linguae personarum ad ea percipienda quae in gymnasio legebantur . . .' Full text of the dedication of Filetico's commentaries on Cicero (to Cardinal Giovanni Colonna) in Pecci, *L'Umanesimo e la 'Cioceria'*, pp. 163–5.

[130] Alessandro de'Alessandri's testimony in Renazzi, I, pp. 217–18.

[131] Biblioteca Angelica, Rome, MS cited in F. Novati, 'Gli scolari romani nei secoli XIV e XV', *Giornale storico della letteratura italiana*, II, 1888, pp. 137–8. I have not been able to check whether MS 88 (8) of Novati's papers deposited with the Società Storica Lombarda, Milan (noted by P. Kristeller, *Iter Italicum*, I, p. 365) includes more material than that in the above article.

[132] Paolo Cortesi, *De Hominibus Doctis*, in P. Villani, *Liber de Civitatis Florentiae famosis civibus* ed. G. C. Galletti, Florence, 1847, p. 230; a reference by Gaspare Veronese is thought by Zippel to refer to Porcelio, *Le vite di Paolo II*, pp. 18–19. On Porcelio see also U. Frittelli, *Gianantonio de'Pandoni detto il 'Porcellio'*, Florence, 1900, pp. 30 ff; R. Avesani, *op. cit.*, above, n. 42, pp. 39 ff; also below, n. 138.

[133] Reg. 118, f. xvi*v*; quoted by Zabughin, I, p. 281.

[134] Sanford, 'Renaissance commentaries on Juvenal' (above, n. 128), pp. 102–5.

[135] D. Gnoli, 'Storia di Pasquino', *Nuova Antologia*, third series, XXV, 1890, pp. 51–75. The pasquinades were printed by Giacomo Mazzocchi, who in 1506 succeeded Etienne Guillery of Lorraine as 'bibliopole academiae Romanae': F. Ascarelli, *Annali tipografici di Giacomo Mazzocchi*, Florence, 1961, p. 15 and *passim*.

[136] See below, n. 140.

[137] On this famous episode see Zabughin, 1, pp. 38 ff; B. Platina, *Liber de vita Christi ac omnium pontificum*, ed. G. Gaida, R.I.S. III, 1, pp. xvi ff.

[138] R. Sabbadini, 'La polemica fra Porcelio e il Panormita', *Rendiconti del Reale Istituto Lombardo di Scienze e Lettere*, 1, Milan, 1917, pp. 495–6.

[139] *Cf.* Sanford, 'Gaspare Veronese' (above, n. 37), pp. 193–4, 198; Zippel, *Le vite di Paolo II*, pp. xxiii–xxix. Andrews (above, n. 34) pp. 9, 23, comments on Gaspare's ommission of reference to these events in the 'lost' fifth book of his papal biography.

[140] Ed. and trans. F. A. Gragg and L. C. Gabel, *Smith College Studies in History*, xxx, Northampton, Mass., 1947, pp. 326–9, 350–6.

[141] Renazzi, 1, p. 124; n. xiii, pp. 282–3.

[142] *Ibid.*, p. 204; *cf.* the cardinal chamberlain's mandate for payment of Filetico, 31 January 1473, to the reformers and 'Episcopo Firmano universitatis studii alme Urbis et Romanae Curiae [*sic*] rectori' in Vatican Archives, Arm. xxix, 38, f. 13*r*.

[143] Renazzi, 1, pp. 204–5; n. xiv, pp. 283–4. On 28 November 1484 a mandate was issued for payment of 200 florins 'Domini Urso episcopo Theanensi Rectori Studii alme Urbis' for two years' salary (A.S.R., Mandati Camerali, 846 = 848, f. 102*r*).

[144] Renazzi, 1, p. 204; *Diario di S. Infessura*, p. 159, no. 1. In 1475 Cillenio of Verona presented a commentary on Tibullus to 'Baptistae Ursino aerarii pontifici custodi et almae Urbis Gymnasii vicerectori': A. della Torre, *Paolo Marsi da Pescina*, Rocca San Casciano, 1903, p. 234.

[145] Renazzi, 1, p. 205; n. xv, p. 284. A salary of 262 *fior. rom.* 10 b. 14 d. was paid him on 12 January 1496 (reg. 126, f. viiii). In 1495, however, some control seemed to have escaped the family: Celso Melino, Bishop of Montefeltro, was then paid as vice-rector 262 *fior. rom.* 14 b. 8 d. (reg. 125, f. 18*r*).

[146] Rashdall, II, pp. 46, 49–50, 53.

[147] G. Zaccagnini, *Storia dello studio di Bologna durante il Rinascimento*, Geneva, 1930, pp. 48–50.

[148] G. Brucker, 'Florence and its university', *Action and Conviction in Early Modern Europe: Essays in Memory of E. H. Harbison*, ed. T. K. Rabb and J. E. Seigel, Princeton, N.J., 1969, pp. 235–6.

FRANCES A. YATES *Warburg Institute*

6

LODOVICO DA PIRANO'S
MEMORY TREATISE

THE CLASSICAL ART of memory was invented in Greece, whence it was passed on to Rome and is described in the Latin treatise on rhetoric known as the *Ad Herennium*, which was supposed throughout the Middle Ages to be by Cicero, or 'Tullius', as he used to be called. It was a mnemonic technique which worked through memorising a series of 'places' on which 'images' were memorised. There were certain rules about what kind of memory 'places' to choose, and what kind of memory 'images'. The anonymous author of *Ad Herennium* gives the fullest exposition of the art, which has come down to us through his exposition of it, but it is also referred to by Cicero and by Quintilian. The Middle Ages knew only the description of the art in *Ad Herennium*, which passed through that period as the authoritative way of committing material to memory. In the thirteenth century the art of memory was formulated anew by Thomas Aquinas and Albertus Magnus, who made the use of it a moral duty and introduced into the rules of *Ad Herennium* subtleties derived from their study of Aristotle on memory in his *De memoria et reminiscentia*.

I begin with this extremely bald summary of a complicated subject, which I have treated at some length in my book *The Art of Memory*,[1] because it must be explained at the outset that Lodovico da Pirano's memory treatise, with which we are concerned here, belongs into the tradition of the classical art of memory. Like the author of *Ad Herennium*, Lodovico da Pirano gives rules for the formation of memory places and memory images. Like Thomas Aquinas, he introduces notions derived from Aristotelian psychology of memory into the rules. Nevertheless, though Lodovico da Pirano is following a well known tradition, there are peculiarities in his memory treatise which make it worthy of fuller attention than I gave it in my book, where it is only briefly mentioned.[2]

The treatise[3] was probably written fairly early in the fifteenth century and can be regarded as an early specimen of a genre which was to become more and more popular as the century progressed. Though we know that in earlier centuries the memory rules were known and were being applied, the genre of the *ars memorativa* treatise begins to become established only in the fifteenth century. The early fifteenth-century treatises are, of course, in manuscript; with the spread of printing, printed memory treatises began to appear, and the genre became very important in the sixteenth century. Practically all known memory treatises base themselves on *Ad Herennium*, and give the traditional rules for places and rules for images, though with variations of many kinds.

Before a full study of the genre can be undertaken a full bibliography of all surviving manuscript treatises is needed. Towards this objective a notable contribution has been made by Paul Kristeller, who in his invaluable *Iter Italicum*[4] has listed a number of hitherto unknown *ars memorativa* treatises discovered by him among the manuscript collections in Italian libraries. By consulting the indices to the volumes of *Iter Italicum*, under 'Memory, artificial', the student of this subject will be led to manuscript material on this topic not listed elsewhere. I am glad to use this article to draw attention to the work which Paul Kristeller has done in this field,

A problem which arises concerning the earlier fifteenth-century memory treatises is the question of whether or not the writers could have been influenced by traditions of classical memory practice, which might have survived from Greek sources or traditions in Byzantium. In the Latin West the Latinised version of the memory rules, derived from Greek sources now lost, had hitherto been the sole source of the tradition, but the fifteenth century might have been able to tap, through the renewed contact with Byzantium, a mnemonic tradition stemming directly from Greek Antiquity.

There was certainly an interest in mnemonics in Byzantium, for a Greek translation of the memory section of *Ad Herennium* exists, made possibly by Maximus Planudes in the fourteenth century or by Theodore of Gaza in the fifteenth.[5] Was there in Byzantium a mnemonic tradition stemming directly from Greek sources, perhaps deriving ultimately from Greek mnemonic practices known to Aristotle, who was certainly interested in an art of memory somewhat similar to the one described in *Ad Herennium*? Among the many importations into Western culture due to the interchange between Byzantine and Latin scholars at the Church Councils early in the century ought we to number a Byzantine tradition for artificial memory which came to join, and complicate, the already existing Latin and Western tradition? I raised this question in my book, without solving it, and I raise it again here, also without solving it. Yet I hope that by giving more information about Lodovico da Pirano's memory treatise I may tempt other scholars to look into the question. For Lodovico da Pirano was certainly in contact with Greek scholars at the Councils, and had some knowledge of Greek. If any new Greek influences came into the memory tradition through the contact with Byzantium they should be apparent in Lodovico's treatise.

Lodovico probably wrote his treatise at Padua, where he was teaching from about 1422 onwards.[6] He was a Franciscan of the province of St Anthony of Padua; he taught theology, philosophy and rhetoric in the university of Padua. He is mentioned for his knowledge of Latin and Greek—

note the 'and Greek'—by Filelfo and by Sicco Polentone. The highlight of his career was his attendance at the Council of Basel, where he spoke in the dispute *in Coena Domini*, and after the transference of the Council to Ferara he was spokesman for the Latins on the *filioque* question in the presence of the Greeks Pletho and Bessarion. In fact Lodovico da Pirano spoke in reply to Bessarion on this burning theological question, the main subject of dispute between the Latin and Greek Churches.

I am not here concerned with Lodovico as theologian, but the placing of him in this conciliar milieu, where momentous contact was made between Byzantine and Latin cultural traditions, is of interest in connection with his memory treatise. Though, as already observed, the treatise certainly belongs mainly to the Latin and scholastic memory tradition, it also contains some unusual features which make one wonder whether Lodovico had picked up, through his knowledge of Greek and contacts with Greek scholars, points from Greek memory training possibly surviving in Byzantium.

In its opening words Lodovico's treatise makes an astonishing departure from the Latin tradition in its choice of the 'inventor' of the art of memory. These opening words, translated from the Latin, are:

The philosopher Democritus, an Athenian, was the first inventor of the artificial memory, who wrote on it in such an obscure manner that no one, until Cicero, understood it.

To the historian of the art of memory there is a novelty here which is positively alarming. In no Latin source is Democritus named as the inventor of the art. The time-honoured 'first inventor' of the art was Simonides of Ceos, who was said to have invented it through noting the places at which guests at a banquet were sitting. The story is told by Cicero in *De oratore*[7] and for the Latin tradition it established Simonides as the inventor of the art of memory. Lodovico da Pirano makes no mention of Simonides; for him Democritus was the inventor of the art of memory. Moreover in this version of the invention of the art of memory, or the artificial memory, as it was usually called, the invention is not presented in mythical form, as in the story of Simonides' discovery of it through his attendance at the fatal banquet. It is a much more concrete statement. Democritus, we are told, had written in a very obscure and difficult way about the art; these writings of his were known to Cicero, who was the first to understand them.

By 'Cicero' Lodovico da Pirano would almost certainly mean the author of *Ad Herennium*, universally supposed to have been written by Cicero. The author of *Ad Herennium* had certainly consulted Greek writings on the art of memory, and in particular he mentions Greek sources when discussing 'memory for words'.

I must briefly explain, referring the reader to my book for further enlightenment, that the author of *Ad Herennium* speaks of two kinds of artificial memory. One is the 'memory for things', or notions; the other is 'memory for words'. In the first method the student aims at memorising only the notions, thoughts, ideas which he will discuss in his speech; for these general notions, or 'things', he forms images to remind him of the 'things' which he memorises on the set orders of 'places' which he has stored in memory. In the second method the aim is to memorise every word in the speech; in this method some image or symbol has to be found for every word, and these images are memorised on the set orders of places. For both types of memory the formation of the memory places is necessary; but in 'memory for things' images of notions are remembered on the places; in 'memory for words' a separate symbol for every word must be memorised on the places.

The author of *Ad Herennium* regards 'memory for words' as a character-istically 'Greek' system. In discussing it he says:

> I know that most of the Greeks who have written on the memory have taken the course of listing images that correspond to a great many words, so that persons who wished to learn these images by heart would have them ready without expending effort in search of them.[8]

He goes on to say that he does not recommend this 'Greek' method, which he thinks too difficult, and advises the student to concentrate on 'memory for things'. It will be enough for him to have in memory the subject matter of his speech, in its right order, and he need not memorise every word in the speech.

I suggest that it may be to this passage in *Ad Herennium* that Lodovico da Pirano is referring when he says that the 'Greek' method of Democritus is very difficult, and was not understood until explained by 'Cicero', that is, by the author of *Ad Herennium*. No writings on memory by Democritus have survived, so we cannot know whether the great philosopher used some peculiarly difficult memory-for-words system for memorising his atomic theory.

Thinking over 'Simonides' and 'Democritus' as rivals for the honour of having invented the art of memory, it may be observed that Simonides (c. 556–468) belongs to an earlier generation, one which almost recedes into a mythical and Pythagorean past, whereas Democritus (c. 460–370) belongs to the rationalising era, being almost contemporary with Aristotle (c. 384–322). Democritus is in fact frequently mentioned by Aristotle. A 'Democritean' memory tradition in Byzantium (if such a thing existed) might therefore have been (1) a difficult memory-for-words tradition or (2) a tradition heavily influenced by Aristotelian psychology of memory.

For what it is worth, this is exactly what we find in Lodovico da Pirano's memory treatise, which concentrates on memory for words, the images in which are to be formed in accordance with Aristotelian theory of association. I do not think that these points are sufficient to *prove* Byzantine influence on Lodovico's memory treatise, but they form an interesting pointer towards future research in these directions.

The existence of Lodovico da Pirano's treatise, in the manuscript in the Marciana library in Venice, was first pointed out by Felice Tocco,[9] who drew attention to the 'Democritus' peculiarity and suggested that it is a mistake for 'Metrodorus' (named by Pliny as perfecter of the art of memory).[10] Baccio Ziliotto, in the introduction to his reprint of the treatise, repeats Tocco's idea and adds the further thought that Democritus' name might have become attached to the memory tradition through the story told by Aulus

Gellius of this philosopher, that he blinded himself to make his inner contemplation more acute. 'Democritus' is sometimes vaguely named as an authority in the alchemical tradition.

The guess now very cautiously put forward is that Lodovico might be repeating some Greek tradition about Democritus and memory of which he had heard through his contacts with Byzantine scholars. The suggestion may be helped by the differences between Pirano's treatise and the Latin memory tradition which might conceivably be due to Greek influence. The problem is, however, obviously a complicated one, and it is possible that other influences may account for the differences. Possibly the fact that Lodovico was a Franciscan, whereas the main Latin memory tradition was shaped by the Dominicans, is an important factor in the situation.

But let us now turn to examine Lodovico's treatise. He gives the rules for 'places' in schematic form, as headings to which he then add explanatory notes. I here give the headings in Latin, followed by abbreviated English translations of the explanations.

Multitudo. Memory places should be sufficient in number to hold all the material to be memorised.

Premeditatio. There should be repeated concentration on the memory places.

Vacuitas sive solitudo. Places should be memorised in unfrequented buildings or districts so that concentration is undisturbed.

Quinto loci signatio. Every fifth place is to be marked with a hand.

Dissimilitudo. Places shall not be too much alike; for example, a series of cells of the brothers are not good as memory places, for they are too similar.

Mediocris magnitudo. Places shall be neither too large nor too small.

Mediocris lux. Places should be neither too brightly lighted nor too obscure.

Distantia. The distance between places should not be too great or too small: Tullius[11] suggests about 30 ft.

Fictio. We may imagine a palace or a temple containing many places, but this is to be done only to exercise the memory.

Multiplicatio. Places may be 'multiplied' by imagining a line running from east to west upon which are placed imaginary towers, as shown in the figure; places may be multiplied through these, that is to say by being changed per *sursum, deorsum, anteorsum, retrorsum, dextrorsum,* and *sinistrorsum.*

With the exception of the last rule on 'multiplication' of places, discussion of which I omit for the moment, all these rules are simply the rules for forming memory places as they are given in *Ad Herennium,* the author of which states that memory places must not be too large or too small, too bright or too dark, that the fifth place should be marked by a hand, and so on.[12] Lodovico is carefully following the classical rules and choosing his places, or memory *loci*, with care. Like the rhetoric students whom the author of *Ad Herennium* taught in ancient Rome, he will wander through buildings and streets, impressing on his memory 'places' chosen in accordance with the rules on which he will later memorise images to remind him of the points of his speech. He is not, however, forming his memory places in ancient Rome but in his monastery. In the classical memory treatise the rule that places must not be too much alike is exemplified by the mention of too many 'intercolumniations' as not suitable for memory places. Lodovico changes this example to 'the cells of the brothers'. Too many cells in a row are too much alike and not suitable to choose as memory places, just as in ancient Rome the spaces in a colonnade were too monotonous and similar.

Lodovico does not give a mystical intensity to the rule about memorising in solitary places, as Thomas Aquinas does.[13] But he expands the rule on *mediocris lux*, that the places are not to be too brightly lighted nor too obscure, with a quotation from Aristotle's *De anima* which he interprets in a mystical direction, as though examining light in a memory place in terms of light in the soul.

In the correct classical manner Lodovico next gives the rules for forming memory images, which he calls *idola*. Here he parts company, to some extent, from *Ad Herennium*, for we hear nothing in his memory rules about choosing images with an emotionally striking appearance, those human images which are actively doing something—the *imagines agentes*[14]—which *Ad Herennium* advises. Lodovico's rules for images are dryly based on the Aristotelian laws of association, through similarity, dissimilarity and contiguity, as laid down in the *De memoria et reminiscentia*. He also gives much attention to 'memory for words', the memorising of every word in a speech through images for each word. The author of *Ad Herennium*, on the contrary, advises the student to memorise 'things' or notions and not to attempt the memorising of every word.[15] These two characteristics of Lodovico's attitude—dependence on Aristotelian association and insistence on memory for words—can be clearly seen in his rules for images. The *idola*, or images to be chosen for use in memory, should be:

In toto simile. That is, exactly like what is to be remembered, as a stone for a stone or Martin himself for Martin.
In toto dissimile per contrarium. As black for white.
In toto dissimile per consuetudinem. As, for Peter, someone who is often with Peter; for a house, a house near it.
In toto dissimile per impositionem. This is to be done either alphabetically, or without the alphabet.

   1 *Per alphabetum*. By using animals or any other class of things as representing letters of the alphabet, as *Asinus*, A; *Bos*, B.[16]
   2 *Sine alphabeto*. In this method images for each word are memorised.

Partim simile per compositionem. As, for example, one may remember 'Mutinensis' by a *mutus* holding an *ensis*. (*Mutinensis* means 'of the city of Mutina'. We are to remember the word by the image of a dumb man holding a sword.) This is a composite image which is 'partly similar' in its components to the sound of the word to be remembered.
Per diminitionem. As 'bertus' for 'Robertus'.

Per transpositionem. As 'maro' for 'Roma'; 'mora' for 'amor'.
Per loquelam. Here we imagine the images to be speaking.

What is missing from Lodovico's rules for images is the classic rule that human images, notably for emotionally exciting qualities, are to be used in 'memory for things'. It was this rule, with its appeal to emotion as a factor in stimulating memory, which gave rise to the effort to invent strikingly beautiful or strikingly hideous human images representing 'things' or notions. Such images, when ranged in the 'places' of memory, would have looked very like inner versions of 'things' constantly seen in medieval didactic art, images of virtues and vices, made strikingly beautiful or strikingly ugly. All this side of the art of memory, so important for its connections with art, seems to be omitted by Lodovico da Pirano. This is partly because he is not interested in 'memory for things' but only in 'memory for words', and in his rules for images he relies on Aristotelian principles of association rather than on the emotionally striking principles recommended in *Ad Herennium.*

Lodovico's three first rules for images, given above, are based on the principles of similarity (*in toto simile*), dissimilarity (*in toto dissimile*) and contiguity. This is purely Aristotelian theory of association, reminding one of a thing by something like it, or by something unlike it, or by something near it. In his fourth rule he is (1) using visual alphabets, or images formed to resemble letters of the alphabet, (2) memorising lists of images for every word.

Lodovico's rules for images are thus directed towards a verbal memory working through associative law and through memorising images for every word. That is to say, he is thinking of a 'memory for words' of the type called 'Greek' by the author of *Ad Herennium,* and of a psychology of memory which is dryly Aristotelian and without the rich, emotional image-forming methods which the Latin tradition had encouraged.

Another interesting point in Lodovico's treatise is that he envisages his memory-for-words method as being used to remember not only Latin words but words of foreign languages, and particularly Greek words. For example, he gives an image through which to remember 'the Greek word for the sea, which is *tellessum* (i.e. θάλασσα).

There are thus in Lodovico's treatise points which distinguish it from the Latin mnemonic tradition. It introduces as inventor of the art of memory Democritus instead of the accepted Simonides. It concentrates on Aristotelian laws of association; the use of Aristotelian psychology from *De memoria et reminiscentia* was characteristic of the Latin scholastic discussion of the art of memory, but Lodovico's rules for images are particularly associative and Aristotelian. It stresses memory for words, and recommends the use of a type of this which *Ad Herennium* rejected and called 'Greek'. It envisages the use of memory for words for remembering Greek or other foreign words, as well as Latin. Have we enough here to justify a guess that Lodovico knew something of Greek mnemonic tradition surviving in Byzantium, through his contacts with Byzantine scholars?

There exists, in a garbled and corrupt form, a Greek treatise on rhetoric
said to have been written by Cassius Longinus, who lived *c.* A.D. 213–73 and
which treats, in a difficult and obscure manner, of the mnemonic through
places and images.[17] It relies on Aristotelian association and may be en-
visaging the use of associative images for memorising words. It certainly has
in mind remembering not only Greek words but also 'the speech of
foreigners'. Is it possible that it is this latest Greek mnemonic tradition,
preserved in Byzantium, that we meet again in Lodovico, with his image
rules taken from Aristotle rather than from 'Tullius', his memory for words
which can apply in several languages?

This suggestion must be left in the form of a guess, as yet unsupported by
evidence. In any case, it is a guess which does not explain 'Democritus', who
is not named as inventor of the art of memory by Cassius Longinus[18] or by
any known Greek source.

There are a few other fifteenth-century memory treatises which also
mention Democritus as inventor of the art. One is by Troilus Boncompagno;
another by J. A. Quirini. Both these manuscripts are in the Marciana at
Venice.[19] Another manuscript treatise which mentions Democritus is the
one by Luca Braga, written at Padua in 1477, of which there is a copy in the
British Museum.[20] Braga, however, also mentions Simonides as inventor
and speaks of Thomas Aquinas as proficient in the art. Since Braga, like
Lodovicus da Pirano, writes in Padua, it is possibly in Paduan circles that
one should look for an explanation of the appearance in the fifteenth century
of Democritus as inventor of the art of memory.

It will be remembered that one of Lodovico's rules for memory places is an
extraordinary one on 'multiplication of places', up and down, backwards and
forwards, to right and to left. Unlike all Lodovico's other place rules, this
one is not to be found in *Ad Herennium*. It is said to work through the agency of
imaginary towers placed on a line running from east to west 'as shown in the
figure'. In the Marciana manuscript from which Ziliotto printed Lodovico's
treatise this figure is not given, but it can be seen in other manuscripts of the
same work, one also in the Marciana,[21] the other in the Vatican.[22]

The figure as seen in these manuscripts consists of two parts: a square
divided into eight sections by vertical, horizontal and diagonal lines; and
nine 'towers' placed on a line with the sun at each end of it, the 'east–west'
line. The towers have doors to them and are clearly memory buildings
divided into many 'places'. The towers are tall, to admit of many rows of
'places', they are very roughly and schematically indicated. The first tower
is, I believe, the memory building before any 'multiplication of places' has
been done on it. The other eight are labelled as intended to show 'multiplication' *per addendo et diminuendo* (not mentioned in the text), and *per sursum,
deorsum, antrorsum, retrorsum, destrorsum, sinistrorsum* (as mentioned in the
text).

'Multiplication of places' is a technique frequently mentioned in the
memory tradition. It is basically quite a simple notion. Once one has grasped

the idea that 'artificial memory' works through memorising many places—usually places in or on buildings—it is clear that when one has used up all the places memorised for remembering one's speech (or whatever material is being committed to memory) there will be no room for remembering any additions made later to the speech, or any other additional material. Therefore one adds—in imagination, of course—another wing or other sets of rooms to the imaginary memory building, which will provide additional places. In its simplest form 'multiplication of places' is no more than this. There are, however, further complications through which the same set of places can be used in different directions for remembering different sets of material or different speeches. I imagine that Lodovico's towers represent this idea, showing places which can be read up and down, inwards and outwards, to left and to right.

Interpretation of the more abstruse memory rules is, however, difficult, nor can one feel quite sure whether they are entirely rational. The 'east–west' line on which the memory towers stand introduces a cosmic, mystical and possibly magical note into Lodovico's system for 'multiplication of places'. One is reminded of the sets of 'memory cubicles', all divided into places, in Robert Fludd's magic memory system; the places are to be memorised in an order proceeding from east to west, following the direction of the sun.[23] Lodovico's 'towers' system, though strictly classical in its use of 'places', may also be verging on occult mnemonics.

The 'towers' system is interesting for the sense of moving through space in memory which it conveys. I have said in my book, when discussing the place rules in *Ad Herennium*, 'what strikes me most about them is the astonishing visual precision which they imply. In a classically trained memory the space between the *loci* can be measured . . .'.[24] Lodovico is extremely conscious, in his rules for places, of measuring the space in memory; and in the 'towers' system he envisages the eye moving up and down, outward and inward, left and right, along the places in memory, in a manner which almost implies that this inner eye sees the places in perspective.

Lodovico da Pirano's memory treatise is interesting not only in itself but because it displays the state of the art of memory at a most important hour in the history of culture, the contact between Western and Byzantine traditions through the theological *rapprochement* in the fifteenth century. The speeches in the meetings of the councils gave an opportunity for something like a revival of the ancient rhetorical tradition, and we have seen that in the case of Lodovico da Pirano the ancient mnemonic tradition was known and was being reformulated. If Lodovico used the mnemonic when making his speech at the Council of Bâle he was using a technique which had been known to Cicero. Whether or not my guesses about the possible influence of Graeco-Byzantine memory tradition on Lodovico will be confirmed, it is at least a fact that we see in Lodovico a man who is in contact with the new Greek scholarship and is using the ancient techniques of the art of memory.

He specialises in memory for words—the technique, almost like a kind of shorthand, which memorised words through sets of arbitrary symbols—and he does not mention the memory-for-things method, the mode of imprinting notions or ideas on memory through striking human images. This does not mean that he did not know that method; his knowledge of *Ad Herennium* and of the scholastic mnemonic descended from it shows that he must have known it. He could therefore, had he wished, have filled the places of his memory towers with strikingly beautiful or hideous image of virtues and vices, with galleries of improving mnemonic allegory.

And that he was aware of the imaginative possibilities of the artificial memory is shown by his inclusion of *fictio* among his rules for places. The author of *Ad Herennium* taught that if the practitioner of artificial memory could not find enough 'real places' in his environment—actual houses, streets and so on to reflect in memory as memory places—he was allowed to invent 'fictitious places', imaginary buildings or backgrounds for his mnemonic technique to use.[25] In Lodovico this suggestion becomes a memory-place rule, *fictio*, that we may imagine palaces or temples as an exercise in memory.

The vast possibilities which this idea opened up for the development of romantic exercises in imaginary architecture, decorated with the images of memory, were thus available to Lodovico da Pirano and his rhetoric students. He opens a phase or a period in memory architecture which is contemporary with the spread of Greek studies in the early Renaissance.

The *ars memorativa* treatises and their curious techniques are as yet a comparatively unworked field of research which can yield material of interest from many points of view. They throw light on a forgotten social habit, once vitally important. In the ages before printing, memorising was an essential activity, and people sought eagerly for the arts which would help towards it. Though all *ars memorativa* treatises are based on the classical rules, which gives them a certain common denominator and a basic similarity, yet each treatise is worth looking into, for they all present variations, give different examples or suggest new light on the universal habit of forming memory places and memory images. The sociologist might learn much from them, for example from the 'hundred memory objects', or things familiar in every-day life, which Lodovico da Pirano, in common with many other writers of memory treatises, recommends as ready-made memory images. The art historian has certainly much to learn from them. It will therefore be useful to make studies of individual treatises such as I have attempted here, and to group them in accordance with their leading characteristics. In this way a quite new approach to the history of man's relation to his environment may be arrived at, and the despised genre of the memory treatise may take on a new importance.

And the effort of the memory artist to learn how to form images and signs through which to simplify the processes of memory was to lead in later ages towards the emergence of scientific methods of notation. Giordano Bruno, in his extraordinary arts of memory, shows knowledge of all the most involved techniques, such as 'multiplication of places', and in the seventeenth century Leibniz was still working within the memory tradition[26] as he moved towards his 'universal characteristic' or language of signs. The memory techniques and their influence on later methods form a subject which is only just emerging above the horizon as an important area of research. A prerequisite for advance in this direction is more adequate study of the *ars memorativa* treatise, its history, its variations, its techniques, its unending efforts to organise and make available the contents of memory.

NOTES

[1] London and Chicago, 1966; paperback edition, Peregrine Books (published by Penguin), 1969. Page references are to the hardback edition.

[2] *Ibid.*, pp. 106–7.

[3] Lodovico da Pirano, *Regulae memoriae artificialis*. The treatise is printed, with an introduction, by Baccio Ziliotto, 'Frate Lodovico da Pirano e le sue *Regulae memoriae artificialis*' in *Atti e memorie della Società istriana di archaeologia e storia patria*, XLIX, 1937, pp. 189–224. Ziliotto prints the treatise from a manuscript in the Biblioteca Marciana, Lat. VI, 274, ff. 5v–15r. The codex contains three other mnemonic treatises. The reference for the manuscript which Ziliotto gives on p. 212 of his article (Marciana, VI, 226) is wrong, or at any rate does not work now. I have seen two other manuscripts of the treatise, Marciana, Lat. XIV, 292, ff. 182r ff; Rome, Vat. Lat. 5347, ff. 1 ff. Only Marciana Lat. VI, 274, names Lodovico da Pirano as the author, but the other two manuscripts are certainly copies of the same treatise. (They are not mentioned by Ziliotto in his article.)

[4] P. O. Kristeller, *Iter italicum*, London and Leiden, I, 1963; II, 1967; other volumes forthcoming.

[5] See H. Caplan's introduction to the Loeb edition of *Ad Herennium*, p. xxvi.

[6] I am indebted to Ziliotto's article for this and other biographical points.

[7] Quoted in *The Art of Memory*, pp. 1–2.

[8] Quoted *ibid.*, p. 15.

[9] Felice Tocco, *Le opere latine di Giordano Bruno*, Florence, 1889, pp. 28–9.

[10] See *The Art of Memory*, pp. 39–41.

[11] I.e. the author of *Ad Herennium*; cf. *The Art of Memory*, p. 7.

[12] See *ibid.*, pp. 7–8.

[13] See *ibid.*, pp. 75–6.

[14] See *ibid.*, pp. 9–12 etc.

[15] On the distinction between 'memory for things' or notions, and 'memory for words' see *The Art of Memory*, pp. 8–9.

[16] This is a reverence to the 'visual alphabets' used in memory; see *The Art of Memory*, pp. 118–20.

[17] See L. Spengel, *Rhetores Graeci*, Leipzig, 1853, I, p. 316; cf. J. M. Edmonds, *Lyra Graeca*, II, 1924, p. 267; L. A. Post, 'Ancient memory systems', *Classical Weekly*, New York, XV, 1932, pp. 107–8.

[18] He gives Simonides as the inventor, in the usual way.

[19] Troilus Boncompagno, *Tractatus super . . . memoria artificiali*, Marciana, VI, 274, ff. 1 ff (immediately followed by Lodovico da Piranos' treatise); J. A. Quirini, *Libro de la scientia de la memoria artificialis*, Lat. XIV, 292, ff. 179 ff.

[20] British Museum, Additional MSS, 10,438, ff. 19 ff.

[21] Marciana, Lat. XIV, 292, ff. 182 ff.

[22] Vat. Lat., 5347, ff. 1 ff.

[23] Robert Fludd, *Utriusque Cosmi . . . Historia*, II; Oppenheim, 1619, *Ars memoriae*, pp. 48 ff. I have discussed the 'memory cubicles' in Fludd's system in my article 'The stage in Robert Fludd's memory system', *Shakespeare Studies*, III, 1967, pp. 156–7.

[24] *The Art of Memory*, p. 8.

[25] *Ibid., loc. cit.*

[26] See Paolo Rossi, *Clavis universalis*, Milan and Naples, 1960, pp. 237 ff; D. P. Walker, 'Leibniz and language', *Journal of the Warburg and Courtauld Institutes*, xxxv, 1972, p. 306.

A. F. C. RYDER *University of Bristol*

7

ANTONIO BECCADELLI: A HUMANIST IN GOVERNMENT

THE LITERARY SENSATION of 1425 in Italy was a pornographic collection of epigrammatic verses entitled *Hermaphroditus*. Published in Bologna, they chronicled the amours and escapades of a thirty-year-old Sicilian law student named Antonio Beccadelli, otherwise known as Panormita, from his birth-place, Palermo. A century earlier the Beccadelli family had emigrated from Bologna, established themselves in Sicily and, through success in business, won a place among the urban patriciate of Palermo. Antonio's father, the most successful member of the family in the second generation, had been knighted.[1] He had intended that his eldest son should make his career as a merchant, but this goal seems never to have been seriously pursued. Instead Antonio, supported by his inheritance and a bursary from his native city, devoted himself to literary studies with the hope of finding a post in one of those courts on the mainland where a man with some literary talent, a good command of elegant Latin and a sound knowledge of the classics might hope for honour and advancement.

A first step towards that goal was taken in 1419 or 1420, when, armed with an introduction to Martin V from his fellow Sicilian Giovanni Aurispa, he went to seek the Pope in Florence. Though the journey put Beccadelli in touch with the burgeoning humanism of Florence and the papal court, it did not secure him any employment, so he decided to improve his qualifications by studying law. He spent almost ten years in that pursuit, peregrinating among the law schools of Siena, Pavia and Bologna; from the latter he obtained his doctorate. Meanwhile he wrote the verses which he gathered together in *Hermaphroditus*, struck up acquaintance and correspondence with many of the leading humanists of northern Italy,[2] and persevered with his efforts to find a suitable niche in some court. Approaches to the Este of Ferrara and to the papal curia having proved fruitless, he decided in 1429—the year in which he transferred his law studies to Pavia—to concentrate his efforts on entering the service of Filippo Maria Visconti, Duke of Milan. This time he met with success; on the strength of his poetic achievement and a promise to write an epic in celebration of Filippo Maria he was named on

1 December 1429 court poet to the duke, with a salary of 400 florins. His
duties included some teaching of rhetoric in the University of Pavia. A further
mark of official recognition came in May 1432, when the emperor Sigismund
for a small fee crowned him poet laureate at Parma.

Although he had seemingly achieved his ambition, Beccadelli was uneasy.
As a poet he found that he had no talent for the epic, and the furtive political
style of Filippo Maria made him an eminently unsatisfactory subject for that
form; so the promised epic was never delivered—probably not even begun.
Apart from many letters the only literary product of the four years spent in
the service of Visconti was an anthology entitled *Poematum et prosarum liber*
which has the merit of being the first, and perhaps the only, humanist
exercise in that form. Most of his creative energy he devoted to studying
Plautus, an author congenial to the man who still bore the reputation of a
witty voluptuary. It was as a defender of the Epicurean philosophy that Valla
introduced Beccadelli into his book *De Voluptate*, written in 1431 when both
men were teaching at Pavia. Filippo Maria let it be known that he was
displeased with the failure of his aulic poet to sing his praises, and that
displeasure led in 1433 to a halving of Beccadelli's salary as a teacher at
Pavia. Another source of discomfort arose from the enmities which his
quarrelsome, intriguing disposition had provoked between himself and his
fellow humanists. The earlier friendship with Valla turned sour, and he had
become involved in polemical exchanges with Pier Candido Decembrio and
Antonio da Ro,[3] both of whom had influence at the ducal court.

Realising that his position was precarious, and that an epicurean could
not live on half-salary, Beccadelli looked around for a new Maecenas. He
found one in Sicily, which had become temporarily the residence of his own
sovereign, Alfonso V of Aragon, a ruler eager for glory and seized with
unbounded enthusiasm for all things classical. Through the good offices of
the royal secretary, Jacme Pelegri, the hopeful humanist, now forty years old,
attracted the king's attention to his prose and verse anthology, which had
been written and dedicated to that end. Early in 1434 he received the
summons that took him back to Sicily and into a service which was to last
until his death.

Historians who have studied Beccadelli's career have all misunderstood
this latter half of it. The majority have, indeed, devoted their attention to the
period which ended with his departure from Milan. All give the impression
that his duties at the Neapolitan court were primarily of a literary character:
instructing the king in Latin, reading classical authors with him, undertaking
diplomatic missions which called for rhetoric in the classic style, recording
his master's virtues in the book *De Dictis et Factis*, and generally promoting
the humanist cause in Naples. Thus Gothein:

Egli era il lettore, il dotto consigliere, il compagno sempre gradito, e gli toccò anche
un posto d'impiegato che gli dava poco da fare.[4]

More recently Resta has expressed essentially the same view, though in more
cautious vein:

Leggendo i vari documenti si apprende che il Panormita ha ricoperto vari incarichi presso la Cancelleria di Alfonso, anche se spesso gli erano assegnati a fini lucrativi più che effettivi.[5]

Such was the impression which Beccadelli himself wished to propagate in his later writings. In fact, like many a humanist, his literary activity belonged mostly to his hours of leisure; those readings of the Roman authors and those philosophical discussions which Panormita conducted for the king took place, as he himself tells us,[6] when the business of the day had been disposed of. And that business, where he was concerned, was the legal affairs of the Crown. He had, it must be remembered, spent ten years studying law, had acquired a doctorate from Bologna, and Alfonso had need of men with legal training to assist him in taking control of the kingdom of Naples. This paper will attempt, therefore, to look more closely at Beccadelli's activities during these years, to show that his government offices did not give him little to do, and to explain why for most of the time he readily devoted himself to bureaucratic duties.

The first office bestowed on him was the post of *gaito* in the Palermo customs. It had fallen vacant on the death of another minor poet, Thomas de Chaula. A *gaito* exercised only petty judicial functions, and it is unlikely that Alfonso intended Beccadelli to perform the duties personally, for he gave him leave to appoint a deputy. The preamble to the letter of appointment,[7] written in eight hexameters, proclaims with a wealth of classical allusion the learning of the new *gaito* in a manner wholly at odds with the character of the post. Although the document bears the signature of the king's principal secretary, Joan Olzina, it is possible that Beccadelli himself took a hand in the composition of the preamble as if to stress that here was a sinecure for a man of letters. That he initially envisaged such a career as a pensioned humanist may also be argued from the annual provision of seventy-five *oncie* which he obtained as a grace from the king at this time. That sum, together with the salary of twenty-five *oncie* as *gaito*, would have enabled him to live in reasonable comfort without the routine burden of any office.

The events of 1435 completely upset Beccadelli's pleasant existence in the court at Palermo and Messina. In February Giovanna II of Naples died, and there began that seven-year struggle between Alfonso and René of Anjou which was to preoccupy the king and turn his court into a perambulating military camp. Furthermore the Aragonese defeat in the naval battle of Ponza (6 August 1435) left Alfonso a prisoner in the hands of the Duke of Milan for several months. Beccadelli had followed the king to the mainland, and, though he escaped captivity at Ponza, found himself employed in a number of offices that gave him a great deal to do.

Initially Alfonso made use of him as a general diplomatic agent. In June 1435, when the Aragonese forces were besieging Gaeta, he was sent to persuade Ottolino Zoppo, the Genoese commander of the garrison, that further resistance would be futile. His arguments convinced Zoppo, but before the agreed terms could be made effective the Genoese was ousted from command. When Gaeta finally fell in December 1435 it was Beccadelli who went by sea to Portovenere to carry the news to Alfonso, returning from his Milanese captivity.[8] In the following year the king despatched him on an embassy to Siena and Florence with the object of explaining the alliance recently concluded between Alfonso and Filippo Maria Visconti, denouncing the hostility of Pope Eugenius IV towards the Aragonese cause in Naples, and persuading those two republics not to support Genoa in its opposition to the king. On this occasion his pleadings failed and Florence remained firmly opposed to the establishment of Aragonese power in Italy.[9]

It must have been soon after his return from Tuscany in 1436 that Beccadelli was appointed a president of the Sommaria, the tribunal responsible for auditing the accounts of receipt and expenditure of all royal officials in the kingdom of Naples. Members of this tribunal were known as *presidentes* and *rationales*, the latter being primarily responsible for the audit proper and the former for the determination of points of law and judgement in legal proceedings that arose from the audit. Hence presidents were always chosen from those holding doctorates of law. The fall of Gaeta had enabled Alfonso to establish there a provisional capital with an embryo administration which he modelled as closely as possible upon that which had served previous kings of Naples. In it the Sommaria, as the principal organ of financial control, played an important role, and there is ample evidence to show that Beccadelli was appointed a president not as a sinecure but in order to make full use of his legal training.

Comparatively little has survived of the once copious records of the Sommaria, so that one cannot follow his career as a president in any detail. His name appears most frequently in a variety of documents emanating from that tribunal in the years 1437 and 1438. Among them is an executory letter—the authorisation of the Sommaria needed to give effect to a privilege —issued by him in Capua on 17 June 1437.[10] In January 1438, while on a mission to the island of Ischia, he was ordered to take possession of a galley in the name of the Crown and send it to the Viceroy of Gaeta.[11] The following month, still in Gaeta, he was commissioned by the Grand Chamberlain, titular head of the Sommaria, to give effect to a contract signed between the Crown and Francesco Longobardo for the farm of certain royal dues in the island.[12] Jumping a few years, we find him on New Year's Day 1444 giving his vote with the other presidents in the trial before the Sommaria of Andrea de Sanctis, treasurer in the Abruzzi provinces, on charges of defrauding the revenue.[13] Later that same year he investigated a petition for remission of tax put forward by the town of Maranola, reported in favour of the petitioners, and countersigned the privilege which granted their request.[14] The name used here and in all other documents until 1455 is Antonio di Bologna, never his humanist appellation, Panormita. As Antonio di Bologna he appears regularly in the lists of presidents of the Sommaria who received annually a quantity of salt as one of the perquisites of office.[15] However, the appearance of a name in these lists is not by itself proof that the president in question was active in his office, for some held the office as a sinecure. Beccadelli, it would seem, ceased to perform the regular duties of a president after 1444, though he continued to draw his salary and other allowances.

Another important responsibility laid on him while the Aragonese administrative headquarters was still in Gaeta was the office of *secretus* and *magister procurator* in that city. As *secretus* he administered the *secrezie* or royal monopolies in the sale of iron, steel, pitch and salt. These commodities were retailed from a storehouse which the *secretus* had to keep stocked and staffed. As *magister procurator* he supervised the collection of customs dues, which in a port as busy as Gaeta entailed much book-keeping and a large subordinate staff. Because of his commitments in the Sommaria it is possible that Beccadelli appointed a deputy to manage the monopolies and customs of Gaeta, paying him out of the salary of 180 ducats a year which the office carried. Even so, ultimate responsibility for the performance of these duties remained with Beccadelli, who had also to present the accounts to the Sommaria.[16] An indication that he did take some interest in the management of the customs of Gaeta is provided by his appointment to a similar office in the city of Naples when it first fell to the Aragonese in June 1442. However, two such offices involving large sums of money laid too heavy a responsibility on one person, so a separate controller was appointed for the Neapolitan customs as from 1 October 1442. Not until June 1444 did Beccadelli present the accounts for those months in which he had administered the customs of Naples,[17] but such delays were not unusual, especially in the earlier years of Alfonso's reign, and so this does not argue any negligence or incompetence in him.

As the Aragonese king developed his administration in the kingdom of Naples he found it necessary to make many *ad hoc* arrangements for offices which served no essential administrative purpose but whose neglect or suppression would have offended powerful Neapolitan interests. One such office was that of the prothonotary, the holder of which ranked as one of the seven principal officers of state. As chief notary of the kingdom the prothonotary had at one time been responsible for drafting public documents of the curia regis, but as it became established custom to bestow the office upon a great noble the functions had passed to a deputy resident at court. Alfonso whittled away the importance of the prothonotary of Naples still further by entrusting most of his secretarial work to the prothonotary and secretaries of Aragon. Nevertheless there remained some classes of documents—such as licences to practise medicine or as a notary—which were peculiarly the business of the Neapolitan prothonotary; and the need not to offend the titular holder, Cristoforo Gaetano, Count of Fondi, necessitated an arrangement to safeguard his prerogatives. Alfonso solved the problem by appointing Beccadelli the locumtenens of the prothonotary. Exactly when he assumed the office is not known, but it was before 17 June 1437, when, in authorising a privilege exempting a Catalan merchant from customs duties, he described himself as 'poete laureati, locumtenentis prothonotarii, Camere nostre Summarie presidentis'.[18] Another privilege exempting the town of Chieti from customs and tolls was issued from the royal camp near Teano on 19 August 1437 by 'Antonium de Bononia poetam laureatum, legum doctorem, camere nostre Summarie presidentem et locumtenentem prothonotarii'.[19]

The latest evidence of his activity as deputy to the prothonotary is a privilege dated 27 December 1438.[20] It is possible, however, that this should read 1437, because the Neapolitan chancery began the new year on 25 December. Unfortunately the records from which Laurenza extracted this information no longer survive, so that it is impossible to ascertain whether he made allowance for the change of date. For six months, or possibly eighteen months, Beccadelli performed the duties of the prothonotary. Although they did not make regular demands upon his time, they involved nonetheless a fair amount of professional labour. Presumably he received some remuneration either in the form of a salary or as a share in the profits of the seals, but we have no details to show whether it represented any substantial addition to his income.

In reviewing those capacities in which Antonio Beccadelli served the king during his first ten years in Alfonso's employment we must finally consider him as a counsellor. He had been given the title *consiliarius* when he first joined the court in Palermo, and that he occasionally attended the royal council is attested by his own account of a meeting held to decide what to do with a large number of women, children and other non-combatants whom the defenders expelled from Gaeta when the king was besieging that city in 1435. He recounts how all those present, himself included, advised that the refugees should be driven back into the city in order to put greater pressure on its dwindling food supplies. After all had spoken the king gave his decision, rejecting their counsel; he ordered instead that the fugitives should be given food and shelter.[21] In later years Beccadelli began to play an important part in the legal work of the council. Alfonso found it convenient to develop the judicial functions of his council in such a manner that it had come by 1440 to constitute a distinct supreme tribunal, with powers extending to all parts of his dominions. In this capacity it acquired the name Sacrum Consilium to distinguish it from the ordinary advisory council. Though membership of the two bodies overlapped, active participation in the Sacrum Consilium was normally restricted to those counsellors with legal training who held some judicial office. The Sacrum Consilium would first consider matters laid before it, usually in the form of petitions, and then delegate the case to one or two of its members to investigate and report back to the full tribunal, which would deliver judgement.

In 1443 the Sacrum Consilium charged its principal legal officer, the Vice-chancellor Battista Platamone,[22] and Beccadelli with an investigation into the alleged insanity of Guillermo del Balzo Orsini, Duke of Andria. After examining the duke himself and a number of witnesses they reported to the king that Guillermo was insane and incapable of managing his affairs. Because legal action was needed to recover part of his estates which had been usurped during his incapacity they advocated that the duke's eldest son, Francisco del Balzo Orsini, be appointed guardian of his father and administrator of all his property and fiefs. The Sacrum Consilium endorsed their findings and authorised a privilege which conferred appropriate powers upon the son.[23]

Another case was handled by Beccadelli alone. It concerned the dowry of Emilia Capice, widow of Tommaso di Sanseverino, Count of Marsico and San Severino, which Emilia and her father were seeking to recover from Tommaso's brother and heir. The case had first been brought in the court of the Vicaria—in effect the high court of the kingdom of Naples—but the plaintiffs had subsequently petitioned the king to revoke it to the Sacrum Consilium. This latter tribunal had then referred the case to Ferrer Ram, prothonotary of Aragon, who in turn handed it over to Beccadelli when the king sent him to Rome. Having gone through the usual procedure of summoning the parties and hearing allegations and counter-allegations, Beccadelli presented his report to the council,[24] which gave judgement in favour of Emilia. He also decided the costs of the case, which the council had ordered should be paid by the defendant.[25] Proceedings in another action involving the profits of the bailiff's court (*gabella baiulacionis*) of Montefusco were likewise entrusted to Beccadelli alone.[26]

To these varied duties as financial administrator, notary and legal counsellor must be added at least one diplomatic mission undertaken in 1440, when Beccadelli went to Savoy to negotiate with the Anti-Pope Felix V for his recognition of the Aragonese claim to Naples.[27] Alfonso hoped in this manner to put pressure upon Eugenius IV, who remained adamantly hostile to him. Moreover it has to be remembered that the records of such bodies as the Sommaria and the Sacrum Consilium have for the most part been destroyed, and that what survives cannot measure the full extent of Beccadelli's participation in the work of those institutions. Enough still remains to demonstrate that in the decade 1434–44 his energies were largely devoted to his work as an official. Despite the care which he took to give pride of place among his titles to that of *poeta laureatus*, his creative literary work virtually ceased. He published no more poetry or prose, nor did he carry his study of Plautus beyond the point it had reached in Pavia. Even his correspondence with humanists elsewhere in Italy became very irregular in this period of his life. Such time as he did devote to language and literature he spent in improving the king's acquaintance with the classical Latin authors.

Alfonso evidently found him a congenial tutor. 'Ab eodem Anthonio complurima iocunde et serio in poesia et oratoria facultate ac philosophia morali et doctrina rei militaris didicerimus et discamus,' states one privilege concerning his annual provision.[28] In another the king praised that 'utilitatem maximam quam ipsum audiendo et legendo percipimus, cum sit orator et eloquentissimus et poeta laureatus'.[29] Elsewhere he refers to him as 'preceptor noster'.[30] Beccadelli himself tells a number of stories about his services as reader to the king. In one of them he relates how, when Alfonso lay ill in Capua, he left Gaeta to visit him, taking some books which he knew the king would enjoy. He chose for reading the life of Alexander by Curtius Rufus, which so fascinated Alfonso that he at once began to recover. Beccadelli continued the reading three times a day until the book was finished and the king wholly cured.[31] Another anecdote tells how, during the siege of Caiazzo in May 1441, Alfonso and Beccadelli were riding through the camp together, discussing the military exploits of Viriatus, the hero of Lusitanian resistance to Rome. Lope Ximenez de Urrea, the Aragonese noble commanding the king's forces, attempted to ride between them, only to be rebuked by Alfonso with the remark that when the discussion concerned learning and antiquity the place by his side belonged not to courtiers but to scholars.[32]

It has been suggested that one of the reasons which led to Beccadelli's literary pursuits being pushed into second place was the pressure exerted by the conquest and administration of the kingdom of Naples upon the king and his entourage.[33] I suspect that another reason may have been the appearance in that same court circle of Lorenzo Valla. Bad blood had already arisen between the newcomer and Beccadelli during the years they had spent in Pavia;[34] it again flared into the open in 1438, when both were in Gaeta. Both had pretensions to be the king's tutor; both represented in the Aragonese court the humanist learning that was capturing the intellectual imagination of Italy. But the contest was an unequal one, for in learning and intellect Valla far outshone Beccadelli. Realising that in this sphere he faced a genius more formidable than his own, the Sicilian may have been that much readier to devote himself to the duties of his various offices.

However, he cannot have been wholly content with his lot, for in the summer of 1444 he gave up his work, returned to Sicily and stayed away from court for some five years. The document which records his resignation as customs officer of Gaeta in September 1444 offers no explanation for his departure.[35] All that is known about this period of his life is that in April or May 1447 he married for the second time.[36] His first wife, Filippa, he had married in Lombardy; his second, Laura Arcella, was a Neapolitan.[37] Alfonso had, according to Beccadelli, opposed the remarriage on the grounds that his studies would suffer but gave his blessing when he learned who the bride was to be.[38] It is reasonable to suppose that, besides getting married, he devoted some of his time to the business of his family estates in Palermo and to the Castello della Zisa, a former royal pleasure resort which the king had given him in 1439.[39] Some time he certainly spent in pressing his claims for payment of his salary from the customs revenues of Palermo, for the money available from that source was never able to satisfy all those who had claims upon it. How seriously he viewed this contest for cash is revealed in a letter written to Alfonso from Palermo. After expressing regret over his delay in returning to Naples he begs the king not to allow a certain Giovanni Marchio to deprive him of his salary from the Palermo revenues; while many had claims on these funds, they were for him, he maintained, his sole source of income.[40] Another of his letters addressed to the king's secretary, Francesch Martorell, may also belong to the years spent in Sicily. In it he asks Martorell to commend him to the king and explain the reasons for his prolonged absence from the court.[41]

Alfonso himself spent almost two of these same years away from his kingdom engaged in war with Florence. When he returned to Naples in November 1448 Beccadelli may have decided that it was time for him too to reappear if he was to retain royal favour. Moreover the court must have

appeared more congenial now that Valla had left it to serve Nicholas V. The
only scholar of any consequence remaining was Bartolomeo Facio, a firm
friend of Beccadelli and his ally in the feud with Valla.[42]

It was probably in 1449 that Beccadelli returned to Naples with his wife
and baby daughter Caterina, though he did not immediately resume his
official duties. A letter written at this time to his friend Aurispa in Rome
announces his marriage to Laura, the birth of his daughter, and the fact
that he is in Naples enjoying a holiday from official business.[43] Whether he
ever returned to the Sommaria as an active president is difficult to ascertain
because of the paucity of documents. He certainly continued to receive his
emoluments as a president, and in October 1454 he obtained the post of
notarius actorum, or chief clerk, in the Sommaria. It had previously been held
by the secretary, Joan Olzina, who was now unable, because of a prolonged
absence in Spain, to supervise effectively the deputy who performed the
duties for him. Beccadelli too was permitted to appoint a deputy, but the
privilege conferring the office on him does lay some stress on the need for the
titular holder to keep a watchful eye on his substitute: '. . . ipsumque officium
ob negotiorum occurrentium exigentiam viri presentia per maxime indigere
cuius solicitudine et diligentia ipsius nostre Camere negotia dirigi valeant'.[44]
The salary of 300 ducats paid to the *notarius actorum* he arranged to draw from
the same Palermo funds that accounted for his other emoluments.[45] His
readiness to rely thus exclusively on a source which had hitherto caused him
such trouble is explained by a privilege which the king had written with his
own hand—a most exceptional mark of favour—on 5 February 1450. It
provided that 'mi consellero e preceptor' should have first call upon the
customs revenue, and was later extended to include the salary as *notarius
actorum*.[46]

The most conspicuous, and probably the most important, use which
Alfonso made of Beccadelli's talents in the years immediately following his
return to court was in the diplomatic sphere. At that time the major objective
of royal policy was to create with Venice and some lesser States of northern
Italy an alliance directed against Florence and Milan. To that end he made
peace with Venice in July 1450. Beccadelli and Luis dez Puig, a Catalan well
versed in the complexities of north Italian politics, were sent to congratulate
the Venetian senate on the ending of a conflict between the king and the
republic that had lasted for more than ten years.[47] The next step was to drive
a wedge between Florence and Milan, and to persuade the Venetians to
attack Milan themselves or else subsidise an attack by the king's forces. In
pursuance of these objectives Alfonso again made use of Beccadelli and Dez
Puig.

Leaving Naples in February 1451, they first visited Rome and Siena to
calm apprehensions and explain that the alliance of Naples and Venice was
open to other States.[48] On 6 March they delivered their embassy in Florence.
The peace of Italy, achieved by the king's endeavours in 1450, was again
threatened, they declared, by the assistance which Florence had given to
Alessandro Sforza. Unless that aid ceased forthwith, Alfonso would be forced

to prohibit the valuable Florentine trade in his dominions.[49] Cosimo de'
Medici took it upon himself to reply eloquently and soothingly, but without
any assurance that Florence would abandon the Sforza. From Florence they
moved to Ferrara, where their task was to persuade Borso d'Este to join the
alliance, though the king expected nothing more than benevolent neutrality.[50]
Having thus sounded opinion in the most important States, they concluded
their mission in Venice, which refused to be hustled into the attack upon
Milan that Alfonso desired.

In each of the States they visited Beccadelli delivered one of those public
orations which had become a notable feature of humanist-dominated Italian
diplomacy in this period. He took particular pride in that which he spoke
before the Venetian senate, and gave a version of it to Facio to include in his
history of Alfonso.[51] The tour also gave him the opportunity to renew his
contacts in the literary world, and to achieve the curious feat of obtaining
from Padua a relic reputed to be an arm of Livy. This he proudly presented
to a grateful king when he returned to Naples in September 1451.[52]

The spring of 1452 saw Beccadelli back in Rome, this time as a member of
a delegation sent to greet the emperor Frederick III, who had come to Italy
in order to be crowned by the Pope and to marry Alfonso's niece, Eleanor of
Portugal. After these ceremonies Frederick and his bride visited Alfonso in
Naples, and it fell to Beccadelli to deliver an oration of welcome when they
crossed the frontier at Terracina. In the following year he was sent to Genoa
in an effort to resolve one of the periodic crises that marked relations between
that republic and the king. It was on this occasion that he delivered the
oration urging the Genoese to unite with other powers in arming a fleet
against the Turks, who had that summer stormed Constantinople.[53]

For the remainder of Alfonso's reign Beccadelli went on no more diplomatic missions. Advancing age—he was now in his sixtieth year—may have
forced him to seek less arduous assignments. His wife too may have influenced
him, for she disliked these journeys that kept him so long from home. In the
course of his last embassy to Venice he wrote asking the king for leave to
return to Naples because his wife was fretting at his absence.[54] But despite
physical and domestic pressures he did pay one last visit to Palermo in 1455.
His private affairs probably led him to make the journey, though it seems
that he looked into the progress of a commissioner whom the king had sent to
Sicily and reported favourably to Alfonso on his return.[55]

He must have been back in Naples by 1 September 1455, the day on which
his appointment as a secretary took effect. Alfonso gave him the office as a
further mark of esteem: 'eundem Antonium inter primos et maiores ac
ordinarios nostros secretarios habemus et prae ceteris pro sua singulari
doctrina ac eloquentia carissimum'.[56] Also it carried a salary of forty *oncie*
and twenty-four *tarini*. But it was no sinecure, as one may see from the number
of letters which Beccadelli wrote as secretary during the last three years of the
reign. Some are concerned with routine administrative business: the letters
to the Sicilian officials mentioned above, for example. Many are addressed
to the rulers of Italian States with the object of justifying Alfonso's diplomatic

manoeuvrings. One of these replies to a letter from Bernardo dei Medici exhorting the king to further the cause of Italian peace and the crusade.[57] A number addressed to Venice, Florence, Ferrara and Milan seek to explain the king's attitude towards the peace negotiations going on between his protégé Jacopo Piccinino and Siena.[58] Others to the Pope, Milan, Venice, Mantua, Ferrara, Urbino and Florence justify Alfonso's stand in his quarrel with Genoa.[59] Letters written by him on 4 October 1455 informed the doge of Venice, the Pope and Cosimo dei Medici of the marriages arranged between the ruling houses of Naples and Milan.[60] In other words, he was given special responsibility for correspondence with the heads of other Italian States for which the king's prestige demanded an elegant latinity. A few other documents, presumably thought to merit a style more elevated than the regular Latin of the chancery, also came from his pen. One example is the privilege appointing the Florentine humanist and diplomat Giannozzo Manetti a president of the Sommaria. It begins 'Tanto evidentius cuiuslibet principis solium sublime conspicitur quanto magis latus eius probis et prudentibus viris atque egregia eruditione et singulari doctrina praeditis consulentibus illustratur'.[61]

In contrast to the legal and financial posts he had held in earlier years, Beccadelli found in his duties as diplomat, orator and secretary a new stimulus to his literary talents. Moreover he now felt secure in his position as grand old man of letters about the court. Brighter lights might come and go, but they did so under his patronage. Theodore Gaza, for example, arrived in Naples bearing a recommendation to Beccadelli from Aurispa, and with the former's assistance obtained a pension of 500 ducats a year.[62] The secretary, who now used the style 'Antonius Panormita', wrote to inform his friend of Theodore's success and urged him to follow as quickly as possible to Naples, where similar rewards awaited him.[63] He likewise played a part in finding a place for Manetti by presenting to Alfonso the work *De dignitate et excellentia hominis*, which Manetti had dedicated to the king.[64] Giovanni Pontano began his career in the Neapolitan chancery in 1451, thanks to a recommendation from Beccadelli to the secretary, Olzina,[65] and he used his influence both within the kingdom and abroad to ensure a favourable reception for Facio's history of Alfonso's exploits in Italy. He asked the vice-chancellor, Battista Platamone, to put in a good word for Facio when he presented the king with the first eight books of his work.[66] While in Venice he praised it to Francesco Barbaro, who wrote to Facio, urging him to finish the remaining two books.[67] By thus using his influence with the king and with numerous exponents of the humanist culture Beccadelli played an important part in establishing the new learning in southern Italy.[68]

Not only did he encourage the activity of others; he too entered on another creative period. It began with the compilation of a work entitled *Vocabolario* written by a team of copyists under his direction. By February 1451, when the treasury paid him 100 ducats for distribution among the scribes, the *Vocabolario* must have been finished, or at least well under way.[69] Presumably it was some kind of word list or dictionary, but its merits we cannot judge, for its present whereabouts are not known. Soon afterwards he began to write another little book, which he published in 1455 under the title *De dictis et factis Alfonsi regis*. In it he celebrated the wit and wisdom of the king in a series of anecdotes following the model of Xenophon's *Memorabilia* and thereby did a great deal to establish Alfonso's reputation as a wise, humane, learned and generous prince.[70] Dedicated to Cosimo de' Medici, the book had an immediate success in Italy. Among its admirers was Aeneas Sylvius Piccolomini, who quickly produced a commentary upon it.[71] Inspired by his success, Beccadelli began work on another book about the king's military prowess, but Alfonso died while he was still engaged on it, and he never completed it.[72] His correspondence too revived as he sought eagerly for talent, manuscripts and news in the humanist circles of Italy.

In every way these years from 1450 to 1458 were probably the happiest of Beccadelli's life: the summit of his official career; the peak of his literary reputation and influence; a time of domestic content and financial ease. Marks of royal favour continued to flatter him: in February 1450 Alfonso gave him the right to quarter the arms of Aragon with his own;[73] in April 1450 he was enrolled in the Seggio di Nido as a life citizen of Naples.[74] The death of the king on 27 June 1458 shattered this pleasant existence. The new king, Fernando, Alfonso's illegitimate son, though not the boorish monster depicted by his enemies' propaganda, did not share his father's passion for the arts. Even had he been that way inclined the attempt of his ex-tutor Pope Calixtus III to deny him the succession, followed by a baronial revolt and Angevin invasion, would still have forced Fernando to concentrate all his energies and resources on the preservation of his kingdom. 'Musae quidem, ne quid in his sperem, cum Alphonso una sepultae iacent,' lamented Beccadelli to the Archbishop of Ravenna.[75] And to Aeneas Sylvius, now Pius II, 'post Alphonsi gloriosissimi regis obitum litteratorum hominum spes omnis extinta est'.[76] To make matters worse, the division of the Aragonese inheritance between Fernando and Juan II of Aragon had once more severed the political link between Sicily and Naples. As a result Beccadelli found that the Palermo customs, his main source of income, were under the control of a foreign king.

So upset was he by this sudden change in his fortunes that he contemplated retiring to Sicily. But Fernando was not insensible to the claims which the aged humanist had upon him, and he found plenty to occupy him as secretary and envoy in the troubled months following Alfonso's death. Soon after it Beccadelli embarked on his last diplomatic mission when he was sent to Milan to confirm Francesco Sforza in his support for Fernando. As a secretary he continued for a time to write letters on the larger political issues to heads of state, in particular he wrote many of those which put Fernando's case before the powers of Italy. As a counsellor he took part in a meeting of the king's council held in Andria in 1459 and advocated action against the Prince of Taranto, the chief fomentor of baronial unrest. Nor did Fernando neglect Beccadelli's pecuniary interests. Thanks to his intercession the new king of Sicily confirmed all the privileges which Alfonso had granted

Beccadelli with respect to his income from the Palermo customs.[77] He was also permitted to retain the Castello della Zisa as a fief, despite a statute which required all tenants-in-chief to reside within the island. To some property which he had acquired in the kingdom of Naples during the reign of Alfonso Fernando added a house seized from the rebel Prince of Rossano. These signs of royal concern sufficed to dissuade him from retiring to Sicily, and he settled down to spend the last years of his life in Naples. In 1463, when he had already relinquished the duties, though not the title, of secretary, he became tutor to Fernando's eldest son, Alfonso.[78] Some other part of his retirement he devoted to writing a *Liber rerum gestarum Ferdinandi Aragoniae*, but still he found this style of work beyond his powers and did not finish it. Greater success attended his efforts to gather together the letters which he wished to preserve as testimony to his skill as a writer and to his standing among the literary and political figures of his age. The publication of the first two books of his letters, the *Epistolae Gallicae* and the *Epistolae Campanae*, was among the first books to be printed in Naples.[79] He died on 19 January 1471 at the age of seventy-six.

The career of Antonio Beccadelli resembled that of many other humanists in its combination of public office and scholarly activity. Indeed, few could manage to devote themselves to the latter pursuit without the support of the former. However, the emphasis laid on one side or the other varied greatly between individuals, so that one needs to examine the evidence very carefully before deciding that an office gave a man much or little to do. Lorenzo Valla, for example, spent eleven years in the court of Alfonso holding the title, but performing none of the duties, of a secretary. During that period of subsidised leisure he conceived and produced his greatest work.[80] Manetti was not required to perform the functions of a president in the Sommaria. Theodore Gaza and Facio received substantial pensions unattached even nominally to any office. In other words, Alfonso was very ready to provide a man of literary or scholarly ability with the means to devote himself, unencumbered by routine duties, to creative work. One can hardly believe that what was granted to so many others would have been refused to Beccadelli had he wanted it. He did in fact enjoy such a period of leisure between 1444 and 1449. It must therefore be assumed that he chose freely the life of the active state official rather than that of the pensioned scholar. His motives in making that choice cannot be determined with any certainty, but his career and character offer some clues. Money and possessions clearly meant a lot to him, and the steady accumulation of offices gave him much more than he could have hoped for from a simple pension or sinecure. Also he was a person of strictly limited creative ability: he possessed a sparkling talent for the vivid sketch of character and incident in verse or prose, but lacked the breadth of vision and power of composition to carry through a major work. His achievement was one of style and form; he had no original ideas to put forward. Such a man could make no creative use of prolonged leisure, and might indeed have become demoralised by it. The very presence of Valla may have driven Beccadelli into a flurry of bureaucratic activity in order that he might be spared humiliating comparison with his rival. Once Valla had gone he was able with greater assurance to raise his head from his ledgers and law books, and to strike a more comfortable balance between his two personae— the man of letters and the government official.

APPENDIX 7.1

A.C.A., Registros, 2700, 97r–v

Illustrissimi principi Francisco Sforcie Vicecomiti Duci Mediolani, Papie Anglerieque Comiti ac Cremone domino amico nostro carissimo.

Rex Aragonum Sicilie citra et ultra farum Valencie Hierusalem. Hungarie Maioricarum Sardinie et Corsice Comes Barchinone etc. Saltem cum intelligerem dux illustris Jacobum Piccininum ad expedicionem contra theucros capessendam perutilem fore tentavi crebro illum cum Sanctissimi domini nostri pape conducere, quove facilius res effici posset stipendiorum partem ipse pollicitus sum. At pontifex, nescio quo christianorum fato hoc ipsum non sua quidem natura que perbenigna est sed malivolorum quorundam suasione, non modo neglexit sed, ut novit excellencia vestra, in eum arma convertit. A quo proposito ut aliquando desisteret et in ea causa et christianorum commodo frequenter Sanctitatem Suam obtestatus sum, verum ille adhuc proposito perstat quo michi nichil esse per hec tempora aut molestius potest aut incommodius. Quare per immortalem inter nos futuram amiciciam vos petimus et rogamus ut nostra gratia et pro christiane religionis commoditate apud Sanctitatem Suam etiam per legatos intercedere velit atque enixissime conari ut ab Jacobo prenominato exercitum revocet illumque quod in manu sua est in gratiam recipiat. Quicquid vero excellencia vestra interprete aut deprecante inter Jacobum et Sanctiatem Suam convenerit nos acceptum ferimus ratumque suscipimus ac firmissimum fore pollicemur. Amplius fraternitati vestre spondemus decetero Jacobum non minus voluntati vestre quam nostre optemperaturum vestrumque perpetuo futurum, hoc cum fraternitas vestra fecerit planum esse incipiet quod clarissimus vir orator vester Albericus de vestra erga Maiestatem nostram benivolencia atque observancia quotidie predicat. De voluntate vero nostra erga Excellenciam vestram hoc maxime argumentum vobis sit quod tam fidenter tamque ingenue hec a vobis petere ausi simus non minora sane beneficia aliquando reddituri quam accepturi. Avetote. Datum in Castellonovo nostro Neapolis die xxii Augusti, Millesimo CCCCLv. Rex Alfonsus.

               Dominus Rex mandavit michi Antonio Panhormita.

A.C.A., Registros, 2700, 100r–v

Sanctissime Pater etc. Pluribus litteris nuper Sanctitatem Vestram etiam atque etiam oravimus ut unum aliquem moribus et gravitate insignem virum ad nos mittere dignaretur qui nomine eiusdem Sanctitatis matrimonio inter incliti Mediolanensium Ducis filiam ac nepotem meum contrahendo interesset, cumque eum summo desiderio aliquandiu expectassemus, cuius dignitate vel auctoritate id sacramentum illustraretur, tandem advenit religiosus vir Marianus multa ex spiritu sancto nobiscum collocutus que tamen omnia tenderent non ad contrahendum, sed potius ad dissolvendum matrimonium. Cuius suasiones velut rationis expertes, cum facile refellissemus, extimavimus ex spiritu sancto potius affinitatem hanc copulandam ac conciliandam esse, spiritum enim sanctum dei amorem esse didicimus ac proinde amicitiis atque concordiis presidere. Enim vero cum ad huiusmodi matrimonium multis et quidem honestissimis rationibus inducamur precipue tamen inducimur ut pax Italie firmior et stabilior permaneat, nam cum intelligent Ducem Mediolani et me non solum amicitia sed etiam necessitudine perpetuo devinctos non ad illum aut ad me quasi discordiarum duces atque fautores ut solebant invicem dissidentes recurrent, sed ex nostra benivolentia condiscent pacem servare odia cohibere et pacifici esse. In hac itaque affinitate pater beatissime tum universam ac perpetuam Italie pacem tum vel maxime sedis apostolice tranquillitatem futuram prospicimus. Ipso igitur spiritu

sancto adiuvante et presente matrimonium hoc quantum in nobis erit perficiemus quod si interim aliquis a Sanctitate Vestra missus affuerit perinde gaudebimus ac si lumen aliquod e celo dimissum repente nobis affulserit. Rex Alfonsus.
Datum in Castellonovo Neapolis xxiiii mensis Septembris MCCCCLv.

Dominus Rex mandavit michi Antonio Panhormita.

A.C.A., Registros, 2661, 136r

Sanctissime etc. Accepi proxime licteras a Petro Duce genuentium et octoviris rei bellice prefectis, quibus in me transferre conantur quod in se nobilitatum est inconstantie vitium nam confectis nuper inter nos induciis, confestim oppida quae in insula Corsice tenebamus invasere diripuere et quod inhumanius est presides et populares nostros crudelissime interemere. Idque cum prius ipsi contra inducias patraverint postea nos levitatis insimulare non verentur. Ego vero licteris suis coactus sum respondere, nam exemplaria licterarum per Italiam dimiserant, quibus satisfacere meque expurgare necessum fuit. Exemplar itaque ad Sanctitatem Vestram mittere decrevimus simul et Beatitudinem Vestram in memoriam revocare volumus conditionem federis inter nos olim percussi ne cui confederatorum scilicet inter genuenses et me sese intromittere auxilium ne prestare liceat.
Datum in Turri Octavi die x Augusti Millesimo CCCCL sexto. Rex Alfonsus.

Dominus Rex mandavit michi Antonio Panhormita.

A.C.A., Registros, 2661, 99r

Magnifico viro Bernardo de Medicis civi florentino amico nostro carissimo.
Rex Aragonum et utriusque Sicilie etc.
Magnifice vir amice noster carissime, Proxime a te litteras accepimus quas illius tue cum apud nos aderas suavitatis atque humanitatis admoniti leto animo perlegimus simul et consilium ac desiderium tuum erga pacem ytalie exosculati sumus. Et ut mentem nostram ipse percipias persuade tibi nihil nobis cordi fixius esse quam pacem et tranquillitatem ytalie. Concordiam itaque dissidencium perobtamus et ad eam perficienciam pro virili nostra laboramus. Sed non Jacobi Piccinini magis causa quam quod intelligimus sublata hac dissensione expedicionem in theucros liberam et expeditam relinqui iis qui suscipere eam concupiscunt. Quare te petimus et rogamus ut quanquidem iam mentem et propositum nostrum deprehendis senatum florencium decetero orteris ut dimicancium et ipse concordiam procuret ut nichil prorsus impediat quominus iniurias in christum et christianos omnis illatas ultum ire festinemus. Vale. Datum in Castellonovo Neapolis die viii Septembris MCCCCLv. Rex Alfonsus.

Anthonius Panormita

NOTES

[1] See G. Resta, 'Antonio Beccadelli', in *Dizionario biografico degli italiani*, VII, Rome, 1965, pp. 400–6, and the bibliography given there.

[2] Among those with whom he corresponded in this period were Gasperino Barzizza, Guarino Veronese, Poggio Bracciolini, Lorenzo Valla and Bartolomeo della Capra. *Cf.* G. Resta, *L'Epistolario del Panormita*, Messina, 1954.

[3] *Cf.* F. Satullo, *La giovanezza di Antonio Beccadelli detto Il Panormita*, Palermo, 1906, p. 116.

[4] E. Gothein, *Il Rinascimento nell'Italia Meridionale* (Italian translation), Florence, 1915, p. 218.

[5] G. Resta, *L'Epistolario*, p. 132.

[6] A. Beccadelli, *De Dictis et Factis Alfonsi Regis*, book IV, 18. This anecdote relates, moreover, to the first year of Beccadelli's service with Alfonso, when the court was still in Sicily.

[7] Printed in R. Starrabba, 'Notizie concernenti Antonio Panormita', *Archivio Storico Siciliano*, new series, XXVII, 1902, pp. 119–20. The privilege is dated Palermo, 14 July 1434.

[8] N. F. Faraglia, *Storia della lotta tra Alfonso e Renato d'Angiò*, Lanciano, 1908, p. 54.

[9] *Ibid.*, p. 62.

[10] V. Laurenza, 'Il Panormita a Napoli', *Atti della Accademia Pontaniana*, XVII, 1936, p. 63.

[11] Archivo de la Corona de Aragon (A.C.A.), Registros, 2651, f. 4*v*.

[12] Laurenza, 'Il Panormita a Napoli', p. 64.

[13] *Ibid.*, p. 70.

[14] A.C.A., Registros, 2906, ff. 99*v*–100*v*, 15 May 1444.

[15] N. Toppi, *De Origine Tribunalium*, Naples, 1659, part I, p. 172, list for 1444. *Ibid.*, p. 173, list for 1446. *Ibid.*, p. 190, list for 1452.

[16] Laurenza, 'Il Panormita a Napoli', p. 68, describes a transaction in February 1442 in which Beccadelli gave the king 400 ducats, partly in cash and partly in red velvet, and was authorised to recover the amount from the *secrezie* of Gaeta.

[17] On 10 June 1444 the Sommaria summoned him to present his accounts. *Ibid.*, p. 70.

[18] Faraglia, *La lotta*, p. 95, n. 3.

[19] A.C.A., Registros, 2914, ff. 141*r*–144*r*.

[20] Laurenza, 'Il Panormita a Napoli, p. 66.

[21] Beccadelli, *De Dictis et Factis*, book I, 15.

[22] Like Beccadelli, Platamone was a Sicilian. See F. Marletta, 'Un uomo di stato del Quattrocento: Battista Platamone', *Archivio storico per la Sicilia*, I, Palermo, 1937, pp. 29–68.

[23] A.C.A., Registros, 2904, f. 115*r*–*v*, 30 December 1443. The privilege bears the annotation 'Mandato regio facto per Babtistam de Plathamone vicecancellarium et Anthonium de Bononia legum doctores consiliarios quibus fuit commissum et has viderunt'.

[24] '. . . facta relacione ex provisione regie in dicto sacro nostro consilio per dictum Antonium de Bononia in quo fuerunt presentes predicti procuratores et advocati partium predictorum ac etiam quamplures nobiles consiliarii ac in iure periti . . .'. (A.C.A., Registros, 2909, ff. 74*v*–78*r*, 12 June 1444.)

[25] *Ibid.*, f. 79*r*–*v*, 23 June 1444. Beccadelli calculated the costs at thirty-one *oncie*, twenty-one *tarini* and fifteen *grana*.

[26] The Sacrum Consilium delivered judgement in this case on Friday 15 May 1444. (A.C.A., Registros, 2906, ff. 94*v*–97*r*.)

[27] J. Ametller y Vinyas, *Alfonso V en Italia y la crisis religiosa del siglo XV*, Gerona, 1903–28, three vols., II, p. 351.

[28] M. Catalano Tirrito, *Nuovi documenti sul Panormita tratti dagli archivi palermitani*, Catania, 1910, p. 175: Gaeta, 1 April 1437.

[29] Catalano Tirrito, *Nuovi documenti*, p. 175. This privilege, dated Capua, 23 May 1438, transferred the provision of seventy-five *oncie* from the oil, wine and salt *gabelle* of Palermo to a weights-and-measures tax in the same city.

[30] E.g. A.C.A., Registros, 2907, f. 1*r*–*v*, 1 October 1444.

[31] Beccadelli, *De Dictis et Factis*, I, 43.

[32] *Ibid.*, I, 42.

[33] *Cf.* above, p. 125.

[34] *Cf.* above, p. 124.

[35] A.C.A., Registros, 2907, f. 1*r*–*v*, 1 October 1444. A privilege appointing Andrea Borromei of Florence to succeed Beccadelli.

[36] Resta, *L'Epistolario*, p. 34.

[37] Beccadelli gives her name as Leonora Aureglia. (*Dictis et Factis*, III, 27.)

[38] *Ibid.*

[39] Catalano Tirrito, *Nuovi documenti*, p. 176.

[40] Beccadelli, *Epistolae Campanae*, 36.

[41] *Ibid.*, 13.

[42] Facio took up the cudgels on behalf of Beccadelli in a polemical exchange with

Valla. *Cf.* P. O. Kristeller, 'Bartolomeo Facio and his unknown correspondence', in *From the Renaissance to the Counter-Reformation,* ed. C. H. Carter, London, 1965, pp. 61–2.

[43] Beccadelli, *Epistolae Campanae,* 26.

[44] Archivio di Stato di Napoli (A.S.N.), Privilegi della Cancellaria, 1, ff. 163r–164r, 11 October 1454. He paid no sealing fee for this privilege 'quia presidens'.

[45] A.C.A., Registros, 2946, ff. 126v–128v.

[46] R. Starrabba, 'Notizie concernenti Antonio Panormita', cited in n. 7 above.

[47] Ametller y Vinyas, *Alfonso V en Italia,* II, p. 683.

[48] A.C.A., Registros, 2697, ff. 81v–82r, 21 February 1451.

[49] A.C.A., Registros, 2697, ff. 82v–83r, 21 February 1451.

[50] *Ibid.,* ff. 85v–86r, 21 February 1451.

[51] B. Facio, *De Rebus Gestis ab Alphonso Primo, Neapolitanorum Rege, Commentariorum,* Lib. 9.

[52] See Laurenza, 'Il Panormita a Napoli', p. 157. A skeleton, assumed to be that of Livy, had recently been discovered in Padua.

[53] This oration is printed with the *Epistolae Campanae.*

[54] *Epistolae Campanae,* 38. The letter is dated 25 June 1450, but 1451 would be a more plausible date.

[55] On 2 November 1455, in his capacity as a secretary, he wrote two letters, one to the president of the council in Sicily and the other to the commissioner in question, informing them that their diligence had been reported to the king. (A.C.A., Registros, 2916, ff. 29v–30r.)

[56] The privilege appointing him a secretary is printed by N. Toppi, *De Origine Tribunalium,* part III, pp. 266–9.

[57] A.C.A., Registros, 2661, f. 99r, 8 September 1455.

[58] *Ibid.,* ff. 120v–121r, 6 June 1456.

[59] *Ibid.,* f. 136r, 10 August 1456.

[60] A.C.A., Registros, 2660, 161r–162r.

[61] N. Toppi, *De Origine Tribunalium,* part III, p. 262, 30 October 1455.

[62] A.C.A., Registros, 2917, ff. 174r–175r, 8 August 1457. The exordium to Theodore's privilege runs: 'Si geste re litteris non commendentur facile perbreviterque defunctis qui ea audiere aut videre memoria in posteros sopitur, sola enim in historia hominum servat memoriam sola mortuos vivere sola absentes semper adesse facit. Perquirendos proinde nobis peritos et historicos ac elegantes viros statuimus et eos habitos beneficiis atque muneribus donare quo ad scribendum ardentius intendant.' One fruit of Theodore's sojourn in Naples was a Latin translation of Aelianus, *De instruendis aciebus.*

[63] Beccadelli, *Epistolae Campanae,* 32.

[64] Beccadelli wrote to inform Manetti that Alfonso had been very pleased with the book. (*Epistolae Campanae,* 34.)

[65] *Cf.* E. Pèrcopo, 'La vita di Giovanni Pontano', *Archivio storico per le province napoletane,* LXI, 1936. Earlier in 1451 Pontano had served as an assistant to Beccadelli and dez Puig in their Italian embassy.

[66] *Epistolae Campanae,* 23.

[67] *Ibid.,* 24. Facio replied that Beccadelli had overpraised a friend, as was his wont. (*Ibid.,* 25).

[68] *Cf.* Resta, *L'Epistolario,* p. 24.

[69] C. Minieri Riccio, 'Alcuni fatti di Alfonso I di Aragona dal 15 apr. 1437–31 magg. 1458', *Archivio storico per le province napoletane,* 1881, VI, p. 411.

[70] *De dictis et factis* has been printed many times: Pisa, 1485; Basel, 1538; Wittenberg, 1585; Amsterdam, 1646; Florence, 1739.

[71] *Commentarius in libros Antonii Panormitae.*

[72] Beccadelli refers to this work in a letter to Theodore Gaza *c.* 1456. See T. de Marinis, *La Biblioteca Napoletana dei Re d'Aragona,* Milan, 1948, five vols., 1947–69, II (1948), p. 3.

[73] Starrabba, 'Notizie', p. 127.

[74] Laurenza, 'Il Panormita a Napoli, p. 11.

[75] Laurenza, 'Il Panormita a Napoli', p. 28.

[76] *Ibid.*

[77] Starrabba, 'Notizie', p. 127. The confirmation is dated 7 January 1460.

[78] Laurenza, 'Il Parnormita a Napoli', p. 31.

[79] Their publication was in about 1474–75.

[80] *De Libero Arbitrio* and *Dialecticae Disputationes* as well as the exposure of the Donation of Constantine belong to this period. Also Valla began *In Novum Testamentum Adnotationes* in Naples.

A. V. ANTONOVICS   *University of Bristol*

8

THE LIBRARY OF CARDINAL DOMENICO CAPRANICA

By HIS LAST will and testament, drawn up on 14 August 1458,[1] Cardinal Domenico Capranica made provision for the foundation of a college—the Collegio Capranica in Rome—and for leaving his books for the use of the scholars of that college:[2] 'quod libri S.R.D. qui sunt necessarii pro dicto collegio ordinentur deputentur et disponantur pro utilitate et commodo studentium in dicto collegio et alii vendantur'. It would appear that the last section of this clause of the will was never put into effect—at least, no record of sales of the cardinal's books has come to light—and when at a later date, in 1486, an inventory was drawn up of books in the library of the college it can be assumed with a fair degree of confidence that this is the bulk of the private library of the cardinal as donated to the college.[3]

The library, as then inventoried, consisted of 387 volumes,[4] with each volume often containing numerous individual works,[5] and was, therefore, one of the largest private libraries of that date and the largest cardinal's library known except the collection of Cardinal Bessarion.[6] All the volumes were in manuscript and the great majority written on parchment, especially in the sections arranged to the right, although many of the legal treatises and other works arranged to the left were on paper.[7] Most were bound in covers of red leather (*corio rubeo*) but a considerable number in other colours or undyed.[8] The books were generally fastened with one, two, three or four chains. The general format of the volumes (*parvum, magnum*, etc) is usually mentioned, but not in any systematic way. Those of special quality are singled out as 'pulchrum' or 'pulcherrimum', etc.[9] The incipits to each volume are recorded.

The volumes were arranged with eleven *banchi* to the right and eleven to the left, with two further volumes listed. Other than this, little has come to light on the original features and lay-out of the library of the college.[10] The general distribution of the volumes among the various sections follows a rough pattern familiar in other libraries of the period—for example, the papal library[11]—but whether it was deliberately modelled on some specific canons, such as those of Tommaso da Sarzana (later Pope Nicholas V), as has been suggested, is less certain.[12]

To the right the first section (vols. 1–17) consisted chiefly of biblical works, commentaries and concordances;[13] a psalter, with gloss; two volumes of the letters of St Paul (vols. 3, 15[14]); a volume of *Legenda Sanctorum*, together with St Bonaventure 'de modo preparandi se ad missam celebrandum';[15] and a few other miscellaneous ecclesiastical works, including a tract 'de visione beata' of frater Johannes Leonis dedicated to Eugenius IV (vol. 16[16]). The second section (vols. 18–31) consisted predominantly of the works of St Augustine (vols. 18, *Vocabulista Augustini et Ambrosii* . . .; 19, *Explanatio . . . in epistolas Johannis*; 20, *de octo questionibus*, etc; 22, *Excerpta de Aug.*[17]; 23, *Retractationes, confessiones*, etc; 24, *de videndo deo*; 25, *55 omelie*;[18] 26, *Octuaginta quatuor sermones* . . .; 27, *Sermones*;[19] 28, *de Trinitate*;[20] 30, *Expositio super psalmos*) and the orations of St Gregory, together with further works of St Augustine (vol. 21) and St Augustine's sermons on the Gospel of St John (vol. 31). The section also contains a volume of the rule of St Benedict (vol. 29).

The third section is equally taken up with works of St Augustine (vols. 32–3, *Milleloquia*;[21] 34, *De Civitate Dei*; 35, *de Trinitate*;[22] 37, *Epistolae*; 38, *de Genesi ad litteram* and St Basil, *Hexaemeron*;[23] 39, *Disputatio super Maximum Arrianum*, etc; 40, *De doctrina Christiana*; 41, *Flores S. Aug. per Franciscum de Maronibus*[24]) and the works of St Ambrose (vols. 36; *Epistolae*, 42–4: three parts *Ambrosiane*, ed. frater Bartholomaeus Sancti Augustini, dedicated to Clement VI;[25] 45, *super Lucam*, etc; 46, *Hexaemeron, De Cain et Abel, De Paradiso, De virginitate*; 47, *De Abraham*, etc; 48, *De paenitentia*; 49, *De Paradiso Dei* and Origen on the Old Testament and other miscellaneous biblical commentaries[26]).

Patristic authors occupy much of the fourth (vols. 50–67) and fifth (vols. 68–86) sections, with works by St Jerome (vols. 50, *super prophetas*;[27] 51 *Dialogus* and *Epistolae*, etc; 52, *Expositio super Esaiam*; 53, *Prologus* . . .; 54, *Explanatio super epistolas Sancti Pauli*; 55, *Hyeronymanus, ed. per Joh. Andree*[28]); Eusebius on St Jerome (vol. 56[29]) and the rules of the Hieronymite Order (vol. 58); Cyprian (vol. 59, *Epistolae*; 76, *ibid.*[30]); Lactantius (vols. 60, *Abbreviatus*;[31] 67, *de ira Dei*[32]); the *Thesaurus* of St Cyrillus (vol. 61[33]); St Gregory (vols. 69, *Moralia*;[34] 70, *39 omelie*; 71, *40 omelie*; 72, *Pastorale*; 73, *Dialogus*, etc; 74, *Flores omnium moralium*; 75, *super Ezechielem*) the *Apolegeticum* of St Gregory of Nazianen (vol. 83[35]); and the works of St John Chrysostom (vols. 77, *Sermones*, with a prologue by Lilio Tifernas to Pope Nicholas V together with the *Pastoralis* of Franciscus Ariminensis (?);[36] 78, *Omelie . . . seu expositio in epistolas Sancti Pauli*;[37] 79, *ad stragilium monachum*; 80, *Expositio in epistolas ad hebreos*, together with the *Enchiridion* and other works of St Augustine;[38] 81, *super actibus apostolorum* and Cassiodorus' first book of the *Institutiones*; and Cassianus' *super Nestorianos de Incarnatione* (vol. 82[39]). Also among these two sections were the Platonic dialogue *Phaedo*, translated by Leonardo Bruni (vol. 67[40]); a work by frater Thome (Naldii) of the Carmelite Order dedicated to Pope Martin V (vol. 68[41]); some volumes of sermons (vols. 64, 85); a *Scrutinium scripturarum* (vol. 84), *Limen confessorum* (vol. 86) and a *Martirologium* (vol. 66) and a volume of St Bernard's sermons *super cantica canticorum* (vol. 63[42]).

The sixth section (vols. 87–100) is mostly taken up with the works of St Bernard (vols. 90–5[43]); a copy of Cassianus' *De Institutis* (vol. 87)[44]; a *Rationale divinorum officiorum* (vol. 88); the letters of Pope Leo I (vol. 89[45]); the sermons of St Zeno, Bishop of Verona (vol. 97[46]); a volume of works by St Ambrose (vol. 98, *Rompertus de sanctificatione et processione sancti spiritus*); St Juvenal(?) *de partibus legis divinae* (vol. 99) and the *Revelationes* of St Bridget of Sweden (vol. 100[47]).

The seventh (vols. 101–16) and eighth (vols. 117–34) sections contained works by Aquinas or commentaries on his works (vols. 105–13, 115–16, 117–22[48]); St Bonaventure (vols. 125–7[49]); Alexander of Hales (vols. 123–4); the *De conformitate Vitae Sancti Francisci* of Bartolomeo of Pisa (vol. 132[50]); a tract *De septem peccatis mortalibus* of Laurentius de Rudolphis (vol. 128[51]); and various sermon collections (vols. 101, 130, 131) and biblical commentaries (vols. 104, 133, 134) and Johannes Scholasticus (vol. 114[52]). The ninth section (vols. 135–52) contained miscellaneous patristic works such as the *Homilie* of Chrysostom and Ambrose *de fuga saeculi* (vol. 135), Josephus (vols. 136, 137[53]); a *Vitae patrum* (vol. 138); the register of St Gregory the Great (vol. 139); the register of Gregory VII (vol. 141); some *Collationes sanctorum patrorum* (vol. 142[54]); Eusebius (vols. 143–5 and a translation of George of Trebizond dedicated to Nicholas V: vol. 147[55]); the *Historia Scholastica* of Petrus Comestor (vol. 147); Dionysius *De celesti hierarchia* (vol. 148[56]); Lactantius (vol. 149[57]); Cassianus *De Institutis* (vol. 151[58]); a tract *De confessione* of St Anthony, Archbishop of Florence (vol. 152[59]); and the popular *Compendium moralium dictorum* of Jeremia da Montagnono (vol. 150[60]).

The works in the tenth section (vols. 153–70) were a miscellaneous collection of ecclesiastical works and tracts such as the decretals collected by St Isidore (vol. 153); his Etymologies (vol. 154) and *De Summo Bono* (vol. 155); Albertus Magnus' *De Laudibus Beatae Virginis* (vol. 156); the *Dialogus* of Ockham (vol. 157); the letters of Pope Innocent III (vol. 158); the tract *De ecclesia potestate* of Peter de La Palu, the French Dominican theologian (d. 1342) (vol. 159); a very mixed volume of tracts (vol. 161); the *De Universo* of Guglielmus Parisiensis (vol. 162[61]); Augustinus Triumphus' *De ecclesiastica potestate* (vol. 163); a *Chronica romanorum pontificum* (vol. 165); the letters of Cassiodorus (vol. 167); a tract against the pragmatic sanction of Bourges (vol. 168); Jacobus de Marchia's *De oppugnatione haereticorum* (vol. 169[62]); and a sermon collection (vol. 170).

The eleventh and final section to the right contained chiefly the works of Aristotle (vols. 173–5) and commentaries and various translations of Aristotle[63] by, for example, Aquinas (vols. 176, 178); Leonardo Bruni's translation of the *Nicomachean Ethics* (vol. 179); Walter Burley on the *Politics* (vol. 182[64]); Henry of Ghent's commentary on the *Ethics* (vol. 188); Johannes Buridan on the same (vol. 190[65]). The section also contained the synodal acts of Pope Adrian I (vol. 172); a volume of Diogenes Laertius (vol. 183[66]); the *Ostensor futurorum* of the Minorite Johannes de Rote (vol. 184); a *Prothemata generalis* to the sermons of St Bonaventure (vol. 191); a collection of pieces on papal rights in the kingdom of Sicily (vol. 189) and a volume of chronicles of the Popes (vol. 192). The section contained two works dedicated to the cardinal: a translation of Aristotle's *De anima* by George of Trebizond (vol. 186[67]) and a volume by frater Gasparis O.P., *Logice* (vol. 180[68]).

What is perhaps most striking about the contents of the library so far surveyed is the number, among the more obvious and traditional ecclesiastical tracts, of works by patristic authors: St Augustine above all, St Ambrose, St Jerome, St John Chrysostom, Lactantius, etc. This clearly reflects the general revival of interest in such authors in the period of Capranica's life, stimulated by the individual interests of scholars such as Ambrogio Traversari and promoted by Popes such as Nicholas V, but also by the debates of the Church councils of the period, above all, the Council of Ferrara–Florence.[69] The role of Cardinal Domenico Capranica in promoting this patristic Renaissance, as important historically as the classical Renaissance and arguably part of the same process, is not well documented,[70] but he appears to have participated with enthusiasm in this revival, which had in turn a bearing on his concern for Church reform and the ideals of the pastoral life revealed by a reading of the patristic authors.[71] Several works in Capranica's library directly reflect these reforming interests.[72] The library, however, contained no works in Greek or Hebrew, although it is arguably only at the end of Capranica's career that a keen interest in works in these languages firmly established itself at the papal Curia.[73]

The works arranged to the left consisted in the first seven sections predominantly of treatises of canon law, legal tracts and collections of legal decisions, miscellaneous ecclesiastical treatises and collections of material on the Schism and the conciliar period. A complete survey of the canon law and other legal treatises would be tedious. Suffice it to say that here we see a typical working library of a fifteenth-century cardinal, who had risen to high ecclesiastical office after a degree in canon law[74] and was subsequently heavily involved in the business of the Curia. Vespasiano da Bisticci has left us a striking account of Capranica in his capacity as Grand Penitentiary (from 1449) when 'every morning and evening he would be obliged to hear numberless pontifical cases',[75] but this was only the climax of a long career in papal administration.[76] It was no doubt with the aid of his legal books, formularies of the Chancery and collections of conciliar material that 'he administered justice with wonderful efficiency'.

The author, indeed, who occupied more volumes than perhaps any other in the library was the late fourteenth-century papal auditor and canon lawyer Gilles de Bellemere (vols. 196–9, 204–5, 211–23, 232–9, 258, 265–6[77]). Also well represented were the collections of Johannes Andreae (vols. 208–9, Novella; 231, 245, 247[78]); Henricus Bohic (vols. 224–5[79]); Francesco Zabarella (vols. 244, 253); Antonio de Butrio (vols. 244, 267, 269, 271–4, 281, 290–4); Dominicus de S. Gimignano (vols. 240–1, 286[80]); Nicolaus

Tudeschi, abbas Siculi (vols. 226–9, 259[81]). Other familiar canonists represented in the library were Innocent IV (vol. 201[82]); Johannes Monachus (vol. 242); Guido de Baysio (vol. 194, *Rosarium . . . super decretum*); Petrus de Braco (vol. 203[83]); John of Legnano (vol. 206[84]); Johannes de Imola (vol. 252) Hostiensis (vol. 275) and Capranica's distinguished contemporary, Juan Torquemada (vol. 200, *Lectura super decretis*). There were also a consider-able number of collections of legal 'consilia'.[85] Individual volumes to note among these sections are a miscellaneous one containing various tracts *ad confitendum*, the *Philobiblon* of Richard de Bury, as well as a tract of Capranica himself *De libris et congregatione librorum suorum* and other works too numerous to list (vol. 282[86]); the *Speculum Iudiciale* of Guillelmus Durantis (vols. 262–3) and Alvarus' *De Planctu Ecclesiae*, with a repertorium made for the cardinal by his familiaris 'Francisco de Tollentino' (vol. 287[87]). Capranica's legations to the March of Ancona are reflected in a copy of the *Constitutiones Aegidianae* with corrections and additions by the cardinal (vol. 279[88]).

The collection of treatises on the Schism and acts of the Councils of Con-stance, Basel and Ferrara–Florence are familiar to students of these events.[89] The copies of the acts of Basel included materials on the personal case of the cardinal regarding the recognition of his promotion to the cardinalate.[90] A fuller discussion of these volumes and their contents is beyond the scope of this survey.

It is the classical works contained in the final sections, the eighth to the eleventh (vols. 301–85) that particularly call for comment in a volume devoted to a scholar of the humanist movement, but there are few surprises. Indeed, the degree of the cardinal's involvement with the humanists remains an elusive subject.[91] Clearly, as a leading Curial figure he could scarcely avoid encountering the humanists in papal service, for example Poggio Bracciolini, with whom some correspondence has been published and several of whose works were in the library,[92] but the degree of involvement is hard to assess: often it entailed merely the furthering of ecclesiastical promotions or cases in which the humanists were involved.[93] There is little evidence that Capranica, like other cardinals of his period, ever sent agents in search of manuscripts,[94] was involved to any great degree in archeological studies, such as those of his colleague and probably close associate Prospero Colonna,[95] or had many works dedicated to him or commissioned by him.[96] This detachment may be the reason for the generally conventional content of the classical sections of his library, although the representation of humanist works is not inconsiderable.

The library contained in its eighth section (vols. 301–19) works of Seneca (vols. 301; *Declamationes*; 301, *De beneficiis*; 302, *Tragedie*; 303, *Epistolae*; 305, *Tragedie*[97]) and Petrarch (vol. 304, *De rebus familiaribus*,[98] *De remediis utriusque fortune*;[99] 309, *De vita solitaria*;[100] 310, *Epithomata*, etc;[101] 311, *Rerum memorandarum*;[102] 313, *Epistolae tres in carminibus*,[103] and Boccaccio's *De casibus virorum illustrium*, etc (vol. 314). Also Aulus Gellius' *Noctes Atticae* (vol. 307[104]); Apuleius' *Golden Ass* (vol. 319), Vegetius' *De re militari* (vol. 317, together with several other works); Egidio Romano's *De regimine principum* (vol. 315[105]), as well as one of the two vernacular works in the library, the *Laude* of Jacopone da Todi (vol. 312). The ninth section contained mainly works of Cicero (vols. 320–4, 328–30[106]); Quintilian's *Institutio oratoria* (vol. 331); Valerius Maximus,[107] with Andrea da Firenze's *De potestatibus romanis* dedicated to Francesco Condulmer (vol. 327[108]); the *De Ingenuis Moribus* of Pier Paolo Vergerio (vol. 318[109]); the *Rhetoricum* of George of Trebizond (vol. 334[110]); an *Ars memorandi* (vol. 325) and various orations *pro insignis doctoratus* (vol. 333). Humanist works included the *De bello punico* of Leonardo Bruni (vol. 334, and other works[111]); the *Vita Ciceronis* and other lives by the Venetian humanist Leonardo Giustiniani (vol. 335[112]); the *Argumenta* on Cicero's orations by Antonio Loschi (vol. 326[113]); Sicco Polenton's *De illustribus scriptoribus linguae latinae* (vol. 336[114]); works by Maffeo Vegio (vols. 331, 341[115]); Gregorio Correr's *De fugiendo seculo* and dialogue *De veritate ad Eustachium fratrem* (vol. 341[116]); works of Poggio, including the tract *De nobilitate*[117] dedicated to Cardinal Gerardo Landriani (vol. 339[118]) and a work of Gasparus Volterranus' *De origine situ et qualitate Urbis Romae* (vol. 342[119]).

The tenth section (vols. 343–66) consisted largely of conventional classical works such as Livy (vols. 343–5); Quintus Curtius' *Historia Alexandri* (vol. 346); a Valerius Maximus (vol. 351); Eutropius' *De strage Romanorum* (vol. 352); Caesar's *De bello gallico* (vol. 355); the works of Virgil (vol. 356[120]) and Servius' commentary (vol. 357); eight comedies of Plautus (vol. 358[121]); Lucan (vol. 360); Statius' *Thebais* (vol. 361); Juvenal and Horace (vol. 362[122]); Ovid's *Metamorphoses* (vol. 365). Among humanist works were Bartolomeo Fazio's Deeds of Alfonso of Naples (vol. 350[123]) and a life of Xenophon dedicated to Alfonso, together with Flavio Biondo's *Roma Instaurata* and Suetonius' life of Caesar (vol. 348[124]); a work in praise of the Visconti Duke of Milan (vol. 359[125]); Francesco Barbaro's *De re uxoria* (vol. 363[126]) and Benvenuto da Imola's *Augustalis*, dedicated to Niccolo d'Este (vol. 364[127]). The section also contained an *Opus de laudibus et vita Pauli apostoli* (vol. 349) and a *Liber hystoriarum* (vol. 347).

The eleventh and final section to the left contained a very mixed set of works, some of which may have been especially intended for the use of the college, for example a volume of vernacular verses on birds, etc (vol. 367); the *Catholicon* of frater Johannes de Ianua of the Dominican Order (vol. 368[128]); a biblical concordance (vol. 369); some *Vocabulistae* (vols. 371–2); volumes of Euclid (vols. 373–4); a *Tractatus de die judicii* (vol. 377); a Dante commentary (vol. 378[129]); Boccaccio's *De montibus* (vol. 379[130]); a formulary of the clerical life based on the *tituli* of the decretals (vol. 379); parts of the *Fons Universalis* of Domenico de Arezzo (vols. 380–3[131]) and a *Chronicon* of Popes and emperors up to Nicholas V (vol. 385). The only humanist work was the translation of Ptolemy by Jacopo Angeli da Scarperia (vol. 370[132]). Two works, some homilies and legends of the saints (vol. 386) and the constitutions of the college, together with a missal (vol. 387), end the inventory.[133]

·　　·　　·

On the formation of Capranica's library little external evidence has come to light. There is no record that he ever sent agents in search of manuscripts.[134] Only a few copyists who were members of his household are known, and it is not certain that they were in regular employment with the cardinal.[135] The well known life of the cardinal by Vespasiano da Bisticci, the Florentine bookseller, indicates some relationships with him, but only one mention of the cardinal appears in the recently published letters of Vespasiano.[136] Some books may have been acquired as gifts while on diplomatic missions or from those seeking his intervention at the Curia; books may have been obtained direct from monasteries, such as those held by the cardinal in commendam,[137] or which he visited as Cardinal Protector of the Franciscan Order or in some other capacity,[138] but no evidence on these matters is forthcoming.

The books themselves are our only guide to their acquisition. A copy of Bartholomaeus de Concordio, *Summa de casibus*, is recorded as having been copied 'in sancto Angelo in Valdo' by Andreas Alberti de Alamania in 1433.[139] The copyist, Johannes de Ghistrelia, was involved in the production of three volumes at least. A volume of Lactantius was copied at Basel in 1436.[140] St Jerome, *Expositiones in epistolas S. Pauli*, completed on 24 September 1437 at Bologna in the cardinal's residence at that date in the Dominican monastery.[141] The same copyist accompanied the cardinal to Ferrara, where the letters of St Leo the Great were transcribed.[142] A volume of St Jerome, *Expositiones in Prohetas minores*, was also written for Capranica at Ferrara, but it is not certain by whom.[143] The volume of Jeremias da Montagnono has the entry 'Alamanus scripsit basuus' and is dated by Tietze to *c.* 1440.[144] The *Confessionale* of St Anthony of Florence was written for the cardinal by Johannes Dorembroch in 1440 (completed on 12 July).[145] A copy of the *Milleloquium* of St Augustine compiled by Bartholomaeus de Carusis was transcribed in 1450 by Bartholomaeus de Magistris or 'de Vice-comitibus'.[146] A volume of Josephus was transcribed by Leonardus Antonii in 1453[147] and the *Thesaurus adversos haereticos* of Cyrillus at Florence by Johannes Caldarifices in 1457.[148] Other volumes may possibly be dated by the general style of the manuscript or illumination. The subject matter of some volumes (for example, those concerned with the Council of Basel and Ferrara–Florence) helps, of course, to determine the date of these. The dedications indicate some *terminus a quo* for others. No certain chronology of acquisitions emerges from this sparse evidence, but one's general impression is of a library built up gradually over the years, with perhaps a concentration of activity in the period after Capranica's return from Basel through to the early 1440s, and then again, with the return from legations to the March of Ancona, in the 1450s up to his death.

The later vicissitudes of Capranica's library are beyond the scope of this article but may be briefly summarised.[149] The library appears to have survived mostly intact through the sack of Rome in 1527[150] and into the later sixteenth century, since a very large proportion of the books inventoried in 1480 were still in the library of the Collegio in the later sixteenth century and in the inventory of 1657 published by Tietze.[151] Some volumes, however, appear already to have been transferred to the Vatican library under Paul V (1605–21) and subsequently under Alexander VII (1655–67).[152] It was in 1842 that a major part of the library of the Collegio Capranica was sold to Gian Francesco De Rossi.[153] When he died in 1854 his widow, Princess Louisa Carlotta of the House of Bourbon, by an act of 6 March 1855 gave the library, at her late husband's wishes, to the Jesuits in Rome.[154] After the occupation of Rome and the threat to suppress certain religious corporations the Austrian emperor in 1873 undertook protection of the Jesuit college, and the books were carried to the Palazzo Venezia, residence of the Austrian embassy to Rome. In 1877 they were sent to Vienna and kept at the Jesuit residence there and were later transferred to the house of the Jesuits at Lainz, where they stayed until the end of the first world war. The Rossiana collection was incorporated into the Vatican Library in 1921.[155]

Capranica's library was but one of a remarkable series of cardinals' libraries in the fifteenth century. It had long been expected of a cardinal that he should be learned and a promoter of learning,[156] but this sentiment was clearly strengthened in the course of the period of Capranica's career. A cardinal busy with curial administration and legal cases needed books for very practical purposes, and Capranica's library in this respect can be compared to other administrator cardinals with book collections, such as Piero Corsini,[157] Jean de Brogny[158] and Amadeo of Saluzzo,[159] to select but a few. In terms of the range of literary works, and especially of classical works, Capranica's library does not perhaps quite match the collections of some of his near contemporaries, for example Giordano Orsini,[160] Nicholas of Cusa[161] and what was perhaps a unique collection for its period, that of Cardinal Bessarion.[162] A fuller comparative study of the cardinals' libraries of the fifteenth century and indeed of many individual collections remains to be undertaken.[163] The college that Capranica founded also, of course, had precedents, perhaps most immediately in the foundation of Niccolò Capocci in the later fourteenth century at Perugia, which Capranica was familiar with,[164] and the colleges established by Cardinal Branda da Castiglione at Pavia[165] and by Niccolò Albergati at Bologna.[166] Capranica's foundation in turn served as an example to later foundations, notably perhaps that of Stefano Nardini in Rome.[167] Concerned to promote a better-educated clergy and one with a pastoral zeal modelled on patristic antecedents, he endowed his college with books to that end: 'divini nominis laudem, orthodoxe fidei propugnationem et Reipublicae utilitatem'.[168] It has already been pointed out elsewhere that in this Capranica acted as one of the heralds of the Catholic revival of the sixteenth century.[169]

APPENDIX 8.1

VOLUMES ON PARCHMENT, VOLUMES ON PAPER, ETC

All the volumes in the *banchi* to the right were written on parchment, except for the following, written on paper (*in papiro*): vols. 8, 14, 65, 70, 84–6, 135, 161–2, 166, 179, 184, 189–90. Doubtful: vols. 165, 182, 186.

Volumes in *banchi* to the left on parchment, except vols. 196–9, 200, 203–6, 211–23,

226–9, 232–41, 243–6, 248–61, 264–74, 280–2, 284, 286, 294, 296, 298–9, 326, 328, 336 ('cum aliquis cartis in pergameno'), 337 ('in pergameno et in papiro'), 340, 346, 349, 357, 375–6, 378, 380–2, 384.

APPENDIX 8.2
BINDINGS AS RECORDED IN INVENTORY OF 1480

All volumes covered 'corio rubeo' except the following.

'Corio pagonatio': vols. 2, 4–6, 14, 17, 23, 25–6, 29, 65, 67–8, 86, 121, 143, 169, 184, 196–9 ('et glaucho'), 205–6, 209, 224, 230–9, 240–1, 259–60, 267–8, 271, 274, 276, 283–4, 295, 299, 301, 305, 310, 315, 318, 326, 328, 340, 353, 366, 370, 375–6, 377, 380–1.

'Corio albo': vols. 10, 13, 19, 30–1, 39, 45, 49, 52, 57, 63–4, 73–5, 92, 106, 111, 116, 125, 131, 134, 138–9, 144, 154, 164, 173, 178–9, 188, 190, 204, 210, 228–9, 244–5, 255, 270, 272, 286–7, 300, 314, 347, 352, 361, 373, 382, 386.

'Corio nigro': vols. 9, 36, 38, 40, 54, 56, 69, 78, 87, 148, 152, 157–8, 165, 172, 185–6, 221–3 ('et pagonatio'), 279, 289–90, 303, 323, 329–31, 350–1, 357, 362, 368, 372.

'Corio viridi': vols. 85, 110, 127, 130, 174, 182, 192, 201, 208, 211–13 ('albo et'), 214–15, 220 ('et pagonatio'), 226, 229, 243, 248, 252–3, 258, 262–3, 265–6, 273, 280, 282, 285, 301, 313, 322, 337, 360, 383–4.

'Celestino': vols. 66, 161, 200, 261, 269, 278, 385.

'Corio rubeo et albo': vol. 202.

'Giallo': vols. 248–51.

'Viridi et giallo': vols. 217–19.

Not known: vols. 84, 349, 355 ('cum tabulis nudis').

According to *Melanges d'Archeologie et d'Histoire*, XLVII (1930), p. 92, 'Il est malheureusement très difficile de retrouver mention des anciens possesseurs à l'interieur des manuscrits, car Rossi leur a imposé a tous une relieure uniforme et beaucoup de notes marginales ou de feuillets de garde disparurent au cours de cette operation.'

NOTES

The following abbreviations will be used hereafter:

Morpurgo-Castelnuovo: M. Morpurgo-Castelnuovo, 'Il Card. Domenico Capranica', *Archivio della Reale Societa Romana di Storia Patria*, LII, 1929, pp. 1–146.

Tietze: H. Tietze, *Die illuminierten Handschriften der Rossiana*, Leipzig, 1911.

Kristeller: P. O. Kristeller, *Iter Italicum*, London and Leiden, 1963, 1967, I, II.

Müntz and Fabre: E. Müntz and P. Fabre, *La Bibliothèque du Vatican au XVe siècle*, Paris, 1887.

Sabbadini: R. Sabbadini, *Le Scoperte dei Codici Latini e Greci ne' Secoli XIV e XV*, Florence, 1905, 1914, I, II.

[1] Vat(ican Library) (Fondo) Lat(ino), 7971, ff. 30–3. A search for the original of this will among the archives of the Ospedale SSmo. Salvatore in the Archivio di Stato, Rome (Fondo Ospedali) and among the notarial records in the same archive failed, but the original will may well exist among these extensive records. The notaries attesting the will were Johannes and Antonius Simbonis. *Cf.* Morpurgo-Castelnuovo, pp. 90 ff.

[2] On the Collegio Capranica I follow the section in Morpurgo-Castelnuovo, pp. 85–116. For the 'constitutiones' see below, n. 133. A brief account of the college in *Dictionnaire d'histoire et geographie ecclesiastique* (hereafter *D.H.G.E.*), art. 'Capranica (College)'. The foundations of the college go back to at least 1456, and properties were handed over to the Ospedale SSmo. Salvatore, the governors of which were to act as trustees and administrators of the college, on 5 January 1457. The transfer to a building adjacent to the Palazzo Capranica—the new building being constructed by

Cardinal Angelo Capranica—was confirmed by Sixtus IV in 1478. See below, n. 10.

[3] There appears to be no clear evidence of additions to the library between 1458 and 1480. The role of Cardinal Angelo Capranica remains somewhat obscure. On his career, *D.H.G.E.*, art. 'Capranica (Angelo)' by R. Mols.

[4] The inventory is in Vat. Lat. 8184, ff. 1–46. Although the volume is headed f. 1, MCCCCLXXXVI, additions on f. 46*v*, i.e. at the end of the inventory dated 25 February 1480 and 5 February 1481 respectively indicate a date *c.* 1480, which is assumed by Morpurgo-Castelnuovo, and earlier in T. Gottlieb, *Ueber mitteralterliche Bibliotheken*, Leipzig, 1890, p. 236.

The entry for 5 February 1481 states, 'Assignati fuerunt suprascripti libri domino Dominico de Neptuna rectori' (with list of witnesses).

There is a gap in the numbers of the volumes when vol. 305 is followed immediately by vol. 307, but earlier a volume after vol. 301 (hereafter to be called vol. 301+) is not recorded by a marginal number.

[5] The individual works in the inventory were separately numbered for the *banchi* to the right and totalled 728, but were not separately numbered for the *banchi* to the left.

The estimate by Giovanni Baptista Poggio that Capranica's library consisted of 2,000 volumes was wrong in terms of the actual volumes but probably not far wrong in the number of works. Life of Domenico Capranica printed in S. Baluze, *Miscellanea*, Lucca, 1761, I, pp. 342–51, with the estimate at p. 350. On other estimates, generally following that of Poggio, Morpurgo-Castelnuovo, p. 117, n. 2.

[6] On the libraries of other cardinals of the period, see further below, n. 148.

An account of the death of Cardinal Marco Barbo in 1491 estimated that his library then consisted of 500 volumes: G. Zippel, 'La jorte di Marco Barbo, cardinale di San Marco', *Scritti Storici in Memoria di Giovanni Monticolo*, Venice, 1922, pp. 195–203, at p. 203.

An excellent general survey of the collections of the period remains that of Sabbadini, I, pp. 183–207.

[7] See appendix 8.1.

[8] See appendix 8.2.

[9] Such notes will be indicated in the more detailed survey of the volumes that follows.

[10] On the architecture of the palace and adjoining college in general, P. Tomei, *L'architettura a Roma nel Quattrocento*, Rome, 1942, pp. 60–3; L. Callari, *I palazzi di Roma*, Rome, 1944, pp. 117–21; T. Magnuson, *Studies in Roman Quattrocento Architecture*, Rome, 1958, pp. 227–9 and especially p. 229, on the new wing built by Angelo Capranica. Virtually no documents have come to light on the construction of the palace either in the time of Domenico or in that of Angelo Capranica.

On library buildings of the fifteenth century in general, B. L. Ullman and P. A. Stadter, *The Public Library of Renaissance Florence*, Padua, 1972, p. 5, with further literature cited.

[11] In the first of the halls of the Vatican Library under Sixtus IV the Latin manuscripts were arranged nine *banchi* to the left and seven to the right, entering from the cortile del Papagallo. R. Devresse, *Le Fonds grec de la Bibliothèque Vaticane des origines à Paul V*, Vatican City, 1965, p. 81, where earlier literature is usefully cited. See further J. Ruysschaert, 'Sixte IV, fondateur de la Bibliothèque Vaticane (15 juin 1475)', *Archivium Historiae Pontificiae*, VII, 1969, pp. 513–24.

[12] As suggested by Morpurgo-Castelnuovo, p. 118. These canons are printed in G. Sforza, 'La patria, la famiglia e la giovinezza di papa Nicolo V', *Atti della Reale Accademia Lucchese di Scienze, Lettere ed Arti*, XXIII, 1884, pp. 359–81. *Cf.* Sabbadini, I, p. 200. The exchange of inventories among scholars and book collectors of the period is known from other sources, P. Kibre, *The Library of Pico della Mirandola*, New York, 1936, pp. 15–16.

[13] Volume 1 is a Bible described as 'pulchrum'. Volumes 5 and 6 are concordances;

vols. 7 and 9, commentaries of Nicolaus of Lyra, the last together with other works; vols. 8, 10, 12–13 are also biblical commentaries. Volume 17 is a *Mammotrectus* probably of Johannes Marchesius.

[14] Volume 3: 'pulchrum'; vol. 15: St Jerome's commentary on the epistles of St Paul, with Prologus. This may be Vat. (Fondo) Rossiano, VIII, 225 (where the present shelf-marks have not been at hand I cite the old numbers). Tietze No. 219 (f. 1, arms of the cardinal), but see later vol. 54.

[15] Possibly = Vat. Rossiano IX, 151. Tietze No. 125. On paper. But *cf.* later volumes of the legends of the saints in the inventory, vols. 386 and earlier vol. 11.

[16] Kristeller, II, p. 445, cites various manuscripts, e.g. Vat. (Fondo) Barb(erini), Lat. 516, but a link with Capranica's library is not indicated.

[17] = Vat. Rossiano IX, 33. Tietze No. 8. Also containing the works of St Anselm.

[18] = Vat. Rossiano VIII, 132. Tietze No. 256 (f. 1, arms of the cardinal).

[19] = Vat. Rossiano VIII, 208. Tietze, p. 118.

[20] = Vat. Rossiano VIII, 133. Tietze, p. 118 and fig. 128 (arms of the cardinal). *Cf.* another copy of the same work, vol. 35.

[21] = Vat. Rossiano VIII, 238a and b. Tietze No. 271. 'Pulcherrimum'. Kristeller, II, p. 466, lists part II as Vat. Rossiano 614 (IX, 304), which seems to be a different copy.

[22] *Cf.* n. 20.

[23] = Vat. Rossiano VIII, 228. Tietze, p. 118.

[24] *Cf.* K. W. Humphreys, *The Library of the Franciscans of the Convent of St Anthony, Padua, at the Beginning of the Fifteenth Century*, Amsterdam, 1966, p. 63, and literature cited.

[25] 'Pulchrum'.

[26] Kristeller, II, p. 465, lists a volume of St Ambrose owned by Capranica, Vat. Rossiano 244 (VIII, 183).

[27] = Vat. Rossiano VIII, 226. Tietze No. 222.

[28] = Vat. Rossiano 294 (VIII, 231). Kristeller, II, p. 465.

[29] Together with various works of St Augustine, Cyrillus on the miracles of St Jerome and the *Dialogus* of St Gregory.

[30] On these *cf.* B. L. Ullman and P. A. Stadter, *op. cit.*, p. 103.

[31] *Cf.* later volume of Lactantius, vol. 149. Volume 60 = Vat. Rossiano VIII, 100). Tietze No. 174.

[32] = Vat. Lat. 223. See A. A. Strnad, 'Studia piccolomineana', in *Enea Silvio Piccolomini Papa Pio II*, ed. D. Maffei, Siena, 1968, p. 328.

On the discovery of the Nonantola manuscript of Lactantius, Sabbadini, I, p. 73. Further literature cited in E. Pellegrin, 'Bibliothèques d'humanistes lombards de la cour des Visconti Sforza', *Bibliothèque d'Humanisme et Renaissance*, XVII, 1955, p. 227, n. 2.

[33] = Vat. Rossiano 451 (IX, 141). Tietze No. 272. Kristeller, II, p. 406. A. A. Strnad, *loc. cit.*, p. 323, n. 115. Ambrogio Traversari's copy was used in the debates with the Greeks at Ferrara, B. L. Ullman and P. A. Stadter, *op. cit.*, p. 11. Nicholas of Cusa had a copy. E. Vansteenberghe, *Le Cardinal Nicolas de Cues*, Paris, 1920, p. 29, n. 6.

[34] = Vat. Rossiano VIII, 185. Tietze No. 153.

[35] One of the patristic authors translated by Ambrogio Traversari. *Cf.* B. L. Ullman and P. A. Stadter, *op. cit.*, p. 137, for Niccoli's copy.

[36] = Vat. Rossiano 213 (VIII, 152). Kristeller, II, p. 468. For Lilius Tifernas see literature cited in L. D. Ettlinger, *The Sistine Chapel before Michelangelo*, Oxford, 1965, p. 116.

[37] Possibly Vat. Rossiano VIII, 107. *Cf.* Tietze, p. 118.

[38] = Vat. Rossiano VIII, 112. Tietze No. 7.

[39] *Cf.* vols. 87, 142, 151.

[40] On this translation, H. Baron, *Leonardi Bruni Aretino. Humanistisch-philosophische Schriften*, Leipzig and Berlin, 1928.

[41] I have not clearly identified the author. See the studies of the Carmelite manuscripts of the Vatican by Graziano a S. Theresa in *Archivum Bibliographicum Carmelitanum*, II–XI, Rome, 1957–69.

[42] *Cf.* vol. 92 and n. 43.

[43] Volume 92 = *sermones super cantica canticorum* and Gislebertus on the same theme = Vat. Rossiano VIII, 125. Tietze No. 127, although it is not there listed as owned by Capranica.

[44] Tietze lists a Rossiano manuscript but owned by Girolamo Grimaldi (VIII, 227), p. 118. *Cf.* Kristeller, II, p. 465, and nn. 58, 39 and 54.

[45] = Vat. Rossiano VIII, 98. Tietze No. 224 (arms of Capranica, f. 1).

[46] On these sermons, found by Guarino da Verona in the chapter library of Verona in 1425, Sabbadini, I, p. 97.

[47] A popular work at the time. Their authenticity was debated at the Council of Basel and defended by Cardinal Juan Torquemada, debates in which Capranica may have been involved. These *defensiones* are also in this same volume. Vat. Rossiano 491 (IX, 181) contains Toquemada's defence, but may be a different volume.

[48] The following volume can be clearly identified: vol. 116: *Summa contra gentiles* = Vat. Rossiano VIII, 176. Tietze No. 104.

[49] Volume 125: *Postilla supra 4^or libris summarum*; vol. 126: *Expositio supra 2° summarum*; vol. 127: *De proprietatibus, Breviloquium*, etc.

[50] = Vat. Rossiano IX, 233. Tietze No. 250 (arms of the cardinal between two *putti*). On the work in general, C. Erickson, 'Bartholomew of Pisa, Francis Exalted, De conformitate', *Medieval Studies*, XXXIV, 1972, pp. 253–74.

[51] 'Parvum et pulchrum'.

[52] This had been translated by Ambrogio Traversari.

[53] Volume 136 = *Antiquitatum . . .* , Vat. Rossiano IX, 270. Tietze No. 268 (arms of the cardinal, f. 1); vol. 137: *De bello judaico libri VII* = Vat. Rossiano IX, 271. Tietze, p. 119.

[54] = Vat. Rossiano VIII, 182. Tietze No. 231 and fig. 124 (arms of the cardinal).

[55] Volume 143: *Cronica Eusebii, Hyeronymi et Prosperis*; vol. 144: *Chronicon*, and continued vol. 145. Possibly = Vat. Rossiano VIII, 111. Tietze, p. 118, or Vat. Rossiano IX, 140 (*ibid.*, p. 119), with the arms of the cardinal. Volume 147 is the *Preparatione evangelica* mentioned in the life of George of Trebizond by Vespasiano da Bisticici.

[56] = Vat. Rossiano 248 (VIII, 187). Described by Kristeller, II, p. 469.

[57] Lactantius Firmiani, *Divinarum institutionum adversus gentes*. *Cf.* earlier, n. 32. This is clearly a different volume. Possibly that in Tietze No. 252 (Rossiano IX, 139)?

[58] *Cf.* earlier, n. 44.

[59] = Vat. Rossiano VIII, 87. Tietze No. 235. Written by Johannes Dorembroch, 1440.

[60] = Vat. Rossiano 429 (IX, 119) (arms of the cardinal, f. 1). Tietze No. 13. Kristeller, II, p. 465.

[61] It is interesting to note that this was borrowed by Capranica from the Vatican Library in 1456. Müntz and Fabre, p. 344.

[62] His tract against the Bogomils of Bosnia. Useful bibliography on this Franciscan in *Histoire de l'Église*, ed. A. Fliche and V. Martin, XIV, Paris, 1964, pp. 534, 649, 1094, 1164.

[63] The individual works are too numerous to list. On translations of Aristotle, useful bibliography and lists of manuscripts in the articles of C. H. Lohr S.J., 'Medieval Latin Aristotle commentaries', *Traditio*, XXIII, 1967; XXVI–XXVIII, 1970–72. Also G. Lacombe, *Aristoteles Latinus*, Rome, 1939–55.

[64] S. H. Thomson, 'Walter Burley's commentary on the *Politics* of Aristotle', *Melanges Auguste Pelzer*, Louvain, 1947, pp. 557–78.

[65] = Vat. Rossiano 785 (X, 165)? Kristeller, II, p. 467. On the work in general, *Tradition*, XXVI, 1970, pp. 161 ff.

[66] On the translation by Ambrogio Traversari, see G. Holmes, *The Florentine Enlightenment, 1400–50*, London, 1969, p. 124.

[67] = Vat. Rossiano 399 (IX, 89). Description in Kristeller, II, p. 469. *Cf.* Tietze No. 221. Kristeller cites another manuscript of the work, Vat. Lat. 2087, II, p. 311.

This translation was undertaken during the pontificate of Nicholas V; see R. Cessi, 'Giorgio da Trebisonda, Poggio Bracciolini e G. Aurispa durante il pontificato di Niccolo V', *Archivio Storico per la Sicilia Orientale*, IX, Catania, 1912, pp. 211–32. *Cf. id.*, *Saggi Romani*, Rome, 1956. Further on the translator, Sabbadini, I, pp. 66 ff. and *Traditio*, XXIV, 1968, pp. 158–9.

Filelfo had brought back a manuscript of the work from Constantinople in 1427.

[68] = Vat. Rossiano 28 (VII a 28). Kristeller, II, p. 465. Capranica became cardinal-priest of Santa Croce in 1444.

[69] For the revival of interest in patristic authors in the Renaissance, P. O. Kristeller, 'Augustine and the early Renaissance', *Studies in Renaissance Thought and Letters*, Rome, 1956, pp. 355–72. Many authors have subsequently commented on it. Literature cited in C. Trinkaus, *In our Image and Likeness*, London, two vols., 1970. Earlier, Sabbadini, I, pp. 87, 90, 119, etc.

The interest is also reflected in other cardinals' libraries of the period, notably those of Giordano Orsini, Nicholas of Cusa and, of course, Bessarion. See below, nn. 159, 160, 161.

[70] E.g. the letter collection of Ambrogio Traversari, ed. L. Mehus, contains only one letter to Capranica, and that on ecclesiastical business.

For Traversari and his contacts, useful summary in G. Holmes, *op. cit.*, pp. 81–4, 96–7, 122–4.

[71] On this connection see H. Jedin, *A History of the Council of Trent*, English translation, London, 1957, I, p. 163.

[72] A tract on the reform of the see of Fermo equally reflects the cardinal's long tenure of this bishopric, after which he was known as the Cardinal of Fermo (*Firmanus*). Capranica held the see probably from 1424. The tract is now in the university library at Bologna, Cod. 2631. According to Morpurgo-Castelnuovo (p. 125 n.) it was composed between 4 Jan. and 24 July 1450. Further, *ibid.*, p. 84.

For Capranica's famous reform memorial in Vat. Lat. 4039, *ibid.*, p. 73ff., and H. Jedin, *op. cit.* p. 120ff. The library did not, it seems, possess a copy.

[73] R. Devresse, *op. cit.*, pp. 7–10, on the slow growth under Martin V and Eugenius IV and the increase under Nicholas V, who had some Greek codices in his library by the end of the pontificate. Other than Bessarion and Isidore of Kiev (*ibid.*, pp. 37–40) no cardinal had substantial collections of Greek manuscripts in the early fifteenth century. The observations of Morpurgo-Castelnuovo on Capranica, p. 119, must be seen in this context.

[74] Morpurgo-Castelnuovo, p. 13, who dates his degree in canon law at Bologna from 1422, and observes that since he was not called 'utriusque iuris doctor' he was probably never similarly qualified in civil law. Capranica studied earlier at Padua, but published works do not, it seems, provide further information on these studies.

[75] *The Vespasiano Memoirs*, trans. W. George and E. Waters, London, 1926, p. 134. More fully on Capranica's period as Grand Penitentiary, E. Göller, *Die päpstliche Pönitentiarie* . . . , Rome, 1911, I, pp. 14–15, 85 ff. (list of office-holders), II, pp. 71–3 (documents). Pastor remains our best authority for the jubilee of 1450.

[76] Capranica held office as clerk of the Camera Apostolica (probably also acting as papal secretary) under Martin V and was employed on various special missions, e.g. the suppression of the revolt of Bologna. After his period at Basel (see n. 89) he acted as camerarius of the Camera of the College of Cardinals 1438–39, 1448–49 and served on several important legations (see n. 88). More fully, *D.H.G.E.*, art. 'Capranica (Domenico)' by J. Toussaint.

[77] H. Gilles, 'Gilles Bellemere et le tribunal de la Rote a la fin du XIVe siècle', *Mélanges d'archéologie et d'histoire*, LXVII, 1955, pp. 281–319, citing further literature.

His works were prominent in the libraries of other administrator cardinals, e.g. Jean de Brogny. See n. 157.

[78] Venice, 1605, etc.

[79] = Vat. Rossiano IX, 283, 284 (two vols.). Tietze No. 61 (arms of the cardinal, f. 219).

[80] The volume cited in Tietze No. 187 came into the library of the college after the inventory of 1480.

[81] On his works, monograph by K. Nörr, *Kirche und Konzil bei Nicolaus de Tudeschis*, Cologne and Graz, 1964. He played a prominent part at the Council of Basel.

[82] = Vat. Rossiano IX, 287. Tietze No. 109.

[83] Repertorium. = Vat. Rossiano IX, 227. Tietze No. 226. Arms of the cardinal, f. 1.

[84] J. P. McCall, 'The writings of John of Legnano, with a list of manuscripts', *Traditio*, XXIII, 1967, pp. 415–37. *Cf.* Müntz and Fabre, p. 17 (1443 papal lib.).

[85] On these collections in general, P. Riesenberg, 'The "consilia" literature: a prospectus', *Manuscripta*, VI, 1962, pp. 3–22.

Kristeller lists several volumes from the Fondo Rossiano in the Vatican Library which may come from Capranica's library, e.g. 1066 (XI, 215) Jo. Caldernius (vol. 255?); 1083 (XI, 224), *ibid.*, Repertorium iuris (vol. 280?); see Kristeller, II, p. 468. *Cf.* Tietze No. 279, Juridici tractatus varii.

[86] Vat. Rossiano, 685.

[87] = Vat. Rossiano IX, 278, 'pulchrum'. Tietze No. 134. Illumination attributed to Niccolo di Giacomo da Bologna.

On the author, N. Jung, *Un Franciscain Théologien du pouvoir pontifical au XIVe siècle: Alvaro Pelayo, évêque et pénitencier de Jean XXII*, Paris, 1931.

Francesco de Tolentino is described in the catalogue as *magister in theologia dignissimus*, once chaplain to the cardinal and now apostolic prothonotary.

[88] Capranica was legate to the March from 10 September 1443 (the date he left Siena) to 14 November 1444; from 11 December 1444 to 31 August 1446 and again from 5 May 1447 to December 1447.

Morpurgo-Castelnuovo identifies the volume as Vat. Lat. 6742, p. 125, n. 5. For further literature on Albornoz see n. 164.

[89] Capranica's copy of the Acts of the Council of Constance (vol. 294 in the inventory), Vat. Lat. 7297, as well as other manuscripts are discussed in the fourth volume of H. Finke, *Acta Concilii Constanciensis*, Münster, 1896–1928.

Kristeller lists a number of manuscripts as coming from Capranica.

The sources for Basel are surveyed in the series *Concilium Basilense*, ed. J. Haller *et al.*, Basel, 1896–1936, especially vol. I. A survey of printed material in A. P. J. Meijknecht, 'Le Concile de Bâle, aperçu général sur ses sources', *Revue d'histoire ecclésiastique*, LXV, 1970, pp. 465–73, although nothing specific on Capranica. One copy of Capranica's of the Acts of Basel is at Florence, formerly Carte Strozziane MS XXXIII. The copy at Venice is noted by Kristeller, II, p. 211 (Marciana, Fondo Antico Lat., 166–7), *cf.* II, pp. 326 (Vat. Lat. 4184–5, 4187), 334 (Vat. Lat. 5600). Vol. 292 in the inventory contains material predominantly on Basel and vol. 295 on Ferrara–Florence.

[90] See, for example, vol. 292. For the Capranica case at Basel, N. Valois, *La Crise religieuse du XVe siècle. Le Pape et le Concile (1418–1450)*, Paris, 1909, I, pp. 184–96, which cites the earlier literature. Also for Capranica role at Basel, where he was present from 1431 to 1435, Morpurgo-Castelnuovo, pp. 30–47. *D.H.G.E.*, art. cit., cols. 936–8.

[91] Morpurgo-Castelnuovo was emphatic in denying Capranica the status of a humanist: 'Certo non partecipo vivamente al movimento umanistico,' pp. 122–3. Other authors refer to him as a 'humanist cardinal', e.g. J. Guiraud, *L'Église et les origines de la Renaissance*, Paris, 1902, pp. 255 ff, at p. 257: 'Les humanistes les plus éminents se groupaient autour de lui comme autour de leur maître'; *D.H.G.E.* art., col. 940: 'il fût un des premiers humanistes'.

[92] E. Walser, *Poggius Florentinus. Leben und Werke*, Leipzig and Berlin, 1914, pp.

316-17, 345-6 and a lament on his death, 552. Also previously in M. Catalanus *De vita et scriptis D. Capranicae cardinalis*, Fermo, 1793.

Works by Poggio listed in the inventory were vols. 161, *de ridis* and the fourth book of *de varietate fortunae*; 337, *de vera felicitatis disputatio*, etc; 339, *de nobilitate*.

[93] For one such example, G. Gualdo, 'Giovanni Toscanella', *Italia medioevale e umanistica*, XIII, 1970, pp. 54-5 (document of 18 April 1445 there printed).

[94] See below, n. 134.

[95] R. Weiss, *The Renaissance Discovery of Classical Antiquity*, Oxford, 1969.

Capranica did, however, have a copy of Flavio Biondo's *Roma Instaurata* in his library (vol. 348). See further on Capranica's relations with Biondo, which may date from the cardinal's stay in Forlì in 1428 but were not close until possibly later, *Scritti inediti e rari di Biondo Flavio*, ed. B. Nogara, Rome, 1927 (see index). For his legation to Genoa in 1453 Biondo wrote for Capranica a speech exhorting the Doge, Pietro di Campofregoso, to join the papal crusading enterprise (*ibid.*, pp. 61-71). Nogara argues that a letter from Rome, 13 September 1446, accompanied by three books of the *Roma Instaurata* (and a promise to send twelve books of the *Historia* (the Decades)) was written to Capranica, but the evidence on this does not seem to be conclusive; *ibid.*, pp. civ, 128.

[96] I have discovered none other than those contained in the library.

[97] Volume 301, 'pulcherrimum volumen'; vol. 302, 'pulcherrimum'.

[98] = Vat. Rossiano 715 (x, 95). Tietze No. 146. Description in F. Petrarch, *Le Familiari*, ed. V. Rossi, Florence, 1933, pp. xvii-xx.

[99] No modern edition has yet appeared.

[100] Also a lengthy list of other works.

[101] = Vat. Rossiano 526. Tietze, p. 105, No. 194.

[102] The edition by G. Billanovich (Florence, 1945), pp. xvii-xxvii, cites two Vatican manuscripts, Vat. Lat. 4526 and 3356, the last from the collection of Cardinal Giordano Orsini.

[103] = Possibly Vat. Rossiano 566 (IX, 256)?

[104] = Vat. Lat. 3452. It subsequently belonged to Fulvio Orsini; see P. De Nolhac, *La Bibliothèque de Fulvio Orsini*, Paris, 1887, p. 224.

[105] Manuscripts of this work are listed by G. Bruni, *Catalogo dei Manoscritti Egidii Romani*, Milan, 1931. I have not identified Capranica's copy.

[106] The Ciceronian works in Capranica's library were vols. 320, 321, *orationes*; 322, *de oratore*; 323, *Epistolae . . .* ; 324, *Epistolae ad Lentulum . . .* ; 328, *Invectiva in Catilinam*; 329, *De legibus*; 330, *Tusculanae quaestiones*, etc.

[107] Also a work entitled *Familie nobiles romanorum et plebes; Tabula R^{mi} eiusdem et Valerii; Summaria eiusdem Valerii per Joannem Andree*, etc.

[108] On this work and the dedication, G. Mercati, *Ultimi contributi alla storia degli umanisti*, fasc. 1: *Traversariana*, Vatican City, 1939, pp. 99-101.

[109] Ed. A. Gnesotto, in *Atti e Memorie della Reale Accademia di Scienze, Lettere ed Arti in Padova*, 1918.

[110] On this work, G. Holmes, *op. cit.*, p. 254.

[111] On the sources of Bruni's version, B. Reynolds, 'Bruni and Perotti present a Greek historian', *Bibliothèque d'Humanisme et Renaissance*, XVI, 1954, pp. 108-14.

[112] On the author, P. H. Labalme, *Bernardo Giustiniani: a Venetian of the Quattrocento*, Rome, 1969 (a study of Leonardo's son), *passim*.

[113] I have not clearly identified this work of Loschi's.

[114] Completed 1433. Sabbadini, I, p. 184. Ed. B. L. Ullman, Rome, 1928.

[115] Volume 341 = M. Veggio's *Dialogus veritatis et Philalitis ad Eustachium fratrem* and Gregorio Correr's *De fugiendo seculo*.

[116] Manuscripts cited by Kristeller, II, p. 336.

[117] See above, n. 92.

[118] On this work, E. Walser, *op. cit.*, pp. 250-1. G. Shepherd, *The Life of Poggio Bracciolini*, Liverpool, second edition, 1837, p. 329.

[119] According to the catalogue, G.V. was an apostolic prothonotary and *orator insignis*. He is almost certainly Gaspare Zacchi di Volterra.

[120] Volume described as 'pulchrum'.

[121] On the history of the manuscripts of Plautus in the Renaissance, and especially the manuscript in the possession of Cardinal Giordano Orsini, E. König, *Kardinal Giordano Orsini . . .*, Freiburg, 1906, pp. 82–108. Poggio's complaint that the cardinal kept it hidden from other scholars in G. Shepherd, *op. cit.*, p. 100 n. C. Questa, *Per la storia del testo di Plauto nell'Umanesimo, 1, La 'recensio' di Poggio Bracciolini*, Rome, 1968.

[122] Volume described as 'pulchrum et longum'. *Cf.* Müntz and Fabre, p. 25 (papal library, 1443).

[123] For the author, P. O. Kristeller, 'The humanist Bartolomeo Facio and his unknown correspondence', *From the Renaissance to the Counter-Reformation: Essays in Honor of Garret Mattingly*, ed. C. S. Carter, New York, 1965, pp. 56–74, with reference to correspondence with Capranica, p. 62 and n. 26 (Vat. Lat. 2906, f. 3*v*) Kristeller dates the *De rebus . . . Alfonsi* 'probably . . . after October 1448' (p. 65).

[124] On the *Roma Instaurata* see above, n. 94.

[125] Possibly the life by Pier Candido Decembrio.

[126] Ed. A. Gnestoto, *Atti e Memorie della Reale Accademia de Scienze, Lettere ed Arti in Padova*, Padua, 1915.

On the work, G. Holmes, *op. cit.*, p. 15. Sabbadini, I, p. 63, n. 122. A letter of Francesco Barbaro, 2 May 1453, to Domenico Capranica concerning the monastery of S. Niccolo in Murano and its privileges is printed in *Archivium Franciscanum Historicum*, XI, 1918, pp. 302–4.

[127] = Vat. Rossiano 373 (IX, 63). Tietze No. 133. Kristeller, II, p. 465.

[128] *Cf.* Müntz and Fabre, pp. 3, 20.

[129] Morpurgo-Castelnuovo, 119. = Vat. Rossiana x, 81.

[130] The entry is noted in V. Branca, *Tradizione delle opere di Giovanni Boccaccio*, Rome, 1958, I, p. 103, where a list of manuscripts is given (pp. 99–103) and this volume listed among 'codici ora irreperibili'.

[131] = Vat. Rossiano 1155–7 (XI, 294*a–c*). Tietze No. 150. Kristeller, II, p. 468.

[132] R. Weiss, 'Jacopo Angeli da Scarperia', *Medioevo e Rinascimento: studi in onore di B. Nardi*, Florence, 1955, II, pp. 803–27. Cardinal Giordano Orsini had a copy of Ptolemy 'portato di Francia'; see Sabbadini, I, p. 56.

[133] The statutes of the college were first printed in Rome in 1708 and then reprinted in 1879; Morpurgo-Castelnuovo, p. 92 and n. 1. Numerous manuscript versions of the 'constitutiones' exist, e.g. Kristeller, II, pp. 118, 584.

[134] As did, for example, other cardinals of the period, such as Giordano Orsini (Sabbadini, I, pp. 110–11 (and monograph cited above, n. 120)) and Nicholas of Cusa (Sabbadini, II, pp. 16–27 (the section on p. 17 on the ways in which Cusa's library was built up is especially instructive)). See further below, n. 160.

For Iacopo Ammanati, one-time secretary to Capranica, and his search for manuscripts, Sabbadini, I, p. 202. On Niccolo Perotti, as one of Bessarion's agents, Müntz and Fabre, pp. 113–14. On a later period, for Antonio Pizzamano, agent of Domenico Grimani, P. Kibre, *op. cit.*, p. 5.

[135] A *familiaris*, Johannes de Lins, is mentioned on a copy of Aquinas's *Summa de virtutibus secundum Aristotelem*. Tietze No. 273. Bernardus de Alb(e)ricis Cumanus, a *familiaris* of the cardinal, was involved in the copying of the letters of St Bernard in 1437. Tietze No. 218. For Francesco de Tollentino see above, n. 86.

[136] G. M. Cagni, *Vespasiano Da Bisticci e il suo epistolario*, Rome, 1969, p. 132, a letter of Giannozzo Manetti to Vespasiano, Rome, 23 November 1454: 'Et io provedero che tu harai le Vite mie che sono 5 in uno volume il quale pochi di fa riebbi da Monsignore di Fermo'. This refers to Manetti's lives of Dante, Petrarch, Boccaccio, Socrates and Seneca. Vat. Rossiano VIII, 148, f. 1, is said to have been bought at Florence.

[137] Perhaps of special interest is the monastery of S. Salvatore di Settimo, a Cistercian house, in the diocese of Florence, resigned by the cardinal in 1441. C. Eubel, *Hierarchia Catholica Medii Aevi*, Münster, ed. altera, 1914, II, p. 6, h. 11 (although wrongly put in the diocese of Ferentino). Apparently Capranica found the monastery in a deplorable state, Morpurgo-Castelnuovo, pp. 81–2, so it is not certain that there was a library there of any consequence. On its contents in a slightly later period, B. L. Ullman and P. A. Stadter, *op. cit.*, p. 26, but referred to there as 'the Benedictine monastery of Settimo'. Was this a separate foundation? See further on Capranica and S. Salvatore a Settimo, in S. Orlandi, *Necrologia di S. Maria Novella*, Florence, 1955, II, p. 317.

Other monasteries held *in commendam* by the cardinal were the monastery of Chiaravalle in the diocese of Sinigallia (S. Maria), a Cistercian house; the Benedictine monastery of San Eustichio in the diocese of Spoleto, resigned 1454; of S. Bartolomeo 'de Campofulone', a Benedictine house in the diocese of Fermo, together with Sant' Anastasio and San Savino in 'Vissiano' in the same diocese. Morpurgo-Castelnuovo, p. 84, and U. Cameli, 'Il monastero di S. Bartolomeo de "Campo Fullonum" e i prelati di Casa Capranica', *Studia Picena*, XI, 1935, pp. 84–6.

[138] On Capranica as Cardinal Protector of the Franciscan Order from 1445 to 1458, P. Riccardo Pratesi, O.F.M., 'Il card. Domenico Capranica, Protettore dei Frati Minori (1445–58) ed una sua lettera alla Congregazione generale di Assissi nel 1445', *Archivum Franciscanum Historicum*, XLVIII, 1955, pp. 197–200. Further material in *ibid.*, XLIX, 1956, I, 1957, pp. 23 ff, 39 ff, and in general Morpurgo-Castelnuovo, pp. 80 ff. There is much material also on his concern for the Clares, e.g. *Archivum Franciscanum Historicum*, XIX, 1926, p. 210 (letter as legate in Perugia, 1430,); *ibid.* XXIII, 1930, pp. 371 ff (at Foligno). Capranica was also Cardinal Protector of the Teutonic Order.

[139] Tietze No. 223.

[140] Tietze No. 216. Joh. de Ghistrella is there called 'clericus Morinensis'. I have found no further information on him.

[141] Tietze No. 219.

[142] Tietze No. 224.

[143] Tietze No. 222: 'in domo R^{mi} cardinalis pro eodem tempore'.

[144] Tietze No. 13.

[145] Tietze No. 235. The same copyist also copied a volume of the Acts of the Council of Basel. See above, no. 89.

[146] Tietze No. 271.

[147] Tietze No. 268.

[148] Tietze No. 272.

[149] The short section on the fate of Capranica's books in Morpurgo-Castelnuovo, pp. 125–6, is regrettably marred by some major errors. A further brief account, more accurate and with bibliography, is in Tietze, pp. xii–xiii.

[150] There is nothing on the Capranica palace and the sack of Rome in L. Pastor, *History of the Popes*, London, 1899, IX, pp. 408, 414.

[151] Tietze, pp. vii–xii. Another inventory of 1578 is to be found in Barb. Lat. 1578. Information kindly supplied from the forthcoming work by Mme Bignami Odier and Mgr J. Ruysschaert.

[152] Morpurgo-Castelnuovo, p. 125, citing I. Carini, *La Biblioteca Vaticana*, Rome, 1892, pp. 76, 83 ff. The account by Felice Contelori, librarian from 1626 to 1632, on the state of the papal library in Vat. Lat. 7763 is published by G. Beltrami in *Archivio della Reale Societa Romana di Storia Patria*, II, 1879, pp. 191–5.

[153] According to Tietze the sale of 1842 consisted of 112 parchment volumes and 112 on paper. De Rossi was the son of the writer Giovanni Gherardo De Rossi (1754–1827).

[154] De Rossi married Louisa Carlotta on 22 July 1838. His wife (b. 1802) married again in 1855 (to Count Giovanni Vimercati), and died in 1857. Vimercati has left an account of her life (Rome, 1855).

[155] J. Bignami Odier, 'Guide au Département des manuscrits de la Bibliothèque du Vatican', *Mélanges d'Archéologie et d'Histoire*, LI, 1934.

[156] For cardinals' libraries in the thirteenth century, R. Mather, 'The codicil of Cardinal Comes of Casate and the libraries of thirteenth-century cardinals', *Traditio* XX, 1964, pp. 319–50. A fuller study is being undertaken by A. Paravicini Bagliani. There is a brief but useful survey of cardinals' libraries in the fourteenth century in B. Guillemain, *La Cour pontificale d'Avignon (1309–1376)*, Paris, 1962, pp. 218 ff.

[157] L. Carolus-Barre, 'Bibliothèques médiévales inédites d'après les archives du Vatican . . . , *Mélanges d'Archéologie et d'Histoire*, LIII, 1936, with list of books, pp. 353–72. An analysis in B. Guillemain', *op. cit.*, p. 219.

[158] L. H. Labande, 'Un légiste du XIVe siècle: J. Allarmet, cardinal de Brogny', *Mélanges Julien Havet*, Par, Le-Puy-en-Velay, 1895, pp. 487–97 (a discussion of the contents). Two inventories survive, one of 1427 listing 171 volumes and one of 1435. M. Fournier, *Les Statuts et privilèges des universités françaises* . . . , II, Paris, 1891, Nos. 1302, 1316. Most of the library was bequeathed to the college which the cardinal founded at Annecy. Jean de Brogny was vice-chancellor to the Avignon obedience after 1394 and then to Popes Alexander V, John XXIII and Martin V in turn.

[159] L. Jarry, 'Testament du Cardinal Amedée de Saluces', *Mémoires de la Société archéologique de l'Orléannais*, XII, 1873, pp. 462–70, especially at p. 465: 'ordinaverimus fieri quamdam librariam Aurelianis et jam ibi plures libros transmiserimus' and further books left to the *studium* at Avignon. Other volumes, including a 'magnum librum conciliorum' were left 'officio camerariatus collegii dd. cardinalium' (an office which the cardinal himself held for many years).

[160] Inventory published in F. Cancellieri, *De secretariis basilicae Vaticanae veteris ac novae libri*, Rome, 1786, II, pp. 906–14. Further information in G. Mercati, *Codici latini Pico Grimani . . . Con una digressione per la storia dei codici di S. Pietro in Vaticano*, Vatican City, 1938. By his will Orsini left his books to the chapter of St Peter's and ordered a library to be constructed for it by his will, printed in E. König, *op. cit.*, pp. 117–20, and n. 119.

[161] On Nicholas of Cusa's library I am much indebted to the stimulating article of P. O. Kristeller, 'A Latin translation of Gemistos Plethon's *De fato* by Johannes Sophianos dedicated to Nicholas of Cusa', *Niccolo Cusa agli inizi del mondo moderno*, Florence, 1970, pp. 175–93, and the literature cited on Cusa's manuscripts, p. 176, n. 3.

[162] Inventory of the books donated to St Marks', Venice, in 1468 printed in H. Omont, 'Inventaire des manuscrits grecs et latins donnés à Saint-Marc de Venise par le Cardinal Bessarion en 1468', *Revue des bibliothèques*, IV, 1894, pp. 129–87; inventory, pp. 149 ff. Since then a great deal of literature has been added. Bessarion's bequest to Venice totalled 746 manuscripts, of which 482 were in Greek. The value of the library was estimated at 15,000 ducats.

[163] Other notable collections were assembled by Antonio Correr (d. 1445), left to the monastery of G. Giorgio in Alga, Venice. M. Foscarini, 'Dei Veneziani raccoglitori di codici', ed. T. Gar, *Archivio storico italiano*, first series, V, 1843, pp. ix–xli, 1–507; Juan Torquemada's books, *Bibliotheca Hispana vetus . . . auctore D. Nicolao Hispalensi*, Madrid, 1788, II, pp. 286–92, and, for manuscripts of his own works, J. M. Garrastchu, 'Los manoscri os del Cardinal Torquemada en lo Biblioteca Vaticana', *Ciencia Tomista*, XXII, 1930, pp. 188–217, 291–322; Jean Jouffroy (d. 1473), Sabbadini, I, pp. 194–5; C. Fierville, *Le Cardinal Jean Jouffroy et son temps*, Paris, 1874, pp. 224–33; A. Mercati, 'Una lettera di Vespasiano da Bisticci a Jean Jouffroy vesc. di Arras e la sua biblioteca romana del Jouffroi', *Mélanges . . . F. Grat*, Paris, 1946, I, pp. 357–66. Some forty-five codices survive in the Fondo latino of the Vatican Library, others at Paris. Francesco Gonzaga (d. 1483) was also a great book collector, as was Guillaume d'Estouteville (d. 1483), who left his books to S. Agostino in Rome, E. Müntz, *Les Arts à la cour des papes* . . . , Paris, 1879, III, pp. 294 ff. I have been unable to consult J. Ruysschaert, 'La bibliothèque du cardinal de Tournai Ferry de Clugny a la Vaticane', *Horae Torncenses, 1171–1971*, Tournai, 1971, pp. 131–41.

[164] The college was founded in 1362. Niccolo Capocci's will has been printed in several works, e.g. A. Ciaconius and A. Oldoino, *Vitae et res gestae Pontificum Romanorum et S.R.E. Cardinalium*, Rome, 1677, II, pp. 511–16. Literature on the college is usefully cited in U. Niccolini, O.F.M., 'San Giovanni da Capistrano, studente e giudice a Perugia', *Archivum Franciscanum Historicum*, LIII, 1960, pp. 44–5.

The foundation of Cardinal Egidio Albornoz (d. 1367) at Bologna may also have been an influence. *The Spanish College at Bologna in the Fourteenth Century*, ed. B. M. Marti, Philadelphia and London, 1966; *El Cardenal Albornoz y el Colegio de España*, ed. E. Verdera y Tuelles, Bologna, three vols., 1972–4. Other important similar foundations of the later fourteenth century were the college established at his birthplace by Cardinal Talleyrand de Périgord (d. 1364), N. Zacour, 'Talleyrand, the Cardinal of Périgord, 1301–64', *Transactions of the American Philosophical Society*, new series, I, part VII, 1960, and the college founded by Cardinal Jean de Dormans in Paris in 1370 and to which he left his books. L. C. Barre, 'Le cardinal de Dormans, chancellier de France, "principal conseiller", de Charles V d'après son testament et les archives du Vatican', *Mélanges d'Archéologie et d'Histoire*, LII, 1935, pp. 318 and text of will at p. 355.

[165] *Codice diplomatico dell'Università di Pavia*, ed. R. Maiocchi, Pavia, 1905–15, II. G. Carotti, 'Gli affreschi dell'oratorio dell'antico collegio fondato dal cardinale Branda Castiglioni in Pavia', *Archivio storico dell'arte*, 1897, pp. 249–75, especially at p. 272, on the documents in the Archivio del Collegio Castiglioni and the cardinal's will of 1429 in favour of the college.

[166] Albergati founded a public library in his episcopal palace at Bologna. *Acta SS.*, Maii II 1866, p. 477. On his books, Sabbadini, I, p. 188, and A. Sorbelli, *La Biblioteca Capitolare . . . di Bologna*, Bologna, 1904, pp. 74–6.

[167] Nardini's will is printed in C. Marcora, 'Stefano Nardini, Arcivescovo di Milano', *Memorie storiche della diocesi di Milano*, III, 1956, pp. 349–52. On the college, *ibid.*, pp. 235 ff. See further the essay on the 'Studium Urbis' in this volume by D. S. Chambers, pp. 68–110.

Niccolo Fortiguerra founded a college and library at Pistoia in 1473. Literature cited in A. A. Strnad, 'Francesco Todeschini-Piccolomini. Politik und Mäzententum im Quattrocento', *Römische historische Mitteilungen*, VIII–IX, 1954–5–1965–6, pp. 175, n. 92, and 176, n. 95.

For the library and college at Toulouse of the French cardinal Pierre de Foix the elder (d. 1465), F. Ehrle, 'Der Cardinal Peter de Foix der Aeltere, die Acten seiner Legation in Aragonien und sein Testament', *Archiv für Literatur- und Kirchegeschichte des Mittelalters*, VII, 1900, pp. 421–514, with the clause of the will, dated 3 August 1464, concerning the college at p. 507.

[168] From the *constitutiones* of the college founded by Capranica, cited by Morpurgo-Castelnuovo, p. 92, where it is noted that the identical words appear in the reform of the statutes of the college founded by Branda da Castiglione at Pavia (above, n. 164).

[169] H. Jedin, *A History of the Council of Trent*, English translation, London, 1957, I, pp. 120 ff.

Interesting comments are made on Capranica and his college in a recent lecture by D. Hay, *Italian Clergy and Italian Culture in the Fifteenth Century*, London, 1973 (Society for Renaissance Studies, Occasional Papers, No. 1).

Additional note

Dr A. A. Strnad of the Austrian Institute in Rome has twice announced his intention of publishing a study of Capranica's library, but to my knowledge this has not yet appeared: *op. cit.* (above, n. 166), p. 145 (n. 135); *Enea Silvio Piccolomini*, ed. D. Maffei, Siena, 1968, p. 349.

9

THE LIBRARY OF
FRANCESCO SASSETTI
(1421–90)[1]

THE LIBRARY OF Francesco di Tommaso Sassetti has recently been the subject of an article by Professor J.-F. Bergier,[2] but it is far from exhausting the interest of this collection. Professor Bergier published Sassetti's book list of 1462[3] for the first time but he did not know that many of Sassetti's manuscripts were included in the 1495 inventory of the Medici books, he did not attempt to make a full examination of the evidence provided by extant manuscripts, and he repeated the old story that Sassetti was a dealer in manuscripts. A study of Sassetti's extant manuscripts and of the style in which they are written and decorated enables us to trace the growth of his collection. It also throws new light on the connection between Sassetti and Bartolomeo Fonzio.[4] In his youth and early manhood Sassetti can be shown to have made a collection of a rather miscellaneous nature. In the 1470s, apparently with the help and advice of Fonzio, the collection was built up with a special care for the works of Cicero, for Latin poets and historians, and for Greek historians in Latin translation. In some cases the new manuscripts which Sassetti commissioned contained texts which he already owned, but perhaps only in inferior copies. However, Sassetti retained the best of his old manuscripts, at least until the late 1480s, when it seems that because of financial troubles he had to sell some of his finest manuscripts. It was chiefly this episode which gave rise to the belief that he dealt in manuscripts.[5]

The three main sources of information on Sassetti's library have all just been mentioned. Firstly, in November 1462 Sassetti made a general inventory of all his assets, including a list of his books with estimates of their value.[6] Secondly, in 1495 an inventory was made of the Medici books which had been confiscated and deposited in San Marco after the flight of Piero di Lorenzo. The listed books included sixty-seven which had belonged to Sassetti, which were returned to his heirs.[7] Thirdly there are the extant manuscripts. Over seventy manuscripts that Sassetti once owned are identifiable.[8] Most of them contain his *ex libris*, usually with one of his mottoes, and sometimes in the manuscripts expressly copied for him his emblems have been incorporated in the decoration. These features will be discussed more fully later. The Sassetti coat of arms—argent, a bend azure bordered in or—is also found in many of the manuscripts.[9]

This is not the place to give a detailed account of Sassetti's life, but it will be useful to set out its bare outlines.[10] Born in 1421 of an old Florentine family, he was sent as a youth to join the branch of the Medici bank at Geneva, probably in the late 1430s. He was rapidly promoted, and in 1447–48 became the manager of the branch. He was based in Geneva, although his business entailed travel in France, until 1459, when he returned to Florence to be assistant to Giovanni di Cosimo de' Medici, who was then general manager of the Medici bank. After Giovanni's death in 1463 Sassetti himself became general manager. He was to remain in control of the bank until his death. He settled down in Florence,[11] having married in 1459, and invested widely in property. He was already rich when he returned to Florence, and his fortune, mostly in investments with various branches of the Medici bank, increased rapidly. In 1462, when he made the inventory of his assets, he was worth nearly 27,000 florins. By 1466 his assets had almost doubled.[12] He was implicitly trusted as manager of the bank first by Piero di Cosimo de' Medici and then by Lorenzo di Piero, but these were difficult years for international finance and unfortunately he does not seem to have kept as strict an eye as he should have done on the management of the various branches of the bank outside Florence. The result, in the mid-1480s, was near disaster, both for the bank and for Sassetti himself. Several of the most important branches had to be liquidated, and the Lyons branch (the successor in 1466 to Geneva) was saved only by Sassetti's personal intervention. The old man went to Lyons in May 1488 to sort things out. He did not return to Florence until October 1489, and died of a stroke soon afterwards, late in March 1490.

In his heyday Sassetti enjoyed his prosperity to the full. He believed in the outward expression of his personal success. He acquired and embellished a fine palace just outside Florence at Montughi which was much admired by his contemporaries,[13] and established in Santa Trinità a splendid burial place for himself and his family which bears witness to his patronage and his philosophy of life. Earlier members of the Sassetti family had been buried in the Dominican church of Santa Maria Novella, but Francesco quarrelled with the Dominicans, partly, it seems, because they understandably objected to the idea of having their main chapel decorated with scenes from the life of St Francis, his patron saint.[14] The Vallombrosan Benedictines of Santa Trinità were more accommodating, and the Sassetti chapel there, with frescoes by Domenico Ghirlandaio and sarcophagi in classical style for Francesco and his wife, Nera Corsi, was completed about 1486.[15] The decorative scheme of the chapel, with its deliberate counterbalancing of Christian and pagan classical themes and its glorification of Sassetti and his Medici patrons, has been much studied.[16] A number of the scenes represented in the sculpted and painted surrounds of the tombs have been shown to have been modelled on surviving classical objects—sarcophagi, coins, etc.[17] Sassetti must have taken an active part in planning the decoration of the chapel, but he was surely helped by his former protégé, Bartolomeo Fonzio. Saxl has shown that Fonzio probably invented the symbolical pseudo-classical inscription which is to be seen on the sarcophagus, used as crib, in Ghirlandaio's altarpiece of the Nativity;[18] it sums up the pagan/Christian reconciliation theme of the whole chapel. Sassetti and Fonzio shared a passionate interest in classical inscriptions. Part of the autograph of Fonzio's epigraphical collection survives, as well as more complete copies of it. From it we learn how he copied down some of the inscriptions in the collection from the originals when he was travelling with Sassetti, and that he collected others with Sassetti's help.[19] Sassetti's own interest in inscriptions is shown in his letters[20] and was probably aroused when he was a young man, travelling on business in Switzerland and France. We know from a letter written to Piero di Cosimo de' Medici in August 1456 that Sassetti was looking out for inscriptions from Lyons for Piero at that time. In his letter he also refers to a 'head of Camilla' and a 'red faun' that he had sent to Piero. These two objects are almost certainly identifiable with two ancient(?) cameos set in rings listed among Piero's precious objects in his inventory of September 1456. Sassetti was waiting for a book that Piero had promised to send him in exchange for the cameos. He had asked for either Cicero's speeches or his letters.[21]

This request for a book is the earliest evidence that we have of Sassetti's book collecting. Was it his searches in France for antiquities for Piero and perhaps other friends that first aroused his own interest in classical Antiquity? We know nothing of his education. It is likely to have been biased to practical business needs. He may well have been apprenticed to a bank in his early teens but nonetheless by that time he would probably have gained a smattering of the usual classical authors studied in school.[22] As a boy in Florence in the early 1430s he may well have met some of the local scholars; for example, if he was already working for the Medici before 1437 he could have known Niccolò Niccoli, who was generous in his encouragement of clever boys and had a magnificent library.[23] It may be no accident that the only known copy of Niccoli's *Commentarium in peregrinatione Germaniae*, a search list of classical texts compiled for the use of two bishops who were visiting Germany in 1431, survives only in a copy bound in at the end of one of Sassetti's manuscripts.[24] The list might have been sent to him by one of his Florentine friends to help him find and identify texts on his journeys in France and Switzerland.

Certainly the 1462 inventory already contains several important manuscripts, which must, therefore, have been acquired by Sassetti before that date, probably in France.[25] The most notable is the ninth-century manuscript which includes Filargirius' commentaries on Vergil (appendix 9.3, No. 26), for which Sassetti paid the equivalent of fifteen florins. Professor Bernhard Bischoff has identified this manuscript as coming from the cathedral library at Lyons, one of the French cities we know Sassetti visited.[26] He also acquired a ninth-century manuscript of Martial which was written in France (No. 72—valued at six florins in 1462) and a superb but puzzling copy of Augustine, *De civitate dei*, the script of which suggests the ninth century and the influence of Tours, while the decoration must be later (No. 2). This manuscript was the most highly valued item in the 1462 list, at forty florins. Other manuscripts of French provenance that Sassetti had acquired by 1462—and he does not seem to have acquired any later—are an eleventh-century miscellany which includes Arator, Avianus and Persius (four florins), Alan of Lille's Anticlaudianus, thirteenth century (two florins?), a fine early fifteenth-century manuscript of Vitruvius, Cato and Varro, originally copied for a friend of the French humanist Jean de Montreuil (ten florins) (Nos. 54, 11, 7), and perhaps also a twelfth- to thirteenth-century Priscian at six florins (No. 28).[27] He had also bought in 'Gallia' a beautiful early eleventh-century illuminated Sacramentary from Regensburg (No. 1). This he valued at only six florins, perhaps the price that he had paid for it.[28] It was probably in Geneva itself that he bought a Terence which had been copied in Italy in 1436 but which had belonged before him to the French cleric and poet Martin Le Franc (1410–61), who became a canon of Geneva in 1447 (No. 22). The 1462 list also includes several other manuscripts which Sassetti had probably bought in the north but which have not been identified: the romance of Tristan in French, Aristotle's *Physics* in French and a Book of Hours 'made in France' (appendix 9.1, Nos. 59, 60, 53).

The other manuscripts listed in 1462 which can be identified all come from Italy. All that are identifiable with certainty date from the fifteenth century and many of them were written in Florence, but most of them must have been bought second-hand. They include a beautiful illustrated Dante copied in Florence about 1410–15 in a good humanistic hand (ten florins: No. 64) and a fine early fifteenth-century Boethius made in Bologna (four florins: No. 59).[29] The books which Sassetti may have bought new include another probably written in Bologna: Benvenuto de' Rambaldi's *Romuleon*, c. 1460, with illumination signed by 'Marsilius Bononiensis' (fifteen florins: No. 48).[30] Sassetti is said by his great-grandson Francesco di Giovambattista to have had many friends in Bologna, and to have visited the city frequently.[31] Two other manuscripts that he may have bought new are simple companion volumes of Cicero's *De finibus* and *Tusculanae* written by one Florentine scribe (Nos. 55, 56, both valued at four florins). There is also a copy of Cicero's *Epistulae ad familiares*, made by a scribe who often worked for Piero de' Medici—perhaps the manuscript sent to Sassetti by Piero in 1456 in exchange for his cameos (No. 31: fifteen florins).

Forty of the sixty-four books listed by Sassetti in 1462 remain unidentified at present.[32] In addition to the three texts cited above which had probably been acquired in France these include an Orosius (four florins) in 'lettere longonbarde', 'ancient' copies of Martianus Capella (ten florins) and Vergil (two florins) and an old Lucan.[33] There was a copy of Cicero's speeches valued at thirty florins—the highest value after the Augustine—which it is tantalising not to be able to identify (appendix 9.1, Nos. 6, 3, 38, 22 or 41, 7). Other comparatively valuable items were a Diodorus Siculus 'di Poggio' valued at fifteen florins,[34] a psalter bound in black velvet at twelve

florins, Benvenuto da Imola's commentary on Dante in three volumes valued
together at thirty florins, Boccaccio's *De casibus* at eight florins,[35] Servius on
Virgil's *Aeneid* on paper at eight florins—a high value for a paper manuscript,
probably because of its length—Macrobius' *Saturnalia*, and Martial, both at
six florins, and Cicero's *De officiis* at five florins—a high value for a short text
(appendix 9.1, Nos. 17, 51, 2, 18, 10, 14, 4, 31). Other texts worth noting are
the *Bucolics* of Calpurnius Siculus (two florins) and 'Francesco d'Arezzo de
calumpnia' (one florin) (appendix 9.1, Nos. 43, 47). The latter was presumably
Francesco Griffolini's Latin translation of the speech by Lucian. The translation was dedicated to John Tiptoft, Earl of Worcester, and given to him just
before he returned to England in 1461—a very new text for Sassetti to have
owned already in 1462.[36] Some of these unidentified manuscripts may have
been new when Sassetti bought them, but the low values put on most of the
remaining items in the list—between one and three florins each—suggest that
they were mainly unpretentious copies which had been bought second-
hand.[37]

It will be seen that the collection of 1462 is predominantly classical, with a
scattering of patristic and other texts. Cicero and the poets, both in Latin
and in the vernacular (Dante and Petrarch), are well represented, often by
more than one copy of the same text. There are four copies of Virgil, but only
one of them contains *Bucolics*, *Georgics* and *Aeneid* together, and two of
commentaries on Virgil; two copies of Dante, plus Benvenuto's commentary;
two of Petrarch, two of Terence, two of Lucan. Such duplication of texts
suggests that Sassetti had been buying any book that took his fancy rather
than systematically collecting texts that he wanted.

We now come to manuscripts known to have belonged to Sassetti which
are not identifiable in the 1462 list. A number of these were surely acquired in
the 1460s.[38] Firstly there are a few Florentine manuscripts, probably copied
in the later 1460s, which Sassetti either commissioned or bought new. There
is Aristeas, *De lxx interpretibus*, in the Latin translation by Matteo Palmieri
dedicated to Pope Paul II (el. 1464), copied by an unidentified scribe who
did further work for Sassetti later (No. 36). There is a simply produced
manuscript containing Poggio's *De varietate fortunae* and Biondo's *Roma
instaurata*. This has a note added later to say that it was commissioned by
Sassetti and cost four florins (No. 58). It is probably the earliest in date of a
series of manuscripts with similar notes, and the fact that it was specially
commissioned reflects Sassetti's interest in Roman antiquities. Finally there
are four manuscripts, three Ciceros and a Caesar, all copied by a scribe called
Hubertus who was working for the bookseller Vespasiano da Bisticci in the
early 1460s but who did a great deal of work for Sassetti, both in the 1460s
and later, as we shall see.[39] Three of these manuscripts, the Caesar and two
containing rhetorical works of Cicero (Nos. 53, 33, 34), can be dated to the
1460s, since they are copied in Hubertus' early style. The other manuscript,
containing Cicero's *Letters to Atticus*, shows a more mature hand, and it was
probably copied about 1470 (No. 32). The three Cicero manuscripts were
decorated by an illuminator whose hand does not appear elsewhere in

Sassetti's manuscripts but who was very closely associated with Vespasiano.[40] It is a reasonable inference that this first group of manuscripts was commissioned from Vespasiano.

There are several books which must have been bought second-hand and are of the same general character as those in the 1462 list but which are not identifiable in it. Probably most of these were acquired in the 1460s. All the books were copied in Italy and all are of fine quality. They include a beautiful twelfth-century copy of the Pauline epistles with gloss (No. 5); a glossed copy of Seneca's *Tragedies* dated 1368 and perhaps written in Verona (No. 17);[41] a fine fifteenth-century Venetian manuscript of Jerome's *Letters*, written in humanistic script and decorated in the style of Cristoforo Cortese (No. 3),[42] and a copy of Leonardo Bruni's *De primo bello punico* made in Milan and decorated by the Master of the *Vitae imperatorum* (No. 44).[43] There are also two comparatively new Florentine manuscripts which must nonetheless have been second-hand: Bruni's *De temporibus suis*, written about 1450–60, with the arms of the Ciampelli family, and Statius, *Thebais*, probably made about 1465–70, to judge from the decoration, but with the erased coat of arms of an owner earlier than Sassetti (Nos. 45, 19).

These manuscripts could, of course, have been acquired by Sassetti later than I have suggested (he almost certainly acquired a few second-hand manuscripts after this date).[44] But an examination of the other manuscripts that he owned suggests that his collecting policy changed radically in the early 1470s: instead of buying ready-made manuscripts he began systematically to commission new ones to complete or improve his collection. To judge from the decoration of the manuscripts concerned, most of this copying was done in the space of only two or three years. Few of the new manuscripts appear to date from much after 1475. The majority are decorated by only two illuminators, who probably worked in close association, and most of the copying was done by only three scribes: Hubertus, who copied ten manuscripts in addition to the four already mentioned;[45] Niccolò Fonzio, brother of Bartolomeo, who copied twelve manuscripts,[46] and Bartolomeo himself, who copied thirteen manuscripts.[47] There remain only eight manuscripts, copied by four other scribes, and these include the only dated one in the group, completed in February 1471–2 (No. 61).[48]

It was probably late in 1471 or early in 1472 that Sassetti took the young scholar Bartolomeo Fonzio under his wing,[49] and it is tempting to see Fonzio's influence behind the new direction that Sassetti's collecting took in the 1470s. I am in no doubt that Fonzio acted for some years as Sassetti's librarian. It has long been known that he had ready access to Sassetti's library; his annotation of and use of Sassetti's manuscripts was already noticed by Marchesi and Sabbadini.[50] A look at Sassetti's collection tells us more. First, the *ex libris*, mottoes and other notes recording prices, etc, which are found in a majority of Sassetti's manuscripts are always written in Fonzio's hand, regardless of when or where a particular manuscript was acquired. Secondly, the chief aim of Fonzio's marginal and other annotations (to be found in many of Sassetti's manuscripts, both those that he owned in about

1470 and those that he acquired later) seems to have been to facilitate Sassetti's own study of his books.[51] Sometimes Fonzio made corrections and added variants from other manuscripts, but far more often he wrote comments on the text and marginal indexes of names and subjects treated. In Sassetti's Dante (No. 64) he added summaries in Italian of the contents of each canto. In the newly commissioned copies of texts which included passages in Greek Fonzio generally wrote in the Greek, of which he often also provided a Latin translation.[52]

We can probably deduce that Fonzio was responsible for another contribution: the rationalising of the contents of Sassetti's library. The library was not to be all-inclusive—the new texts which were copied almost all fall into the categories of poetry and history which Fonzio himself declared to be Sassetti's chief interests.[53] It was probably Fonzio who weeded out the inferior or duplicate copies which appear only in the 1462 inventory and who commissioned new, perhaps more legible, manuscripts to replace some of them,[54] and to fill gaps in the collection. The fact that most of the work on the new manuscripts was done by only three scribes, including Fonzio and his brother, and only two illuminators, suggests that he organised it himself, without having recourse to a bookseller such as Vespasiano da Bisticci. Some of the new manuscripts produced were 'portmanteau' volumes in which a number of shortish texts on a similar subject were put together. These collections include speeches extracted from classical authors and a series of lives of classical philosophers and poets (Nos. 30, 67). Some of these collections apparently existed already.[55] To compile others Fonzio probably drew on his own *zibaldoni*, or notebooks, into which over the years he copied rare texts and items which attracted his interest.[56] A manuscript listed below (No. 77) may represent a middle stage in the process of collecting the texts together. It originally contained Pellegrino Allio's translation of the *Vita Homeri*, and Allio's own Latin poems, copied by an unidentified scribe. To these Fonzio added, in his own hand, further collections of lives, including P. C. Decembrio's lives of poets and Pomponio Leto's life of Lucan. The Decembrio and Leto lives are both to be found in Fonzio's *zibaldoni*.[57] All the lives collected in the manuscript (but not Allio's poems) were included in a manuscript copied for Sassetti by Hubertus (No. 67).

Hubertus copied all the large collections, including Cicero's philosophical works, and a number of other substantial texts, such as Aulus Gellius, Josephus, and Quintilian (the last-named copied from the 1470 printed edition: No. 27). Niccolò Fonzio copied mostly history and geography, much of it in recent Latin translations from the Greek,[58] also original works by Filelfo and Galeotto Marzio. Bartolomeo Fonzio concentrated on the poets, including Petrarch. The only manuscript in prose that he copied included Francesco Griffolini's Latin translation of the letters of Pseudo-Phalaris, a popular text which he had himself translated into Italian a few years before.[59]

The *ex libris* which Fonzio added to Sassetti's manuscripts are of several kinds. First, and by far the most common, is 'FRANCISCI SASSETTI[60] THOMAE

FILII CIVIS FLORENTINI', always accompanied by Sassetti's motto, 'MITIA FATA MIHI'. This is found in at least twenty-six manuscripts,[61] always written on a flyleaf, sometimes at the beginning of the manuscript, more often at the end. These manuscripts include all those that Sassetti probably acquired in France and the north and all the second-hand Italian manuscripts that he appears to have acquired during his early years in Florence. It seems that Fonzio added this *ex libris* to most of the manuscripts that he found when he first took charge of Sassetti's library. Only three manuscripts probably or certainly datable to the 1470s have the *ex libris*. One is the copy of Aristotle's *Politics* in Latin, dated February 1471–2 (No. 61). Another is the copy of Aristotle's *Ethics* in Latin (No. 60). These manuscripts both have borders incorporating Sassetti's emblems, and are decorated by the same artist, Antonio di Niccolò di Lorenzo, one of the two illuminators who did most of the work for Sassetti which I would attribute to the early 1470s.[62] Since these manuscripts have this particular *ex libris* they may be the earliest of the '1470s' group. The third manuscript, the collection of astronomical texts (*Aratea*, etc: No. 65), I attribute to the 1470s with some hesitation. It could be earlier, but the star diagrams appear to have been executed by Bartolomeo Fonzio, probably at the time that the manuscript was made.

The other common *ex libris* is 'FRANCISCVS SASSETTVS[63] THOMAE FILIVS (CIVIS FLORENTINVS)[64] FACIVNDVM CVRAVIT'. It is found now in eleven manuscripts,[65] but may originally have been in more.[66] It is always written on an end flyleaf, and it is always accompanied by one of two mottoes, either 'MITIA FATA MIHI' (six times) or 'SORS PLACIDA MIHI' (five times).[67] The exception, with no motto, is the manuscript of Poggio and Biondo already mentioned. This note, which I am sure should be taken to mean that Sassetti commissioned a manuscript for his own use, not acting for others as an entrepreneur as has sometimes been suggested, is found in two types of manuscript. Firstly there are four manuscripts which, to judge from the style of their script and decoration, are unlikely to have been copied later than about 1470. These are the manuscript of Poggio and Biondo, and three manuscripts of works of Cicero copied by Hubertus (Nos. 58, 32–4). The second group consists of four 'later' manuscripts copied by Hubertus (three of them being of the 'portmanteau' type) and three copied by Niccolò Fonzio (Nos. 6, 27, 30, 47, 50, 67, 68). The 'early' manuscripts were perhaps given this *ex libris* by Fonzio to distinguish them from 'new' manuscripts already in Sassetti's collection when he took over which had not been commissioned specially. Sassetti must have provided Fonzio with records of his purchases, for a number of the *ex libris* are accompanied by longer notes written by Fonzio in minuscule and, alas, usually completely erased.[68] The few surviving or partly legible examples[69] show that the notes recorded the price paid by Sassetti for the manuscript and sometimes other information as well. The best example is the note in the Filargirius (No. 26): 'Hic Servius quem e Gallia mecum attuli pretii est aureorum largorum quindecim— duc. xv.'[70]

Six '1470s' manuscripts, three of them copied by Niccolò and two by Bartolomeo Fonzio, have, or once had, the simple *ex libris* FRANCISCI SASSETTI written by Bartolomeo on the front flyleaf.[71] This leaves eleven manuscripts copied by Bartolomeo, four by Niccolò and five by Hubertus with no *ex libris* at all.[72] In some cases, but not always, this may be because flyleaves have been lost. Some of the manuscripts with no *ex libris* are late, and were perhaps copied after Fonzio had left Sassetti's service. Others have decoration which incorporates Sassetti's emblems as well as his arms, and perhaps it was considered that the manuscripts did not need further identification.

Six manuscripts have on the verso of their front flyleaves, in addition to one of the *ex libris* described above, elaborate painted designs.[73] Some of these pages are fully painted, some are executed in pen and wash, but using gold as well (plate 9.3). No two are exactly alike but the designs all incorporate certain features: 'FRANCISCI SASSETTI' in a roundel, a scroll with the motto 'A MON POVOIR', never found with Sassetti's ordinary *ex libris*, and the family emblem of pebble or stone ('sasso') in a sling of David, drawn to look rather like a basket, with its cords twisting upwards to form part of the design. The page in Sassetti's copy of Aristotle's *Ethics* (No. 60) is especially elaborate. It is painted to simulate a piece of parchment pinned to the page, and the sling is supported on either side by a centaur, Sassetti's assertive emblem to match the proud French motto, which is found repeatedly in the decoration of his chapel in Santa Trinità (*c.* 1480–6) but only once elsewhere in his manuscripts.[74] The Aristotle, and Sassetti's copy of Bruni's *History* of Florence, perhaps new when the special pages were painted in, but the other manuscripts—the two volumes of Cicero's letters, the *De oratore* and the Caesar—are all earlier. There may have been similar *ex libris* pages, now lost, in other manuscripts, but probably not many. These texts must have been ones by which Sassetti set special store. I suspect that some, perhaps all, of these decorative pages were painted by Bartolomeo Fonzio. There are similarities of detail in some of the drawings in the autograph of his epigraphical collection, in the drawing of 'Calumny' in the presentation copy of his Italian translation of Lucian's *De calumnia*, and in the astronomical drawings in Sassetti's *Aratea*, in which the names and other written matter are certainly in Fonzio's hand.[75]

Sassetti's French motto A MON POVOIR, used in these *ex libris* pages, is also found in the illuminated borders of five of his manuscripts.[76] Three of these were apparently decorated in the 1470s, but two (Nos. 23, 71A) are probably later. Two of the manuscripts were decorated by Antonio di Niccolò di Lorenzo, who was probably the first artist to include Sassetti's emblems in his borders. Indeed, most of the borders which include the emblems are attributable to him. His borders are generally quite simple, and the Sassetti emblems are so subtly incorporated into the design that it is easy to overlook them. The *putti* playing in the borders or flanking the coat of arms carry (and sometimes use) slings. Often the ropes of the sling are used as an edging to the coat of arms, with the sling holding its pebble hanging below;[77] occasionally interlaced slings frame the coat of arms, in the roundel where normally one would find a laurel wreath (Nos. 16, 18, 57); once a pattern of slings runs all along the bottom border (No. 60). Antonio was fond of including animals in his borders but surprisingly he only once used Sassetti's emblem of the centaur: a pair flank the coat of arms in one of the few really elaborate borders that he painted for Sassetti—in the collection of speeches from classical authors (No. 30). One of the striking features of Sassetti's manuscripts, when compared, for example, with those being prepared for members of the Medici family in the same years, is the simplicity of their decoration. Only six of the manuscripts, two of them very late, have painted borders filling all four margins of the first page of text,[78] although such borders were a commonplace in the manuscripts which were being produced at this time for rich collectors. Six more manuscripts, four of them late, have first pages with quite elaborate decoration, but only in three margins.[79] Only one of these manuscripts, a late one, has a painted title page which formed part of the original decoration,[80] as opposed to the added *ex libris* pages which have already been discussed.

Most of Sassetti's '1470s' manuscripts are simply decorated with borders on three sides in the humanistic 'vine stem' style, a few have transitional borders, mixing the vine-stem style and the new flower style which was soon to replace it, and a few have borders of flowers only. The decoration of seventeen manuscripts can be attributed with some confidence to Antonio di Niccolò di Lorenzo.[81] In almost all these manuscripts Antonio includes Sassetti emblems in the decoration. By an odd contrast another fine artist, who to judge from his style was closely associated with Antonio, decorated possibly eleven manuscripts for Sassetti[82] but never used any of his emblems. Several other illuminators, one of whom may have been associated with Antonio, decorated one or two each of the 'early 1470s' manuscripts, and occasionally included Sassetti's emblems.[83] A few of the manuscripts copied by Hubertus and Niccolò Fonzio have later-looking decoration which one would attribute to the mid- or late 1470s. One of these (No. 67) was decorated by Antonio di Niccolò; the decoration of three, all bearing Sassetti emblems, is attributable to the priest Ser Benedetto di Silvestro;[84] one was decorated by Francesco Rosselli and one by a follower of his.[85] There are in addition two manuscripts which may have been copied as late as the 1480s—the splendid large *Aenid* perhaps decorated by Boccardino Vecchio (No. 23), and the small *Aeneid* copied by Bartolomeo Fonzio (No. 71A).

By the mid 1470s, it seems, Sassetti's library had assumed its final form. After this there were to be only occasional second-hand purchases,[86] the odd new commission such as the Virgil, and of course dedication copies of their works presented by his humanist friends.[87] Two small works of this kind, by Antonio Benivieni and Filelfo, survive in what may be the dedication copies (Nos. 79, 80). Oddly enough, both are concerned with means of combating the plague, and were presumably composed during the plague which broke out in 1478. It is not clear for how long Sassetti's special protégé, Bartolomeo Fonzio, remained closely associated with his household, but it was probably until at least 1478. In that year Fonzio's edition of Celsus, the *editio princeps*, was printed in Florence by Niccolò di Lorenzo (Hain 4835). In his preface to the edition Fonzio said that Sassetti had helped him to get hold of manuscripts to supplement the mutilated text that was available to him, including 'vetusta exemplaria e Gallia conquisita'. The meaning of this phrase has long been debated. Fonzio used no manuscripts from France, but he did use the ancient Laur. 73, 1, which Sassetti probably borrowed for him from Bologna, where it then was.[88] Fonzio may have been acting as tutor to Sassetti's young sons in the 1470s, in addition to his other activities, for in April 1478 he wrote to the merchant Francesco Gaddi in Rome, reminding him of ancient coins which he had promised to send to Cosimo Sassetti (b. 1463).[89] Fonzio was described as a teacher ('rhetoricae professor') in the notarial protocols of his friend Piero Cennini when he appeared as a witness in 1479.[90] He certainly had private pupils later.[91] His close ties with the Sassetti family, though not his friendship, had probably ended by 1481, when he was appointed to a public lectureship in the *Studio*.[92]

Sassetti had large investments in the various branches of the Medici bank, and his personal fortune seems to have been seriously affected by the crisis in the affairs of the bank in the late 1480s.[93] At just this time, in 1487 or 1488, the humanist Taddeo Ugoleto came to Florence looking for manuscripts that he could buy for King Matthias Corvinus of Hungary.[94] By the time Sassetti left for Lyons in May 1488 to try and save the Medici branch there, he had sold Ugoleto his ancient manuscript of Martial, and an ancient Valerius Flaccus as well.[95] These two manuscripts appear never to have reached the king's collection, but a number of fifteenth-century manuscripts which had once belonged to Sassetti did reach it.[96] The probability is that these manuscripts were sold to Ugoleto for the king at the same time as the others. The manuscripts which certainly entered the Corvinus library include those containing the three 'portmanteau' collections of history, and the collected philosophical works of Cicero. All are comparatively late manuscripts which Sassetti may not have minded parting with but which would have been useful to anyone building up a library.

In 1491, the year after Sassetti's death, his heirs handed over ('commodaverunt') to Lorenzo de' Medici some sixty-seven manuscripts; not his entire collection as it then survived, but probably a large proportion of it. As a result the manuscripts were confiscated with the Medici private library after Piero de' Medici's flight from Florence in 1494, and were included in the inventory of the confiscated Medici books deposited in San Marco which was made in October 1495. In February 1497/8 Bartolomeo Fonzio succeeded in claiming these sixty-seven manuscripts back on behalf of the Sassetti heirs, and they were deleted from the inventory.[97] They include a high proportion of the still identifiable Sassetti manuscripts which had remained in Florence. Only nine are missing of those that he probably still owned at the time of his death;[89] the most notable absentees are the Filargirius and the Augustine, *De civitate dei*. There were probably not many more. The 1495 inventory included some Sassetti manuscripts now lost or still unidentified:

Asconius Pedianus, the *Rhetorica ad Herennium*, Calpurnius Siculus (this already appeared in the 1462 list), two volumes of commentaries on Dante, and second copies of Seneca's Tragedies and Dionysius Halicarnassus.[99] The latter was perhaps a copy of Lampugnano Birago's complete translation, dedicated to Pope Paul II. Sassetti's known copy is of the incomplete version dedicated to Pope Nicholas V.[100] Another manuscript listed as 'Vita Homeri ex Herodoto et quedam alia' is probably identifiable with No. 77 below, which has not previously been associated with Sassetti.

The later history of the Sassetti books is not clear at present. Certainly most of them, at least sixty-two, passed into the Medici collection and so were kept together. It has been said that Francesco's second son Cosimo (d. 1527) gave these manuscripts to the Medici Pope, Clement VII.[101] If this is so, it may be that he was really making restitution to the Medici family for the books that had been claimed back by Fonzio in February 1497/8, for we do not know under what conditions—pledge, sale, loan or gift—these had originally been handed over to Lorenzo.[102] Whatever the truth may be, not all Sassetti's manuscripts were handed over, for at least two, the Dante and Petrarch, still belonged to the Sassetti family in the mid-sixteenth century.[103] It may be significant that they are both texts in the *volgare*.[104]

Sassetti's collection as we now know it was not large by the standards of his time. If one adds up all the manuscripts, identified and unidentified, that he is known to have owned at any time the total is still only just over 120 volumes, scarcely more than the number of identified manuscripts owned by Coluccio Salutati nearly a century before.[105] The total number of manuscripts owned by Sassetti was probably in fact rather larger than the sum of those known to us, for he may have sold other manuscripts, now lost, to Matthias Corvinus,[106] and perhaps to other collectors as well. We must also remember that the 1495 inventory did not include all the manuscripts that he still owned at the time of his death. Yet it is clear that his library was choice rather than large. He owned some ancient manuscripts whose rarity or beauty would have made any library outstanding—the Filargirius and the Martial, the Sacramentary and the Augustine—and many other handsome manuscripts written in more recent times, apart from those that he had commissioned himself. His newly commissioned manuscripts are not ostentatiously decorated—those later acquired by Corvinus stand out in the Corvinus library because of their comparative simplicity—but they are all on parchment. Indeed, the few manuscripts in Sassetti's list of 1462 which were then specified as being on paper appear to have been weeded out or replaced later.[107] No printed books once owned by Sassetti are known to me,[108] and it may be that he deliberately avoided collecting them, despite the links of his friend Fonzio with several printers.[109] Why else did he have his manuscript Quintilian (No. 27) copied from Campanus' printed edition? Clearly not because he could not afford to buy the latter. It could be, though it seems unlikely, that he could not find a copy for sale. The less precious parts of Sassetti's library, strong in fields in which he was especially interested, seem to have been intended to be used while at the same time giving a discreet pleasure, with their decorous script and decoration. It is clear from the manuscripts themselves that they really were used. Sassetti does not appear to have owned any manuscripts in Greek, but he owned many Greek texts in Latin translation. This fits the functional aim of his library that I have suggested: he clearly knew Latin and was sufficiently in the humanist swim to want his Latin texts in the original, but he is unlikely to have had an opportunity to learn Greek. Fonzio translated several texts into Italian[110] but none was intended for Sassetti, whose name, 'Saxettus', was used instead as the title for Fonzio's collection of Latin poems.[111] More than one contemporary praised Sassetti for the devotion he showed to study despite his business cares,[112] and it seems that such praise was not mere hyperbole. Indeed, it may be that he should have been criticised for devoting too much time to his studies instead of attending to his business!

APPENDIX 9.1

LIST OF SASSETTI'S MANUSCRIPTS IN NOVEMBER 1462

(Archivio di Stato, Florence, Carte Strozziane, ser. II, 20, Ricordanze of Francesco Sassetti. Printed by J.-F. Bergier, 'Humanisme et vie d'affaires . . .' in *Mélanges F. Braudel*, I, 1973, pp. 117–18. I shall note my principal divergences from his edition, citing his readings as B. The numbering on the left has been added for convenience of reference.)

f. 3*v*

+Mcccc°lxii

Libri in latino. Ci troviamo deono dare per li infrascripti libri stimati questo di*a* p[rim]o di novembre

(1)[113]	1°Agostino de civitate dei di lett. anticha bellissimo*b* coperto di chuoyo azurro	fl. 40
(2)	3 volumi della esposition[e] di Dante di Benvenuto da Imola coperti*c* di rosso	fl. 30
(3)[114]	1 Marziale [*sic*] Capella fornito anticho	fl. 10
(4)	1 altro Marziale coperto di biancho	fl. 6
(5)[115]	1 Vetruvio et Chato de Re Rusticha et Marco Varro de agricoltura coperto di rosso	fl. 10
(6)	1 Paolo Orosio in lett. longonbarde	fl. 4
(7)	1 libro d'orationi di Tulio costo fl. 25 la(rghi)*d*	fl. 30
(8)[116]	1 libro di pistole*e* di Tulio	fl. 15
(9)[117]	1 S[er]vio*f* grande sopra tutte l'opere di Vergilio	fl. 15
(10)	1 altro S[er]vio*f* in papiero sopra l'Eneida*g*	fl. 8
(11)[118]	1 Lattantio coperto di rosso	fl. 10
(12)[119]	1 messale antichissimo	fl. 6
(13)[120]	3 libri cioe—1° Boetio d[e] consolatio[ne] fl. 4,	
(14)	1° Macchobrio [*sic*] de saturnalibus fl. 6	
(15)	1° comento sopra.lla rettoricha d[i] Tulio in papiero fl. 2 In t[utt]o	fl. 12
(16)	1 V[er]gilio coperto di rosso cioe l'Eneidos	fl. 6
(17)	1 Diodoro Sichulo di Poggio coperto di paonazzo	fl. 15
(18)[121]	1 de casibus virorum illustrium del Bocchaccio	fl. 8
(19, [122] 20[122])	2 libri di Terentio, 1° bianco 1° paonazzo	fl. 12
(21,[123] 22[124])	II 1° Prisciano anticho fl. 6, 1° Luchano v[ecchi]o fl. 1	fl. 7

(*a*) die B. (*b*) bellissima B. (*c*) coperto B. (*d*) id est B. (*e*) d'espistole B. (*f*) F[ilargi]-rio B. (*g*) Eneide B.

(23)[125]	1 Marziale chuocho[a] anticho coperto di rosso	fl. 6
(24)[126]	1 Tulio de finibus bonorum et malorum	fl. 4
(25)[127]	1 Arator in versi con molte cose	fl. 4
(26)	1 Salustio coperto di rosso	fl. 2
(27,[128] 28[129])	11 1º Vegietio et Frontino, 1º de bello gotorum	fl. 9
(29)[130]	1 de primo bello punico	fl. 4
(30)	1 V[er]gilio Eneidos piccholino coperto d[i] rosso	fl. 6
(31)	1 Tulio de offitiis coperto di rosso	fl. 5
(32, 33)	8 1º Ovidio de arte amandi fl. 3, 1º Beda fl. 3,	
(34,[131] 35)	1º Tulio de tuschulanis fl. 4, 1º Oratio fl. 3,	
(36, 37,[132] 38)	1 Statio fl. 3, 1º Claudiani [sic][b] fl. 2, 1º V[er]gilio	
(39)	anticho fl. 2, 1º Tibullo fl. 1º. In [tutt]o	fl. 21
(40)	1 vangielista et appochalisse	fl. 3
(41,[133] 42[134])	4 1º Luchano anticho fl. 3, 1ª buccholicha con[c] gieorgicha	
(43,[135] 44[136])	fl. 3, 1ª buccholicha d[i] Calfurno[d] fl. 2, 1ª[e] spera fl. 2,	
(45[137])	1º de amicitia et sene[c]tute fl. 2	fl. 12
(46, 47[138])	4 1º Persio fl. 1, 1º d[i] Fr[ancesc]o d'Arezzo de calum-	
(48, 49[139])	pnia fl. 1, 1ª carta da navichare fl. 4, 1º licano[f] fl. 5	fl. 11
(50[140])	1 Romoleon delle storie di Roma	fl. 15
(51)	1 Salterio coperto di velluto nero	fl. 12
(52)	1 altro Salterio coperto di verde	fl. 4
(53)	1 libriccino di donna fatto in Francia	fl. 7
(54)	1 libriccino di storie[g] abreviato con Regola[g]	fl. 1

Somma in tutto vaglono i detti libri stimati e rivisti detto
di[h] primo di novembre posti[j] in questo a[c] 2   fl. 370

f. 4

+ Mcccc°lxii

Libri schritti di contro deono avere adi[k] x di novembre 1472
fl. ccclxx posto valsente debbi dare in questo a[c] 2 pe' libri
dirinpetto de' quali si fene poi altro inventario e altro
ritratto com'appare al mio libro bianco coperto di chuoyo
a[c] 51—fl. ccclxx

f. 4v

+ Mcccc°lxii[l]

Libri in volgare. Ci troviamo deono dare per li infrascritti
libri stimati questo di[m] primo di novembre

(55)[141]	1º Dante bello coperto di rosso	fl. 10
(56)	1 Petrarcha coperto di rosso	fl. 4
(57)[142]	1 de trionphi coperto di paonazzo	fl. 1
(58)	1 de primo bello punico in papiero	fl. 1
(59)[143]	1 libro di Tristano[n] in francioxo[o]	fl. 1
(60)[144]	1 libro della phisicha d'Aristotele in francioso[p]	fl. 3
(61)	1 Dante piccholino	fl. 1

Somma in tutto vaglono i detti libri fl. xxi stimati detto
di[m] primo di novembre posti[q] in questo a[c] 2   fl. xxi

f. 5

+ Mcccclxii

Libri schritti di contro deono avere adi[k]x di novembre 1472
fl. xxi posto valsente debbi dare in questo a[c] 2 pe' libri

(a) Marziale, chuocho B. (b) Claudiano B. (c) et B. (d) Calfurnio B. (e) 1º B. (f) sic
leg. litano? (g) 'Peu lisible' B. (h) die B. (j) posto B. (k) a die B. (l) Mccccxii B.
(m) die B. (n) Justiano B. (o) franciexo B. (p) francieso B. (q) posto B.

dirinpetto de' quali faremo questo di altro inventario e
altro ritratto com'appare al mio libro biancho coperto d[i]
chuoyo a[c] 51   fl. xxi

APPENDIX 9.2

THE SASSETTI MANUSCRIPTS INCLUDED IN THE 1495 INVENTORY
OF THE MEDICI BOOKS

(Taken from E. S. Piccolomini's edition (*Arch. stor. ital.*, third series, xx, 1874, 51–80)
of the inventory made 20 October 1495 of the Medici books consigned to S. Marco.
The entries for the sixty-seven Sassetti MSS were deleted when they were reclaimed for
the family in February 1497/8. The first numbers are the running numbers given to
the items in the Medici inventory by Piccolomini. The numbers in brackets at the
ends of items refer to the list of MSS in appendix 9.3 below. Piccolomini based his
edition on the copy of the inventory in the Archivio di Stato, Florence, Archivio
Mediceo avanti il Principato, Filz. LXXXVII. I have noted the more important
divergences in the copy in Filz. LXXXIV, 273, the only copy that I have seen. This is
the copy with Bartolomeo Fonzio's autograph note of receipt of sixty-seven Sassetti
books, dated 16 February 1497(/8) on f. 438*v* (Piccolomini, document XVI: *Arch. stor.
ital.*, third series, XIX, 1874, 288).)

(Piccolomini, p. 63—'Sexta Capsa')

(241)   626[a] Valerius Flaccus, in menbranis—La. [*i.e. in Latin*] (No. 25)

(Piccolomini, p. 70—'Decima Capsa')

(436)   —Arator in Bibliam in carminibus[b] in menbranis. n. 734—La. (No. 54)
(440)   —Anticlaudianus (in LXXXIV and CIV only), n. 733—La. (No. 11)

(Piccolomini, p. 73,—'Capsa XIII')

(511)   735 Victruvius de Architectura in menbranis[c]—La. (No. 7)

(Piccolomini, pp. 74–6—'In primo scrinio nigro hoc est in eadem Capsa 14[a]'.
Piccolomini says that in Filz. CIV is a note that all the cancelled books in this chest
were returned to Bartolomeo Fonzio, acting for the sons of Francesco Sassetti, 16
February 1497/8. In Filz. LXXXIV, 273, f. 436*v*, the note 'Saxetti' has been added
at the beginning of the section.)

(528)   Lucretius in menbranis sine numero—La.   (No. 13)
(529)   Epistole[d] Hieronymi, in menbranis, absque numero—La.   (No. 3)
(530)   Boetius de consolatione, in menbranis, absque numero—La.   (No. 59)
(531)   Ovidius de arte amandi[e], in menbranis, absque numero—La.   (No. 15)
(533)   Quintus Curtius, in menbranis absque numero—La.   (No. 41)
(534)   Scipionis et Hanibalis vite per Donatum Acciaiuolum translate[f]—La.   (No.
        51)
(535)   Polytica Aristotelis per Donatum Acciaiuolum translata[g], in menbranis,
        absque numero—La.   (No. 61)
(536)   Virgilii Eneys, in menbranis, volumine magno et pulchro, sine numero[h]—La.
        (No. 23)
(537)   Phalaridis epistole in volumine parvo, in menbranis[j], translate per Fran-
        ciscum Aretinum—La.   (No. 29)

(*a*) *corr. to* 627 *in LXXXIV.* (*b*) *in carminibus om. LXXXIV.* (*c*) . . . *gallicis litteris LXXXIV.* (*d*) . . . *sancti LXXXIV* (*e*) *de arte amandi om. LXXXIV.* (*f*) . . . *in
membranis LXXXIV.* (*g*) *per Leonardum translata LXXXIV.* (*h*) *volumine . . . numero
om. LXXXIV. The omission of* sine *or* absque numero, *usual in LXXXIV, has not normally
been noted.* (*j*) *in volumine . . . membranis om. LXXXIV.*

(538) Lactantius, in menbranis—La. (No. 4)

(539) Cicero de natura deorum, in menbranis[a] (No. 62)

(541) Iosephus de bello iudaico, in menbranis—La. (No. 46)

(542) Plautus in pergameno[b]—La. (No. 16)

(543) Historia rerum Romanorum, a quodam iuniore scripta ignoto auctore,[c] in pulcro volumine in menbranis—La. (No. 48)

(544) Comentaria primi belli punici Leonardi Aretini in menbranis.—La. (No. 43 or 44)

(545) Fragmentum Arati translatum, in menbranis.—La. (No. 65)

(546) Vegetius de re militari, in menbranis.—La. (No. 75?)

(547) Livii prima decas, in menbranis—La. (No. 37)

(548) Conciones Titi Livii, excerte, in pulcro volumine[d] et alia quedam,[e] in menbranis—La. (No. 30)

(549) Lucanus, cum glosulis, in menbranis—La. (No. 74?)

(550) Senece tragedie, in menbranis—La.

(551) Iustinus historicus,[f] in menbranis—La. (No. 47)

(552) Poggius de varietate fortune, in menbranis—La. (No. 58)

(553) Silius Italicus, in menbranis—La. (No. 18)

(554) Claudianus poeta,[g] in menbranis—La. (No. 9)

(555) Priscianus, codex antiquus,[h] in menbranis—La. (No. 28)

(557)[j] Epistole Platonis per Leonardum Aretinum[k] translate, in menbranis—La. (No. 57)

(558) Cicero, orator,[l] in menbranis—La. (No. 33)

(561) Comentaria primi belli punici, per Leonardum, in pergameno[m]—La. (No. 43 or 44)

(562) Cicero de oratore, in menbranis—La. (No. 34)

(563) Cicero de finibus bonorum et malorum, in menbranis—La. (No. 55)

(564) Catullus et Propertius, in menbranis—La. (No. 10)

(567) Asconius Pedianus in orationes Ciceronis.[n]

(569) Tusculanae Ciceronis, in menbranis.[o] (No. 56)

(570) Dyonisii Alicarnasei, originum Romani populi, translatus,[p] in menbranis—La. (No. 52?)

(573) Sylve Statii, in pergameno[q]—La. (No. 20)

(574) Rhetorica Ciceronis ad Herennium, in menbranis—La.

(575) Mathei Palmerii florentini[r] de septuaginta interpretibus, in menbranis—La. (No. 36)

(579) Vita Homeri ex Herodoto translata et quedam alia, in menbranis—La. (No. 77?)

(583) Leonardi Aretini de temporibus suis, in pergameno[s]—La. (No. 45)

(586) Calphurnii egloge,[t] in menbranis—La.

(Piccolomini, pp. 76–9. 'Capsa xv id est in 2° scrinio nigro'. Filz. LXXXIV: 'Saxetti'.)

(597) Historie florentine[u] Leonardi Aretini, in menbranis. (No. 42)

(598) Danthes florentinus,[v] in menbranis—Vulgare.[w] (No. 64)

(599) Comentum super Danthem, in menbranis—Vulgare.[w]

(a) ... —La. *LXXXIV*. (b) ... in membranis *LXXXIV*. (c) ignoto auctore *om. LXXXIV. In margin:* Credo esse Romuleum. (d) in pulcro volumine *om. LXXXIV*. (e) *For* quedam *LXXXVI and CIV read* in Rhetoricis. (f) historicus *om. LXXXIV*. (g) poeta *om. LXXXIV*. (h) codex antiquus *om. LXXXIV*. (j) *556 is not noted as uncancelled by Piccolomini, but is not cancelled in LXXXIV and is not identifiable among Sassetti's surviving books.* (k) Aretinum *om. LXXXIV*. (l) de oratore *LXXXIV, clearly a mistake.* (m) in membranis *LXXXIV*. (n) ... in membr.—La. *LXXXIV*. (o) ... La. *LXXXIV*. (p) translatus *om. LXXXIV*. (q) in membranis *LXXXIV*. (r) Mattheus Palmerius *LXXXIV*. (s) in m[embranis] *LXXXIV*. (t) Calphurnius eglogarum *LXXXIV*. (u) florentinorum *LXXXIV*. (v) florentinus, *om. LXXXIV*. (w) Vulgare *om. LXXXIV*.

(600)   Commentaria Caesaris, in menbranis.   (No. 53)
(601)   Livius de bello macedonico, in menbranis—La.[a]   (No. 39)
(602)   Livius de secundo bello punico, in menbranis—La.   (No. 38)
(603)   Tucidides translatus a Laurentio Valla.[b]   (No. 40)
(604)   Statii Thebay,[c] in menbranis—La   (No. 19)
(607)   Herodotus translatus a Laurentio Valla,[d] in menbranis—La.   (No. 49)
(608)   Expositio in tertiam partem Danthis, in menbranis—La.
(609)   Ethyca Aristotelis translata ab[e] Argyropolo, in menbranis—La.   (No. 60)
(611)   Diodorus Syculus per Poggium translatus, in menbranis—La.   (No. 50)
(612)   Epistole Pauli apostoli[f] cum glosulis, in menbranis—La.   (No. 5)
(614)   Tragedie Senece et[g] cum glosulis, in menbranis—La.   (No. 17)
(615)   Ciceronis epistole ad Attichum, in menbranis—La.   (No. 32)
(616)   Francisci Phylelphi convivia, in menbranis—La.   (No. 35)
(618)   Quintilianus, in menbranis—La.   (No. 27)
(623)   Manlii Astronomicon Liber ad Cesarem Agustum,[h] in menbranis—La. (No. 8)
(624)   Liber[j] Galeotti[k] de homine, in menbranis—La.   (No. 63)
(625)   Terentius latinus,[l] in menbranis—La.   (No. 21 or 22)
(641)   Leonardus de bello Goctorum, in menbranis—La.   (No. 76?)
(667)[m] Dyonisii Alicarnassei de origine Rome, in menbranis—La.   (No. 52?)

(a) La. om. *LXXXIV both here and subsequently*. (b) Valensi in m(embranis) *LXXXIV*.
(c) Thebais Statii *LXXXIV*. (d) Valensi *LXXXIV*. (e) translata om. *LXXXIV and per
for* ab. (f) apostoli om. *LXXXIV*. (g) et om. *LXXXIV*. (h) ad Cesarem Agustum *om
LXXXIV*. (j) Liber om. *LXXXIV*. (k) Galeottus *LXXXIV*. (l) latinus om. *LXXXIV*.
(m) Piccolomini (p. 76, n. 2) lists No. 657 as the last of the deleted items, but this was
probably a mistake for 667, which is deleted in LXXXIV at least.

APPENDIX 9.3
THE SURVIVING COLLECTION OF SASSETTI

A   *Types of* ex libris *and mottoes*

These are written in capitals by Bartolomeo Fonzio, with the exception of type (vi).

(i)   FRANCISCI SASSETTI (*or, rarely,* SAXETTI) THOMAE FILII CIVIS FLORENTINI. Cited in
descriptions as FSTFCF. See Nos. 1–5, 7, 11, 17, 19, 21–2, 24, 26, 28, 43–5, 48, 54–6,
59–61, 64–5.

(ii)   FRANCISCVS SASSETTVS THOMAE FILIVS (CIVIS FLORENTINVS *or vice versa*) FACIUNDVM
CVRAVIT. Cited as FSTF(CF *or* FC)FC. See Nos. 6, 27, 30, 32–4, 47, 50, 58, 67, 68.

(iii)   FRANCISCI SASSETTI (*or*, rarely, SAXETTI). Cited as FS. See Nos. 16, 25, 42, 49, 52, 71.
Also found in flyleaf designs: see p. 168 above.

(iv)   MITIA FATA MIHI. Cited as MFM. See Nos. 1–6, 7, 11, 17, 19, 21–2, 24, 26–8, 30, 36,
43–5, 48, 53–6, 58–61, 64–5, 67–8, 70.

(v)   SORS PLACIDA MIHI. Cited as SPM. See Nos. 32–4, 47, 50.

(vi)   A MON POVOIR. Cited as AMP. Found only in illuminated borders and painted
flyleaf *ex libris* designs. See Nos. 23, 27, 31–2, 34, 40, 42, 53, 60–1, 71A.

B   *Manuscripts certainly from Sassetti*

MSS that I have seen are marked *. MSS of which I have seen photographs or reproduc-
tions are marked †. 1462 = the list of Sassetti's books in appendix 9.1. 1495 = the
Medici list; see appendix 9.2. BBB = the MS was described for me by Bruce Barker-
Benfield. Bandini = A. M. Bandini, *Catalogus codicum latinorum Bibliothecae Mediceae
Laurentianae*, five vols., Florence, 1774–78. D'Ancona = P. D'Ancona, *La miniatura
fiorentina*, 1914, II (descriptions of MSS). All MSS except No. 79 are on parchment.

†(1) *Bologna, Biblioteca Universitaria 1084*, Sacramentary (A. Ebner, *Quellen und Forschungen zur Gesch. und Kunstgesch. des Missale in Mittelalter. Iter italicum*, Freiburg im Breisgau, 1896, pp. 6–12, with plates; L. Frati in *Studi ital. di filol. class.* XVI, 1908, 306, No. 588 (wrongly described as Gallican Missal); R. Bauerreiss, 'Bayerische Handschriften der Jahrtausendwende in Italien, I', *Studien und Mitteilungen zur Gesch. des Bened. ordens* LXX, 1959, 187–8; Sabbadini, addenda to *Scoperte*, I, p. 165, in new edition, 1967, p. 273). Early eleventh century. Made at Regensburg, perhaps for the nunnery of Niedermunster. 189 leaves, 295 × 205 mm. Fine illuminated pages. Folio 189, in Fonzio's hand: 'Hoc Missale quod e Gallia mecum attuli pretii est aureorum largorum [... *longish erasure*]. MFM. FSTFCF.' 1462 No. 12: fl. 6. Later in the private library of Pope Benedict XIV (1740–58), who gave the MS to the Bologna library in 1755. I am indebted to Dott. M. Fornieri, acting director of the library, for information about the MS.

*(2) *Florence, Biblioteca Medicea Laurenziana 12, 21*, Augustine, *De civitate Dei* (Bandini i, col. 25; A. de Laborde, *Les MSS à peintures de la Cité de Dieu*, I, 1909, p. 89; M. T. Gibson, *Journ. Theol. Studies*, new series, XX, 1971, 436). Ninth or eleventh to twelfth centuries? Region of Tours? For MSS of this kind from Angers see J. Vezin, 'Les "scriptoria" d'Angers au XIe siècle', École Nationale des Chartes, *Positions des thèses . . . 1958*, 131–8. 293 written leaves, 350 × 263 mm. Fine white parchment, regular, Tours-like script, rather barbaric illumination, including *incipit* page with portrait of Augustine. The script could be ninth-century but may be later (eleventh- or twelfth-century?), since the decoration must be later. Professor Bernhard Bischoff, in a letter and on the basis of a photographic reproduction only, described the MS to me as 'ein höchst problematisches Stück'. M. Jean Vezin (in a similar letter) pointed out links between the decoration of the MS (which appears to be original) and that of an eleventh-century MS from Tours. Folio 1v, note in Fonzio's hand, partly erased: 'Hunc vetustum emendatumque librum Augustini de civitate dei . . .' and: MFM. FSTFCF. End paste-down: '3'. 1462 No. 1: fl. 40.

*(3) *Laur. 19, 15*, Jerome, *Letters*, etc (Bandini i, col. 549–53). Venice, second quarter of the fifteenth century. 249 written leaves, 380 × 250 mm. Distinctive humanistic script. Fine initials in the style of Cristoforo Cortese (see n. 42). Some headings and notes written by Fonzio. End flyleaf, recto, longish erasure, followed by MFM. FSTFCF. End paste-down: '54'. 1495 No. 529.

*(4) *Laur. 21, 4*, Lactantius, *Div. inst., De ira dei, De opif. dei* (Bandini i, col. 664). Florence, c. 1450–60(?). 300 written leaves, 273 × 190 mm. Odd semi-humanistic script, Greek written in by Giorgio Antonio Vespucci (de la Mare, *Handwriting of Italian humanists*, I, 1, p. xvi). Simple vine-stem initials. End flyleaf, recto: MFM. FSTFCF. End paste-down: '203(?)'. A few marginalia by Bartolomeo Fonzio. 1462 No. 11: fl. 10. 1495 No. 538.

*(5) *Laur. 23, 13*, Pauline Epistles with gloss 'Pro altercatione' and other glosses, including some attributed to Lanfranc (Bandini i, col. 718; Sabbadini, *Scoperte*, I, p. 165, calls the MS French). Fine twelfth-century Italian MS. 337 written leaves, 310 × 220 mm. Some initials drawn in coloured inks (purple (mostly), green, yellow), others illuminated. Folio 338, longish erasure, followed by: MFM. FSTFCF. Traces of number on end paste-down, illegible. 1495 No. 612.

*(6) *Laur. 29, 35*, Solinus (Bandini ii, col. 53; D'Ancona No. 852). Florence, early 1470s. 137 written leaves, 240 × 155 mm. Copied by Niccolò Fonzio (see n. 46) in his cursive hand. Vine-stem initial joined to flower border with Sassetti arms, perhaps by artist of No. 9. End flyleaf, long erasure, followed by: MFM. FSTFFCFC (not noted by Bandini).

*(7) *Laur. 30, 10*, Vitruvius, Cato, Varro (Bandini ii, col. 73–4; Sabbadini, *loc. cit.*; *Mostra storica nazionale della miniatura*, Rome, 1954, No. 454 and plate XCVII; G. Billanovich in *Italia med. e um.* VII, 1964, 345–6: perhaps copied for a friend of Jean de Montreuil; M. Meiss, *French Painting in the Time of Jean de Berry*, I, 1967, p. 360, as workshop of the 'Virgil master'). France, early fifteenth-century. 117 written leaves, 388 × 280 mm. Skilled cursive book hand, fine miniatures. Folio 118, erasure, perhaps ending: 'decem aureis', followed by MFM. FSTFCF. Annotations and Greek in an Italian hand —not Fonzio. 1462 No. 5: fl. 10. 1495 No. 511.

*(8) *Laur. 30, 15*, Manilius, *Astronomicon* (Bandini ii, col. 75–6; D'Ancona No. 290). Florence, early 1470s? Ninety-four leaves, 270 × 173 mm. Copied by Bartolomeo Fonzio (see n. 47). Simple vine-stem border with Sassetti arms, perhaps by artist of No. 9. 1495 No. 623.

*(9) *Laur. 33, 1*, Claudian (Bandini ii, col. 87–9; D'Ancona No. 292). Florence, early 1470s? 188 leaves, 270 × 174 mm. Copied by Bartolomeo Fonzio. Vine-stem border with Sassetti arms, by artist close to Antonio di Niccolò di Lorenzo (see n. 82). 1495 No. 554. See plate 9.1.

*(10) *Laur. 33, 11*, Catullus, Propertius, Tibullus (Bandini ii, col. 99; D'Ancona No. 293). Florence, early 1470s? 173 leaves, 275 × 182 mm. Copied by Bartolomeo Fonzio. Vine-stem border by Antonio di Niccolò di Lorenzo (see n. 81), including *putti* with slings, Sassetti arms framed in rope with pebble below. 1495 No. 564.

*(11) *Laur. 33, 16*, Alan of Lille, *Anticlaudianus* (Bandini ii, col. 101–2). Italy or southern France? Thirteenth-century. Seventy-five written leaves, 208 × 121 mm. Fourteenth-century glosses in a French-looking hand. Folio 1v (front flyleaf): MFM. FSTFCF. End paste-down, erasure, and '82' (or '32'?). Perhaps 1462 No. 37: fl. 2. 1495 No. 440.

*(12) *Laur. 34, 2*, Horace, Juvenal, Persius (Bandini ii, col. 145–6; D'Ancona No. 296). Florence, early 1470s? 258 leaves, 270 × 183 mm. Copied by Bartolomeo Fonzio. Vine-stem border by Antonio di Niccolò di Lorenzo, with Sassetti arms as in No. 10.

*(13) *Laur. 35, 28*, Lucretius (Bandini ii, col. 209; D'Ancona No. 308). Florence, early 1470s? 143 leaves, 312 × 204 mm. Copied by Bartolomeo Fonzio. Faceted initial with pearls on decorated ground, joined to vine-stem border with Sassetti arms, perhaps by artist of No. 9. 1495 No. 528.

*(14) *Laur. 36, 1*, Ovid, *Met.* and *Fasti* (Bandini ii, col. 227; D'Ancona No. 309). Florence, 1472 or later. 240 leaves, 301 × 193 mm. Copied by Bartolomeo Fonzio. Vine-stem border by Antonio di Niccolò di Lorenzo, with *putti* with slings, Sassetti arms as in No. 10.

*(15) *Laur. 36, 2*, Ovid, *Ars amatoria*, etc (Bandini ii, col. 227–9; D'Ancona No. 310). Florence, 1472 or later. 255 leaves, 299 × 189 mm. Copied by Bartolomeo Fonzio. Vine-stem border by Antonio di Niccolò di Lorenzo, with *putti* with slings, Sassetti arms as in No. 10. 1495 No. 531.

*(16) *Laur. 36, 38*, Platus, twenty plays (Bandini ii, col. 24³; D'Ancona No. 312; BBB). Florence, early 1470s? 273 leaves, 339 × 241 mm. Copied by Niccolò Fonzio in his formal hand. Vine-stem border by Antonio di Niccolò di Lorenzo, including *putto* with sling, Sassetti arms with outer frame of slings. Front flyleaf, verso: FS. 1495 No. 542.

*(17) *Laur. 37, 6*, Seneca, *Tragedies*, with elaborate gloss written by scribe which cites Trevet (Bandini ii, col. 249–50; Sabbadini, *Scoperte*, I, p. 165, as probably French). Italy 1368(?). 189 written leaves, 270 × 202 mm. Small gothic script, illuminated initials. Folio 186, obscure colophon of scribe in verse (printed by Bandini), possibly stating that the MS was copied by or for 'Franciscus' (Minerbanus ?) from (or at the same time as) the copy of Antonio del Gaio, and completed on 6 June 1368(?). A few notes and corrections in a different fourteenth-century hand. Front flyleaf, verso: MFM. FSTFCF. 1495 No. 614.

*(18) *Laur. 37, 17*, Silius Italicus (Bandini ii, col. 255; D'Ancona No. 317). Florence, early 1470s? 227 leaves, 310 × 205 mm. Copied by Bartolomeo Fonzio. Vine-stem border by Antonio di Niccolò di Lorenzo with Sassetti arms as in No. 10 and with outer frame of interlacing slings instead of a laurel wreath. No original flyleaves. 1495 No. 553.

*(19) *Laur. 38, 2*, Statius, *Theb.*, *Achill.* (Bandini ii, col. 259–60; D'Ancona No. 860). Florence, c. 1465–75. 168 leaves, 242 × 155 mm. Humanistic cursive hand. Flower border perhaps by Ser Benedetto di Silvestro includes erased arms (not Sassetti) and *putto* holding column with scroll 'DEI VOLVNTAS'. Folio 169 (flyleaf): MFM. FSTFCF, followed by erasure beginning: 'Hunc . . .'. End paste-down: '75'. 1495 No. 604.

*(20) *Laur. 38, 13*, Statius, *Sylvae* (Bandini ii, col. 263; D'Ancona No. 318). Florence, 1472 or later. 105 leaves, 220 × 148 mm. Copied by Bartolomeo Fonzio. Vine-stem border by artist of No. 9, with Sassetti arms. 1495 No. 573.

*(21) *Laur. 38, 15*, Terence, *Comedies* (Bandini ii, col. 266–7; D'Ancona No. 319). Florence, February 1448/9. 108 written leaves, 240 × 163 mm. Distinctive humanistic hand. Folio 108, colophon in red, partly erased: 'Liber [. . . *erased part not legible now but read by Bandini as* mei Iohannis de Albizzis] quem propria manu transcriptum reddidit. Quarto nonas februarii Mº CCCCº XLVIII'. Simple vine-stem initials. Folio iiv (front flyleaf): MFM. FSTFCF. 1462 No. 19 or 20. 1495 No. 625?

*(22) *Laur. 38, 23*, Terence, *Comedies* (Bandini ii, col. 271; Sabbadini, *Scoperte*, 1, p. 165). Reggio (Emilia or Calabria?), October 1436. 111 leaves, 257 × 182 mm. Semi-humanistic hand. Folio 108v, colophon: '. . . propria manu Gabrielis de Donelis civis notariique Regini. Finis deo dante fuit imponitus anno domini Mccccxxxvi prima die octobris.' Illuminated initials in gothic style. A few corrections in an Italian gothic hand which also wrote the note at the end of the MS recording the visit of the emperor Frederick of Austria to Geneva on 23 October 1442 and departure on the 27th. End paste-down, erased notes in a French hand, not previously noticed, include: 'Martinus le Franc S.mi d.n. pape Felicis quinti secretarius prepositus Lausaneum', also '11' and erasure in Fonzio's hand ending: '. . . ducatis quatuor largis— duc. 4'. Folio iv (flyleaf): MFM. FSTFCF. 1462 No. 19 or 20. 1495 No. 625? For Martin Le Franc, c. 1410–61, best known as a French poet, see A. Piaget, *Martin Le Franc, Prévot de Lausanne*, Lausanne, 1888. He became provost of Lausanne in September 1443 and a canon of Geneva in 1447.

†(23) *Laur. 39, 6*, Virgil, *Aeneid* (Bandini ii, col. 301; D'Ancona No. 861; G. Biagi, *Cinquanta tavole in fototipia da codici della R. Bibl. Med. Laur.*, 1914, plate XXXVI; *Mostra nazionale della miniatura*, 1954, No. 485; B. L. Ullman, *The Origin and Development of Humanistic Script*, 1960, p. 122). Florence, c. 1480–90? 177 leaves, 335 × 223 mm. Fine humanistic hand, attributed by Biagi to Antonio Sinibaldi but perhaps identifiable with Alessandro Verazzano. Elaborate borders perhaps by Boccardino Vecchio, the first with acanthus, jewels, cameos, vignettes, etc, Sassetti arms, device of sling and pebble and scrolls with motto AMP incorporated in the border. 1495 No. 536.

*(24) *Laur. 39, 25*, Virgil, *Buc.* and *Georg.*; Ovid, *Ep. Sapph.* (Bandini ii, col. 312). Florence, c. 1435–45? Sixty-seven leaves, 215 × 141 mm. Good humanistic hand. Simple vine-stem initials. End paste-down: 'Francisca Gianfigliaz[i]a', written twice (fifteenth-century). Also '28'. Folio 69 (flyleaf): MFM. FSTFCF, followed by erasure. One note (f. 5) perhaps written by Sassetti and a scribble (f. 68) written by the scribe of No. 65. Probably 1462 No. 42: fl. 3.

*(25) *Laur. 39, 36*, Valerius Flaccus (Bandini ii, col. 316; D'Ancona No. 329; Marchesi, *B. della Fonte*, p. 139; E. Courtney, preface to Teubner edition of Valerius Flaccus, 1970, pp. xxix–xxx). Florence, early 1470s? 118 leaves, 250 × 168 mm. Copied and annotated by Bartolomeo Fonzio (first identified by Marchesi). A descendant of Niccoli's transcript of the complete text. Vine-stem border with Sassetti arms, perhaps by the artist of No. 9. At the beginning was FS, cited by Bandini but now lost. 1495 No. 241.

*(26) *Laur. 45, 14*, Filargirius and Servius on Virgil (Bandini ii, col. 345–50; Sabbadini, *Scoperte*, I, p. 165; G. Funaioli, *Esegesi virgiliana antica* (Pubbl. Univ. Cattolica del Sacro Cuore, fourth series, IX), Milan, 1930, pp. 8–9). France, first half of the ninth century. 228 leaves, 360 × 275 mm. Written by several scribes. Top of f. 1: 'Expositio Servii super Virgilium' (thirteenth- or fourteenth-century, written in a hand identified by Professor Bernhard Bischoff (in a letter) as that of a cathedral librarian at Lyons. However, he says that the MS was written not at Lyons but possibly at Luxeuil). Front flyleaf, verso, erased: MFM. FSTFCF. Folio 229 (end flyleaf), written by Fonzio: 'Hic Servius quem e Gallia mecum attuli, pretii est aureorum largorum quindecim—duc. xv.' End paste-down: '46'. 1462 No. 9: fl. 15.

*(27) *Laur. 46, 6*, Quintilian, *Instit. orat.* (Bandini ii, col. 381–2; D'Ancona No. 349; M. Winterbottom, 'Fifteenth-century MSS of Quintilian', *Classical Quarterly*, XVII, 1967, 343; Bergier, 'Humanisme', plate III: detail of f. 1). Florence, August 1470 or later: copied from the edition by Campanus pr. Rome, August 1470, and including his preface at the end. 239 written leaves, 355 × 235 mm. Copied by Hubertus (see n. 38), with Greek by Fonzio. Vine-stem border by Antonio di Niccolò di Lorenzo with *putti*, vignettes, etc. Sassetti arms as in No. 10 with motto AMP. Folio 240 (flyleaf): FSTFCFFC. MFM. 1495 No. 618.

*(28) *Laur. 47, 4*, Priscian, *De octo partibus, De accentibus* (Bandini ii, col. 390; Sabbadini, *Scoperte*, I, p. 165, as French; M. T. Gibson in *Scriptorium*, XXVI, 1972, 110). Italy or France? (see n. 27). Twelfth- or thirteenth-century? 142 leaves, 240 × 173 mm. Illuminated initials. Notes in several thirteenth- and fourteenth-century hands, including, in red (thirteenth-century), running headings, foliation by books and alphabetical numbering by leaves, clearly copied from another MS and used for purposes of cross-reference in glosses to the text. At the end of the text, note of scribe: 'xviii caterni', and (fourteenth-century): 'detur Priscianus minor pro duobus florenis'; also an erasure on end flyleaf. Front flyleaf, verso: MFM. FSTFCF. End paste-down: '10'. 1462 No. 21: fl. 6. 1495 No. 555.

*(29) *Laur. 47, 25*, Letters of Ps.-Phalaris and Brutus in Latin translations of Francesco Griffolini and Rinuccio Aretino (Bandini ii, col. 414–16; D'Ancona No. 867). Florence, early 1470s? 115 leaves, 187 × 112 mm. Copied by Bartolomeo Fonzio. Simple flower border by same artist as Nos. 35, 78, with Sassetti arms. 1495 No. 537.

*(30) *Laur. 47, 35*, speeches taken from Livy, Quintus Curtius, Sallust; Gasparino Barzizza, letters and formulary; speeches from the *Aeneid* (two sets), Lucan, and Ovid, *Met.* (Bandini ii, col. 422–3; D'Ancona No. 355; Sabbadini, *Scoperte*, I, p. 165; Warburg, 'Verfügung', p. 362; Bergier, 'Humanisme', plate I: detail of lower border of f. 1, enlarged.) Florence, early 1470s? 282 leaves, 318 × 216 mm. Copied by Hubertus. Corrections by Fonzio. Folio 1, elaborate border by Antonio di Niccolò di Lorenzo, partly vine-stem, partly of flowers and coloured panels, with vignettes, animals, birds, *putti* (some with slings and pebbles) and two centaurs with shields, flanking the Sassetti arms as in No. 10. At end: FSTFFCFC. MFM. 1495 No. 548. The first collection of speeches has the same *incipit* as the collection in MS Berlin, lat. fol. 99, Florence, 1460s, from the library of King Matthias Corvinus but

probably originally copied for Archbishop Janos Vitéz (*Bibliotheca Corviniana*, 1969, No. 128 and plate LXXXVIII).

*(31) *Laur. 49, 2*, Cicero, *Epp. ad fam.* (Bandini ii, col. 461–2; D'Ancona No. 368; Marchesi, *B. della Fonte*, p. 132). Florence, *c.* 1460–65. 177 leaves, 300 × 213 mm. The scribe is identifiable as Julianus Antonii de Prato, who signed Laur. 21, 11, sermons of St Leo with *ex libris* of Piero de' Medici, and copied a number of other MSS for Piero. Vine-stem border with Sassetti arms by an illuminator who decorated many of the MSS prepared by Vespasiano da Bisticci for the Badia of Fiesole in the early 1460s. Folio *iv* (flyleaf): 'FRANCISCI SASSETTI T. F.' (partly erased) and long note on Ptolemy, king of Egypt (and the death of Pompey), both written by Fonzio, with, below, a pen and wash drawing incorporating Sassetti notes FS and AMP and emblem of sling with pebble (plate 9.3). Annotations and Greek by Fonzio (first pointed out by Marchesi). Perhaps 1462 No. 8: fl. 15. Was this MS sent to Sassetti by Piero de' Medici (see above, pp. 162, 163)?

*(32) *Laur. 49, 22*, Cicero, *Epp. ad Brut., Q. Frat., Att.; Somn. Scip.; Leg.* (Bandini ii, col. 478–9; D'Ancona No. 373). Florence, *c.* 1470. 231 written leaves, 320 × 225 mm. Written by Hubertus. Fine vine-stem border by an unidentified follower of Francesco d'Antonio (see n. 40), with Sassetti arms. Folio ii*v* (flyleaf), elaborate full-page drawing incorporating FS, emblem of sling and motto AMP in a roundel supported by *putti*, all in an elegant freely drawn monumental frame with the Sassetti arms, tied to a laurel garland, dangling on either side. Folio 232: FSTFFCFC. SPM. Corrections and Greek by Fonzio. 1495 No. 615.

*(33) *Laur. 50, 36*, Cicero, *Orator, Brutus, Partit. orat., Topica* (Bandini ii, col. 520; D'Ancona No. 378). Florence, late 1460s? 165 written leaves, 241 × 173 mm. Copied by Hubertus. Simple vine-stem border with Sassetti arms, by same artist as No. 32. Folio 166 (flyleaf): FSTFFCFC. SPM. A few marginalia by Fonzio. 1495 No. 558.

*(34) *Laur. 50, 42*, Cicero, *De oratore* (Bandini ii, col. 522; D'Ancona No. 380). Florence, late 1460s? 166 written leaves, 243 × 175 mm. Copied by Hubertus. Simple vine-stem border with Sassetti arms by artist of No. 32. Folio *iv* (flyleaf), drawing incorporating FS in gold, sling with pebbles lying below and motto AMP. Folio 167 (flyleaf): FSTFFCFC. SPM. Some notes and corrections by Fonzio. 1495 No. 562.

*(35) *Laur. 53, 5*, Filelfo, *Convivia* (Bandini ii, col. 603; D'Ancona No. 872). Florence, early 1470s? 123 written leaves, 240 × 165 mm. Copied by Niccolò Fonzio. Flower border by same artist as Nos. 29, 78, with Sassetti arms and sling below. 1495 No. 616.

*(36) *Laur. 54, 17*, Aristeas, *De lxx interpretibus* in Latin translation of Matteo Palmieri dedicated to Pope Paul II (1464–71); letters of Hippocrates and Diogenes in Latin translations of Rinuccio and Francesco Aretino (Bandini ii, col. 657–8; D'Ancona No. 391). Florence, *c.* 1465–70? 109 written leaves, 199 × 129 mm. Humanistic hand, same as in Nos. 42, 60. Simple vine-stem border with Sassetti arms. Folio 111 (flyleaf): erasure, followed by MFM. End paste-down: '93'. A few notes by Fonzio. 1495 No. 575.

*(37) *Laur. 63, 7*, Livy, Dec. I (Bandini ii, col. 688; D'Ancona No. 396; A. de la Mare, 'Florentine manuscripts of Livy in the fifteenth century', in *Livy*, ed. T. A. Dorey, 1971, p. 185). Florence, early 1470s? 234 leaves, 352 × 240 mm. Copied by Giovanfrancesco Marzi. Vine-stem border by Antonio di Niccolò di Lorenzo, with Sassetti arms. Rubrication, copious marginalia and corrections by Bartolomeo Fonzio. 1495 No. 547.

*(38) *Laur. 63, 8*, Livy, Dec. III (Bandini ii, col. 688; D'Ancona No. 397; de la Mare, *loc. cit.* and p. 188, n. 5). Florence, early 1470s? 218 leaves, 355 × 240 mm. Folio 218 (caps.): 'Finis. Iohannes Franciscus Martius Geminianensis

transcripsit.' Vine-stem border with Sassetti arms as in No. 37. Rubrication, marginalia and corrections by Bartolomeo Fonzio, who also added Boccaccio's life of Livy ('Pauca de T. Livio a Johanne Boccaccio collecta') on the verso of the front flyleaf. 1495 No. 602.

*(39)　*Laur. 63, 9*, Livy, Dec. IV and epitome (Bandini ii, col. 689; D'Ancona No. 398; de la Mare, *art. cit.*, p. 185), Florence, early 1470s? 196 leaves, 344 × 240 mm. Copied by Giovanfrancesco Marzi. Vine-stem border as in Nos. 37, 38, with Sassetti arms. Front flyleaf, verso (red caps.): 'FRANCISCI SASSETTI THOMAE FILII', followed by note of contents also in red and written by Fonzio. He rubricated, annotated and corrected the MS. 1495 No. 601.

*(40)　*Laur. 63, 32*, Thucydides, translated by Valla (Bandini ii, col. 704–5; D'Ancona No. 405; BBB). Florence, early 1470s? 250 leaves, 322 × 236 mm. Copied in formal hand of Niccolò Fonzio. Vine-stem border by same artist as No. 57, with Sassetti arms, *putti* holding up stones, and Sassetti motto AMP in Medici-type diamond ring with three feathers. No original flyleaves. 1495 No. 603.

*(41)　*Laur. 64, 30*, Quintus Curtius (Bandini ii, col. 722; D'Ancona No. 414). Florence, early 1470s? 183 leaves, 255 × 175 mm. Cursive hand of Niccolò Fonzio. Simple vine-stem border by Antonio di Niccolò di Lorenzo with Sassetti arms as in No. 10, and *putti* with slings. Annotated and corrected by Bartolomeo Fonzio. No original flyleaves. 1495 No. 533. See plate 9.2.

†(42)　*Laur. 65, 8*, L. Bruni, *Historia florentina* (Bandini ii, col. 731; D'Ancona No. 880; BBB). Florence, early 1470s? 273 leaves, 310 × 216 mm. Copied by the same scribe as Nos. 36, 60. Elaborate flower border by a follower of Ser Benedetto di Silvestro includes *putti* with slings, Sassetti arms. Folio i*v* (flyleaf), FS in Fonzio's hand, and below painted *ex libris* with FS, motto AMP on scroll, and sling. Some notes perhaps by Fonzio. 1495 No. 597.

*(43)　*Laur. 65, 11*, L. Bruni, *De primo bello punico* (Bandini ii, col. 732; D'Ancona No. 421). Florence, *c.* 1455–60. 135 written leaves, 208 × 138 mm. Good humanistic hand, same as No. 76. Vine-stem borders by early Francesco d'Antonio with half-erased arms (divided, not Sassetti). Folio i*v* (flyleaf): MFM. FSTFCF. End paste-down: '102'. Probably 1462 No. 29: fl. 4. 1495 No. 544 or 561.

*(44)　*Laur. 65, 16*, L. Bruni, *De primo bello punico*, etc (Bandini ii, col. 735). Milan, second quarter of the fifteenth century. Fifty-six written leaves, 242 × 165 mm. Semi-humanistic script. Fine decoration by the Master of the *Vitae imperatorum* (see n. 43). Folio 57 (flyleaf), erasure, followed by: MFM. FSTFCF. A few notes by Fonzio. 1495 No. 544 or 561.

†(45)　*Laur. 65, 19*, L. Bruni, *De temporibus suis* (Bandini ii, col. 736; BBB). Florence(?), *c.* 1450–60. Forty-eight leaves, 191 × 133 mm. Good humanistic hand. Folio 2, vine-stem initial and border with arms of Ciampelli of Florence, wrongly attributed to Sassetti by Bandini (or, a bend voided and two roundels sable). Folio 1, erasure: 'liber [. . .]ugonis'; f. i*v*: MFM. FSTFCF. 1495 No. 583.

*(46)　*Laur. 66, 7*, Josephus, *De bello iudaico*; *De vet. iud.* (Bandini ii, col. 785–6; D'Ancona No. 881). Florence, mid to late 1470s. 251 written leaves, 320 × 223 mm. Written by Hubertus, in a rather uncertain hand. Elaborate flower and acanthus border with medallions, *putti*, Sassetti arms as in No. 10, and 'portrait' of the author in the initial, by a follower of Francesco Rosselli. End paste-down '71'. 1495 No. 541.

*(47)　*Laur. 66, 11*, Justin (Bandini ii, col. 787; D'Ancona No. 435). Florence, early 1470s? 200 written leaves, 253 × 170 mm. Written in cursive hand of Niccolò Fonzio. Simple vine-stem border with Sassetti arms. Folio 201 (flyleaf), erasure followed by: FSTFFC. SPM. Many annotations by Bartolomeo Fonzio. 1495 No. 551.

*(48) *Laur. 66, 29,* Benvenuto de' Rambaldi of Imola, *Romuleon* (Bandini ii, col. 806; G. Mariani Canova, *La miniatura veneta del Rinascimento,* 1969, cat. No. 64 (with earlier bibliography) and fig. 75). Bologna, *c.* 1450–60? (For this attribution see n. 30.) 325 written leaves, 260 × 183 mm. Good humanistic hand. Vine-stem border framed in laurel, with *putti,* vignettes, Sassetti arms (clearly original), initial 'P' formed partly of *putti* standing on columns, and monsters, the upper part in a faceted frame; a scroll beside reads: 'MARSILIVS BOLOGNE[N]SIS FECIT'. Subsequent initials in similar style, some with flowers. Front flyleaf: MFM. FSTFCF. End paste-down: '22' and erasure in Fonzio's hand which may partly read: 'Pretii [aureorum viginti . . .?] fl. [20?]'. Probably 1462 No. 50: fl. 15. 1495 No. 543.

*(49) *Laur. 67, 2,* Herodotus, translated by Valla (Bandini ii, col. 815; D'Ancona No. 442; BBB). Florence, early 1470s? 260 written leaves, 322 × 222 mm. Written in formal hand of Niccolò Fonzio. Good vine-stem border, by the artist of No. 9, with Sassetti arms. Folio iv (flyleaf): FS. Some notes and corrections by Bartolomeo Fonzio. 1495 No. 607.

*(50) *Laur. 67, 7,* Diodorus Siculus, translated by Poggio (Bandini ii, col. 819–20; D'Ancona No. 882). Florence, early 1470s? 220 written leaves, 270 × 180 mm. Cursive hand of Niccolò Fonzio. Folio 1, vine-stem initial joined to good flower border with Sassetti arms, perhaps by the artist of No. 9. Folio 221 (flyleaf): FSTFFC. SPM. Annotations by Bartolomeo Fonzio include notes on Roman measures and money, on f. 220v (*cf.* n. 49, p. 195). 1495 No. 611.

*(51) *Laur. 67, 20,* Donato Acciaiuoli, lives of Scipio, Hannibal and Charlemagne (Bandini ii, col. 827; D'Ancona No. 446). Florence, *c.* 1470? 100 written leaves, 226 × 155 mm. Written by Hubertus. Good vine-stem border by Antonio di Niccolò di Lorenzo with Sassetti arms as in No. 10, *putti* with slings. Annotations by Bartolomeo Fonzio. 1495 No. 534.

*(52) *Laur. 67, 23,* Dionysius of Halicarnassus, *Antiq. Rom.,* books I–II, translated by Lampugnano Birago, ending incomplete. The earlier version, dedicated to Pope Nicholas V, beginning: Quum nec rationes vellem, without the preface (Bandini ii, col. 829; D'Ancona No. 447). Florence, early 1470s? 152 leaves, 219 × 150 mm. Formal hand of Niccolò Fonzio. Vine-stem border by a follower of Antonio di Niccolò di Lorenzo with Sassetti arms. At the beginning was: FS, cited by Bandini, but now lost. A few notes and corrections by Bartolomeo Fonzio. 1495 No. 570 or 667 (two copies of text listed). For the *incipit* of the earlier version of the translation see Kristeller, *Iter* I, pp. 342, 348; II, p. 309. The first edition, Treviso, 1480 (Hain 6239), is of the version dedicated to Pope Paul II.

*(53) *Laur. 68, 14,* Caesar (Bandini ii, col. 843–4; D'Ancona No. 795; Marchesi, *B. della Fonte,* p. 132; V. Brown, *The Textual Transmission of Caesar's 'Civil War'* (*Mnemosyne,* suppl. 23), Leiden, 1972, p. 55). Florence, late 1460s? 199 leaves, 325 × 230 mm. Copied by Hubertus. Vine-stem border perhaps by Ser Benedetto di Silvestro with Sassetti arms. Folio ivv (flyleaf), *ex libris* page with FS in gold, emblem of sling, and AMP. End flyleaf: MFM, followed by Sassetti *ex libris,* erased. Annotations by Bartolomeo Fonzio, first identified by Marchesi. 1495 No. 600.

*(54) *Laur. 68, 24,* Arator, *De actibus apost.;* Avianus; *Ilias latina;* Bede, *De arte metrica, De figuris;* Persius (Bandini ii, col. 850–1; Sabbadini, *Scoperte,* I, p. 165, as French; A. P. McKinley, *Arator, the Codices,* Cambridge, Mass., 1942, pp. 52–3, No. 84; A. Guaglianone in introduction to *Aviani 'Fabulae'* (Corpus Script. Lat. Paravaniorum), 1958, pp. xiv–xv). Rather poor parchment. France, eleventh century. 119 written leaves, 241 × 127 mm. Erasures on f. 119 and end paste-down, where there is also: MFM. FSTFCF. The section containing Bede has a few notes by Fonzio. 1462 No. 25: fl. 4. 1495 No. 436.

*(55)   *Laur. 76, 5*, Cicero, *De finibus* (Bandini iii, col. 88–9). Florence(?), *c.* 1440–50.
         Eighty-four leaves, 242 × 160 mm. Humanistic script (the same scribe wrote
         No. 56 and Oxford, Bodl. MS Laud Lat. 48, Cicero, Speeches, on paper,
         dated 1450 (Pächt, Alexander, *Illum. MSS in Bodl. Lib.* 2, No. 335 and plate
         XXXI). Simple vine-stem initial. End flyleaf, upside down, erased: MFM.
         FSTFCF. Front flyleaf, upside down: '106'. 1462 No. 24: fl. 4. 1495 No. 563.

†(56)   *Laur. 76, 10*, Cicero, *Tusc. quaest.* (Bandini iii, col. 90–1; BBB). Florence,
         c. 1440–50. Eighty-eight leaves, 239 × 162 mm. Same scribe and decoration
         as No. 55. Folio iv (flyleaf): MFM. FSTFCF. End paste-down: '10', and erasure
         in Fonzio's hand: 'Pretii au[re]orum l[ar]go[rum . . .]duc.[i?]iii'. Annota-
         tions and Greek perhaps in Fonzio's hand. 1462 No. 34: fl. 4. 1495 No. 569.

*(57)   *Laur. 76, 42*, Plato, *Letters*, Xenophon and Basil, translated by Bruni;
         Onosander, translated by Niccolò Sagondino (Bandini iii, col. 113–14;
         D'Ancona No. 456). Florence, early 1470s? 200 written leaves, 207 × 135
         mm. Written by Hubertus. Vine-stem border by same artist as No. 40 with
         Sassetti arms framed in two slings; initial in later-looking style. 1495 No. 557.

*(58)   *Laur. 76, 50*, Poggio, *De varietate fortunae*; Biondo, *Roma instaurata* (Bandini
         iii, col. 119–20). Florence, *c.* 1460–70? (after 1462). 183 written leaves,
         205 × 140 mm. Good humanistic cursive. Simple vine-stem initial and
         border with space for arms left blank. At end, in Fonzio's hand, partly
         erased: 'Hunc librum in quem quattuor aureos largos impendit Francisscus.
         Fr. Saxettus Thomae filius civis florentinus faciundum curavit' then MFM.
         The Biondo text has many notes and corrections by Fonzio. 1495 No. 552.

†(59)   *Laur. 78, 16*, Boethius, *De consol. philos.* (Bandini iii, col. 165; D'Ancona
         No. 30; BBB). Bologna, early fifteenth century. Fifty-eight leaves, 341 × 236
         mm. Round semi-gothic script showing humanistic influence, Fine histori-
         ated initial. Folio 58*v* (caps.): 'Explicit liber Boecii. Deo G[ratias] A[gimus].
         Matheus s[crip]s[it].' Front flyleaf, recto: 'GYIDO PONTECELO' (early
         fifteenth-century?), followed by a notarial (?) sign; verso: MFM. FSTFCF. End
         paste-down: '84'. Probably 1462 No. 13: fl. 4. 1495 No. 530.

†(60)   *Laur. 79, 1*, Aristotle, *Ethics*, translated into Latin by Argyropulos; L.
         Bruni, *Isagogicon*; Ps.-Aristotle, *Econ.*, translated by Bruni (Bandini iii, col.
         169–71; D'Ancona No. 459; painted *ex libris* page reproduced Warburg,
         'Verfügung', plate XX, 37, and see pp. 152–4; Bergier, 'Humanisme', plate
         IV). Florence, early 1470s? 127 leaves, 331 × 225 mm. Copied by same scribe
         as Nos. 36, 42. Elaborate vine-stem border by Antonio di Niccolò di Lorenzo,
         including Sassetti arms as in No. 10, *putti* with slings, etc. Folio iv (flyleaf),
         elaborate painted *ex libris* (see reproductions), painted as though it were
         a piece of parchment pinned to the page, incorporating roundel with
         FS, scroll with AMP, and two centaurs flanking the Sassetti pebble and sling.
         At end: MFM. FSTFCF, erased. (Not mentioned by D'Ancona.) 1495 No. 609.

†(61)   *Laur. 79, 24*, Aristotle, *Politics*, translated into Latin by Bruni (Bandini iii,
         col. 181; D'Ancona No. 466; Bergier, 'Humanisme', plate II (detail of lower
         border of f. 1); BBB). Florence, February 1471/2. 160 written leaves, 264 ×
         170 mm. Distinctive humanistic cursive hand. Folio 1, vine-stem border by
         Antonio di Niccolò di Lorenzo with Sassetti arms as in No. 10, accompanied
         by scroll with motto AMP, flanked by *putti* with slings. Folio 160: 'Finis.
         D.E.O. G.R.A.T.I.A.S. Anno M.cccc.lxxi°. Mense Februarii. Die Lune
         Hora Paulo ante vigesimam.' Front paste-down, cursive, fifteenth-cen-
         tury(?): 'Sassetti'; f. iv (flyleaf): MFM. FSTFCF. Folio i, erasure of two lines in
         Fonzio's hand, beginning: 'Hunc l[. . .]'. End paste-down: '32'. 1495 No.
         535.

*(62)   *Laur. 83, 6*, Cicero, *De nat. deorum, De div., De fato* (Bandini iii, col. 208–9,
         identified the arms; Ullman, *Origin and Devel. of Hum. Script*, p. 94, No. 9,
         does not mention the arms). Florence, *c.* 1410–12. 127 leaves, 274 × 179 mm.

Folio 118 (caps.): 'Ioannes Arretinus scripsit'; f. 127 (caps.): 'Bernardo [. . .]ortin[. . . *altered to* Portinârio] Ioannes Arretinus plurimam salutem dicit. Vale diu felixque sis.' Written in Giovanni's stiff, early hand, of *c.* 1410–12. Contemporary vine-stem initials. On f. 1, wreath with Sassetti arms in small flower border, added *c.* 1475 or later. End paste-down: '95'. 1495 No. 539.

*(63) *Laur. 84, 27,* Galeotto Marzio, *De homine* (Bandini iii, col. 255–6; D'Ancona No. 474). Florence, early 1470s? 119 written leaves, 273 × 173 mm. Written in formal hand of Niccolò Fonzio. Vine-stem border with Sassetti arms, perhaps by artist of No. 9. 1495 No. 624.

*(64) Florence, *Bibl. Nazionale Banco Rari 215 (Pal. 320),* Dante, *Divina commedia* (D'Ancona No. 172; L. Gentile, *I codici palatini* (*Catt. dei MSS della Bibl. Naz. cent. di Firenze,* ed. A. Bartoli, 1), Rome, 1889, pp. 534–5; *Mostra naz. della miniatura,* 1954, No. 352; B. Degenhart and A. Schmitt, *Corpus der ital. Zeichnungen 1300–1450,* 1, 2, 1968, No. 186; P. Brieger, M. Meiss and C. S. Singleton, *Illum. MSS. of the Divine Comedy,* 1970, 1, pp. 248–9 and fig. 14 (f. ii); 11, plates 14 (f. iv), 33 (f. iiiv)). Florence, *c.* 1410–15. 234 leaves (wrongly numbered 224), 252 × 152 mm. Fine early humanistic script, strongly influenced by Poggio. Contemporary vine-stem initials. Series of miniatures: f. ii, portrait of Dante perhaps added later; those on f. iiiv, iv (for *Inferno*), 78v (for *Purgatorio*), are probably original, since they appear to have been annotated by the scribe. Front flyleaf: MFM. FSTFCF, and note (also written by Fonzio): 'Hunc ego Dantem aureis largis decem emi—duc. x.' Followed by *ex libris* dated 1560 of Lorenzo d'Alessandro de' Bardi, conte di Vernio: '. . . olim fuit Galeazzi Sassettii civis florentini sui avunculi' and 'Poi del Canonico Michel Dati'. Sassetti arms (erased) in vine-stem border added on f. 1. Carefully annotated by Bartolomeo Fonzio, with a summary in Italian at the beginning of each canto. 1462 No. 55: fl. 10. 1495 No. 598. The Galeazzo Sassetti mentioned was the eldest son of Francesco's son Teodoro; his sister Margherita married Alessandro de' Bardi (see Passerini's family tree in *Arch. stor. ital.* IV, 2, 1853, cx). In 1846 the MS belonged to Contessa Baldovinetti.

*(65) London, *British Museum, Add. 15819,* fragment of *Aratea,* deriving from the lost MS discovered by Poggio; Aratus, etc (F. Saxl and H. Meier, *Verzeichnis astrol. und mythol. illust. HSS. . . . III,* London, 1953, 1, pp. 51–3; 11, plate LXXIX, 205 (detail of f. 30v); W. Y. Fletcher, *Foreign Bookbindings in the B.M.,* 1896, plate VIII; T. De Marinis, *La legatura artistica in Italia nei secoli XV e XVI,* 1970, 1, No. 1038). Florence, *c.* 1465–75? Seventy-one written leaves, 237 × 170 mm. Good humanistic cursive hand. The scribe also wrote ff. 3–4 of No. 72 below, and a scribble in No. 24. Folio 1, vine-stem border with Sassetti arms. Diagrams with figures perhaps drawn by Bartolomeo Fonzio. His annotations form an integral part of the drawings, e.g. on f. 3 (see plate 9.4), and there is a strong affinity with the figure drawing in Oxford, Bodl. Lat. misc. d. 85, Fonzio's autograph epigraphical collection (for bibliography see Pächt, Alexander, *Cat. of Illum. MSS in Bodl. Lib.* 11, No. 329; many of the drawings are reproduced by Saxl, 'The classical inscription', *cit.*: Ashmole MS). Cf. also the drawing of 'Calumnia' in the copy of Fonzio's Italian translation of Lucian, *De calumnia,* sent to Ercole d'Este in July 1472: Berlin Kupferstichkab. 78 c 26 (former Hamilton 16) (reproduced by Trinkaus, 'A humanist's image', plate facing p. 132; see pp. 132–3 for bibliography). Original binding in dark brown leather, blind-stamped; edges gilt and gauffered; traces of four clasps with ivy-leaf-shaped metal catches and corner bosses. Folio 77 (flyleaf), erasure, followed by: MFM. FSTFCF (see fig. 9.1). Annotated by Fonzio. 1495 No. 545. Bought by British Museum from Techener, Paris, 1846.

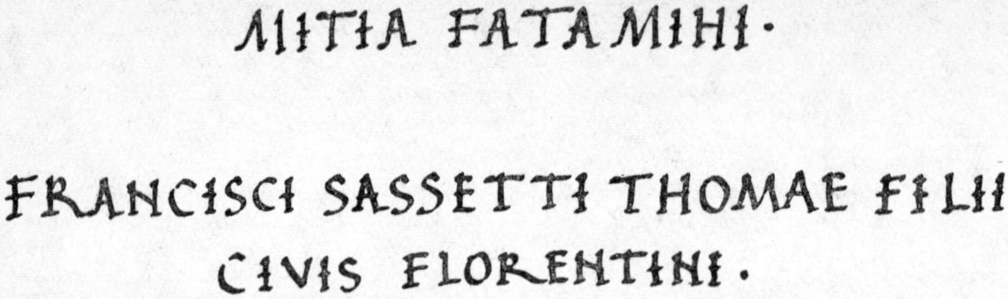

ΛΙΙΤΙΑ FATA MIHI·

FRANCISCI SASSETTI THOMAE FILII
CIVIS FLORENTINI·

FIG. 9.1   *Aratea*, etc. London, B.M. Add. MS 15819, f. 77. Sassetti *ex libris* in the hand of Bartolomeo Fonzio. See No. 65

*(66) *Manchester, Chetham's Library 27900*, Aulus Gellius (*Bibl. Corviniana*, No. 70 (with bibliography) and plate XXIV: Sassetti's arms are not identified). Florence, early 1470s? 251 written leaves, 333 × 225 mm. Written by Hubertus. Vine-stem border by Antonio di Niccolò di Lorenzo with Sassetti arms as in No. 10, partly erased, and *putti* holding slings. Greek etc, by Fonzio. Corvinus binding (see Anthony Hobson, *The Book Collector*, 1958, 265–8).

*(67) *Milan, Bibl. Trivulziana 817*, collection of lives of philosophers and poets: Diogenes Laertius, translated by Traversari; Ps.-Herodotous, *Vita Homeri*, translated by Pellegrino Allio; Donatus, life of Virgil; P. C. Decembrio, *Vitae poetarum*; Pomponius Infortunatus (i.e. Leto), life of Lucan; extracts from Eusebius, *De temporibus* and Quintilian, *Instit. orat.* (*Bibl. Corviniana*, No. 71 (with earlier bibliography) and plate XXV). Probably in part a fair copy of No. 77 below, Florence, 1470s. 202 written leaves, 329 × 224 mm. Written by Hubertus. Elaborate, late-looking framed border by Antonio di Niccolò di Lorenzo; however, subsequent initials in vine-stem style. Corvinus arms, painted over with another coat of arms. Folio 203 (flyleaf), erased inscription of five lines, followed by: FSTFFCFC. MFM. Corvinus binding.

*(68) *Modena, Bibl. Estense Lat. 437 (a.Q.4.15)*, miscellany: Cornelius Nepos; Florus, epitome of Livy; Lodovico Guasti, epitome of Pliny; Pomponius Mela; 'Zombini grammatici clerici Pistoriensis, Abbreviatio de situ orbis' (perhaps an extract from the Chronicle of Sozomeno of Pistoia); (Cornelius Nepos) life of Pomponius Atticus; Sextus Rufus, *Breviarium* (*Bibl. Corviniana*, No. 79 and Plate XXXIII). Florence, 1470s? 156 leaves, 360 × 243 mm. Written by Hubertus. Flower borders by Ser Benedetto di Silvestro include Sassetti device of sling, and *putti* holding pebbles, Corvinus arms, in one case (f. 69) clearly painted over Sassetti arms. Folio 157 (flyleaf), erasure of four lines, followed by: MFM. FSTFFCFC. Pomponius Mela annotated by Fonzio.

*(69) *Modena, Bibl. Estense Lat. 472 (a.X.1.10)*, Strabo, in Latin translation of Guarino (*Bibl. Corviniana*, No. 86 and plate XLI). Florence, 1470s. 249 written leaves, 398 × 272 mm. Written in formal hand of Niccolò Fonzio. Flower border by a follower of Francesco Rosselli. Arms of Matthias Corvinus apparently painted over Sassetti arms (a bend is visible). A few marginalia and some Greek written in by Bartolomeo Fonzio.

*(70) *New York, Pierpont Morgan Library M. 497*, Cicero, *De nat. deorum*, *De div.*, *De officiis*, *De amicitia*, *Paradoxa*, *De senectute*, *De acad.*, *Timaeus*, *Somn. Scip.*, *De leg.*, *De fato*; Niccolò Niccoli, *Commentarium* (large biblio. includes: T. De Marinis, *Cat.* XII, 1913, No. 10, plates III–IV; A. de Hevesy, *La bibl. du roi Mat. Corv.*, 1923, No. 76; G. Fraknoi *et al.*, *Bibliotheca Corvina*, 1927, No. 76; Pierpont Morgan Lib., *Exhib. of illum. MSS held at New York Publ. Lib.*, 1934, No. 124; W. Allen, 'The four Corvinus MSS in the U.S.', *Bull. New York Publ. Lib.* XLII, 1938, 321–3; exhib., *Italian MSS in the Pierpont Morgan Lib.*, 1953,

No. 72; *Bibl. Corviniana*, No. 99 and plate LIII). Florence, 1470s. I + 270 leaves, 320 × 210 mm, surviving. Written by Hubertus. The *Commentarium*, ff. 269*v*–271, was added in a distinctive humanistic cursive. Painted title page and flower borders by Ser Benedetto di Silvestro. All the borders once contained Sassetti's arms and pebble emblem. On ff. 1 and 98 the arms, and on f. 1 the emblem, have been painted over with those of King Matthias Corvinus. On two other leaves (ff. 175, 195), other heraldic elements were added to Sassetti's arms: on f. 195 two lions; on both leaves three fleurs de sable added to the bend. These led to the suggestion that the MS was originally made for the family of Chyurlia da Lizzano, whose arms are not, however, identical. Hevesy and others cite the Sassetti *ex libris*: 'M[ITI]A FATA MIHI. FRANCIS[CUS SASSETTUS]' (perhaps the beginning of *ex libris* type (ii)) but there is no trace of this in the MS now, nor of any erasure. However, Mr William Voelkle of the Pierpont Morgan Library, to whom I am indebted for much information about the MS, made a careful examination of it at my request and found that the last quire is imperfect (it was already like this when the MS was acquired in 1912) so that a flyleaf may have been lost.

*(71) *Oxford, Bodleian Library, Montagu d. 32 (S.C. 25401)*, Bruni, Life of Petrarch; Petrarch, *Canzoniere* and *Trionfi* (Pächt, Alexander, *Catalogue of Illuminated MSS in Bodl. Lib.* II, No. 315 and plate XXIX (detail of f. 7); the MS will be fully described by Nicholas Mann in his census of Petrarch MSS in Great Britain to be published in *Italia medioevale e umanistica*, XVII, 1974). On f. 188*v* is a note that the 'Rerum vulgarium fragmenta' were copied from the MS in the hand of Leonardo Giustiniani (see *Mostra di codici petrarcheschi laurenziani*, Florence, 1974, p. 48). Florence, early 1470s? 228 original written leaves, 251 × 106 mm. Written by Bartolomeo Fonzio. Vine-stem border by the artist of No. 9, Sassetti arms. Front flyleaf, verso: FS, then erasure. On recto: 'est nunc Francisci et Filippi Joannis Bapt.ae T[eodo]ri Francisci de Saxettis cuius possessio [primu]m fuit'. Eighteenth-century *ex libris* of Marchese Giovanni Gerini. Binding by Ellis for A. J. Hanrott (d. 1842).

†(71)A See addenda, p. 200.

†(72) *Vat. Lat. 3294*, Martial (E. Chatelain, *Paléog. des classiques latins* II, Paris, 1894–1900, plate CLII; Sabbadini, *Scoperte*, I, p. 143; *Survie des classiques latins* (Vatican Library exhibition), 1973, No. 67; V. Branca in *Venezia e Ungheria nel Rinascimento*, ed. V. Branca, 1973, pp. 346–7; BBB). Mid-ninth century, written in France (Professor Bischoff says perhaps at Auxerre). Ninety-nine leaves, approx. 220 × 195 mm. Folio 101 (flyleaf), erasure of five lines later written over. 1462 No. 23: fl. 6. Many corrections and additions in a fifteenth-century hand, perhaps Ugoleto. Folio ii, *ex libris*: 'Val. Martialis . . . Thadaei Ugoleti Parmensis'. Folios 1–4 are fifteenth-century additions, ff. 1–2 possibly in the hand of Ugoleto. Folios 3–4 (the *Epigrammaton Liber*) are in the same hand as No. 65 above. On f. 3 an unidentified coat of arms between cornucopiae: argent, a rampant creature with a lion's body and man's head, holding a gold ball or disc (fifteenth- to sixteenth-century). Poliziano referred to this MS of Martial, which had been bought by Ugoleto from Sassetti (*Miscellanea*, pr. September 1489, cap. xxiii; *Secunda centuria*, ed. Branca, Pastore Stocchi, Florence, 1972, cap. 35, 5). It is also presumably the MS referred to in Ugoleto's letter *cit.* under No. 82 below. Belonged in the sixteenth century to Fulvio Orsini.

*(73) *Venice, Bibl. Naz. Marciana Lat. X 31 (3585)*, historical collection: Suetonius, *De xii Caesaribus*; Ps.-Pliny, *De viris*, with *Brevis adnotatio* of Giov. Mansionario; Eutropius; Paulus diaconus, *Hist. Rom.*; Petrarch, *De viris*; Domizio Calderini, life of Suetonius; extract from Sicco Polentone, *De illustribus scriptoribus* (E. Casamassima, 'A Corvin Kodexek . . .', *Magyar Könyvszemle* 81, 1965,

111, fig. 14 (detail of notes by Fonzio); *Bibl. Corviniana*, No. 130 and plate xci). Florence, 1470s. 168 leaves, 358 × 240 mm. Written by Hubertus. Fine flower border by Benedetto di Silvestro with Sassetti emblem of sling with pebble hanging from the initial. Sassetti arms painted over with those of King Matthias Corvinus. Suetonius annotated by Fonzio.

c *Manuscripts probably or possibly from Sassetti's collection*

*(74) *Florence, Laur. 35, 15*, Lucan (Bandini ii, col. 206). Twelfth-century. Ninety-three written leaves, approx. 231 × 154 mm. Fourteenth-century glosses and additions. No original flyleaves. Annotated by Bartolomeo Fonzio. Probably 1462 No. 22 or 41. 1495 No. 549?

*(75) *Laur. 45, 21*, Vegetius and Frontinus (Bandini ii, col. 358–9; D'Ancona No. 347). Florence, c. 1460. 149 leaves, 240 × 170 mm. Good humanistic hand; colophon (f. 149v): '. . . EXPLICIT. LEGE FOELICITER. F.I.N.I.S. Τελδσ. Silvester Pisanus Palmeriorum sanguine natus scripsit'. Folio 5, simple vine-stem border with space for arms left blank. Heavily annotated and corrected by Bartolomeo Fonzio. Probably 1462 No. 27. 1495 No. 546? For further mss signed by the scribe see Kristeller, *Iter ital.* ii, pp. 57, 442.

*(76) *Laur. 65, 10*, L. Bruni, *De bello italico adv. gothos* (Bandini ii, col. 732; D'Ancona No. 420). Florence, 1459. 120 leaves, 210 × 140 mm. Written by the same scribe as No. 43. Folio 120v (caps.): 'Finis. Scripsit [M *or* Ia(?) . . . ii *erased*] filius anno aetatis sue xvii ab incarnatione vero domini salvatoris nostri MCCCC°LVIIII°'. Good vine-stem border by early Francesco d'Antonio in same style as in No. 43, with similar erased arms, divided. A few notes perhaps by Fonzio and one (f. 25) perhaps by Sassetti himself. Probably 1462 No. 28. 1495 No. 641?

*(77) *Laur. 65, 52*, ff. 3–24, Pellegrino Allio, *Vita Homeri* translated from Ps.-Herodotus, and eleven Latin poems; f. 25, 'Vitae quorundam Latinarum poetarum a P. Candido editae'; f. 28, 'Pomponii Infortunati [*i.e. Pomponio Leto*] in M. Annei Lucani vitam'; f. 31, extracts on poets from Eusebius, *De temporibus*; f. 36, extract on poets from Quintilian, *De instit. orat.* (Bandini ii, col. 774). Florence, c. 1465–75? Thirty-eight leaves, 195 × 114 mm. Folios 3–24, unidentified humanistic cursive hand; ff. 1–2v (contents), 25–38v, in the hand of Bartolomeo Fonzio, who also foliated the ms and wrote the heading on f. 3. Simple vine-stem initial and border on f. 3. Erasure on end paste-down. Probably 1495 No. 579. *Cf.* the almost identical collection of texts in No. 67.

??*(78) *Laur. 73, 4*, Celsus, complete text (Bandini iii, col. 24; D'Ancona No. 887; Sabbadini, *Storia e critica dei testi latini* (first edition, 1914), reprinted Padua, 1971, pp. 222, 232–4. He suggested that the ms was written in northern Italy; *A. Cornelii Celsi quae supersunt*, ed. F. Marx (*Corpus Medicorum Latinorum*, 1), Leipzig, 1915, pp. lvii, No. 19, lxiii). Florence, early 1470s? 263 leaves, 267 × 181 mm. Written in formal hand of Niccolò Fonzio. Flower border by same artist as Nos. 29, 35; original arms painted over with a later coat of arms, erased. From an offset on the front flyleaf it appears that the first coat of arms was that of King Matthias Corvinus of Hungary (for another ms of Celsus owned by him see *Bibl. Corviniana*, No. 88). Many notes and corrections (some specifically from a 'vetus exemplum') by Bartolomeo Fonzio, who used L (Laur. 73, 1, ninth to tenth century), as Sabbadini pointed out. Marx says that the ms was copied from Niccoli's copy (Laur. 73, 7), and that it was used for Fonzio's edition of 1478.

*(79) *Laur Ashb. 922 (853)*, (*a*) ff. 1–25v (with early foliation 216–39), Antonio Benivieni, *De peste*, with preface to Francesco Sassetti (Della Torre, *Storia dell'Accad. Plat. di Firenze*, p. 781, n. 6; Kristeller, *Iter*, i, p. 85); (*b*) ff. 26–32, extracts attributed to Fazio degli Uberti. The last (ff. 31v–2) is *Dittamondo*

Lib. II, cap. 30, lines 82–108. Part (*a*) was probably written *c.* 1478–79 during the plague. On paper, watermarks: in (*a*) a ladder, Briquet No. 5907 or 5911; (*b*) an angel(?) holding up two fleur de lys, not in Briquet. 205 × 140 mm. Part (*a*) is written in a humanistic cursive with gothic features; part (*b*) was written by Bartolomeo Fonzio, who also wrote a few notes in part (*a*). Presumably the dedication copy; Benivieni apparently dedicated the work to Lorenzo de' Medici as well (Kristeller, *Iter*, I, p. 90: Laur. Ashb. 781 (712), ff. 1–11*v*).

*(80) *Florence, Bibl. Naz. Magl. XV 190 (former Strozzi 4to No. 283)*, beginning (f. 1): Rimedii efficacissimi contro la peste . . . (P. O. Kristeller, *Supplementum Ficinianum*, Florence, 1937, I, p. xxiii; II, pp. 175–82: edition of the text). Probably written *c.* 1478–79. Four leaves, 226 × 164 mm. Semi-humanistic cursive hand. Front flyleaf (sixteenth-century): 'Ricepte contro alla peste composte dalla viva voce di M.o Marsilio Ficino fiorentino medico e filosofo ex.mo a stanza di Franc.o di Tomaso Sassetti cittadino fiorentino e scritta di mano di M. Bart.o Fontio'. The hand of the text does not look like Fonzio's, but a few annotations may be in Sassetti's hand. There is no reference to Sassetti in Ficino's *Consiglio contro la pestilenza*, first printed Florence, Ripoli, 1481 (Hain 7082).

*(81) *Oxford, Bodleian Library Rawl. C.748*, Isaac, *De dietis universalibus* and *Practica* (G. D. Macray, *Richardi Rawlinson Codicum classem tertium* [*Cat. Codd. MSS Bibl. Bodl.* v, 2], 1878, col. 387). Written in Italy, twelfth or thirteenth century. 113 written leaves (ff. 113–3*v* contain medical recipes and verses in a slightly later hand), 183 × 108 mm. Folio 113: 'Emi hunc librum a Bianco die 3ª Novembris 1439'. Folio ii*v* (flyleaf): 'Thadaei Ugoleti parmen[sis]', written over an erasure of two lines, ending 'F', which may have been in Fonzio's hand. Marginalia by Fonzio, including, f. 98, 'Epydimia'. Also marginalia in a hand of the thirteenth to fourteenth centuries.

?*(82) *Vatican Library, Vat. Lat. 3277*, Valerius Flaccus (Chatelain, *Paléog. class. lat.* II, plate CLXV; Sabbadini, *Scoperte*, I, p. 151; II, p. 257; E. Courtney, preface to Teubner edition of Valerius Flaccus, 1970, pp. vi–viii, x; *Survie des classiques latins*, No. 93; V. Branca in *Venezia e Ungheria . . .*, pp. 347–52). Ninth century, from Fulda. 140 leaves, 190 × 150 mm. The MS was perhaps in Italy by 1429, though not necessarily, since Niccoli's copy (from which another was made in 1429), was apparently not copied directly from it. In the sixteenth century the MS belonged to Fulvio Orsini. Since no other complete early MS of Valerius Flaccus is known, it has been assumed that this is the MS 'très vieux' of Valerius Flaccus that Taddeo Ugoleto bought from Sassetti, with a Martial, for King Matthias Corvinus. He mentioned the two MSS in an undated latter to the king, the present whereabouts of which is not known (A. Del Prato, 'Librai e biblioteche parmensi . . .', *Arch. stor. prov. parm.*, new series, IV, 1904, 12, quotes a French translation of the letter, which was apparently first printed by S. Hegedus in J. Abel and S. Hegedus. *Analecta nova*, Budapest, 1903, pp. 458–9, not available to me). Poliziano, in his *Miscellanea*, pr. 19 September 1489 (Hain 13221), also mentions the MS 'pervet[us]' of Valerius Flaccus, belonging by then to King Matthias Corvinus, and in the hands of Ugoleto (see reference in Courtney). However, he also refers to the MS in his *Secunda centuria* (ed. Branca, Pastore Stocchi, cap. 2, 11): '. . . Eumque mihi librum, tunc quoque sic perversum Taddaeus Ugoletus parmensis olim commodavit, cuius in marginibus Nicolai Nicoli florentini manus agnoscitur'. As Branca points out, there are no annotations attributable to Niccoli in the present MS (*ed. cit.*, I, p. 23, n. 45). Nor are there any traces in it of the ownership of Sassetti or Ugoleto. So was there another complete early MS of Valerius Flaccus (descended from this one) circulating in Florence in the fifteenth century and now lost, or was Poliziano mistaken in his reference to Niccoli? If this *was* the MS owned by Sassetti he probably acquired it late in his life, since it does not appear in the 1462 list, and Fonzio's transcript of the text, made for Sassetti (No. 25 above) was not copied from it but is a descendant of Niccoli's copy.

Rejected MSS

Three MSS have coats of arms which have been said to be Sassetti's but which are not in fact his:

> (a) *Florence, Laur. 43, 15*, Petrus de Crescentiis, *De agricultura*, in Italian (D'Ancona No. 342). Florentine MS of *c.* 1460–70. The arms are Capponi of Florence.
>
> (b) *Laur. 45, 12*, Servius on Virgil, *Buc.* and *Georg.* (Bandini ii, col. 344; D' Ancona No. 344). Fine Florentine MS of *c.* 1430–40. The arms are Alamanni of Florence.
>
> (c) *Laur. Strozzi 94*, Boccaccio, *De montibus* (D'Ancona No. 901). Florentine MS of late fifteenth century, on paper. Arms azure, a bend argent, perhaps Buonaveri of Florence.

NOTES

In preparing a study of this kind one incurs many debts. I would especially like to thank Mr Bruce Barker-Benfield, who described for me a number of MSS which I had not time to see for myself and checked others; Dr Richard Hunt, who kindly read and criticised my draft; the staff of the Biblioteca Medicea Laurenziana for their kindness and patience, and for help with enquiries, Dr Jonathan Alexander, M. François Avril, Professor Bernhard Bischoff, Dott. M. Fornieri, Dr Margaret T. Gibson, Mr Michael Reeve, Monsignor José Ruysschaert, M. Jean Vezin and Mr William Voelkle.

[1] For Sassetti's life see first R. de Roover, *The Rise and Decline of the Medici Bank, 1397–1494*, Cambridge, Mass., 1963, pp. 361–4 and *passim* (with family tree on p. 389); J.-F. Bergier, *Genève et l'économie européenne de la Renaissance*, Paris, 1963, pp. 288–291 and *passim*. These authors correct mistakes in the earlier, still indispensable studies: A. Warburg, 'Francesco Sassettis letzwillige Verfügung', originally published in 1907 and reprinted in his *Gesammelte Schriften*, I, Leipzig and Berlin, 1932, pp. 129–158, 353–65 (additional notes), henceforth cited as 'Verfügung'; F. Edler de Roover, 'Fransesco Sassetti and the downfall of the Medici banking house', *Bulletin of the Business Historical Society*, XVII, 1943, 65–80. Warburg, pp. 130–4, reprints the account of Sassetti by his great-grandson Francesco di Giovambattista, a useful source but also the origin of later mistakes. For a detailed family tree and genealogical notes see Passerini in *Archivio storico italiano*, IV, 2, 1853, cx–cxii.

[2] 'Humanisme et vie d'affaires. La bibliothèque du banquier Francesco Sassetti', in *Mélanges en l'honneur de Fernand Braudel*, I, *Histoire économique du monde mediterranéen 1450–1650*, Toulouse, 1973, pp. 107–21.

[3] This list was already known to Warburg ('Verfugüng', p. 133, n. 4).

[4] 1446?–1513. See especially C. Marchesi, *Bartolomeo della Fonte*, first edition, Catania, 1899. This is very rare, but includes an appendix of letters not in the edition of 1900; F. Saxl, 'The classical inscription in Renaissance art and politics', *Journal of the Warburg and Courtauld Institutes*, IV, 1940–41, 19–46; C. Trinkaus, 'A humanist's image of humanism: the inaugural orations of Bartolomeo della Fonte', *Studies in the Renaissance*, VII, 1960, 90–147. The family name was probably della Fonte but Bartolomeo always referred to himself as 'Fontio' or 'Fontius' and his contemporaries usually did the same.

[5] For example, Marchesi, *op. cit.*, pp. 80, 130, calls Sassetti 'l'Aurispa della seconda generazione umanistica'. The mistaken belief was reinforced by the note 'Franciscus Sassettus faciundum curavit' found in a number of manuscripts: see above, p. 167.

⁶ Appendix 9.1. Bergier printed the list in his article cited n. 1, which appeared when I was already preparing to publish it in the present study. Since I do not agree with all his readings I decided to include it nonetheless.

⁷ Appendix 9.2. The full inventory was printed by Piccolomini in his study of the Medici library, but I have listed the deleted items in this appendix for convenience of reference.

⁸ Listed and described in appendix 9.3. Descriptions in this appendix will be cited simply as 'No. 1', etc. Most of them are already identifiable in Bandini's catalogue of the Latin manuscripts of the Medici collection in the Biblioteca Laurenziana, published in the 1770s. Several more were added by D'Ancona in his book on Florentine illumination, published in 1914. A few of their attributions are mistaken: see above, p. 190.

⁹ See plates 9.1–2 and reproductions cited of Nos. 23, 27, 30, 48, 61, 71. All but one of the former Sassetti MSS known to me have been rebound, but many still retain their original end paste-downs, and on these is often to be found a number, written in arabic numerals, in a fifteenth- to sixteenth-century hand, in the upper right-hand corner and framed on the left by a semi-circle. This is apparently a Medici numbering. For example, '72' written in this way is found in MS Laur. 21, 13, which has the *ex libris* of Piero di Cosimo de' Medici.

¹⁰ Based on the authorities cited in n. 1.

¹¹ After his return he held a number of suitable public offices: member of the Signoria, January–February 1468/9 (G. Cambi, *Istorie* [*Delizie degli eruditi toscani*, ed. I. di San Luigi, xx], 1785, p. 491); *arroto* for Balìe of 1471, 1480 (N. Rubinstein, *The Government of Florence under the Medici, 1434–94*, Oxford, 1966, pp. 307, 313); one of the 'officiales Banchi' for eight months from May 1467; official of the Monte for a year from March 1467/8; one of the 'conservatores legum' for six months beginning 25 September 1471 (Florence, Arch. di Stato, Tratte 81, ff. 151, 65*v*, 53); official of the Studio for a year from November 1484 (*ibid.*, Tratte 82, f. 49).

¹² Sassetti's account of his assets in 1462 and 1466 is analysed in detail by F. Edler de Roover in her article cited in n. 1.

¹³ Warburg, 'Verfügung', pp. 133–4, 143; G. Carocci, *I dintorni di Firenze*, I, Florence, 1906, p. 183. Sassetti acquired the palace from the Macinghi in 1460. It was sold to Piero Capponi by Sassetti's son, Teodoro, in 1546 but was still known as 'Il Sassetto' in Carocci's time. Apparently only traces of Sassetti's building now remain: see A. Chastel, *Art et humanisme à Florence au temps de Laurent le Magnifique*, Paris, 1959, pp. 170–1.

¹⁴ Warburg, pp. 135–8.

¹⁵ There still seems to be some doubt about the dates when Sassetti acquired rights over the chapel in S. Trinità and when its decoration was completed, although the dates already suggested by Warburg for the decoration of the chapel—1480–86—appear to be the correct ones. The document concerning masses for St Francis to be celebrated in the chapel and the endowment of the chapel (Warburg, 'Bildniskunst und Florentinisches Burgertum 1', *Gesamm. Schriften* 1, p. 97 n. 1: Florence, Arch. di Stato, Arch. Not. Antecosmiano A.381 [Ser Andrea d'Agnolo da Terranova, 1482–88], ff. 269–75), is dated 1 January 1486/7, not 1486 as sometimes stated, and refers to the decoration and tombs as completed. Warburg ('Verfügung', p. 138, n. 1) also cites a document of February 1479 which shows that Sassetti had acquired the rights over the chapel by then. However, a published letter of Sassetti's, 18 April 1478 to Francesco Gaddi, which shows that he was still negotiating then to acquire the right to the chapel (for as little as possible), does not seem to have been noticed (exhibition catalogue, *Il Quattrocento negli autografi e negli incunaboli della Bibl. Nazionale di Roma*, 1950, No. 136).

¹⁶ Apart from Warburg's two articles see, for example, E. Borsook, *The Mural Painters of Tuscany*, London, 1960, pp. 159–60 and plates 80–4; C. de Tolnay, 'Two frescoes by Domenico and David Ghirlandaio in Santa Trinità in Florence', *Wallraf-*

Richartz Jahrbuch, xxiii, 1961, 237 ff; W. Welliver in *Art Quarterly*, xxxii, 1969, 269 ff; Artur Rosenauer, 'Ein nicht zur Ausführung gelangter Entwurf Dom. Ghirlandaios für die Capella Sassetti', *Festschrift Otto Demus und Otto Pacht (Wiener Jahrbuch für Kunstgesch.* xxv), 1972, 187 ff.

[17] Some of the examples identified by him and others are cited by Warburg, 'Verfügung', pp. 154–5; see also Saxl, 'The classical inscription', p. 28; de Tolnay, *op. cit.*, p. 239.

[18] Fonzio may also have devised the inscriptions on the tombs of Sassetti and his wife ('The classical inscription', pp. 27–9). Did he suggest as well Sassetti's adoption of the centaur as a personal emblem? Warburg pointed out that the idea could derive from Ciriaco of Ancona's collections of inscriptions and drawings of classical monuments ('Verfügung', p. 155). Fonzio's epigraphical collection is largely derived from collections of Ciriaco (Saxl, pp. 30–7).

[19] The autograph MS (which formerly belonged to Professor Bernard Ashmole), now Oxford, Bodl. Lat. misc. d. 85, is described in detail by Saxl, *op. cit.* Note f. 55: 'Hoc ego ex proprio loco assumpsi e Roma rediens cum Fr. Saxetto'; f. 55*v*: '. . . hoc e Roma rediens cum Fr. Sassetto comperi et ex equo descendens transcripsi'; f. 64*v*, an inscription 'nuper inventum a nobis' at Ripoli, near Florence; ff. 65, 92*v*, inscriptions sent to Sassetti by Filippo Martelli, the second specifically 'e Roma'. This was probably Filippo di Ugolino Martelli (1438–73), who was a factor of the Medici bank in Rome, 1455–66 (de Roover, *Rise and Decline of Medici Bank*, p. 388). Saxl (p. 30, n. 2) lists a number of inscriptions from Lyons and Nîmes which are not known in collections earlier than Fonzio's, and suggests that he could have got them from Cosimo Sassetti, Francesco's son, who was with the Medici branch at Lyons in the 1480s. They are more likely to have come from Francesco himself, since all but one come in the earlier part of Fonzio's MS, between ff. 62–71*v*.

[20] E.g. to Francesco Gaddi in Rome, 18 April 1478: '. . . Raccomandovi tutto e recordovi medagle, sculpture, epigrammi o se altro vi capita . . .' (letter *cit.* above, n. 15); to the same in France, 4 March 1478–9: '. . . investigate di qualche epigramma antico, che ne debbe essere nel paese del quale vi fate parte . . .' (ed. T. De Marinis and A. Perosa, *Nuovi documenti per la storia del Rinascimento*, Florence, 1970, p. 24). See also *Protocolli del carteggio di Lorenzo il Magnifico* . . ., ed. M. Del Piazzo, Florence, 1956, p. 165 (12 September 1481): 'Al signore di Faenza. Risposta, e mandossi li epitafii del Sassetto.' For Francesco d'Agnolo Gaddi, who also owned a fine library, see especially L. Sozzi, 'Lettere ined. di Philippe de Commynes à Francesco Gaddi', *Studi . . . in on. di T. De Marinis* iv, 1964, 205–62; C. Bec, 'La bibliothèque d'un grand bourgeois florentin, Francesco d'Agnolo Gaddi (1496)', *Bibl. d'Humanisme et Renaissance* xxxiv, 1972, pp. 239–47.

[21] '. . . Attendo se arete mandato questo libro mi promettesti in cambio della testa di Cammilla et in cambio di quello fauno rosso. Bisongna orationii o pistole di Tulio et poi sarete quito et chancellato. Annosi a dare altri amici[?]. Io ò bene a mente quell'altre teste et se nulla ci chapitera di buono a merchato raxonevole non me le lascero schappare. Anchora ò a mente quelli epitaffi ma bisongnami essere a Lione. Non abbiate pensiero ch'io dimentichi nessuno vostro fatto, così prego che me et i mieii abbiate a richordo per che sono pure vostro et vostra creatura et con voi ò a vivere et morire . . .', from Geneva, 24 August 1456. (Florence, Arch. di Stato, Arch. Med. avanti il Principato, Filz. xvii, 127. The first part of the letter was cited in detail by Bergier, *Genève*, p. 303, but he misunderstood this passage and thought that Sassetti was sending books to Piero.) For Piero's inventories see E. Müntz, *Les Collections des Médicis au XVe s.*, Paris, 1888, p. 16 (15 September 1456): 'Uno anello leghatovi un chammeo con una testa di Chamilla . . . Uno anello leghatovi un chammeo et corniuola con una testa d'un Fauno'. Beside both items is noted in the margin 'Di rilievo leghate in oro'. The rings appear again in Piero's inventory of 20 January 1464/5, where the second cameo is further described as 'di diaspro' (Müntz, p. 38), but they are not identifiable in the 1492 inventory of Lorenzo.

[22] See C. Bec, *Les Marchands écrivains à Florence 1375–1434*, Paris, 1967, especially part III, ch. II, pp. 383–415, 'Formation intellectuelle et culture des marchands'. It seems that boys destined to commerce generally left school at fourteen or fifteen to be apprenticed (p. 391).

[23] B. L. Ullman and P. A. Stadter, *The Public Library of Renaissance Florence*, Padua, 1972, especially part II, pp. 59–104; A. C. de la Mare, *The Handwriting of Italian Humanists*, I, I, 1973, No. 4, Niccolò Niccoli, p. 48.

[24] No. 70 below. For bibliography on the *Commentarium* see N. Rubinstein, 'An unknown letter by Jacopo di Poggio Bracciolini on discoveries of classical texts', *Italia medioevale e umanistica*, I, 1958, 383–4. The addition is written in a humanistic cursive hand of the second half of the fifteenth century (not Fonzio's), and another possibility is that it was written after the MS had entered the collection of King Matthias Corvinus of Hungary, perhaps by Taddeo Ugoleto, who searched Europe for manuscripts to buy for the king (for Ugoleto see below, n. 94).

[25] Sabbadini, who did not know the 1462 list, listed Sassetti books which had probably come from France but indeed the Pauline Epistles and Seneca, Nos. 5, 17, app. 9.3, which are certainly Italian (*Le scoperte dei codici latini e greci nei secoli XIV e XV*, I, Florence, 1905 (reprinted with Sabbadini's addenda, ed. E. Garin, Florence, 1967), p. 165, and addenda, p. 273 (the Bologna MS: No. 1, appendix 9.3).

[26] See 1456 letter *cit.* n. 21, also Bergier, *Genève*, p. 330: on 24 April 1455 Sassetti and his colleagues applied for citizenship of Lyons to help their business there and in the rest of France. The Medici branch at Geneva was moved to Lyons in 1466.

[27] The Priscian is difficult to place. It may have been written in Italy but has French-looking decoration.

[28] What did Sassetti (or Fonzio) mean by 'Gallia'? Sabbadini suggested that when Fonzio used the word in the preface to his edition of Celsus he meant 'Cisalpine Gaul' (see below, n. 88). The same interpretation may apply here. Perhaps Sassetti acquired the south German MS in Geneva from a visiting agent who knew of his book collecting.

[29] The first, historiated, initial in this MS is close to the style of 'Zebo da Firenze': *cf.* O. Pächt and J. J. G. Alexander, *Catalogue of Illuminated MSS in the Bodleian Library*, II, Oxford, 1970, plate XIII, No. 131. The gothic script of the MS shows humanistic influence. The earlier owner of the MS, 'Gyido Pontecelo', was probably a member of the Ponticelli family of Bologna.

[30] Oddly enough, the scholars who have cited the MS did not identify the text, although Bandini already named Rambaldi as the author. The MS is generally assigned to Venice, because Marsilius worked there later, but the decoration is very close to that in MSS made in Bologna in the 1450s, for example for Cardinal Bessarion. *Cf.* Venice, Bibl. Naz. Marciana, *Cento codici bessarionei*, exhibition catalogue, 1968, No. 96 (1453), plate 57; No. 98, plate 58; also Pächt and Alexander, *Cat.* II, plate LXIV, Nos. 661, 666.

[31] He also says that Sassetti and his family were granted citizenship of Bologna in 1484 by public decree (Warburg, 'Verfügung', p. 131).

[32] I have tried many 'possibles' in the Medici collection in the Biblioteca Medicea Laurenziana, where most of the identified Sassetti MSS are to be found, but with no success so far. Probably many of the less valuable MSS were disposed of in the 1470s, and others sold in the late 1480s.

[33] Two old copies of Lucan are listed in the inventory (appendix 9.1, Nos. 22, 41). One of these is probably identifiable with No. 74 below.

[34] Sassetti's known copy of Poggio's translation of Diodorus Siculus is too late (No. 50). A Greek MS of Diodorus Siculus on paper, N.B. Vienna, Suppl. gr. 20, copied by Johannes Skutariotes in Florence in 1442, probably belonged at one time to King Matthias Corvinus of Hungary, who bought a number of Sassetti's MSS in the 1480s (C. Csapodi and K. Csapodi-Gárdonyi, *Bibliotheca Corviniana*, Shannon, 1969, No. 166). Could it be—by a long stretch of the imagination—that this MS once belonged to Poggio (i.e. 'di Poggio') and later to Sassetti? The inventory made after Poggio's

death listed 'Diobeus [*i.e.* Diodorus?] in papiro' (E. Walser, *Poggius Florentinus*, 1914, p. 423). Perhaps Corvinus also acquired Sassetti's expensive MS of Cicero's speeches. No MS of his containing the speeches has been identified, but it is a text that he is likely to have owned.

[35] Could this be the Corvinus MS, Budapest, Nat. Mus. Clmae 425, copied in Florence in 1422 (I. Berkovits, *Illuminated manuscripts from the library of Matthias Corvinus*, Budapest, 1964, No. 35 and fig. 1; *Bibl. Corviniana, cit.*, No. 38)?

[36] For the translation, first printed at Nürnberg *c.* 1475 with Griffolini's translation of the letters of Diogenes (Hain 6192), see G. Mancini, *Francesco Griffolini cognominato Francesco Aretino*, Florence, 1890, p. 30; E. P. Goldschmidt, 'Lucian's *Calumnia*', in *Saxl Memorial Essays*, ed. D. J. Gordon, London, 1957, pp. 235–7. Mancini and Saxl between them list four MSS containing the *De calumnia* translation: Cambridge, St John's Coll. 61; London, B.M., Arundel 277; Munich, clm. 414, and Florence, Laur. 53, 21. The first three belonged to John Gunthorpe, the Pirckheimers and Hartmann Schedel respectively. The fourth could be Sassetti's copy. Lucian comes on ff. 24–36 but was originally a separate MS, much earlier in date than the first part of the volume as it now stands, which contains Carlo Aldobrandi, *Libellus ad rationem studendi* dedicated to Lorenzo de' Medici, decorated in late fifteenth-century style and probably the dedication copy. The Lucian is a simple MS in a good humanistic cursive with vine-stem initials, and could easily have been made as early as 1462. There are no original flyleaves. The MS of Calpurnius Siculus may be Florence, Ricc. 724, on parchment, twenty-seven written leaves, approx. 196 × 130 mm. with simple Florentine vine-stem initials of *c.* 1450–60. On f. 24*v* is a marginal bracket in red, apparently in the hand of Bartolomeo Fonzio.

[37] There is no room here to go into the complicated question of the prices that were paid for books in the fifteenth century. The price could be affected by many factors: length, materials, age, type of decoration, rarity of the text, provenance. On the whole the first owner bore the brunt of the cost of a book; second-hand books usually cost comparatively much less than new copies of the same text, and MSS on paper cost much less than the same texts copied on parchment.

[38] Between 1462 and 1466, when Sassetti reassessed his property (but without making a new list of his books), the estimated value of his books had risen from 391 to 500 florins (F. Edler de Roover, 'Francesco Sassetti . . .', p. 70). This could represent between ten and twenty new MSS.

[39] I shall discuss and list the work of Hubertus fully in my forthcoming book on Vespasiano da Bisticci. There is one signed MS, Laur. Fies. 19, Augustine on Psalms (Bandini does not cite the colophon), produced by Vespasiano for Fiesole in 1464. Folio 252: 'Deo gratias. Hubertus scripsit.' Hubertus' early hand, as found in the Fiesole MS, has many gothic features. By about 1470 these have mostly disappeared, but he never abandoned the single-compartment 'a'. For some reproductions of his hand (unfortunately there is none of the early type) see under Nos. 27, 30, 66, 67, 68, 70, 73, appendix 9.3.

[40] He is an artist very close to Francesco d'Antonio del Cherico, who specialised in decorative borders rather than miniatures and who, for want of a better name, I call the master of the pear-shaped *putti*. He first appears about 1460, and is active until at least the early 1480s. Many examples of his work have been reproduced, both in the 'vine stem' and the later flower styles. For a few examples of his early style see *Bibl. Corviniana, cit.*, plates XLIII, XCVI, XCVIII; Berkovits, *op. cit.*, plates III, VI, VII, XII.

[41] The verse colophon is very obscure, but it certainly mentions Antonio Gaio, i.e. perhaps Antonio del Gaio or da Legnano, the chancellor *c.* 1369 of Cansignorio della Scala (d. 1385), for whom see G. Billanovich, 'Dal Livio di Raterio al Livio del Petrarca', *Italia med. e um.* II, 1959, 160–2, 166–9.

[42] For the bibliography on Cortese (d. *c.* 1445) see C. Huter, 'The Novella master: a Paduan illuminator around 1400', *Arte veneta*, XXV, 1971, n. 55. For some examples of his work see Pächt and Alexander, *Cat.* II, Nos. 443, 449, etc, but the present MS

is decorated in a more humanistic style, similar to the Dyson Perrins Cicero (Warner, *Cat.*, No. 70), sold Sotheby's 29 November 1960, lot 126.

[43] For a recent study of this master see A. Stones, 'An Italian miniature in the Gambier–Parry collection', *Burlington Magazine*, CXI, 1969, 7–11.

[44] See n. 86 below.

[45] Nos. 27, 30, 46, 51, 57, 66, 67, 68, 70, 73,

[46] Nos. 6, 16, 35, 40, 41, 47, 49, 50, 52, 63, 69, 78. I shall also discuss the work of Niccolò Fonzio in my book on Vespasiano. His hand is very close to that of his brother, Bartolomeo, and sometimes hard to distinguish from it. My identification is again based on one signed MS: Laur. Ashb. 1052 (983), letters of Ps.-Phalaris in the Italian translation of Bartolomeo Fonzio (P. O. Kristeller, *Iter italicum*, I, 1963, p. 93). Folio 60*v*: 'Scripte per Nicholo Fontio adi xv di luglio Mcccclxviii'.

[47] Nos. 8–10, 12–15, 18, 20, 25, 29, 71, 71A. Fonzio too signed only one MS: Munich, Bayerisches Staatsbibl., clm., 15738, Macrobius, *Saturnalia* and *Comment. in Somn. Scip.*, copied for his Hungarian friend Petrus Garazda (reproduced by C. Trinkaus, 'The unknown Quattrocento Poetics of Bartolomeo della Fonte', *Studies in the Renaissance*, XIII, 1966, 42, 43: he analyses Fonzio's hand on p. 122), but his *zibaldoni* in the Biblioteca Riccardiana in Florence, already studied in detail by Marchesi and Sabbadini, have long been accepted as his autographs (for some reproductions see I. Maier, *Ange Politien*, Geneva, 1966, pp. 50–1, 54–5). For some reproductions of other MSS copied by Bartolomeo see *Bibliotheca Corviniana*, plates XVIII, XXVI, XXXV, CXXVIII.

[48] The eight MSS are: No. 61, Aristotle, *Politics*; Nos. 42 and 60, Bruni's *History of Florence* and Aristotle, *Ethics*, copied by the scribe who (probably earlier) copied Aristeas (No. 36); No. 65, Germanicus, *Aratea*, etc, copied in a good humanistic cursive. This MS could be earlier but is decorated in the same style as one of the Niccolò Fonzio MSS (No. 47); Nos. 37–9, Sassetti's set of Livy, copied by Giovanfrancesco Marzi, who seems to have been a Livy specialist; No. 23, Sassetti's splendid Virgil, copied *c.* 1480 or even later.

[49] Fonzio had been in Ferrara (probably from early 1469, rather than 1467 as Marchesi suggests), but returned to Florence after the death of Borso d'Este in August 1471. He had hoped to go to Hungary, but that plan fell through. It was probably in the spring of 1472 that he accompanied Sassetti on their visit to Rome (for which see above, n. 19), for he described such a visit in a letter to Battista Guarino dated April 1472 (Bart. Fontius, *Epist.*, ed. L. Juhász, Budapest, 1931, Ep. I, 16). Fonzio wrote an account of Roman weights and measures, in response to Sassetti's repeated requests, in the form of a long letter (Ep. III., 7, earlier version: see pp. 50–3). He rededicated it later, *c.* 1510–11, to Francesco Ricci). Delayed 'ob innumeras occupationes', he dated the letter Cal. Jan. 1472, i.e. probably January 1473, when he was on a mission to Foviano with Donato Acciaiuoli (A. Della Torre, *Storia dell'Accademia Platonica di Firenze*, Florence, 1902, pp. 421–2). Fonzio accompanied Acciauoli on another mission, to France, in October to December 1473 but pined for the Sassetti family and Montughi (Bart. Fontius, *Carmina*, ed. I. Fogel and L. Juhász, Leipzig, 1932, I, 3, pp. 2–3; Della Torre, *op. cit.*, p. 412, n. 1). Fonzio's letter to Piero Cennini (Ep. I, 18) describing how he had been taken up by Sassetti after his other hopes of patronage had failed must be dated to August 1473, rather than 1472 as in the MS and edition (Della Torre, *loc. cit.*).

[50] See Nos. 31, 53, 78, appendix 9.3.

[51] Books which Fonzio actually owned were much more heavily annotated by him, often at several different dates, and the notes are full of specific cross-references to his other books. For an example of such annotations see his twelfth-century Horace, Florence, Ricc. MS 700.

[52] For some examples of his notes, etc., see plate 9.3, also *Bibl. Corviniana*, plates XXIV (Greek only), XCI; E. Casamassima in *Magyar Könyvszemle*, LXXXI, 1965, 111, fig. 14.

[53] See his poem addressed to Sassetti (*Carmina, cit.*, I, 5, p. 5):

... Totque inter curas et tanta negotia semper
Intendens animum nobilibus studiis,
Quaecunque historici, quicquid scripsere poetae
Estque Leontina quicquid in arte, vides,
Colligis et veterum praecepta et scripta novorum,
Doctorum releves ut monumenta virum ...

⁵⁴ E.g. appendix 9.1, Nos. 31 and 45, 32, 35 and 46, 36, 39, 56–7, were probably replaced by appendix 9.3, Nos. 70, 15, 12, 19 or 20, 10, 71. The replacement of appendix 9.1, Nos. 16 and 30, by appendix 9.3, Nos. 23 and 71A?, probably occurred later.

⁵⁵ Part of the collection of speeches already appears in a rather earlier MS: see No. 30, appendix 9.3.

⁵⁶ Florence, Bibl. Riccardiana, MSS 62, 151–4, 646, 667(?), 673, 819, 837, 893, 907 (see Marchesi, *B. della Fonte*, pp. 101–12; Trinkaus, 'A humanist's image ...', pp. 131–2; Kristeller, *Iter*, I, *passim*. Some of the MSS were known to and used by Sabbadini. I understand that a detailed study of the *zibaldoni* will be published shortly in Florence.

⁵⁷ In Ricc. 907, f. 137*v*, and ff. 152, 148 (Kristeller, *Iter*, I, pp. 208, 188). Domizio Calderini's Life of Suetonius, in Ricc. 153, f. 100 (*ibid.*, p. 188) is included in No. 73 below. Is the 'Abbreviatio de situ orbis' attributed to Sozomeno of Pistoia in No. 68 the same as the geographical names 'ex Zombino' in Ricc. 673, f. 132 (*ibid.*, p. 196)?

⁵⁸ Herodotus and Thucydides, translated by Valla; Diodorus Siculus, translated by Poggio; Strabo, translated by Guarino; Dionysius of Halicarnassus, translated by Lampugnano Birago.

⁵⁹ The translation had been made by 15 July 1468 (see n. 46 above). The first printed edition (Hain 12903) is dated 1471. See also Clough's essay in this volume, p. 57.

⁶⁰ Sometimes spelt 'SAXETTI'.

⁶¹ See appendix 9.3, A (i), (iv). Nos. 36, 53, 70, in which the *ex libris* is (or was) partly erased, may have been the same, but they could have had the 'faciundum curavit' version.

⁶² See above, p. 169.

⁶³ Sometimes spelt 'SAXETTVS'.

⁶⁴ These two words are often reversed. They are omitted in Nos. 47, 50.

⁶⁵ See appendix 9.3, A (ii).

⁶⁶ E.g. those cited in n. 61, and others where flyleaves are lost.

⁶⁷ For a discussion of Sassetti's mottoes see Warburg, 'Verfügung', pp. 153–4.

⁶⁸ The process of obliteration has usually been completed by the use of reagent on the erasures.

⁶⁹ See Nos. 1, 2, 7, 19, 26, 48, 56, 58, 64.

⁷⁰ *Cf.* the almost identical note in No. 1. The note in No. 64 is also written in the first person.

⁷¹ See appendix 9.3, A (iii). Nos. 31, 39 have 'FRANCISCI SASSETTI T[HOMAE] F[ILII]'.

⁷² Nos. 8–10, 12–15, 18, 20, 29, 35, 40–1, 46, 51, 57, 63, 66, 73.

⁷³ Nos. 31–2, 34, 42, 53, 60.

⁷⁴ In the first border to No. 30. Reproductions of the page in the Aristotle are cited under No. 60.

⁷⁵ For references see No. 65.

⁷⁶ Nos. 23, 27, 40, 61, 71A.

⁷⁷ Nos. 10, 12, 14–15, 18, 27, 30, 41 (plates 9.2–3), 46, 51, 60–1, 66. This is often the only way in which the emblem is used in the decoration.

⁷⁸ Nos. 23, 27, 30–1, 67, 71A. See also No. 78, which may not have belonged to Sassetti. The only complete page reproduced by Bergier is of a MS from this group (no. 27). This gives a misleading impression of the type of MS that Sassetti owned.

⁷⁹ Nos. 42, 46, 60, 68, 70, 73.

[80] No. 70.

[81] Nos. 10, 12, 14–16, 18, 27, 30, 37–9, 41 (plate 9.2), 51, 60–1, 66–7. For documentation on Antonio, 1445–1527, see M. Levi D'Ancona, *Miniatura e miniatori a Firenze dal XIV al XVI secolo*, 1962, pp. 19–22 and plate 2. I base my attribution to him of MSS decorated in humanistic style on her identification of his hand in a Hebrew biblical MS dated 1467 (now Yale Univ. MS 409), sold at Sotheby's on 9 July 1969, lot 63, with plate. Many of his MSS have been reproduced. For a few examples see references under Nos. 27, 30, 60–1, 66–7; and for an example of his flower style, British Museum, *Reproductions from Illuminated Manuscripts*, third series, London, 1908, plate XL (Add. MS 15246).

[82] Nos. 6(?), 8(?), 9 (plate 9.1), 13(?), 20, 25(?), 49, 50(?), 52, 63(?), 71. The attribution of the six indicated by a question mark is not completely certain because there are no figures in the decoration. This illuminator's *putti* are fatter and softer than Antonio's, which are usually quite thin and muscular-looking. For a reproduction of a rather more elaborate MS decorated by the second artist see T. De Marinis, *La biblioteca napoletana dei re d'Aragona*, III, Milan, 1947, plate 158.

[83] Nos. 40 and 57 are decorated in the vine-stem style by a feeble artist strongly influenced by Antonio; Nos. 47 and 65 have simple vine-stem borders perhaps by a follower of Ser Benedetto di Silvestro; Nos. 29, 35 and 78 are decorated in the new flower style by another artist perhaps influenced by Benedetto. No. 42 is decorated in a similar style by an artist even closer to Benedetto.

[84] Nos. 68, 70, 73. For Ser Benedetto, an artist closely associated with Francesco d'Antonio and often confused with him, see Levi D'Ancona, *Miniatura*, pp. 65–9 and plate 9.

[85] No. 69 is decorated by Rosselli and No. 46 by his follower. Rosselli was identified by M. Levi D'Ancona, 'Francesco Rosselli', *Commentari*, XVI, 1965, 56–76.

[86] For example, the Cicero copied by Giovanni Aretino (No. 62), to which a border with the Sassetti arms was added in the style of the mid-1470s or later, and Sassetti's ancient MS of Valerius Flaccus, perhaps identifiable with No. 82. Bartolomeo Fonzio used a fifteenth-century text to make his copy of Valerius Flaccus for Sassetti (No. 25): he would surely have used the old one, at least for corrections, if Sassetti had already owned it then. No. 81 is another MS which Sassetti may have acquired at this time.

[87] Apart from the poems and letters of Fonzio we have a letter to Sassetti from Ficino (*Opera*, Basle, 1576, p. 799), and poems by Ugolino Verino (*Epigrammata*, book VII, 28 and 29: f. 77v in MS. Laur. 39, 40). Alessandro Braccesi dedicated the first version of his *Amores* to Sassetti. (See A. Perosa in the introduction to his edition of Braccesi's *Carmina*, Florence, 1943. B. Agnoletti, *Aless. Braccesi*, 1901, pp. 38–9, says this dedication cannot be later than 1473.)

[88] See the bibliography under No. 78. Sabbadini suggested that by 'Gallia' Fonzio meant Cisalpine Gaul rather than France only, and that he was referring not only to Laur. 73, 1, which he borrowed from Bologna, and which had been discovered earlier in Milan, but also to Laur. 73, 4 (No. 78), which he certainly used for the edition. Unfortunately Laur. 73, 4 was copied in Florence, not Milan as Sabbadini supposed.

[89] Printed by Marchesi, *B. della Fonte*, p. 194, n. 1. The original letter, with an added note by Sassetti, is Florence, Bibl. Naz. MS Magl. XXIV 108, f. 2. For Fonzio's continuing association with Sassetti see also *Protocolli . . . di Lorenzo il Magnifico, cit.*, p. 65: 6 August 1478 'Al re di Francia, a Giannetto Ballerini, ordinò Francesco Sassetti, scripse il Fontio'. In a letter of February 1479(/80?) to Antonio Calderini, Fonzio made excuses for Sassetti, who had not answered a letter because he was too busy (*Ep.* I, 21, p. 21).

[90] Florence, Arch. di Stato, Arch. Notarile Antecosmiano c. 395, f. 127. In November 1480, when he acted for the printer Niccolò di Lorenzo in an agreement, he was described as 'literarii ludi magister' (*ibid.*, f. 138v).

[91] Marchesi, *B. della Fonte*, p. 72.

[92] For Fonzio's appointments in the Studio see Trinkaus, 'A humanist's image', pp. 91–4; A. F. Verde, *Lo studio fiorentino, 1473–1503*, II, Florence, 1973, pp. 84–5.

[93] This is clear from the 'will' which Sassetti addressed to his sons before he left for Lyons in 1488 (printed by Warburg, 'Verfügung, pp. 140–4), which is full of talk of retrenchment and possible ruin. See also de Roover, *Rise and Decline*, pp. 362–3.

[94] On Ugoleto see A. Del Prato, 'Librai e biblioteche parmensi del sec. XV', *Arch. stor. per le prov. parmensi*, new series, IV, 1904, 12–18, 36–56 (he prints the inventory of Ugoleto's library made after his death in 1516); F. Rizzi, 'Un umanista ignorato: Taddeo Ugoleto', *Aurea Parma*, XXXVII, 1953, 3–17, 79–91; A. Ciavarella, 'Un editore e umanista filologo: Taddeo Ugoleto detto Della Rocca', *Arch. stor. prov. parm.*, fourth series, IX, 1957, 133–73; V. Branca, 'Mercanti e librai fra Italia e Ungheria', in *Italia e Ungheria nel Rinascimento*, ed. V. Branca, Florence, 1973 (Fondazione G. Cini, Civiltà Veneziana, Studi 28). The precise date of Ugoleto's visit is not known. It is generally (even by Ciavarella) given as 1485, but Rizzi's suggested date of 1487–88 is more convincing, especially since in his letter to King Matthias of January 1488/9 Fonzio describes Ugoleto's recent visit (Ep. II, 12).

[95] See notes under Nos. 72, 82 below. The Martial has the *ex libris* of Ugoleto. A twelfth-century MS of Isaac, *De dietis* and *Practica* (No. 81), which also has Ugoleto's *ex libris*, has a few annotations by Bartolomeo Fonzio. This suggests that Ugoleto may have bought it (from Sassetti?) at the same time. Sabbadini (*Scoperte* II, 1914, p. 255, followed by Ciavarella) cites Del Prato for another purchase from Sassetti, of a Tertullian. I cannot find the reference in Del Prato.

[96] Nos. 66–70, 73, 78(?). A letter of Fonzio's dated 1509 apparently refers to the fact that some Sassetti books had gone to Hungary (Ep. III, 5).

[97] E. S. Piccolomini, 'Delle condiz. e delle vicende della Libreria Medicea Privata dal 1494 al 1508', *Arch. stor. ital.*, third series, XIX, 1874, 267–8, docs. XV–XVI. For the list of books see appendix 9.2.

[98] Nos. 2, 6, 12, 14, 21 or 22, 24, 26, 31, 71. Nos. 1 and 71A could already have been sold, since they are not now with the Medici books.

[99] Appendix 9.2, Nos. 567, 574, 586, 599, 608, 550, 570, or 667.

[100] See under No. 52. The fact that there are two versions and dedications of the translation does not seem to have been generally noticed. It is not mentioned in the account of Birago by M. Miglio in *Diz. biog. degli italiani* x, 1968, pp. 596–7.

[101] Mario Rossi, *Un letterato e mercante fiorentino del secolo XVI: Filippo Sassetti*, Città di Castello, 1899, p. 7, n. 3. He gives no reference. Several Sassetti MSS are certainly identifiable in a list of some Medici books made some time before May 1536: *Index bibliothecae Mediceae*, ed. E. Alvisi (*Collez. di opere ined. e rare*), Florence, 1882 (very rare). For example, appendix 9.3 No. 54 is identifiable on p. 15 ('. . . liber pervetustus') and No. 7 on p. 16 ('. . . literis Gallicis').

[102] It could be that the Sassetti brothers had really sold the MSS to Lorenzo and that Fonzio claimed them back to preserve them against the return of the Medici family to Florence.

[103] The Dante (No. 64) belonged in 1560 to Francesco's great-great-grandson, Lorenzo d'Alessandro de' Bardi, Conte di Vernio. The Petrarch (No. 71) has the *ex libris* of Filippo and Francesco di Giovambattista Sassetti, his great-grandsons.

[104] In the fourteenth and fifteenth centuries, at least, texts in the vernacular were often retained by a family when the main part of a library was bequeathed elsewhere. For some examples see A. Mazza, 'L'inventario della "parva libraria" di Santo Spirito e la biblioteca del Boccaccio', *Italia med. e. um* IX, 1966, 4–5.

[105] 111 (not all certain) are listed by B. L. Ullman, *The Humanism of Coluccio Salutati*, Padua, 1963, pp. 138–203. I have listed eight more (*Handwriting of Ital. Humanists* I, 1, 1973, pp. xv, 41–3) and it seems likely that others have been or will be found.

[106] For some suggestions see nn. 34–5 above.

[107] The only MS on paper known to me which probably belonged to him is No. 79.

[108] Francesco di Giovambattista Sassetti, writing a century later, described the books as 'la maggior parte scritti in penna' (Warburg, 'Verfügung', p. 133), but he cannot have known the library at first hand, and many of his other statements are inaccurate.

[109] For one such link see n. 90 above. Fonzio had most of his own works printed. He commissioned some work (including an edition of Statius, *Sylvae*, in 1479–80) from the Ripoli press in Florence, and is perhaps identifiable as the 'ser Meo' who was working for them as a corrector in 1478 (Ripoli accounts, ed. Roediger, *Bibliofilo*, VIII, 1887, 174–5; IX, 1888, 95, 121; E. Nesi, *Diario della stamperia di Ripoli*, 1903, pp. 17, 20–1, 23, 36, 40–1, 46–7, 61–2). He was also a close friend of Ser Piero Cennini, who helped his father Bernardo with his famous edition of Servius, printed in Florence in 1471–72 (Hain 14707).

[110] The translations were all made in his youth when he was seeking rich patrons. All are Italian versions of Greek texts which had already been translated into Latin. (i) Letters of Ps.-Phalaris, dedicated to Francesco Baroncini, a Florentine merchant. Made by July 1468 and first printed 1471 (see n. 59). (ii) Aristeas, *De lxx interpretibus*. Dedicated first to Duke Borso d'Este, probably *c.* 1468, before Fonzio's visit to Ferrara. The autograph dedication copy is MS. Vat. Ross. 407; secondly to King Ferrante of Naples, presumably after Borso's death in 1471. Dedication copy: MS. Vat. Ottob. Lat. 1558, corrected by Fonzio. (iii) Lucian, *De calumnia*, sent to Duke Ercole d'Este in 1472 (see under No. 65 below). It is worth noting that Sassetti owned copies of all these texts in Latin. The Ps-.Phalaris (No. 29) was copied by Fonzio himself, too late to have been used for the translation, but he could have borrowed the Lucian (see appendix 9.1, No. 47 and n. 36 above) and the Aristeas (No. 36) if he already had access to Sassetti's library in the 1460s.

[111] The poems are given this title in Wolfenbüttel, Herzog August Bibl. MS. 43 Aug. fol. (*Bibl. Corviniana*, No. 168 and plate CXXVIII), the autograph collection of Fonzio's works which he made for King Matthias Corvinus, probably in 1489.

[112] For Fonzio see the poem *cit.* in n. 53 above, also the letter from Rome, 1485, to Sassetti about the discovery of the perfectly preserved body of a Roman girl (*Ep.* II, 7, and see Saxl, 'The classical inscription', pp. 26–7). See also Alessandro Braccesi, Epig. XIV, in *Carmina*, ed. Perosa, pp. 87–8.

[113] Appendix 9.3, No. 2. Eleventh-century(?), written in France.

[114] Presumably Martianus Capella.

[115] Appendix 9.3, No. 7. Early fifteenth-century, written in France.

[116] Probably appendix 9.3, No. 31. Fifteenth-century, written in Florence.

[117] Appendix 9.3, No. 26, Filargirius, etc, is headed 'Servius . . .' and cost Sassetti fifteen ducats. Ninth-century, from France.

[118] Appendix 9.3., No. 4, Fifteenth-century, written in Florence.

[119] Appendix 9.3, No. 1. Early eleventh-century, written in Germany, but brought by Sassetti 'e Gallia'.

[120] Appendix 9.3, No. 59. Early fifteenth-century, written in Bologna.

[121] See n. 35 above.

[122] Appendix 9.3, No. 21, written in Florence, 1448–49, or 22, written at Reggio 1436, but probably bought by Sassetti in Geneva. Both second-hand.

[123] Appendix 9.3, No. 28. Twelfth- or thirteenth-century. Possibly acquired in France.

[124] This MS, or No. 41, is probably appendix 9.3, No. 74.

[125] Presumably appendix 9.3, No. 72. Ninth-century, written in France.

[126] Appendix 9.3, No. 55. Fifteenth-century, written in Florence.

[127] Appendix 9.3, No. 54. Eleventh-century, written in France.

[128] Probably appendix 9.3, No. 75. Florentine MS of *c.* 1460.

[129] Probably appendix 9.3, No. 76. Florentine MS dated 1459.

[130] Probably appendix 9.3, No. 43, a companion volume to appendix 9.3, No. 76, rather than No. 44.

[131] Appendix 9.3, No. 56. Fifteenth-century, written in Florence. Companion volume to No. 55.

[132] The misspelling of the name suggests that appendix 9.3, No. 11 may be intended: Alan of Lille, *Anticlaudianus*, thirteenth-century, written probably in France.

[133] See No. 22 above.

[134] Probably appendix 9.3, No. 24. Florence, second quarter of the fifteenth century. Second-hand.

[135] I.e. Calpurnius Siculus; *cf.* appendix 9.2, No. 586. See above, n. 36.

[136] Perhaps Dati's poem, rather than a star map as suggested by Bergier, 'Humanisme', p. 114.

[137] I.e. the works by Cicero.

[138] Probably Franceso Griffolini's Latin translation of Lucian; see above, n. 36.

[139] A litany?

[140] Appendix 9.3, No. 48. Mid-fifteenth-century, probably written in Bologna.

[141] Appendix 9.3, No. 64. Early fifteenth-century, written in Florence, and bought for ten ducats.

[142] I.e. the *Trionfi* of Petrarch.

[143] Presumably one of the French versions of the Tristan romance.

[144] I have not been able to find a French translation of the *Physics*.

Addenda

Page 177, No. 3. Probably identifiable as the hand of Nicolaus de Salveldia, who signed MS Laur. Edili 215 at Venice in 1441.

Page 178, No. 7. Also *Mostra della biblioteca di Lorenzo nella Bibl. Med. Laur.* (Onoranze nazionali a Lorenzo il Magnifico nel V centenario . . .), Florence, 1949, No. 124 and plate XI.

Page 178, Nos. 14 and 15. Mr Michael Reeve tells me that these MSS were copied from a combination of the 1471 Rome and 1472 Bologna editions of Ovid.

Page 179, No. 20. Later emended from the 1475 edition (information from M. Reeve).

Page 180, No. 25. Also E. Casamassima, *art. cit.* under No. 73, p. 111, fig. 15.

Page 184, No. 55. Also British Museum, Add. MS 10965, Cicero, *Partit. orat., D or., Orator.*

Page 184, No. 58. There are corrections in the Poggio text which appear to be in the hand of Jacopo di Poggio Bracciolini (*cf.* his note in Vat. Lat. 3245, copied by Poggio and given by Jacopo to Bernardo Bembo).

Page 186, No. 70. The *Somnium Scipionis* has some corrections by Fonzio.

Page 187, No.† 71A. Paris, *Bibliothèque Nationale*, Lat. *8456A*, Virgil (*Aeneid, Catalogue des manuscrits en écriture latine portant des indications de date, de lieu ou de copiste*, ed. C. Samaran and R. Marichal, III, 1974, p. 622). Florence, *c.* 1480–90? 313 leaves, 138 × 90 mm. Copied by Bartolomeo Fonzio. Folio 2, Sassetti arms, possibly painted over earlier border in the style of Boccardino with Sassetti arms, slings, AMP, hinds, medals, etc. *Ex libris* of Francesco del Nero. Given to Roger de Gaignières in 1709 by the abbé de Castres. I am indebted to M. François Avril, who examined this MS for me.

Page 188, No. 75 end. Also Paris, B.N. Lat. 6451A (*Catalogue des manuscrits en écriture latine . . . ,* II, 1962, p. 504); Dresden, Dc 175a.

Page 190, Rejected MSS, (b). Probably written for Andrea Alamanni: see the scribe's monogram, NOTANDREA, on f. 73.

Page 190, n. 4. I have not been able to consult *Lo scrittoio di Bartolomeo Fonzio,* ed. G. Carusi and S. Zamponi, with a note by E. Casamassima, Milan, 1974, which was published after this article had gone to press.

Page 192, n 19, end. Another possibility is Paulus Aemilius of Verona: see his undated letter to Fonzio apparently sending him copies of inscriptions from Lyons for his collection. The letter is probably datable to the mid-1470s, since it refers to the closeness to Sassetti of Fonzio, 'quem in ore die noctuque tanta cum laude et benivolentiae testificatione versari video' (ed. Verde, *Studio fior.*, *cit.*, II, p. 87).

Page 194, n. 38. Probably at some time before 1467 Antonius Pellotus wrote some verses to Sassetti in which he asked for copies of his Priscian (probably appendix 9.1, No. 21; appendix 9.3, No. 28), Servius (probably appendix 9.1, No. 9; appendix 9. 3, No. 26) and Pliny's *Natural History* (Oxford, Bodl. MS Lat. misc. e 81, f. 71: see P. O. Kristeller, *Studies in Renaissance Thought and Letters*, Rome, 1956, p. 155). The Pliny work figures neither in the 1462 inventory nor among unidentified MSS from Sassetti; if he really owned it he presumably acquired it during this period in the 1460s.

Page 194, n. 41. For the MS see now Guido Billanovich, 'Appunti per la diffusione di Seneca Tragico e di Catullo', in *Tra latino e volgare. Per C. Dionisotti*, Padua, two vols., 1974, pp. 148–55.

Page 195, n. 47. See also, no doubt, *Lo scrittoio di Bartolomeo Fonzio, cit. supra.*

Page 196, n. 11 end. Renewed for another year in 1485 (A. F. Verde, *Lo studio fiorentino 1473–1503*, I, Florence, 1973, p. 277).

Page 196, n. 56. In other words, *Lo scrittoio di Bartolomeo Fonzio, cit. supra.*

M. E. MALLETT   *University of Warwick*

IO

SOME NOTES ON A FIFTEENTH-CENTURY *CONDOTTIERE* AND HIS LIBRARY: COUNT ANTONIO DA MARSCIANO

IT HAS OFTEN been suggested that warfare in fifteenth-century Italy was affected, as were so many other respects of life, by a conscious classicism, that the leading *condottieri* were steeped in the study of Antiquity. It was from this source, and particularly Vegetius, that they are often thought to have drawn their interest in field fortifications; Frontinus and Vegetius are said to have taught them the arts of deception and the complicated tactics to which they were so addicted, while Onosander and Vegetius instructed them in the importance of leadership qualities. Paolo Giovio, in fact, attributed some of the military failures of Italian captains to a misplaced and unrealistic imitation of classical precedents.[1]

There were, of course, many examples of *condottieri* who were both cultured classicists and bibliophiles. Federigo da Montefeltro is only the best known example of the educated soldier patron. In his own generation Francesco Sforza showed a great interest in the Visconti library, which he inherited along with the Milanese State, and had a new inventory made for it; his brother Alessandro was an avid collector of books for his library in Pesaro.[2] Sigismondo Malatesta founded a public library in Rimini, and his brother, Malatesta Novello, built the Biblioteca Malatestiana in Cesena.[3] Giovanfrancesco Pico della Mirandola, another founder of a fifteenth-century library, was a soldier of some repute. Ludovico Gonzaga was a pupil of Vittorino da Feltre and an active collector of manuscripts. He was associated with the first printing venture in Mantua and himself edited the text of Virgil's *Georgics*.[4] In the previous generation Ludovico's father, Gianfrancesco Gonzaga, had been the patron of Vittorino, who was his librarian, and collected Greek manuscripts, while both Pandolfo and Carlo Malatesta were noted and respected for their classical learning.[5] Among subsequent *condottieri* Renato and Gian Jacopo Trivulzio and Antonio Giacomini stand out as book collectors.[6]

However, there is little evidence to be found, either in the inventories of the libraries which these men collected or in a study of their own military exploits and writings, that classical inspiration was a major source of their military techniques. None of the libraries assembled by these *condottieri* showed a marked bias towards military works; they were, on the whole, humanist collections of a standard pattern. They were the libraries of the princes which many of these men had become, rather than of the soldiers which they had been and occasionally still were. Of course, knowing what books a man possessed is not necessarily a guide to what he read or what interested him, but if we know the books he did not possess we can reasonably assume that his interests did not lie in those directions. The fact that few of the serious *condottiere* bibliophiles had an extensive collection of the classical military literature would seem to suggest that they did not, on the whole, seek instruction from that source in their professional careers. Nor were there many signs of a conscious classicism in warfare. The explanations for the growing use of field fortifications lie deeply bedded in the practical requirements of the wars in Lombardy between 1425 and 1454. Practical experience seems to have been more important than humanistic example to fifteenth-century soldiers. They may have been surrounded by humanist chancellors and sycophants; they may, like Sforza and Piccinino, have been compared to Hannibal and Scipio;[7] but it was the examples of their immediate masters and contemporary colleagues which affected them more than those of ancient heroes. As Pier Paolo Vergerio remarked in *De ingenuis moribus*, 'The art of war can only be rightly acquired by constant experience in the field, but such books as have been written by great soldiers on their calling must not be overlooked'.[8] Valturio's *De re militari* may be the best known Italian military treatise of the fifteenth century but it tells us little about contemporary warfare. His restatements of classical precepts must have seemed curiously irrelevant to the literate captains of the second half of the fifteenth century, whose approach to war was much more accurately expressed by Orso Orsini and Diomede Caraffa in their treatises.[9]

Having said all this, however, one must mention one *condottiere* library which does show an interesting and quite exceptional degree of specialisation in military works as well as an awareness of contemporary intellectual trends. This was the library of Count Antonio da Marsciano, which was described in his will of 1476.[10] Count Antonio was an Umbrian who spent all his active life in the service of Venice, and who, as well as being an interesting example of a cultured *condottiere*, was also a prototype of the fifteenth-century professional soldier. Here was a man who was a genuine soldier–scholar, but, as we shall see, even here it was contemporary experience rather than classical example which really shaped his military career.

The Counts of Marsciano claimed to be able to trace their ancestry back to ancient lords of Chiusi. In 1281 they had sold Marsciano itself to Perugia, and their estates by the fifteenth century were concentrated in the hill country to the south of Lake Trasimene. It was in the family castle at Migliano that Antonio was born on 20 December 1429.[11] His father, Count Ranuccio, had married Angela, the daughter of Beccarino di Brunoro da Leonessa, a noted soldier in the early years of the century who had been

executed by Tartaglia in Toscanella in 1419. Angela's brother was Gentile
da Leonessa, and her cousin, Giacoma, was the wife of Gattamelata; this
connection was to be a crucial one for the young Count Antonio, as it linked
him to one of the leading *condottiere* clans of the fifteenth century—the
Gatteschi. Count Ranuccio was not an active soldier; he was Podestà of
Rieti in 1436 but otherwise seems to have spent his life in relative obscurity
as an Umbrian country noble. But Antonio's great-uncle, Guerriero da
Marsciano, had an active military career; he was a close associate of
Gattamelata and followed him from papal to Venetian service in 1434. By
1437 he had a Venetian *condotta* for 100 lances and he fought in the campaigns against Niccolò Piccinino in 1438–39, being captured in August
1438.[12] Venice quickly obtained his release by exchanging him, which was
some indication of his importance to the Venetian army, but early in 1440
he was killed in action. However, his company was kept in being so that his
young sons could eventually inherit it, and as late as 1453 the Venetian senate
was still discussing ways of helping the family of this faithful old soldier.[13]

At some moment when he was quite young Count Antonio also took
service with Venice, almost certainly amongst the troops of his uncle Gentile
da Leonessa. Gattamelata himself retired from active service late in 1440,
although he continued to retain the title of Venetian captain general, and
thereafter the command of his troops was shared by his cousin Gentile and
his young son Gian Antonio. Antonio da Marsciano was betrothed at the age
of ten to one of Gattamelata's daughters, Todeschina, and although the
marriage was not solemnised until the late 1450s it is clear that much earlier
than this he had joined the Gatteschi companies in Venetian service.[14]
Another son-in-law of Gattamelata was Tiberto Brandolini, the son of
Gattamelata's old brother in arms Count Brandolino Brandolini, and until
his desertion of Venice in 1452 his powerful company fought alongside that
of Gentile and Gian Antonio, and formed part of the Gattesco tradition. At
the battle of Caravaggio in 1448 the Gatteschi contributed over 1,500
cavalry to the Venetian army, and this battle may have been Count
Antonio's first real taste of action.[15]

At this point one must pause briefly to consider the nature of this Venetian
army which Antonio joined and in which he spent most of the rest of his life.
The true nature of military organisation in most fifteenth-century Italian
States has been a good deal obscured by the strong current of vilification of
the *condottieri* which started in contemporary humanist writing and was
carried on by Machiavelli and Guicciardini. As a result the impermanence
and infidelity of the captains and the ineffectiveness of their methods have
been considerably exaggerated. Part of the confusion has stemmed from a
tendency to telescope the whole Italian mercenary experience of the fourteenth and fifteenth centuries into one phenomenon—a transition from a
reliance on foreign mercenary companies to one on independent, Italian
mercenary captains. What is missing from this picture is the emergence of the
permanent standing army in most of the Italian States by the late fifteenth
century.[16]

Prior to 1404 Venice had only limited interests on the mainland of Italy and had been largely untouched by the military developments of the fourteenth century. With the war against the Carraresi of 1404–05 and the occupation of Verona, Vicenza and Padua, she became a mainland power with a concern for the permanent defence of a Terraferma empire. From that moment she took the lead in the creation of a permanent army.[17] Venetian *condottieri* who won the approval of the senate were encouraged to remain in Venetian service by offers of additional cash rewards, fiefs, Venetian citizenship and palaces in Venice. The length of their contracts was extended to a common two years in the first instance, and renewals of the contracts became a formality. Peacetime service with reduced companies became an accepted part of the system, and the permanent *condottieri* received permanent winter quarters in and around the new subject cities of the Terraferma. Each company was allotted to one of the city treasuries for its pay, and a strong military administration grew up based on *collaterali* in each of the main subject cities. This was the background to the phenomenon of the *Marcheschi*, the faithful Venetian *condottieri* who formed a coherent and continuing group in the Milanese wars of the 1430s and 1440s. By the time of the peace of Lodi and the Italian League, when large standing forces were written into the terms of the *entente*, Venice had a cadre of *condottieri* who had been in her service for periods of up to twenty years, and an efficient military administration to support them.

The new permanent forces were not just *condottiere* cavalry companies. Another feature of this period was the emergence of bodies of cavalry employed directly by the State as permanent troops. These were the so-called *lanze spezzate*. These troops were usually recruited from the remnants of *condottiere* companies whose captain had died or retired after a long period of faithful service. They gradually won the reputation of being crack, veteran troops as they became the most permanent feature of cavalry organisation. Their commanders were appointed by the State with the rank of governor of the *lanze spezzate*.

Venice in 1454 already had large numbers of *lanze spezzate*. The seasoned company of Roberto Paganelli da Montalboddo, who had died about 1448, was transferred into the *lanze spezzate*, and in 1451 when Bartolomeo Colleoni deserted some of his best troops were retained in the same capacity. But one of the largest elements in the *lanze spezzate* during the next thirty years was the Gatteschi. Gentile da Leonessa had been killed at the siege of Manerbio early in 1453, and only a few weeks earlier Gian Antonio di Gattamelata had been severely wounded in the head by a hand-gun shot, though his life was miraculously saved by the doctors.[18] For three years Gian Antonio di Gattamelata remained commander of the Gatteschi companies, although he seems to have been a permanent invalid. In 1456 he finally died without male heirs, and, as Gentile da Leonessa had had no legitimate heirs either, there was no obvious successor to the command of the Gatteschi. Venice therefore took the opportunity to enrol them into the *lanze spezzate*, but the company was kept together under the title of the Società di San Marco, and Antonio, Count of Marsciano, was appointed to command it in 1459.[19]

For the next twenty-three years Antonio was governor of the Società, and was also senior commander in the *lanze spezzate*. During this time the Venetian army had a remarkably static character. Bartolomeo Colleoni was captain general for most of the period, until his death in 1476, and his troops provided the forward frontier garrison, based on his headquarters at Malpaga, near Bergamo. Carlo Fortebracci, the son of Braccio da Montone, was the second-in-command until his death in 1479, and he was almost continuously based in Brescia. Antonio da Marsciano spent most of the period in and around Verona, while Deifebo dall' Anguillara, when he joined Venetian service after being driven into exile by Paul II in 1465, spent the next fifteen years as senior commander in Friuli. But for the long war with the Turks between 1463 and 1479 the Venetian army in this period would have looked even more stable. But in 1463 large numbers of troops were sent to the Morea, where both Bertoldo d'Este and Cecco Brandolini were killed, and where in 1464 Sigismondo Malatesta was temporarily brought in to command the detached army. This brief period was the one occasion when considerable numbers of Italian troops were used in the Balkans, but the heavy losses and a realisation of the greater effectiveness and lesser expense of Greek and Albanian stradiots in this warfare led to the experiment being abandoned. However, Turkish pressure in Friuli necessitated a large part of the army being concentrated in that area in the 1470s, and the losses of senior commanders continued.[20]

But Antonio da Marsciano and the Society of St Mark were moved only once from the Veronese, and that was for the siege of Trieste in 1463. This Venetian expedition consisted of 1,400 cavalry and 3,000–4,000 infantry, and Count Antonio was the senior commander.[21] He was wounded in the leg during the siege by a hand-gun shot, and when the truce was signed in the autumn he was moved with his company back to the Verones. By this time he had been allowed to take over the castle at Sanguinetto, south-east of Verona, as his headquarters and residence for his family. Sanguinetto, strategically placed guarding the crossing of the Po, was one of the estates given by Venice to her *condottieri* either in fief or on a less permanent basis as part of her policy of providing for the defence of her frontiers. It had belonged to Carmagnola and later to Alvise dal Verme, and then in 1451 was given to Gentile da Leonessa.[22] Bertoldo d'Este, who had married one of Gentile's illegitimate daughters, had occupied it briefly, but in 1461 Antonio da Marsciano moved in and there his elder children were born.[23]

Throughout the 1460s Antonio's troops formed the core of the standing forces in the Veronese, and a contingent of them was garrisoned in the city itself. In addition to the Società di San Marco, which he commanded in the name of the republic, he had a *condotta* for 105 cavalry of his own, and this was increased to 150 during the 1467 emergency created by Colleoni's dealings with the Florentine exiles.[24] However, there is no indication that he joined Colleoni in the Molinella campaign. In 1471 he was alerted by

Venice and moved with his troops towards the Mantuan frontier to counter any aggressive moves by Milan and Mantua, which Venice suspected might follow the death of Borso d'Este in Ferrara.[25] In November 1472 he was directed to move with part of his troops and take command of the garrison in the citadel of Verona. This move into the city entitled him to increased pay for his men, and for the next ten years he lived with his family in the citadel.[26]

The outbreak of the Pazzi war and the simultaneous increase of Turkish pressure in Friuli in 1478 made additional demands on Venice's military strength. Count Antonio and the Gatteschi were designated for the Friuli emergency, and the company was moved into camp in the Trevigiano while a part actually went to the eastern front.[27] In April 1479, after a truce had been signed with the Turks and some of Venice's best troops had been moved from Friuli to Tuscany, Antonio took over command of the army in Friuli as governor-general.[28] In the autumn of that year he was described as one of the most faithful of the republic's captains and was authorised to increase his own *condotta* by 100 cavalry.[29] However, he did not in fact see active service again until the war of Ferrara, when his troops were among the first to be mobilised, and he played an important role in the early stages of the campaign. By this time, in 1482, Antonio was one of the last surviving senior Venetian commanders who had seen service in the Milanese wars prior to the Peace of Lodi. Colleoni and Carlo Fortebracci were both dead, although their companies were still very much in being, the latter's being now commanded by his son Bernardino. The new captain general was Roberto da Sanseverino, and Antonio, despite his unique record of service, still commanded only 400 cavalry of his own. This, however, was an entirely normal situation in the Venetian army, and while the lack of promotion slightly irked him there is no evidence of his having sought to break out of the system.[30]

Antonio and his troops were among the first to cross Roberto da Sanseverino's causeway into the Ferrarese on 2 May 1482.[31] He was given the task of guarding Melara as the main army moved south-eastwards along the Po to strike at Ficarolo. Then, having been moved once more into the vanguard, he began to build a bastion at Polesine di Casaglia, below Figarolo, to cut off the now besieged town from Ferrara. Here on 6 June he was overwhelmed by a vigorous Ferrarese counter-attack and captured. For a short time he was held prisoner in the castle at Ferrara, where amongst the officers appointed to guard him was the Milanese historian Bernardino Corio.[32] Then he was taken to Milan and probably exchanged in the next year for Ugo da Sanseverino, who had been captured by the Venetians at the battle of Argenta.

By the time Antonio was released the situation had changed in a number of respects. His eldest son, Ranuccio, had taken command of the Gatteschi and was distinguishing himself in the fighting round Lagoscuro.[33] More important, Sixtus IV had abandoned his alliance with Venice and joined the league against her, bringing down an Interdict on the city. Antonio was a religious man and it may be that a reluctance to fight against the Pope dictated his next action, which was to abandon his long association with Venice and take service with Florence. Or it may have been that his services were really no longer required by Venice, as his son was successfully leading his company. His *condotta* with Florence was negotiated by Bernardo Rucellai, the Florentine ambassador in Milan, and was for a company of 150 men-at-arms (600 cavalry) and twenty-five mounted crossbowmen in time of war.[34] Antonio was to receive 20,000 florins a year for this company, and by September 1483 he was in Pisa preparing for the campaign in the Lunigiana against the Genoese to recover Sarzana. It is interesting that in the final stages of the war of Ferrara Antonio was not used against the Venetians. He had to borrow money to fit out a new company for himself[35] but he seems to have been the commander of this affair, which culminated in the following year with the siege of Pietrasanta. Corio described him as Florentine captain general, and the documents, although not explicit about this, do seem to indicate that he was senior to Niccolò Orsini, Count of Pitigliano.[36] He was certainly leading an assault on Pietrasanta on 31 October 1484 when he was hit in the stomach by an artillery shot and killed. His body was taken back to Pisa, where he was buried in S. Michele fuori le Mura.[37]

Such was the military career of Antonio, Count of Marsciano; it was not a spectacular career and it has little in common with the normal vision of the *condottiere*. But at the same time Antonio was by no means an insignificant figure, and his role as a long-serving professional captain was in fact more characteristic of Italian warfare of the period than the careers of men like Jacopo Piccinino or Roberto da Sanseverino. Furthermore Antonio was something more than just a soldier; he was described by Ughelli as 'molto versato nelle belle lettere, curioso indagatore nella venerenda antichità'; he was in fact a scholar, a man of letters and bibliophile.[38] Whilst in Florentine service he was an active correspondent of Lorenzo de' Medici, and the two appear to have had long discussions together when Lorenzo was in Pisa in September 1483.[39] Antonio's letters are ornate and full of Latin tags, but the most complete evidence of his scholarly interests lies in the description of his library which forms part of his will, drawn up in 1476.

Antonio da Marsciano, at this moment some eight years before his death, had a library of forty items; of these thirty-two were manuscripts and eight printed books.[40] Most of the printed books were probably from Venetian presses, including what were almost certainly copies of Jensen's 1470 Justinus, his 1471 Caesar and the 1472 *Scriptores Rei Rusticae*. The copy of Walter Burley's *Super arte porphyrii* was presumably that printed by Cristoforus Arnoldus in Venice.[41] However, it is the subject matter of the collection which is of particular interest. The military bias is clearly apparent, with manuscripts of Vegetius and Frontinus, the two most influential classical military writers, and a good selection of classical military historians. Antonio's manuscript of Sallust's *De bello Jugurthino* was written in his own hand, and he also had manuscripts of Livy, Procopius, Caesar and Polybius, together with a now lost military treatise of Cato. This historical, military interest was further borne out by the standard classical biographical collections which he possessed; Suetonius' *Lives of the Caesars*, Plutarch's *Lives*, the *De viribus illustribus* once ascribed to Pliny and Curtius Ruffus' life of Alexander the Great all found their place on the count's shelves.[42] He also possessed a Vitruvius *De Architettura*, two manuscripts of collected medical works, including the *Remedia* of Antonio Cermisone, the influential Paduan doctor who had treated Gattamelata for the stone, and Petrus de Abano's treatise on poisons, and two medieval works on marshalling and the care of horses.[43] Perhaps most interestingly of all, Antonio had a copy of Valturio's *De re militari* with illustrations. Roberto Valturio's collection of classical military lore had been completed in the 1450s for Sigismondo Malatesta, and many copies of it circulated during the succeeding years. Some were commissioned by Sigismondo himself to give to his military colleagues, but there is no knowing whether Antonio's copy originated in this way.[44] This copy has in fact been recently identified as that which is now in the British Museum.[45]

But Valturio was by no means the only near contemporary author represented in Antonio's library. He clearly had an interest in humanistic educational writings, as he had copies of Pier Paolo Vergerio's *De ingenuis moribus*, Guarino's Latin translation of the pseudo-Plutarchan treatise *De liberis educandis*, Francesco Barbaro's *De re uxoria* and works by Valla and Matteo Palmieri. Bruni's edition of the pseudo-Aristotelian *Oeconomicorum* and two Cicero manuscripts confirmed the civic caste of his humanist interests. But there was yet another side to Antonio's interests, and this was country life. He increased the family estates in southern Umbria in addition to his interests in the Veronese, and on his shelves were two collections of classical agricultural tracts, a treatise on the training of birds and Pliny's *Natural History*. Finally the pious side of Antonio's character, which led him to make bequests to a mass of small Umbrian churches, comes out in his books. The inventory starts with St Ambrose's *De Offitiis* and the *Transitus* of St Jerome, the latter written in the count's own hand.

Antonio da Marsciano's will was drawn up in the citadel at Verona on 13 December 1476. Among the many executors named were Ermolao Barbaro the younger and Ludovico Nogarola, the nephew of the celebrated Isotta. Antonio had been stationed for years in the Veronese and spent at least ten years living in Verona itself. The intellectual life of Verona in this period, under the aegis of Bishop Ermolao Barbaro, was active and advanced, and the collecting of manuscripts was a particular feature of it.[46] Closely connected with the bishop were his secretary, Giovanni Antonio Panteo, poet, Greek scholar and teacher, who had an active circle of disciples, and his treasurer, Antonio Beccaria, who had for a time been secretary to Duke Humphrey of Gloucester. Other prominent figures in Veronese intellectual circles of the time were Pier Donato Avogaro, the humanist notary, Giovanni Mario di Francesco Filelfo, who had a school in the city, and Cristoforo Lanfranchini, jurist, poet and bibliophile. Pomponio Leto probably visited Verona in 1480, and a number of native Veronese scholars who spent most of their lives out of the city maintained continuing contacts with this circle. Felice

Feliciano, Martino and Jacopo Rizzoni and Leonardo Montagna were all sometimes to be seen in the city, and Fra Giocondo, the military architect, and Bartolomeo Cepolla, the Paduan jurist whose classical military treatise formed the framework for the better known work of Paride dal Pozzo, were also linked to the city and to the interests of Count Antonio.

The exact links between Antonio and these circles in Verona have yet to be discovered, but it is hard to believe that so erudite a soldier lived for ten years in the citadel with no such contacts. Had he perhaps, as the possessor of a manuscript of Valturio, something to do with the first printing of that work in Verona in 1472? Were some of the Veronese bibliophiles involved in assembling this interesting soldier's collection? By what means did Antonio acquire the eight very recently published books which figured in it? All these are questions which remain to be answered. However, it is clear that when Antonio wrote in one of his letters to Lorenzo de' Medici, '. . . it only remains for me to remind Your Magnificence with reverence that to conceal one's secrets from the enemy and at the same time to uncover his secrets can be regarded as a most potent factor in ultimate victory', he was not just paraphrasing from the Frontinus in his library.[47] He was expressing one of the principal, practical precepts of fifteenth-century warfare, and any of his *condottiere* colleagues would have agreed with him, particularly had he served for thirty years under the watchful eye of the Venetian Council of Ten.

APPENDIX 10.1

THE LIBRARY OF ANTONIO, COUNT OF MARSCIANO, AS
DESCRIBED IN HIS WILL OF 13 DECEMBER 1476.

Bibliothecam preterea (si qua nunc dici phas est) seu libros omnes nostros historiarum, et quarumcumque facultatum, prout tempore mortis meae reperientur, hique in praesentiarum, Divina concedente clementia, sunt. In primis in uno volumine quarti folii, quinternorum quindecim membranorum, cum parmulis tabulatis, alboque cohopertis, *Sanctus Ambrosius de Offitiis*; atque etiam exinde *Sancti Hieronymi transitus*, mea propria manu scriptus: necnon et *De vita, et obitu Beatorum Floridi, et Amantii*, sub eodem volumine alligati: item *una Dechadum Titi Livii ab Urbe condita de gestis Romanorum*, in uno volumine pleni folii, quinternorum triginta duorum membranorum: item *una alia Dechadum Titi Livii subsequenter de gestis Romanorum*, ut supra; *De secundo bello punico*; in uno alio volumine pleni folii, quinternorum viginti unum membranorum. Item in uno alio volumine quinternorum duodecim membranorum quarti folii, cum parmulis tabulatis, rubeoque cohopertis, *Chrispus Salustius de seditione Lutii Catilinae contra Senatum*; ac *De Bello Jugurthino*; mea propria manu. Item in alio volumine quarti folii, quinternorum viginti trium membranorum, cum parmulis tabulatis, rubeoque cohopertis, *Flavius Vegetius De re militari*; atque *Vibius Equestris de fluminibus, fontibus, lacubus, nemoribus, paludibus, montibus, gentibusque*. Item in uno alio volumine quarti folii, quinternorum novem membranorum, cum parmulis tabulatis, rubeoque cohopertis, *Iulius Frontinus De re militari, scilicet Stratagemarum militarium*; et *Marcus Cato de re quoque militari*; atque etiam *Historia fabulosa Griseldis, per disertissimum vatem D. Franciscum Petrarcam: Passaggiumque exinde ultra mare D. Godofredi Bolionis in acquisitione Civitatis Ierusalem, totiusque Terrae Sanctae*: idque passaggium mea manu propria subiunxi. Nec non et alia quoque *Fabulosa Historia Bochatii de Sigismonda, per D. Leonardum Arethinum, ex vulgari in Latinum versa*; omnes pariter in eodem alligatae volumine. Item in alio volumine quarti folii, vel parvioris, quinternorum novem membranorum cum parmulis tabulatis, rubeoque cohopertis, *Echonomicum Aristotelis de re familiari*; scilicet, *Super eo Commentariolum per D. Leonardum Arethinum editum*; atque etiam *Ysagogicum moralis disciplinae*, sub eadem ligatura, mea propria manu. Item in alio volumine quarti, vel parvioris folii, quinternorum octo membranorum, cum parmulis tabulatis, rubeoque cohopertis, *Iacomellus Traugurinus, De disciplina avium*, in vulgari. Item in alio volumine quarti folii, quinternorum decem, et duarum cartarum pecudinarum, seu edorum, cum parmulis tabulatis, rubeoque cohopertis, *Leonardus Arethinus super Polibio De bello Gothorum, Italico*: additis etiam in fine *Duabus Epistolis; altera ad Alphonsum Aragonum Regem; altera ad Chiriacum Anconitanum*. Item in alio volumine quarti folii, quinternorum sex bonbicinarum, cum parmulis tabulatis, rubeoque cohopertis, ac bullis aliquibus super infixis, *Marcus Tullius Cicero, De Amicitia. De Senectute. Et De paradossis in eodem compendio*. Item in alio volumine folii magni quinternorum triginta membranorum cum parmulis tabulatis, rubeoque cohopertis, ac aureis, scilicet aeris bullis superinfixis, *Robertus Valturius De re militari, ad Ill. Sigismundum Pandulphum de Malatestis Ariminensem*; cum picturis machinarum, militari maxime disciplinae attinentium. Item in alio volumine quinternorum decem membranorum quarti folii, cum parmulis tabulatis, rubeoque cohopertis, *Leonardus Arethinus super Polibio de gestis Romanorum, de primo bello Punico*. Item in alio volumine quarti folii, quinternorum decem novem, et cartharum quatuor membranarum, cum parmulis tabulatis, rubeoque cohopertis, *Q. Curtius Ruffus De gestis Alexandri Magni Macedonis*. Item in alio volumine quarti folii, quinter . . . membranorum cum parmulis tabulatis, rubeoque cohopertis, *L. Vetruvius Cerdo de Architectura*. Item in alio volumine quarti folii, quinternorum septem membranorum, cum parmulis tabulatis, rubeoque cohopertis, *Epithomata Decadum Titi Livii ab Urbe condita de gestis Romanorum*. Item in alio volumine quarti folii quinternulorum octo membranorum cum parmulis tabulatis, rubeoque cohopertis, *L. Anneius Florus De gestis Romanorum ab Urbe condita*. Item in alio volumine quarti, sive minoris folii, quinternulorum octo membranorum, cum parmulis tabulatis, rubeoque cohopertis, *Opus morale super ludo Scachorum, et De offitiis nobilium, plebeiorumque*. Item in alio volumine quarti, minorisve quinternulorum quatuordecim membranorum, cum parmulis tabulatis, rubeoque cohopertis, *Franciscus Barbarus De re uxoria*; atque *Guarinus Veronensis De liberis educandis*; necnon et *Petrus Paulus Vergerius De ingenuis moribus, et liberalibus studiis adolescentulorum*. Item in altero volumine parvo quinternulorum trium, et cartarum sex membranarum, cum parmulis tabulatis, rubeoque cohopertis, *Laurentius Valla De situ Italiae*. Item in altero volumine quarti folii, quinternorum quindecim, et cartarum quoque sex membranarum, cum parmulis tabulatis, rubeoque cohopertis, *Palladius Rutilius de Agricultura*, idemque *Palladius De insitione, ad Pasisulum virum doctissimum; aliquibus etiam Carminibus in fine additis*. Item in alio volumine folii maioris quinternorum quadraginta novem, et cartarum quattuor membranarum, cum assidibus, seu parmulis tabulatis, croceoque colore cohopertis, aerisque bullis superinfixis, *C. Plinius secundus De naturali historia*. Item in alio volumine folii maioris cartarum ducentarum nonaginta octo bombicinarum cum assidibus, seu parmulis tabulatis, rubeoque cohopertis, *Plutarcus De vita Illustrium virorum a Theseo, Romuloque usque ad Sertorium*. Item in alio quoque volumins folii maioris, ut supra cartarum . . . bombicinarum cum assidibus, seu parmulis tabulatis, nigroque cohopertis, idem *Plutarcus de Vita Illustrium Virorum a Sertorio supradicto, Cimone, Lucullo, continuando exinde ad Karolum Magnum usque*. Item in altero volumine quarti folii, quinternorum sexdecim membranarum, cum assidibus, seu parmulis tabulatis, rubeoque cohopertis, *Virgilius Poeta*, videlicet, *Eneidos* tantum. Item in alio volumine quarti folii, quinternorum quatuordecim bombicinarum, in stampa, cum assidibus, sive parmulis tabulatis, nigroque cohopertis, *Iustinus in Trogum Pompeum, scilicet ipsius Trogi historias*. Item in alio quoque volumine eiusdem magnitudinis, et coloris, quarti folii, ut supra, quinternorum quindecim bombicinarum in stampa, cum assidibus, seu parmulis tabulatis, nigroque cohopertis, *C. Suetonius De vita duodecim Caesarum*. Item in altero volumine communis folii quinternorum quatuordecim bombicinarum in stampa, cum assidibus, sive parmulis tabulatis nudis, seu discohopertis, *Tractatus in Sacra Pagina De restitutionibus usurarum, excommunicationibusque*.

Item in altero volumine quarti folii quinternorum decem novem membranorum, cum assidibus seu tabulis, rubeoque cohopertis, bullis aliquibus superinfixis, *Marcii Tulii Ciceronis Epistolae*. Item in alio volumine folii magni quinternorum triginta bombicinarum, scilicet cartarum trecentarum in stampa, cum assidibus, seu parmulis tabulatis, nigroque cohopertis, *L. Iunius Moderatus, Columella, Palladius, Rutilius; enarrationesque priscarum vocum Marci Catonis; atque Marcus Cato priscus; et Marcus quoque Terrentius Varro; omnes de re rustica,* sub eodem volumine compaginati. Item in altero volumine quarti folii, ac minoris, cartarum centum sex membranarum, cum parmulis tabulatis, quodam rubeo cohopertis, quod pavonacium vocant, *Plinius De Viribus Illustribus; Aemilius Probus De Viris excellentibus exterarum gentium; Plutarcus De Fortuna Alexandri, aut virtute*; idemque *Plutarcus de Romanorum virtute, ac fortuna*. Item in alio volumine folii communis cartarum quinquaginta quatuor bombicinarum cum assidibus, seu parmulis tabulatis nudis, sive discohopertis, in eoque, *De vita, et moribus Philosophorum veterum*; et exinde *De aliquibus epistolis*, atque etiam *De nonnullis Constitutionibus Pontificum*; et *Declamationes Colutii*. Item in altero volumine quarti folii, cartarum octoaginta bombicinarum cum assidibus, sive parmulis tabulatis, rubeoque cohopertis, *Magister Petrus de Abbano de venenis*; atque exinde *Magister Arnaldus De cognoscendis venenis*; seu et *D. Valascus de Tarenta Prothomedici De Epidemia*; *nec non et Remedia quaedam ad praeservandum tempore pestis ab ea*; *et alia quoque remedia nonnulla contra pestem, annotata per eximium Medicorum Monarcam Magistrum Antonium Cermisonum*. Item in alio volumine quarti folii cartarum centum triginta quatuor bombicinarum, cum assidibus, rubeoque cohopertis, *Magister Alexander cochus solemnissimus De epulis ad convivandum, sive ad parandum diligenter convivia*; in vulgari; atque etiam *De aliquibus nonnullis aliis Receptis, Consiliisque medicinalibus, Virtutibusque herbarum, et aliis etiam pluribus, et diversissimis causis, et materiis, seu rebus notandis diversimode de die in diem ad notitiam habitis, ibidemque per ordinem prout in eo paulatim additis, et adiunctis*. Item in alio volumine folii communis cartarum quadraginta duarum bombicinarum cum assidibus, rubeoque cohopertis, *D. Magister Iordanus Ruffus de Calabria miles, et mareschalchus optimus, atque famosissimus Serenissimi Imperatoris Federici Barbarossa, De natura equorum, nutritione, et Maschalcia*, in vulgari; atque etiam *aliae exinde nonnullae Receptae, et Medecinae equorum illius. . . .* Item in alio volumine folii mezani cartarum centum quadraginta sex bombicinarum in stampa, cum assidibus, sive parmulis tabulatis, rubeoque cohopertis. *C. Iulius Caesar*, videlicet, *Commentariorum suorum gestorum de bello Gallico, civilique Pompeiano, Alexandrino, Affrico, et Yspalensi*. Item in altero volumine quarti folii, cartarum septuaginta octo bombicinarum in stampa, cum assidibus, sive parmulis tabulatis nudis, seu discohopertis, *M. Paulus de Venetiis in Sacra Pagina, scilicet ad introitum, et cognitionem sacrae Theologiae*; hoc videlicet est *Logica quaedam compendiosa, et valde utillima ad perdiscendum*. Item in altero quoque volumine eiusdem formae, et materiae praedictae quarti folii, ut supra, cartarum scilicet septuaginta octo bombicinarum, et in stampa, cum assidibus, seu parmulis tabulatis, et nudis, ut supra, idem *Magister Paulus de Venetiis in Sacra Pagina, videlicet quaedam Logica compendiosa utillima ad perdiscendum*. Item in altero quoque volumine quarti folii, cartarum centum quatuordecim bombicinarum in stampa, cum assidibus, sive parmulis tabulatis nudis, sive discohopertis, *Gualterius Burleus Anglicus super arte Porphirii, et Aristotelis, videlicet de Praedicamentis*. Item in alio volumine folii communis, sive mezani, quinternorum membranorum, cum assidibus, seu parmulis tabulatis ... cohopertis, *Matheus Palmerius Florentinus De temporibus*. Item in alio volumine quarti folii quinternorum duodecim membranorum cum assidibus, seu parmulis tabulatis . . . cohopertis, *Magister Laurentius dictus Nucius, famosissimus, atque optimus Mareschalchus de Urbe, super natura, et cognitione, seu qualitatibus equorum, ac de Maschalcia, aegritudinibusque cognoscendis, et remediis eorundem*; valde bonus.

NOTES

I am most grateful to both Dr Cecil Clough and Dr Dennis Rhodes for their comments and suggestions on the material in this article.

[1] P. Giovio, *Opera*, III, *Historiarum*, ed. D. Visconti, Rome, 1957, pp. 126–7.

[2] D. Robathan, 'Libraries of the Italian Renaissance', in *The Medieval Library*, ed. J. W. Thompson, New York, second edition, 1957, pp. 556–8. An inventory of the library of Alessandro's grandson, Giovanni, was published by A. Vernarecci, 'La libreria di Giovanni Sforza, Signore di Pesaro', *Archivio storico per le Marche e per l'Umbria*, III, 1886, pp. 501–23; the library has been discussed by C. H. Clough, 'A note of purchase of 1467 for Alessandro Sforza's library in Pesaro', *Studia Oliveriana*, XIII–XIV, 1966, pp. 171–8.

[3] A. Domeniconi, *La Biblioteca Malatestiana*, Udine, 1962.

[4] Robathan, *op. cit.*, p. 533. On the Gonzaga library see also C. H. Clough, 'The library of the Gonzaga of Mantua', *Librarium*, XV, 1972, pp. 50–63; *Mostra dei codici gonzagheschi: La Biblioteca dei Gonzaga da Luigi I ad Isabella*, ed. U. Meroni, Mantua, 1966.

[5] C. Yriarte, *Un condottiere au XVe siècle. Rimini: études sur les lettres et les arts à la cour des Malatesta*, Paris, 1882, pp. 54–70.

[6] E. Motta, *Libri di casa Trivulzio nel secolo XV*, Como, 1890.

[7] It was the humanist Gian Antonio Porcellio who described the wars of 1451–52 in strictly classical terms (see J. Burckhardt, *The Civilisation of the Renaissance in Italy*, London, 1951, p. 63). The study of warfare in fifteenth-century Italy still depends largely on the old authorities E. Ricotti, *La storia delle compagnie di ventura in Italia*, second edition, Turin, 1893, and G. Canestrini, 'Documenti per servire alla storia della milizia italiana', *Archivio storico italiano*, XV, 1851. However, for more recent surveys see P. Pieri, *Il Rinascimento e la crisi militare italiana*, Turin, second edition, 1952, pp. 205–56, and M. E. Mallett, *Mercenaries and their Masters: Warfare in Renaissance Italy*, London, 1973. For remarks on the lack of serious classicism among Italian captains see F. L. Taylor, *The Art of War in Italy, 1494–1529*, Cambridge, 1921, p. 178.

[8] W. H. Woodward, *Vittorino da Feltre and other Humanist Educators*, Cambridge, 1897, translates Vergerio's work at pp. 96–118; for the extract quoted see p. 116.

[9] P. Pieri, 'L'arte militare italiana nella seconda metà del secolo XV negli scritti di Diomede Caraffa, conte di Maddaloni', *Ricordi e studi in memoria di Francesco Flamini da suoi discepoli*, Naples, 1931, pp. 87–103; *id.*, 'Il "Governo et exercitio de la militia" di Orso degli Orsini e i "Memoriali" di Diomede Caraffa', *Archivio storico per le provincie napoletane*, new series, XIX, 1933, pp. 99–212.

[10] F. Ughelli, *L'Albero e istoria della famiglia dei conti di Marsciano*, Rome, 1667, pp. 128 ff. The section which contains a description of the library is reprinted here in appendix 10.1.

[11] Ughelli, *op. cit.*, p. 32.

[12] Archivio di Stato, Venice (hereafter referred to as A.S.V.), Senatus Secreta, XIII, f. 86, and XIV, f. 70v. Report of his capture in 1438 comes in Cristoforo da Soldo, *Cronaca*, ed. G. Brizzolara, in L. A. Muratori, *Rerum italicarium scriptores*, new series, Bologna, twenty-four vols., 1900– , XXI, part 3, p. 13. For reference to Guerriero's earlier service in the papal army see Archivio Segreto Vaticano, Armadio, XXII, ff. 85–87 (23 October 1433).

[13] A.S.V., Senatus Terra, III, f. 82 (28 September 1453), and R. Predelli (ed.), *I libri commemoriali della repubblica di Venezia: Regesti*, V, *Monumenti storici della R. Deputazione veneta di storia patria*, first series, *Documenti*, vol. X, 1901, p. 82.

[14] Ughelli, *op. cit.*, pp. 35–7. Todeschina brought Antonio a dowry of 600 florins. In 1478 a senate minute referred to Antonio 'qui a puero ad hanc etatem militavit ad nostram stipendiam'. (A.S.V., Senatus Secreta, XXVIII, f. 78.)

[15] For details of the Venetian army about this time see Cristoforo da Soldo, *Cronaca, cit.*, pp. 77 and 98.

[16] For discussion of this question see Mallett, *Mercenaries and their Masters, cit.,* *passim.*

[17] M. E. Mallett, 'Venice and its *condottieri,* 1404–54', in *Renaissance Venice,* ed. J. R. Hale, London, 1973, pp. 121–45, provides detailed discussion and references for the creation of Venetian standing forces.

[18] G. Eroli, *Erasmo Gattamelata da Narni: suoi monumenti e sua famiglia,* Rome, 1876, pp. 41–2; Cristoforo da Soldo, *Cronaca, cit.,* pp. 115–17.

[19] A.S.V., Senatus Secreta, xx, f. 89 (19 May 1456), and Ughelli, *op. cit.,* p. 33.

[20] The material for a study of the Venetian army in this period lies mainly in the Senatus Secreta and Senatus Terra, and will be discussed in a forthcoming book on the Venetian army by J. R. Hale and M. E. Mallett.

[21] M. Sanuto, *Vite dei duchi di Venezia,* in L. Muratori, *Rerum italicarum scriptores,* Milan, twenty-five vols., 1723–57, xxii (1733), p. 1178.

[22] Mallett, 'Venice and its condottieri', *cit.,* p. 129.

[23] Ughelli, *op. cit.,* p. 33.

[24] A.S.V., Senatus Terra, v, f. 185v (31 May 1467).

[25] A.S.V., Senatus Secreta, xxv, ff. 48–9 (11 July 1471).

[26] A.S.V., Senatus Terra, vi, f. 187v (27 November 1472) and f. 192v (4 January 1473).

[27] A.S.V., Senatus Terra, vii, f. 197v (9 February 1478); viii, f. 10v (30 Mary 1478); viii, f. 41 (25 February 1479); viii, f. 66 (11 October 1479).

[28] A.S.V., Senatus Secreta, xxix, f. 10 (20 April 1479).

[29] A.S.V., Senatus Terra, viii, f. 64 (29 September 1479).

[30] A.S.V., Senatus Secreta, xxix, f. 54 (15 November 1479).

[31] *Cronaca di Anonimo Veronese (1446–88),* ed. G. Soranzo, in *Monumenti storici pubblicati dalla R. Deputazione veneta di storia patria,* third series, iv, 1915, pp. 370 and 373; M. Sanuto, *Commentari della guerra di Ferrara tra li veneziani e il duca Ercole d'Este nel 1482,* Venice, 1829, pp. 17 and 21; E. Piva, *La guerra di Ferrara nel 1482,* Padua, 1893; R. Cessi, 'Per la storia della guerra di Ferrara, 1482–3', *Notizie degli archivi di Stato,* viii, 1948, pp. 63–72, and in *Archivio Veneto,* lxxix, 1950, pp. 57–76; Bernardino Zambotti, *Diario Ferrarese,* ed. G. Pardi, *Rerum italicarum scriptores,* new series, xxiv, part 7 (1937), pp. 108 and 145.

[32] B. Corio, *Storia di Milano,* Milan, three vols., 1855–57, iii, p. 384.

[33] Sanuto, *Commentari, cit.,* pp. 91–3. Sanuto also reports (p. 33) that Girolamo, a younger son of Antonio, was killed during this war by a spingard shot at Castel Guglielmo. Ranuccio da Marsciano continued to serve Venice until 1487, when he joined the Florentines with 100 lances. He served bravely during the Pisan war and was killed at the siege of Capua in 1501. He married Giovanna, the daughter of Roberto Malatesta.

[34] For the *condotta* see Archivio di Stato, Firenze, X di Balià, Deliberazioni, condotte e stanziamenti, 27, ff. 110–17 (12 September 1483).

[35] Archivio di Stato, Milan, Autografi, 205, fasc. 34.

[36] Corio, *op. cit.,* iii, p. 384.

[37] Ughelli, *op. cit.,* p. 37.

[38] *Ibid.,* p. 4.

[39] The surviving letters of Antonio da Marsciano to Lorenzo are in the Archivio di Stato, Florence, Archivio Mediceo avanti il Principato, xxvi, 306 (21 Spetember 1483); xl, 411 (27 November 1483); xxxix, 95 (4 March 1484); xl, 100 (10 March 1484). The last letter is that described in the printed catalogue as xxxix, 112, but the collocation has been changed. Two other letters attributed to Antonio in the printed catalogue present certain difficulties; xxvi, 305 is clearly not written by Antonio da Marsciano but by Antonio 'de Curte', and xl, 267 has been lost.

During the same period Lorenzo wrote at least ten letters to Antonio (see *Protocolli del carteggio di Lorenzo il Magnifico,* ed. Marcello del Piazzo, Florence, 1956).

[40] There is no mention of this library in the standard works, i.e. C. Frati, *Dizionario*

bio-bibliografico dei bibliotecari e bibliofili italiani del sec. XIV al XIX, Florence, 1933, and T. Gottlieb, *Über mittelalterliche Bibliotheken*, Leipzig, 1890.

[41] The first Italian edition of Burley is usually recorded as undated but probably 1476–78 (*Catalogue of Books printed in the Fifteenth Century now in the British Museum*, v, *Venice*, London, 1963, p. 206). However, the fact that Antonio had a copy in 1476 suggests that this is the last possible date for this edition.

[42] It is interesting to note that all the works regarded as forming the literary sources for Machiavelli's *Arte della Guerra* were present in Antonio's library; see L. A. Burd, 'Le fonti letterarie di Machiavelli nell'Arte della Guerra', *Atti della R. Accademia dei Lincei, Memorie della classe di scienze morali, storiche e filologiche*, fifth series, iv, 1897, pp. 187–261.

[43] The works of Pietro da Abano were particularly popular in the fifteenth century and were recommended by Nicholas V for every library; see P. Kibre, 'The intellectual interests reflected in libraries of the fourteenth and fifteenth centuries', *Journal of the History of Ideas*, vii, 1946, p. 286. For further remarks on the popularity of this work see the introduction to *Il trattato 'de venenis' di Petrus de Abano*, ed. A. Bendicenti, Florence, 1949.

[44] A. F. Massera, 'Roberto Valturio; "omnium scientiarium doctor et monarcha" (1405–75)', *Monografie dell'Istituto tecnico 'R. Valturio' di Rimini*, i, Faenza, 1958.

[45] E. Radakiewicz, 'Who was the first owner of the London manuscript of Valturius?' in *Studi Riminesi e bibliografici in onore di Carlo Lucchesi*, Società di Studi Romagnoli, Rimini, 1952, pp. 187–91.

[46] Vespasiano da Bisticci spoke highly of Bishop Ermolao Barbaro; see *Vite di uomini illustri del secolo XV*, ed. P. Ancona and E. Aeschlimann, Milan, 1951, p. 144. S. Maffei, *Verona illustrata*, Verona, 1732, ii, 'Degli scrittori veronese', libro iii, provides material on many of the Veronese humanists of the period; for more recent comment see particularly M. Carrara, 'Scritture veronesi del secolo XV', *Atti e memorie dell' Accademia di agricultura, scienze, lettere di Verona*, sixth series, viii, 1956–57; C. Perpolli, 'L'Actio Panthea e l'umanesimo veronese', *ibid.*, fourth series, xvi, 1915; G. P. Marchi, 'Martino Rizzoni: allievo di Guarino', *ibid.*, sixth series, xvii, 1965–66; R. Avesani and B. M. Pebbles, 'Studies in Piero Donato Avogaro of Verona', *Italia medievale et humanistica*, v, 1962. On Veronese libraries and book collections of the fifteenth century see M. Carrara, 'Opere di classici in librerie veronesi del secolo XV. La biblioteca di Lorenzo Stagnolo', *Atti e memorie dell'Accademia ... di Verona*, sixth series, vi, 1956; G. P. Marchi, 'Libri e biblioteche del Quattrocento', *Studi storici veronesi di Luigi Simeoni*, xvi–xvii, 1966–67; M. Lecce, 'Biblioteche e prezzi di libri a Verona alla fine del Medioevo', *Economia e storia*, viii, 1961; A. Avena, 'I libri del notaio veronese Bartolomeo Squarceti da Cavaion', *Bibliofilia*, xiii, 1911.

[47] '... non restando etiam da ricordare reverentemente a Vostra Magnificentia chel nascondere del secreto a lo inimco et attingere el suo se puote reputar casone potissima per una parte de la victoria....' (Archivio di Stato, Florence, Archivio Mediceo avanti il Principato, xxxix, 95 (4 March 1484.)

NICOLAI RUBINSTEIN *Westfield College, London*

II

MICHELOZZO AND NICCOLÒ MICHELOZZI IN CHIOS
1466–67

IN HIS LIFE of Michelozzo Michelozzi Vasari writes that one should not follow Michelozzo's example in having 'bisogno negli ultimi anni [di sua vita] d'andarsi procacciando miseramente il vivere'.[1] Michelozzo died in 1472, and until now the only contemporary evidence we possessed concerning his activities during the last years of his life was a contract he concluded, on 16 May 1464, at Ragusa, where he had spent three years in the employment of the republic.[2] In this contract he agreed to serve the Mahona of Chios 'bene fedelmente ad uso di buon maestro' for a yearly salary of 300 gold ducats, and to leave for Chios within eight days.[3] Milanesi states that it is not known whether Michelozzo really went.[4] Philip Argenti, in his book on Chios under Genoese rule, concludes that 'nothing is known of his activities on the island',[5] and Harriet Caplow, in a recent article which sheds new light on Michelozzo's activities at Ragusa, asks, 'Did Michelozzo actually go to Chios?' and, despite extensive researches in the island itself, is equally unable to answer this question.[6] A group of corrected drafts and copies of letters written in Latin by Michelozzo's son Niccolò, which forms part of a miscellaneous manuscript in the Biblioteca Nazionale in Florence,[7] however, allows us to answer it in the affirmative, and at the same time to confirm Vasari's account of Michelozzo's economic difficulties in his old age.

Niccolò Michelozzi, who was later to become Lorenzo de' Medici's secretary, had joined his father in Chios in 1466, having embarked at Pisa in May of that year.[8] They left the island to return to Florence in the following year.[9] During his stay on Chios he tried to help his father to improve a difficult financial situation, from which he too was to suffer, by using his humanist training in writing in his father's name or on his behalf. The year before he had been corresponding with Alessandro Braccesi, Naldo Naldi and other humanist friends about works of classical literature and had been praising the epistolary style and the poems of his correspondents;[10] now he had to deal with the professional and financial problems of Michelozzo. The first piece of the *copiario* is an undated draft, in Niccolò's hand, of a letter by

Michelozzo to Matthias Corvinus, king of Hungary, in which, after praising in enthusiastic terms the king's exploits against the Turks, Michelozzo offers his services.[11] Michelozzo had learned, he writes to the king, from Florentine merchants on their way from Hungary, 'quasdam esse in tuo amplissimo regno cavernas, ex quibus auri atque argenti vectigalia inclita tua Maiestas recipere solita erat', which had been flooded 'aquarum rapacissima vi'. He now offers the king, as 'remedium optimum ac securissimum', an invention of his on which he had been working since his youth and which he had just brought to its final completion:

ut maturari iuventus nostra cepta est, instrumentum quoddam animum ipsum ac fantasiam nostram iactare incepit, quod ego excogitando ac magnopere laborando summo studio, ingenti cura, non parvo etiam sumptu, omni denique mente quatraginta iam annis sum prosecutus ac tandem nuper, cum Chii moram traherem, ad optatum ac suum optimum exitum perduxi.

This 'instrumentum' could be 'ad quoslibet aquarum impetus reperiendos et ad ipsas quo velis inducendos . . . aptissimum'; moreover, 'minimo quidem sumptu confici potest absque ullo iumentorum auxilio'.[12] It would bring the king 'presidium . . . non parvum presertim in bellis, quorum sumptus maximos esse constat'. He finally expresses the hope that he will be given an opportunity to demonstrate to the king 'architecturae artem, quae nobis semper scopon veluti sagictatori, ut Greci dicunt, extitit', and informs him that he will spend the winter in Chios, after which he intends to leave for Italy, stay a few months at Ancona, and from there return to Florence. In fifteenth-century Italy engineering formed part of the architect's craft,[13] and Michelozzo could well consider himself specially qualified to offer his services as an engineer in view of his work at Ragusa, where, as has been recently shown, he was employed not as architect but 'pro ingeniario Comunis' to supervise the new fortifications of that city.[14]

This is the last we hear of the project. The other three letters written by Niccolò on his father's behalf are written in his own person to Adoardo Giustiniani. The Giustiniani formed the Mahona of Chios, and Adoardo was one of the two Giustiniani in whose names the contract with Michelozzo had been concluded at Ragusa.[15] It emerges from these letters that Michelozzo had not received the salary which was due to him under his contract, and that he—and for that matter Niccolò himself—were in dire financial straits. His father, Niccolò writes in the first, undated letter,[16]

tuo primum dehinc consociorum tuorum hortatu consilioque ex Ragusio, Exclavonie urbe, in qua quidem summo ob industriam suam honore non parvaque utilitate triennia vita degerat, in hanc ob habitantes illic Ianuenses nobilissimam quidem et mercature aptissimam insulam deductus est, existimans hanc sibi fortunam meliorem futuram quam Ragusiensis illa bona fuerit.

His expectations had, however been disappointed: 'melior quidem fuisset fortuna, si eam suorum laborum mercedem, quam vobiscum pactus est, eidem solveretur'. Things were so bad that after Niccolò's arrival money had more than once been lacking to buy the necessary food. He therefore begs

Adoardo Giustiniani, at that time in charge of the island's financial administration ('cumque in presentia eo fungaris magistratu qui quidem et
communia vectigalia colligat et communes sumptus cotidianos efficiat'), to
see to it 'ut Michaeloz[o] parenti carissimo suoque labori fiat satis'.

One cannot help wondering whether the fault was entirely on the Mahona's
side. In Ragusa too Michelozzo had got into trouble with his employers and
had been criticised, even reprimanded in 1463, for not attending to his
duties regularly.[17] From another letter to Adoardo Giustiniani[18] it emerges
that Michelozzo had not yet been paid his full salary, and Niccolò paints a
sombre picture of their desperate situation. He witnesses his father, 'quondam
suavissimum iocundissimumque, continuo quodam merore vestra quidem,
qui Chium regitis, causa adeo laborare, ut die nullam, noctu vero minimam
quidem requiem adipisci posse conspiciam'; indeed, he fears for his life 'ob
continuas ingentissimasque calamitates atque anxietates'. If he had been
paid the salary that was owed him they would have left 'cum navi de
Anchona' which had sailed to Italy the day before. But now another ship of
the same origin was expected from Pera before the end of the month, 'quius
iam decem dies absumsimus', and Niccolò begs Adoardo Giustiniani to see
to it that 'quod semel futurum est fiat quamprimum'. Michelozzo, 'cuius sibi,
cum senex sit, maxima penuria est', must not delay his departure any longer,
'nonnihil tempus hic conteret', since he had, 'sui ingenii artificio', agreed to
work elsewhere, 'nonnulla alibi . . . depactus sit'. Niccolò's appeal seems to
have been successful, for, as he writes in a third letter to Adoardo Giustiniani,
Adoardo had informed him through a Florentine compatriot named
Benedetto, 'Benedictus florentinus'—possibly Benedetto Dei, who was at
that time in Chios[19]—'promptissimum esse atque paratissimum ad id
maxime conficiendum' that what he and others owed Michelozzo, 'quamprimum solvant'. Overjoyed by this news, Niccolò gratefully assures Adoardo
that he had never doubted his good intentions, 'sed maxime et animo et
menti nostre fixum steterat et in presentia maxime prestat te eiusdem animi
voluntatisque semper fuisse'. Even so, he reminds him, 'licet nequaquam
opus sit', to let action follow words without further delay. 'Vides enim non
modo in dies, sed in horas, a patrono navim anconitanam expectari'; if they
miss the transport to Italy, 'quod aliud expectandum nobis sit ignoro penitus'.
This letter may have been written around 13 April, on which day he informs
Pietro Cennini[20] of their impending return to Italy and that they are
expecting 'in dies' 'navim quandam ex Ancona' belonging to Andrea
degli Agli.[21] On 29 April, however, Niccolò writes to Alessandro Braccesi[22]
that on the same day two ships are leaving Chios, and that he will send his
letter with one of them to Italy, while he and his father will sail with the
other to Constantinople, 'Constantinopolim usque'; Braccesi may expect
him back in Florence at the beginning of August.[23] In the end he and his
father returned to Italy together with Florentine merchants who were
returning from Constantinople 'cum anconitanis navibus',[24] one of which
belonged to Andrea degli Agli.[25] But as we shall see presently, this was not
the end of their troubles.

Niccolò seems to have taken an instant dislike to Chios and its inhabitants, and not surprisingly, this dislike was increased by his experiences on the island. In his first letter from Chios to Alessandro Braccesi, of 13 September 1466,[26] he affirms his belief 'homines omni humanitate penitus exutos esse, qui quieto volentique animo his in locis moram minimam quidem trahere possint', and laments his fate, which forced him, against his will, to stay there. 'Primum quidem locorum omnium nulla amenitas est'; it may be enough to say that in the summer the earth is scorched by torrid sun, while in the winter it is flooded by continuous rain to such an extent 'ut nusquam fere progredi liceat'. Practically nothing grows on the island except mastic, which is incredible considering the fact that it is so much frequented by ships and merchants.[27] And the worst is that 'conservatio nobis necessaria habenda cum est inhumanis quidem Grecorum reliquiis, quod genus hominum superbum, quam ineptum, quam insulsum, quam denique et verbis et re ipsa ab omnium ceterorum hominum consuetudine remotum sit', he does not even dare to write. The winter he spent in Chios seems to have confirmed the poor opinion he had of the island and its inhabitants. In a letter of 14 February 1467[28] to the Bishop of Chios, Antonio Pallavicino, he condoles with him that so wise a man should have come to the island as pastor 'non ovium, sed potius hircorum fetentium, qui nullis quidem neque blanditiis neque flagellis ad stabula perduci possint', such as the Greeks of Chios, 'quas quippe gentes inhumanas esse et a cunctis humanis divinisque moribus abhorrere manifeste apparet'. Making allowances for rhetorical exaggeration, Niccolò's letters seem to reflect a genuine distaste for Chios and its Greek population, and his experiences with the Genoese of Chios made him conclude that they had adopted some of the ways of the island's Greeks. If he were to speak the truth, he continues in his letter to Antonio Pallavicini, 'hi qui nequaquam Greci sunt, nec ab vera religione abhorrent', had assumed, 'quamquam ex nobilissimo Ianuensium genere existant . . . nonnullos ex Grecorum moribus, fortasse ob crebram cum eis conversationem'.

In the circumstances his absence from Florence and from his Florentine friends must have weighed heavily on him. He may also have been anxious not to lose contact with possible sources of employment there. Before he left for Chios Niccolò had done some temporary work in the Florentine chancery on behalf of his friend, Alessandro Braccesi,[29] and his request to Braccesi, in his last letter to him from Chios, of 29 April 1467, to remember him to the chancellor, Bartolomeo Scala,[30] may not have been without some practical considerations. His letters to Alessandro Braccesi and Naldo Naldi voice his disappointment at not hearing from them. On 23 October 1466 he bitterly complains to Braccesi that it is four months and twenty-eight days since he received his last letter at Pisa before embarking for Chios.[31] In the absence of later news the letters he had received from Braccesi while waiting for his ship to leave 'quotidie in manibus versantur, eas solum legendo animum quietum consolatumque reperio'. He similarly complains to Naldo Naldi, shortly before his departure from Chios,[32] that he had not received any letters from him, not even greetings to inform him 'ut valeas, quidque agas,

quid Muse post meum istinc discessum tecum agant negocii'. However, in
this case Niccolò himself was not blameless, for he had not written to Naldi
since he had left Pisa: but at least, he adds, he had sent him many greetings.[33]
On 13 April 1467, which may have been the day on which he wrote this
letter, he also wrote to Pietro Cennini[34] that he had not received any letters
from him, although he would have had much to say, 'que scribi debeant
digna'. Now Niccolò only wants to inform him of their impending return to
Florence, 'qui cunctis nostris de te lamentationibus finem imponet'.

Much as he disliked Chios and its inhabitants, Niccolò must have been
aware of the advantages the island possessed for collecting news of military
operations in Greece and beyond at a time when Venice was trying to stop
the Turkish advance and Skanderbeg was putting up a desperate resistance
to the Turks in Albania. He may also have felt that by conveying such news
to Alessandro Braccesi he would render himself useful to the Florentine
government, as well as showing his qualifications as a 'military correspondent',
and thus improve his chances of future employment in the chancery. Unfortunately his information was not always accurate or sufficiently precise.
In his letter of 13 September 1466[35] he describes Mohammed II's invasion of
Albania in spring 1466 but evidently does not know the name of Skanderbeg's
fortress, Kruje, which the Turks besieged in vain.[36] He puts the size of the
Turkish army at 80,000 ('ut aiunt'), which may in fact be nearer the truth
than contemporary estimates of 200,000 to 300,000;[37] but he does not seem
to know the name of the Christian traitor who provided 'adytum in reliquas
eius provincie partes' and thus enabled Mohammed to devastate Albania;
nor does he name the 'munitissimum . . . castellum' the Sultan had built as a
military base before returning to Constantinople.[38] In October Niccolò
reports on the Venetian campaign of that year in the Morea, which after
initial successes ended in disaster, and in the execution of the Venetian
provveditore of the Morea, Iacopo Barbarigo, whom Niccolò wrongly calls
'totius classis princeps',[39] and of Michael Raul, or Ralli, a prominent Greek
supporter of Venice.[40] 'Sicque victoria potiti sunt,' he ends his account of the
Venetian defeat, 'tanta nostrorum strage Christianorum, ut absque dolore
ingentissimo maximaque Venetorum miseratione a nobis scribi nequaquam
possit.' He was soon to have reason to be less sympathetic to the Venetians.

On 29 April 1467 Niccolò wrote to Alessandro Braccesi that he and his
father were leaving that day for Constantinople, and that if they were to see
'que memoria digna putemus, tua potissimum causa annotabimus atque
tibi, quamprimum facultas dabitur, litteris significabimus'.[41] In a subsequent letter to Braccesi[42] he informs him that after their departure from
Chios they had sailed on a Cretan ship, 'quatuor dierum navigatione,
Neptuno et Eolo secundis', to Crete. In order to continue 'quod ceteris nostris
litteris ceptum est, ut scilicet te de cunctis que viderim locis certiorem
faciam', he describes how he visited 'nobilissiman Iovis insulam' and 'nobilissi-
mum promontorium iuxta Canducam civitatem ad quartum lapidem, cuius
cacumen facies hominis longe prospicientibus apparet, quam quidem
effigiem dicunt esse Iovis. In huius montis radicibus Boream versus collis

est subtus omnino vacuus, quod sepulchrum maximi Iovis asserunt extitisse.'[43] One can enter the mountain 'eo longo foramine', but, 'ceptas iam ruinas timentes', they did not dare go any farther. Beyond the mountain could be seen a labyrinth 'penitus inextricabilis' and Knossos, said to be the 'antiquissima civitas' of Minos but now 'deleta penitus'.[44] In the same letter in which he describes his visit to Crete he also informs Braccesi that the ship in which he was returning home had been captured by the Venetian navy, and that he and his father, as well as the Florentine merchants who were travelling to Florence from Constantinople on the ships from Ancona, had been taken as prisoners to Venice. Braccesi would have already heard from the merchants who had proceeded to Florence 'quo modo excepti et quibus tormentis sevissimis quidem affecti sint'.

The story of this incident can be told from the public records of Florence and Venice. On 13 September 1467 the Florentine government wrote to the Venetian Signoria[45] in order to complain that two ships, which were returning from Thracia to Italy, and which, although they belonged to inhabitants of Ancona, carried many precious commodities belonging to Florentine merchants, had been captured by the Venetian navy, taken to Modon and despoiled of their cargo.[46] According to the Florentines the ships did not carry anything prohibited by the Pope, only the goods of Florentine merchants with which they were returning home from enemy territory, and they therefore expressed the hope that if Venice had not yet restored everything she would do so forthwith. To this the Venetians replied on the 22nd[47] that they were at war with the Turks, and having been informed that ships from Ancona had been carrying to the enemy 'spreto Dei timore . . . arma, pulveres et . . . munitiones, quibus nostri carent', they had asked Ancona to stop sending her ships to the Straits. Ancona had promised to do so, and had told them 'quod si qui inobedientes . . . eorum cives . . . contra facere auderent', the Venetians, 'quorum intererat', were to take the necessary measures. Accordingly, as the ships from Ancona did not desist, 'a navigatione consueta et sceleratis comertiis', the Venetians had seen themselves compelled 'ingenti impensa armare IIIIᵒʳ naves', with orders to retain any such ships 'in Strictum navigantes'. This had now happened, and the captured ships with their passengers had been ordered to be taken to Venice.

The Florentine government thereupon expressed its relief[48] that the interception of the ships from Ancona 'minime propter Florentinos cives et mercatores extitisse': nevertheless 'maximo detrimento est mercatoribus nostris pecunias et mercimonia Florentinorum trahi istuc', i.e. to Venice; the Venetians would no doubt show their justice and humanity by releasing the Florentine citizens and their goods. But the intercepted ships did not arrive in Venice until the end of December. On 7 December the Senate[49] ordered the captain of the navy to bring the captured ships from Ancona to Venice, with the exception 'navis magne anconitane', whose merchandise and passengers were to be taken there on Venetian ships; and the passengers were to be kept 'sub bona custodia' until the Signoria, 'audito capitaneo,

de eis constituerit'. As emerges from a reply to the Florentine ambassador in
Venice, Tommaso Soderini, the ships arrived at the end of that month;[50]
and on 2 January 1468 the Senate decided to appoint three of its members to
examine the matter of the captured ships, 'quum processus formatus per
capitaneum nostrum navium armatarum contra navim Andree de Aliis' and
others which had been captured 'redeuntes ex Constantinopoli, satis longus
est'. The matter was referred to the Council of Ten, and on 23 January the
Ten decided,[51] moved by 'reverentia . . . in summum pontificem, qui tam
efficaciter instat et intercedit', that, although 'naves ipse iustissime capte
sint', they should be handed back to their owners, who could leave Venice
with them 'libere ab omni datio'. On 27 January the Ten conveyed their
decision, to which they had been prompted by letters from Rome, to the
senate,[52] and specified that 'res et mercationes Florentinorum ac An-
conitanorum et aliorum reperte super navibus anconitanis . . . libere restitui
debeant illis quorum sunt'.

Niccolò Michelozzi's *copiario* does not reveal how he and his father fared
in Venice; but on the verso of a letter written by him most probably during
his stay in that city[53] we read the initial words of another, unfinished, draft
which seems to refer to the restitution of Florentine property decreed by the
Ten: 'A voi M. co Messer Polo Morosini delle robe di me Michelozo architecto
fiore[ntino]'.[54] The letter is addressed on the recto 'Iohanni Flor[entino?]',[55]
and in it Niccolò refers to a convivial meeting his father had in Giovanni's
house on 10 January.

Rettulit autem ad nos Michaelozus mihi suavissimus pater, cum ad IIII° Idus
Ianuarii apud vos convivaret, cum multa prius tecum racionatus esset, in eum te
sermonem incidisse, ut mentionem faceres de scriptore quodam anglico, cuius nomen
memoria decidisse dixit, qui, ut tu aiebas, optimum quidem stilum in dicendo
obtinuisse. Id nomen, et quoniam scriptorum omnium semper curiosus extiti et
quoniam audivi sepius nullum ex iis locis qui dicendi stilo floreret oriundum fuisse,
mirum in modum desidero tuis litteris aut verbis percipere.[56]

Even at a time when he must have been under great stress Niccolò did not
forget his humanist interests. But, no doubt anxious for his future, he also
remembered the importance of keeping in touch with men of influence, and
asked Giovanni to recommend him to Tommaso Soderini, the Florentine
ambassador in Venice and one of the leading followers of Piero de' Medici.[57]

APPENDIX II.1

[f. 39*v*] Alex[andr]o Braccensio Florentiae

Litteras meas ex Petro Matheio Florentino, qui hinc cum triremibus nostris mercatoriis[a] istuc se[b] omnino protulit,[c] iamdiu te accepisse arbitror,[d] quae te et locorum
omnium et temporum, quibus huc usque adnavigavimus, certiorem facere potuerunt.
Quod autem ea loca, quae meis litteris perscripta fuerant, gratissima tibi acciderint,

(*a*) triremibus nostris mercatoriis *ex* triremibus mercatoribus Florent *corr*.
(*b*) se *ex* sese *corr*.
(*c*) protulit *vel* contulit.
(*d*) iamdiu—arbitror *ex* accepisse te arbitror *ex* te accepisse arbitror *corr*.

nihil est quod dubitem; te enim harum rerum semper cupidum repperi et curiosum.[e] Eapropter etiam nunc cetera quae meis litteris annotata nequaqam fuerant loca, que hanc insulam Bizantiumque media interiacent, ac aliqua[f] de Constantino-politane ipsa urbe verba facere animo staret sententia, si tempus ipsum, quod in presentia datur brevissimum, pateretur. Festinat enim e portu solvere navis, que heri ex Rodo Chion concesserat, iamque eius carinae prora Occidentem prospicit, venti ipsi in horas eius cursum secundare videntur, linthea antemnis complicata ad mals summitatem consurgunt, anchora, que[g] arenis herentia immotam solent nec ventii parentem reddere navim, ad prorae summitatem suspensa esse cernuntur. Eo fit ut eorum locorum descriptio, quae tibi ingentissime foret iucunditati, in aliud quidem tempus nobis invitis differatur. Quare si brevior ero et temporis angustie et[h] Zephiro adeo iter ipsum ad Italiam secundanti ascribas velim,[i] non mihi, qui longior tecum esse cuperem, quandoquidem quanto longiores sunt mee litterae, tanto maiorem tibi laetitiam afferre solite sunt. Ea navis, ut naute ipsi asserunt, Venetias concedet; hinc littere Florentiam portabuntur et te mihi summa quadam et insolita obstrictum benevolentia nequaquam animo penitus quietum ob meam istinc absentiam con-solationi esse poterunt, presertim cum tibi referent statim elapso quod instat hieme, quo tempore, ut te non latet, navim equoreo ipsi monstro committere periculosissi-mum est, simul cum parente proprio Italiam patriam nostram reversurum, ac que verba nunc a nobis per litteras fiunt, ore proprio ab utroque nostrum esse futura. Quod autem mihi non parvam prebuerit anxietatem, postea quam in portu ipso Pisano primum ventis linthea prebuimus, hoc maximum extat quod iam menses quatuor dies XXVIII° preteriere, quibus nullas a te litteras accepi, quamobrem que nobis[j] sit expectatio tuarum litterarum tu ipse ob consolidatissimam amicitiam nostram non minus ac ego cognoscis; nec ulla datur alia de te mihi consolatio preterquam littere tue, quas, cum Pisis moram traherem, ad me scripsisti. He quotidie in manibus versantur, eas solum legendo animum quietum consolatumque reperio; quod si alteras nuper a te scriptas accepero, non dubito quum mira quadam letitia exiliam. Nuper circiter Nonas Augusti Venetorum classis ingentissima, que unis et quadraginta triremibus[k] grippereis aliisque naviculis bello aptis nonagesimum post centesimum impleret[l] numerum, in eam Grecie partem, que vulgo Morea dicitur, applicuit terroremque ingentissimum Turchis[m] eorumque capitaneo Sangiacobbei nomine, qui ei provincie preerat, incussit, adeo ut cum nequaquam se tutum urbe Patras nominis eius provincie principaliori arbitraretur ob Grecorum multitudinem, relicta urbe montana loca urbi[n] propinqua naturaque munita exercitu suo Tur-chorum, qui mille quingenti equites extiterant, possedit. Interea circitum [sic] IIII Augusti Venetorum classis generalis dux Iacobus Barbarighus Venetus, sumpto sibi comite Ralli Greco (hic princeps peditum eius provincie erat), ingentissimo exercitu, ut put[ant] qui peditibus decem milibus, equitibus vero trecentis constaret, urbem ipsam Patras aggressus est victoriaque minimo quidem tempore nullaque difficultate potitus est; quam ingressus, erectis Venetorum vexillis, non satis fore existimans urbem cepisse statuit eodem tempore Turchorum castra adoriri. Sangiacobbei autem prospiciens tam grande exercitum in se suosque irruere, cum pugnare statuisset, quoniam locorum natura vivaretur [sic], fugam simulans exercitum suum (hi mille

(e) semper—curiosum *ex* semper repperi et cupidum et curiosum *corr.*
(f) aliqua *ex* alia *corr.*
(g) ante *del.*
(h) Eolo *del.*
(i) velim *ex* velis *corr.*
(j) quamobrem—nobis *ex* quid quamobrem quanta nobis *corr.*
(k) et *del.*
(l) impleret *ex* implebant *corr.*
(m) qui *del.*
(n) urbi *ex* urbique *corr.*

quingenti equites erant) bifariam divisit ac in insidiis, quas iamdudum hosti paraverat, latuit. Veneti vero utpote victoria bacchantes parvique seu potius nihili inimica castra facientes, in ea inciderunt arctissima loca, que ferocissimis Turchorum militibus [f. 40r] undique cingebantur, ibique, insidiis palam factis concursuque facto, cum ferocissimi undique circumstarent Turchi, Veneti effranguntur et in fugam miser-abiliter vertuntur. Venetorum ad octingenti cesi totidem fere captivi, inter quos et Iacobus Barbaricus totius classis princeps et Ralli peditum dux extitere, quorum alter postmodum pelle nudatus, alter palo affixus, miserabiliter quidem vitam finiere. Reliqua deinde turba Venetorum naves usque fugata paulumque per mare navibus insectata est, que Venetias tanto suorum damno tantoque Christianorum omnium dedecore postmodum redivit. Turchi vero, cum ad urbem redirent, ipsam in dedi-tionem receperunt sicque victoria potiti sunt tanta nostrorum strage Christianorum, ut absque dolore ingentissimo maximaque Venetorum miseratione a nobis scribi nequaquam possit nec sine lachrimarum multarum abundantia excogitari queat. Mahumeth vero maximus Turchorum omnium princeps IIII° Idus Septembris [cum] omni suo exercitu, quem primo⁰ vere in Albaniam duxerat quique ex mortifero ipso cum Christianis bello supererat, Constantinopolim rediit secumque duxit ex Albanis aliorumque locorum hominibus captivorum ac servorumᵖ duodecim millia, qui dehinc tanquam oves per omnem Phrygiam miserrime quidem venditi sunt, eorum quoad vixerint exuti libertate. Nihil est aliud impresentia quod ad te scribam preterquam de amicitia nostra, quam tibi maximopere commendo. Vale et me Florentie vere saltem adulto om[ni] dubitatione seposita futurum expectato. Interim valitudinem cura diligenter et ama.

Chii X° Kalendas Novembris 1466.

APPENDIX II.2

Eidem

Scripsi ad te alias de itinere omni nostro a portu ipso Pisano queque nobis videnda acaderint adusque Chion insulam, in qua ut in presentia vitam degam necessitas facit quodque aliquamdiu futurus sim, nobis invitis accidit. Existimo enim eos homines omni humanitate penitus exutos esse, qui quieto volentique animo his in locis moram minimam quidem trahere possint. Primum quidem locorum omnium nulla amenitas est; qua de re hoc mihi dixisse satis sit, quod estatis tempore torrentissi-mo quidem siccatur sole, hieme vero adeo continuis imbribus ablutus omnis humus, ut nusquam fere progredi liceat. Rerum dehinc omnium quis humana sibi doleat natura negatisᵃ caritudo, cum nihil fere preter masticum in insula procreetur ultra quam cuiquam credibile sit, cum frequentatissimus locus sit et navibus et mercatori-bus. Preterea, quod potissimum est, conversatio nobis necessaria habenda est cum inhumanis quidem Grecorcum reliquiis, quod genus hominum superbum quam ineptum quam insulsum quam denique et verbis et re ipsa ab omnium ceterorum hominum consuetudine remotum sit, scribere nequaguam ausim: longissimum enim opus aggrederes atque adeo fastidiosum, ut idem nec ad exitum perducere animus sufficiat, et tibi et ceteris consilio quodam preditis fastidio potius quam iucunditati foret. Sed his hactenus. Mahumet Ottomanli maximus princeps Turchorum circiter Kalendas Maias ingentissimum exercitum suum octoginta milium ut aiunt hominum in Albaniam deduxit, quam ingressus provinciamᵇ discurrereᶜ depredarique incipiens, ut moris sui est, cum ad locum quendam arctissimum naturaque munitum devenisset, Christianorum exercitum ea loca custodientem, duce viro fortissimo Scanderbech nomine principe eius provinciae, presto habuit obviam, quorum tanta vis tantaque

(*o*) quem primo *ex* quem in Alb primo *corr.*
(*p*) secumque—servorum *ex* secumque captivos duxit Christianos ac servos *corr.*

(*a*) tanta *del.*
(*b*) provinciam *ex* provincias *corr.*
(*c*) discurre *MS.*

solertia fuit, ut non ingentissimo ferocissimoque Turchorum ecercitui resistere, verum etiam hostium vires effringere et nonnullos ex principibus simul cum Turchorum non parva turba neci tradere potuerunt. Obque id sevissimus Turchorum princeps ceteras Albaniae partes discurrere*d* depredarique eius arctissimi loci obstaculo nequaquam potuit; cumque alium eius provincie aditum inquireret, Christianum castelli cuiusdam dominum perfidem quidem repperit,*e* a quo, conditione sue salutis promissa, adytum in reliquas eius provincie partes recepit. Sicque ingressu potitus omnem provinciam discurrens depredatus est, [f. 40*v*] homines partim sevissimis tormentis cesi ad eorum vindictam, qui superiori bello necati fuerant, reliqui capti et servi in Frigiam missi ad vitam agendam morte ipsa nefandiorem. Rediens postmodum adverso latere locum ipsum arctissimum, qui suos antea debellaverat Christianorum solertia, nulla pugna (Christiani enim cum nequaquam se pares arbitrarentur ad urbes*f* munitissimaque loca vallo menibusque circumdata perfugerant) nullaque difficultate cepit; quo in loco aiunt eum in presentia munitissimum quoddam castellum edificare, ut sibi alias, cum eam provinciam aggredi volet, in omnes Albanie partes aditus pateat. Hec sunt, suavissime*g* Alexander, que ad te de his, que nuper his in locis acta sunt, scribere potui; queque in dies succedent curabo, ut quam diligentissime meis litteris cognoscas. Vale.

Chii Idibus Septenbris 1466.

(*d*) discurrerere *MS.*
(*e*) perfidum quidem repperit *ex* rep perfidum quidem *corr.*
(*f*) ad urbes *ex* ad caste *corr.*
(*g*) suavissime *ex* carissime *corr.*

NOTES

[1] *Le Vite de' più eccellenti pittori scultori ed architettori*, ed. G. Milanesi, II, Florence 1878, p. 431.

[2] Not two years, as has been generally assumed: see Harriet McNeal Caplow, 'Michelozzo at Ragusa: new documents and revaluations', *Journal of the Society of Architectural Historians*, XXXI, 1972, pp. 108–19 (p. 111), and below, p. 217.

[3] The text of the contract was first published by A. Neri, 'Michelozzo a Scio', *Giornale Ligustico di Archeologia, Storia e Letteratura*, x, 1883, pp. 457–60, and most recently by P. Argenti, *The Occupation of Chios by the Genoese and the Administration of the Island, 1340–1561*, Cambridge, 1958, II, pp. 442–4. The Mahona of Chios governed the island under Genoese rule.

[4] Vasari, *op. cit.*, p. 449, n. 2.

[5] *Op. cit.*, I, p. 561.

[6] *Op. cit.*, p. 115.

[7] Palat., 1158, ff. 38*r*–53*v*. Unless otherwise indicated, all references are to this MS, and for a description of it see A. Saitta Revignas, *I manoscritti palatini della Biblioteca Nazionale Centrale di Firenze*, III, fasc. 4, Rome, 1955, pp. 315–17.

[8] On 23 October 1466 he writes to Alessandro Braccesi from Chios (MS *cit.*, f. 39*v*; see above, p. 219): 'postea quam in portu ipso pisano primum ventis linthea prebuimus hoc maximum extat quod iam menses quatuor dies XXVIII° preteriere, quibus nullas a te litteras accepi'.

[9] See above, p. 218

[10] These letters, in Latin, which are contained in an autograph *copiario* (Florence, Bibl. Naz., Magl. VIII, 1421), have been published by C. Marchesi in an appendix to his *Bartolomeo della Fonte* (first edition only, Catania, 1899), pp. xxii–xxxiii; they date from January to November 1465. On Niccolò's subsequent correspondence with Braccesi see P. O. Kristeller, 'An unknown correspondence of Alessandro Braccesi with Niccolò Michelozzi, Naldo Naldi, Bartolomeo Scala, and other humanists (1470–1472) in MS Bodl. Auct. F. 2, 17', in *Classical Mediaeval and Renaissance Studies in Honor of Berthold Louis Ullman*, ed. C. Henderson, Jr., Rome, 1964, II, pp. 311–59.

[11] Folio 38r–v. There is no heading, but the identity of the addressee results from the contents of the letter. *Inc.*: 'Eximia fama atque incredibilis splendor admirabilium virtutum tuarum'.

[12] On fifteenth-century inventions of hydraulic constructions see F. D. Prager and G. Scaglia, *Mariano Taccola and his Book* De ingeniis, Cambridge, Mass., 1972, pp. 38–9, 222–3. The earliest detailed description of mine pumps is to be found in Georgius Agricola's *De re metallica* of 1533 to 1553 (see W. B. Parsons, *Engineers and Engineering in the Renaissance*, Baltimore, 1939, pp. 181, 188–9).

[13] See F. D. Prager and G. Scaglia, *Brunelleschi: Studies of his Technology and Inventions*, Cambridge, Mass., 1970. *Cf.* Leon Battista Alberti, *De re aedificatoria*, ed. G. Orlandi and P. Portoghesi, Milan, 1966, prologue.

[14] See Caplow, *op. cit.*, p. 110 and doc. 14.

[15] See the text in Argenti, *op. cit.*, II, p. 442.

[16] Folio 40v. No heading.

[17] Caplow, *op. cit.*, p. 114 and doc. 31.

[18] Folio 47r, n.d. 'Adovardo Justiniani'.

[19] Folio 44r. See his letters between May 1466 and July 1467, ed. P. Orvieto, 'Un esperto orientalista del '400: Benedetto Dei', *Rinascimento*, IX, 1969, pp. 232–48.

[20] See below, n. 34.

[21] On 1 July 1467 Benedetto Dei writes from Chios that 'del mese di marzo capitò qqua i Llevante la nave fiorentina degli Agli, partita d'Ancona con panni e drappi', etc. (Orvieto, *op. cit.*, p. 241.)

[22] Folio 46r. 'Alexandro Brachiensio'. 'Chii IIIo Calendas Maias.'

[23] '. . . et me Florentie Kalendis saltim Augusti futurum expectato.'

[24] To Alessandro Braccesi, n.d., f. 47v: 'simul cum ceteris mercatoribus nostris, qui ex Constantinopoli cum anconitanis navibus Florentiam redeuntes . . . '; see above, p. 221.

[25] See above, pp. 220–1. On 9 June Benedetto Dei wrote to his brother in Florence that he was hoping to return to Italy 'o colla nave degli Agli o colla nave di Dionigi, qual prima partirà di questo porto'. (Ed. Orvieto, *op. cit.*, p. 241.)

[26] Folio 40r–v. 'Chii Idibus Septenbris 1466'. Appendix 11.2. In Niccolò's *copiario* this letter follows on that to Braccesi of 23 October 1488 (ff. 39v–40r), and must therefore be a copy and not a draft. The first five letters of Niccolò's *copiario* as contained in MS Palat. 1158, of which this letter is the third—the second is addressed by him to his father, with whom he had quarrelled—are in a separate fascicle (ff. 35r–40v; 35r–37v are blank).

[27] Mastic was one of the chief products of Chios; see Girolamo Giustinian, *History of Chios*, ed. P. Argenti, Cambridge, 1943, pp. 206–9.

[28] Folio 41r. 'Ant[oni]o Paravisino Reverendissimo Chiensium episcopo.' 'Chii XVI Kalendas Martias.'

[29] See his letter to Antonius Stephorus of 7 July 1465, ed. Marchesi, *op. cit.*, p. xxv: during Braccesi's absence in the Casentino 'me suo cancellariae officio fungi precepit'.

[30] Folio 46r. See below, n. 57.

[31] Folios 39v, 40r. 'Chii Xo Kalendas Novembris 1466.' Appendix 11.1.

[32] Folio 41v, n.d. 'Naldo de Naldis, Florentie.'

[33] 'Neminem enim pretermisi quem quidem ad vos perventurum putarem, cui litteras non dederim, in quis curavi salutes esse quamplurimas ad te meo nomine perferendas.'

[34] Folio 53r. 'Nicolaus Michaelozius Petro Cenninio S.P.D.' 'Chii Idibus Aprilis MCCCCLXVII'. He writes that they are expecting daily ('in dies') 'navim quandam ex Ancona' belonging to Andrea degli Agli, 'civis florentinus, licet plurimum sue vite Ancone degerit'. *Cf.* his letter to Naldi, *loc. cit.*: 'Andreas Allius, civis florentinus, licet Ancone plurimum sue vite degerit, hic propediem simul cum navi sua futurus est'.

[35] Appendix 11.2.

[36] A. Gegaj, *L'Albanie et l'invasion turque au XVe siècle*, Louvain, 1937, pp. 142–3.

[37] *Ibid.*, p. 142. *Cf.* L. Pastor, *History of the Popes*, trans. F. I. Antrobus, IV, London, 1900, p. 86.

[38] Its name was Valma or Valmora: Gegaj, p. 143. The news had reached Venice the middle of August: *cf. Cronaca di Anonimo Veronese*, ed. G. Soranzo (*Monum. stor. pubbl. dalla R. Dep. Veneta di st. p.*, third series, IV, 19), p. 236.

[39] The Venetian Captain General *del Mar* was Vettore Capello. Niccolò calls the Turkish governor of the Morea 'Sangiacobbei'. In fact his name was Omar Beg. *Sanjak Bey* was the title of Ottoman officers who governed districts which included important cities. (A. H. Libyer, *The Government of the Ottoman Empire in the Time of Suleiman the Magnificent*, Cambridge, Mass., 1913, p. 103.)

[40] On the Venetian campaign of 1466 see C. Hopf, *Geschichte Griechenlands*, II, Leipzig, 1868, p. 156; N. Jorga, *Geschichte des osmanischen Reiches*, II, Gotha, 1909, pp. 133–4; F. Babinger, *Mehmed der Eroberer und seine Zeit*, Munich, 1953, pp. 275–6.

[41] Folio 46r; see above, p. 218. From his letter to Braccesi of 23 October 1466 (appendix 11.2) it appears that Niccolò had already visited Constantinople on his journey to Chios. Chios was in fact one of the possible ports of call for Florentine galleys on their return voyage from Constantinople; M. Mallett, *The Florentine Galleys in the Fifteenth Century*, Oxford, 1967, p. 67. In a letter to Niccolò Michelozzi of 1497 Bonsignore Bonsignori refers to Niccolò having visited Constantinople; E. Borsook, 'The travels of Bernardo Michelozzi and Bonsignore Bonsignori in the Levant (1497–98)', *Journal of the Warburg and Courtauld Institutes*, XXXVI, 1973, p. 145, n. 3, and appendix, 5. For a further reference to Niccolò's visit to Constantinople see R. Cardini, *La critica del Landino*, Florence, 1973, p. 251, n. 8.

[42] Folio 47v, n.d. 'Florentie. Alexandro Brach[iensio]'. See also above, p. 221.

[43] Servius, *Ad Aen.* VII, 180: 'apud Cretam esse dicitur Iovis sepulcrum.' *Cf.* Cristoforo Buondelmonti, 'Descriptio insulae Cretae', in F. Cornaro, *Creta Sacra*, Venice, 1755, I, p. 97 (*cf.* p. 10): a cavern 'in cuius capite sepulcrum Iovis Maximi cognoscimus cum epitaphyo, tam deleto quod vix literam cognoscere potuimus aliquam, sed quia per omnem insulam ita esse provulgatum cognovi, quod omnia credere difficile non fuit . . . Effigiem ibi et a longe faciei habet, in cuius fronte Templum Iovis usque ad infimum deletum dimisi . . . '; see R. Weiss, *The Renaissance Discovery of Classical Antiquity*, Oxford, 1969, p. 136.

[44] *Cf.* Buondelmonti, *op. cit.*, pp. 102–4.

[45] Archivio di Stato, Florence (A.S.F.), Signori, Missive, la Cancelleria, reg. 45, ff. 169v–170r.

[46] In a letter of 9 June 1467 from Chios Benedetto Dei had warned his brother in Florence, on the basis of information he had received from Venice, 'E ffa' sopra tutto che tu non venissi o mandassi nulla per le nave d'Ancona, perche in Vinegia armiamo 4 nave, e ggià n'è uscito fuori 2 per aspettarle alla bocca'. (Ed. Orvieto, *op. cit.*, p. 240.) On 7 November he writes, rather belatedly, to Lorenzo de' Medici from Messina, where he had stopped on his way back to Florence, that ships from Ancona, among them that of the Agli, had been 'prese a Modone a l'armata e istate istraziate, rubate e vilipese . . . contro ogni debita ragione'. (*Ibid.*, p. 250.)

[47] Archivio di Stato, Venice (A.S.V.), Senatus Secreta, XXIII, f. 75r.

[48] A.S.F., Signori, Miss., la Canc., reg. 45, ff. 170r–v (28 September).

[49] A.S.V., Senatus Secreta, XXIII, f. 90v.

[50] *Ibid.*, f. 92v, 28 December: no decision could be taken concerning 'res Florentinorum suorum' before the ships had arrived; as they have now arrived, the Senate will do so.

[51] A.S.V., Consiglio dei Dieci, Misti, 17, f. 83r.

[52] *Ibid.*, f. 83v.

[53] Folio 42v, n.d.

[54] A few years earlier Paolo Morosini had written his description of the Venetian government to Gregory of Heimburg. (Ed. G. Valentinelli, *Biblioteca manuscripta . . .*, Venice, 1868–73, II, pp. 231–64.)

[55] Folios 42r–v, n.d. 'Flor[entino?]' *ex* 'Fior[entino?]'.

[56] The 'scriptor anglicus' may have been John Free, who in 1464 presented to Paul II his translation of Synesius' *De insomniis*, which was probably written by him. (R. J. Mitchell, *John Free*, London, 1955, pp. 128–30.)

[57] 'Et me plurimum conmendato Thomasio equiti dignissimo ac pro Illustrissimo Florentie populo oratori excellentissimo.' Among Niccolò Michelozzi's letters in MS Palat. 1158 there are two versions of a consolatory letter to Braccesi on the premature death of their friend Antonio Clementi, another in which Niccolò complains about not yet having received the letter Braccesi had promised to write 'ob Antonii nostri obitum', and a third in which he replies to Braccesi, whom he had failed to comfort (ff. 48r–v and 52r, 49r–v, 50r; n.d.). These letters are copied in a different fascicle from those written in Chios and on paper with a different watermark, and may therefore belong to a later period. Naldo Naldi's elegy on Antonio's death has been dated between 1471 and 1473. (*Elegiarum libri III*, ed. L. Juhász, Leipzig, 1934, pp. 60–2; see A. Perosa, 'Storia di un libro di poesie latine dell'umanista fiorentino Alessandro Braccesi', *Bibliofilia*, XLV, 1943, pp. 167–8.) Antonio Clementi belonged to Niccolò's humanist circle in Florence; two short poems by him are included in one of the manuscripts of Braccesi's *Carmina* (ed. Perosa, Florence, 1943, p. 160), and Braccesi praises Antonio, in a poem addressed to him (*ibid.*, p. 94), as 'lyrico carmine nobilem'.

Niccolò Michelozzi must have returned to Florence early in 1468, when he became assistant to the First Chancellor, Bartolomeo Scala. His hand appears in the *minutario* of the letters of the Signoria for the first time on 8 April (see the forthcoming Lorenzo di Piero de' Medici, *Le Lettere*, I, ed. R. Fubini, letter No. 109, n. 1).

S. A. JAYAWARDENE *Science Museum Library, London*

12

THE 'TRATTATO D'ABACO' OF PIERO DELLA FRANCESCA

1 INTRODUCTION

IN HIS BIOGRAPHY of Piero della Francesca, Vasari accused Luca Pacioli of having plagiarised the works of Piero on perspective, arithmetic and geometry.[1] In the absence of any evidence to support it, this accusation was considered unjust by many. However, with the discovery of two manuscripts of Piero's—'De prospectiva pingendi' and 'De quinque corporibus regularibus'—the question of plagiarism had to be considered afresh.[2] In 1903 it was established by Pittarelli that Part III of Pacioli's *Divina proportione* was an Italian version of the 'De quinque corporibus regularibus'.[3] Since then another work of Piero's has come to light—a manuscript containing a book of practical arithmetic.

Girolamo Mancini, in his edition of Vasari's lives of Piero della Francesca, Alberti, Francesco da Giorgio, Signorelli and De Marcillat (1917), drew attention to a manuscript of an unknown author in the Biblioteca Laurenziana in Florence, Ashburnham 359*, which he identified as being an autograph manuscript of Piero della Francesca.[4] It was one of the numerous manuscripts, formerly owned by Guglielmo Libri, which the Italian government bought from Lord Ashburnham in 1884 for the Laurenziana. In fact an extract from it, ff. 62–79v, is found in volume III of Libri's *Histoire des sciences mathématiques en Italie*.[5] Although Mancini established the authorship of the work and described its contents in 1917, not much notice of it was taken by historians of mathematics until Gino Arrighi, while preparing the manuscript for publication, gave a short account of it in *Physis* in 1967.[6] The work has since been published by the Domus Galilaeana in Pisa,[7] and it is on a study of this edition that the present article is based.

2 PRACTICAL ARITHMETICS AND THE 'MAESTRI D'ABACO'

Practical arithmetics or algorisms, using Hindu-Arabic numerals, written for the use of merchant apprentices, were common in Renaissance Italy. The commercial activity of the Italian cities encouraged the composition of these works. They were usually written by teachers of arithmetic (then called *maestri d'abaco*) who drew their inspiration from the arithmetic of Leonardo of Pisa.[8] Their popularity is evident from the large number of algorisms in manuscript that have been preserved to our day. The activity of these teachers continued late into the sixteenth century, for more than a hundred practical arithmetics were published in Italy during the years 1478–1600.

Leonardo's work, the 'Liber abaci', written in 1202, was a treatise on arithmetic which introduced the Hindu-Arabic numerals and the rules of algebra to Italy. It was an extensive work, written in Latin and not suitable for the use of merchant apprentices.[9] It was mainly for their use that the practical arithmetics were written. The practical arithmetic—*practica d'arismetricha* or *trattato d'abaco*—was a simplified *liber abaci* written in Italian. In general the topics dealt with in such a book were: reading and writing of the Hindu-Arabic numerals; four fundamental operations with integers; fractions; the rule of three; mercantile arithmetic (price of goods, barter, partnership, alligation, exchange, interest); recreational arithmetic; rule of false position; roots; continued proportion (i.e. geometrical progression); geometry (mensuration); rules of algebra. The book contained numerous problems—*ragioni*. It differed from the modern textbook in that the author gave the solution of every problem stated. The extent to which algebra was treated varied. Some authors did not include it at all.

Among the *maestri d'abaco* who lived before the invention of printing were Paolo dell'Abbaco (Dagomari) of Prato, Antonio Mazzinghi of Peretola, Giovanni di Bartolo, all of whom taught at the Bottegha dell'abacho a Santa Trinità in Florence; Raffaele Canacci, Benedetto da Firenze, Luca da Firenze, Paolo Gherardi, who had schools elsewhere in Florence; Massolo da Perugia, Frate Lionardo da Pistoia. Some of them are known to us by their works preserved in manuscript and others are mentioned in the works of their successors.[10] Printing was introduced to Italy about 1465, and the first arithmetics to be published in Italy were an anonymous work now known as the Treviso Arithmetic (1478) and the arithmetics of Pietro Borghi (1484), Filippo Calandri (1491) and Luca Pacioli (1494).[11] They were all written by teachers of arithmetic. That of Pietro Borghi of Venice was the most popular: at least seventeen editions of it were printed before 1600. Calandri, a Florentine, dedicated his work to Giuliano de' Medici; there is in fact an illuminated manuscript of this work specially written for him.[12] Pacioli's book, the *Summa de arithmetica, geometria, proportioni et proportionalita* (Venice, 1494) was dedicated to the young Duke of Urbino, Guidobaldo da Monte-feltro, whose father had been Piero's patron.

3 LUCA PACIOLI

Luca Pacioli and Piero were contemporaries, Piero being about twenty-five years older. They both came from Borgo San Sepolcro. There is no evidence to support Vasari's statement that Pacioli had been Piero's pupil. He spent some years in Venice as tutor to the sons of a Venetian merchant, and studied at the school of Domenico Bragadino. After joining the Franciscan Order he spent a life of peregrination, teaching mathematics in various cities of Italy. He wrote three books of arithmetic, none of which was published;[13] they apparently served as sources for his *Summa*, published in 1494. It was an encyclopaedic work containing the mathematical knowledge of the time; as such it was studied by successive generations of Italian mathematicians. It contained treatises on theoretical and practical arithmetic, book-keeping and geometry. It was the first printed work to give an account of the rules of algebra. Pacioli admitted to having borrowed freely from Euclid, Boethius, Sacrobosco, Leonardo of Pisa and others. He made no mention of the arithmetic of Piero, although in the dedicatory letter to the Duke of Urbino he referred to Piero's work on perspective, calling him 'el monarcha ali tempi nostri de la pictura.'[14]

4 PIERO'S 'TRATTATO'

Piero's work differed from the majority of practical arithmetics in that he did not devote any space to explaining numeration or the fundamental operations. His was rather a collection of problems than a textbook. He did, however, include the rules of algebra, and the greater part of his problems were solved by using the algebraic method.

The manuscript originally had no title, but the words 'Trattato d'abaco' have been lettered on the spine after rebinding. It consists of 128 leaves and was probably written for a member of the Pichi family of San Sepolcro.[15] In my analysis of the work I have divided the text into chapters; in fact the blank spaces in the text suggest that the author had intended doing so.

Folios 3–4v. [*Chapter I. Fractions.*] The text begins with a few prefatory remarks which suggest that the author is not a *maestro d'abaco*: 'Having been requested by a person whose requests are, to me, commands, to write [a manual] on the arithmetic necessary to merchants; not being presumptuous, but in order to obey him, I shall try to satisfy his wishes, namely by writing on commercial problems such as barter, interest and partnership, beginning with the rule of three, followed by the rule of false position, and, if it pleases God, some algebra; dealing first with fractions [and operations with them].' The author assumes a knowledge of the elements of arithmetic. He explains the application of the four fundamental operations (multiplication, division, addition, subtraction) to fractions. Several examples follow.

Folios 5–15v. [*Chapter II. Rule of three.*] The rule of three, based on the doctrine of proportion, is believed to have originated in India as a rule of thumb necessary to merchants for their business transactions. Like the majority of authors, Piero states the rule without any explanation and proceeds to give examples of the application of the rule. The various problems used for illustrating it are: price of goods, profit and loss, barter, partnership, alligation, mixtures, cistern problem, 'too much and not enough'.

·   ·   ·

Folios 16–23v. [*Chapter III. Rule of false position.*] The method known as the 'rule of false position' (*hisab al-Khataayn* or *el cataym*) seems to have been brought to Europe from India by the Arabs.[16] A large number of arithmetical problems, if solved by the methods of algebra, lead to solving equations of the type $ax + b = 0$. At a time when symbolic notation had not been developed mathematicians used the rule of false position to solve such problems. They used the 'rule of single false' when the result (m) increased or diminished in the same proportion as the unknown quantity (x), that is, $ax = m$. Assuming a value x' for x and the corresponding value of m to be m', we have $ax' = m'$. That is,

$$x = \frac{m}{m'} x'.$$

If the problem is such that the result does not increase in the same proportion as the unknown quantity, but reduces to an equation such as $ax + b = m$, we use the 'rule of double false', where we place two false quantities in the problem. We make two guesses (positions) for the unknown quantity, say x', x''; the corresponding values of m are $m + e'$, $m + e''$, where e', e'' are the errors. We then have:

$$ax' + b = m + e'$$
$$ax'' + b = m + e''$$
$$ax + b = m$$

Eliminating a and $b - m$, we have

$$\begin{vmatrix} x & 1 & 0 \\ x' & 1 & -e' \\ x'' & 1 & -e'' \end{vmatrix} = 0$$

or

$$x(e' - e'') = e'x'' - e''x'$$

that is

$$x = \frac{e'x'' - e''x'}{e' - e''}$$

In common language, the product of the first error and the second position diminished by the product of the second error and the first position and the result divided by the difference between the errors gives the quantity whose value is required.

Piero explains the rule of double false briefly and gives a number of examples. The following is one. 'Two men wish to buy a horse worth thirty-five ducats and neither can buy it alone. The first says to the second, "Give me half your money and I will buy the horse." Says the second to the first, "Give me a third of your money and I will buy the horse." How much does each have?'

First position. Suppose the first had 15, then the second would have 40 in order that the first might buy the horse with his money and half the second's.

The second, on receiving a third of the first's money, will have 45. So the error here is 10.

Second position. Suppose the first had 24, then the second would have 22 in order that the first might buy the horse with his money and half the second's. The second, on receiving a third of the first's money, will have 30. So the error here is −5.

The quantity required is

$$\frac{(10 \times 24) + (5 \times 15)}{10 + 5}$$

that is, 315/15 or 21, which is what the first had. The second gave the first fourteen to buy the horse; the amount the second had was therefore twenty-eight.

The different types of problem illustrating the rule of false are: two men buying a horse, 'too much and not enough', buying two kinds of the same commodity, division of money, the two birds and other recreational problems.[17]

Folios 24–33. [*Chapter III. §1. Rules of algebra.*] Piero starts by explaining the terms *root* and *square*. Then he states the standard types of algebraic equations, three simple and three composite, following the usage of Leonardo of Pisa. He then gives the rules for solving them. The equations, in modern notation, are:

1	$ax = b$
2	$ax^2 = bx$
3	$ax^2 = b$
4	$ax^2 + bx = c$
5	$ax^2 + c = bx$
6	$ax^2 = bx + c$

After that he explains the addition, subtraction, multiplication and division of roots and binomials containing roots. Then he deals with the multiplication and division of algebraic quantities. Then he gives the rules for solving sixty-one algebraic equations, including 1–6 above:[18]

7	$ax^3 = b$
8	$ax^3 = \sqrt{b}$
9	$ax^3 = bx$
10	$ax^3 = bx^2$
11	$ax^3 = bx^2 + cx$
12	$ax^3 = bx + c$
13	$ax^3 = bx^2 + c$
14	$ax^3 = bx^2 + cx + d$
15	$ax^3 + bx^2 = cx$
16	$ax^3 + cx = bx^2$

17    $ax^4 = b$
18    $ax^4 = bx$
19    $ax^4 = bx^2$
20    $ax^4 = bx^3$
21    $ax^4 = bx^2 + c$
22    $ax^2 = \sqrt{b}$
23    $ax^2 = b + \sqrt{c}$
24    $ax + bx^2 + cx^3 = d$
25    $ax + bx^2 + cx^3 + dx^4 = e$
26    $ax^2 + bx^3 + cx^4 = \sqrt{d}$
27    $\sqrt{(ax^2 + bx + cx^4)} = \sqrt{(d + ex^3)}$
28    $ax = \sqrt{b}$
29    $a = \sqrt{(bx^2)}$
30    $a = \sqrt{(bx^3)}$
31    $ax = \sqrt{(bx)}$
32    $ax^2 = \sqrt{(bx)}$
33    $ax = \sqrt{(bx^3)}$
34    $ax^2 = \sqrt{(bx^2)}$
35    $ax^2 = \sqrt{(bx^3)}$
36    $ax^3 = \sqrt{(bx^2)}$
37    $ax^4 = \sqrt{(bx^2)}$
38    $ax^3 = \sqrt{(bx^3)}$
39    $ax^3 = \sqrt{(bx^2)}$
40    $ax^4 = \sqrt{(bx^4)}$
41    $a = \sqrt{(bx)}$
42    $ax^3 = bx^2 + cx$
43    $ax^4 + bx^3 = cx^2$
44    $ax^4 + bx^2 = cx^3$
45    $ax^4 = bx^3 + cx^2$
46    $ax^4 + bx^2 = c$
47    $ax^4 + b = cx^2$
48    $ax^4 = bx^2 + c$
49    $ax^3 + bx^2 + cx = d$
50    $ax^4 + bx^3 + cx^2 + dx = e$
51   [Repetition of 29]
52   [Repetition of 8]
53    $ax = \sqrt{(bx^2)}$
54–9 [Repetition of 34–40]
60    $ax + bx^2 + cx^3 + dx^4 + ex^5 = f$
61    $ax + bx^2 + cx^3 + dx^4 + ex^5 + fx^6 = g$

Folios 34–79v. [*Chapter III. §2. Problems solved by the rules of algebra.*] The author now gives a number of problems illustrating the rules for solving the equations 1–20 and 22–5.

In the case of the cubic equations 12, 13, 14 and 24 and the quartic equations 25 and 26, the rules given for solving them are incorrect. These incorrect rules are not peculiar to Piero. They are found in the *trattati d'abaco* of some of his predecessors.[19] Luca Pacioli stated in the *Summa de arithmetica* that the cubic equation could not be solved. It was only in the first half of the sixteenth century that Scipione del Ferro and Ludovico Ferrari found methods of solving these equations.[20] However, the problems illustrating equations 24 and 25 are correctly solved with the aid of the rules, as the resulting equations are special cases and could be reduced to the forms $(x + p)^3 = q$ and $(x + p)^4 = q$.

Folios 68–79v contain miscellaneous problems solved by the methods of algebra.

Folios 80–120. [*Chapter IV. Mensuration. Plane and solid figures.*] The geo-metrical part of the work consists of a number of problems dealing with mensuration which are solved by means of the methods of algebra. The figures treated are: triangle, square, rectangle, parallelogram, regular pentagon, regular hexagon, regular octagon, circle, tetrahedron, cube, sphere, truncated tetrahedron, truncated cube, dodecahedron, icosahedron, octahedron, pyramid.

Folios 120v–127. [*Chapter V. Miscellaneous problems.*] The last few pages of the manuscript deal with more arithmetical problems—division of money, continued proportion, number puzzles. Most of them are solved by the methods of algebra.

5 THE ARITHMETICAL PROBLEMS

The arithmetical problems of the *trattato* are typical of those found in the arithmetics of Leonardo of Pisa and the Italian *maestri d'abaco*. They fall into three main groups: (1) problems relating to events of day-to-day living; (2) fictitious problems woven into incidents of daily life; (3) purely recreational problems.

Comparative studies by D. E. Smith and Vera Sanford have brought out the similarity of the problems in the arithmetics of different origin—China, India, Islam, Germany, Italy and others.[21] More detailed studies have been made by Kurt Vogel in his edition of the *Rechenbuch* of the Benedictine Abbey of St Emmeram, in which he has classified the problems according to their content.[22] Since then he has published critical editions of two late Byzantine arithmetics and a Chinese work of the Han period.[23] In classifying Piero's problems I have adapted Vogel's classification. I have given below (in translation) the problems which are representative of each class and cited the arithmetics of Leonardo of Pisa, Pacioli and a few others where similar problems can be found.[24]

§1. Price of goods, services (*Preisberechnungen*), ff. 5–7v. [13]

(f. 5) *A pound of silk costs 5 lire 3 soldi. What is the cost of 6 ounces?*

Cf. Leonardo of Pisa, pp. 83–94; Pacioli, ff. 57–63.

§2. Profit and loss (*Gewinn und Verlust*), ff. 7, 51*v*. [4]

(f. 7)　*I bought a piece of cloth for* 172 *ducats. For how much should I sell it in order to make a profit of* 19 *per cent?*

Cf. Leonardo of Pisa, p. 281; Paolo dell'Abbaco, 32; Pacioli, ff. 63–65*v*.

§3. Barter (*Stich; Warentausch*), ff. 8–9*v*. [11]

(f. 8)　*Two men barter. One has linen and the other wool. The first barters a roll of linen worth* 15 *ducats for* 20 *ducats but wants a third of the price in cash. A hundred pounds of wool is worth* 7 *ducats. At what price should the second man barter his wool so that neither is the loser?*

(f. 9*v*)　*Two men barter. One has skins worth* 12 *ducats a hundred* [*pounds*] *which he charges at* 16 *ducats and gives* 13 *months' time. The other has shellac which he charges at* 32 *ducats a hundred and gives* 7 *months' time. What would a hundred* [*pounds*] *of shellac have cost if they were to make an equal barter?*

Cf. Leonardo of Pisa, pp. 118–27; Paolo dell'Abbaco, 33; Pacioli, ff. 161–7.

§4. Partnership (*Gesellschaftsrechnung*), ff. 10–12, 38*v*. [11]

(f. 11)　*Three men enter into a partnership. The first puts in* 58 [*ducats*], *the second* 87; *we do not know how much the third puts in. Their profit is* 368, *of which the first gets* 86. *What shares of profit do the second and third receive and how much did the third invest?*

(f. 11)　*Three men enter into a partnership. The first invests* 234 *ducats on March* 1, *and on July* 1 *he withdraws* 50 *ducats; the second invests* 286 *ducats on May* 1 *and on August* 1 *he withdraws* 80 *ducats; the third invests* 368 *ducats on June* 1 *and on October* 1 *he withdraws* 100 *ducats. On December* 1 *they find that they have made a profit of* 568 *ducats. What is the share of each?*

Cf. Leonardo of Pisa, pp. 135–43; Pacioli, ff. 150–9. The problem on f. 38*v* is found in Pacioli, f. 150*v* (6).

§5. Alligation, mixtures (*Munzlegierungen, Mischungsrechnungen*), ff. 12*v*–14*v*. [14]

(f. 13*v*)　*I have* 12 *pounds of* 19 *carat gold. If I convert it into* 22½ *carat gold, how many pounds of gold will I get?*

(f. 14*v*)　*A bell founder wishes to cast a bell in five metals; the first costs* 16 *lire, the second* 18 *lire, the third* 20 *lire, the fourth* 27 *lire and the fifth* 31 *lire per* 100 *pounds. The bell is to weigh* 775 *pounds and the cost of the metal is* 162¾ *lire. How much of each metal does he need?* [This is an indeterminate problem and can have several solutions.]

(f. 14*v*)　*I have grain of five different kinds, costing* 16, 15, 13, 11 *and* 7 *soldi per staio. I wish to make* 30 *stai of a mixture which will cost* 10 *soldi per staio. What quantity of each kind do I need?* [Indeterminate problem.]

Cf. Leonardo of Pisa, pp. 143–59, 161, 164; Pacioli, ff. 182*v*–186. The second problem above is found in Leonardo of Pisa, p. 164 (Campane ex quinque metallis) with two different solutions.

§6. Interest (*Zins und Zinseszins*), ff. 51*v*, 67–71*v*, 77–8. [21]

(f. 67)　*A man lends another* 100 *lire. At the end of three years he returns* 150 *lire* [*interest and capital*]. *What is the monthly interest per lira?*

Cf. Leonardo of Pisa, pp. 270–3; Pacioli, ff. 173*v*–182*v*. Ten of the above problems (ff. 68, 69, 69*v*, 70*v*, 71, 77, 77*v*) are found in Pacioli, ff. 180 (34), 180*v* (35), 180 (32), 179 (26), 181*v* (46), 180*v* (36), 180*v* (39), 180 (33), 179 (28), 181*v* (45).

§7. Calculation of wages (*Arbeitslohn*), ff. 43*v*, 52. [3]

(f. 43*v*)   *A gentleman employing a servant offers him* 25 *ducats a year and a horse. At the end of two months the servant wishes to leave and asks to be paid. The master gives him the horse and says, 'Give me* 4 *ducats and we shall be quits.' What was the horse worth?*

(f. 52)   *A man contracts with a builder to pay* 10 *florins for digging a well* 4 *ells deep. On finding no water at a depth of* 4 *ells, the man asks the builder to continue digging and earn another* 11 *florins. How deep does he dig?*

Cf. Paolo dell'Abbaco, 58, 102.

§8. Work and time (*Arbeitsleistung*), f. 127. [1]

(f. 127)   *Of three workmen the second and third can complete a job in* 10 *days. The first and third can do it in* 12 *days while the first and second can do it in* 15 *days. In how many days can each of them do the job alone?*

Cf. Paolo dell'Abbaco, 23. A variation of this is the cistern problem (§18).

§9. Problems of pursuit (*Bewegungsaufgaben*), f. 40. [1]

(f. 40)   *Two men at a distance of* 25 *miles from each other start walking in the same direction. One walks* 25 *miles each day. The other walks* 1 *mile the first day,* 2 *miles the second,* 4 *miles the third and so on, doubling the distance walked the previous day until he reaches the first. In how many days will they meet?*

Cf. Leonardo of Pisa, p. 182; Paolo dell'Abbaco, 118; Pacioli, ff. 41*v*, 42*v*. The identical problem is found in Pacioli, f. 41*v* (20).

§10. Exchange (*Geldumrechnungen*), ff. 62, 72*v*. [2]

(f. 72*v*)   *A man receives* 26 *grossi and* 26 *pizzoli in exchange for* 1 *florin. There are as many pizzoli in a grosso as there are grossi in a florin. How many pizzoli are there in a grosso?*

Cf. Leonardo of Pisa, p. 105; Paolo dell'Abbaco, 116; Pacioli, ff. 167–173*v*.

§11. Fractions ('*Haurechnungen,*), ff. 17, 18*v*, 23, 37, 40, 41*v*. [6]

(f. 17)   *A fish weighs* 60 *pounds; the head weighs three-fifths of the breast and the tail one-third of the head. How many pounds does the breast weigh?*

(f. 18*v*)   *On being asked the time a man says, 'A third and a quarter of the hour that has struck is a fifth and a sixth of the hour that is going to strike.' What is the time?*

Cf. Leonardo of Pisa, p. 177; Paolo dell'Abbaco, 43, 83. The problem on f. 18*v* is found in Pacioli, f. 105 (8).

§12. Division of money (*Geben und Nehmen*), ff. 21, 21*v*, 38, 41–3, 53, 72–76*v*, 120–122*v*. [28]

(f. 53)   *A sum of* 90 *lire is divided equally among a number of men. Afterwards three others join them and demand their share. Each of the first group gives the newcomers* 5 *lire, so that they all have the same amount of money. How many men were there at first?*

(f. 73*v*)   *Two men have some money. The first says to the second, 'Give me half your money, then I will have six.' The second says to the first, 'Give me a third of your money, then I will have* 6 + $\sqrt{6}$.' *How much does each have?*

Cf. Leonardo of Pisa, p. 190; Paolo dell'Abbaco, 69, 126; Calandri, [i8]; Pacioli, ff. 189–193*v*.

Twelve of the above problems (21*v*, 41, 43, 72, 72*v*, 73, 74*v*, 75, 75*v*, 76, 76*v*, 120*v*,

122v) are found in Pacioli, ff. 105 (23), 193 (31), 193 (30), 188v (2), 188v (3), 188v (5), 189 (9), 189 (10), 189 (7), 193 (28), 190 (18), 190 (17).

§13. 'One alone cannot buy' (*Einer kann nicht allein kaufen*), ff. 16, 17v, 22, 36v, 39, 39v, 40v, 44v. [10]

(f. 17v)   *Three men wish to buy a horse costing 30 ducats, but neither of them can buy it alone. The first says to the second, 'Give me one-third of your money and I will buy the horse.' The second says to the third, 'Give me a quarter of your money and I will buy the horse.' The third says to the first, 'Give me a fifth of your money and I will buy the horse.' How much money does each have?*

Cf. Leonardo of Pisa, p. 228; Pacioli, f. 192v.
The problem on f. 40v is found in Pacioli, f. 193v (37).

§14. Business trips (*Die Torwächter im Apfelgarten*), ff. 37v, 58, 60. [3]

(f. 37v)   *A man leaves Borgo with a certain amount of money. He goes to Pesaro, doubles his money, then goes to Ancona where he spends 11 ducats. With what remains he goes to Racanati where for every ducat he makes 3; then to Fermo where he spends 47 ducats; then to Ascoli where he doubles his money and spends 34 ducats. With the rest he goes to Aquila and spends 16 ducats and he is left with nothing. How much did he start with?*

Cf. Leonardo of Pisa, pp. 258–66; Pacioli, ff. 93v, 105v, 186–188.

§15. Buying equal quantities of different commodities (*Einkauf gleicher Mengen verschiedener Sorten*), ff. 7, 7v. [2]

(f. 7v)   *I wish to spend 464 lire on equal quantities of three different commodities. The first costs 3 lire 4 soldi [per pound]; the second 7 lire 5 soldi, and the third 9 lire 17 soldi.*

Cf. Pacioli, f. 99v.

§16. The labourer (*Der Arbeiter im Weinberg*), ff. 17, 38. [2].

(f. 17)   *A man promises to do a job of work in 30 days, and asks to be paid 16 shillings for each day he works. The employer agrees provided that the man pays back 15 shillings for each day he does not work. At the end of the 30 days neither of them owes the other any money. How many days did the man work and how many days did he not work?*

Cf. Leonardo of Pisa, p. 323; Calandri, 1v; Pacioli, f. 99.

§17. 'Too much and not enough' (*Zuviel und Zuwenig*), ff. 15v, 16v, 37, 52v. [4]

(f. 15v)   *A woman after selling figs for 6 shillings said: 'If I had given 2 less for every penny, I would have made so many pennies more as the number of figs I would have sold.' How many figs did she sell for a penny?*

(f. 16v)   *Two men have equal amounts of money. If the first buys 13 ells of cloth, he will have 15 ducats left. The other buying 20 ells at the same rate will need 28 ducats. What is the cost of an ell of cloth and how much money does each have?*

Cf. Calandri [i3].

§18. The cistern problem (*Brunnenaufgaben*), ff. 14v. [1]

(f. 14v)   *A fountain has two basins one above and one below, each of which has three outlets. The first outlet of the top basin fills the lower basin in 2 hours; the second in three hours and the third in 4 hours. When all these three outlets are shut, the first outlet of the lower basin empties it in 3 hours, the second in 4 hours and the third in 5 hours. If all the outlets are opened how long will it take for the lower basin to fill?*

Cf. Leonardo of Pisa, pp. 183 ff.

§19. Linear simultaneous equations, ff. 16*v*, 18*v*, 19, 23, 37*v*, 38*v*. 42*v*, 44. [9]

(f. 16*v*)   *A merchant has two kinds of cloth, costing* 15 *and* 12 *lire per canna. A customer wishes to spend* 100 *lire on both kinds, buying in all* 7 *canne. How much will he buy of each?*

(f. 19)   *Three melons less one water-melon cost* 6 *soldi;* 7 *melons and* 10 *water-melons cost* 28 *soldi at the same rate. What are the respective costs of a melon and a water-melon?*

(f. 19)   *A man goes to the market and spends* 86 *soldi on* 3 *chickens,* 4 *partridges and* 5 *geese. A partridge costs* 2 *soldi more than a chicken, and a goose costs* 3 *soldi more than a partridge. What is the cost of each?*

The first problem (f. 16*v*) is identical with Pacioli, f. 99*v* (19). Pacioli, f. 104*v* (6) is similar to the third problem above.

The problems of §12 fall into this category.

§20. Indeterminate problems (*Unbestimmte Analytik*), ff. 19*v*, 20*v*, 122*v*, 123*v*, 124*v*, 125. [8]

(f. 20*v*)   *A gentleman giving his daughter in marriage needs* 100 *precious stones in order to complete a necklace: pearls, rubies, sapphires and balas rubies. He calls his steward, gives him* 100 *ducats and says, 'Go to Genoa, and with these* 100 *ducats buy pearls, rubies, sapphires and balas rubies. See that you buy* 100 *stones in all and do not spend more than one third-of a ducat for a pearl, half for a ruby,* 1 *for a sapphire and* 3 *for a balas-ruby. How many stones of each kind does he buy?*

(f. 122*v*)   *Find me a number which is divisible by* 7, *but which when divided by* 2, 3, 4, 5 *or* 6 *leaves a remainder* 1.

(f. 124*v*)   *Find me three squares, such that their sum is a square and the sum of the first two is also a square.*

Cf. Leonardo of Pisa, I, pp. 161, 164, 165, 281; II, pp. 216–18, 254, 256, 272, 279; Paolo dell'Abbaco, 190. The first problem above (f. 20*v*) is essentially the same as Pacioli, f. 105 (17), except that the latter is the case of a steward going to the fair to buy sheep, goats, pigs and asses. The solution is exactly the same as Piero's. The second problem above (f. 122*v*) is an abstract version of the problem of the broken eggs; see Marliani IV and Algorismus Ratisbonensis, 349.

Some of the problems of §5 also belong to this group.

§21. Division of a number into two (or three) parts (*Zerlegung einer Zahl in zwei Summanden*), ff. 34–36, 48, 49–51, 55*v*–58. 59*v*, 73*v*, 74*v*, 77, 78*v*. [38]

(f. 34)   *Divide* 10 *into two parts such that the difference between* 4 *times the first and* 5 *times the second is* 3.

(f. 50)   *Divide* 10 *into two parts such that the sum of the squares of the parts divided by the difference between the squares is equal to* 26.

(f. 57)   *Divide* 10 *into two parts such that their product is equal to the square of their difference.*

Cf. Leonardo of Pisa, pp. 207–12, 410, 437.

§22.   Find me a number . . ., ff. 36, 43*v*, 45–46, 47, 48*v*, 49, 58*v*, 60. [13]

(f. 47)   *Find me a number such that when a third and a fourth of it are taken away, and the remainder squared, the result is* 12.

Cf. Paolo dell'Abbaco, 84, 85; Pacioli, f. 99 (9, 10).

§23. Find me two (three) numbers in the ratio . . ., ff. 45–47, 48, 48*v*, 58*v*, 60, 61, 62–66*v*, 125. [30]

(f. 46v) *Find me two numbers in the ratio 4 : 5 such that the sum of their squares is 369.*

(f. 63) *Find me three numbers in the ratio 3 : 4 : 5 such that the cube of the first number is equal to the third number plus the square of the second.*

Cf. Paolo dell'Abbaco, 174–176.

§24. Geometrical progression (*Geometrische Reihen*), ff. 123, 124v, 125v–127v. [7]

(f. 124v) *The sum of four numbers in geometrical progression is 50; the sum of the first two is 20. Find the numbers.*

Cf. Leonardo of Pisa, p. 181; Pacioli, ff. 78v, 91, 92, 95v–96v. Four of these problems (ff. 123, 127, 127v) are in Pacioli, ff. 96v (32 and 31), 93v (18), 96 (29).

§25. Geometrical problems (*Algebra in der Geometrie*), ff. 22, 44, 53, 55, 59, 60v, 65, 79, 79v. [11]

(f. 22) *On a plain there are two towers, one 40 ells high and the other 50 ells high. The distance between them is 100 ells. Two birds, one on each tower, descend at the same time to drink water, flying equal distances to a point on the ground where there is a spring. What is the distance of the spring from each tower?*

(f. 44) *A ladder is standing against a wall. When the foot of the ladder is displaced 6 ells, the top of the ladder is lowered 2 ells. What is the length of the ladder?*

Cf. Leonardo of Pisa, 331; Paolo dell'Abbaco, 160, 167; Calandri, 08v.

§26. Unclassified problems, ff. 53v, 59, 60v, 124, 126v. [6]

These are problems which do not fall into any of the above groups—mainly number puzzles.

6 THE GEOMETRICAL PART OF THE 'TRATTATO'

One feature which distinguishes this work from other practical arithmetics and confirms one's belief that the author was not a *maestro d'abaco* is that it contains a large number of geometrical problems. These problems, solved by algebraic methods, relate mainly to the mensuration of plane figures and the properties of regular and semi-regular polyhedra. They have been arranged as follows:

  (i) Area, sides, height of a triangle. [8]
  (ii) Area, sides, diagonal of a square. [8]
  (iii) Area, sides, diagonal of a rectangle. [15]
  (iv) Area, sides, diagonal of a parallelogram. [4]
  (v) Regular polygons (5, 6, 8 sides). [11]
  (vi) Circle. [6]
  (vii) Plane figures (triangles, circles, etc) contained in or containing other plane figures. [14]
  (viii) Intersection of a plane figure by a straight line so that its area is divided in a given ratio. [15]
  (ix) Regular and semi-regular polyhedra. [56]

It would seem that this part of the manuscript was the main source of books I–III of Piero's 'De quinque corporibus regularibus' (Codex Vat. Urb. lat. 632), for the majority of the problems in groups (ii), (v), (vi), (viii) and (ix) are found in this work, sometimes with errors corrected. Most of the problems in groups (iii), (iv), (vii) and (ix) are found in the geometrical part of Pacioli's *Summa de arithmetica*.[25] Those in group (ix) appear once again in his *Divina proportione*.

At the end of the manuscript, immediately after the geometrical problems, there are several miscellaneous problems (ff 120v–127v) which seem to be out of place. This confirms Gino Arrighi's view that the author intended revising the manuscript. Without further research it is not possible to say exactly when or where Pacioli had occasion to see it. A total of 105 problems of the *Summa* can be traced to Piero's arithmetic.

7 CONCLUSION

The *trattati d'abaco* of Renaissance Italy not only give us an insight into the history of standard problems of arithmetic but they also provide us with important source material for the history of algebra. In its early stages algebra was a method of solving arithmetical problems. It was introduced to Italy by Leonardo of Pisa at the beginning of the thirteenth century. The many extant manuscript copies of his 'Liber abaci' are evidence of the wide influence it had on his fellow countrymen. That many of the *maestri d'abaco* who came after Leonardo devoted a few chapters of their books to the rules of algebra may be seen in the manuscripts of their works that have been preserved. Among the printed works to contain a treatment of the methods of algebra were the arithmetics of Pacioli, Ghaligaio, Cardano, and Tartaglia.[26] They all show the influence of Leonardo of Pisa and the *maestri d'abaco*. Cardano's treatise on algebraic equations, the *Ars magna*, is itself not free from problems of practical arithmetic.[27] Only with the publication of Bombelli's *Algebra* do we see the subject treated as an independent discipline.[28] However, my study of a manuscript of this work shows that Bombelli too was influenced by the *maestri d'abaco*.[29]

A study of the arithmetical books of the Renaissance is therefore necessary in order to appreciate the development of algebra in its early stages. This is especially true for the period that lies between Leonardo of Pisa and Luca Pacioli, as it has been neglected by historians.[30] We must be grateful to Gino Arrighi for his edition of Piero della Francesca's arithmetic, as it helps us to fill the gaps in our knowledge of this period and reveals another source of Pacioli's *Summa de arithmetica*.

APPENDIX 12.1

PROBLEMS COMMON TO (*a*) PIERO'S 'TRATTATO D'ABACO', (*b*) PIERO'S 'DE QUINQUE CORPORIBUS REGULARIBUS' (I)–(III) (*c*), PACIOLI'S 'SUMMA DE ARITHMETICA . . . TRACTATUS GEOMETRIE'

(*a*)	(*b*)	(*c*)
81v	(I) 6	–
83–84	14–21	–
84v–87	–	18–20v [12]
88v–89	29, 30, 34, 35	
90	36, 28	

(a)	(b)	(c)
91v–94	37–40, 42–47, 49	
95, 95v		56v (51), 57 (52)
97–98		57 (53)–57v (55)
100	8	
101–103v	11–13, 22, 23, 25, 24	
104v	55	
105	(II) 4	
105		68v (2)
105, 105v	5, 6	68v (3, 4)
105v		69 (5)
106	18	69 (6)
106, 106v	–	69 (7–10)
106v, 107	(III) 15, 16	69 (11–14)
	(II) 3, 16	
107–109v	–	69 (15)–70 (20)
110–113v	(II) 28–36	70 (21)–71v (30)
114	(II) 21, 22	71v (32, 33)
114	–	71v (34)
114v–115v	(II) 26, 11, 8–10	72 (35–39)
115v	–	72 (40)
116–117v	(III) 7, 12–14, 18, 17, 20, 19, 22, 21	72v (41)–73 (50)
118–119v	(III) 23–29	73 (51)–73v (56)
		[7]

Note. The figure in square brackets indicates the number of problems.

NOTES

[1] G. Vasari, *Le vite de piu eccelenti architetti, pittori et scultori italiani*, Florence, 1550, pp. 360, 361, 365.

[2] *Petrus Pictor Burgensis de prospectiva pingendi. Nach dem Codex* [1576] *der Königlichen Bibliothek zu Parma* . . ., ed. C. Winterberg, Strassburg, 1899; G. Mancini, 'L'opera *De corporibus regularibus* di Pietro Franceschi, detto Della Francesca, usurpata da fra Luca Pacioli', *Memorie delle classe di sc. mor. e fil. della R. Accad. dei Lincei*, fifth series, XIV, 1915, pp. 446–77.

[3] G. Pittarelli, 'Luca Pacioli usurpò per se stesso qualche libro di Piero de' Franceschi?' *Atti dei IV Congresso internazionale dei matematici* (*Roma, 6–11 aprile 1908*), Rome, 1909, III, pp. 436–40.

[4] Vasari, *Vite cinque annotate da Girolamo Mancini* (*Franceschi–Alberti–Francesco di Giorgio–Signorelli–De Marcillat*) . . ., Florence, 1917, pp. 210–14.

[5] Paris, 1840, III, pp. 302–49.

[6] 'Note di algebra di Piero della Francesca', *Physis*, IX, 1967, pp. 421–4.

[7] Piero della Francesca, *Trattato d'abaco; dal Codice Ashburnhamiano 280* (*359*–291**) *della Biblioteca Medicea Laurenziana di Firenze*, ed. Gino Arrighi, Pisa, 1970.

[8] Also known as Leonardo Fibonacci. His works were published by Baldassare Boncompagni: *Scritti di Leonardo Pisano*, Rome, two vols., 1857–62. The arithmetic or *Liber abaci* is in vol. I.

[9] See Kurt Vogel's article on Leonardo in *Dictionary of Scientific Biography*, New York, 1971, IV, pp. 604–13.

[10] G. Arrighi, 'Nuovi contributi per la storia della matematica in Firenze nell'età di mezzo', *Rendiconti dell'Istituto Lombardo, Classe di Scienze* (A), CI, 1967, pp. 395–404; D. E. Smith, *Rara arithmetica*, New York, 1908, pp. 435–40, 443–6, 459–63, 464–5, 468–470. In recent years Gino Arrighi has published studies of several *trattati d'abaco* in Italian libraries; see n. 9 in Piero della Francesca, *Trattato d'abaco*, 1970, p. 13, and notably

G. Arrighi, 'Piero della Francesca matematico', *Atti e Memorie della Accademia Petrarca di Lettere, Arti e Scienze*, new series, 1968–69 (1970), pp. 144–57, which adds little.

[11] These works and others are described in Smith, *Rara arithmetica*.

[12] Recently published: Filippo Calandri, *Arithmetica secondo la lezione del Codice 2669 (sec. XV) della Biblioteca Riccardiana di Firenze*, Florence, Cassa di Risparmio, 1969.

[13] A manuscript of one of these works is in the Vatican Library: Codex Vat. Lat. 3129.

[14] Pacioli, *Summa*, f. 2 [preliminaries].

[15] E. Rostagno and T. Lodi, *I codici Ashburnhamiani della Biblioteca Medicea Laurenziana di Firenze*, Rome, I, fasc. 6, 1948, pp. 462–7.

[16] George Peacock, 'Arithmetic', in *Encyclopaedia Metropolitana, Pure Sciences*, London, 1845, p. 468.

[17] See classification pp. 235–40.

[18] Piero's algebraical analysis needs a separate study. However, it may be mentioned that not all the rules are correct; for example, the rules given for solving equations of the third, fourth and fifth degrees are valid only for special cases of these equations. The rule for solving the equation of the sixth degree is altogether incorrect.

[19] British Museum, Add. MS 8784, ff. 57–59; G. Arrighi, 'Metodi di calcolo in un codice lucchese del trecento', *Bollettino della Unione Matematica Italiana*, third series, XVIII, 1963, p. 439.

[20] *Dictionary of Scientific Biography*, IV, pp. 586–8, 595–6.

[21] D. E. Smith, *History of Mathematics*, Boston, Mass., 1923–25, II, pp. 532–91; Vera Sanford, *History and Significance of Certain Standard Problems in Algebra*, New York, Teachers' College, 1927.

[22] K. Vogel, *Die Practica des Algorismus Ratisbonensis*, Munich, 1954, pp. 155–83.

[23] K. Vogel, *Ein byzantinisches Rechenbuch des frühen 14. Jahrhunderts*, Vienna, 1968; Chiu Chang Suan Shu, *Neun Bücher arithmetischer Technik. Ein chinesisches Rechenbuch . . . aus der frühen Hanzeit*, Braunschweig, 1968. H. Hunger and K. Vogel, *Ein byzantinisches Rechenbuch des 15. Jahrhunderts* (*Österreichische Akademie der Wissenschaften*, philos.-hist. Klasse, Denkschriften, LXXVII, 2 Abh.), Vienna, 1963.

[24] I have given Vogel's description in round brackets. As the problems in the *Trattato* have not been numbered, I have given the folio numbers of the manuscript. The total number of problems in each group is given in square brackets. The works cited are: Leonardo of Pisa, *Liber abaci*; Pacioli, *Summa*; Paolo dell'Abbaco, *Trattato d'Aritmetica*, Pisa, 1964; F. Calandri, *De aritmetica opusculum*, Florence, 1491; Arrighi, 'Giuochi aritmetici in un Abaco del Quattrocento'; il matematico milanese Giovanni Marliani', *Rendiconti dell'Istituto Lombardo*, classe di scienze (A), XCIX, 1965. In the case of Leonardo of Pisa all references are to the *Liber abaci* unless otherwise stated. In Paolo dell'Abbaco the problems have been numbered in one sequence. In Pacioli the problems in some chapters have numbers; these I have given in round brackets.

[25] See appendix 12.1.

[26] Francesco Ghaligai, *Summa de arithmetica*, Florence, 1521; Girolamo Cardano, *Practica arithmetice, et mensurandi singularis*, Mediolani, 1539; Niccolò Tartaglia, *La prima-sexta parte del general trattato di numeri et misure*, Vinegia, 1556–60.

[27] Cardano, *Artis magnae sive De regulis algebraicis liber unus*, Norimbergae, 1545.

[28] Rafael Bombelli, *L'algebra parte maggiore dell'arimetica divisa in tre libri*, Bologna, 1572.

[29] 'The influence of practical arithmetics on the *Algebra* of Rafael Bombelli', *Isis*, LXIV, 1973, pp. 510–23.

[30] Gino Arrighi's studies in recent years have helped to improve the situation. See n. 10.

CHARLES B. SCHMITT *Warburg Institute*

13

AN UNSTUDIED FIFTEENTH-CENTURY LATIN TRANSLATION OF SEXTUS EMPIRICUS BY GIOVANNI LORENZI
(Vat. Lat. 2990)

IT HAS LONG been recognised that one of the most significant contributions of the fifteenth-century Italian humanists was their discovery, editing, translating and diffusing of previously unknown or little known writings of classical Antiquity. The story of the discovery and diffusion of such texts as Lucretius' *De rerum natura* and Cicero's *Letters to Atticus* is well known, as are the recovery and impact of the writings of Greek authors too numerous to mention. Though the general outline—and, indeed, many of the specific details—of this process has been well known, thanks to the research of many scholars, especially the magisterial studies of Sabbadini,[1] further specific investigations are required before we can have a comprehensive picture of this cultural phenomenon. Additional study is necessary particularly with regard to philosophical, medical and scientific texts, which have not been so carefully studied by modern scholars as have works of more purely literary orientation. Nevertheless, now that a systematic start has been made in assembling all the relevant material concerning the translation and commentaries based on classical texts[2] we should be able to look forward to eventually having a full survey of the diffusion of these during the Middle Ages and Renaissance.

One ancient writer whose *fortuna* illustrates very well the changes which the Renaissance brought is the Greek philosopher Sextus Empiricus (fl. A.D. 200).[3] Though not an original thinker in his own right, Sextus was an accurate compiler of the major teachings of the ancient sceptical schools of philosophy deriving from Pyrrho of Elis (*c.* 360–270 B.C.). Since the original writings of the whole group of sceptics before Sextus have been lost, his writings contain the fullest and most accurate extant account of the teachings and opinions of this important philosophical tradition which had flourished for five centuries before him.[4] For this reason the compendia from Sextus' pen which have survived are of great importance, not only in so far as they allow us to reconstruct with some historical accuracy various developments of Greek philosophical thought, but in as much as they gained a renewed life, exerting a distinct influence on Renaissance and early modern thought after their recovery and assimilation through the efforts of the Renaissance humanists.

Owing to a specific set of historical circumstances nearly all the writings about the sceptical school failed to survive Antiquity. Even those which did—such as Sextus Empiricus and parts of the writings of Cicero, Diogenes Laertius and Ptolemy—all but disappeared from view during the Middle Ages and certainly had little role in the development of the Western medieval tradition.[5] Though there was some continuity of interest in scepticism, as well as in the writings of Sextus Empiricus, among Byzantine scholars,[6] Western knowledge seems to have been confined to a single Latin translation of Sextus extant in two manuscripts, which was apparently read but little or not at all.[7]

Thus for all intents and purposes ancient sceptical philosophy found no direct continuity through the Middle Ages, though certain other developments quasi-sceptical in orientation did flourish. There are clear parallels, for example, between some of the epistemological criticisms of Nicolaus of Autrecourt or of certain mystical and religious writings of the Western Middle Ages and some key ideas of ancient scepticism.[8] These, however, seem to be purely incidental similarities, and thus far no convincing evidence has been brought forward[9] to support the influence of ancient sceptical writings on medieval thought.

The real revival of the ancient sceptical tradition began in the sixteenth century, building on the foundations established by the fifteenth-century Italian humanists. The major details of this have been set forth in recent years and there is no need to reiterate it here,[10] other than stressing a few significant factors. First of all, the text of Sextus Empiricus did not appear in print until 1621,[11] though Latin translations were available in printed versions in 1562 and 1569,[12] and there were a substantial number of Greek manuscripts available by the sixteenth century.[13] As early as 1520, however, various sceptical doctrines deriving from Sextus Empiricus found their way into print in the *Examen vanitatis doctrinae gentium* of Gianfrancesco Pico, who had access to Greek manuscripts of Sextus.[14] Though little use was made of this major ancient source of sceptical doctrine—with the exception of Pico and a few others who used it in a more limited way—before the first printing of the translations of Sextus, various manuscripts of his writings had already appeared in Italy during the early years of the Quattrocento.

Knowledge of Sextus and his writings was relatively limited in Western Europe during the fifteenth century, though the existence of this material was known to a wider group than has perhaps previously been realised. Though manuscripts of Sextus' writings were known to a number of Italian Quattrocento humanists—but not outside Italy as far as can be determined—relatively little use was made of them. In fact no one in Italy before Pico,[15] so far as I have been able to determine, showed the least interest in the destructive philosophical and scientific critique to be found in Sextus' writings.

The first Sextus manuscript was brought to Italy from Constantinople about 1427 by Francesco Filelfo.[16] Filelfo himself made use of the manuscript frequently in his writings, but largely for the information it brought to him about classical Antiquity rather than for the philosophical ideas it contained.[17] Giovanni Aurispa, who himself did so much to bring Greek culture to Italy in the early years of the Quattrocento, apparently did not personally come across a Sextus manuscript during his Eastern travels, for in 1441 we find him requesting Filelfo to borrow his copy.[18] In 1452 Filelfo himself, in an effort to improve his own codex, wished to get hold of a manuscript in the hands of Cardinal Bessarion,[19] a copy which ultimately found its way into the Biblioteca Marciana in Venice.[20] By 1459 a copy of Sextus had come into the hands of the Medici, for at that time, as has only recently been shown, Guarino da Verona wrote to Piero di Cosimo de' Medici asking for a copy of that manuscript.[21] A Sextus manuscript was in the Vatican as early as 1475,[22] and we know that later a copy came into the hands of Giovanni Pico della Mirandola[23] and that Angelo Poliziano copied a number of excerpts from Sextus.[24] Attempts to translate the writings into Latin were not lacking, though none of the fifteenth-century efforts succeeded in popularising the Greek sceptical treatises. Besides Giovanni Lorenzi, with whom we are here primarily concerned, there is another partial translation extant in mutilated form,[25] and we know that no lesser a figure than Girolamo Savonarola advocated having a complete translation of Sextus made.[26] Though no evidence has hitherto come to light to indicate that this project was actually carried out, we do know that a Sextus manuscript was to be found in the Florentine convent of S. Marco during Savonarola's time.[27]

This, in brief outline, is the diffusion of knowledge of the writings of Sextus Empiricus in Italy before 1500, and, as already mentioned, no attention whatever seems to have been paid to that author elsewhere in Western Europe during the fifteenth century. It seems certain that further details will come to light when we have been able to investigate all the previously mentioned material more fully. Particularly important would be a careful study of the *provenance* of all known extant manuscripts[28] and the publication of characteristic abstracts from the extant Latin translations with accompanying analysis. In the present paper I shall publish sections from one of the fifteenth-century Latin translations, that of Giovanni Lorenzi.[29] Before considering the translation itself it might be well to provide a rapid summary of Lorenzi's life and activities.

The basic facts of Lorenzi's life[30] can be set forth quite briefly.[31] He was born in Venice about 1440 of a humble family. Of his early education we know very little, though he did attain the level of proficiency necessary to allow him to enter the *Studio* of Padua and to take a degree there *in utroque jure* on 28 August 1469. Among the witnesses to his degree were Niccolò Lelio Cosmico and Demetrios Chalcondyles, who besides being among Lorenzi's teachers were also two of his closest friends at Padua. In addition to legal studies Lorenzi also studied Greek with Chalcondyles, one of the most distinguished teachers of that language in late Quattrocento Italy, and later carried on a fruitful correspondence with him. After taking his degree Lorenzi remained in Padua until early 1472, at which time he entered the service of Cardinal Marco Barbo (1420–91).[32] Lorenzi accompanied the apostolic legate on a diplomatic mission to Germany, Bohemia, Hungary and Poland in an attempt to restore peace to the empire. Barbo returned to Rome in 1474, with Lorenzi still in his service. There the latter acted as a secretary to the cardinal, who took up offices in the recently completed Palazzo Venezia.

The remainder of the Venetian humanist's life was spent in Rome, where he came into contact with many of the leading scholars who congregated around the papal court during the fifteenth century. He rose steadily through the ranks of papal bureaucracy, being named *scriptor apostolicus* in 1479 and apostolic secretary in 1484. We also know that during this time Lorenzi continued his own studies, making use of the growing collection of manuscripts and printed books housed in the Vatican Library, Greek manuscripts especially attracting his attention. Such literary pursuits were given further opportunity for development when, with the accession of Innocent VIII (1484–92) and the subsequent death of Cristoforo Persona, Lorenzi was named papal librarian on 13 December 1485. He held that position until the death of the pontiff, when his successor, Alexander VI, named his own candidate to the librarianship. The remaining years of Lorenzi's life were spent in Rome, where he apparently continued his studies until his death about 1501.

Though Lorenzi's activities included a broadly based study of various classical authors—and the manuscript researches of several scholars show this[33]—he apparently wrote relatively little. Besides a number of letters, some of which have now been published, he also wrote a substantial *Consolaria* to Francesco Tarsio on the death of a younger brother[34] and made Latin translations of a number of Plutarch's *Moralia*,[35] most of which were never printed.[36]

Having said this much, let us now turn to a consideration of Lorenzi's translation of Sextus Empiricus. As far as can be determined, this translation was made from a manuscript which was in the Vatican during his period as librarian but which has subsequently disappeared from view. Such a manuscript, written on vellum, appeared in the library inventory of 1475, as well as in later ones of 1481, 1484, 1518 and in the inventory of Greek works of about 1517–18.[37] The manuscript is missing, however, from later inventories, made between 1533 and 1555, perhaps vanishing with the sack of Rome.[38] The existence of a Sextus manuscript in the Vatican during Lorenzi's time is also attested by the fact that Gioacchino Turriani, General of the Dominicans from 1487 to 1500, borrowed it from the library in 1494.[39] Though at present there are a number of Greek manuscripts of Sextus in the Vatican Library, most of them date from the sixteenth century or later.[40] There appears to be but a single fifteenth-century Sextus manuscript in the Vatican at present, and that came to the collection later and, moreover, contains only a portion of the works translated by Lorenzi.[41] Consequently, in the absence of more concrete evidence, the safest hypothesis is that Lorenzi made his translation from the copy of Sextus to which he had easiest access, viz. the codex which was in the Vatican Library during the fifteenth century, but which has since been lost sight of.

At what date did Lorenzi make his translation? The manuscript itself carries no clear evidence which would help us to date it directly. If Mercati's[42] identification of the scribe as the German humanist Jakob Questenberg is correct—and I can see no reason to doubt the conclusion of that excellent scholar—the earliest date possible for the transcription is 1485, when Questenberg arrived in Rome.[43] Mercati went further and argued, on the basis of the handwriting of the section of the manuscript containing the Sextus translation (which was originally separate from the other treatises contained in the present-day Vat. Lat. 2990), that it was made by Questenberg soon after he arrived in Rome, before he adapted his handwriting to the current Roman model, which can be seen in later examples of his hand.[44] Such a hypothesis with regard to the dating is also consonant with other evidence. While Giovanni Lorenzi borrowed manuscripts from the Vatican Library both before and after becoming librarian and duly recorded this information in the 'register of loans', during his tenure of office he did not record himself as using books from the collection, though his name appears often as the one responsible for lending books to other readers.[45] This would seem to indicate that he read the translated Sextus Empiricus while he was papal librarian. Consequently, in the absence of further evidence, the probable date for Lorenzi's translation of Sextus Empiricus as found in Vat. Lat. 2990 must be taken to be sometime shortly after 1485.[46]

There is no evidence that Lorenzi's translation was read by any contemporaries and, as far as we have been able to discover, it was not mentioned in print before Mercati published his note in 1920 and then amplified his findings thirteen years later.[47] Since then there have been several references to the translation in print, but no one has thus far gone beyond Mercati's meagre comments on it, nor has anyone published the text.[48] There is, in fact, relatively little to be said about it, though it does seem worthwhile to get sections of it into print so that scholars may be able to compare it more easily with other translations of the same author.

Lorenzi's translation does portray a number of peculiarities, and there are various points which call for comment. First of all, it should be noted, though it is hardly evident from the sections here edited, that generally quotations from other authors found in Sextus' writings are left untranslated (i.e. in Greek) by Lorenzi.[49] On a few other occasions he does translate such passages.[50] When Sextus uses Greek terms to illustrate some point or other the translator sometimes garbles them to such an extent that they could scarcely be intelligible to the Latin reader. In many places the translator fails to catch the meaning of the Greek text, often producing a Latin version which is very far indeed from conveying the meaning of the original.[51] Sometimes one can see what the translator is getting at only after seeing the Greek text, but at other times the Latin remains opaque even then.

Obviously, in Lorenzi's time the sceptical philosophical vocabulary was not entirely fixed in Latin and Lorenzi was allowed a certain latitude of which later writers could not avail themselves. A few examples should suffice. At one point λόγος is translated simply as *sermo*, where the meaning would seem to call for a term such as *ratio*,[52] though the precise meaning of the passage is perhaps debatable, and Hervet rendered it as *oratio*.[53] Perhaps more serious is the case in the same passage where the technical meaning of two key sceptical terms, ἐπέχειν and ἀκαταληπτεῖν, is missed and quite non-technical renderings, *obtinet* and *non percipiat* are given.[54] This is, we might mention, in spite of the fact that Cicero had long ago rightly understood the specific meaning of these terms in the *Academica* and elsewhere.[55]

This, however, is not the place to dwell on such matters, nor are we yet in a position to discuss all of this in detail. Before that is possible further work is necessary on other translations of Sextus, including the editing of excerpts from the Venice translation as well as the publication of further extracts from the medieval translation[56] along with a collation of the Paris and Madrid manuscripts of it. In the present paper we have merely attempted to make a beginning towards a comprehensive analysis of the *fortuna* of Sextus Empiricus in the Quattrocento.

DESCRIPTION OF THE MANUSCRIPT AND EDITING PROCEDURE

There is little of direct importance to us here to be added to the description of the manuscript already made by Mercati,[57] but it might help to reiterate the essential facts. It is a paper manuscript of 384 folios, probably in the hand of Jakob Questenberg. It was originally in three parts, but was later bound together and a general table of contents added to it. This was apparently done already in the fifteenth century, for the table of contents seems clearly to be a fifteenth-century hand. According to Mercati, the hand of the table of contents, as well as of the remainder of the manuscript, is that of Questenberg, though various sections date from different times. Today the manuscript has a single pagination, but a second serial numbering also appears on the pages containing the translation of Sextus (ff. 1–116). The manuscript is made up entirely of fifteenth-century humanist translations of philosophical works and contains the following: Aristotle, *De anima*, trans. Georgius Trapezuntius (ff. 3–57); Alexander of Aphrodisias, *Problemata*, trans. Theodorus Gaza (ff. 61–141*v*); (Pseudo-) Aristotle, *Magna moralia*, trans. Gregorius Tiphernas (ff. 142–265); and Sextus Empiricus, *Contra mathematicos* [incomplete], trans. Io[annes] L[aurentius] (ff. 266–381). All the translations, save the one by Lorenzi, are well known and are extant in numerous manuscript and/or printed copies.

The attribution of the translation to Lorenzi rests on the table of contents prefaced to the manuscript, for nowhere else is there any indication of who the translator might have been. The table of contents, which according to Mercati is attributable to Questenberg, reads in part as follows: 'Sexti Emperici contra professores artium interprete Io. L.' Mercati[58] has argued convincingly that the form 'Io. L.' was commonly used as an abbreviation for Lorenzi's name. The fact that Questenberg was closer to Lorenzi than to any of the other translators whose works are contained in the manuscript also helps to explain why Lorenzi's name is written in a more intimate form while those of Trapezuntius, Gaza, and Tiphernas are written in more conventional form.

In editing the text I have tried to transcribe it as accurately as possible, normally retaining the orthographical peculiarities of the manuscript. In a few instances in which there seems to have been an obvious scribal slip of the pen I have corrected these, but indicate the manuscript reading in the apparatus. The letters 't' and 'c', as well as 'u' and 'v', which are not distinguished in the manuscript, have been transcribed in accord with modern usage. On the other hand, where the scribe writes 'y' in place of the more conventional 'i' I have retained this spelling. More frequently than not the dipthong 'ae' is written as 'e', in which cases I have retained the spelling of the manuscript. Upon occasion, especially towards the end of the Sextus section of the manuscript, 'ę' or 'ae' is found, and in these cases I have transcribed it as 'ae'. If Mercati's hypothesis about Questenberg's having altered his handwriting after coming to Italy is correct, this may be an indication that a gradual change was taking place as he was transcribing the Sextus translation.[59] As Mercati has already noted,[60] though some sections of Vat. Lat. 2990 contain ample marginal annotations, especially in the section devoted to Trapezuntius's translation of the *De anima*, there are very few indeed in the Sextus translation. Those few which occur in the sections we here edit have been noted in the apparatus.

There seems to be little point at present in editing the entire Sextus translation, but we have tried to select characteristic sections of it. We have especially attempted to print parts which express key sceptic ideas and to include some sections from each of Sextus' works which Lorenzi has translated. Moreover we have carefully included in our edition substantial *incipits* and *explicits* of each work, even though on occasion these are among the most difficult sections of the manuscript to read, owing to the fact that the ink has soaked into the paper, leaving a very blurred result. Most difficulties of reading the text we have been able to resolve, for we have constantly had before us the Teubner edition, the Loeb edition with accompanying English translation, and Fabricius' edition with Hervet's Latin translation.[61] We have tried to present as intelligible an edition of the excerpts as possible, though, for the reasons mentioned above, there are still sections very difficult to understand without reference to the Greek text or other more intelligible translations. To provide an understandable text we have altered the punctuation and have capitalised in accord with modern editorial practice.

[SEXTI EMPERICI CONTRA PROFESSORES ARTIUM]

[Liber I]

[266r] [1] [C]ontra eos qui disciplinas profitentur arguere communiter Epicurei et Pyrrhonei non tamen eodem medio animique impulsu affecti, fuisse videntur.

2 Pyrrhonei: pyrhronei *cod.*

Epicurei nanque tanquam nihil ad perfectam sapientie cognitionem afferrent aut, ut quidam coniectantur, quandam excusationem ignorantie sue pretendentes contradixisse videntur. In multis enim indoctus omnino Epicurus deprehenditur, adeo ut neque in communi locutione eliminatus sit. [2] Fortasse etiam inimicitia quadam in Platonicos Aristotelicosque ac eorum similes multiplici disciplina preditos incitatur. Neque omnino a vero discrepat contra eum (ad huiusmodi contradictionem provectum fuisse) Nausiphanis, qui Pyrrhonis ipsius auditor fuit, inimicitia incensum. Multos enim ex adolescentibus Nausiphanes insectatores habebat et disciplinarum, ac precipue rhetorice, studiosus erat. [3] Cum enim Nausiphanis dyscipulus fuisset etiam Epicurus, ut a seipso et non ab alio doctus et quasi natura formatus philosophus videretur, se eius auditorem fuisse omnino negabat omnemque eius famam obscu [266v] rare nitebatur, cumque Nausiphanis gloria celebraretur, multis in accusandis disciplinis erat, quarum precipue causa Nausiphanis nomen clarissimum erat. [4] Scribit enim in epistola ad eos qui Mytylene philosophabantur de Nausiphane in hec verba, 'Equidem existimo miseros quosdam putare me discipulum pneumonis et inter adolescentulos quosdam ebrios et crapulantes,' ipsum audivisse Nausiphanem scilicet pneumonis nomine tanquam stultum et insensatum taxans. Et rursus in eadem epistola, cum pluribus verbis in hominem invectus fuisset, latentur eius in disciplinis profectum significare videtur. 'Erat enim,' inquit, 'vir pessimus et circa huiusmodi studiorum genus versabatur ex quibus impossibile erat ad rectam sapientiam pervenire occulte,' intelligens de disciplinis. [5] Epicurus quidem, quantum coniectura assequi possumus, huiuscemodi occasionibus irritatus bellum disciplinis omnibus denuntiverat. Pyrrhonei vero non ea de causa, quod scilicet nihil ad sapientiam conducerent, disciplinis contradixerunt, esset quippe contra eorum professionem assertiva oratio, [267r] neque rursus propter disciplinarum ignorantiam ad contradicendum provecti sunt. Nam simul cum institutione et doctrina maxime ex omnibus philosophis expertissimi et ad gloriam ex vulgarium opinione aucupandam omnino indifferenter se habent. [6] Inimicitiarum autem contra aliquos causa ad contradicendum provectos, qui eorum modestiam noverit, omnino negabit (longe enim ab eorum mansuetudine huiuscemodi malum abest), sed tale quidam in disciplinis quale in universa philosophia passi sunt. Quemadmodum enim ad eam percipiende veritatis desyderio se contulerunt, ita propemodum equali contradictionis inordinatione ac pugna rebus ipsis accurentes se continuerunt. Eadem quoque ad disciplinarum ipsarum veritatem capessendam cupiditate illecti, cum easdem dubitationes invenissent, non occultaverunt. [7] Quapropter et nos ipsi eandem institutionem secuti, omni contentionis specie remota, ea, quae diligenter contra huiusmodi disciplinas excogitata sunt, colligere tentabimus. Docere autem in presenti unde huiuscemodi studiorum genera encyklia cognominata fuerint quotque sint [267v] enumerare supervacuum existimo, cum presertim huiuscemodi nominibus ab eo tempore quo docebamur nobis ipsis aures tinniant. Id vero, quod in presenti maxime necessarium existimamus, demonstrandum erit—[8] scilicet eorum que contra disciplinas dicuntur, alia quidem in universum contra omnes, alia vero tanquam contra singulas dici consuevere. In universum enim

---

6 sit *suprascr. cod.*
12 dyscipulus: dysciplus *cod.*
17 ex epistola epicur *cod. add. in marg.*
17 fuisse *cod. add. in marg.*
18 pneumonis: *Gr.* πλεύμονος, *sed cf. ed. Mau,* pp. 1-2, *ubi codd. A et B* πνεύμονος *habent.*
20 pneumonis: *Gr.* πλεύμονα
38 capessendam: capestendam *cod.*
42 liberalium scientiarum *cod. add. in marg.*

dicimus verbi causa, cum arguuntur nullam omnino esse disciplinam, particularius vero cum contra grammaticos de dictione aut elementis, contra geometras quod principia ex presuppositionibus accipi non debent, contra musicos vero 50 nihil esse vocem aut tempus, disputare solemus. Videamus igitur prius commenti ordine universaliorem contradictionem.

[Caput I] *An sit aliquod discipline genus.*

[9] Cum apud philosophos plures et varii de disciplina tractatus et dissonantie fuerint, de illis iudicare presentis non est institutionis. Sufficit enim hoc interea 55 presupponere, quod, si quid scibile est et hoc [268r] homini comprehensibile sit, quatuor ante omnia confiteri oportet: quod scilicet res imprimis sit que doceatur, deinde qui doceat, discypulus et tradende doctrine modus. Cum vero, neque quod doceatur, neque doctor, neque addiscens, neque docendi modus sit, ut inferius demonstrabimus, et nullum igitur erit discipline genus. 60

[273v] [Caput 1] *De grammaticis*

[41] Principio igitur nobis sit statim cum grammaticis questio, quoniam ab infantia et a primis, ut ita loquamur, incunabulis grammatice dedicamur, quippe que ad aliarum doctrinarum disciplinam, quasi ianua sit ultraque omnes disciplinas, temeraria quadam audacia insignis Sirenarum, [274r] 65 quodammodo pollicitationem profitetur. [42] Ille enim, cum scirent natura innatam esse homini curiositatem ac eius in pectore precipuum quoddam agnoscende veritatis desyderium residere, non solum divinis quibusdam concentibus navigantes demulcere, verum etiam rerum scientiam eos se docturas pollicebantur. Aiunt enim: 70

> O decus Argoli cum quin puppim flectit Ulixes,
> Auribus, ut nostros possis agnoscere cantus.
> Nam nemo hec unquam est transvectus cerula cursu.
> Quin prius asciscerit vocum dulcidini captus
> Post variis avido saccatus pectore musis 75
> Doctior ad patrias lapsus pervenerit oras,
> Nunc grave certamen belli clademque canemus.
> Grecia quam Troye divino numine vexit,
> Omniaque elatus regum vestigia terris.

[43] Grammatica autem simul cum ea parte, que ex fabula historiarumque 80 ratione diffinitur, etiam circa linguam artificiosumque loquendi modum et lectiones maxime iactabunda incredibile sui ipsius desiderium audientibus excitat. Sed, ne extra ianuam vagari videamur, ostendemus [274v] nobis est et quot sint grammatice genera et de quo ipsorum nobis querendum proponamus.

[Caput II] *Quot modis grammatica accipiatur* 85

[44] 'Grammatice' igitur secundum equivocationem communiter et proprie dicitur. Communiter quidem secundum qualiscunque litterature cognitionem significatur, quam communi loquendi consuetudine 'grammaticen' appellamus;

61 De grammaticis: *Gr.* Πρὸς γραμματικους
71 Argoli: *Gr.* Ἀχαιῶν
74 asciscerit: ascicerit *cod.*
75 saccatus: sacatus *cod.*
71–9 Homer, *Od.* XII, 184 ff.
87 qualiscunque: qualiuscunque *cod.*
88 *Gr. add.* ἐάν τε Ἑλληνικῶν ἐάν τε βαρβαρικῶν *post* significatur

proprie vero sumpta ea intelligetur que a Crathete, Aristophane atque Aristarcho perfecte elaborata est. [45] Videtur autem utraque facultas pari nomine a 90 quadam aperta significatione cognominata: prima etenim a litteris quibus articulatas voces signare consuevimus; secunda vero fortasse, ut quidam affirmaverunt, quasi ordinatius distribuita a priore deducitur. Hec enim prioris pars quedam est, et quemadmodum 'iatrice', que latine 'medicina' interpretatur, ab extrahendis e vulnerato corpore sagittis antiquitus dicta est; in presenti vero, 95 cum longe ad curandas alias egritudines artificior sit, priscum tamen retinuit [275r] nomen. [46] Et, uti 'geometria' a terrae commensuratione cognomen a principio vendicavit, nunc autem et in speculatione rerum naturalium ordinata veterem appellationem servat. Sic perfecta 'grammatice', primum a litterarum cognitione nominata, etiam in argutioribus ac longe magis artificiosis earundem 100 litterarum considerationibus idem nomen obtinuit. [47] Et fortasse, ut Asclepiades affirmat, hec posterior a litteris quidem, sed non ab eisdem a quibus hec illa communior. Illa enim, ut diximus, ab elementis, hec autem ab operibus, que per litteras elaborantur, cognominatur. Opera enim huiuscemodi littere appellabantur, qua loquendi consuetudine documenta 'publicas litteras' appella- 105 mus et, cum aliquem doctum significare voluerimus, multarum litterarum cognitione preditum esse dicimus.

[279r] [65] Quod, si non solum eorum, que apud poetas et scriptores dicuntur, peritia est, describere eam ex eo, quod ipsi in parte accidit, minime oportebat. Sed dimissa tum subtili [279v] sermocinatione, ut polliciti sumus, an possibile 110 sit in huiusmodi suum grammaticen finem aliquem sustinere, consyderemus. [66] Cum igitur 'eam peritiam ut plurimum esse eorumque a poetis et scriptoribus' dicuntur, asseveraverint an omnium, an aliquorum; velim dicant non vere ut in plurimis sed omnium erit, quod si omnium, etiam in infinito erit (sunt enim hec infinita). Infinitorum vero peritia nulla est. Quapropter neque grammatica 115 aliqua erit. Quod si aliquorum, postquam etiam vulgares ipsi nonnulla, que a poetis et scriptoribus dicuntur, scientes, grammatices peritiam non habent; neque hec grammatice appellanda erit. [67] Nisi forte quispiam propter id quod dictum est, ut in plurimis, ea ratione dictum fuisse affirmat, ut differentia quedam in omnium dubitatione, et quantum ad vulgares attinet, subintelligatur. 120 In hoc enim vulgari grammaticus distabit, inquantum non paucorum, ut ille, sed plurimum, que apud poetas et scriptores dicuntur, peritus est; a cognitione autem omnium, que fortasse impossibilis est, separatus erit; postquam non omnia sed plura ex eis cognoscere se profiteatur. [280r] [68] Hec autem, non defendentis, sed malis mala coacervantis, nec amplius mediocriter sed funditus 125 novas dubitationes provocantis, erunt. Primum igitur quemadmodum multa indefinita sunt et acervum dubitationum generant; its eodem modo etiam plurima. Quapropter aut hec nobis circumscribant ostendantque usque ad quem terminum cognitionum ea, que apud poetas et scriptores dicuntur, accipienda sint aut, si in professione indefinitorum persistentem plurima se cognoscere 130 affirment, interrogatiunculam parvam etiam suscipere non graventur. [69] Circumscripto enim plurimi numero, si quis unum detrahat, plurimus adhuc remanebit, nam omnino absurdissimum erit unitatis adiectione hunc, alterum vero nullo modo, plurimum appellare. Ac propterea unitate adiecta numerus ille, qui apud eos plurimus appellatur, ad id necessario deveniet ut non amplius 135 plurimus sit, et propter hoc neque etiam grammatice erit, quod dubitationis coacervative conclusio est. [70] Quis enim negare posset grammatice ruditatis

---

89 Crathete: *Gr.* Κράτητα τὸν Μαλλώτην
94 ιατρικη *cod. add. in marg.*
101–2 Asclepiades: Asclipiades *cod.*
123 separatus: seperatus *cod.*

revera esse, si que numero infinita sunt plurima appellentur? Quemadmodum
[280v] enim modicum ad aliquid refertur et secundum plurimi positionem
intelligitur, sic et plurimum secundum positionem ad modicum considerabitur. 140
Si igitur plurimorum, que apud poetas et scriptores dicuntur, peritiam habent
grammatici, paucorumque reliqua sunt non habebunt; [71] si vero adiectum
plurimum et dimissum minimum est, non amplius illud, quod omne est, infinitum erit. Verumtamen, ne de huiuscemodi diligentius disseramus, hoc tantum
dicimus falsum omnino esse quod grammaticus plurima eorum, que apud poetas 145
et scriptores dicuntur, cognoscat. Parvula enim omnino particula est eorum que
cognoscit, si consyderetur ad reliqua et plurima, que non novit, quemadmodum
questione procedente ostendemus.

[328v] [305] ... Videbitur fortasse grammaticis in honorem eius hoc dictum et
propter philosophi dignitatem atque splendorem. Alius autem e contrario surgens 150
dicet [329r] pugnabitque exempla a Phliasio de Pyrrhone inducta scepticae
voluntati nullo modo quadrare, si quidem sol que prius non videbantur claritate
sua illustrans ostendit. Pyrrhon autem e contrario, que nobis manifesta et in
propatulo erant, prius ad incertitudinem obscuritatemque, quasi violenta
quadem, deducit. [306] Si quis vero hoc diligenter philosophiceque considerabit, 155
sensum aliter habere inveniet; ait enim quod, scilicet solis locum obtinet,
Pyrrhon ex eo, quod quemadmodum Deus recto intuitu oculos in eum iacientes
debilitat atque obscurat; sit etiam et scepticus sermo, si diligentius quispiam
eum introspicere voluerit, mentis oculum omnino confundat, ita, ut de uno
quoque per dogmaticam temeritatem affirmato[?] exposito non percipiat.   160

[331v] [320] ... Sed iam contra eos, qui ab hac disciplina deducuntur, hec
dixisse sufficiat; ab alio igitur principio exordientes [332r] que etiam contra
oratores dicere oporteat consyderemus.

SEXTI EMPERICI DE GRAMMATICA

[Liber II] *Sequitur eiusdem de rhetorica.*   165

[1] Posteaquam ea que de grammatica dicenda erant percurrimus, consequens
est ut etiam de rhetorica dicamus, quae virilior fortiorque existimatur,
utpote cuius virtus in foro subselliisque quasi trutina quadam expenditur atque
examinatur. Verum quia non subsistentie ac subsistentie commune signum est
notio, nec alterum istorum, nisi prius quesitum preocupaverimus quale sit, 170
queri possit: age quid nam sit rhetorice consyderemus, dic eas que maxime a
phylosophis celebrate sunt descriptiones vicissim apponamus. [2] Plato igitur
in *Gorgia*, secundum diffinitivam ex appositione doctrinam, talem ex rethori-
ces[!] diffinitionem ex appositione enuntiasse videatur. 'Rhetorica,' inquit,
'orationis ministerio persuasionis magistra est, in ipsa oratione vim potestatemque 175
persuasibilem, non doctrinalem habens.' Quod autem 'orationis ministerio' addidit adeo fortasse fecit, quoniam pluraque apud homines [332v] semota oratione
persuasionem facere consueverunt, quemadmodum: auctoritas, divitiae, voluptas
et pulchritudo sunt. [3] Seniores etenim Troyanorum, quamquam undique
bello premerentur ac animo adversus Helenem utpote calamitatis causam 180
omnino alieno et irato essent, eius tamen pulchra elegantique forma persuasi.

[353r] [106] Et ut summatim concedamus has esse rhetoricae partes. Postquam
iustum quod iustum sit, et utile quod utile, et honestum quod honestum similiter
sit, demonstraverit. Instabitur, quod demonstratio nihil est, neque rhetorica talibus nixa partibus subsistet, quod autem nihil sit demonstratio diligentius in 185
Scepticis Commentariis demonstratum est; brevius autem et summatim etiam

174–6 *Cf. Gorgias* 453a.
184–6 *Cf. Pyr. hyp.* II, 134ff.

nunc attingemus. [107] Si enim oratio nihil est neque demonstratio quae orationis qualitas est. Aliquid est nihil autem est oratio, ut ostendimus, quoniam scilicet nec in vocibus, neque in incorporeis dicibilibus subsistentiam habet, neque demonstratio igitur est; [108] quod, si est, [353v] aut manifesta aut 190 incerta erit. Sed manifesta non est, incertum enim aliquid circa se habet, ac propterea discordat, cum omnis res quae non convenit et concors non est incerta sit. [109] Relinquetur igitur ipsam omnino esse incertam. Quod, si hoc aut ex seipsa aut ex demonstratione assumetur, sed neque ex se ipsa assumi potest, incerta enim erat. Incertum autem ex seipso assumptum fidem non facit, neque 195 rursus ex demonstratione propter processum in infinitum, non igitur aliqua est demonstratio. [110] Generali autem nulla existente demonstratione, neque specialis aliqua demonstratio erit, quemadmodum animali non existente, neque homo erit. Generalis autem demonstratio, ut ostendimus, non est, nulla ergo earum que specie consistunt erit. Postquam enim incerta est, ut paulo ante 200 ratiocinati sumus, per aliquam constitui debet. Per quam igitur? Per generalem aut per specialem. [111] Non per specialem, quoniam nondum generalis stabilem habet subsistentiam; neque etiam per generalem, ipsa enim est quae adhuc in dubitationem vertitur. Non igitur [354r] generalis aliqua demonstratio est. Ex quo sequitur neque specialem subsistere. Et aliter, si generalis demonstratio 205 assumpta aliqua ad que refertur habet, neque generalis est; si non habet, nihil probabit; et multo magis neque sui ipsius subsistentiam. [112] Preterea demonstratio, alterius demonstrationis faciens fidem, aut de ea queritur, aut non queritur. Sed, quod talis sit, ut de ipsa non queratur, propter superius enumeratas causas, esse non poterit; si de ea queritur, ab alia probari debet, et illa rursus 210 ab alia, usque in infinitum. Non igitur aliqua est demonstratio. [113] Sed postquam ad rhetoricam continentia theoremata satis diximus, ab alio rursus principio eas, quae ad geometras arithmeticosque pertinent, dubitationes attingamus.

[Liber III] *Sexti Emperici contra geometras*   215

[1] Quoniam geometrae, dubitationum eos persequentium numerum perspicientes, ad rem, que periculi nihil et securitatis in se plurimum habere videtur, ex suppositione videlicet geometriae [354v] principia petendo confugere solent, optimum erit, si et nos quoque in ea quam facturi sumus contradictione de suppositionis ratione principium faciamus. [2] Nam et Timon in his que *Contra* 220 *physicos* scripsit hoc ante omnia querendum existimavit: si ex suppositione videlicet assumendum aliquid esset. Quapropter etiam nos hoc quasi posito fundamento in his, que contra disciplinarum professores pervenimus[?], itidem facere conveniens erit. [3] Ordinis autem causa illud presupponendum est, quod licet alias multipliciter suppositio cognominetur; in presenti eam tripliciter accipi 225 satis erit. Primo autem modo pro scaenicae temeritatis argumento appellatur (secundum quem loquendi usum et tragicam et comicam suppositionem, ac apud Dicearchum quasdam suppositiones ex Euripidis Sophoclisque fabulis esse dicimus); nihil aliud quam tragedie argumentum suppositionem appellantes. [4] Altero significationis modo suppositio in rhetoricis eorum que particularia 230 sunt questio dicitur (secundum quod et sophiste [355r] sepenumero in auditoriis 'ponatur supplicio suppositio' dicere consueverunt). Secundum tertiam partitionem suppositiones[?] demonstrationum principium intelligimus[?], ut ea[?] scilicet petitionem ad alicuius propositionem.

---

205 si: Sm *cod.* (*Gr.* εἰ δὲ); *correxi.*
230–4 *cod. non liquet*
233 suppositiones: suppositionenda (?) *cod., sed non liquet*

[357*r*] [17] ... Quod igitur hi, qui disciplinas profitentur, ex suppositione 235
demonstrationis principia sumentes ac in uno quoque theoremate 'detur hoc' in
susurrantes non bene faciunt, ex his satis demonstratum esse existimamus. [18]
Deinceps igitur ad cetera transeuntes, quod falsa impersuasibiliaque artis eorum
principia sint, doceamus; et licet multa, [357*v*] quemadmodum narrationis
principio nostre significavimus, circa hec dici possent, ea in dubitatione hac 240
inducemus, quibus eversis et reliqua simul evertuntur. Postquam autem in
suspicionem calumniamque deductis eorum principiis neque particulariter
eorum demonstrationes procedere possunt, ea que ad principia quadrare videntur, interea percurramus. [19] Statim igitur, tanquam principale aliquid ac ut
ita loquamur quasi maxime elementale quiddam, nos docere volunt quod trinas 245
dimensiones—longitudinem videlicet, latitudinem, profunditatemque—habeat
corpus: esse quarum prima longitudinis dimensio a superiori ad inferiorem
protenditur partem; secunda, que latitudine constat a dextris ad sinistra; tertia
vero, que profunditate conficitur a prioribus ad posteriora deducitur. Ita, ut ex
tribus his, sex, due scilicet ex una quaque dimensiones fiant: prioris quidem 250
superiorem inferioremque, alterius dextram sinistramque, tertie priorem
posteriorem fieri. Ex puncti etiam fluxu lineam fluere, e linea superficiem, ex
superficie autem corpus solidum constare aiunt. [358*r*] [20] Unde et punctum
impartibile indivisibileque signum aut lineae extremum, lineam vero absque
latitudine, longitudinem aut superficiei terminum superficiem corporis, itidem 255
terminum aut sine profunditate latitudinem describentes dicunt. [21] Ordine
igitur haec reasummentes, de puncto primum, postea de linea, de superficie
corporeque disseramus. Hic enim eversis neque geometria ars esse poterit, utpote
tum ea, ex quibus eius compositio procedere videtur, non habeat.

[375*v*] [116] ... et in commentariis contra physicos grammaticosque[?] osten- 260
dimus. Non igitur geometris aliquid ex linea aufferre[?] secareque possibile est.

[Liber IV] *Contra arithmeticos*

[1] Quoniam quod ad quantum attinet, aliud in continuis corporibus et
magnitudo appellatur circa quam precipue versatur geometria, aliud vero in
discretis continetur ex ea que numerus constituitur circa quem arithmetica 265
insumatur, a geometricis principiis theorematibusque distendentes etiam ea, que
ad numerum pertinent, consyderemus.

[381*r*] [31] ... Quod vero neque per additionem, si secundum dubitationum
analogiam progrediemur, facile ostendere poterimus. Nam unitate addita
decadi, aut integre decadi aut ultime decadis parti additio <non> fieri dicamus. 270
Sed, si integre decadi superadditur unitas, posteaquam tota decas cum omnibus
particularibus unitatibus intelligitur, oportebit factam unitatis additionem
omnibus decadis singularibus unitatibus accedere, quod quidem absurdum est.
[32] Sequetur enim ex unitatis additione decadem vigesimam fieri, quod
de genere impossibilium est. Non igitur totae decadi unitatem superaddi 275
dicendum est. Atqui neque ultime decadis parti fiet, siquidem decas non augebi-
tur, quoniam propter unius partis augmentum non statim totius decadis augmentum fiet. [33] Et in universum ac in omnibus aut manenti decadi aut non
manenti superadditur unitas. Sed manenti numquam superaddi posset, [381*v*]
siquidem non amplius manebit decas, neque etiam non manenti, rei enim a 280
principio non consistenti nec additio fieri poterit. [34] Si igitur numerus per
additionem et ademptionem consistere intelligitur, ut diximus,—ostendimus

260–7 *cod. non liquet*
270 non *add. cod., sed Gr. particulam neg. non habet.*

autem nos neutrum istorum esse posse numerum—nihil penitus esse dicendum est. Quapropter his contra geometras arithmeticosque dubitando decursis, ab alio rursus principio etiam contra mathematicos redargutionem faciamus. 285

CONTRA ARITHMETICOS

[Liber V] *Eiusdem contra astrologos*

[text breaks off here]

NOTES

[1] Especially R. Sabbadini, *Le scoperte dei codici latini e greci ne' secoli XIV e XV*, Florence, 1905–14; reprint ed. E. Garin, 1967.

[2] *Catalogus translationum et commentariorum: Mediaeval and Renaissance Latin Translations and Commentaries. Annotated Lists and Guides*, ed. P. O. Kristeller *et al.*, Washington, D.C., I, 1960, II, 1971.

[3] Of the large literature on Sextus and Greek scepticism the following are among the more important works: V. Brochard, *Les Sceptiques grecs*, Paris, 1887; second edition, 1933; A. Goedeckemeyer, *Die Geschichte des griechischen Skeptizismus*, Leipzig, 1905; M. dal Pra, *Lo scetticismo greco*, Milan, 1940; L. Robin, *Pyrrhon et le scepticisme grec*, Paris, 1944; and among more recent books, C. Stough, *Greek Scepticism*, Berkeley and Los Angeles, 1969, and A. E. Chatzilysandros, *Geschichte der skeptischen Tropen ausgehend von Diogenes Laertius und Sextus Empiricus*, Munich, 1970.

[4] Other important sources include Cicero, especially the *Academica* and the *De natura deorum*; Diogenes Laertius' *Vita Pyrrhonis*; and Ptolemy's *De criterio*.

[5] These topics are dealt with much more fully in my *Cicero Scepticus: a Study of the Influence of the 'Academica' in the Renaissance*, The Hague, 1972, and 'The recovery and assimilation of Ancient Scepticism in the Renaissance', *Rivista critica di storia della filosofia*, XXVII, 1972, pp. 363–84, where references to further literature are to be found.

[6] In addition to my paper cited in the previous note see also J. A. Fabricius, *Bibliotheca graeca*, ed. Harles, Hamburg, 1790–1809, V, pp. 527–28; A. Elter and L. Radermacher, *Analecta graeca*, Bonn, 1899; and D. M. Nicol, 'The Byzantine Church and Hellenic learning in the fourteenth century', *Studies in Church History*, V, 1969, pp. 23–47, especially 43.

[7] The translation was made from a Greek manuscript now lost and has thus been useful in establishing the modern critical text of Sextus Empiricus. See Sexti Empirici *Opera*, ed. H. Mutschmann, I, Leipzig, 1912, pp. X–XII. The two known manuscripts of the translation are presently Paris, B.N. lat. 14,700, and Madrid, B.N. 10,112. The former has been known for some time and served Mutschmann for his edition. For further information see also C. Jourdain, 'Sextus Empiricus et la philosophie scolastique', in Jourdain's *Excursions historiques et philosophiques à travers le moyen âge*, Paris, 1888, pp. 201–17; C. Baeumker, 'Eine bisher unbekannte lateinische Übersetzung der Πυρρώνειοι Ὑποτυπώσεις des Sextus Empiricus', *Archiv für Geschichte der Philosophie*, IV, 1891, 574–7; and H. Mutschmann, 'Zur Übersetzertätigkeit des Nicolaus von Rhegium (zu Paris lat. 14,700)', *Berliner Philologische Wochenschrift*, XXII, 1911, pp. 691–2. The Madrid MS was described by J. M. Millás Vallicrosa, *Las traducciones orientales en los manuscritos de la Biblioteca Catedral de Toledo*, Madrid, 1942, pp. 211 f, who failed to connect the anonymous text of the manuscript with Sextus Empiricus. The identification of the text was first made by Professor Kristeller, who also has pointed out to me Millás Vallicrosa's description of the manuscript. *Cf.* R. H. Popkin, *History of Scepticism from Erasmus to Descartes*, revised edition, New York, 1968, p. 17, n. 2. I plan to study the Paris and Madrid MSS further in a subsequent publication.

[8] See J. Lappe, *Nicolaus von Autrecourt*, Münster, 1908, and J. R. Weinberg, *Nicolaus of Autrecourt: a Study in Fourteenth-century Thought*, Princeton, N.J., 1948; K. Michalski, *La Philosophie au XIVe siècle: six études*, ed. K. Flasch, Frankfurt, 1969, which reprints Michalski's important papers dating from 1922–37.

⁹ See especially the remarks made by A. Maier, 'Das Problem der Evidenz in der Philosophie des 14. Jahrhunderts', in her *Ausgehendes Mittelalters*, Rome, 1964–67, II, 367–418.

¹⁰ See Popkin (n. 7), my publications cited in n. 5, and my *Gianfrancesco Pico della Mirandola (1469–1533) and his Critique of Aristotle*, The Hague, 1967.

¹¹ *Opera omnia quae extant*, Geneva, 1621.

¹² *Pyrrhoniarum hypotypōseōn libri III* . . . *latine nunc primum editi interprete Henrico Stephano*, Paris, 1562, and *Adversus mathematicos* . . . *graece numquam latine nunc primum editum, Genriano Herveto Aurelio interprete* . . ., Paris, 1569.

¹³ See the information cited below in n. 40.

¹⁴ For details see Schmitt, *Gianfrancesco Pico* . . .

¹⁵ But see below, n. 26.

¹⁶ Sabbadini (n. 1), I, p. 48.

¹⁷ For details of the various writings in which Filelfo used Sextus see A. Calderini, 'Ricerche intorno alla biblioteca e alla cultural greca di Francesco Filelfo', *Studi italiani di filologia classica*, xx, 1913, pp. 204–424, especially 389–90.

¹⁸ In a letter dated 10 June 1441 Filelfo agreed to lend his MS to Aurispa. See *Carteggio di Giovanni Aurispa*, ed. R. Sabbadini, Rome, 1931, p. 97.

¹⁹ Calderini (n. 17), p. 189. *Cf. Francisci Philelfi* . . . *Epistolarum familiarum libri XXXVII* . . ., Venice, 1502, f. 71.

²⁰ H. Omont, 'Inventaire des manuscrits grecs et latins donnés à S. Marc par le Cardinal Bessarion en 1468', *Revue des Bibliothèques*, IV, 1894, pp. 129–87, at 165.

²¹ L. Capra, 'Contributo a Guarino Veronese', *Italia mediovale e umanistica*, XIV, 1971, pp. 193–247, especially 244–7. Three Sextus manuscripts are listed in the inventory of the Medici Library made by Janos Lascaris at some time before the death of Lorenzo de' Medici in 1492. See K. Müller, 'Neue Mittheilungen über Janos Lascaris und die Mediceische Bibliothek', *Zentralblatt für Bibliothekswesen*, I, 1884, pp. 333–412. There is but a single Sextus MS listed, however, in the inventory made on 20 October 1495. See E. Piccolomini, *Intorno alle condizioni ed alle vicende della Libreria Medicea privata*, Florence, 1875, p. lxxxiii, item 174 [also printed in *Archivio storico italiano*, third series, XIX (1874) and XXI (1875)].

²² R. Devreesse, *Les Fonds grecs de la Bibliothèque Vaticane des origines à Paul V*, Vatican City, 1965 = Studi e testi, 244, p. 55.

²³ P. Kibre, *The Library of Pico della Mirandola*, New York, 1936, Nos. 673 and 104.4

²⁴ I. Maier, *Les Manuscrits d'Ange Politien*, Geneva 1965, pp. 117–23, 229.

²⁵ Venice, Marciana Lat. x, 267 (3640). This MS seems to contain nearly a complete translation of the *Outlines of Pyrrhonism*, as well as extracts from other works. The best printed description is in P. O. Kristeller, *Iter Italicum*, I, II, London and Leiden, 1963–1967, II, p. 252. I plan to study this manuscript in detail and to edit excerpts from it in a future publication. Popkin (n. 7) attributes the translation to Petrus de Montagnana but does not indicate upon what evidence he bases this attribution. As Professor Kristeller suggests to me (private communication), it will be necessary to compare the hand of this manuscript with other manuscripts known to be by Petrus. There were, however, several individuals who went by the name of Petrus de Montagnana. See P. Sambin, 'La formazione quattrocentesca della Biblioteca di S. Giovanni di Verdara in Padova', *Atti dell'Istituto Veneto di Scienze, Lettere ed Arti*, CXIV, 1955–56, pp. 263–80, at 267–8, 278–9. An interesting side note to this is that one of the men of this name was the father of Pietro Pomponazzi's second wife (Ludovica da Montagnana); see B. Nardi, *Studi su Pietro Pomponazzi*, Florence, 1965, pp. 214, 225, 227.

²⁶ This is brought out in chapter II of Gianfrancesco Pico's *Vita Savonarolae*. See the text in *Vitae selectorum aliquot virorum* . . ., ed. W. Bates, London, 1681, pp. 107–40, at 109. *Cf.* D. P. Walker, *The Ancient Theology*, London, 1972, pp. 59–62. I hope to look into this matter more carefully on another occasion.

²⁷ B. L. Ullman and P. A. Stadter, *The Public Library of Renaissance Florence: Niccolò Niccoli, Cosimo de' Medici and the Library of San Marco*, Padua, 1972, pp. 257 [No. 1142],

277 [M. 94]. This is a Greek MS, which is given the title *Sexti Empyrici Piromorum* [sic] *dogmatum libri decem* in the catalogue of *c.* 1499–1500 and is called *Pyrrhoniorum hypotyposes et Sextus Empiricus in Pyrrhonios* in the inventory of *c.* 1545. This MS therefore presumably contained all the extant works of Sextus. It is now apparently lost, for the editors of the above-cited work were unable to identify it with existing Sextus MSS.

[28] A rapid survey based on the lists of Mutschmann and Mau gives the following information on the dates of known Sextus MSS:

Tenth-century	one
Fourteenth-century	two
Fourteenth- or fifteenth-century	one
Fifteenth-century	seven
Sixteenth-century	twenty-one
Seventeenth-century	four

See Mutschmann (n. 7) and the same author's 'Die Überlieferung der Schriften des Sextus Empiricus', *Rheinisches Museum für Philologie*, new series, LXIV, 1909, pp. 245–83; *Sexti Empirici Opera*, III (*Adversus Mathematicos* I–VI), ed. J. Mau, Leipzig, 1961.

[29] Contained in MS Vat. Lat. 2990, ff. 266–381. For further details of the manuscript and knowledge of it see below.

[30] Among the forms of his name which we have encountered are the following: Joannes Laurentius, Joannes Venetus, Joannes de Venetiis, Joannes de Dionysiis, and Giovanni Lorenzi.

[31] My summary is based on the following sources, where references to further literature on Lorenzi, especially to contemporary or near-contemporary accounts, may be found: A. M. Albareda, 'Intorno alla fine del bibliotecario apostolico Giovanni Lorenzi', *Miscellanea Pio Paschini* [*Lateranum*, new series, *an.* 14–15], Rome, 1948–49, II, pp. 191–204; M. Bertòla (ed.), *I due primi registri di prestito della Biblioteca Apostolica Vaticana: codici Vaticani Latini 3964, 3966*, Vatican City, 1942, p. 84 and *passim*; G. Cammelli, *I dotti bizantini e le origini dell'umanesimo*: III. *Demetrio Calcondila*, Florence, 1954, *ad indicem*; G. Mercati, *Opere minori*, Rome, 1937–41 (= *Studi e Testi*, 76–80), IV, pp. 107–8 ['Una traduzione di Giovanni Lorenzi da Sesto Empirico', from *Bessarione*, XXXVI, 1920, 144–46], 437–61 ['Questenbergiana' from *Rendiconti Pontific. Accademia di Archeologia*, third series, VIII, 1933, pp. 249–69]; H. Noiret, 'Huit lettres inédites de Démétrius Chalcondyle', *Mélanges d'archéologie et d'histoire*, VII, 1887, pp. 472–500; P. de Nolhac, 'Giovanni Lorenzi bibliothécaire d'Innocent VIII', *Mélanges d'archéologie et d'histoire*, VIII, 1888, pp. 3–18; P. Paschini, 'Un ellenista veneziano del Quattrocento: Giovanni Lorenzi', *Archivio veneto*, fifth series, XXXII–XXXIII, 1943, pp. 114–46; P. Paschini, *Il carteggio fra il card. Marco Barbo e Giovanni Lorenzi (1481–90)*, Vatican City, 1948 (= *Studi e Testi*, 137); and V. Rossi, 'Niccolò Lelio Cosmico', *Giornale storico della letteratura italiana*, XIII, 1889, pp. 101–58, especially 106–7, 112–15. I have not been able to consult G. della Santa, 'Una lettera di G. Lorenzi a D. Calcondila', *La Scintilla*, IX, 1895.

[32] For a brief summary of Barbo's life and activities with further references see the article by G. Gualdo in *Dizionario Biografico degli Italiani*, VI, 1964, pp. 249–52.

[33] See especially the works of Albareda, Bertòla, Mercati, Nolhac and Paschini cited in n. 31 and P. O. Kristeller, *Iter Italicum* (n. 25) *ad indices*.

[34] Mercati (n. 31), IV, p. 452.

[35] On this see especially Paschini, 'Un ellenista . . .' (n. 31), p. 140, and G. Resta, 'Antonio Cassarino e le sue traduzioni da Plutarco e Platone', *Italia medioevale e umanistica*, II, 1959, pp. 207–83, at 230, 232, 236, 241.

[36] Several of Lorenzi's translations were published after his death. They are included in the following volumes: *Plutarchi Libellus aureus quomodo ab adulatore discernatur amicus. Joanne Laurentio Veneto viro doctissimo interprete nuper ad utilitatem legentium summa diligentia publicatus*, Romae, 1514; *Plutarchus Cheroneus de bona valitudine interprete Jo. Laurentio Veneto*, Romae, 1514; *Plutarchi opusuclum de nugacitate ab Ioanne Laurentio*

Veneto, (Romae, 1523; and *Plutarchus Chaeroneus. De curiositate. Item de nugacitate. Interprete Ioanne Laurentio Veneto*, Romae: in aedibus F. Minitii Calvi Novocomensis anno 1524 mense Aprili). The first three publications are given detailed descriptions in F. Ascarelli, *Annali tipografici di Giacomo Mazzocchi*, Florence, 1961, Nos. 73, 84, 163. I have been able to see none of them. The fourth I have inspected in the British Museum copy (shelf mark 8405.dd.29). It seems as though these printed versions are less well known to Lorenzi scholars than are the manuscript copies of his translation. See the previous note.

[37] R. Devreesse (n. 22), 55, 91, 129, 197, 251. Though the earlier inventories give us little detail concerning the specific writings contained in the MS, the Greek inventory says specifically that the *Contra mathematicos* were included. Devreesse was unable to identify the manuscript with any one currently in the Vatican.

[38] *Ibid.*, pp. 264–482.

[39] Bertòla (n. 31), p. 84. *Cf.* p. 61, n. 2, for information and further bibliography on Turriani.

[40] Mutschmann, 'Die Überlieferung . . .' (n. 28), pp. 246–8. This is the fullest listing of extant Sextus MSS, but is not complete, for Vat. Ross. 979 (XI, 129; gr. 24), a sixteenth-century MS which came to the Vatican with the De Rossi MSS after having been in the Biblioteca Angelica, is not included. For further information on that MS see G. Mercati, *Note per la storia di alcune biblioteche romane nei secoli XVI–XIX*, Vatican City, 1952 (= Studi e Testi, 164), pp. 31, 38. Further new MSS not known to Mutschmann at the time he wrote his article cited in n. 28 are added by him and other editors in the Teubner edition of Sextus.

[41] Barb. gr. 248 (*cf.* Mutschmann, *art. cit.*, 249) contains only the first two books of the *Contra mathematicos*.

[42] Mercati, *Opere minori* (n. 31), IV, pp. 452–3.

[43] F. Güldner, *Jakob Questenberg, ein deutscher Humanist in Rom* (Wernigerode a. H., 1905), p. 9. According to Mercati, *Opere minori*, IV, p. 437, n. 1, Güldner's thesis is also printed in *Zeitschrift des Harz-Vereins für Geschichte und Altertumskunde*, XXXVIII, 1905, though the separate printing gives no indication of this fact. There is a copy of the latter in the library of the Warburg Institute, London.

[44] *Opere minori*, IV, p. 453.

[45] The evidence is in Bertola (n. 31). Lorenzi borrowed various books up to 6 October 1485 (p. 35), but there were no further loans in his name until 24 December 1494 (p. 83). Lorenzi was designated Papal Librarian on 13 December 1485 (see Paschini, 'Un ellenista. . .', p. 127).

[46] I am not entirely happy with the probability of the argument here and must confess that I am not fully convinced by Mercati's supposition about Questenberg's handwriting. The first dated sample of July 1486, reproduced in Bertòla, p. 65, is quite different from what we find in the Sextus translation. The latter has certain stronger similarities to what is found in the first part of Vat. Lat. 2990 (especially the final 's' and the double 's' ligature). For a sample see Mercati, *Opere minori*, IV, p. 461, These, however, are matters which must be dealt with by paleographers more expert than myself.

[47] Cited above, n. 31.

[48] The MS is listed in Kristeller, *Iter Italicum*, II, p. 358, and cited by Popkin (n. 7), p. 17, n. 3, and Schmitt, *Gianfrancesco Pico* (n. 10), p. 49, n. 49.

[49] E.g. the quotations from Callimachus (I, 48; cod. f. 275) and Homer (I, 101; cod. f. 286v). Here and subsequently my references to Sextus give the book of the *Contra mathematicos* followed by the section number, which is printed in all standard editions of that author.

[50] One notable case is the long quotation from Homer at 1, 42. *Cf.* lines 71–9 of our text.

[51] E.g. lines 93–5 (1, 45), where it is argued that the Greek word ἰατρική ('medicine') is derived from ἰός ('poison' or 'arrow'). The translator adds to the text

' "iatrice" que latine "medicina" interpretatur' to aid his reader, but then writes 'sagittis' with no reference to the Greek original, so the whole point of the argument is lost. In the next section (1, 46) the same problem occurs, when 'geometria' is related to 'terra', a connection which comes across in Greek but is lost in Latin translation (*cf.* lines 97–8).

[52] Line 158.

[53] Sextus Empiricus, *Opera, graece et latine* . . . *notas addidit Jo. Albertus Fabricius*, Leipzig, 1718, p. 284.

[54] Lines 156, 160.

[55] *Acad.* II, xviii, 59, and II, vi, 17–18 and elsewhere in Cicero's works. On the general question see H.-J. Hartung, 'Ciceros Methode bei der Übersetzung griechischer philosophischer Termini', Hamburg University dissertation, 1970.

[56] Brief extracts based on the Paris MS are published in Jourdain (n. 7), pp. 204–5, and in the Teubner edition of Sextus Empiricus (n. 7), I, pp. 209–10.

[57] Mercati, *Opere minori*, IV, pp. 107–8, 452–3. *Cf.* Kristeller (n. 25), II, p. 358, who also gives *incipit*s and *explicit*s.

[58] Mercati, *Opere minori*, IV, p. 108.

[59] Certainly the dipthong is generally indicated in the other sections of Vat. Lat. 2990, which Mercati argued were written after the Sextus translation. See the sample in Mercati, *Opere minori*, IV, p. 461.

[60] *Ibid.*, pp. 452–3.

[61] Cited above in nn. 28 and 53; *Sextus Empiricus with an English Translation by R. G. Bury*, London, four vols., 1933–49.

PHILIP McNAIR *University of Birmingham*

14

POLIZIANO'S
HOROSCOPE

THIS ARTICLE ARISES from a little difficulty which I encountered in Florence during the summer of 1971, and I trust that the reader will forgive me if I write it in the first person.

Having been invited to edit a selection of the poems of Angelo Poliziano, I was beginning to embark on the customary biographical introduction when I discovered a very curious thing: there were two different traditions about the humanist poet's birth date which were quite independent of each other. More surprising still, nobody appeared to have noticed the fact before. Nor was this a question of remote history, or a survival from a less critical age, but a cleavage of opinion which seemed to bedevil the standard monographs of our own day; for without realising it every biographer of Poliziano in the last fifty years has retailed one or other of the two alleged dates of birth, without so much as a nod in the direction of the rival tradition or any acknowledgement of its existence.

To give an example from two homonymous scholars (one Italian and the other French) of high academic reputation who have written important books on Poliziano in the last decade: Bruno Maier, a distinguished professor and literary critic who teaches at Trieste, in an edition of Poliziano's poems published at Novara in 1969, gives the date of his birth categorically and without comment as 5 May 1454, as indeed he had already given it in an influential study which came out in 1956;[1] on the other hand, Ida Maïer of the Sorbonne, in her valuable volume devoted to the formation of Poliziano as a humanist poet, published by Droz of Geneva in 1966, states with equal assurance and absence of documentation that he was born on 14 July 1454.[2]

Here was an obstacle which lay at the very threshold of my biographical introduction, and obviously I should have to clear it out of my way before I could proceed. Between 5 May and 14 July 1454 yawned a discrepancy of ten weeks: which of the two dates was right, or were they both equally arbitrary and unfounded? How did the rival traditions arise, and what were their sources?

To judge from his writings, Poliziano himself appears to have been the source of neither tradition. Although fully conscious of the importance of dates in his adult life, he was not one of those poets who tell us all about the circumstances of their birth in their poems. Unlike his great friend Giovanni Pico della Mirandola, who described the conjunction of the planets at the moment of his own nativity in Latin verse, the author of *Le stanze per la giostra* does not record the name of the star he was born under; indeed, he is conspicuously reticent about his childhood in Montepulciano, darkened by the savage murder of his father in a blood feud—in marked contrast to a later Italian poet, Giovanni Pascoli, in whose verse the assassination of his father became a recurring theme. As far as I know, the only time Poliziano refers to his birth is in the fifth stanza of the first book of his unfinished masterpiece, where he claims that he was consecrated to Lorenzo de' Medici from the cradle:

> Deh, sarà mai che con piú alte note,
>   se non contasti al mio volar fortuna,
>   lo spirto delle membra, che devote
>   ti fuor da' fati insin già dalla cuna,
>   risuoni te dai Numidi a Boote,
>   dagl' Indi al mar che 'l nostro celo imbruna,
>   e posto il nido in tuo felice ligno,
>   di roco augel diventi un bianco cigno?

Yet if it had been left to Messer Angelo to choose there is little doubt that he would have preferred to have been born in the first week of May, in time to gather 'la bella rosa del giardino mentre è piú fiorita'; by the same token, if dating his birth were a matter of personal choice we could well understand that a citizen of France such as Ida Maïer might prefer her *Fête Nationale* to the day of Napoleon's death; but no such fanciful preference springs to mind to account for the choice of 5 May by a modern Italian editor of the humanist poet's *cose volgari* such as Bruno Maier. The facts of the case are, of course, rather more prosaic. It is the privilege of scholars to build upon each other's work, for scholarship is nothing if not cumulative; and as I began to probe beneath the surface I discovered that Bruno Maier and Ida Maïer were only the latest spokesmen of two established biographical positions, and that the two traditions they represent were parallel lines which not only never meet but never even catch a glimpse of one another.[3]

When I realised this bizarre fact, I mentioned it to Professor Alessandro Perosa of Florence University, who is without doubt one of the two most erudite Poliziano scholars alive in Italy today. I asked him if he knew anything about this difference of opinion regarding so cardinal a question as the date of the poet's birth: he answered no, he had never noticed anything, but had always taken the birth date for granted. I also consulted our congratuland himself, who was visiting Florence in the latter part of June 1971. From our conversation it was evident that here was a neglected corner of the field of Poliziano studies which should be explored. So I began to investigate the two rival traditions, and this is what I found.

The source of the 5 May tradition—which had been supported by no less a critic than Gaetano Trombadori—I traced with little difficulty to an un-documented statement in a book on Poliziano which was published as recently as the first world war. Its author was Pietro Micheli, who was born in 1865 and taught Italian literature in his native Livorno until his retirement in 1927. His modest claim to scholarship consists in more than twenty publications, including two novels, some verses entitled *Fantasia*, a few occasional pieces such as *I cani nella letteratura* and *Letteratura che non ha senso* (chastely catalogued in the National Library in Florence as *Letteratura che non ha sesso*), and a panegyric on wine. His little book *La vita e le opere di Angelo Poliziano* was published in the *Biblioteca degli Studenti* at Livorno in 1917. On its first page Micheli states: 'Angelo Ambrogini nacque a Montepulciano il 5 maggio 1454 [. . .]': what inspired him to do so we shall probably never know. (In Florence's Biblioteca Marucelliana I found the inscribed copy of his book which he presented to Isidoro Del Lungo, the prince of Poliziano's biographers; but the aged author of *Florentia* had made no marginal comment on Micheli's hieratic pronouncement.)

Does Poliziano himself offer any oblique confirmation or denial of the 5 May tradition? The only clue that I have discovered in his writings is negative. For most men their fortieth birthday is an event which does not pass unobserved, yet we find him writing to Piero Dovizi from his Villa Bruscoli at Fontelucente on 5 May 1494 without any hint that this day marked a personal milestone for him, which would have been unusual in one so date-conscious as the mature Poliziano.[4]

At first sight, the 14 July tradition seemed to have an immeasurably stronger case, for it boasts a long line of editors, biographers and critics of Poliziano in its support, including such heavyweights as Giosue Carducci (1863), Vincenzo Nannucci (1814) and Pierantonio Serassi (1747). But I had to go back to 1736 to find any bibliographical indication of the evidence on which the tradition is based. In his monumental *Historia vitae et in literas meritorum Angeli Politiani*, published at Leipzig that year, Friedrich Otho Mencke tells us: 'Natum esse Politianum anno C[hristi] MCCCCLIV, pridie Idus Quintiles, Scriptores omnes inter se conveniunt.' He annotates the second half of this statement with the affirmation 'Neque de anno, neque de die quicquam ab ullo scriptorem movetur dubii', and for both halves he furnishes a bibliography of nine works of reference, the earliest of which issued from the press in 1580.[5]

In that year Abraham Bucholzer (1529–84), in amplification of his *Isagoge chronologica* of 1577, published at Frankfurt an der Oder his Protestant *Index chronologicus a mundo condito ad annum Christi 1580 deductus*, the fruit of seventeen years' work, which was brought up to date—first by his son Gottfried and then by his grandson Abraham—in successive editions until the year 1634. In the 1616 edition I came across the following entry recorded under the year 5424 from the foundation of the world (which, according to the chronological premises adopted, converts at A.D. 1454): 'ANGELVS POLITIANVS Philosophus, Poeta & Orator, qui Herodianum latine inter-pretatus est'—it is quaint what famous people were famous for in earlier centuries—'& cuius Epistolae extant, nascitur 14 Iulii, hora 1. minutis 28. post merid. in monte Politiano Hetruriae.' This commendably exact notice is followed by the one cryptic and abbreviated reference 'Cardan'.[6]

That was just the clue I had been looking for. In another connection I had already acquired an interest in the life of Gerolamo Cardano (1501–76), the mathematician, astrologer and physician from Pavia who was born two years before Nostradamus and died ten years after him, for he gives his name not only to the cubic equation but also to two humdrum parts of the common-or-garden motor car. Now I began to search his works, which in the Lyons edition of 1663 fill ten folio volumes, and in the fifth I came upon his astrological case book *De exemplis centum geniturarum*, first published at Nürnberg in 1547 (the year, incidentally, in which Nostradamus began his series of predictions). As its title suggests, this work purports to give the horoscopes of 100 notable people or events. They turn out to be an odd assortment in which Cicero and Erasmus rub shoulders with Luther, Dürer, Charles V, Paul III, George of Trebizond, the Effoeminati, the Oculus Privatus, Cardano himself and other members of his family, big and little.[7]

Sandwiched between the nativities of Andreas Vesalius and Jacob Moltzer at No. 94 of the hundred I found the horoscope of Angelo Poliziano, which gives the time of his birth with startling precision as '1454. die 14 Iulij, hora 1. mi. 28. Secun. 12.' (fig. 14.1).[8] Here is the source of the 14 July tradition, and indeed of the common acceptance of 1454 as the year of Poliziano's birth, for Bucholzer (whether father, son or grandson) relies on Cardano, Mencke on Bucholzer, and every subsequent biographer until 1917 on Mencke.

While I was still studying this horoscope I received an invitation to address a conference on humanism at Montepulciano, so I thought to myself, what more appropriate topic could I treat than the date of birth of that city's most famous son? (In parenthesis I should say that the little Tuscan town is not so proud of her poet as we might imagine; if you ask the average *poliziano*—as every native of Montepulciano is called to this day—to name the illustrious men and women from his city's past he will be sure to answer, 'St Agnese, St Robert Bellarmine and Pope Marcellus II,' in that order, devoutly forgetting the humanist who died in so strong an odour of unsanctity in September 1494.)

In preparing my paper for this conference I realised that the crux of the argument must be the teasing problem of interpretation which makes Poliziano's horoscope unique: what on earth did its caster mean by 'Secun. 12.'? It is a curious fact that out of the whole series of 100 genitures contained in Cardano's *De exemplis centum geniturarum*, plus more than fifty further examples scattered through his other astrological writings, it is only in Poliziano's case that this expression is used. At first, quite naturally, I took it to mean 'secunda duodecim', and understood the caster to be pinpointing the poet's birth at 1.28 *ante meridiem* and 12 seconds.[9] But I was aware that even in English the word 'second' is polysemous (as Dante would say) and has proved a punster's pitch.[10] The Latin abbreviation, too, seemed to be patient of other interpretations; and the more I thought about it, the more

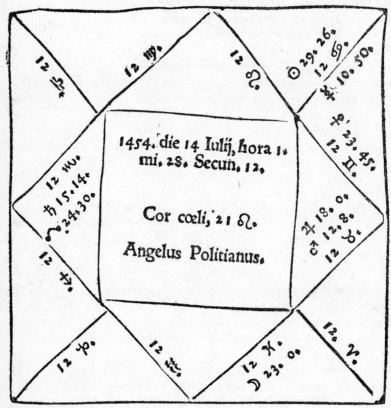

HIBR. CARDANI LIB.
XCIIII.

1454. die 14 Iulij, hora 1. mi. 28. Secun. 12.

Cor cœli, 21 ♌.

Angelus Politianus.

Hic Regulum habuit in corde cœli, & ob id clarissimus fuit temporibus suis. Saturnus in ascendente, pertinaciam cum draconis capite dedit in studendo, unde clarus orator, mellifluus poeta, eloquentissimus scriptor euasit, ut cum Plinio secundo Cæcilio, epistolis suis fœliciter decertet. Mars dominus ascendentis, cum Ioue, in septima, fœlicem ac perpetuam moram extra patriam decernit. Mercurius optime positus erat in trino ascendentis, & sextili domini illius, Luna etiam in sextili Iouis, in trinoق Solis. Sol etiã in sextili Iouis, & Luna in trino Saturni, omnesق in aqueis signis, gloriam quantam quisق alius, & in uita & post mortem, donec magna coniunctio in aqueis signis, præstant, gratiaق illum apud Principes euehunt, mirum tamen est, si articulari morbo non laborauit. Mortuus est anno 1509, die 24 Septembris.

FIG. 14.1   Poliziano's horoscope, from G. Cardano's *De exemplis centum geniturarum,* Nürnberg, 1547, f. 178v.

preposterous the idea appeared that this sixteenth-century astrologer should be making an exception of Poliziano, uniquely calculating *his* birth in terms of seconds as though it were a lunar eclipse. Therefore when I gave my paper that August I argued that 'Secun.' must be an abbreviation of 'secundum', which the author was using in the familiar Latin sense of 'following', and that 'secundum duodecim' here meant *after midday*, as we have seen Bucholzer understood it.[11]

After I had spoken, however, there followed a lively discussion on this point, and I found that I was in the presence of experts—such as Professor Gino Arrighi, the eminent mathematician from Lucca—who were of the firm and insistent opinion that the caster of the horoscope here means *twelve seconds*. One palaeographer said that 'Secun.' was an impossible abbreviation of 'secundum' in the sense of 'following', and could only be unabbreviated as 'secunda' or 'secundae'. In short, I was persuaded to reconsider the entire evidence on which I had based my argument, and in doing so I have had to modify my conclusions in the light of the following three discoveries.

First, by controlling Cardano's use of the abbreviation 'secun.' in some of his other writings I have found that it is invariably employed for seconds in the measurement of time;[12] hence it now seems to me reasonably certain that 'Secun. 12.' in Poliziano's horoscope means precisely *twelve seconds* rather than *post meridiem*.

My next discovery is nothing more than a hint from horological history. For the *second*, as the sixtieth part of a minute, was the notional invention of the Babylonians, and was, of course, known to exist in theory during the Middle Ages, although it could not be measured accurately in practice— at least not domestically. Medieval scientists distinguished between the *minuta prima*, which we call the minute, and the *minuta secunda* (or *minutum secundum*, for the neuter was also used), which we call the second. As late as 1670 we find John Wilkins, Bishop of Chester, writing 'Four flames of equal magnitude will be kept alive for the space of sixteen second minutes'.[13] (Radiotelevisione Italiana still maintains this medieval terminology, and will announce after the commercials for shampoo and *pasta* in the morning, 'Sono le ore sette e tre minuti primi'.) The first known mention of seconds in English goes back to 1391, when Geoffrey Chaucer, in *A Treatise on the Astrolabe*, after naming the twelve signs of the zodiac, adds, 'But understand wel that these degres of signes ben everich of hem considered of 60 mynutes, and every mynute of 60 secundes, and so furth into smale fraccions infinite, as saith Alkabucius'.[14]

In practice, however, seconds could not be determined or recorded with any accuracy in a domestic setting until long after the lifetime of Cardano, who died in 1576. Although it was before 1602 that Galileo discovered the value of the isochronism of the pendulum for the exact measurement of time,[15] and demonstrated it in 1641 by devising the first mechanism to employ a pendulum for controlling clockwork, yet clocks with seconds hands were not in regular production until after 1670, when William Clement introduced his anchor escapement, which made it practicable to market domestic clocks housing a pendulum with a period of a second. Nevertheless the very first timepiece known to have recorded seconds—with whatever degree of approximation—was constructed before Galileo was born, and it must surely be accounted a striking coincidence that it was made in the same place and about the same time as the publication of Poliziano's horoscope in the *De exemplis centum geniturarum*. This exquisite example of mid-sixteenth-century German craftsmanship is described by Lloyd as 'a little chamber clock about nine and a half inches high, dating from about 1550, which is the earliest known to record hours, minutes and seconds on separate dials'.[16] It is preserved in the Germanisches National-Museum in Nuremberg, the probable city of its manufacture.

In the lifetime of Cardano Nuremberg (with Augsburg as its closest rival) was the world's leading centre of clock making, with a wide reputation for skill and ingenuity. Here Peter Henlein was generally believed to have invented the pocket or portable watch (the Nuremberg egg) about 1510, until Professor Enrico Morpurgo proved in 1954 that the *orologio tascabile* had been in use in Italy in the second half of the fifteenth century.[17] And although other centres came to the fore when the city declined in the seventeenth century, a generation after Cardano's death Fynes Moryson of Cadeby, that inveterate traveller and quondam Fellow of Peterhouse, Cambridge, could still write, 'I must confesse that the Germans of Nurenberg in those parts are esteemed the best workmen for clockes and some like thinges.'[18]

Indeed, in this enquiry all roads seem to lead to Nuremberg, which was a centre not only of clock making but also of mathematics, astrology and scientific publishing: and of all the scientific publishers in Nuremberg the most enterprising and prestigious was Johannes Petreius, alias Hans Peterlein, who was born about 1497, graduated from the new University of Wittenberg, and plied his press in the city of Dürer from the early 1520s until his death in 1550. His output proves his industry. Beside the editions of Erasmus, Luther, Melanchthon and Zwingli that jostled one another through those busy years we find the astrological treatises of Camerarius, Gaurico and Regiomontanus. Great classics of Italian humanism also issued from his press: in 1532 came Pico's *Conclusiones nongentae*, and in 1538 the text of Poliziano' *Nutritia*, with a learned commentary by Johann Ludwig Brassicanus (1509–49).[19] But by far his greatest claim to perpetual fame is that in 1543 he first gave the world one of the most epoch-making volumes in the history of the universe, the *De revolutionibus orbium coelestium libri VI* by Nicholas Copernicus.

Cardano's association with Nuremberg began in 1539 in the following way. Earlier that year his *Practica arithmetice & mensurandi singularis* had been printed by Bernardino Caluschi in Milan with a *cri de cœur* from the author that a prophet was not without honour save in his own country, and with the open hint that he had other books to publish. The invitation was taken up by the canny Petreius, who offered to print any manuscript that Cardano cared to send him. The offer was brought to Milan by Andreas Osiander (1498–1552), the leading Nuremberg Reformer whose niece Thomas Cranmer had married in the clockwork city seven years before (and was said to have smuggled into the celibate realm of Henry VIII in a chest). Not only would Petreius print but Osiander would exercise a watching editorial brief on any of Cardano's potential publications, just as four years later he was to pilot through the press the *magnum opus* of Copernicus, adding in the process the infamous notice *Ad lectorem de hypothesibus huius operis* which prefaces the treatise. Of his acceptance of this double offer Cardano later recorded (in the *Libellus de libris propriis, cui titulus est, Ephemerus*) that it was the beginning of his glory.[20]

Petreius began to publish Cardano's writings in 1543, when he brought out his *Libelli duo* (later reprinted in his *Libelli quinque*); the following year came his *De sapientia libri quinque*, and in 1545 his greatest mathematical work under the title *Artis magnae, sive de regulis algebraicis, liber unus*: the dedication is to Osiander. Two years later it was Petreius who published his astrological case book *De exemplis centum geniturarum*, and hence printed Poliziano's horoscope for the first time.

Cardano's fascination with clockwork is plain to anyone who scans his writings. It is apparent from one of his major treatises, the *De subtilitate libri XXI*, which was first published in part by the firm of Petreius at Nuremberg, and thereafter more fully at Paris in 1551. It is even more apparent from his *De rerum varietate libri XVII* (Basel, 1557), the forty-seventh chapter of the ninth book of which is largely concerned with clockwork and proffers instructions in clock making.[21] As its name suggests, the cardan shaft—a method of mechanical drive where the two centres are not in line—was his invention, and was utilised in the astronomical clock which Eberdt Baldwein, alias Eberhart Baldwin, made for Landgraf Wilhelm IV of Hesse between 1559 and 1561.[22] Clocks also had their place in Cardano's practice of medicine: in 1552 he came to Scotland and prescribed a strict dietary regimen for John Hamilton, the last Catholic Archbishop of St Andrews, whom he treated for asthma; but no regimen is effective unless it is adhered to punctiliously, 'ideo bonum erit ut habeat exactissimum horologium et grande, nam omnes principes in Italia habent et etiam plura et bona'.[23]

In view of this fascination with clockwork and association with Nuremberg we might have argued that the two events—the casting of Poliziano's horoscope and the construction of the Nuremberg three-dialled clock which recorded seconds—were connected by some invisible cardan shaft, and that the unique expression 'secunda duodecim' in the one betrayed the caster's compulsive interest in the seconds hand of the other. But there would have been two fatal flaws in our argument, for first there is no record that Cardano ever went to Nuremberg in person,[24] and secondly the horoscope of Poliziano which he included in his *De exemplis* was not cast by him.

'The sources for his nativities have never been investigated, and it is not to be excluded that in this case he is drawing on an earlier unprinted horoscope which has not yet come to light.' So I wrote in June 1971.[25] Now that unprinted source *has* come to light. I made this third and most radical discovery when I studied his case book again at greater length and with

greater care in January 1973. Beneath the horoscope of Cornelius Agrippa
(No. 67 of the hundred) I found the following admission which had escaped
me before:

Iam non desino dicere, cuncta necessitate quadam evenire, dum enim de adiiciendis
genituris cogitarem, forte fortuna Georgius Ioachimus in Italiam ex Germania venit,
vir humanus et in mathematicis haud mediocriter eruditus, sed in primis primo more
officiosus ac syncerus. Hic clarorum virorum genituras, quas secum habebat, mihi
obtulit ultro: Vesalii, Ioannis Monteregii, Cornelii Agrippae, Politiani, Iacobi
Mycilli, Osiandri: quarum aliquot addidi huic operi ad centenarium explendum:
dubias enim omnes reieci.[26]

Here, if one sought it, was the living link with Nuremberg. As a mathematical genius who turned his hand to astrology Georg Joachim Rheticus
(1514–74) was at least Cardano's equal, and played an even more important
role in the history of science.[27] Born on 16 February 1514 at Feldkirch in
Vorarlberg (in the Roman province of Rhaetia—hence his cognomen
Rhäticus, Rhetikus or Rheticus), at the age of fourteen he went to study
under Oswald Myconius (1488–1552) at Zurich before entering the
University of Wittenberg in 1532. As a student he so distinguished himself in
mathematics that Melanchthon appointed him to a lectureship in 1536, the
year of his graduation. It was during the first two years he lectured in
Wittenberg that Rheticus became convinced of the truth of the Copernican
theory, which was anathema to Luther, Melanchthon and the Protestant
Establishment.

In October 1538 he set out on his travels. First he went to Nuremberg,
where he called on Petreius and the globe-making astrologer Johann
Schöner (1477–1547), at the same time seeking the acquaintance of the
mathematician Johann Hartmann (1489–1545), who had lived many years
in Rome. From Nuremberg he journeyed to Ingolstadt, and from Ingolstadt
to Tübingen, where he arrived in January 1539.

Still early in 1539, Rheticus went east to visit Copernicus at Frauenburg in
Prussia. He arrived unheralded and uninvited to become not only the great
man's most enthusiastic disciple but also his most effective public relations
officer. For in March 1540 he had printed by Johann von Werden in Danzig
the first considerable published account of the Copernican theory, and it was
probably the favourable reception with which this *Narratio prima* met that
persuaded Copernicus to allow his revolutionary treatise to be printed in
the closing year of his life.

Copernicus entrusted his manuscript to his friend Bishop Tiedemann
Giese (1480–1550), who in turn forwarded it to Rheticus, who in October
1541 had returned to lecture in Wittenberg. In May of the following year
Rheticus paid a second visit to Nuremberg, where he arranged for its
publication by Petreius; but since he was called to a Chair at Leipzig that
autumn he handed over the responsibility of editing the treatise to Osiander.

In the late summer of 1545 Rheticus began his long visit to Italy, where his
beloved Copernicus had passed nine years of his early manhood. He called
on Luca Gaurico (1476–1558)—all too optimistically called 'the last of the

astrologers'[28]—and he stayed with Gerolamo Cardano in Milan. The stay was evidently of some little duration, for the two mathematicians had much in common: many hours of it were spent in playing chess (and probably dice, for Cardano was an inveterate and self-confessed gambler). Rheticus's biographer regrets that there is practically nothing to show for this period of his life,[29] but in his *Aphorisms* Cardano has left us this lively description of their common interest in horoscopy:

Cum Georgius Ioachimus Rheticus, syderalium motuum peritissimus, Mediolani moram per hos dies trahens, audisset à me saepius, posse hac arte, nuper à me inuenta & tradita, oblata genitura, de figura corporis, de moribus, de magnis euentibus, incognito illo, cuius esset genesis, multa ac praeclara praedici, periculumque iam bis, sucae dente euentu, feasset, tandem die 21 Martij, 1546 ad me uenit, cum hac genitura,[30] suppresso nomine, ac homine, cum neque ipse tum nomen sciret, rogauitque, ut aliquid de ea dicerem, magnum in ea euentum acadisse dicens: Tertiam autem partem Aquarij in ascendente statuerat, non 17 cum non ex dato tempore, sed iuxta sua placita, tempus contraxisset. Tunc ego inspiciens dixi, uir hic Saturninus est, ac melancholicus, tum ille, unde hoc? tum ego, quia ascendenti praeest Saturnus, & illius oppositam partem tenens, ipsum respicit, estque Saturnus in Leone, qui tristitiam auget. Inde subiungo, Habet autem blanda uerba & leuia, uideturque mitis & placidus. Tum ille, cur hoc? Quia (respondi ego) Aquarius humanum est signum (etc).[31]

Like Cardano, Rheticus was a practising astrologer from the outset of his career. When he was lecturing at Wittenberg from 1536 to 1538 one of his students called Nikolaus Gugler took notes of three of his lectures. The third of these was devoted to astrology, and was illustrated by a series of thirty-two nativities of famous people from the Bible, secular history and his own times: one was an autohoroscope of the lecturer himself, another was of Albrecht Dürer—significantly different from the example given in Cardano's case book.[32] It is an interesting fact that Poliziano's horoscope is not included in this series contained in Gugler's notes, which are preserved in the Bibliothèque Nationale in Paris.[33] And yet when Rheticus visited Italy in 1545 he brought with him a collection of nativities of various people, of whom Cardano (as we have seen) names Vesalius, Regiomontanus, Cornelius Agrippa, Poliziano, Jacob Mycillus and Osiander:[34] and of these six, only Poliziano was Italian.

It is not very likely that Rheticus himself cast the horoscope for Poliziano, as the occasion would hardly have arisen for him to do so; and even if it had arisen, it may reasonably be supposed that the relevant data would not have been available to him. What, then, was his channel of supply? When, where and from whom did he obtain the nativity which he offered to Cardano? As it does not figure in Gugler's notes, the time of its acquisition would appear to have been between 1538 and 1545. The place may well have been Nuremberg, which had welcomed many travellers from Rome, Florence and Milan since the birth of Poliziano. Here Johann Müller (1436–76), better known as Regiomontanus, from his native town of Königsberg in Franconia, had settled in 1471, well versed in the ways of Italy, where he had spent seven years;[35] and although it is improbable that this great astronomer-mathematician—who drew nativities in his day[36]—brought back the horoscope of the 'teen-age Poliziano, nevertheless he was only one of numberless scientists and scholars who had visited both Florence and Nuremberg between 1454 and 1545.

Indeed, the possible channels through which Rheticus may have received Poliziano's horoscope are legion and invite speculation. It may have come into his hands from Hartmann, or from Schöner, who in 1539 presented Gugler with the horoscope he had cast for him four years before;[37] it may have reached Nuremberg through Brassicanus (whose 1538 commentary on Poliziano's *Nutritia* we have already noted), for he had travelled in Italy and was a Doctor of Laws from Padua. But there is a still more attractive hypothesis open to us: Rheticus may have obtained it from Copernicus, who had entered the University of Bologna in 1496 and is said to have lodged in the house of the Professor of Astronomy, Domenico Maria da Novara (1454–1504).

But speculation remains speculation in default of evidence; what we know for certain is that nativities pullulated in that second half of the fifteenth century in which Poliziano was born. Practically every man of consequence in Latin Christendom willy-nilly had his horoscope cast, and many such horoscopes have survived. Perhaps nowhere was the practice of horoscopy in greater evidence than in Medicean Florence. It is curious that in no collection that I have examined have I found a nativity for Lorenzo il Magnifico himself, but Paolo Giovio (1483–1552) tells us that Marsilio Ficino, 'who was an astrologer of great authority', cast the horoscope of Lorenzo's son Giovanni and foretold that one day he would become Pope.[38] Other members of the Platonic Academy followed his lead. Pico's horoscope was drawn by Girolamo Benivieni, who also cast his own.[39] In 1481 Cristoforo Landino, commenting on Dante's *Veltro*, published his own prophecy of a major reform in Christendom from the conjunction of Saturn and Jupiter on 25 November 1484 'a hore xiii et minuti xli'—missing Luther's birth by a mere twelve months and fifteen days.[40] Besides these known facts there could be said to exist an inherent probability that the mutual casting of horoscopes was the kind of activity which enlivened the leisure of the Ficino circle.

Poliziano's horoscope is more likely to have been cast during his lifetime than after his death, and it is more likely to have been cast by Ficino—who hailed the 'Homericus adolescens' in 1473—than by anyone else. But whether it was Ficino, Landino or Benivieni who cast it, the horoscope seems to have disappeared without trace until Rheticus gave it to Cardano fifty-one years after Poliziano's death.

Did its presumed fifteenth-century caster record the time of Poliziano's birth in seconds? This seems to me most unlikely. There were four schools of thought among practising astrologers of the Renaissance on the moment of parturition, according to whether the time of birth was taken from the appearance of the head, the emergence of the feet, the cutting of the cord, or the first cry of the baby; but in 1454 it would have been impracticable to have recorded any of these events in terms of seconds, nor would any fifteenth-century horoscopist have attempted to do so. It is more likely that Cardano and Rheticus, who evidently enjoyed experimenting with horoscopes together, added this problematical detail of 'Secun. 12.' as a *jeu d'esprit* in Milan in 1545–46. Or was it a Protestant printer's protest in the publishing house of Petreius?

On what shaky foundations stand so many of our inherited historical assumptions! And yet the horoscope, for all its bogus pretensions, could be the historian's friend; for in an age when both ordinary and extraordinary people believed in astrology (encouraged by philosophers as prestigious as Pomponazzi, scientists as illustrious as Kepler), they had strong motive for recording with some care the time of birth of their children, and the horoscope drawn in reasonable proximity to the event constitutes more cast-iron historical evidence, and more cogent historical testimony, than the biographical memoir or even the baptismal register.[41]

NOTES

[1] A. Poliziano, *Stanze per la giostra, Orfeo—Rime*, ed. B. Maier, Novara, 1969, p. 23; B. Maier, 'Agnolo Poliziano' in *Letteratura italiana: I Maggiori*, Milan ,1956, p. 245.

[2] I. Maïer, *Ange Politien: la formation d'un poète humaniste (1469–80)*, Geneva, 1966, p. 419.

[3] The substance of this paragraph is taken from my article 'On the date of Poliziano's birth' in *Civiltà dell'umanesimo: Atti del VI, VII, VIII Convegno del Centro di Studi Umanistici 'A. Poliziano'*, Florence, 1972, pp. 179–99, which contains some of the material in the first part of the present contribution.

[4] A. Poliziano, *Prose volgari inedite*, ed. I. Del Lungo, Florence, 1867, pp. 83–4.

[5] F. O. Mencke, *Historia*, Leipzig, 1736, pp. 21–2.

[6] *Index chronologicus, monstrans annorum seriem a mundo condito usque ad annum nati Christi 1616*, Frankfurt a. O., 1616, p. 406.

[7] *Hieronymi Cardani [...] libelli quinque [...] I. De supplemento Almanach: II. De restitutione temporum & motuum coelestium: III. De iudicijs geniturarum: IIII. De reuolutionibus: V. De exemplis centum geniturarum*, Nürnberg, 1547. This book was placed on the Spanish *Index* of 1559. On Gerolamo Cardano see H. Morley, *Jerome Cardan: the Life of Girolamo Cardano, of Milan, Physician*, London, two vols., 1854; L. Thorndike, *A History of Magic and Experimental Science*, New York, six vols., 1923–41, V, pp. 563–79; A. Bellini, *Gerolamo Cardano e il suo tempo (sec. XVI)*, Milan, 1947; O. Ore, *Cardano the Gambling Scholar*, Princeton, N.J., 1953; A. Mondini, *Gerolamo Cardano: matematicomedico e filosofo naturale*, Rome, 1962.

[8] *De exemplis centum geniturarum*, ed. cit., f. 178v (the whole page is shown here in our reproduction). The legend reads: 'Hic Regulum habuit in corde coeli, et ob id clarissimus fuit temporibus suis. Saturnus in ascendente, pertinaciam cum draconis capite dedit in studendo, unde clarus orator, mellifluus poeta, eloquentissimus scriptor evasit, ut cum Plinio secundo Caecilio, epistolis suis foeliciter decertet. Mars dominus ascendentis, cum Iove, in septima, foelicem ac perpetuam moram extra patriam decernit. Mercurius optime positus erat in trino ascendentis, et sextili domini illius, Luna etiam in sextili Iovis, in trinoque Solis. Sol etiam in sextili Iovis, et Luna in trino Saturni, omnesque in aqueis signis, gloriam quantam quisque alius, et in vita et post mortem, donec magna coniunctio in aqueis signis, praestant, gratiaque illum apud Principes evehunt, mirum tamen est, si articulari morbo non laboravit. Mortuus est anno 1509, die 24 Septembris.' A smaller-scale reproduction of this horoscope was printed in *Hieronymi Cardani Opera omnia*, ed. Carolus Sponius (Charles Spon), Lyons, 1663, V, p. 500. Other horoscopes of Poliziano, probably derived from this one but differing in detail, in which 'Secun. 12.' is replaced by 'P.M.', will be

found in Luca Gaurico, *Tractatus astrologicus*, Venice, 1552, f. 64v (reproduced in an altered form in Gaurico's *Opera astrologica*, II, Basel, 1575, p. 1663) and Francesco Giuntini, *Speculum astrologiae*, I, Lyons, 1581, p. 462. There is also a manuscript horoscope of Poliziano, among others which almost certainly derive from Cardano's *De exemplis*, at the back of a copy of *Albohali Arabis astrologi antiquissimi ac clarissimi de iudicijs natiuitatum liber unus* (ed. J. Heller), Nuremberg, 1546, preserved in the Bibliothèque Nationale in Paris (see L. Thorndike, *op. cit.*, VI, p. 105).

[9] In his *De exemplis* Cardano as a rule either uses the twenty-four-hour clock (No. 54: 'hora 17 horologij'; No. 55: 'hora 23 horologij'; No. 59: 'ho. 17 mi. 30 horologij') or indicates the second half of the day by *post meridiem*.

[10] As, for example, in Thomas Hood's *The Duel*, in which two men agree to fight over a girl,

> But first they sought a friend apiece,
> This pleasant thought to give—
> When they were dead, they thus should have
> Two seconds still to live.

See T. Hood, *Whimsicalities and Warnings*, ed. Julian Ennis, London, 1970, p. 44.

[11] My paper was called 'La data di nascita del Poliziano' and was given in Italian; an English version of it entitled 'On the date of Poliziano's birth' appears as the article already cited in n. 3.

[12] For instance, in chapter XI of his *De supplemento Almanach*, Nuremberg, 1547, p. 19B, we find the typical passage: 'Exemplum, sit Luna in gra. 19. min. 25. capricorni, & sit in longitudine media, ubi semidiameter eius est, mi. 16. secun. 30. & in gradibus 19. mi. 8. capricorni, est borealior sinistrae spatulae sagittarij. Differunt igitur in min. 17. & quia semidiameter Lunae est min. 16. secun. 30. & semidiameter stellae magnitudinis quintae, est min. 1. erit igitur longitudo semidiametrorum min. 17. secun. 30. & hoc est plus minutis distantiae qui sunt 17. igitur dicemus quod se tangunt.'

[13] Quoted in H. Alan Lloyd, *The Collector's Dictionary of Clocks*, London, 1964, p. 156.

[14] Part I, para. 8, in *The Works of Geoffrey Chaucer*, ed. F. N. Robinson, Boston, Mass., second edition, 1957, p. 547.

[15] But not when he was an undergraduate at Pisa in the 1580s, as was claimed by his first biographer, Vincenzio Viviani. 'Following the fashionable hagiographical style of his day, Viviani seriously misrepresented Galileo's early interests by claiming that he had discovered the isochronism of the pendulum and the law of uniform acceleration of falling bodies by performing experiments while still a student at Pisa'; see William R. Shea, *Galileo's Intellectual Revolution*, London, 1972, p. 3.

[16] H. Alan Lloyd, *Some outstanding Clocks over Seven Hundred Years, 1250–1950*, London, 1958, p. 38: plates 32 (a) and (b) between pp. 32 and 33 reproduce photographs of this clock.

[17] E. Morpurgo, *L'origine dell'orologio tascabile*, Rome, 1954.

[18] Quoted from Moryson's *Itinerary* in Carlo M. Cipolla, *Clocks and Culture, 1300–1700*, London, 1967, p. 62 (reprinted with *Guns and Sails* in Carlo M. Cipolla, *European Culture and Overseas Expansion*, Harmondsworth, 1970, p. 137).

[19] *In Angeli Politiani Nutritia commentarii*, auth. Ioan. Ludouico Brassicano iuris utriusque consulto.

[20] *Hieronymi Cardani Opera omnia*, I, p. 104: '[. . .] cum tunc esset Andreas Osiander Norimbergae, vir Latinae, Grecae, Hebraicaeque linguae peritus, tum Typographus Ioan. Petreius, bonis literis, si quis alius, fauens, inito consilio totis viribus mecum agere coeperunt, vt aliquod opus illis traderem vt imprimerent. Atque ita initium gloriae nostrae, si qua deinceps fuit, hinc ortum habuit. Ergo primum librum De astrorum iudiciis auctum edidi.'

[21] Liber IX, cap. XLVII, pp. 362–72: Cardano's clearest diagram of clockwork is on p. 365.

²² See H. Alan Lloyd, *The Collector's Dictionary of Clocks*, pp. 32–3.

²³ *Hieronymi Cardani Opera omnia*, IX, p. 228. Cardano's cure was triumphantly successful: Hamilton was free from asthma when he mounted the scaffold at Stirling in 1571.

²⁴ The city is not mentioned in chapter XXIX of his autobiography, which gives the itinerary of his travels.

²⁵ The article cited in n. 3, p. 189.

²⁶ *De exemplis centum geniturarum*, f. 163r.

²⁷ See K. H. Burmeister, *Georg Joachim Rhetikus, 1514–74. Eine Bio-Bibliographie*, Wiesbaden, three vols., 1967.

²⁸ See E. Percopo, 'Luca Gaurico ultimo degli astrologi', in *Atti della R. Accademia di Archeologia, Lettere e Belle Arti*, XVII, 1893–96, pp. 3–102.

²⁹ Burmeister, *op. cit.*, I, p. 90.

³⁰ The horoscope referred to is of Francesco Marsilio Ro, born in 1505.

³¹ *Aphorismorum astronomicorum segmenta septem*, published by Petreius together with the *Libelli quinque*, Nürnberg, 1547, ff. 298v–299r.

³² *De exemplis*, f. 182v.

³³ MS Lat. 7395, pp. 323–30 (I am grateful to Mlle Evelyne Hanquart, who at my request kindly consulted this manuscript for me). See Burmeister, *op. cit.*, pp. 6–7, 30 and 169.

³⁴ Nos. 93, 89, 67, 94, 95 and 92 respectively of *De exemplis centum geniturarum*.

³⁵ See E. Zinner, *Leben und Wirken des Joh. Müller von Königsberg, genannt Regiomontanus*, Osnabruck, second edition, 1968.

³⁶ See his horoscope for Emperor Maximilian I (1459–1519), cast in 1459, in Zinner, *op. cit.*, plate 8.

³⁷ See Thorndike, *History of Magic*, V, p. 368.

³⁸ 'ferebant etiam Marsilium Ficinum, qui eximiae authoritatis fuisset astrologus, ex fortunata & regia genesi, ei sacrorum principatum, quum adhuc esset, puer, nec planè sacris initiatus, omnino detulisse'; see *Vita Leonis Decimi*, book III, p. 64, in *Pauli Iovii Novocomensis Episcopi Nucerini Illustrium Virorum Vitae*, Florence, 1551.

³⁹ See P. O. Kristeller, 'Giovanni Pico della Mirandola and his sources' in *L'opera e il pensiero di Giovanni Pico della Mirandola nella storia dell'Umanesimo*, Florence, two vols., 1965, I, pp. 35–142: Pico's horoscope is reproduced on plate V, facing p. 112; see also pp. 50–1, n. 56. For Benivieni's autohoroscope see my article cited in n. 3, pp. 189–91.

⁴⁰ *Comento di Christophoro Landino fiorentino sopra la Comedia di Danthe Alighieri poeta fiorentino*, Florence, 1481, unpaginated but glossing *Inferno*, I, 105: 'Sara adunque elueltro tale influentia laquale nascera tra cielo et cielo. Oueramēte quel principe elquale da tale influentia sara prodocto. Onde dira disotto chio ueggio certamente et pero el narro. Et certo nellanno M. cccc. lxxxiiii. nel di uigesimo quinto di nouembre et a hore. xiii. et minuti. xli di tale di sara la coniunctione di Saturno et di Ioue nello scorpione nellascendente del quinto grado della libra: laquale dimostra mutatione di religione: Et perche Ioue preuale a Saturno significa che tale mutatione sara inmeglio. Ilperche non potendo essere religione alchuna piu uera che la nostra ho ferma speranza che la rep. christiana si ridurra a optima uita e gouerno.'

⁴¹ Had, for instance, the first Earl and Countess of Mornington believed in astrology, the hour, day and place of the birth of the first Duke of Wellington in 1769 would not now be the subject of conjecture.

D. M. Bueno de Mesquita *Christ Church, Oxford*

15

THE DEPUTATI DEL DENARO
IN THE GOVERNMENT
OF LUDOVICO SFORZA

PECUNIA NERVUS BELLI, and of much else too. So far as governments were concerned in the fifteenth century it was a commodity in chronically short supply. Hence in France and England, for example, the need for an efficient and flexible system of determining priorities in the distribution of cash can be recognised as an element in the history of financial administration.[1]

The Camera of the Dukes of Milan, as it evolved in the second half of the fourteenth century, seems to have had responsibility under the duke for all matters relating to the duke's revenues. The term was often used in the singular in the fifteenth century, but the Camera comprised two virtually independent departments, under the direction respectively of the Masters of the ordinary and of the extraordinary revenues: the Magistri utriusque Camere, as they were sometimes called. Closely linked to the Camera was an office for the recipt and disbursement of cash, the Treasury, under a Treasurer General.[2]

The financial history of the duchy under the Visconti and the Sforza can never be fully written, for the records kept by the Camera in its office in the corte dell'Arengo in Milan have not survived. The lengthy standing orders issued for the Camera in the name of Filippo Maria Visconti in 1445 describe its functions in some detail. They were essentially those of an accounting office with jurisdiction, a bureaucratic department well stocked with auditors and dominated by paper.[3] Other records too show signs of the rigidity inherent in medieval administrative institutions, as custom and routine, reflecting in some measure the interests both of the prince and of his servants, gained a self-perpetuating hold. It seems unlikely that such a department could readily adapt itself to the urgent and changing needs of its master. The practice of other States suggests that the daily problem of relating inadequate resources of cash to the needs of court, government and policy called for a more informal and dynamic instrument. Whether any other channels for financial decision and action existed under Filippo Maria Visconti and the first two Sforza dukes is a question still to be investigated. For the last two decades of the fifteenth century, when Ludovico Sforza governed the duchy first as lieutenant-general for his nephew and then as duke, the answer is to be found in the work of a small committee, usually described as the Prefecti rei pecuniarie or Deputati del denaro.

Ludovico Sforza himself has given us the evidence in his 'political testament', the instructions he prepared between 1497 and 1499 for the government of the duchy in the event of his death. Having described the functions of the Masters of the two branches of the Camera, he devoted quite a long paragraph to the Deputati del denaro. In spite of the collective plural of the title, this was a magistracy, a committee, 'magistrato trovato da noi in le difficultà et pressure de guerra'. It was, in principle at least, a temporary expedient, designed to cope with the emergencies of wartime; 'cessando la guerra, et reducte le intrate al netto', it was to be absorbed into the 'magistrato ordinario delle entrate'. Its main functions were to prepare an annual civil and military budget, and to exercise sole control over the assignment of revenue to meet expenses. Its members might be chosen from among the Masters of the revenues; 'habijno credito, et experientia: et sopra el tutto sijno fidati al stato'. They must also be rich. Finally, there were not to be more than three of them, in view of 'la potestà se li da ampla'.[4]

This paragraph has evoked remarkably little curiosity among historians. Malaguzzi Valeri summarised it in a brief and, as it happens, misleading sentence. Santoro did not mention the Deputati directly in her account of the administrative structure of the duchy, though she referred to one of their letters. Benaglio, who wrote before the testament was published, knew nothing of them.[5] Yet hundreds of letters that refer to the work of the Deputati and testify to its importance have in fact survived in the archives of the Cancelleria segreta which now form the core of the Archivio Sforzesco. It is possible to trace the origins of the committee, to see something of the manner in which it fulfilled its duties, to identify at least some of its members, and to draw some conclusions about its place in the pattern and methods of government of the most powerful 'despotic state' of Italy in the Renaissance.[6]

A ducal letter of 27 November 1480 enregistered in the Cancelleria segreta contains the first specific mention I have found of the Deputati, eo nomine. The letter instructed the Commissario generale sopra le genti d'arme to render account of the fines he exacted both to the Treasurer General and to 'li spectabili deputati sopra le intrate nostre'. When the Chancery issued a letter at the request of another department the clerk who copied it into the register normally noted the names of the initiators. Thus the names are recorded at the foot of this letter: 'Petrus Franciscus Vicecomes. Antonius Marlianus'.[7]

Pierfrancesco Visconti and Antonio Marliani were in fact the 'deputati sopra le entrate'. This is clear from an earlier letter in the same register, which supplies the exact date of the creation of the Deputati, and a first definition of their functions:[8]

Petro Francisco Vicecomiti et ⎫
D. Antonio Marliano   ⎬ Consiliariis
                           ⎭

Como sapeti, dopo lo acerbissimo caso della morte del quondam Illmo. Sigre. nostro consorte et patre, ce sonno occorse tante spese de guerre,[9] et per molte altre diverse cagione, che fin adesso non solo l'intrate del anno presente, ma ancora quelle de l'anno futuro quasi tutte sonno consumate, et ogni giorno ne occorreno de novi carichi; alli quali essendo necessario fare provisione: per la prudentia integrità et longa experientia vostra, nè manco per la fede et devotione singulare havete ad nuy et alle cose nostre, ve commettemo et volemo che insieme con Aluysio Becchetto,[10] li magistri de l'entrate et Thesaurario nostro generale,[11] examinati diligentemente ogni nostro debito et credito; et cum ogni studio et diligentia investigati et cerchati tutte le vie et modi seranno expediente per provedere a queste nostre graveze et alla satisfactione de quilli che da nuy debbeno havere; et consultata et examinata fra vuy et epsi Aloysio, Magistri et Thesaurario quella forma et via ve parirà alla giornata de prehendere così in recatare dinari ad interesse como ancora se vi occorrarà alcuna megliore via, per expeditione de queste nostre graveze, quale tanto ne premeno. Et strenzati quilli sonno deputati ad simile cura ad attenderli cum tanta più vigilantia et accurata opera quanto chiaramente intendite richedere questo nostro bisogno, per esserci sopragionti queste intorerabile spese, alle quale cum quello megliore modo si può è necessario fare provisione; tenendone avisati de quello ve occorrarà tractare alla giornata circa ciò, nè permettendo se vegna ad alcuna conclusione senza nostra participatione. Mediolani xxi oct. 1480.

B[artholomeus] C[halcus]

Per Phi[lippum] Co[mitem]

The date places the appointment within the framework of the final struggle for power between Ludovico Sforza and the widowed Duchess Regent Bona of Savoy. On 7 October Ludovico had contrived to transfer his nephew, the eleven-year-old Duke Giangaleazzo, from his mother's care into the custody of his 'governatori' in the Rocchetta, the inner fortress of the Castello di Porta Giovia. After a vain struggle to maintain her rights, Bona surrendered the regency and left Milan on 2 November. In the intervening weeks her enemies had made much of the financial dilapidation of the State during her regency. A series of discussions between Bona and the party of the Rochetta opened on 18 October. It seems likely that the appointment of Visconti and Marliani emanated from these discussions, and that its implicit recognition of financial mismanagement brought Ludovico Sforza a step closer to supreme power.[12]

The financial crisis, however, was a reality as well as a pretext, and the commission to Visconti and Marliani remained in force after Bona had left Milan. It was reissued at the beginning of 1481, with the same preamble but a fuller and more detailed delegation of powers:[13]

Vi commettemo et volemo debiati vedere et examinare bene tutte le intrate pertinente ad la camera nostra, così de datii como de sale, et tracta de biade, taxe de cavalli, et de qualunca altra natura se sia; et intendere tutti li debiti che essa nostra camera ha, et le assignatione facte sopra epse nostre intrate, graveze et spese che li[14] havemo ogni anno così de salariati como de altra natura; havendo da voi per vostra instructione quelli magistri de le intrate nostre, thesaureri, resonati et caduno altro parerà ad voi per informatione vostra. Et quando havereti bene visto et inteso el tutto, fategli tutte quelle provisione che ve parerano megliore per regulare et governare bene tutte le dicte intrate, et augumentarle dove cum honestà se puosseno augumentare. Et per extinguere et per exeguire li debiti et dare bona forma alle dicte graveze et spesa, vi damo possanza così de cassarle como moderarle et redurle alla necessità, como parerà allo prudentissimo iudicio vostro; drizando omne pensiere et mente vostra al bon governo et stabilmento et bene de l'intrate nostre, et del stato nostro, como in voi amplamente se confidamo. Concedendovi arbitrio et facultà di potere tore dinari ad interesse così ad longo tempo como breve, et fare omne altra provisione che ad voi meglio parerà, perchè del tutto se reposamo sopra la fede integrità experientia et prudentia vostra. Et tutto quello fareti et ordinareti disponemo habia loco, et sia rato et fermo, e per le presente lo approbamo collaudamo et ratificamo. Volendo che tutte le ordinatione et conclusione vostre pertinente ad intrate tantum, le faciate annotare et expedire dal egregio Filippo Ferruffino secretario nostro electo sopra le dicte intrate,[15] el quale volemo sia asistente presso voi. Et de le cose de qualche importantia daritene notitia inante che vegnate ad conclusione d'epse. Commandando per tenore de le presente ad tutti li magistri de le intrate nostre utriusque camere, commissarii de cavalli, commissarii et administratori sopra'l sale, deputati sopra le biade, referendarii, thesaurerii, canevari de sale, et ad caduno altro officiale et subdito nostro dependente da le entrate nostre così presente como futuri, che ve obediscano non altramente che la persona nostra propria, et faciano et adimpiiscano quanto per voi circa predicta serà ordinato. Mediolani ii Januarii 1481.

B .C.

Per Rozascum

Jo. Galeaz Ma. Dux Mli. ss.

Thus the Deputati received full warrant for that 'potestà ampla' to which Ludovico Sforza referred in his testament. This letter, compared with that of the previous October, conferred larger powers in a more clearly defined form. All financial departments and officers, from the Masters of the Camera downwards, were now placed in explicit subordination, required to obey and implement the instructions of the Deputati. The duke approved and ratified their decisions in advance. Only the will of Ludovico Sforza, reflected in the instruction to refer 'le cose de qualche importantia' to the duke, limited their complete freedom of action in the financial sphere. The Deputati were inserted as a new element between the prince on the one hand and the established channels of government on the other. The new regime was ready to try new measures.

According to a usually well informed chronicler, jewels and plate 'maximi pretii et inextimabilis valoris', part of the treasure of Galeazzo Sforza, were sold at the end of 1480 in order to pay debts due to allied princes and to *condottieri*[16]—one of the first fruits, perhaps, of the work of the Deputati. They were told in March 1481 that it was their business to recover the jewels and other valuables of Antonio Tassino, forfeit to the Camera.[17] An authorisation to Pierfrancesco Visconti 'ed altri' to dispose of certain *dazi* or excise duties may have been addressed to the Deputati.[18] But there is, on the whole, disappointingly little evidence to be found, for the years 1481–82, of the manner in which they used their large powers.

The heavy military expenditure incurred during the war of Ferrara in 1482–84 put a fresh strain on the financial resources of the State. It seems likely that the war gave a decisive impetus to the nature and scope of the committee's operations. Its own letters were now normally subscribed 'Prefecti rei pecuniarie', though a good deal of variety still existed in the usage of the Chancery.[19] Whatever the formula, a growing body of evidence shows that the Deputati del denaro exercised a detailed and daily control during the years 1483–85 over all the business arising from the raising and disbursement of money for the duke. In June 1483, for instance, they wrote to Ludovico Sforza that they had seen his letter 'per la quale Quella richede ducati 1000. Noi li habiamo ad omne possanza subito apparegiati, et cusì li mandemo per lo presente cavalario alla Signoria vostra.'[20] A month later Ludovico sent a message to Bartolomeo Calco 'che avisati li deputati sopra li dinari ad apparechiare 3M ducati senza dimora', to pay the troops in the Cremonese.[21] Emergency measures against the plague,[22] the pay of diplomatic agents going abroad,[23] the complaints of Castellans that their men were starving for lack of pay[24] or of useful Swiss clients that their pensions were overdue,[25] the repair of fortresses and the replenishment of their supplies,[26] the claims of farmers of the *dazi* that they were entitled to a rebate[27]—all passed through the hands of the Deputati.

There seems to have been no hard and fast distinction between the kinds of business dealt with by the committee and by the Camera. The arrangement of 'subventiones', the payments made by those who were appointed to office in the dominion, normally formed part of the duties of the Maestri delle entrate. In one such case at the end of 1484 the Deputati were negotiating with three candidates, and Ludovico Sforza left the final choice to them. The fact that the bidding was exceptionally high probably accounts for their intervention.[28] The Deputati could in fact intervene at any time to promote the interests of the Camera, or indeed to guard it against the credulity of the prince—witness their reluctance to comply with Ludovico Sforza's order to refund the subvention of a protégé of Lorenzo de Medici who had held office in the dominion until he had cleared his accounts at the Camera. 'Luy forse se ne renderà renitente, per havere mal manegiato li denari de la camera, et ritrovarsi molto gravato de debiti sì con la camera, como etiandio con altre persone.'[29]

Orders for the payment of cash sometimes went to Filippo Ferruffino, the Secretary for the ordinary revenues who had been placed at the disposal of the Deputati by the terms of their commission of 2 January 1481. Ferruffino's own words show that he could do no more than press the Deputati to take action: 'la Dominica non ne ho possuto parlare ad questi magnifici deputati; quali ho mandato admonire siano qua domatina per questa quanto per altre expeditione'.[30] There may be a hint of exasperation here; the Deputati already had a reputation for dragging their feet. A month earlier Ludovico Sforza had written to Bartolomeo Calco, 'Dicemo maravegliarne asai de li deputati della pecunia che essendoli stato scripto facessero provisione ad Ambrosio Ferraro[31] de dinari per fornir el lavorerio de Domossula, non l'habino facto; e sequendo el ricordo vostro, nuy li scrivemo de qui opportunamente.'[32] The Deputati promised to provide the money within the next two weeks. Calco took the opportunity to put in a word at the same time for the *cavallari*, the post riders who carried government mail. Their pay was sadly in arrears. His messenger reported that 'fin a qui non ho havuto se non bone parole', and two days later: 'essendo stati essi deputati insema heri e hogi, holi facto instantia a fare qualche provisione perchè si potesse havere dinari. Tandem non ho poduto havere se non bone parole como ho havuto per il passato; et così harò per l'avenire se altra provisione non si fa.'[33]

By 1485, then, the Deputati del denaro had come to play a crucial part in government, and one that called for a detailed knowledge of all aspects of finance and taxation. They continued to perform these functions, in peace and in war, until the flight of Ludovico Sforza from Milan in 1499. The instructions issued to Filippo Ferruffino when he was appointed Secretary in November 1480 contained no reference to the newly created Deputati. The instructions for Filippo's son Alberto, who succeeded him in 1490,[34] have not come to light. Alberto died in 1496, and the office was granted to Giangiacomo Ferruffino, who had been trained under Filippo, 'tam etsi juvenilis adhuc sit etatis'.[35] He took charge of a busy department, with eight assistants and thirteen *cavallari* under his direction in 1499,[36] but his instructions make it clear that he and his staff were entirely at the disposal of the Deputati del denaro. Six out of ten clauses were concerned with matters that he was to refer to the Deputati or on which he was to take no action without their consent. Two dealt with the internal running of the department, and one directed him to keep an eye on the Masters of the ordinary revenues at such times as he was not required to attend on the Deputati. The tenth clause, 'per concludere ogni cosa', expressed the guiding principle to which all his actions should conform:

che non faci expeditione de cosa alcuna de momento senza saputa de li deputati overo de uno o duy de loro. Perchè benchè l'officio sia data alla persona tua, se siamo risolti farlo perchè habiano havere questa impresa, et sia sua cura che l'officio vadi bene et fidelmente governato.[37]

The records of the activities of the Deputati between 1486 and 1499 embrace all the kinds of business in which we have already seen them involved. They were called on to determine the methods of raising money[38] and to negotiate substantial loans in Genoa.[39] They were the experts to whom queries about taxation were referred,[40] the general administrators of the property of the Camera,[41] and the guardians of its interests.[42] We shall come back to some of the implications of their activities. The manifold business of taxation and finance, the many legal disputes and petitions that arose from it, the complex system of accounts to be kept and audited left plenty of scope still for the expertise of the Masters of the revenues. But supreme responsibility for the financial solvency of the State and the detailed oversight of every aspect of financial administration now rested with the Deputati. The Masters of the ordinary revenues were clearly subordinate to them, but they also concerned themselves, as we shall see, with the profits of criminal jurisdiction, the main business of the other branch of the Camera. When Ludovico Sforza wrote his testament, at a time of spiralling military expenditure, the prospect of absorbing the Deputati into the Camera must have seemed on any realistic count a distant one.

.   .   .

What sort of men did Ludovico Sforza choose for these high responsibilities?

Visconti and Marliani, the first Deputati, were members of the Consiglio segreto, appointed primarily, it seems, for their political experience and reliability. Pierfrancesco Visconti was a soldier of some repute. He sat in the Consiglio del castello, the inner council that played an important part in government during the regency of Bona of Savoy. He cannot have served actively as a Deputato for very long, for he was in command of the Sforza troops in the field against Venice in 1483, and he died in 1484.[43] Marliani's career is difficult to reconstruct, but he had probably had financial experience as a Master of the revenues before he was promoted to the council.[44] He was certainly still alive in 1489, but there is no evidence to show how long he remained a Deputato.

The Deputati, writing at the end of 1484 to inform Ludovico Sforza of a decision they had taken, stated that 'cusì tutti noy siamo concorsi in questa deliberatione, excepto el Thexaurero generale quale non ha voluto dare la voce sua'.[45] The committee must by then have numbered at least three, and had acquired in Antonio Landriani a member who as Treasurer General had already held a major post in the financial administration for ten years. His presence on the committee served to strengthen the element of technical knowledge that the developing nature of its work increasingly demanded.

The Landriani were an old and prominent noble family, traditionally associated with the Ghibelline interest. Antonio's father had been a leading figure in the Ambrosian Republic. Little is known of Antonio's career before Galeazzo Sforza appointed him in 1474 to the office of Treasurer General, which he held for twenty-five years. He also served in those years as a *commissario delle monete*, as a Master of the extraordinary revenues, and on the Consiglio segreto.[46] Already in high office in 1480, he does not seem to have established particularly close personal relations with Ludovico Sforza, but he attached himself closely to Ludovico's political interests, acted as spokesman for his claims on the death of the duke Giangaleazzo, and stiffened his resolution to resist the French both in 1495 and in 1499.[47] He was certainly believed to have played a large part in extorting the means to do so. The Capitano di Giustizia of Milan sent one of his men to the Duomo on a September morning in 1495: 'ha trovato uno scritto alla porta che dicea, finchè non se amazza Antonio da Landriano mai non cessarano li presti in Milano. Amazemelo amazemelo'.[48] The exhortation was fulfilled on 30 August 1499, and whatever personal motives may have prompted the murder, the people rejoiced, and two days later Ludovico Sforza fled from Milan.

Bergonzio Botta and Marchesino Stanga had certainly joined Landriano on the committee by May 1490,[49] and may already have been on it for some years. Thereafter they are often to be found acting jointly as Deputati, and occasionally in association with Landriani as well.

The Botta were one of the leading families of Tortona. Bergonzio, born about 1453,[50] entered the financial administration in the footsteps of his father, and had become a Master of the ordinary revenues as well as a Deputato by 1490.[51] By then his brother was Bishop of Tortona, and his marriage to Marietta Spinola had brought him into contact with the circle of disorderly but politically useful nobility whose lands straddled the Genoese border of the dominion. If we may judge by a jocular interchange of letters about his ailments, he was on fairly close personal terms with Ludovico Sforza.[52] It was a natural obligation of a man influential at home and at court to receive Isabella of Aragon at his palace when she passed through Tortona on her way to Milan to become the bride of Giangaleazzo Sforza; and the ballet that Bergonzio staged to mark the occasion has earned him a modest place among patrons of the arts.[53] But his popular reputation was as unsavoury as Landriani's. One chronicler bracketed them together as the 'duo canes rapaces' responsible for the 'subsidium intollerabile' imposed in 1497.[54] Unlike Landriani he escaped the fury of the mob in 1499 by taking shelter in the Castello, and when it surrendered he made terms with the French and came out openly as a Guelf.[55] He paid a large price when Ludovico Sforza returned to the dominion,[56] but he had backed the winning side in the long run, and he consolidated his position by marrying his daughter into the great family of the Borromeo. He died in Milan in 1504.

Marchesino Stanga of Cremona belonged, like Botta, to the wealthy provincial nobility who tended to gravitate towards Milan. Marchesino attached himself in his youth to Ludovico Sforza,[57] and became one of his most trusted friends. He was appointed 'prefectus annone' some time in the 1480s—that is, put in charge of the measures to ensure adequate supplies of grain in the dominion—and he seems to have discharged his duties conscientiously and with success.[58] He may already have been a Deputato in 1489, when he passed on to Bartolomeo Calco some instructions for cuts in government expenditure.[59] The rather vague descriptions that writers gave of his financial office in the 1490s probably stemmed from his dominant position on the committee; Tristano Calco called him 'supremus [?rei] pecuniarie minister', and Niccolò Lucari, who dedicated to him an edition of the De remediis of Petrarch, 'aerarii tribunus cum secretiori sigillo'.[60] Marchesino was in fact far more than a successful civil servant. His marriage to a daughter of Count Giovanni Borromeo in 1491 was a great occasion. He embellished his native city of Cremona, built a villa at Bellagio—one of the first on the Lakes—and his palace in Milan, though still unfinished, was already one of the sights of the city in 1492, testimony to his eminence among 'li primi che habbia il Duca'.[61] Artists like Giancristoforo Romano,[62] men of letters like Lucari, Antonio Perotto and Bernardo Bellincioni enjoyed or sought his patronage.[63] It is not surprising that Ludovico used him as a channel of communication with the artists working for the court: with Amedeo, and with Leonardo da Vinci.[64] 'Vir in primis elegans', he was not, it seems a soldier; he equipped a contingent for the joust in honour of Ludovico's marriage but did not lead it himself.[65] But he was a friend of princes; he spread his talents widely in government, diplomacy and patronage; and perhaps few men stood closer to Ludovico Sforza. Ludovico used him increasingly on diplomatic business from 1496 onwards, and if he kept his place as a Deputato he can have given little time to it. He accompanied Ludovico to Germany in 1499, but was back in Milan before the year was out, partly to save his property from confiscation by the French but perhaps too with Ludovico's consent.[66] He threw in his lot with the Sforza again when they returned in 1500, was imprisoned after their final defeat, and died in Milan in August 1500.[67]

One further name can be added to the list of the Deputati: that of Gualtiero Bascapè. The Bascapè, though not one of the great Milanese families, were quite prominent among the Ghibelline nobility.[68] 'Messer Gualtero', as he was usually called, lacked the personal flair and probably the wealth of Marchesino Stanga, but within a more limited sphere he followed much the same paths. Born about 1458, he too began his career in the personal service of Ludovico Sforza,[69] as one of his chamberlains when we first come across him in 1483, and already dealing with money, for the pay of the troops.[70] He was promoted to the office of Giudice dei dazi in Milan in 1488.[71] He also appears as a Deputato delle monete along with Antonio Landriani in 1489 and 1490.[72] An order to Stanga in 1494 to pay cash 'senza Gualtero' suggests that they normally worked together, so he may already have become a Deputato del denaro by that date.[73] A few references to his activities in financial affairs during 1495 have survived, and he appears specifically as a Deputato early in 1496, though he continued to hold the office of Giudice dei dazi (probably delegating the duties to a lieutenant) and to use the title Camerario.[74] As Stanga became increasingly occupied with other affairs Bascapè took charge of the daily business of the office, and references to individual Deputati in 1497 and 1498 are almost always to Bascapè, sometimes associated with Botta and more rarely with Landriani as well. He became a Master of the ordinary revenues at the beginning of 1499, yielding the office of Giudice dei dazi to his brother,[75] and he also appears as a Commissario del sale in a salary list for 1499, but there is no reason to suppose that he gave up his duties as a Deputato.[76] Already a busy career, then, but many other miscellaneous tasks devolved upon him. He conveyed personal messages for Ludovico Sforza;[77] he took delivery from Ambrogio da Predi of works of art for Bianca Maria Sforza to take to Germany at the time of her marriage to Maximilian;[78] he supervised the return to the Duomo of valuables that Azzo Visconti had appropriated 150 years before;[79] after the death of the Duchess Beatrice he was charged with the collection of the revenues from her estates.[80] He sat on a committee for the cleaning up and embellishment of Milan, and was probably the leading spirit in it; Francesco Tanzio, dedicating to Ludovico Sforza his edition of Bernardo Bellincioni's poems, referred to 'prelibato tuo et mio Gualtiero', and in the context of Ludovico's plans for the improvement of Milan wrote of 'l'umano, fidele, prudente et sollicito esecutore de li toi comandamenti Gualtiero, instrumento del tuo ingegno'.[81] Antonio Perotto wrote epigrams for Bascapè as well as for Stanga and other members of the court,[82] and Bellincioni, the Florentine rhymester imported into the court to civilise the rough tongue of Lombardy, dedicated a sonnet to him 'domandandogli un piacere', as indeed he dedicated one to Botta and Stanga 'venendo loro una notte da

Pavia e con clamori domandandomi'.[83] Bascapè also supervised the decoration of the Castello of Milan, along with Ambrogio Ferrario, the Commissario
generale dei lavori, and with 'Maestro Leonardo'.[84] Leonardo has left a
note of an idea for a sketch showing Ludovico Sforza and 'messer Gualtieri
con riverente atto'.[85] It sums up Bascapè's place beside Stanga as an un-
obtrusive and ubiquitous agent of Ludovico's dream of Milan as a great
centre of art and learning. When all his hopes collapsed in 1499 Bascapè went
to Germany with him, was rewarded for his loyalty in February 1500, and
was captured and imprisoned by the French when they recovered Milan.[86]
He came to terms with them in the end, and died in Milan in 1508.[87]

The Deputati del denaro, then, were men experienced in financial
administration; their tentacles spread widely and no doubt of set purpose
through most of the central offices of government concerned with the
revenues of the duke. But their links with the court and their personal
relations with Ludovico Sforza were perhaps no less vital to the fulfilment
of their duties. It is difficult to judge what they made out of it for themselves.
Stanga, born to riches, lived splendidly and died a wealthy man.[88] Of
Bascapè we know only that, at the time of the flight from Milan in September
1499, 'fo tolto una cassa a Gualtero, havia assà danari dentro'.[89] A more
sinister report reached Venice early in 1498, but in a form too garbled to
command complete confidence. 'Bergonzo di Landriano', a strange hybrid
described as 'exatore di danari', had paid 40,000 ducats, according to
Sanuto, to buy off a demand that he should render account of his administration.[90] It may have meant no more than that the duke's needs were
pressing and all who could must help.

Not many months later, Bascapè apparently made a personal protest
against a general letter of criticism sent out to the duke's officials. Ludovico
Sforza assured him that the letter was meant 'solum per dare lume a li
altri' and that neither he nor Bergonzio need pay any attention to it, 'perchè
sapemo cum quanta diligentia et studio l'uno et l'altro se exhibisce non solo
in quelle cose che importano ma etiam in quelle che tochano qualche altro
privato particolare'.[91]

Was this full expression of confidence misplaced? Given the general
standards of public administration, it is probably fairer to look at the service
the Deputati gave rather than at what they may have illicitly gained from it.

The financial agents of a ruler were expected to be ready to dip into their
own pockets to meet the financial imperatives of the prince. When Ludovico
Sforza was urgently enlisting troops for the 'impresa del Patrimonio' in 1486
the Deputati were told to find the money forthwith 'se ben dovessero im-
prestarli de li suoi'.[92] Or again, writing to the Deputati from Piacenza in 1494:

Havendo noi bisogno al presente de cinque mille ducati, volemo che trovati de
haverli et ne li mandati senza dimora. Et quando non li havesti de nostri così in
prompto che se li potesti mandare subito, voi ve stringereti insieme, et fra voi li
recatareti de vostri, non interponendoli momento de tempo, tolendoveli poi voi de
li primi che venerano. . . . Et provedeti in modo che domani li habiamo qua in
omne modo.[93]

On one such occasion they reported that 'li havemo tolti in prestito da nostri amici'.[94] One can see why Ludovico declared that the Deputati must be rich.

Most of the surviving correspondence about the work of the Deputati is concerned with *expeditiones*: that is, the payment of cash to those authorised to receive it. Ludovico Sforza was a notoriously dilatory paymaster. There was in fact never enough cash to go round. The reasons for what the Deputati described at the end of 1484 as 'lo grande bisogno del dinaro vedemo havere al presente la Camera vostra'[95] cannot be examined here. It was a reality they had constantly to wrestle with, and they shared the odium that it aroused among the creditors of the duke.

It was in the nature of political priorities that large sums often took precedence over small ones. Giovanni Colli, arriving in Milan with orders from the duke, presented himself to Bascapè, who took him straight off to see Botta and Landriani, 'et se prehesce ordine che domane me inviarò al camino mio cum tuta la summa de li 12,500 ducati'.[96] Whithersoever he was bound, he might well have felt surprise at such prompt dispatch. A month earlier Bascapè had explained that Raimondo Raimondi, who should have been on his way back to England, 'non è stato expedito, havendo prima atexo a le expeditione del S. Marchese di Mantua et de le giente d'arme, per le qual è stato necessario rechatare de molti dinari'. The Deputati confirmed this on the following day.

Nuy non l'habiamo expedito, non perchè non sapiamo l'importantia de l'andata ma per non havere possuto più presto, per li altri gran carichi havemo havuti; che doppoy che la v. Ex. andò alla monstra de Melegnano in qua trovamo che havemo speso circa ducati 60,000, et tutti li havemo recatati como havemo possuto.[97]

The lesser men in the duke's service probably fared worst. We have heard of the plight of the *cavallari* in 1485. Bartolomeo Calco was writing about it again to Ludovico Sforza in 1490. 'Se la Signoria vostra fa pensiere che siano adoperato cavallari, La gli può provedere como gli piace.' But the *cavallari* were again without their pay in 1495.[98] A newly appointed Commissario of Bormio, urgently needed at his post, was delayed for at least three weeks in Milan; Calco wrote that the Deputati 'non fanno altra demonstratione de volerlo spazare'; the sum involved was sixteen ducats.[99] A disillusioned Commissario of Domodossola wrote bitterly to the Duke, 'La Ex. v. commesse a li deputati che me volesseno remunerare, mha me tegneteno a Milano su l'ostaria uno mese cum duoi cavalli, et poi me mandoreno cum le man piene de mosche.'[100] Even in those days the cost of staying in Milan was abnormally high.[101] An agent sent by the Bishop of Chur to collect his unpaid pension was kept waiting for at least six weeks 'sopra l'ostaria' in Milan, in spite of two letters from Ludovico Sforza to the Deputati.[102]

That was in peacetime. The signing of the Holy League against France on 31 March 1495 brought mobilisation for war and more problems for the committee. The *collaterali cavalcanti*, who travelled around the dominion to hold musters of the armed forces, apparently went on strike for lack of pay;

the Deputati were told to provide 'per modo che nel avenire alli tempi soi habino ad cavalcare.'[103] Ludovico Sforza, after a brief visit to the camp of Galeazzo Sanseverino, the commander of the western front, summoned Botta and Stanga to Vigevano on 18 April. He wrote to the Deputati next day to remind them of the orders he had given; 'solicitando m. Galeazzo ogn'hora queste cose, ve ne faremo novo ricordo'. Two days later four further notes on the subject went off from Vigevano, three for the Deputati and one personally for Botta and Stanga.[104] Antonio Missaglia, the head of the biggest armaments firm in Milan, chose this moment to send a long tirade to the duke about the 'mali trattamenti a me facti per li magci. deputati de la pecunia'. The government owed him enormous sums. He had been promised assignments of 12,000 lire on revenues for the current year, but he had not received them; he had been unable to collect about 36,000 lire from assignments over the past eight years that had proved worthless; he had been encouraged to expand his labour force in order to increase production for the government, and as a result he was now on the verge of ruin. Marchesino's answer on behalf of the Deputati was lame and unpromising; they had not yet got round to making any assignments for the year, but when they did so 'non se mancharà anchora de dare loco a la sua'.[105] Meanwhile Bernardino da Sarzana, a soldier commissioned to raise a force of 300 infantry, was waiting 'como desperato' in Milan for the money he needed to enlist his men. 'Anchora questi deputati non me hanno spazato de li denari quale me ha prestati v. S. per soa gratia.' Waiting upon the Deputati, he suffered a change of heart. Three letters of the duke to his Ministers had produced nothing. Too ashamed to seek leave beforehand, he wrote sadly and apologetically to tell the duke that he had entered a monastery: 'sono andato religioso'.[106] The needs of the army might seem to have the highest priority, but Galeazzo Sanseverino's agent in Milan had the usual story to tell him. 'Cognosco che in loco de expeditione ho da questi deputati parole.'[107]

Bartolomeo Calco, who so often found himself caught in the tangled relations between Ludovico Sforza, the duke's creditors and the Deputati, could be sharply critical, but he was aware of the committee's difficulties and was prepared to remind Ludovico of them.

Ho sollicitato, et facto sollicitare presso questi deputati sopra el dinaro. Ma io non ne vedo effecto alcuno più l'uno dì che l'altro; perchè se bene epsi deputati per rechatarli faciano tutto quello che possono, nientedimeno per non haverli loro il modo non ne reuscisce altra provisione.[108]

Many times he asked Ludovico to write personally to the committee, but this solved no problems and usually had little effect. Calco put the issue in general terms. 'Seria pur bene che la S. vra. facesse fare qualche provisione perchè quando accadeno simili bisogni, se li possa provedere senza perdere tanto tempo.'[109]

That call for a fresh approach apparently went unheeded. There is no evidence to suggest that the Deputati ever envisaged or proposed any radical changes. Instead they did what they could within the limits of the existing system. They lost no opportunity to exact or borrow money, and carefully scrutinised every claim made on the Camera. They cavilled over trivial matters such as the payment of an extra allowance to the *cavallari* attached to the court,[110] the entitlement of agents travelling on the duke's business,[111] the currency in which Bianca Maria Sforza's dowry was to be paid to Maximilian of Habsburg,[112] the terminal dates at which subsidies were due to the Swiss.[113] Why pay a pension 'secundo el consueto', as Ludovico ordered, when it could simply be charged against a larger debt that the pensioner owed to the Camera?[114] They would not implement a questionably valid act of generosity without a formal order countersigned by Ludovico himself.[115] They chivvied him when he granted a delay in the payment of a large fine they had imposed; they had already assigned the money.[116] The commune of Como, assessed at 5,000 ducats for the war subsidy of 1495, made an offer of 2,000; Ludovico would not press them—there were rumours of an attack by the Swiss, and he did not want to encourage discontent in that area; but as soon as the rumours were dispelled the Deputati put the matter before him again.[117] They applied informal blackmail on Giovanni Aldighieri, already under threat of *disgrazia* and loss of office for failing to comply with an order, when he refused a request to lend 1,500 ducats to the duke; unless he changed his mind forthwith, 'meteresti in compromisso le cose vostre, che non saria poi in facultà nostra de darvi remedio'.[118]

If the Deputati never got to the roots of the problem they worked hard to find palliatives. Ludovico Sforza often complained of their dilatory execution of his commands, but a notable measure of patience accompanied his protests; he too, like Calco, understood the difficulty of their task. He continued to entrust the 'interesse de la camera nostra' to their hands. They could impose fines for non-payment of debts to the Camera.[119] They had large discretionary powers in the sale of offices,[120] in the detection and prosecution of frauds against the Camera,[121] and in devising expedients to satisfy creditors for whom cash could not be found. In the formal words of the Chancery, in one such case, 'ne remettemo a quanto per voi se farà cum dicti datieri, essendo certi che non fareti se non partito che sia cum avantazo et ceda ad utilità nostra, como seti soliti fare'.[122] When Ludovico decided to allocate the profits from the sale of all property forfeit to the Camera for the payment of his debts, he left it to the Deputati to determine priorities: 'distribuereti a li creditori che a vuy parerà'.[123] All these powers could obviously be turned to their own advantage if they chose.

There can be no doubt that the Deputati del denaro existed as a corporate body with collective functions. They operated, like all the departments of government, within a framework of standing orders issued by the duke.[124] Their ruling might be accorded precedence even over that of the Consiglio segreto, in terms of dignity at least the supreme magistracy of the State.[125] While the main body of the council met in the Corte dell'Arengo, the Deputati seem to have had an office in the Castello itself, along with the Chancery.[126] An order given by Ludovico Sforza when he was away from

Milan suggests that the Deputati attended with the councillors at the reading of diplomatic dispatches.[127] At a moment of crisis when the French army had already crossed the western borders of the dominion in 1499, the Ferrarese ambassador Costabili went up to the Castello at his usual time one morning and made his way to the chapel 'dove se sole congregare el consiglio'. He found, on one side of the chapel, the secretaries reading some letters to the assembled councillors. On the other side Ludovico was discussing business with the Deputati.[128] It is a rare glimpse of Sforza government in operation at the highest level.

Nevertheless an element of ambiguity hung over the committee's status, above all perhaps because of the principle that it existed only on a temporary basis to meet an emergency, so that it was never recognised as an established part of the civil service. Its members were apparently not appointed, like other officers, by letters patent—at least, none has come to light. They showed a tendency, though it was by no means a rule, to use other titles than that of 'Deputato' in legal documents. A record of an exchange of land in which the duke was one of the parties names his *procuratores et mandatarii* as Antonio Landriani, Councillor and Treasurer General, Bergonzio Botta, Master of ordinary revenues, and Gualtiero Bascapè, Giudice dei dazi. The deed was transacted in the Castello, and Giangiacomo Ferruffino was one of the witnesses.[129] But we cannot be sure that this was an example of the Deputati at work, performing a normal part of their duties as guardians of the welfare of the Camera, because the document gives no hint that the committee as such had anything to do with it.

This account of the activities of the Deputati raises a number of questions about the financial methods and policy of the Sforza that cannot be answered here. At least it may have served to show that the Deputati took first place in the mechanism to which Ludovico Sforza looked for the solution of his financial problems, and that he pinned great hopes on them. To play their part effectively they needed and received a rather special measure of his confidence. In that lay both the strength of their position and their vulnerability.

There is a well known account in Ambrogio da Paullo's chronicle of 'li favoriti dil Moro' who surrounded him during the last years of his reign and caused his downfall—most of them 'vili et abietta, ma per favore del Moro erano fatti grandi'. The favourites, according to da Paullo, could be called the true lords of the dominion

perchè regevano il Stato a suo modo, et il Moro ad ogni loro malfare assentiva, che fu poi causa della sua rovina et nostra disfazione et così de tutta Italia, perchè con il consiglio de loro il Moro misse il prestito alli gentilomini et artesani de tutte le città del dominio, et così fora a li castelli et ville; a li contadini mandolli li fanti in possessione, se non pagavano a li termini postoli, che fu principio et causa de ogni gran mal successo.[130]

Paullo's sympathies lay on the one hand with 'il povero duca' Giangaleazzo Sforza, and on the other with 'li omini da bene de nobil sangue de Milano' who had been ousted from their due place by the upstart favourites. His account of the men who decided Ludovico's fiscal policy, and of the consequences of their work, is certainly not in itself a complete explanation of the collapse of the dynasty. But he wrote with some knowledge of what went on at court, for he had served in the ducal household. He went on to give a list of the favourites. 'Li infrascritti, zoè m. Antonio di Landriani tesorer, m. Bregonzo Botta delli maestri delle entrate, m. Marchesino Stanga capo delli maestri sopra l'officio delle biave, uno Gualterino secretario. . . .'

Five more names follow, those of men more diverse in function but who are all known to have had a place in the intimate circle of the court; a sixth, added as an afterthought, is that of a son-in-law of Antonio Landriani. It was, of course, no secret that the four men who can be identified as Deputati del denaro in the latter part of Ludovico's rule had a large responsibility in fiscal matters. Was it by chance that Paullo put these names at the head of his list of the hated favourites?

The word recurs in Sanuto's diary when he records the news of the death of Marchesino Stanga 'olim favorito dil signor Ludovico'.[131] The opinion finds some support in a more impartial source than Paullo. It is to be found in Sanuto's summary of the relation made to the senate by Marco Lippomano in August 1499, after he had served for two years as Oratore at the court of Milan. 'Poteva con il ducha 4 quali tiravano danari, zoè misier Antonio di Landriam thesoriere, misier Bergonzio Bota, misier Marchesin Stanga et misier Gualtier.' He went on to describe an angry scene that had occurred in Ludovico Sforza's presence. Francesco Bernardino Visconti, who was to be the leader and spokesman of Milan in the negotiations with the French after Ludovico's flight, declared that he would not ride against the duke's enemies, 'perchè l'havia 4 quali lo voleno ruinar dil stado con tuor dai populi e farseli inimici, e misier Bergonzio li parlò contra, unde ditto misier Francesco Bernardin li disse te farò tajar la testa via da uno de miei famiglii'.[132]

If we accept Lippomano's story—and there seems no reason to doubt it— the incident sets Paullo's testimony in a more precise context. In terms of social status none of the four Deputati could be called 'vili et abietti' by any standards other, perhaps, than those of the great land-owning families of the dominion such as the Visconti, the Pallavicino, the Borromeo. Landriani and Bascapè were indeed 'omini de nobil sangue di Milano'; Botta and Stanga, though some Milanese might have looked on them with distaste as *forastieri*, belonged to families no less eminent in their own cities, and after Ludovico's fall they were both able to make use of their social ties with the Milanese nobility. The tensions and resentments that found expression in the word *favoriti* were the product of functional and political rather than of social antipathies. It is true that the populace, 'le stolte arme plebee',[133] hounded the favourites when their chance came. Given the nature of the Sforza regime, it probably mattered more in purely political terms that Ludovico had destroyed the coherence of the Ghibelline nobility, the traditional allies of the dynasty who had come out in his favour in 1479. Corio, the most informative of the Milanese historians of the time, commented on the favour Ludovico showed to the Guelfs, though in terms too vague to be easily related to the politics and personalities of the time. He also includes among the misdeeds of Ludovico's government what Paullo spelt out at greater length: 'quanta esaltazione di gente vile, quante deposizioni di nobili'.[134] Certainly there was a dissident element among the Ghibelline nobility in the late summer of 1499, and Francesco Bernardino Visconti was at the head of the dissidents. When, backed by the Borromeo, he led them into an alliance with the chief Guelf families, headed by the Trivulzi, he is said to have excluded the Ghibelline Pusterla and Landriani from his party.[135] The shifting align-ments of noble families in search of power were not, of course, confined to States under autocratic rule in Italy at the time, though the jealousies which flourished in the atmosphere of a court probably heightened their intensity. Visconti's championship of an over-taxed population may not sound wholly convincing, but his attack on the Deputati del denaro and the fiscal policies attributed to them, backed by the evidence of Paullo, should not be ignored as a pointer to the causes of aristocratic discontent.

The Sforza were deeply committed to an aristocratic structure in their State. Rightly or wrongly—and they may have had little practical choice—they felt bound to accept the established position of the Lombard nobility, in the hope that it would bolster the very slim sanctions on which their own authority rested and help to confirm their place in the eyes of the world. The price they paid, in the limitation of their public power, is written large in the records of their government.[136] The prince had to rely on a constant and delicate adjustment of personal relationships in order to control a society of this kind and not be dominated by it. In this uneasy balance the Deputati del denaro were set apart from their social equals, like all those whom men called favourites (and the word was in common use), by the special trust of the prince, by the power and the opportunities his trust conferred, by the jealousies that their power aroused, and in the case of the Deputati by the peculiarly sensitive field in which their authority lay. The court, the civil service and the nobility can be seen as three distinct though overlapping circles, vying with one another for the ear of the prince. The bureaucratic establishment restored by Francesco Sforza in 1450 had at least the prestige of custom, of recognised procedures and of its innate conservatism to commend it.[137] The Deputati operated outside this structure, or at best on the periphery of it, with no evident checks upon them. Tradition, so far as we can judge, still formed the basis of the ideas of political wisdom and sound government natural to the subjects of the Sforza, and the Deputati had no traditional place in the order of government. Though many men must have had dealings with them as a committee, it seems to have been as men of the court who abused the confidence of the prince, and as interlopers in government, that they came under fire. Ludovico's choice of associates in his court did much to alienate the Milanese nobility from him. The association of the Deputati with the court helps to explain the bitterness of Francesco Bernardino's attack on them.[138]

So the perfectly sensible experiment of 1480 contributed something in the end to the collapse of 1499. Nor is it easy to find any compensating achievement to set to the credit of the Deputati. They did what they could to keep Ludovico Sforza financially afloat, and judging by the reliance that he continued to place on them they achieved some success, in his eyes at least, and they attracted upon themselves a good deal of the opprobrium that his policies aroused. They never put the finances of the State on a sound basis, and were probably never in a position to do so. The terms of appointment of Pierfrancesco Visconti and Antonio Marliani in 1480 might have been taken as an occasion for a thorough review and overhaul of the whole financial system. By the time the war of Ferrara ended, if not before, the Deputati had become deeply absorbed in the endless minutiae of financial administration. Even if they had had the time and the will to stand back from the daily details and look at the problem as a whole, it is unlikely that any effective general measures they proposed would have been accepted. Only the serious co-operation of the prince could impose a strict control of expenditure related to available resources, and there is little sign that Ludovico Sforza had any of the consistent concern for good husbandry that marked his contemporary Henry Tudor.

On the other hand the appointment of the Deputati in October 1480, one of the first acts of power that can be attributed to Ludovico Sforza, was a not unpromising start. Ludovico's thoughts on government were certainly far from radical, but he had some understanding of the need to keep the mechanism of government up to date and to improve its capacity to meet the growing demands on the State. There are other indications that he liked to use small, carefully chosen and rather informal committees, created without limit of time or guarantee of permanence, to deal with specific problems. He was ready to adapt his methods to the circumstances. But his temperament did not incline him to persevere with intractable problems, and the way in which the Deputati evolved suggests that as he became inured to the tasks of ruling he readily postponed any prospect of comprehensive solutions in favour of short-term and very imperfect expedients.

The Sforza certainly clung to an experiment that seems to have established itself as a part of their thinking on government. There are traces of the Deputati, with Botta among their number, during Ludovico's brief restoration early in 1500; and Massimiliano revived the office in 1513–15.[139] No record of its survival under foreign domination has yet come to light. It may not have been well suited to serve the needs of a foreign master. Yet it deserves some record among the institutions of the Sforza, for its brief history throws a good deal of light on the nature of their government and on the internal politics of their time.

NOTES

[1] For a recent general comment see B. Guenée, *L'Occident aux XIVe et XVe siècles: les États*, Paris, 1971, especially pp. 203–4.

[2] C. Santoro, *Uffici del dominio Sforzesco*, Milan, 1948 (henceforth cited as *Uffici*), pp. xxv–xxix (and also in the Treccani degli Alfieri, *Storia di Milano*, VII, Milan, 1956, pp. 526–8).

[3] Published by C. Santoro, *Studi in onore di Amintore Fanfani*, III, Milan, 1962, pp. 465–92. For a summary of the earlier history of the Camera and the ducal revenues see F. Cognasso in *Storia di Milano*, VI, Milan, 1955, pp. 495–503.

[4] G. Molini, *Documenti di storia italiana*, I, Florence, 1836, pp. 319–21.

[5] G. Benaglio, *Relazione istorica del Magistrato delle ducali entrate straordinarie . . .*, Milan, 1711; F. Malaguzzi Valeri, *La corte di Lodovico il Moro*, I, Milan, 1913, p. 108; Santoro, *Uffici*, p. xviii, and *Storia di Milano*, VII, p. 521.

[6] The series in the Archivio di Stato of Milan used for this paper are cited as Reg(istri) Duc(ali); L(ettere) Miss(ive); and Cart(eggio) Sf(orzesco), followed by the number of the register or, in the latter case, of the *cartella*. My thanks are due to the Director, Professor A. R. Natale, and to the staff of the Archivio for their unfailing courtesy and help.

[7] L. Miss. 152, f. 114*v*.

[8] *Ibid.*, f. 63. I have kept the original spelling of documents but have expanded the contractions, modernised the punctuation and added accents.

[9] This must refer to the war of the Pazzi conspiracy and the campaigns to recover Genoa. Compare the 'pressure di guerra' in Ludovico's testament.

[10] Financial secretary in the Cancelleria segreta. He was devoted to Bona, and joined her after her withdrawal from Milan. He had been confirmed in office three days after the 'reductio ad Rochetam' by letters patent which reflect the confusion and uncertainties of these weeks: Reg. Duc. 114, ff. 202*v*–3.

[11] Antonio Landriani, for whom see *infra*.

[12] This account is based mainly on the evidence published by C. de' Rosmini, *Dell'Istoria di Milano*, IV, Milan, 1820, pp. 187–9, nn. 15–17. One would expect a letter conferring powers of this kind to have been countersigned *manu propria* by the *Duces* Bona and Giangaleazzo.

[13] L. Miss. 152, ff. 153–4.

[14] 'Accadeno' cancelled.

[15] Appointed 15 November 1480. See also *infra*.

[16] 'Cronica gestorum in partibus Lombardie', in L. A. Muratori, *Rer. Ital. Script.*, new series, XXII, part 3, p. 90. A check had been made on the 'vasselli' in the castello of Pavia in July: L. Miss. 150, f. 201, 20 July, to the Castellan.

[17] L. Miss. 152, ff. 243*v*–4, 23 March 1481, to Visconti and Marliani. For Tassino see Rosmini, *op. cit.*, IV, pp. 178–85, nn. 8–13.

[18] A letter to Pierfrancesco Visconti 'ed altri', mentioned by A. Ceruti in his edition of Ambrogio da Paullo, *Cronaca Milanese*, in *Misc. di stor. ital.*, XIII, 1871, p. 100, n. 1.

[19] Half a dozen or so variants can be found in L. Miss. 162 and 163, and in Cart. Sf. 1088 and 1089. The only danger of confusion arises from the existence of Deputati or Commissarii delle monete, responsible for the enforcement of the currency regulations.

[20] Cart. Sf. 1087, 23 June 1483, subscribed 'Prefecti rei pecuniarie'.

[21] *Ibid.*, 25 July 1483, Giovanni Ambrogio (da Perego) to Calco.

[22] *Ibid.*, 6 September 1483, the Prefecti to the Deputati dell'Ospedale Maggiore; L. Miss. 162, f. 239*v*, 4 October 1484, to the Prefecti; Cart. Sf. 1089, 28 September 1485, 'Philippus Eustachius Castellanus et Prefecti rei pecuniarie' to the duke.

[23] E.g. Cart. Sf. 1089, 1 October 1485, Prefecti to Lud. Sforza, for Gianfrancesco Visconti going to 'Alamania'.

[24] L. Miss. 162, f. 242*v*, 6 October 1484, to the Prefecti, for the Castellans of Voltaggio and Fiaccone (Alessandrino).

[25] *Ibid.*, f. 255, 12 October 1484, for the Bishop of Chur; f. 256*r–v*, 13 October, for George Count of Werdenberg.

[26] Cart. Sf. 1089, 4 December 1484, Deputati to Lud. Sforza; and 2 November 1485, Lud. Sforza to Calco; both concerning Domodossola.

[27] L. Miss. 160, ff. 262*v*–3, 6 April 1484, to the Deputati.

[28] Cart. Sf. 1089, 7 December 1484, two letters of the Deputati, one to Lud. Sforza and one to Calco; and 9 December to Lud. Sforza.

[29] Cart. Sf. 1087, 21 June 1483. For the official concerned, Giuseppe Colombino, see Santoro, *Uffici*, p. 507.

[30] Cart. Sf. 1089, 4 December 1485.

[31] He was Tesoriere generale or Commissario generale sopra lavorerii.

[32] Cart. Sf. 1089, 2 November 1485.

[33] *Ibid.*, 3 and 5 November 1485, Gianpiero Casati (the Ufficiale dei cavallari at the Chancery) to Calco.

[34] Filippo's instructions are in Reg. Duc. 114, ff. 237*v*–8*v*. Santoro, *Uffici*, p. 51, n. 6, puts the date of Filippo's death too late, and (p. 52) does not recognise Alberto as his successor.

[35] From the letters patent of appointment: Reg. Duc. 189 ff. 119–20, 17 September 1496.

[36] Santoro. *Uffici*, p. 52, n. 7, and the article there cited.

[37] L. Miss. 204, ff. 138–140*v*, 12 October 1496.

[38] Cart. Sf. 1134, in the folder for January 1496, a joint letter of the Archbishop of Milan, Calco and Bernardino Corte, summoning the Deputati post-haste to deal with an urgent call for money from the duke. The day and month are now lost.

[39] L. Miss. 199, ff. 118*v*–19 (to the Deputati) and f. 144*v* (to Bergonzio Botta and Marchesino Stanga), 5 and 8 April 1495. Cart. Sf. 1120, 2 April 1495; 1122, 4 May 1495; 1139, 25 April 1498, all from the Deputati to the duke.

[40] Cart. Sf. 1120, 24 March 1495, Agostino Calco to Bart. Calco.

[41] For instance, they proposed the sale of property to repay a large subvention: Cart. Sf. 1120, 27 March 1495, to the Duke. They had 'special cura de advertire a li beni de li ribelli': Cart. Sf. 1122, 25 September 1495, also to the duke.

[42] 'Tractandosi del interesse de la camera nostra, la mandiamo ad voi.' L. Miss. 199, f. 80, 31 March 1495, to the Deputati.

[43] Santoro, *Uffici*, p. 12, n. 2, and the article of Lazzeroni there cited. *Acta in Consilio secreto Mediolani*, ed. A. R. Natale, I, Milan, 1963, p. xxiii.

[44] Santoro, *Uffici*, pp. 65, 76, 13 and 78 (references in chronological order). They raise problems that cannot be discussed here.

[45] Cart. Sf. 1089, 9 December 1484, the Prefecti to Lud. Sforza.

[46] There is a sketch of his career by F. Calvi in *Rendiconti dell'Istituto Lombardo*, second series, xv, 1882, pp. 681–6; a summary in Malaguzzi Valeri, *op. cit.*, I, pp. 480–1.

[47] B. Corio, *Storia di Milano*, ed. E. de Magri, III, Milan, 1857, pp. 583–4 (for 1495), 683–4 (for 1498–99). Also A. Grumello, *Cronaca*, in *Raccolta di Cronisti e Documenti storici lombardi*, ed. G. Müller, I, Milan, 1856, p. 28.

[48] Cart. Sf. 1122, 17 September 1495, Alberto Bruscolo to the duke.

[49] Cart. Sf. 1092, 8 May 1490, Bart. Calco to Lud. Sforza, refers to the Deputati going to Vigevano; *ibid.*, 9 May, Agostino Calco from Vigevano to Bart. Calco, in the same context mentions Botta and Stanga.

[50] E. Motta, 'Morti in Milano, 1452–1552', *Arch. stor. lomb.*, XVIII, 1891, p. 285. There is a brief note on Bergonzio in A. Giulini, 'Nozze Borromeo nel Quattrocento', *ibid.*, XXXVII, part I, 1910, p. 264, n. 1.

[51] The earliest reference I have found is a letter to him in L. Miss. 181, f. 61, 18 August 1490; *cf.* Santoro, *Uffici*, p. 67, n. 3. For his father Giovanni, *ibid.*, pp. 66, 68.

[52] Malaguzzi Valeri, *op. cit.*, I, p. 194.

[53] *Ibid.*, p. 536. K. Trauman Steinitz, 'The voyage of Isabella d'Aragon from Naples to Milan', *Bibliothèque d'Humanisme et de Renaissance*, XXIII, 1961, p. 22 and n. 1.

[54] F. Muralto, *Annalia*, ed. P. A. Doninio, Milan, 1861, pp. 53–4.

[55] L. G. Pélissier, *Louis XII et Ludovic Sforza*, II, Paris, 1896, pp. 283, 292.

[56] *Ibid.*, p. 151 (from Sanuto, *Diarii*, III, p. 135).

⁵⁷ 'Ab adolescentia': Reg. Duc. 92, f. 53, 10 January 1492. For accounts of Marchesino see F. Arisi, *Cremona literata*, I, Cremona, 1702, pp. 376–84; R. Renier, 'Gaspare Visconti', *Arch. stor. lomb.*, XIII, 1886, pp. 802–6. I have not seen Ildefonso Stanga, *La famiglia Stanga*, Milan, 1895.

⁵⁸ A letter of Lud. Sforza to Bart. Calco authenticated 'Marchesinus' and concerned with grain supply, in Cart. Sf. 1138, folder for December 1497, is in fact dated 15 December 1488. Marchesino was 'secretarius noster predilectus': L. Miss. 149, f. 309, 23 March 1491, to the Maestri delle entrate straordinarie, but he was not on the staff of the Cancelleria segreta (*cf.* Santoro, *Uffici*, p. 52): the title seems to have been attached to the 'prefectura annone': Reg. Duc. 189, ff. 175v–6, 25 May 1497, confirmation of his appointment.

⁵⁹ Cart. Sf. 1091, undated, in the folder for December 1489; but part of the instructions were passed on to the Camera on 14 February 1489: L. Miss. 149, f. 223.

⁶⁰ Tristani Chalci Historiographi *Residua*, Milan, 1644, p. 110. R. Renier, 'Gaspare Visconti', *Arch. stor. lomb.*, XIII, 1886, p. 802, n. 4, for Lucari. In 1496 Marchesino held one of the corniole or privy signets of the duke: L. Miss. 204, f. 138v, the instructions for Giangiacomo Ferruffino. Bartolomeo Calco held another one.

⁶¹ C. A. Vianello, 'Testimonianze venete su Milano . . .,' *Arch. stor. lomb.*, new series, IV, 1939, p. 414.

⁶² A. Luzio and R. Renier, 'Relazioni di Isabella d'Este con Ludovico e Beatrice Sforza', *ibid.*, XVII, 1890, p. 118.

⁶³ For poems and epigrams addressed to him by Perotto and others see P. O. Kristeller, *Iter Italicum*, I, London, 1963, pp. 113–14; II, 1967, p. 354. For Bellincioni see *infra*, n. 83.

⁶⁴ E. M[otta], 'Per l'Amedeo', *Arch. stor. lomb.*, XXX, part 1, 1903, p. 488. C. C[antù], 'Aneddoti di Lodovico il Moro', *ibid.*, I, 1874, pp. 483–4.

⁶⁵ Tristano Calco, *op. cit.*, p. 95; and p. 111, for his elegance.

⁶⁶ Sanuto, *Diarii*, II, p. 1373, and *cf.* Pélissier, *op. cit.*, II, p. 291.

⁶⁷ News of his death reached Bassano on 28 August: Sanuto, *Diarii*, III, p. 681.

⁶⁸ B. Corio, *op. cit.*, II, p. 487.

⁶⁹ 'Ab ineunte adolescentia': Santoro, *Uffici*, p. 148. E. Motta, 'Morti in Milano', *Arch. stor. lomb.*, XVIII, 1891, p. 286, for date of birth. His father was Battista: see the document referred to *infra*, n. 129. I know of no account of his career.

⁷⁰ Bart. Calco to 'm. Gualtero': Cart. Sf. 1087, 26 June 1483; *ibid.*, 22 June, Battista Landriani to Lud. Sforza, addressed 'in manibus Gualterii'.

⁷¹ Santoro, *Uffici*, p. 148.

⁷² L. Miss. 177, f. 44, to Gregorio Panigarola, 18 September 1489; in the margin, 'minuta est in filza signat. Deputat. super monetis viz. Antonius Thex., Gualterius.' Cart. Sf. 1094, 4 December 1490, draft of a letter to Raffaello Gambarana, subscribed 'Antonius Thes. Gualterius'.

⁷³ 'Volemo che ti senza Gualtero provedi de presente de denari . . .' (11 May 1494): L. Beltrami, *Castello di Milano*, Milan, 1894, p. 485.

⁷⁴ Witness list in Reg. Duc. 63, f. 93v, 14 January 1495 ([*sic*] on f. 92, but 'Indictione XIV, die Jovis' points to 1496), as prefectus nummarius and judex datiorum. *Ibid.*, ff. 177v, 239v, 247, he witnessed as *camerarius* and *judex datiorum* on the same day. His *locum tenens* as Giudice dei dazi, Antonio Bascapè, is mentioned in a legal record: Cart. Sf. 1140, 28 November 1498.

⁷⁵ Santoro, *Uffici*, pp. 67, 148.

⁷⁶ *Id.*, 'Contributi alla storia dell'amministrazione sforzesca', in *Arch. stor. lomb.*, new series, IV, 1939, p. 2 of doc. 4.

⁷⁷ Eg. Cart. Sf. 1139, 12 February 1498, Alberto Bruscolo to the duke (one of two letters of that date); *ibid.*, 16 June 1498, Lud. Sforza to Bart. Calco.

⁷⁸ Malaguzzi Valeri, *op. cit.*, III, p. 7, 7 December 1493.

⁷⁹ L. Beltrami, *op. cit.*, pp. 504–5, 16 December 1497.

⁸⁰ L. Miss. 206 *bis*, ff. 162v–3, 30 June 1497, to Bascapè.

[81] *Le rime* di Bernardo Bellincioni, ed. P. Fanfani, Bologna, 1876, I, pp. 5–7. For the committee see C. Santoro, *Registri delle lettere ducali del periodo sforzesco*, Milan, 1961, pp. 257–8: Reg. 6, Nos. 115, 118–19.

[82] Kristeller, *op. cit.*, I pp. 113–14.

[83] *Le rime*, ed. cit., I, pp. 242–3, 179–80.

[84] L. Beltrami, *op. cit.*, pp. 511–12 (letters of 20 and 21 April 1498).

[85] *Literary works* of Leonardo da Vinci, ed. J. P. Richter, London, third edition, 1970, I, p. 383.

[86] L. G. Pélissier, *op. cit.*, II, p. 133. G. Andrea de Prato, 'Storia di Milano', *Arch. stor. Ital.*, III, 1842, p. 247.

[87] *Inv. e Reg. del R. Archivio di Stato in Milano* III, Milan, 1920, p. 329 (Reg. 24, No. 220), 22 February 1507, in favour of Gualtiero and his brother Battista.

[88] For his will see A. Noto, *Amici dei poveri di Milano, 1305–1964*, Milan, second edition, 1966, p. 212.

[89] Sanuto, *Diarii*, II, p. 1311. Leonardo da Vinci mentions a property at Candia near Alessandria belonging to 'Messer Gualtieri': *Literary Works*, ed. cit., II, p. 195.

[90] Sanuto, *Diarii*, I, p. 881.

[91] Cart. Sf. 1140, 28 October 1498, a draft of Ludovico's letter.

[92] Cart. Sf. 1090, 1 March 1486, Lud. Sforza to Bart. Calco and Luigi Terzago.

[93] Cart. Sf. 1469 (*Potenze Sovrane: Lud. Sforza*), 20 October 1494 (a draft).

[94] Cart. Sf. 1120, 25 April 1495.

[95] Cart. Sf. 1089, 9 December 1484, one of two letters of that date to Ludovico Sforza.

[96] Cart. Sf. 1140, 26 August 1498, G. Colli to the duke.

[97] *Ibid.*, 8 and 9 July 1498, both to the duke. I have not been able to identify or date the 'mostra di Melegnano'. For Raimondi's mission see *Calendar of State Papers, Milan*, ed. A. B. Hinds, I, London, 1912, pp. 343–51.

[98] Calco's letter in Cart. Sf. 1092, 8 May 1490. Also Cart. Sf. 1094, 15 December 1490, Calco to Lud. Sforza; Cart. Sf. 1122, 2 May 1495, Tommaso Brasca to Calco; L. Miss. 199, f. 200v, 1 May 1495, to the Deputati.

[99] Cart. Sf. 1092, 20 April 1490, to Lud. Sforza; and again, 26 April, *ibid.*

[100] Cart. Sf. 1157, 5 February 1498, Traversa to the duke.

[101] 'Se compra ogni cossa fin al sole in Milano.' Cart. Sf. 1139, 27 March 1498, Antonio Trotto to the duke.

[102] Cart. Sf. 1091, 28 April and 16 May 1489, Calco to Lud. Sforza.

[103] L. Miss. 199, f. 116, 5 April 1495.

[104] For Ludovico's projected visit to the camp see Luzio and Renier, *art. cit.*, *Arch. stor. lomb.*, XVII, 1890, p. 624, n. 4. Cart. Sf. 1120, 18 April 1495, the Deputati to the duke; 19 April, the duke to the Deputati, and the four letters of 21 April are drafts.

[105] *Ibid.*, 24 (Missaglia) and 30 April (Stanga), both to the duke.

[106] *Ibid.*, 18 and 28 April 1495, Bernardino's letters; and 30 April, the draft of a letter to Filippino Fieschi, for Ludovico's message in reply.

[107] Cart. Sf. 1122, 9 July 1495, Andrea Birago to Sanseverino.

[108] Cart. Sf. 1091, 2 (or 5?) December 1489, to Lud. Sforza (in the folder for September 1489).

[109] Cart. Sf. 1092, 25 May 1490, to Lud. Sforza.

[110] Cart. Sf. 1120, 1 April 1495, Tommaso Brasca to Calco; L. Miss. 199, ff. 97v–98, 2 April 1495, to the Deputati.

[111] L. Miss. 199, ff. 171r–v, 177, 185v–6, 24, 26, 28 April 1495, all to the Deputati, for Bernardino Imperiale. Cart. Sf. 1094, 18 November 1490, Calco to Lud. Sforza (for Gianpiero Pietrasanta and Battista Sfondrati). Cart. Sf. 1139, 4 April 1498, the Deputati to the duke (for Niccolò Maleta).

[112] Cart. Sf. 1091, 9 and 10 May 1489, Calco to the duke.

[113] Cart. Sf. 1122, 20 September 1495, the Deputati to the duke.

[114] Cart. Sf. 1141, 14 March 1499, Calco to the Deputati, and their reply written below.

[115] Cart. Sf. 1122, 7 August 1495, Stanga to the duke.

[116] The case of Taddea Malaspina Signora di Scaldasole. Cart. Sf. 1120, 21 and 24 March and 27 April 1495, the Deputati to the duke. Cart. Sf. 1141, folder for March 1499, contains the draft of a letter of the duke to the Deputati, 24 March 1495, on the same subject.

[117] Cart. Sf. 1122, 3 August 1495, the Deputati to the duke.

[118] Cart. Sf. 1140, 27 September 1498, the draft of their letter; *ibid.*, 26 September, the draft of a ducal letter to Aldighieri. He may still have been administrator of the salt monopoly in Parma, a post he held in 1480 and 1485.

[119] Their letter of 21 March 1495 referred to in n. 116.

[120] See *supra*, p. 280, and n. 28. Some other instances in L. Miss. 172 *bis*, f. 14*v*, 17 July 1488, and L. Miss. 199, f. 175*v*, 25 April 1495, both to the Deputati; Cart. Sf. 1157, 28 July 1496, Giangiacomo Madregnano to the Deputati.

[121] E.g. Cart. Sf. 1120, 17 April 1495, the Deputati to the duke.

[122] L. Miss. 199, f. 71*v*, 30 March 1495, to the Deputati, in reply to a letter of theirs in Cart. Sf. 1120, 28 March. *Cf.* also their letter, *ibid.*, 27 March.

[123] Cart. Sf. 1122, 8 December 1495 (in the folder for September 1495), draft of a ducal letter to the Deputati.

[124] 'Noi non sapemo che li deputati del denaro haviano ordini da noi de non fare assignatione. . . . Sapemo bene che hanno ordini di non fare assignatione se non sono tuti insiema.' Cart. Sf. 1090, 4 September 1486, Lud. Sforza to Calco.

[125] L. Miss. 206 *bis*, f. 182, 11 July 1497, to the Consiglio about a case before them, seems to uphold an 'inhibitione' imposed by the Deputati. On the other hand, a letter to the Podestà of Milan told him to obey the Consiglio in spite of a 'relatione facta nomine deputatorum nostrorum rei pecuniarie': *ibid.*, f. 100*v*, 22 May 1497.

[126] Cart. Sf. 1087, 6 September 1483, 'ducales Prefecti rei monetarie Castri' (to the Deputies of the Ospedale Maggiore). Cart. Sf. 1090, 23 April 1486, Lud. Sforza to Calco and Luigi Terzago: 'quelli deputati sopra el dinaro lì in castello'. L. Miss. 177, f. 43*v*, a note from the Deputati to Calco, 'ex castro porte Jovis Mli. 17 Sept. 1489'. Cart. Sf. 1137, 9 February 1497, the Deputati to Calco 'ex camera', is ambiguous; *cf. ibid.*, 19 July 1497, Bascapè to Andrea Borgio 'ex curia', which suggests that Bascapè may have worked from an office (perhaps that of the Giudice dei dazi) in the Corte dell'Arengo alongside the Camera.

[127] Cart. Sf. 1122, 30 September 1495, Lud. Sforza from the siege of Novara to Calco, enclosing a summary of diplomatic mail: 'se partecipi alli consilieri et deputati'.

[128] Costabili's report, 16 August 1499: L. G. Pélissier, 'Textes et fragments inédits relatifs à l'histoire des moeurs italiennes, 1498–1500', *Revue des langues romanes*, fourth series, x, 1897, pp. 522–3. 'Da l'altro canto de la capella era il signor duca cum li deputati a fare facende.'

[129] A. Caimi, 'Di un documento in cui è ricordato Leonardo da Vinci', *Bollettino della Consulta Archaeologica*, pp. 115–17, in *Arch. stor. lomb.*, II, 1875.

[130] Ed. Ceruti, in *Misc. di stor. Italiana*, XIII, 1871, pp. 105–6. Malaguzzi Valeri, *op. cit.*, I, p. 481, quotes the list, adding the secretaries of the Cancelleria.

[131] Sanuto, *Diarii*, III, p. 681.

[132] *Ibid.*, II, p. 1033.

[133] G. Andrea de Prato, 'Cronica', *Arch. stor. Ital.*, III, 1842, p. 222. See also B. Corio, *op. cit.*, III, p. 692.

[134] *Ibid.*, p. 471. For his references to Guelfs and Ghibellines see pp. 351–2, 404–5, 423, 429, 687. He does not explain the meaning of the terms.

[135] According to Sanuto, *Diarii*, II, p. 1210.

[136] See, for instance, D. M. Bueno de Mesquita, 'Ludovico Sforza and his vassals', in *Italian Renaissance Studies*, ed. E. F. Jacob, London, 1960, pp. 184–215. F. Catalano, 'Scorci Machiavelliani', *Nuova rivista storica*, XLIX, 1965, pp. 545–6, reasserts his schematic views on the neglect of the bourgeoisie. More fundamental is G. Chittolini,

'La crisis delle libertà communali e le origini dello Stato territoriale', *Rivista storica ital.*, LXXXII, 1970, pp. 99–120.

[137] The government constantly underlined its adherence to 'il consueto': D. M. Bueno de Mesquita, The place of despotism in Italian politics', in *Europe in the Late Middle Ages*, ed. J. R. Hale *et al.*, London, 1965, pp. 318–23.

[138] In his relation Lippomano also named Galeazzo Sanseverino (regarded by many as a foreigner) and Bernardino Corte (also named by Paullo) as men who 'poteva con il ducha'. 'Ins' and 'Outs', 'court' and 'country'?

[139] C. Santoro, *Gli offici del commune di Milano* (*Archivio della Fondazione Italiana per la storia amministrativa*, VII), Milan, 1968, pp. 336, 403–4.

PAUL LAWRENCE ROSE   *James Cook*
University of North Queensland

16

BARTOLOMEO ZAMBERTI'S FUNERAL ORATION FOR THE HUMANIST ENCYCLOPAEDIST GIORGIO VALLA

THE HUMANIST Giorgio Valla of Piacenza (1447–1500), apparently a relative of the more famous Lorenzo, is well known for his translations of Greek literary, philosophical, medical and mathematical texts; for his spectacular library of Greek manuscripts; and for his encyclopaedia *De Expetendis Rebus et Fugiendis*, posthumously published at Venice by Aldus in 1501.[1] After studying with Constantine Lascaris at Milan in the early 1460s Valla went on to pursue medicine and mathematics at Pavia under Giovanni Marliani. In the following years Giorgio himself became a notable teacher of humanities at Pavia, Milan and Genoa before finding his final niche at Venice in 1485 as public professor of Latin.[2] His residence there was marred by his imprisonment on suspicion of treason for some months in 1496, but he was acquitted and released. The humanist died in January 1500 (new style). As his correspondence shows, Valla was acquainted with many leading humanists, including Ermolao Barbaro (who had been instrumental in Valla's coming to Venice), Jacopo Antiquari, Poliziano, Francesco Filelfo, Giovanni Pico, Ficino, Pietro Barozzi, Niccolò Leoniceno and Aldo Manuzio.[3] Surprisingly, however, his role in the formation of the Venetian *cultura filosofica* of the sixteenth century has been little studied.

Valla's main achievements lie in the translation and editing of classical texts. Among his philosophical and literary writings are commentaries on Cicero, Pliny and Juvenal and notes on the *De Orthographia* of Giovanni Tortelli.[4] There is also a translation of the *Problemata* of Alexander of Aphrodisias done, according to Valla, at the suggestion of Giovanni Marliani, his teacher at Pavia.[5] Marliani may also be considered a dominant influence on Valla's numerous medical translations, which include works of Galen, Hippocrates and other Greeks. Several of these are printed in a miscellany of Valla's translations published at Venice in 1498 and dedicated to the Duke of Urbino.[6] This important collection includes also several Latin versions of Greek mathematical works, among them Aristarchus of Samos, Proclus (*De Astrolabo*), Cleomedes (*Musica*) and Euclid–Hypsicles, book XIV.

Valla's preoccupation with mathematics is attested by the public lectures on humanities that he was giving at Venice in the 1490s. According to Cademosto's life of his adoptive father, the humanist often lectured on astronomy and geometry on festivals and during vacations.[7] In 1492 Valla apparently gave courses of lectures on Euclid and Vitruvius, as well as on such properly humanistic topics as Plautus and Cicero's *De Oratore*.[8] While reading the second book of the *Historia Naturalis* of Pliny, Valla decided to elucidate its obscure astronomical sections with fresh mathematical notes.[9]

The mathematical part of Valla's splendid collection of Greek manuscripts is outstanding. Among the extant mathematical manuscripts that he seems to have owned are Greek texts of the Aristotelian *Mechanica*, Euclid, Apollonius, Ptolemy and Proclus. After Valla's death his manuscripts were incorporated into the Carpi family library, whence they passed in great part to the Biblioteca Estense, where many of them are still to be found.[10] One of the most interesting of Valla's Greek manuscripts, however, has been lost since the mid-sixteenth century. This is the famous Codex A of Archimedes, which had attracted a great deal of humanist interest during the 1490s. Valla's Archimedes was seen by Janus Lascaris at Venice *c.* 1490;[11] in 1491 it was examined by Poliziano, who arranged to have a copy forwarded to Florence.[12] In 1492 an emissary of Ercole I d'Este tried to borrow the codex on behalf of his master, but Valla was loth to let such a treasure out of his hands, although willing to allow a copy of it to be made.[13]

Codex A and other mathematical manuscripts of Valla's figure prominently in his *De Expetendis Rebus*. Here appear for the first time in print excerpts translated from Apollonius, Archimedes, Eutochius and Heron, as well as Valla's own commentaries on Euclid.[14] It is also possible that Valla intended translating Codex A anew *in toto* to replace the earlier Renaissance translation of Archimedes done by Jacobus Cremonensis *c.* 1450.[15]

Valla's *De Expetendis Rebus* has been little studied to date, yet it is a source of some importance for the state of humanist studies around 1500.[16] The work is an enormous humanistic encyclopaedia compiled largely from fresh translations and paraphrases of classical authors: medieval and Arabic works are generally excluded. Of medieval translators Valla seems to have had a poor opinion, to judge by the critical remarks with which he prefaced his 1496 translation of the *Magna Moralia* of Aristotle.[17] In content, therefore, Valla's *De Expetendis Rebus* marks a departure from medieval encyclopaedias.

The same may be said of the form of Valla's work. Although its design is a little obscure,[18] it is possible to interpret the encyclopaedia as a fusion of mathematics, medicine and natural philosophy (subjects in which Valla's translations reveal a special interest) with the *studia humanitatis*.[19] In this scheme mathematics holds pride of place. The first of the forty-nine books[20] defines philosophy and establishes the place of mathematics in philosophy. Books 2–19 treat the mathematical sciences, starting with arithmetic and moving on to music, geometry and astronomy. Physics is disposed of in books 20–3, medicine in books 24–30. Books 31–41 comprise the humanities (grammar, dialectic, poetry, rhetoric and moral philosophy). There follow sections on economics and politics (books 42–5) and physiology and psychology (books 46–8), rounded out by a conclusion (book 49). Thus the first thirty books attend to Valla's primary divisions of philosophy, while the second group (books 31–48) pertains to the humanist study of man, whether in the active or in the contemplative sphere. Through the device of re-constituting traditional *philosophia* into a tripartite framework of mathematics, medicine and natural philosophy, Valla successfully abandoned the typical structure of the medieval encyclopaedia. To this reformed *philosophia* (books 1–30) he then added a new layer of humanist learning (books 31–48). The *De Expetendis Rebus* represents, therefore, a remarkable attempt at forming a humanist encyclopaedia totally different in both form and content from that of the Middle Ages.

The importance attached to mathematics by Valla left an imprint upon Venetian humanist thought.[21] As Nardi has pointed out, the predominantly Aristotelian Scuola di Rialto took a surprisingly strong interest in mathe-matics from the middle of the fifteenth century;[22] perhaps its foremost alumnus in this respect was the mathematician Luca Pacioli, who was later to oppose Valla's disciple, Zamberti. However, the importance of the Rialto school has obscured the role of the more humanistic Scuola di San Marco in bringing a mathematical flavour to Venetian humanism. Yet it is not surprising that the San Marco Platonists, represented by Valla, should have shared an interest in mathematics. One major influence on Valla had, of course, been his teacher at Pavia, the mathematician Giovanni Marliani. But it seems that as early as 1475 our humanist was expounding Cicero's remarks on the mathematical *Timaeus* of Plato.[23] Certainly Valla's philo-sophical attitude to mathematics has far more in common with the *Timaeus* than with the somewhat dry mathematical thought of the scholastic Marliani.[24]

Valla died on 23 January 1500,[25] but his brand of mathematical Platonism found an enthusiastic continuator in his student, the Venetian Bartolomeo Zamberti. Little is known of Zamberti except that he seems to have been born in 1473 and died after July 1539, the date of his latest known work.[26] Active as a lawyer and a humanist, Zamberti had a particular interest in Alexander of Aphrodisias, whose logical works he translated between 1511 and 1524.[27] (It will be remembered that Valla had earlier translated the *Problemata* of Alexander.)

Perhaps the chief project of Zamberti was to restore mathematics to an eminent position in *cultura filosofica*, thus following in the footsteps of Valla.[28] This theme is rehearsed in Zamberti's main preface to the Latin translation (from the Greek) of Euclid that he published at Venice in 1505. Much of this preface comes from Proclus and Ammonius and consists of a short history of Greek geometry in which Plato emerges as the figure who conjoined mathematics with moral and natural philosophy. To emphasise the relation-ship between mathematics and natural philosophy Zamberti confuses Euclid the geometer with Eucleides of Megara, the Platonistic philosopher.[29] These themes are reiterated in the six subsidiary prefaces interspersed through the volume. While the volume as a whole is dedicated to Valla's patron, Duke Guidobaldo of Urbino, the shorter prefaces are addressed to local personages, including Lorenzo Loredano, Paolo Pisano, Lodovico Mocenigo, Giovanni Zamberti (Bartolomeo's brother), Giovanni Antonio Abiosi and Marino Giorgi.

Zamberti's Euclid of 1505—which he tells us he worked on for seven years —was the first translation from the Greek to appear in print.[30] The *Elementa* had previously been published in the Arabo-Latin redaction of Campano (Venice, 1482) which attracted the humanist wrath of Zamberti: originally a perfectly designed work, the *Elementa* had been translated by Giovanni Antonio Campano without the least good judgement. In his hands Euclid had been barbarously obscured, preposterously and perversely confused, and corruptly and ignorantly destroyed. The *Elementa* in this version should be retitled *Chaos*. Zamberti has now tried to rescue the work from its obscurity and render it accessible not only to mathematicians but also to logicians and physicians. Under the patronage of the Duke of Urbino, the translator hopes, the volume will be received into the schools.[31] Later Zamberti speaks of the wondrous ghosts, dreams and fantasies which pervade the version of Campano—'ille interpres barbarissimus'. As relief from this tediousness Zamberti invites the weary student to turn to the more humane ('ad humaniora') pleasures of the present translation.[32] Here one will not find barbarisms such as Campano's use of the word *helmuain* in a Latin text and his mistranslation of the fifth definition of book v.

Zamberti's ferocious edition soon provoked a defence of Campano by Fra Luca Pacioli of Borgo San Sepolcro. In the 1460s Pacioli had studied mathematics under Domenico Bragadino at the Scuola di Rialto in Venice. He himself taught in the Adriatic city and later at Perugia, Florence, Milan and Rome. In 1494 Pacioli published his *Summa de Aritmetica* at Venice, dedicating it to that ubiquitous patron of mathematical learning Duke Guidobaldo of Urbino. During a later sojourn in Venice Pacioli delivered a public lecture on the fifth book of Euclid at the church of San Bartolomeo (August 1508). The lecture (which reveals Pacioli's own Platonist sympathies despite his earlier affiliation to the Rialto school) was attended by a notable audience of scholars. Among the ninety-four named by Pacioli are G. B. Egnazio, Fra Giocondo, Janus Lascaris, Bernardo Bembo, Sebastiano Foscarini, Marino Sanuto, Aldo Manuzio and Bernardo Rucellai, the Florentine.[33] The following year Pacioli brought out at Venice a revised edition of the Campano *Elementa* intended as a defence of the medieval author. The title page of the 1509 Euclid acclaims Campano as 'interpres fidissimus' and blames the errors of the medieval redaction not upon its author but upon careless copyists. In revising the redaction—particularly the diagrams therein—Pacioli portrays himself as a *castigator* of a different sort from Zamberti, whom he chides (without naming) for having ignorantly shown off at the expense of Campano. The dispute, as it happened, was not finally decided in favour of either party. For in 1516 Jacques Lefèvre d'Etaples reconciled the two translations in a composite volume; and both versions were later made obsolete as a result of the publication of the Greek *editio princeps* at Basel in 1533 and the superlative Latin translation of Federico Commandino (Pesaro, 1572).[34]

Besides his Euclid, Zamberti also completed in 1539 a Latin translation of Proclus' commentary on that author (Munich, MS Lat. 6).[35] This was not published, but the first translation of the commentary to be printed was by a Venetian successor of Zamberti's, Francesco Barozzi (Padua, 1560). Barozzi also devoted much effort to expounding the number passages of Plato's *Republic*, as well as to the study of mathematics proper. It is therefore possible to extend Valla's influence on Venetian humanists and mathematicians into the second half of the sixteenth century.

The document printed below may help to illustrate the ideas of both Zamberti and Valla. Zamberti's funeral oration for Giorgio Valla is at present preserved in an early sixteenth-century manuscript in *scrittura libraria*, at the Biblioteca Nazionale Marciana, Venice, MS Lat. xi, 6 (3811).[36] As far as I know, Professor Kristeller has given the only printed notice to date of this item.[37]

Cademosto does not mention Zamberti's delivering the oration at the funeral of Valla (d. 23 January 1500).[38] Moreover Zamberti prefaces his *éloge* with a dedication, dated *iii Kalendas Aprilis M.D.I.*, to Lorenzo Loredano (who later received one of the dedications of the Zamberti Euclid of 1505).[39] But Zamberti does use the explicit title *In funere Georgii Valae . . . oratio*, suggesting that it was indeed delivered at the funeral.

In general Zamberti corroborates Cademosto's account of the humanist, though in a less precise way. One point of interest is the claim to Giorgio's family connection with Lorenzo Valla (f. 4). But the general import of the oration is Valla's contribution to the renaissance of learning, a revival that includes the restoration of mathematics. Thus at f. 3*v* Zamberti laments the decay of learning, singling out as examples grammar, physiology and the extinct mathematical disciplines. At ff. 4*v*–5 Valla's role in bringing about a revival is elaborated: in mathematics Valla's efforts were so distinguished that in him Nicomachus, Euclid, Archimedes and Ptolemy were deemed to have come to life again (*reviviscere*). The case of Giorgio Valla may serve to illustrate a central point made by Professor Kristeller some years ago: in the Renaissance there was no automatic antagonism between humanism and mathematics.[40]

EDITING PROCEDURE

The manuscript is neither foliated nor paginated; the foliations given are the editor's. Abbreviations and contractions have been expanded, while the original orthography has been retained. In several places the punctuation has been modernised, and capital letters have been supplied.

BIBLIOTECA NAZIONALE MARCIANA, VENICE, MS LAT. XI, 6 (3811)

BARTHOLAMEUS ZAMBERTUS VENETUS LAURENTIO LAURETANO
PATRICIO VENETO VIRO ERVDITISSIMO SALUTEM DICIT AETERNAM

A maioribus nostris instituta usque ad nostra tempora propagata consuetudo tenuit Laurenti uir longe doctissime, ut quocumque nouo anno, quem non nulli martijs, nonnulli Januarijs kalendis incipere censuerunt, qui perpetuo uincti essent beniuolentiae uinculo se adinuicem aliquo munusculo salutarent. Te igitur, quem ob egregiam animi tui clementiam praeclarasque uirtutes non modo diligo sed uehementer amaui, eo existimaui munere salutandum, quod et tibi a me dari, et abs te accipi oporteret. Nolui enim ad te mittere id quod multi nostrae aetatis qui uiuunt ineptiores ineptia tribuunt, scilicet edulia aut aurum siue argentum, quae animos hominum potius corrumpere et effoeminari solent, quam ad aliquam uirtutem impellere. Quam igitur in funere Georgij Vallae Placentini philosophi praestantissimi nostrique; praeceptoris eximij orationem contexui ad te mitto, scilicet ut ea fit quae et nostrorum maiorum instituto satisfaciat et mei in te [f. 1v] amoris argumentum sit immortale. Quam si tibi non displicuisse intellexero aliquod aliud ingenio excultum, elaboratum industria, nitidum ellegantia excudam quod tuo uirtutum sacrario emancipabo, ut admirabilis illa humanitas tua quanti Laurentium Lauretanum semper existimauerim exactissime cognoscere possit. Hoc igitur munusculum uidebis mi Laurenti: et cum quid tibi otij superfuerit legere etiam ne pigeat. Quod si feceris abs te mihi cumulate satisfactum fuisse censebo. Et fortasse quod illud admirabile ingenium tuum tam publicis quam priuatis negotijs tandem expeditum: cum huiusmodi se senserit studiorum nostrorum rudimentis lacessitum emittet eos flores quos suffundere solet, omni splendore clariores, omni elegantia insignes, omni suauitate redolentes, qui sane facillime effecerunt ut ea tibi sim deuinctus beniuolentia, qualem nullum tempus obliuioni mandare possit. Munusculum igitur candidissime Laurenti accipias et ualeas aeternum dulce mei dimidium iii kalendas Aprilis. M. D. I. [f. 2r]

FUNERE GEORGII VALAE PLACENTINI PHILOSOPHI PRAESTANTISSIMI
ORATIO

Posteaquam hunc ornatissimum locum ad dicendum amplissimum sic iniqua sors tulit, grauissimi patres caeterique auditores praestantissimi, ut Georgij Vallae philosophi eximij nostrique saeculi rarissimi ornamenti laudes explicaturus conscenderem. Si ea quae de illo praeclara nullisque saeculis audita facinora dici possunt ieiuniori exiguaque oratione minus quam parest recensuero, clementioris animi uestri magnitudinem praestantiamque singularem quaeso atque obtestor, ut id et moerori maestitiaeque, quibus adeo animus noster consternitur, ut uix sui compos esse uideatur, et imbecilitati nostrae ad id oneris subeundi attribuendum putetis. Quandoquidem lachrymae quibus oculi, et singultus quibus pectus abundant silentium rumpere minime permittant: ac unicuique exactissimum sit, tantas talesque uirtutes, tanta rutilantis gloriae ornamenta in illo enituisse, ut ununquenque et in omni dicendi genere [f. 2v] consumacissimum facillime deterrere posset. At cum illud animo mecum circumuoluo Georgium scilicet Vallam tali amore me prosequutum fuisse, ut omni solertia, omni studio curaque inuigilauerit. Quo efficeret ut teneros suscipiens annos sinu socratico ex tenebris ad lucem ex senticosis confragosisque locis ad uerae uirtutis fastigium se duce facillime aspirarem. Omni sane ingratitudini et uitiorum omnium pessimo obnoxius facillime existimari possem, nisi eorum quae iecisset seminum si minus uiuendo, attamen supremo funeri maesto ac plorabundo aliquos fructus reportaret. Vnde sane effectum est ut tametsi paruitate ingenij detentus efficere tamen nequiuerim, quin et obseruantiae quam erga illum habebam maximam satisfacerem, et Joannis Petri necnon et Hieronymi eius necessariorum luctus maerorem ac maestissimos planctus aliqua ex parte demulcerem. Tametsi minime inficias iverim multos in hoc grauissimorum sapientissimorum uirorum coetu adesse illius discipulos. Et me quidem omnium minimo longe peritiores qui huiusmodi prouintiam liberius ac expeditius aequis possent uiribus substinere. Sed quoniam suorum erga me meritorum magnitudo ita exigit eiusque necessarij sic referendum censuere permittamus uela uentis et oram soluentibus iuxta illud Quintiliani [f. 3r] bene precemur. Illud in primis refferendo quae sint omnes nostri cogitatus irridendi, quae uanae et fallaces prorsus omnium spes mortalium, quandoquidem illum

Georgium Vallam pridieque uitam cum morte commutaret nitide facunde atque
eleganter de animae immortalitate quaestionibus tusculanis M. Tullij ducibus
audiuerimus disputantem, seque accingentem intellexerimus quo die ad superos ex
humanis secessit, ut epicurea deliramenta platonicorumque rectius philosophantium
instituta Lucretio epicureo Timaeoque ducibus patefaceret, importuna morte ex
mortalium oculis sublatus: illam omnibus saeculis deplorandam: illam diem in quo
totius Italiae rutilanti extincto illo sidere plurimum sit ingemiscendum: illam diem non
solum nobis maestissimi auditores, uobisque Ioannes Petre et Hieronyme: sed uniuerse
ciuitati tristem ac peraccerbam. Quandoquidem omnes nunc prorsus disciplinae cum
uno Georgio Valla extinctae facillime existimari possint. Qua igitur oratione, qua
ellegantia, qua uerborum politie uos nunc praestantissimi auditores demulcerem:
presertim cum ego potius consolabundus huc aduenerim quam ut alios consolarer:
tum etiam cum tanta taleque et omnibus saeculis mauditam iacturam perpessi sitis,
quantum aut qualem animo unusquisque uix concipere posset. Mortua nunc [f. 3v]
grammatica: extinctae mathematicae disciplinae: e medio mortalium sublata
physiologia: ac uniuersa philosophia miro squalore confecta: luctuoso pullo atque
obscuro palio circunuoluta in tenebris et caligine iacet foedissime plorabunda. Quibus
igitur lachrymis, quo fletu, aut planctu lugubrem hunc diem persequi poterimus,
grauissimi auditores: nullis. Nam nullae lachrymae aut luctus huic tam graui iactura
mederi posse existimandae sunt. At quam lachrymis fatum nec flectitur ullis: illud
sane recta intellectus trutina cognoscendum est ιὸ ζβροζεις ἀπασιμ χαζθανεῖν
ὁ φειλεται illudque assidue uoluendum animo quod *Irheitius cecinit* [?] Orpheus
aeternum scilicet fieri nihil. Nam naturae cedens Georgius Valla, et cum nobis
minime persuaderemus non solum uos Ioannes Petre et Hieronyme iuuenes integerrimi, uerum etiam et omnes discipulos ac totam ciuitatem tanti uiri praesentia
exultantem miro squalore confecit. Heu sortem aduersam cum sic Deo optimo
maximo placitum sit, ut uoluptati moeror, laetitiae tristitia, risui luctus comes
consequatur. Sed ne uos humanissimi auditores diuturniori quae parest et incompta
quidem orationem detineam. Quae huiusmodi sit quae uestros eruditissimos uultus
potius formidare [f. 4r] debeat quam ex nostro pectore prodire: illud quod mihi dicendum superest citius quam fieri poterit absoluam ac breui percurram. Georgius igitur
Valla Placentia antiquissima ciuitate honestissimaque Vallarum familia oriundus
quanta doctrina inter mortales enituerit morumque sanctitudine illuxerit unicuique
constare liquido existimauerim. Cuius uirtutes admirabilisque doctrina effecerunt,
ut phama quam Vallarum familiae prius Laurentius ille Valla, qui sua tempestate
latinae linguae delitiae appellatus est, praestiterat, Illustrior, Clarior atque Spetiosior
fieret. Et ea mehercule splendescentis gloriae magnitudine, ut ad coelos ipsos Vallarum
familia uno omnium iudicio elata esse latissime censeatur. Placentiae igitur prima
grammatices rudimenta cum suscepisset, epithalamium quoddam publice adolescen-
tulus ad huc recitauit: qua re adeo illius aetatis adolescentes omnes excellere uisus
est, ut totius ciuitatis oculos in se conuerteret. Vnde illum suasus pater Mediolanum
misit longe praestantioribus doctoribus erudiendum altioribusque disciplinis imbuendum. Qua in ciuitate cum humanioribus studijs operam daret Georgium
Tiphernatem utriusque linguae peritissimum habuit praeceptorem. Sed quoniam illi
uisum est ieiuna nullaque [f. 4v] prorsus esse latina studia, nisi eis graecarum litterarum fontes suffragarentur, se graecis litteris Constantino Lascari Bysantio longe
ferme omniu doctissimo tradidit imbuendum. In quibus sibi comparandis labores
contempsit, uoluptates neglexit aliosque discipulos excessit, et adeo ut litterarum
graecarum peritiam sibi quaesitam uendicauerit: et uendicatam cognouerit: et
cognitam denique illustrauerit. Vni Georgio immortales igitur habendae gratiae.
Quandoquidem foedissima barbarie expulsas Italia graecas litteras, ex Graecia in
Italiam deduxerit. Et deductas auxerit: et auctas illustrauerit: et illustratas aeterni-
tati donauerit. Expulit igitur barbariem Georgius Georgius [*sic*] disciplinas suis
studijs et uigilijs suscitauit: Georgius bonas litteras pene intereuntes et intermortuas
reuiuiscere fecit: Georgius ellegantiam peperit: Georgius denique quo aduixit romani

sermonis maiestatem tutatus est. Testes uos omnes citauerim grauissimi auditores quantis uiribus conaretur cum profitebatur, ut uandalica uocabula lutulentamque barbariem deijceret iam nimia nonnullorum inscitia tumescentem ac ferme per uniuersam Italiam longe lateque uagantem. At cum Georgius animaduerteret nihil esse posse hominibus manifestum, nisi rerum causae omnium naturalium [f. 5r] innotescerent priusque ad eas perscrutandas animum conuerteret, humanioribus studijs relictis, paulo altioribus studijs deditus Arithmeticae, Geometriae, Musicae nec non Astrologiae sibi peritiam uendicauit. Quae mathimata Georgius Valla adeo consumate intellexit, ut nihil esset quin omnes faterentur Nicomachum, Euclidem, Archimedem ac Ptolemaeum reuiuiscere. Verum enimuero cum apprime Georgius intellexisset nihil fieri posse sine causa: posteaquam illis disciplinis quas commemorauimus id studij quod recensuimus cum adhuc esset Mediolani suppeditauit, Papiam petere statuit ut scilicet physicis rebus inuestigandis operam daret. Habuit igitur cum Papiae esset in physicis Ioannem Marlianum illius quidem tempestatis praestantissimum philosophum. Quo praeceptore sic physiologiam adeptus est, ut omnes uno ore faterentur unum in terris Platonem uitam ducere. At quoniam, sicut ad Haerenium scribens inquit M. Tullius, omnis in omni disciplina infirma est artis praeceptio sine summa exercitationis assiduitate, talem tantamque physiologiae sibi comparandae operam prestitit quantam aut qualem animo perpendere difficile esset; unde effectum est ut ad medicinae studio conuertere animum non dubitauerit. Qua disciplina tantum gloriae: tantum laudis ac [f. 5v] splendoris sibi comparauit, quantum nullis saeculis obliuioni mandari possit, et ea quidem amplitudine gloriae qua non solum tempestate illa uerum etiam in praesentia sibi omnes facillime persuadere possent Gallenum, Hippocratem, Aetium, Dioscoridem, Paulum gmetam [?] atque Alexandrum in terris uitam ducere a morte regressos. Posteaquam igitur physiologiae splendorem medicinaeque maiestatem Georgius Valla sibi comparauit: phama tanti uiri in sublime elata per omnium ora diffusa est. Quae ciuitas igitur, quae oppida, quae gymnasia, quae demum philosophantium scholae in uniuersa Italia, quibus Georgij Vallae splendor non illuxerit atque sonitus eloquentiae non intonuerit. Ex illo igitur rutilanti gloriae splendore moti Papienses eum publico stipendio conduxere, ut scilicet is esset qui iuuenum animos lasciuientium corrigeret atque ad uirtutes disciplinasque capescendas excitaret. At cum per aliquot annos Papiae summa cum gloria uitam duxisset, Ienuensibus obnixe rogantibus non potuit non satisfacere, scilicet quin Ienuam peteret. Relicta igitur Papia maiori a Ienuensibus stipendio conductus Ienuam petijt. In qua ciuitate quid feceret illud sane exactissimum argumentum est nam Ienuensium animos alioqui mercaturae et nauigationi deditos Georgius Valla [f. 6r] a mari ad patriam deduxit, a sedicionibus ad pacem reuocauit, a mercatura ad litterarum studia capescenda excitauit, a uitijsque ad uirtutes pellexit. Ienuenses igitur Georgius Valla exornauit, at uirtutibus exornauit, praeclaris institutis exornauit: moribus exornauit. Quid est igitur quod Ienuenses illi non tribuant? Quid est quod Ienuenses illi concedi oportere non existiment? Quod cum ita sit quis quaeso sane mentis negauerit pulchrum esse digito monstrari et dicier: hic est. His igitur tam splendide rebus gestis Mediolanenses exciti nulli stipendio pepercerunt nostro efficeret ut qui Papiam exornauerat. Ienuam illustrauerat: Mediolanum quoque nobilitaret. Georgius igitur Valla quandoquidem id obnixe ibant. Mediolanenses, Ienua relicta Mediolanum adijt. Quem uirum quanti existimarent Mediolanenses in praesentia non est quod dicam, nam indubitatissimi testes citari possunt ipsi Mediolanenses ipsi uobis exarent hic astantes, ipsi dicant, ipsi loquantur, ipsi uos Georgium Vallam Mediolani profitentem bonarum litterarum semina disseminasse reddant certiores. Quorum quidem operum phama cum iam per omnium ora uolitaret, Venetorum inclyta res publica et totius Italiae Regina illum tanti existimauit, ut dignum censuerit eum sibi perpetua beniuolentia deuinciri. Conductus igitur [f. 6v] Georgius publico stipendio ut Venetijs profiteretur tanta animi clementia talibus moribus talique doctrina discipulos undique conuolantes sibi deuinxit, ut omnes discipuli unum Georgium audirent, unum Georgium immutarentur, unum Georgium suspicerent atque intuerentur argute atque enucleate disputantem. Venetijs igitur per aliquot annos cum uixisset Georgius statuit nec uigilijs, nec laboribus parcere, quo linguam latinam uberiorem efficeret, et phamam de se posteritati relinqueret immortalem. Cum igitur iunioris ad huc etatis esset commentaria in satyras Juuenalis, nec non in libros topicorum de uniuersitate, de fato, M. Tullij Ciceronis non minore facundia quam ellegantia composuit. At qui Commentaria in librum de uniuersitate legit facillime sibi persuadet non Georgium Vallam sed Platonem illum diuinum de rerum natura audire disputantem. Libellum etiam de argumentis contexuit. At maioribus postmodum uigilijs et laboribus deditus admirabilem illum de expetendis fugiendisque rebus librum quadraginta et octo uoluminibus complexus est. In quo facile est intueri atque audire omnium prorsus scholas philosophantium dissidentes. At cum senex adhuc esset linguam latinam augere cupiens multos Graeciae praeclarissimos auctores in Italiam deductos latinis legendos tradidit. Nam Alexandri aphrodisiei [f. 7r] problemata eiusdemque libellum de causis febrium latinis donauit: praeterea Nicephori logicem: Euclidis quartum decimum elementorum librum nec non et Hypsiclem quarti decimi Euclidis interpretem: Nicephorum de astrolabo: Proclum diadocum de astrolabo: Aristarchi librum de magnitudinibus et distantijs Lunae ac solis: Timaeum de mundo: Cleonidis musicem: non nullas Eusebij pamphili theologicas quaestiones: Cleomedem de mundo: Athenagoram philosophum de resurrectione. Praeterea coelum, ethicem, nec non et poeticem Aristotelis: Rhazem de pestilentia: Galenique medici praestantissimi libellos de inequali distemperantia, de bono corporis habitu de corporis humani confirmatione de presagitura, de presagio, tum etiam Galeni introductorium. ac Pselum de uictu humano. Librum praeterea uenationum importuna morte correptus, reliquit, Sed eius uita quid speciosius, quid clarius, quid rutilantius? In omnibus namque rebus nihil ab ipso peccatum est nil temere aut leuiter commissum, nihil denique uno omnium iudicio non circunspectissime actum siue indicatum depraehenditur. Testes igitur non solum uos humanissimi auditores estis, ante quorum oculos Georgius uixit, uerum etiam tota ciuitas quae illo sidere sublato in [f. 7v] lachrymas est deuoluta. Nec mirum est tamen in illo tantam fuisse prudentiam in quo maxima esset temperantia nam singulari laetabitur fragilitate, et adeo ut uictus tenuitate et cibi simplicitate ualetudini potius consuleret quam ulli luxuriae insecuiret. Quis est, quaeso, qui in eo aliquod incontinens factum uiderit aut conspexerit. Non dicam quanta erat leuitate affabilis, nam angustia temporis id consulto relinquo. Legem igitur sibi indixit Georgius ut molitie omnique foedissimo luxu expulso religiosissimam uitae sanctimoniam sequeretur. Tali etiam constantia enituit ut nullis diuitijs moueretur ac nullis aduersis moueretur quo minus uno eodemque uultu semper inter discipulos uersaretur. Quod cum ita habeat, uos alloquor imprimis Ioannes Petre et Hieronyme, iuuenes integerrimi, tristes expellite lachrymas, dolori pausam facite; at durum est ab hijs quos dilexerimus abstrahi, accerbum est atque luctuosum tali uiro orbatos esse. Verum non est quod diu non exaudientem uocemus, aut non rediturum queramus. Viuunt omnia deo optimo maximo; facessant igitur lachrymae, humanissimi auditores: discedant fletus; expellatur luctus; quandoquidem non mortuus est Georgius Valla, sed uiuit, nam illud exactissimum est, illos qui cum uirtute uitam cum morte [f. 8r] commutat minime interire. Gratulemur igitur Georgio Vallae quod ex hijs tenebris, ex hoc carcere et ualle miseriae solutus et phamam de se posteris reliquerit immortalem et, ad lucem ueram coelique regias aulas, ac ad perpetuam felicitatem euolauerit bene anteacta uita acquisitam. Cuius animam Deum optimum maximum parest, humanissimi auditores, iugiter praecemur ut perpetuis gaudijs frui permittat.

NOTES

[1] J. L. Heiberg, *Beiträge zur Geschichte Georg Vallas und seiner Bibliothek* [*Zentralblatt für Bibliothekswesen*, XVI], Leipzig, 1896, pp. 3–44, prints with commentary and additional documents the life of Valla written by the humanist's adopted son,

Giampietro Cademosto Valla. For supplementary data see Remigio Sabbadini's review of Heiberg in the *Giornale Storico della Letteratura Italiana*, XXIX, 1897, pp. 525–7. *Id.*, 'Briciole umanistiche. LII. Giorgio Valla', *Giornale Storico della Letteratura Italiana*, L, 1907, pp. 34–71, at 50–2. *Catalogus Translationum et Commentariorum: Medieval and Renaissance Latin Translations and Commentaries*, ed. Paul Oscar Kristeller, Washington, D.C., 1960, I, p. 126. Other recent notices of Valla appear in Giovanni Forlini, 'Una lettera di Giovanni Pico all'umanista piacentino Giorgio Valla', *Atti e Memorie della Deputazione di Storia Patria per le antiche Provincie Modenesi*, ninth series, IV–V, 1964–65, pp. 315–18. Cesare Vasoli, 'Ricerche sulle dialettiche quattrocentesche', *Rivista Critica di Storia della Filosofia*, XV, 1960, 265–87, at pp. 276 ff. Paul Lawrence Rose, 'Humanist culture and Renaissance mathematics: the Italian libraries of the Quattrocento', *Studies in the Renaissance*, XX, 1973, pp. 46–105, at 94–8. Other references may be found in M. E. Cosenza, *Biographical and Bibliographical Dictionary of the Italian Humanists and of the World of Classical Scholarship in Italy, 1300–1800*, Boston, Mass., six vols., 1962–67, IV, 3549–9. See addenda, p. 310.

² Sabbadini, *Giornale Storico*, XXIX, 1897, pp. 525–7, establishes the dates of Valla's teaching as follows: Pavia, 1466–76; Genoa, 1476–81; Milan, 1481–82; Pavia, 1483–84; Venice, 1485–1500. Valla is said to have visited Greece in 1486. See p. 310.

³ The correspondence is published by Heiberg, *Vallas Bibliothek*, pp. 44 ff, from Vaticana MS Vat. Lat. 3537. For a more complete version of the important letter to Antiquari of 1492 on the translation of Greek mathematical texts (Heiberg, pp. 87–8) see Giovanni Battista Vermiglioli, *Memorie de Jacopo Antiquari*, Perugia, 1813, pp. 418–21, who prints it from Biblioteca Trivulziana, Milan, MS 803, ff. 59–60*v*. *Cf.* Caterina Santoro, *I codici medioevali della Biblioteca Trivulziana*, Milan, 1965, p. 211.

⁴ Bibliography in Heiburg, *Vallas Bibliothek*, pp. 36–41. *Cf. Catalogus Translationum*, I, pp. 125, 130, 165, 223. On Tortelli see the series of studies by O. Besomi and Marcangela Regoliosi, '[Lorenzo] Valla e Tortelli', in *Italia Medioevale e Umanistica*, IX, 1966, pp. 75–189; XII, 1969, pp. 129–96; XIII, 1970, pp. 95–137; also R. P. Oliver, 'Giovanni Tortelli', in *Studies presented to David Moore Robinson*, St Louis, 1953, II, pp. 1257–71.

⁵ *Alexandri Aphrodisei Problemata per Georgium Vallam in Latinum conversa*, Venice, 1488, sig. a. ii *rv*; see *Catalogus Translationum*, I, p. 130.

⁶ *Hoc in volumine hec continentur: Nicephori Logica . . .*, Venice, 1498. For Guidobaldo, Duke of Urbino, see below.

⁷ Cademosto, *Vita Georgii Vallae*, ed. Heiberg, *Vallas Bibliothek*, p. 4.

⁸ Valla's letters of July–August 1492 in Heiberg, *Vallas Bibliothek*, pp. 87–8. *Cf. ibid.*, p. 25.

⁹ *Ibid.*, p. 70. See Giampietro Cademosto Valla, *Commentaria in Ptolomaei Quadripartitum, in Ciceronis Partitiones et Tusculanas Quaestiones, in Plinii Naturalis Historiae Lib. II*, Venice, 1502.

¹⁰ For Valla's library see the inventory of the Carpi library published by Heiberg, *Vallas Bibliothek*, pp. 107 ff, from Vatican MS Barb. Lat. 3108, Also G. Mercati, *Codici Latini Pico, Grimani, Pio . . . e i Codici Greci Pio di Modena*, Studie e Testi, 75, Vatican City, 1928, pp. 203–45 and *passim*. Anon., *Cenni Storici della Reale Biblioteca Estense in Modena*, Modena, 1873. V. Puntoni, 'Indice dei Codici Greci della Biblioteca Estense di Modena', *Studi Italiani di Filologia Classica*, IV, 1896, pp. 379–536.

An unnoticed inventory of 1558 of the mathematical codices in the Carpi library is Vaticana, MS Barb. Lat. 304, ff. 163*rv*.

¹¹ K. K. Müller, 'Neue Mittheilungen über Janus Lascaris und die Mediceiische Bibliothek', *Zentralblatt für Bibliothekswesen*, I, 1884, pp. 333–412, at 383–4. For this and the following references see Rose, 'Humanist culture', pp. 94–8.

¹² Müller, 'Lascaris', p. 356. Angelo Fabroni, *Laurentii Medicis Vita*, Pisa, 1784, II, pp. 284–6. J. L. Heiberg, *Archimedes: Opera Omnia*, second edition, Leipzig, 1910–15, III, p. xii.

[13] Giulio Bertoni, *La Biblioteca Estense e la coltura ferrarese ai tempi del duca Ercole I (1471–1505)*, Turin, 1903, pp. 119–20.

[14] J. L. Heiberg, 'Die Handschriften Georg Vallas von griechischen Mathematikern', *Jahrbücher für classische Philologie*, supplement, XII, 1881, pp. 375–402.

[15] For Valla's contemplated translation of Archimedes see the letters printed by Heiberg, *Vallas Bibliothek*, pp. 47, 69–70, 85, 87–8. For Jacobus Cremonensis see Heiberg, *Archimedes*, III, pp. lxxiii ff.

[16] The only serious treatment of Valla to date is that of Heiberg. As might be expected, M. Gukovski, 'Italian encyclopaedists of the thirteenth to the sixteenth centuries' (in Russian), *Akademiia Nauk S.S.R. Institut Knigi, Dokumenti, Pis'ma. Trudy*, II, 1932, pp. 43–64, at 53–5, is a Marxist account. The humanistic importance of the *De Expetendis Rebus* seems to have been missed by Vittorio Cian, 'Contributo all storia dell'enciclopedismo nell'eta della Rinascita: *Il Methodus Studiorum* del card. Pietro Bembo', in *Miscellanea di studi storici in onore di Giovanni Sforza*, Lucca, 1920, pp. 289–330, who regarded it (p. 299) as anachronistic in organisation. See addenda, p. 310.

[17] Quoted by Heiberg, *Vallas Bibliothek*, p. 34.

[18] According to Giampietro Cademosto, his adoptive father died before he could revise and edit the whole work so as to reveal its design clearly. See Giampietro's dedication of the *De Expetendis Rebus* and the remarks in his *Vita Georgii Vallae*, ed. Heiberg, *Vallas Bibliothek*, p. 5.

[19] See Valla's remarks on the place of mathematics in philosophy in the letters to Antiquari of 1489–90, 1491 and 1492, in Heiberg, *Vallas Bibliothek*, pp. 54–61, 64–5, 68. *Cf. ibid.*, pp. 33–4.

Valla's unpublished *Venationes* (Vaticana, MS Vat. Lat. 3537, ff. 10–143) is an interesting attempt at constructing a humanistic philosophy linked to mathematical and medical learning.

For Valla's conjoining of poetry and mathematics see Heiberg, *Vallas Bibliothek*, p. 20. Jacob Bernays, *Gesammelte Abhandlungen*, Berlin, 1885, II, pp. 337–8.

On Medieval encyclopaedism see Vittorio Cian, 'Vivaldo Belcalzer e l'enciclopedismo italiano delle origini', *Giornale Storico della Letteratura Italiana*, Supplemento, V, 1902, *La Pensée encyclopédique au moyen âge*, ed. M. de Gandillac, Neuchâtel, 1966, pp. 1 f; S. Viarre, 'Le Commentaire ordonné du monde dans quelques sommes scientifiques des XII et XIIIe siècles', in *Classical Influences on European Culture, A.D. 500–1500*, ed. R. R. Bolgar, Cambridge, 1971, pp. 203–15; B. Stock, *Myth and Science in the Twelfth Century*, Princeton, N.J., 1972.

[20] For the evolution of the *De Expetendis Rebus* from a *corpus* of translations to the unified encyclopaedia of 1501 see Valla's letters of the period 1491–98 in Heiberg, *Vallas Bibliothek*, pp. 82, 69–70, 77, 90, in that sequence. By 1494 (pp. 69–70) Valla had settled on a canon of forty-nine books. The last book was finished in 1498 (p. 90), In 1498 also (pp. 90, 92) Valla decided on the Epicurean title of *De Expetendis Rebus*. although he had used the phrase earlier in connection with his translation of Alexander of Aphrodisias' *Problemata*, 1488, sig. a. iiv. See addenda, p. 310.

[21] For sixteenth-century Venetian interest in mathematics see Paul Lawrence Rose, 'The Accademia Venetiana: science and culture in Renaissance Venice', *Studi Veneziani*, XI, 1969, pp. 191–242.

[22] Bruno Nardi, 'Letteratura e cultura veneziana del Quattrocento', in *La civiltà veneziana del Quattrocento*, Fondazione G. Cini, Venice and Florence, 1957, pp. 99–145. *Id.*, 'La Scuola di Rialto e l'umanesimo veneziano', in *Umanesimo europeo e umanesimo veneziano*, ed. Vittore Branca, Venice and Florence, 1963, pp. 93–139. The latter is reprinted in Nardi's *Saggi sulla cultura veneta del Quattro e Cinquecento*, Padua, 1971, pp. 45–98.

[23] Heiberg, *Vallas Bibliothek*, pp. 103–4.

[24] *Cf.* Marshall Clagett, *Giovanni Marliani and Late Medieval Physics*, New York, 1941.

[25] Heiberg, *Vallas Bibliothek*, p. 41. Valla was born in 1447. (*Ibid.*, p. 6.)

[26] See *Catalogus Translationum*, I, p. 90, for a short bio-bibliography. Zambertis'

latest autograph manuscript is the translation of Proclus, *Commentary on Euclid I*, Bayerische Staatsbibliothek, Munich, MS Lat. 6, at f. 154v.

Contrary to *Catalogus Translationum*, 1, p. 90, Zamberti did not translate Apollonius. This slip derives from E. A. Cicogna, *Delle iscrizioni veneziane*, Venice, 1824–42, IV, p. 510, who misread a sentence in Francesco Maurolico, *Cosmographia*, Venice, 1543, sig. a. iiv.

[27] *Catalogus Translationum*, 1, pp. 89, 103, 121. The translations are in Munich, MSS Lat. 117, 120, 121.

[28] *Cf.* Valla's letter to Antiquari in Heiberg, *Vallas Bibliothek*, pp. 54–61. Addenda, below.

[29] *Euclidis Megarensis Philosophi Platonici Mathematicarum Disciplinarum Janitoris. . . . Elementorum Libros XIII cum Expositione Theonis*, trans. Bartolomeo Zamberti, Venice, Tacuinus, 1505 (reissued Venice, 1510). See the general preface at sigs. 1–6v. Addenda, below.

[30] See J. L. Heiberg, *Euclidis Opera Omnia*, Leipzig, 1883–1916, v, cii–civ. H. Weissenborn, *Die Übersetzungen des Euklid durch Campano und Zamberto*, Halle, 1882. Thomas Heath, *The Thirteen Books of Euclid's Elements*, second edition, Cambridge, 1908, I, pp. 98–9.

[31] Zamberti, *Euclides*, sig. 5v–6.

[32] *Ibid.*, sig. CC iiiir.

[33] *Euclidis Opera. . . .*, ed. Luca Pacioli, Venice, Paganinus, 1509, f. 31rv.

[34] Maurolico, *Cosmographia*, sig. a. iiv, condemns Zamberti's translation. But Commandino attributed its failing to dependence upon a poor Greek text, according to Bernardino Baldi, *Cronica de'matematici*, Urbino, 1707, pp. 99–100.

[35] See Zamberti, *Euclides*, sig. 6v. *Cf.* B. Boncompagni, 'Intorno al comento di Proclo sul primo libro degli *Elementi* di Euclide', *Bullettino di Bibliografia e di Storia delle Scienze Matematiche e Fisiche*, VII, 1875, pp. 152–65.

The *Somma della Opere* projected by the Accademia Venetiana (Venice, 1559), f. 13v, announces a new translation of Proclus. This is probably the Barozzi version.

[36] I am grateful to Professor Giorgio E. Ferrari, the former director of the Marciana, for kindly supplying me with a microfilm of the manuscript.

[37] P. O. Kristeller, *Iter Italicum*, London and Leiden, 1967, II, p. 238.

[38] For the funeral see Cademosto, *Vita Georgii Valla*, ed. Heiberg, *Valla's Bibliothek*, p. 6, who mentions some *carmina* at the tomb.

[39] Zamberti, *Euclides*, 1505, sig. x iiiv.

[40] P. O. Kristeller, *Studies in Renaissance Thought and Letters*, Rome, 1956, pp. 580–2.

Addenda

Page 308, n. 1 end. See also J. L. Heiberg, 'Nachträgliches über Georg Valla', in *Zentr. für Bibliotheksw.*, XV, 1898, pp. 189–97, while further allied information will be in my book *The Italian Renaissance of Mathematics*, Geneva, 1975, pp. 46 ff.

Page 308, n. 2 end. C. Borsetti, *Historia almi Ferrariae gymnasii*, Ferrara, 1735, II, p. 45, states that Valla studied astronomy, mathematics, and natural philosophy at Ferrara under Pietro Bono Avvogaro, Lodovico Jusberti Heremita, and Niccolò Leoniceno respectively.

Page 309, n. 16 end. For the influence of *De Expetendis Rebus* on Copernicus see L. A. Birkenmajer, *Stromata Copernicana*, Cracow, 1924, chapter 4.

Page 309, n. 20 end. The title *De Expetendis Rebus* was also used for a draft encyclopaedia in 1481, see Heiberg, 'Nachträgliches . . .', pp. 191–3.

Page 310, n. 28 end. For Zamberti's use of mathematics as a bridge between nature and theology see E. W. Strong, *Procedures and Metaphysics*, Berkeley, Calif., 1936, pp. 192–201, while pp. 62 f unnecessarily separated Valla's and Zamberti's views on the matter. Venetian humanistic interest in Euclid may explain Scipio Carteromachus's annotated text of Euclid in the Vatican Library MS Gr. 1295.

Page 310, n. 29 end. It seems that Zamberti's 'seven years' extended from 1493 to 1500, and hence the translation would have been under the influence of Valla.

MARTIN KEMP   *University of Glasgow*

17

'OGNI DIPINTORE DIPINGE SE': A NEOPLATONIC ECHO IN LEONARDO'S ART THEORY?

ON AT LEAST seven occasions Leonardo expressed his conviction that all painters automatically tend to produce figures which 'resemble their masters';[1] that is, a series of unwitting self-portraits. This notion remained with Leonardo over a considerable period of time: the earliest reference can be dated reasonably accurately to 1492 and the latest probably to the period after 1510.[2] And there is no evidence to suggest that he ever seriously doubted its validity.

In MS A we are told that 'a painter who has clumsy hands will paint similar hands in his works . . . any part that may be good or poor in yourself . . . will be partly shown in your figures'.[3] Similarly in MS Ashburnham I Leonardo notes that 'you [the artist] might be mistaken and choose figures which have conformity with yours. For it would often seem that such conformity pleases us; and if you should be ugly you would select faces that are not beautiful and you would make ugly faces like many painters. For the figures resemble the master.'[4] The theory of auto-mimesis is expounded at greatest length and with greatest sophistication in two passages in the lost *Libro* A, both of which merit extended quotation:

The painter should make his figure according to the rules for a body in Nature, which is commonly known to be of praiseworthy proportions. In addition to this, he should have himself measured to see where his own person varies much or little from that termed praiseworthy. With this information he must studiously oppose falling into the same shortcomings, in the figures he makes, that are found in his own person. Be advised that you must fight your utmost against this vice, since it is a failing that was born together with judgement, because the soul, the mistress of your body, naturally delights in works similar to that which she produced in composing her body. And from this it comes about that there is no woman so ugly that she does not find a lover, unless she is monstrous.[5]

Figures often resemble their masters . . . because judgement is that which moves the hand to the creations of lineaments of figures through varying aspects until it is satisfied. And, because judgement is one of the powers of the soul, by which it composes the form of the body in which it resides, according to its will, thus having to reproduce with the hands a human body, it naturally reproduces that body which it first invented. From this it follows that he who falls in love naturally loves things similar to himself.[6]

Leonardo emphasised that auto-mimesis is a matter of no small consequence: it is the 'greatest defect of painters';[7] it is not a symptom of one particular man's egotism, narcissism or desire for self-advertisement, but a defect which comes from the deepest nature of each man's soul; it is a matter which lies at the very heart of artistic invention; it is inseparably related to the faculty of judgement; and judgement provides the key (albeit largely unrecognised) to Leonardo's theory of beauty. On these grounds auto-mimesis deserves serious attention. This it has begun to receive in the hands of André Chastel.

As Chastel has shown, the catch phrase 'ogni dipintore dipinge se' was recorded on a number of occasions during the Renaissance.[8] In a group of aphorisms associated with Poliziano it is attributed to Cosimo de' Medici, while Savonarola noted in a more general manner that 'si dice che ogni dipintore dipinge se medesimo'.[9] Vasari attributed a similar opinion to Michelangelo: 'ogni pittore ritrae se medesimo'.[10] The aphorism may have been relatively commonplace, repeated in a off-hand and often unconsidered manner—as aphorisms so often are.

Chastel interprets Leonardo's adoption of the notion as an echo of Ficino's Neoplatonism.[11] The aphorism certainly seems to have been known in Neoplatonic circles, and Leonardo's elaborate statements of automimesis in *Libro* A indicate that a 'philosophical' interpretation is not unreasonable. But, as I hope to show, Leonardo's formulation and development of the theory are highly at variance with Ficino's philosophy in particular and with Neoplatonic thought in general. In attempting to tackle this problem I believe that we shall be lead to reconsider vitally important aspects of Leonardo's art theory—the problem of judgement in particular.

I

On a general level it may be possible to reconcile the proposition that 'ogni dipintore dipinge se' with a theory of creation in which the artist realises in paint the forms which are within his mind—the 'Ideas' which are ultimately essential for any Neoplatonic theory of art. In such a reconciliation we may say that each painter would reveal his inner self, mind and soul, rather than directly reflecting external Nature.

For his part Leonardo was ready to accept that a form of inner invention played a legitimate role in the production of a painting. During his first Milanese period he acknowledged that the painter could usefully concern himself with 'notable things composed by subtle speculation', things which the faculty of 'invention made first in your imagination'.[12] And, in two early passages in the *Tratatto*, he almost appears to be moving in the direction of a Neoplatonic theory of art: 'Whatever exists in the universe through essence, presence or imagination, he [the artist] has it first in his mind and then in his hands, and in these are of such excellence that within a certain space of time they produce a proportioned harmony, seen in a single glance'.[13] 'The divinity which is the science of painting transmutes the painter's mind into a resemblance of the divine mind. With free power it reasons concerning the generation of the diverse natures of the various animals, plants . . .'[14]

When Leonardo states that the things which the artist has 'first in his mind' correspond to 'whatever exists in the universe' he might appear to be expressing a theory which bears some resemblance to Ficino's epistemology, in particular to the concept of *adaequatio* (correspondance, affinity, underlying conformity perceived intuitively through a form of resonance).[15] Leonardo's statement that 'he who falls in love naturally loves things similar to himself' is also a form of *adaequatio* and is undeniably close to Ficino's interpretation of love as a form of affinity.[16] It is through *adaequatio*, according to Ficino, that the divine harmonies of the *formulae* within the soul are activated in contact with certain external objects:

Every mind praises the round figure when it first encounters it in things, and knows not why it praises it. So too in architecture we praise the symmetry of the walls, the disposition of its stones, the forms of its windows and doors; and in the human body, the proportions of its members; or in a melody, the harmony of its tones. If every mind approves of them . . . it can only be because of a natural and necessary instinct . . . The reasons for these judgements are, therefore, innate in the mind itself.[17]

It is not difficult to reconcile Ficino's *adaequatio* with Alberti's earlier assertions concerning the judgement of beauty: 'the judgement that you make that a thing is beautiful does not proceed from mere opinion but from a secret argument and discourse implanted within the mind itself; which plainly appears to be so from this, that no man beholds anything ugly or deformed without immediate hatred and abhorrence'.[18] Whenever a 'beautiful whole . . . offers itself to the mind, either by the conveyance of sight, hearing or any of the other senses, we immediately perceive this congruity . . . nor does this congruity arise so much from the body in which it is found, or from any of its members, as from itself and from Nature, so that its true seat is in the mind and reason'.[19]

So far so good. We do indeed appear to have discerned an echo of Neoplatonism in Renaissance art theory and, perhaps, in Leonardo's thought— an echo which can be reconciled with the interpretation of auto-mimesis as the reflection of the innate qualities of the soul. But if we begin to look more closely at Leonardo's conception of auto-mimesis in relation to invention, judgement and Nature, the echo singularly fails to resonate in a Neoplatonic manner.

Leonardo, it will be remembered, considered that auto-mimesis was a cardinal sin for the painter. If auto-mimesis really consisted in the realisation of inner Ideas (elevated notions for Neoplatonism), why should it be so undesirable? We might answer, in a manner which has become routine in Leonardo studies, that Leonardo was not a Neoplatonist at heart and had little faith in Neoplatonic Ideas as vehicles of truth. This vague answer ultimately contains a germ of truth, but it misses the real point of the theory of auto-mimesis in Leonardo's thought. A more directly relevant answer lies within an examination of the original premise that auto-mimesis can be identified as a Neoplatonic component in Leonardo's thought.

At its simplest, the bald statement 'ogni dipintore dipinge se' means that the painter would for some reason or other tend to produce figures that resemble his own person in external appearance. This is what Leonardo usually understood by auto-mimesis. Exceptionally, on one occasion, he extended this to include aspects of the artist's behaviour and personality, such as briskness in movement, piety in demeanour, idleness or insanity.[20] This interpretation bears some resemblance to Savonarola's conviction that each work of art automatically reveals its author's moral and spiritual state.[21] However, in all his other notes on this subject Leonardo pays exclusive attention to the defects of ugliness and disproportion which reflect the artist's own bodily appearance. If, for instance, Socrates had practised as a painter he would in Leonardo's view have tended to produce figures which would have deviated considerably from the norms of ideal beauty—to judge from the extant portraits and Alcibiades' description of Socrates' odd appearance.[22] The uglier the artist, the greater would be his difficulties!

I suspect that a Neoplatonist would have found such an interpretation of auto-mimesis hard to swallow. But, faced with Leonardo's proposition, a Neoplatonist could assert that the proper avoidance of bodily imitation consisted in the artist's recourse to the imitation of inner *formulae* and to the more invariable potencies of the soul's higher faculties. The ideal figures produced by such a recourse to higher Ideas would (to adapt an analogy from Plato's *Symposium*) be like the perfect statuettes of gods contained within the hollow shell of a naturalistic statue of Socrates: 'he [Socrates] bears a strong resemblance to those figures of Silenus in statuaries shops; they are hollow inside, and when they are taken apart you see that they contain little figures of gods'.[23]

Leonardo, however, did not believe that the realisation of inner Ideas provided the solution to the problem of avoiding the imitation of one's own features. The artist's faculty of invention, according to Leonardo, is inseparably dependent upon the faults to be found in his own person. And— horror of horrors for the Neoplatonists—these faults result from the variability of *all* the innate qualities of the soul. His line of argument runs as follows.

First, *the soul forms the body*. This notion may ultimately be derived from Aristotle (though not expressed by Aristotle in very clear terms). It was certainly adopted by Thomas Aquinas, whom the Neoplatonists may have followed in this respect. In this tradition the soul generally corresponds to the 'essence' of the body; and 'form' is understood in a largely metaphysical manner.[24] By contrast, Leonardo's interpretation of this formula is far more literal and basic. According to Leonardo the soul precisely determines the individual characteristics and peculiarities of each man's body. To use our earlier example, Socrates' soul, as the template of his organic body, would have contained the potentiality of his ugly features as an integral and essential part of its structure and creative potential. This literal account of the soul directly producing the detailed form of each individual body does not appear to reflect the Neoplatonic (essentialist) version of the form-creating soul, but rather a straightforward (materialist) version of the Hippocratic theory of generation, as transmitted to Leonardo by Avicenna: 'here Avicenna supposes that the soul begets the soul and the body and every member, *per errata*'.[25] And the great variety of bodily forms generated by human souls bears witness to the fact that every soul is—at the most fundamental level—individually variable in its productive potency.

Secondly, *the soul forms the judgement*. From the arguments above it follows that judgement must also be individual and variable, qualities which separate it radically from judgement as conceived by Alberti and *adaequatio* as conceived by Ficino. For Alberti, judgement shares none of the variability of 'mere opinion': 'There are some who will . . . say that men are guided by a variety of opinions in their judgement of beauty and of buildings; and that forms and structures must vary according to every man's particular taste and fancy, and not be tied down to any rules of art. A common thing with the ignorant to despise what they do not understand.'[26] Innate judgement pertains, in Alberti's sense, to the Platonic qualities of knowledge and reason rather than belief and opinion. For Leonardo, however, judgement possesses no such absolute qualities of certainty; there are as many variations in judgement as there are variations in bodily form, because both variations originate from the 'organic' variability of souls.

Thirdly, *judgement directs invention*. Since the painter's inventions, in Leonardo's theory, cannot be other than subject to judgement, and since judgement exhibits individual variations—variations which correspond precisely to the forms of the body created by each soul—it follows that the 'inventions' will inevitably 'resemble their masters' in external appearance.

It is difficult to equate these concepts of judgement and invention with a Neoplatonic theory of Ideas in relation to creativity. All of which suggests that too much weight should not be placed upon the apparently Neoplatonic passages from the *Trattato* quoted above. These excerpts, considered in isolation, provide a very misleading impression of Leonardo's art theory during the 1490s. Nor are they representative of the direction in which his thought was later to move, when the derivative and inconsistent aspects of his early theories become less apparent.

In an intellectually opportunist fashion rather characteristic of Renaissance art theorists, Leonardo was quite prepared to exploit certain philosophical ideas in a manner which was hardly justified by their original context. Thus he praises the 'divine' inventive power of the artist—for the sake of the glory which it reflects on his art—and accepts that the history painter must necessarily be a master of inner invention.[27] But his conception of the utter fallibility of artistic invention and judgement which lies behind his formulation of auto-mimesis certainly does not place the painter in the position of a Neoplatonic philosopher speculating transcendentally upon cosmic truth.

In judging Leonardo's art theory we must be careful not to fall into the habit of interpreting his ideas in terms of modern notions of creativity; we should bear in mind that none of the terms which he exploits rather un-systematically in connection with the production of a work of art can neces-sarily be taken as synonymous for *creazione*. He rarely uses *creazione* or *creare* to denote the artist's production of a composition,[28] preferring to exploit *fare, comporre, inventare, partorire, nascere* and *generare*, the last three of which carry biological associations entirely appropriate for his 'Hippocratic' theory of auto-mimesis. The historian should be very cautious before he makes any substitution of the modern terminology of artistic creation for Leonardo's preferred vocabulary—an illicit form of substitution which occurs all too frequently, not only in Leonardo scholarship but also in studies and translations of Alberti. The term *invenzione* should be treated with special care.

In marked contrast to most post-Romantic attitudes, the classical traditions tended to link artistic invention with the rational faculties of the mind. Cicero, for example, defined invention as the 'discovery of topics either true or probable' and considered that it 'is the first and most important part of rhetoric'.[29] Alberti very probably bore this rhetorical tradition in mind when he formed a division of labour between *inventione*, which he limited to the literary–poetic conceptions behind paintings (i.e. Cicero's topics), and *compositio*, which he applied to the formal aspects of each work.[30] No such distinction between invention of content and composition of form is readily apparent in Leonardo's art theory. The manner in which he discusses invention and imagination depends less upon Alberti than upon the strong tradition of Aristotelean faculty psychology in the Middle Ages.

In his variations upon the medieval systems of mind he granted imagina-tion the ability to operate rationally in conjunction with the rational capacities of thought in the second ventricle of the brain, as opposed to imagination, which in medieval theory resided in the first ventricle and was both a 'coffer or repository' for sensory images and the originator of fantasies.[31] The second ventricle in his rearrangement of the medieval schemes was also the seat of judgement and of the soul.[32] Thus, at the very centre of cerebral activity, imagination and judgement and the soul are together responsible for the errors which result in auto-mimesis during the process of artistic invention.

Like his theory of artistic invention, Leonardo's theory of love is not in practice developed in a Neoplatonic manner, in spite of some early similarities to Ficino's ideas. Ficino's theory concentrated metaphysically upon the spiritual resonance between compatible souls. He considered love to be one of the most elevated and eternal powers granted to man. For Leonardo, however, love dubiously shares the status of auto-mimesis; both tendencies depend upon the individual variations of judgement which result from the idiosyncrasies of the individual soul. Affinity in love is thus queerly character-ised by the mutual attraction of people who resemble each other in appearance.

However, in common with Neoplatonic theory Leonardo believed that the artist should strive towards a higher goal than imitation of (and love for) his own features; he should strive towards something truer. But if the painter cannot appeal Platonically to any of the higher faculties of the soul in order to remedy the grave defect of auto-mimesis, what can he do? How can he overcome the falibility of his judgement?

II

The answer for Leonardo lies outside the mind of man—in Nature. His remedy in Nature is the self-effacing search for the true systems of human proportions; and such a search occupied considerable space in his Milanese notebooks.[33]

The overriding anxiety which he expressed when discussing auto-mimesis was that it resulted in figures with defective proportions, in deviation from the norm or norms of beauty. This means that the remedy in Nature could not be, as Sir Ernst Gombrich has implied, a study of those forms in other men which stand at the furthest extreme from the painter's own features; that is, in the study of grotesque figures and in the practice of caricature.[34] Nor is the remedy to be found, as Chastel has suggested, in the artist's identification of himself with other figures, completely losing himself in them.[35] To be sure, Leonardo insistently required that the history painter should be able to encompass a wide variety of figures—and one result of auto-mimesis would be lack of variety—but total imitation (or exaggeration) of other, individual figures would not necessarily provide closer access to true beauty than imitation of one's own features.

The painter could legitimately take a number of steps towards the re-formation of his innately defective judgement of proportions. One of the most important was self-awareness. If, again for example, our painter-Socrates correctly ascertained the deviant character of his features he could 'studiously oppose falling into the same shortcomings . . . in the figures he makes'.[36] To this end the painter should measure his own figure to see how it deviates from the norm of proportioned beauty. But self-awareness does not solve the problem of how the artist is to find the norm itself.

In answer to this problem Leonardo resorts partly to a kind of average or general norm; 'different judges of similar intelligence will form a great variety of judgements amongst themselves. And you must be between one and the other of their selections.'[37] A consensus of opinions would be useful: 'the painter should make his figure according to the rules for a body in Nature which is *commonly known* to be of praiseworthy proportions'.[38] This implies that each individual's idiosyncrasies would tend to be cancelled out by those of other men and that something equivalent to a 'common will' might emerge—something close to the truth.

Leonardo's procedure also contains strong echoes of the Zeuxian form of selection: 'consider and take the best parts of many beautiful faces, of which the beauty if confirmed more by public fame than by your own judgement'.[39] It should be remembered that the Zeuxian procedure of selection (by now a commonplace of humanist 'art criticism') had earlier been given a highly respectable, Socratic pedigree by Xenophon.[40]

Alberti, specifically citing the Zeuxis anecdote, had advocated a similar method.[41] His early statements in *De pictura* leave some doubt as to the relationship between judgement and Nature, but by the time of *De re aedificatoria* Allberti is confident that the artist, in selecting the best parts from erring Nature, would be guided by innately *certain* judgement in the depths of his mind. This is not to say that complete certainty was easily realised in practice; the artist must study 'keenly and assiduously' to fashion true beauty from the thinly dispersed beauties of Nature.

Leonardo's Zeuxis would also have studied assiduously. But in an inductive manner—studying proportion in Nature as the absolute corrective for his innately *defective* judgement. Alberti and Leonardo shared their faith in the rule of number and proportion (which ultimately relates to the Pythagorean and Platonic traditions) but the manner in which the artist's all-important judgement directs the perception and recreation of a mathematically harmonious world differs radically in their theories of art.

During his first Milanese period Leonardo devoted considerable energies to procedures designed to cultivate a 'free and good judgement; since good judgement is born of good understanding, and good understanding derives from reasons drawn from good rules, and good rules are the daughters of good experience, the common mother of all sciences and arts'.[42]

The artist could call upon certain 'aids' to modify his judgement: he could look at his painting in a mirror; he could leave his painting for a period; he could stand farther back from his work; and he could solicit the 'advice of anybody', because anybody's judgement differs usefully from his own.[43] Leonardo sought procedures which would give the artist what we might call a 'fresh perspective', a perspective less tainted by his personal prejudices. Above all, the study through 'experience' of the mathematical rules of Nature (and therefore of art) would be essential in overcoming prejudice and cultivating sound judgement. In training the faculty of judgement along mathematical lines the study of Nature could be supplemented by mental exercises, such as visual contests, in which each participant attempts to judge the length of a distant line, continually checking his results and attempting to improve the accuracy of his judgements.[44]

An induced grasp of mathematical judgement could never on its own be a substitute for deficient inventive powers when composing figures;[45] but, equally, no amount of inventiveness could overcome defective judgement. Invention born of imagination and sound judgement born of mathematical understanding should go hand-in-hand in the production of a painting.

In general, Leonardo's conception of the predominantly inductive relationship between the mathematics of Nature and the painter's understanding of rules closely reflects the tradition of 'experience' in medieval science. This is not to ignore the importance of certain elements from Albertian aesthetics; in particular, Leonardo derived his notions of proportional harmony from the Albertian tradition, accepting that beauty is susceptible to mathematical analysis and synthesis. But the way in which he expressed man's intellectual comprehension and judgement of the mathematics of Nature is largely dependent upon what is generally called Aristotelean natural philosophy.

In the hands of Roger Bacon and John Peckham, amongst others, we find that the methodology of Aristotle's science has been interwoven with a Pythagorean-cum-Platonic reverence for the 'divinity' of mathematics. Bacon undoubtedly regarded himself as a follower of Aristotle, but he adopted a theory of numbers which, on his own admission, depended upon such non-Aristotelean sources as Ptolemy, Euclid and Boethius.[46] Bacon considered (in an 'almost' Neoplatonic manner) that geometrical knowledge 'is almost innate, and as it were preceded the discovery and learning, or at least is less in need of them than other sciences . . . for the people at large and those wholly illiterate know how to draw figures and compute and sing, all of which are mathematical operations'.[47] However, fundamentally unlike a Neoplatonist, Bacon exploited mathematical principles in what he considered to be an empirical manner in his investigations of physical phenomena in the natural world. For him the truth of mathematics was inseparably united with 'experience' and always confirmed by practice.[48]

It is only a short step from the principles and methods behind such medieval science to Leonardo's conception of the relationship between Nature and the mathematical beauties of art—whereas a methodological chasm separates the principle of Ficinian *adaequatio* from the inductive correction of aesthetic judgement which is so essential for Leonardo's theory of beauty. The hypothesis that the medieval science of 'experience' provides an important antecedent for Leonardo's induction of mathematical beauty from Nature is reinforced by the close correspondence between the inventive process in his theory of art and the two-stage procedure of Paduan Aristotelianism—the procedure of *resolutio* and *compositio* which has also been discerned in Bacon's science.[49]

The highly scientific process through which the artist produces beautiful images seems to operate as follows, according to Leonardo. The painter derives the underlying rules (causes or laws) from his study of Nature in the context of those supremely certain truths which can be mathematically demonstrated and which have been rigorously verified by long experience. Perspective and proportion are products of such study. These rules are then impressed upon the mind in such a way as to override the innate quirks of individual judgement which would otherwise result in auto-mimesis. When the artist subsequently wishes to compose a picture he invents the composition in his imagination, and his up-graded faculty of judgement directs the realisation of his invention so that it accords with the laws of Nature. Figures so composed will conform to the true rules of proportion; they will not conform to the appearance of their master.

Taking Alberti's *De pictura* as the starting point for Renaissance art theory, and as a probable source of inspiration for Leonardo, we may say that Leonardo legitimately developed the Aristotelean aspects of Alberti's optics in the direction of medieval science, adopting the basic tenets of Baconian and Paduan methodology.[50] Alberti's notions of proportion and harmony are less legitimately developed in a similarly 'Baconian' direction, and Alberti's fundamental confidence in the God-given perfection of man's innate

judgement is abandoned. In both developments of the Albertian tradition
Leonardo thus moves away from rather than towards a Neoplatonic theory
of art—although Alberti's theory of beauty would seem to lead more
naturally in a Neoplatonic direction.

Leonardo's interpretation of the maxim that 'ogni dipintore dipinge se' is
directly dependent upon his characterisation of judgement as a variable
factor, which is in turn dependent upon his conception of the variability of
souls as manifested through the variety of bodies which the souls Hippo-
cratically form. The echo of the aphorism 'ogni dipintore dipinge se' thus
strikes a notably un-Platonic note in Leonardo's theory of beauty. Like so
many other aphorisms of comparably brevity, it could easily be pressed into
the service of a number of different causes. Leonardo's particular exploitation
of the notion in the cause of his form of empiricism is a far cry from the
philosophy of the Neoplatonic circles in which it appears to have been
current, while sharing much in common with the concept of experience in
Aristotelean natural philosophy.

NOTES

[1] *Trat.* 137 (B.N. 2038, f. 27r; McMahon 276), *Trat.* 105 (ms A, f. 23r; McMahon
85), *Trat.* 108 (McMahon 86), *Trat.* 109 (*Libro* A, 28; McMahon 45), *Trat.* 186
(*Libro* A, 37; McMahon 273), *Trat.* 282 (*Libro* A, 28; McMahon 438) and *Trat.* 296
(*Libro* A, 15; McMahon 437). *Trattato* references are to H. Ludwig, *Leonardo da Vinci.
Das Buch von der Malerei*, Vienna, two vols., 1882. McMahon numbers refer to A. P.
McMahon, *Treatise on Painting by Leonardo da Vinci*, Princeton, N.J., two vols., 1956.
For *Libro* A see C. Pedretti, *Leonardo da Vinci on Painting: a Lost Book* (*Libro A*), London,
1965.

[2] ms A, and B.N. 2038 (Ashburnham 1) were originally part of the same ms and are
dated 1492. The lost *Libro* A has convincingly been given a late date by Pedretti,
A Lost Book, pp. 11 ff. Some notes on water from *Libro* A were copied by Leonardo in
the Codex Leicester, probably datable *c.* 1509.

[3] Folio 23r (Richter 586): 'quel pittore che avrà goffe mani le farà simili nelle sua
opere . . . ogni parte di bono e di tristo che ài in te, si dimostrerà in parte in nelle tue
figure'. Richter numbers refer to J. P. Richter, *The Literary Works of Leonardo da Vinci*,
London, third edition, two vols., 1970.

[4] B.N. 2038, f. 27r (Richter 587): 'ti potresti ingannare togliĕdo visi che avessino
cõfromità col tuo, perchè spesso pare che simili cõformita ci piacino, e se tu fussi
brutto eleggieresti volti nõ belli e faresti brutti volti comme molti pittori, che spesso
le figure somigliano il maestro'.

[5] 28 (45), Pedretti, *A Lost Book*, p. 53: 'debbe il pittore fare la sua figura sopra la
regola d'un corpo naturale il quale communemente sa di proporzione laudabile.
Oltre di questo, fa misurare sè medisimo e vedere in che parte la sua persona varia,
assai o poco, da quella antidetta laudabile. E fatta questa notizia, debbe riprare con
tutto il suo studio di non incorrere nei medesimi mancamenti, nelle figure da lui
operate, che nella persona sua si trova. E sappi che questo vizio ti bisogna sommamente
pugnare, conciossiachè egli è mancamento ch'è nato insieme col giudizio; perchè
l'anima, maestra del tuo corpo, è quella che [fe'] il tuo proprio giudizio; e volontieri
si diletta nelle opere simili a quella ch'ella operò nel comporre del suo corpo. E di qui
nasce che non è si brutta figura di femmina che non trovi qualche amante, se già non
fussi mostruosa.'

[6] 15 (11), Pedretti, *A Lost Book*, p. 35: 'le figure spesso somigliano alli loro maestri
. . . chè il giudizio nostro è quello che move la mano alle creazione de' lineamente

d'esse figure per diversi aspetti, in sino a tanto ch'esso si satisfaccia. E perchè esso giudizio è una delle potenze dell' anima nostra, con la quale essa compose la forma del corpo dov'essa abita, secondo il suo volere, onde, avendo co'le mani a rifare un corpo unmano, volentieri rifà quel corpo di che essa fu prima inventrice. E di qui nasce che chi s'innamora volontieri s' innamorano di cose a loro simiglianti.'

[7] *Trat.* 108 (McMahon 86): 'massimo diffetto de pittori'.

[8] A. Chastel, *Art et humanisme à Florence au temps de Laurent le Magnifique*, Paris, 1961, pp. 102–3; also C. Gutkind, *Cosimo de' Medici*, Oxford, 1938, p. 234.

[9] A. Poliziano, *Tagebuch, 1477–79*, ed. A. Wesselski, Jena, 1929, p. 72, n. 150; and G. Savonarola, *Prediche sopra Ezechiel*, Venice, 1517, f. 71*v*.

[10] G. Vasari, *Le vite de'piu eccellenti pittori, scultori ed archittetori*, ed. G. Milanesi, Florence, 1906, VII, p. 260. This was Michelangelo's caustic answer to the question of why 'some painter or other had produced a picture in which the best thing was an ox'.

[11] *The Genius of Leonardo da Vinci; Leonardo da Vinci on Art and the Artist*, New York, 1961, p. 225; and *Art et humanisme*, p. 103.

[12] B.N. 2038, f. 26*r* (Richter 496 and 502): 'cose notabili da sottili speculatione côpresse'; la īuentione fatta ī prima nella tua imaginatiua'. Richter misleadingly translates 'invention' as 'idea'.

[13] *Trat.* 13 (McMahon 35): 'et in effetto, ciò, ch'è nell uniuerso per essentia, presentia o'immaginatione, esso lo ha prima nella mente, e poi nelle mani; e quelle sono di tanta eccellentia, che in pari tempi generano una proportionata armonia in un' solo sguardo'. *Cf. Trat.* 30 (McMahon 43) and *Trat.* 27 (McMahon 28) for statements on proportioned harmony.

[14] *Trat.* 68 (McMahon 280): 'la deità, ch'è la scientia del pittore, fa che la mente del pittore si trasmutta in una similitudine di mente diuina, imperoche con libera potesta discorre allà generatione di diuerse essentia di uarij animali, piante . . .'. *Cf.* Chastel, *Art et humanisme*, p. 421.

[15] See P. O. Kristeller's unrivalled discussion of affinity in Ficino's epistemology in *The Philosophy of Marsilio Ficino*, trans. V. Conant, New York, 1943, pp. 48 ff and 231 ff.

[16] Kristeller, *Ficino*, pp. 110 ff. *Cf.* Leonardo's unusually Neo-platonic claim in MS Triv., f. 6*r* (*c.* 1487–90; Richter 1202): 'Muouesi l'amante per la cosa amata come il sense e lo sensibile, e cō seco s'uniscie e fassi una cosa medesima; l'opera è la prima cosa che nasce dall'unione; se la cosa amanta è vile, l'amate si fa vile. Quando la cosa unita è cōueniēte al suo vnitore, le seguita dilettatione e piacere e soddisfatione.' ('The lover is moved by the thing loved as is the sense by sensible things, and they unite and make one and the same thing; the work is the first thing born of this union; if the thing loved is base the lover becomes base. When the united object suits that which unites it, there follow delight and pleasure and satisfaction.') This early statement may justifiably be regarded as a Neoplatonic echo. (Leonardo listed Ficino's *Theologica platonica* . . . as one of the books in his possession [C.A. 210*r*].) The same notion is found in Savonarola; see D. Weinstein, *Savonarola and Florence*, Princeton, N.J., 1970, p. 193. But for Leonardo's non-Platonic development of this Ficinian theme see p. 316.

[17] *Theologica Platonica*, XI, 5, f. 255 (trans. P. O. Kristeller).

[18] *De re aedificatoria*, IX, 5 (ed. J. Leoni, reprinted London, 1955).

[19] *De re aed.*, IX, 5 (Leoni, p. 195).

[20] *Trat.* 108 (McMahon 86): 's'egli è pronto nel parlare e ne'moti, le sue figure sonno il simile in prontitudine; e s'el maestro è diuotto, il simile paiano le figure con lor colli torti; e s'el maestro è da poco, le sue figure paiono la pigritia ritratta al naturale; e s'el maestro e sproportionato, le figure sue son simili, e s'elgi c pazzo, nelle sue istorie di dimostra largamente, le quali sono nemiche di conclusione' ('if he is quick in his speech and movements, his figures are similar in quickness; and if the master is pious, his figures seem the same with their necks bent; and if the master is

good-for-nothing, his figures seem idleness portrayed from life, and if he is dispropor-
tioned, his figures are similar, and if he is mad, this will be comprehensively shown in
his narratives, in which his figures make no sense').

[21] See Chastel, *Art et humanisme*, p. 103.

[22] As recorded in Plato's *Symposium*, 39, 40 and 44.

[23] *Symposium*, 39.

[24] Aristotle, *De anima*, 421*b*, 10: 'what is soul? . . . It is the substance which corresponds to the definitive formula of a thing's essence. That means it corresponds to the
essential "whatness" of a body. This is interpreted by Thomas Aquinas in his commentary on *De anima* to mean that "the soul is a substance in the manner of a form
that characterises a particular sort of body" (221) and that "the soul . . . is the form
of the living body" (271).'

[25] Windsor 19097*v* (*c*. 1490). *Cf*. Windsor 19115*r* (*c*. 1510): Nature 'places within
them [the embryos] the soul of the body which forms them; that is the soul of the
mother, which first constructs in the womb the shape of the man and in due time
awakens the soul that is to be its inhabitant'. For Leonardo's artificial construction
of the human body to accommodate the Hippocratic notions see M. Kemp, '*Il
concetto dell'anima* in Leonardo's early skull studies', *Journal of the Warburg and Courtauld
Institutes*, XXXIV, 1971, pp. 125–6.

[26] *De re aed.*, VI, 2 (Leoni, 113). Sir Anthony Blunt, *Artistic Theory in Italy, 1450–1600*,
Oxford, 1964, p. 17, rightly stresses the invariability of judgement in Alberti's theory,
but (pp. 27 ff.) he does not clearly differentiate Leonardo's definition. Chastel, *Art et
humanisme*, p. 423, and *The Genius of Leonardo*, p. 225, equates judgement with 'l'énergie
subconsciente' and 'the intervention of the subconscious in the painter's activity'.
E. H. Gombrich, 'Leonardo's grotesque heads: prolegomena to their study', in
Leonardo saggi e richerche, Rome, 1954, p. 211, characterises the action of judgement in
a similar manner. Such modern equations are more misleading than helpful. Judgement was an innately intellectual measuring power (accurate in Alberti but faulty in
Leonardo), bearing little resemblance to the subconscious or unconscious in modern
psychology.

[27] See E. H. Gombrich, 'Leonardo's method of working out compositions', in
Norm and Form, London, 1966, pp. 58–63; and Kemp, 'Early skull studies', pp. 13–32.

[28] An example is *Libro* A, 15; see n. 6. Panofsky's statement that this instance is
unique (*Renaissance and Renascences*, Stockholm, 1960, p. 188, n. 3) is untrue, as I
intend to show in a forthcoming article.

[29] *De inventione*, I, 5, and II, 59.

[30] This application of invention specifically to content occurs in the opening para-
graphs of book III of *De pictura* (ed. and trans. C. Grayson, *Leon Battista Alberti 'On
painting' and 'On sculpture'*, London, 1972, pp. 94–7). See also E. Verheyen, *The
Paintings in the 'Studiolo' of Isabella d'Este at Mantua*, New York, 1971, pp. 22–9, where
a similar usage is found in Isabella's letters on artistic matters.

[31] For medieval imagination see Avicenna *De anima*, I, 5, and R. Bacon, *Opus Majus*,
V, 2. A useful introduction to medieval psychology is provided by M. W. Bundy,
The Theory of Imagination in Classical and Medieval Thought, Illinois, 1927, pp. 179 ff.
Leonardo's conception of artistic imagination is discussed in my 'Early skull studies',
pp. 132–4.

[32] Windsor 19019*r*: 'the soul appears to reside in the seat of judgement, and judgement in the place termed the *sensus communis*, where all the senses converge'. In 'Early
skull studies' I failed to emphasise the extent to which his notion of imagination and
the *sensus communis* departed from medieval theory (e. g. Bacon and Avicenna, for
whom the *sensus* was a lowly mechanism for co-ordinating sense impressions in the first
ventricle).

[33] Leonardo's detailed exploration of the mathematic's of art reached its peak during the 1490s, as witnessed by the notes on perspective in MS A and B.N. 2038 and the
proportional studies on early sheets at Windsor (e.g. Nos. 19130–40, 12601, 12607,

19057r and 19058v). His search for a limited number of proportional systems appears to have occupied relatively less of his time during the sixteenth century, and his demands for variety become more insistent (e.g. MS G, 5v; Richter 503).

[34] 'Leonardo's grotesque heads', pp. 199–219.

[35] *Art et humanisme*, p. 104.

[36] *Libro* A, 28 (45); above, n. 5.

[37] *Libro* A, 44 (95); Pedretti, *A Lost Book*, p. 78 (*Trat.*, 141; McMahon 279): 'li vari giudici di pari intelligenza le giudicheranno di gran varietà infra loro; e sarai [or esserui] tra l'un l'altro delle loro elezioni'.

[38] *Libro* A, 28 (45); above, n. 5. *Cf.* Alberti's recommendation in *De Statua* to study 'many bodies considered to be most beautiful by those who know' (ed. Grayson, 134–135).

[39] B.N. 2038, 27r (Richter 587): 'guarda a torre le parti bone di molti volti belli, le quali belle sieno cõferme piv pubblica fama che per tuo givditio'.

[40] Xenophon, *Memorabilia*, II, 3, 11: 'in portraying ideal types of beauty, seeing that it is not easy to light upon any one human being who is absolutely devoid of blemish, you call from many models the most beautiful traits of each'. This same section (from Socrates' conversation with the sculptor Parrhasius) also contains a statement on 'il concetto dell' anima' which Leonardo would have found particularly congenial: 'as through some chink, or crevice, there pierces through the countenance of man, through the very posture of his body as he stands or moves, a glimpse of his nobility or freedom, or again something in him low and grovelling'.

[41] *De pictura*, III (ed. Grayson, pp. 98–9), probably based upon Cicero, *De inventione*, II, 1, and Pliny, *Hist. Nat.*, XXXV, 36. The Zeuxis story is discussed by M. Baxandall, *Giotto and the Orators*, Oxford, 1971, pp. 35 ff. A history of 'selective imitation' is provided by E. Panofsky, *Idea: a Concept in Art Theory*, trans. J. Peake, Columbia, S.C., 1968.

[42] C.A. 221v (*c.* 1490; Richter 18); 'uno libero e bono giuditio jnperochè 'l bono giuditio nascie dal bene intēdere, e 'l bene intēdere diriua da ragione tratta da bone regole e le bone regole sono figliole della bona speriēta: comvne madre di tutte le sciēte e arti'. It should be noted that 'libero' means free from personal taint rather than from absolute controls.

[43] These aids are discussed on B.N. 2038, 28r (Richter 530), and 26r (Richter 532).

[44] B.N. 2038, 26v (Richter 507).

[45] C.A. 221v (Richter 18): 'queste regole sono da vsare solamēte per ripruova delle figure jnperochè ogni omo nella prima cõpositione fa qualque errore . . . se tu volessi adoperare le regole nel cõporre non verresti mai acapo e faresti confusione nelle tue opere' ('these [mathematical] rules are only of use in correcting figures, since every man makes several mistakes in his first composition . . . if you try to apply the rules in the composition you will never reach the end and you will make confusion in your works').

[46] *Opus Majus*, IV, 1, 2 f.

[47] *Ibid.*, IV, 1, 3.

[48] *Ibid.*, VI, 1, 1 f, where experience is praised as the factor without which 'nothing can be sufficiently known'. Bacon subsequently used optics to prove his point. Leonardo's conception of experience in relation to mathematics is discussed in my 'Dissection and divinity in Leonardo's late anatomies', *Journal of the Warburg and Courtauld Institutes*, XXXV, 1972, p. 222.

[49] Kemp, 'Early skull studies', pp. 129–31.

[50] For Aristotelean aspects of Alberti's optics see S. Y. Edgerton, Jr., 'Alberti's colour theory: a medieval bottle without Renaissance wine', *Journal of the Warburg and Courtauld Institutes*, XXXII, 1969, pp. 109–34.

C. MALCOLM BROWN *Carleton University, Ontario*

18

'LO INSACIABILE DESIDERIO NOSTRO DE COSE ANTIQUE': NEW DOCUMENTS ON ISABELLA D'ESTE'S COLLECTION OF ANTIQUITIES

THE PHRASE 'lo insaciabile desiderio nostro de cose antique' is found in a letter that Isabella d'Este wrote in 1507. She had just received two alabaster portrait busts from Niccolò Frisio and looked forward to the possibility of obtaining reliefs of the Labours of Hercules. This was not the only time when Isabella had occasion to refer to her insatiable desire for antiques. In 1499 a Roman agent was reminded 'sapeti quanto siamo apetitose de queste antiquità'; Cristoforo Chigi was thanked in 1508 for the gift of an antique intaglio that 'non poteva già esserni più charo et accepto di quello che l'è . . . per el continuo desiderio che havemo de cose antique, quale summamente ne piaceno et delectano'. Some years earlier, in 1502, she had sought Cardinal Ippolito d'Este's assistance in the negotiations for an *all'antica* Cupid and a 'Venere antiqua de marmo picola.'[1] She looked forward to their acquisition because 'io che ho posto grande cura in recogliere cose antique per honorare el mio studio desideraria grandemente haverli'. The letter from which this passage comes also specifies that both the antiques and their modern counterparts, small-scale reproductions or variations on classical themes, were required for a *studio* or *studiolo* in the Ducal Palace in Mantua. Isabella d'Este's collection was eventually housed in a suite of rooms known collectively as the Appartamento della Grotta, or individually as the Studiolo and the Grotta. These rooms were originally located in the Torretta di San Nicolò in the Castello. In 1522 the collection was transferred to more ample quarters on the ground floor of the nearby Corte Vecchia.[2] In their first setting the rooms were arranged in a vertical alignment, with the Studiolo above the Grotta. A horizontal arrangement was possible in the Corte Vecchia whereby the Studiolo served as an antecamera to the Grotta (plates 18.1–2). Allegorical paintings by Andrea Mantegna, Pietro Perugino, Lorenzo Costa and Correggio were hung in the Studiolo.[3] The *raccolta d'antichità*, the *pietre dure* vases, the engraved gems and the gold, silver and bronze medallions were housed in the Grotta together with the reliefs and the marble and bronze statues.

An inventory, and letters from the files of Isabella's correspondence document the contents of both rooms. The archival evidence assumes a greater importance for the Grotta than for the Studiolo, as the main collection was housed in the former and fewer than a dozen of these objects can now be identified. Many of the relevant documents were published in the nineteenth century by the archivists Carlo D'Arco, Antonio Bertolotti and Alessandro Luzio.[4] Their pioneering examination of the Renaissance materials of the Mantua archives has formed the basis for most subsequent research, including the recent studies by Jan Lauts, Andrew Martindale and the late Roberto Weiss,[5] who have discussed Isabella's collection of antiquities in a sensitive and intelligent manner. These scholars, however, did not attempt to verify from the originals the correctness or the completeness of the published documents. Indeed, there has been a general tendency on the part of scholars to use what was printed in the nineteenth century, rather than to examine the actual *carteggi*, despite the fact that the published material is scattered unsystematically in numerous books and recondite articles. It is true that the general outline of Isabella's patronage of the arts as portrayed by the publications of the archivists, and by the synthesis drawn from them by such scholars as Lauts and Weiss, may not be drastically altered as a result of a re-examination of the sources. Yet such a task if accompanied by full documentation will enable one to discern striking details hitherto unknown.

The present study seeks to justify the above conclusion. Its main purpose is to make available thirty-six unknown letters from Isabella d'Este's correspondence files, which are published in an appendix. The preceding paper is focused on the contents of the Grotta and the Studiolo, taking its evidence from the correspondence files (and especially the thirty-six letters) and an inventory of 1542.

Knowledge of the extent of the collection and the precise manner in which it was displayed comes from the inventory that Odoardo Stivini compiled in 1542.[6] Information concerning individual acquisitions and documentation of the manner in which negotiations were conducted come from the correspondence files. The inventory and the correspondence files are therefore complementary; the one treats of the end results, and the other the means by which these were realised. Nonetheless neither can be used to the exclusion of the other. The following example will demonstrate why this is the case. The inventory catalogues some seventy-two *pietre dure* vases and at least twelve bronze statuettes by modern sculptors. The correspondence files refer, however, to the acquisition of a single vase and only three bronzes. In any number of instances an object may be documented in one or the other source but not in both. There are several possible explanations. The inventory was limited to the contents of two rooms, the Studiolo and the Grotta. It did not catalogue objects Isabella acquired but displayed elsewhere, either in the Ducal Palace or in her suburban villas.[7] Furthermore not all of the correspondence she wrote and received has been preserved. Apart from the loss of individual documents by chance over the years, there remains the destruction of all of Isabella's *Libri dei Copialettere* for 1525–27 (the period of her residence in Rome), which were lost in the aftermath of the sack. Moreover verbal transactions would, of course, remain unknown save in the few instances where there is evidence providing some indirect reference to them.[8] Finally the account books of the court were wilfully destroyed in the nineteenth century.[9]

The documentation that exists for six of the more important objects from the collection which have survived will demonstrate how the inventory and the correspondence may be used, and how the one complements and supplements the other. The works in question include two reliefs (Proserpina, Two Satyrs) and the portrait bust of Faustina, all still in the Ducal Palace in Mantua (plates 18.6, 18.5, 18.3), a cameo now in Leningrad (plate 18.4), a cameo vase now in Braunschweig (plate 18.7) and a bronze statuette now in Vienna (plates 18.8–9).[10] The Proserpina relief is discussed in both sources. Its location in the Studiolo, embedded in the wall beneath the window, is recorded in the inventory, while its acquisition in 1523–24 is documented in the correspondence files. The second relief, the Hellenistic portrayal of Two Satyrs, is not mentioned by Stivini, although it is known to have entered the collection in 1501 (appendix 18.1, document 1). The Faustina portrait, like the Proserpina relief, is mentioned in both sources. The correspondence files indicate it as a 1506 purchase, which Stivini saw to the right of an Octavian bust over the central cabinet in the Grotta. The Leningrad cameo has been identified with the first entry in the inventory: 'Uno cameo grande fornito d'oro con due teste di relievo di Cesare e Livia legato in oro con una gherlanda incirca con foglie di lauro smaltato di verde, con una perla de sotto, et da roverso lavorato a niello, et una tavola con il nome della Illustrissima Signora Madamma di bona memoria.'

No indication of date of manufacture is provided in the inventory, either for this classical piece or for the Roman Faustina. Stivini did occasionally describe a certain item as modern or antique, the latter being used to describe the Proserpina relief. The correspondence files do not refer either to the Leningrad cameo or to the late antique cameo vase in Braunschweig, but they do mention the 'Hercules and Antheus' bronze, which Stivini locates on the lower moulding in the Grotta. The Viennese statuette can be attributed to L'Antico and the inscription 'D. Isabella M. Mar.' is found under its base. Although modern, the statue is based on an antique prototype.[11] Accordingly it fits into the aesthetic and intellectual framework of Isabella's collection. The relationship between the antique and the modern was best expressed by the sixteenth-century connoisseur and collector Marc' Antonio Michiel. In his discussion of the bronzes in Marco of Mantua's collection in Padua he wrote, 'le figurette de bronze sono moderne de diversi maestri e vengono dall'antichità come el Giove che siede'.[12] This description could aptly be applied to that portion of Isabella's collection which was displayed on the ledge above the wainscot in the Grotta, as will be discussed in due course.

Before considering in more detail the inventory which allows one to reconstruct the collection, it is helpful to have some notion of the collection's dispersal. This will afford an opportunity to introduce two other statues, which may originally have come from the Grotta. The contents of Isabella's apartments appear to have been kept intact at least until the end of the sixteenth century. Yet by 1630 little of them, if anything, remained in the rooms that had housed the collection or elsewhere in the Ducal Palace of Mantua. A major portion of the artistic patrimony of the Gonzaga court was sold to Charles I of England in 1627-28.[13] This included several items from the Grotta, the most notable being the Michelangelo and Praxiteles Cupids which Stivini located on either side of the window. The Studiolo allegories had already been shipped to France as a present for Cardinal Richelieu.[14] The correspondence of Charles's agents does not specify that bronzes were included in the sale. Yet there is reason to believe that Isabella's 'Hercules and Antheus' had been shipped to England at this time. It was purchased there by Ludwig Wilhelm and it then passed, together with the rest of his collection, into the Kunsthistorisches Museum in Vienna.[15] The knowledge that one object from Wilhelm's collection came from Mantua suggests the possibility that other pieces may have a similar provenance. There are statues of Leda and Venus (plates 18.12, 18.11) reproduced in the 1735 catalogue of the collection on the same page that displays the 'Hercules and Antheus' (plate 18.10).[16] Can they be identified with the 'due figure di marmoro moderne cioè una Leda et una Venere' which Stivini locates on the cornice above the door in the Grotta? The bronze Mercury to the right of the Leda on this page of the 1735 catalogue is also now in Vienna and can be attributed to L'Antico.[17] The Viennese statuette, of which there are several versions, seems to be related to the Stivini entry which records 'Un Mercurio che insegna a leggere a Cupido'. No version of the Cupid is known and, unlike the Hercules group, the Mercury does not have Isabella's name inscribed under the base.[18] Even so, one can postulate a Mantuan provenance for Wilhelm's Mercury.

Two years after the sale to Charles the imperial forces entered Mantua. General Aldringen ordered the sack, which the chronicler Brusoni described as 'cosa deplorabile il vedere consumate e sparse in un baleno tutte le delizie, le pompe, li fasti, le ricchezze e le glorie dell'inclita Casa Gonzaga, raccolte per lo spazio di quasi trecent'anni da que' Principi e Signori'.[19] Although this account does exaggerate the dispersal of the collection in consequence of the sack, it should be noted that many objects of value, including items from Isabella's collection, were presumably still in Mantua at the time of the sack, since they had not been included in the sale. The cameo vase, claimed in the name of Franz Albrecht of Lauenberg, eventually found its way into the Braunschweig museum.[20] It is not known who removed the Leningrad cameo to Prague.[21] It may have been taken by Rudolf, Graf Colloredo, who laid claim to four paintings of Gonzaga triumphs from the Palazzo di San Sebastiano, or by General Aldringen, who removed Lorenzo Costa's 'Triumph of Duke Federico'.[22] Apart from the items already discussed, nothing certain is known of the rest of Isabella's collection subsequent to its partial sale and the sack of Mantua. For instance, the Michelangelo and Praxiteles Cupids which went to England are presumed to have been destroyed during the fire at the Whitehall Palace, of 4/14 January 1698.[23] It is, of course, possible that objects from the Grotta still exist in public or private collections, but can no longer be identified as such because their provenance is now unknown. Unlike Lorenzo de' Medici, Isabella is not known to have engraved her initials on her *pietre dure* vases or on her cameos. [24] It would accordingly be reckless to attempt to say which, if any, of the Quattrocento heads of *putti* that are known can be identified with the Stivini entry which reads 'una figure di Venere di marmo antica sopra alla porta a sedere con un vaso in mano *con due teste di putini di bronzo una per lato*'. [25]

What details are furnished by the 1542 inventory, which lists a total of 1,620 objects in 235 entries? First 1,240 items were coins and medallions, 119 were of gold, 1,012 of silver, while the rest, consisting of 110 bronze medallions, were mounted on twenty-two plaques in groups of five. [26] Isabella owned a total of seventy-two vases, flasks and cups, fifty-five of which were of *pietre dure*. This included fourteen in agate and a like number in jasper. Most of them were fitted with gold covers, handles and pedestals which ran the gamut from simplicity to the bizarre. One of the chalcedony vases is described as having a 'coperto, manico et piede de oro, cioè il piede a triangolo con tre arpie e tre perle sopra le testa d'esse arpie et tre zoglie nel petto, cioè diamante, rubino, e smeraldo, con dui manichi fatti a scartozzi con due figurine et in cima al coperto un diamante in ponta'. Twenty-nine of the forty-six engraved gems were cameos, and three of the statuettes were of *pietre dure*. Of the remainder, forty-eight were in bronze and seventeen of marble, while there were thirteen portrait busts, and three reliefs. In addition to the nine allegorical paintings the collection contained several watches, inlaid boxes, an astrolabe and such rarities as a unicorn horn, several pieces of coral and 'un dente di pesce sopra la fenestra lungo tre palmi'. [27]

Most of the collection was displayed in the Grotta, since the allegorical pictures were the principal decoration in the Studiolo. Nonetheless this latter room contained several antique objects in addition to its tables, which seem to have been made from slabs of classical columns. There were, for instance, the busts of Brutus and Caracalla, set on either side of a window—that very one below which the Proserpina relief was located. The ledges formed by the cornices of the door frames, which gave access to the Studiolo, as well as those of the door frames between the Studiolo and the Grotta, supported three vases and two *putti* heads in the first instance, and three alabaster vases in the second. An astrolabe, a lead mirror in its walnut case, a metal inkstand and various inlaid boxes were found on the aforementioned tables.

Forty-two of the forty-eight bronzes were displayed on the two mouldings in the Grotta. The seventeen on the ledge at the springing of the vault are somewhat vaguely described: 'fra figure e mezze figure e teste antiche et moderne di brongio'. The twenty-five set slightly above eye level on the cornice of the wainscot are individually catalogued. These include the Vienna Mercury and the 'Hercules and Antheus' which have already been discussed. The 'Apollo simil a quello di Roma', the 'nudo dall spina', the 'duoi nudi dal bastone' and the 'Cupidine con un arco in mano', the latter set on the window ledge, can also be attributed to L'Antico. [28]

L'Antico's repertory is not known to have included such subjects as the Laocoön (of which Isabella owned two versions), the 'duoi satiri che servono per candeglieri' or the 'Neptuno sopra un monstro col tridente'. All the known versions of the latter have been attributed to Severo da Ravenna, while Stivini's description of the satyrs suggests that Isabella owned statuettes executed in the Riccio workshop.[29] The authorship of both the statuettes of the Laocoön is more problematic.[30] Normally one would assume that the 'mano di brongio picciola' must have been antique. In this instance such a supposition might be erroneous, not only because so many of the bronzes on the lower moulding were demonstrably modern, but also because of the number of 'fragments' which were produced in Paduan and Venetian work-shops in the late fifteenth and early sixteenth centuries.[31] Indeed, Stivini, whose use of the terms 'modern' and 'antique' is too erratic to be relied on, reserved the latter for the 'figura antica nuda e li mancha un brazzo' and for the lamp 'con una figuretta a cavallo, qual lucerna è suso una testa di cavallo con vernice verde'. The mounting for the lamp was unquestionably modern, while Stivini may have been misled by the damaged statue, since several such statuettes of female nudes of Quattrocento vintage are known.[32]

The 'Hercules and Antheus', the Apollo Belvedere and the Laocoön, like the marble 'Dying Cleopatra' set above the cupboard to the right of the window, are all copies of antique statues in the Vatican Belvedere.[33] The lower moulding which housed the twenty-five bronzes was broken by the door which gave access to the room. Above its cornice were located an antique Venus with two bronze *putti* heads set on either side, and also the modern Leda and Venus which have already been discussed. Portraits of Lucius Verus, an old man (not otherwise specified and unidentified), Claudius, Livia, Germanicus the Younger and Faustina the Elder, as well as 'una figura di marmo de una donna a sentare', were set on the moulding above the wainscot on either side of the door in the north-west wall. This, according to Stivini, was the 'seconda faccia della Grotta'. The doorway itself was a major work of art, as its frame and lintel contained inlays of semi-precious stones and historiated marble *tondi*.[34] Busts of Octavian, Lucilla and Faustina were located on the moulding above the three cup-boards of the 'prima faccia', that is, the north-east wall which faces the window. This suggests that the twenty-five bronze statuettes previously discussed were set along the south-east wall which faces the entrance. The aforementioned cupboards housed the bulk of the collection; the cameos, vases and silver objects. The unicorn horn was placed above the cabinets, 'sopra due rampini torti di fuor via'.[35] The bronze coins were located, however, in a cupboard to the left of the window, while the remainder of the medallions were placed in the corresponding cabinet to the right. These cabinets housed respectively the marble cupids by Praxiteles and Michel-angelo, with the 'Dying Cleopatra' located above the latter. Two small tables were located in front of each. An antique arm, a porphyry vase and two ivory caskets were set on the floor beneath the table on the right, while under the other table were three antique marble feet, six terracotta vases and several caskets. Portraits of Tiberius and Mark Antony were set on either side of the window, the former being framed by a statuette of a seated Pan and the aforementioned Cupid holding a bow, the latter by a

Mars and the second Laocoön. A Leda, a Silenus and an antique foot were presumably also located on the window ledge. Detached from the wall and perhaps placed towards the centre of the room was a porphyry table set in a wooden frame, and a walnut chair. Various objects were arranged on this table, among them the Marchesa's inkstand, several watches and inlaid boxes, including one of walnut which contained ninety-five gold and silver coins.

The *intarsia* wainscots of Federigo da Montefeltro's Studioli in his palaces of Urbino and Gubbio are famous, and appear of higher quality than the *intarsia* work executed by the Mola brothers for Isabella's Studiolo and Grotta; however, there is no evidence as to the existence of *objets d'art* in the rooms of Federigo da Montefeltro. In the case of Lorenzo de' Medici's *scrittorio*, which certainly contained items of greater value than were to be found in Isabella's collection, the precise location of the objects in the room is not known.[36] In comparison it would be possible to execute sketches to show both the decoration (in broad terms, since the *intarsia* is now much mutilated) and for the years after the transference of 1522 the exact position of the *objets d'art* in Isabella's Grotta (on the basis of Stivini's inventory of 1542)—this room, by the way, like her Studiolo, was generally accessible to visitors during her lifetime.[37] Giangiorgio Trissino, one such visitor, was clearly not exaggerating, or merely indulging in correct etiquette when he wrote:

Chi meglio, e piú volentieri di costei sa spendere nelle cose lodevoli, e spendere dove il bisogno conosce; e questa sua liberalità si puo chiaramente comprendere dalle splendide sue vestimenta, da i paramenti di casa magnifici, e dalle fabriche bella dilettevole, quasi divine, con alcuni dolcissimi camerini pieni di rarissimi libri, di pitture bellisime, di antique sculture meravigliose, e di moderne, che si avicinano a quelle, di Camei di tagli, di Medaglie, e di gemme elettissime: et in somma di tante altre cose pretiose e rare abondevoli sono, che ad un tempo diletto grandissimo, e non piccola meraviglia porgono a i riguardanti.[38]

The documentation of the acquisition of many individual items which Trissino saw, and which Stivini catalogued, is to be found in the correspondence files. These contain some 300 letters dealing with negotiations for antiques, which can be catalogued according to the individual items and arranged chronologically. All in all, information is provided for some sixty objects. Obviously not all the letters relating to an item are of equal importance, and their transcription is not necessary when they represent merely reminders, or repetitions of earlier communications. The importance of the other correspondence is twofold. It serves to document many of the facets both of Isabella's successful and of frustrated negotiations to build up her collection over a period of some thirty-five years. No corpus of comparable depth exists for any other collector or collection during the second half of the fifteenth or the first half of the sixteenth centuries. Indeed, given the fact that the Gonzaga archives seem to be more completely preserved than those for other courts, these *carteggi* have often been called upon to fill in the gaps that exist elsewhere. Thus, by way of example, several acquisitions made by Pope Julius II for the Vatican sculpture garden (the Belvedere) are best or uniquely documented by letters written by Mantuan agents to Isabella d'Este.[39] Likewise the fate of a portion of the Lorenzo de' Medici collection of *pietre dure* vases is known from the Gonzaga *carteggi*, which also document one of the gems Piero was constrained to sell in 1503.[40] It is tempting to exaggerate the importance of the Gonzaga archives, but in the light of the select examples just cited it would be equally wrong to relegate them to a lesser role than they merit.

The ensuing discussion of Isabella d'Este's correspondence seeks to provide a chronological picture of how the collection grew. The survey is based on all available material, both published and unpublished. It differs, therefore, from the previous published accounts such as those by Lauts and Weiss which were mentioned earlier.

Isabella appears to have decided to form a comprehensive *raccolta d'antichità* only about 1497. The correspondence from the years 1490–96 deals almost exclusively with the acquisition of antique *intagli* and with the commissions for engraved semi-precious stones from Venetian craftsmen.[41] The shift away from this concentration on gems towards a more all-inclusive approach, which included bronzes and marbles, is first detected in several letters, notably those Isabella wrote on 7 March and 4 April 1498. In the former she thanked Ludovico Agnelli for the gift of a 'brazo de una figura de bronzo antiquo . . . *per ornare uno studio principiato*'. The second letter was addressed to Giovanni Andrea del Fiore and it advised him that 'voressimo altro cha chamei. Ve respondemo che nui desideramo anchora molto piú de havere qualche figurette et teste de bronzo et marmore.'[42] Thus the foundations for a collection to be housed in the Studiolo date from precisely the same moment when the decision had been taken to commission a series of allegorical pictures for the same room.[43] Eventually the antiques were moved from the Studiolo to the Grotta, the lower room in the Torretta di San Nicolò in the Castello. This arrangement was maintained after the move from the Castello to the Corte Vecchia, as is known from the Stivini inventory.

No evidence exists to suggest that Isabella had put the room below the Studiolo to any practical use prior to 1508. It was in fact only in April of that year that she asked for antiques specifically for this room because 'la grotta nostra è finita'.[44] The wooden ceiling, with its *imprese*, was set in place in April of the preceeding year. Yet on 7 March 1498 Niccolò da Correggio spoke of his desire to enter 'a la solinga grotta', and two months later the Marchesa dated a letter to her husband 'in grandissima pressia—in la Grotta'.[45] In 1503 and again in 1505 and 1506, before any evidence exists of work undertaken to provide the room with a wainscot and an inlaid ceiling, Isabella received or was offered antiques for the Grotta.[46] Yet prior to 1508, and certainly as late as 1506, Isabella herself always asked for antiques for the Studiolo.[47] There is only one plausible explanation for the confusion in names, unless one is willing to believe that Isabella and her correspondents were talking at cross-purposes—that she adamantly insisted on placing in the room called the Studiolo those antiques which their donors intended for the

Grotta. It is that the word Grotta could be applied both to the suit of rooms themselves and also to one specific unit in the group. Raphaello Toscano, writing in 1586, had in fact spoken of the five rooms in the Corte Vecchia 'che la grotta il mondo appella'.[48] He singled out two for special comment. These were the rooms Stivini called the 'studio apresso la Grotta' and the Grotta. It would be interesting to follow up Hirschfeld's intelligent suggestion that the 'bella grotta' described by Boiardo in his *Orlando Innamorato* is related directly or indirectly to Isabella's decision to use the word for her *gabinetti*.[49] This is not the place, however, to enter further into the problem of the precise meaning of the word Grotta, which had never been used before and was never to be used again as an alternative to *studio*, *studiolo* or *scrittorio*. When it gained popularity in the mid-sixteenth century it was used almost exclusively to refer to a type of garden decoration; an artificial cave decorated with shells. It would, in any event, be too great a simplification to suggest that the name Grotta was suggested to Isabella by the low vault of the room below the Studiolo, or by the *grotta* in which Vulcan's workshop is located in Andrea Mantegna's *Parnassus*—a painting which was installed in the Studiolo in July of 1497 (plate 18.13). Nonetheless neither Isabella d'Este nor her friends could have overlooked the intended similarity between the vases displayed on Vulcan's forge and those which formed part of her collection.

1497–1506. This period opens with that shift in interest, which has already been described, away from *intagli* and towards marble and bronze statues required for the express purpose of decorating a *studiolo*. As a result of selective purchases and a number of gifts Isabella was well on the way to realising her ambition to achieve a representative collection when she wrote to Gian Cristoforo Romano on 6 August 1506 that 'cossi a poco poco andarimo facendo un studio'. She had just acquired an agate vase at an auction of the Vianello collection in Venice and had purchased the Faustina bust from her court painter, Andrea Mantegna.[50] The modest tone of her comment to Romano is all the more unjustified when it is recalled that the Michelangelo *all'antica* Cupid entered the collection in 1502, while the Praxiteles version arrived four years later. They were singled out for special praise by Leandro Alberti in 1550 and figured prominently in the negotiations between Vincenzo Gonzaga and Charles I's agent, Daniel Nys, in 1627–28.[51]

Isabella d'Este's initial contact with the Agnelli brothers, Ludovico and Onorato, in February 1497 led to no fewer than six gifts by September 1501.[52] These included a 'brazo de una figura de bronze antiquo', busts of Jove and Hercules, and several slabs from an antique column as well as the relief of the Two Fauns. The correspondence with Onorato for the antique columns is contemporary with the negotiations with Antonio Maria Pico della Mirandola for 'la tavola de pietre'. This correspondence provides ample testimony to the difficulty of exporting antiques from Rome. Not even an export licence from the Pope could ensure success with the Conservators.[53]

The negotiations in 1498 with the executors of the Venetian Domenico di Piero's estate throw light on the extent of Domenico's collection, portions of which are catalogued in the letters.[54] There is nothing in the correspondence, however, to indicate that any purchases resulted, and the same comment can be applied to both of Isabella's attempts (in 1498 and 1502) to obtain *objets d'art* through her brother, Cardinal Ippolito d'Este.[55] Isabella's bid in 1502 to claim an 'intaglio de uno nudo' that had belonged to her sister Beatrice failed because the item had been lost or destroyed, while the negotiations in the same year for several *pietre dure* vases from the Medici collection failed to produce the desired results owing to a disagreement over the price and the means by which payment was to be made. She had, however, received an antique marble vase in 1499 from a Roman correspondent.[56]

It was with Guidobaldo da Montefeltro's express consent that the Marchesa negotiated with Cesare Borgia for the Michelangelo Cupid and the 'Venere antiqua de marmo picola' that had been appropriated after the Montefeltro had been ousted from Urbino in June 1502; Guidobaldo's attempt to reclaim these objects with Borgia's fall in 1503 was to no avail. Cesare Borgia's agent had brought the marble statues to Mantua on 21 July 1502.[57] Several months later, on 2 October, the Marchesa reaffirmed her intention 'de havere uno Cupido antiquo quale è de li figlioli de quondam Messer Guido Bonatto, li quali ce lo darianno ogni volta che uno de lor fratelli havessino uno beneficio de cento ducati o qui o in Roma'. The negotiations for the Cupid, attributed to Praxiteles had began in 1498, and were not concluded until December 1505, by which time the price of the benefice Isabella sought to obtain from the Pope had increased to 150 ducats.[58]

In the summer of 1502 the Marchesa of Crotone sent Isabella a 'locerne per cose antique' and a 'Hercule quale dicono che è Libico'. The following year, on 23 March 1503, Isabella received twenty antique medallions from the same source.[59] Isabella's response to the offer of a cameo from the Medici collection for 200 ducats is not documented, although it is known that she did not follow up Lorenzo da Pavia's suggestion that she should purchase a Rhodian bronze in 1503.[60] It was Lorenzo da Pavia who discouraged her from purchasing the antiques in the Zoan Andrea del Fiore collection, presumably she took his advice.[61] In September of that same year, 1503, the Marchesa received 'una figuretta de bronze de la grandeza del puttino dal spine'. The commission for a companion piece for the Spinario, the statuette L'Antico cast in March in 1501, was made because 'voria mettere sopra una cornice da uscio al incontro de quello putino per darli conformità, essendo li ussi de una proportione'.[62] The Spinario which Stivini saw on the lower moulding in the Grotta in the Corte Vecchia was therefore originally located above the door in the Studiolo in the Castello.

In February 1505 Isabella was the recipient of a medallion that had been discovered in digging the foundations of a new palace in Urbino, but she rejected as modern the 'testa anticha de avolio' Giovanni Gonzaga had purchased in her name for ten ducats. 'Havendola vista Messer Andrea Mantinea e Zo. Christophoro [Romano] non la judicano antiqua nè bona.'[63] The Marchesa thought to profit from Romano's visit to Rome to enlarge her holdings, and she gave him specific instructions to examine the collection that Giovanni Ciampolini had assembled.[64] If anything resulted, no trace of it remains in the available documents. The Bonatto Cupid arrived in Mantua in February of 1506 together with 'una testa antiqua', and Isabella received several more the same year from the Marchesa of Crotone. Two of these were restored by L'Antico, who identified one as a Minerva in his letter of May 1506.[65] The Faustina, that Isabella purchased from Mantegna for 100 ducats in August 1506, has already been mentioned, as have the 'duoi teste de alabastro' of Antonia and Faustina, which had belonged to Antongaleazzo Bentivoglio, the Protonotary, and presumably been abandoned during the families' flight in October 1506 and was acquired for Isabella by Niccolò Frisio prior to 27 November.[66] The outcome of her advancing rights to a 'Cupido fatto per morto' owned by Cardinal Federico Sanseverino is known; she failed because he did not die, as anticipated, in the October of the same year.[67]

1507–14. On 5 July 1507 Isabella learned of the arrival of the antiques Fra Sabba da Castiglione had shipped from Rhodes. It was the first of two such shipments of Greek originals. The second reached Venice exactly a year later, in July 1508. In addition to several medallions the cases contained 'uno corpo senza testa, bracchia et gamba di marmore stato novamente trovato in una vigna al Lyndo', a marble vase and 'un monstro marino parimente di marmo, grande circa un cubito che con lascivo atto fa vezzi a un Nimpha, quale esso tiene con un braccio stretta', which had been found at Halicarnassus. The 'due testaiuole de amazone' had the same provenance. Although nothing came of Fra Sabba's starry-eyed plans to ship a Mausoleum to Mantua, he had been able, with Isabella's assistance, to overcome the obstacles Amalrico d'Amboise, the Grand Master of the Order of St John in Rhodes, placed in the path of the shipment of the other objects.[68]

Gregorio di Negroponte was frustrated in his desire to send Isabella antiques from Rome in May 1507. Price and competition were the two main obstacles. Yet two years earlier Ludovico Canossa had encouraged her to visit Rome because 'qua è bona condition de cose antique per essare le moderne in maior pretio fusseno mai, et forsi non seria male che de Signora deveniste mercante'![69] In November 1507 Isabella consulted L'Antico on the authenticity of several objects offered her by a Milanese merchant. His response is not preserved.[70] The following year she was sent 'una testa antica et un putino et una capra' by Cardinal Sanseverino. Several months earlier she had been offered a 'cosa unica' by her brother-in-law, Cardinal Sigismondo Gonzaga. This unique piece turned out to be another goat.[71] The Chigi brothers, Agostino and Cristoforo, presented her with an *intaglio* in July of 1508, and on Gian Cristoforo Romano's advice the son of the former Mantuan ambassador to Venice paid twenty ducats for a cameo in December 1509.[72] Emilia Pio had expressed the hope that Isabella might purchase objects from the collection of the recently deceased Galeotto Franciotti della Rovere, Cardinal of San Pietro in Vincoli (who had died on 11 September 1507), but the outcome is not known.[73] Giovanni Andrea di Casale sent ten medallions in 1508, while Gian Francesco Valier shipped her a marble head which had arrived in Venice from Rhodes in 1511.[74] In October an agent in Rome proposed the purchase of 'una testa di Ariadna con una corona de vida in testa', a marble satyr and an antique cornelian. Isabella rejected the offer, claiming that 'adesso havendo nui da spendere troppo in la fabricha di la casa che havemo principiata, non poteme attendere ad altre spese'.[75] This did not, however, prevent her from spending fifteen ducats in 1502 for a so-called Plato bust that belonged to the Bellini family in spite of the fact that her agent had cautioned against the purchase.[76]

1514–24. Shortly after L'Antico had restored an otherwise undocumented statue of Mars, Isabella left Mantua for Rome, where she went 'ogni giorno vedendo queste antiquiade quale ogni dí ni pareno piú mirande'.[77] In spite of this, and despite the reception she received after entering the city on 18 October 1514, the Marchesa returned to Mantua the following March 'in tutto privo'. She sought to rectify the situation, and to appease her desire to augment her collection, by enlisting the services of Giovanni Gonzaga. Through him Isabella brought to a successful conclusion her negotiations with the Duke of Milan for objects from the collection of Galeazzo Sforza of Pesaro. Among the antique busts was a portrait of Hadrian for which Bishop Ludovico Gonzaga was reputed to have once offered 400 ducats. The outcome of Isabella's negotiations to purchase other items in the collection which were to be sold remains uncertain.[78] L'Antico's response to a request in 1515 for an expert opinion on a 'quadro marmoro' is not known, and it therefore remains uncertain whether its purchase resulted.[79] Count Niccolò Maffei gave her 'due belle teste antica' and 'alcune medaglie et altri intaglii' in 1517, and the Mantuan ambassador in Venice, Giovanni Battista Malatesta, sent a terracotta vase in 1522.[80] Three years earlier Isabella sought to obtain casts of several statuettes from L'Antico; among them was the 'Hercules and Antheus' now at Vienna.[81] She appears not to have acted on Alfonso Faccino's suggestion that she should spend 400 ducats on a statue of Cybele which had been unearthed in Rome.[82] In 1524, the Proserpina relief arrived in Mantua, sent to Isabella as a gift from her son, who had obtained it from Pope Hadrian. It is the fragment from a Roman sarcophagus, which had been sold to Pope Leo X, who is reputed to have given 500 ducats to the unnamed Roman who had discovered it in Trastevere.[83]

1527–29. It is not difficult to believe that Isabella received various presents and that she made numerous purchases during her two-year stay in Rome (1525–27). Documentary evidence in support of the notion, however, is difficult to come by, in part because of the loss of her 'Libri dei Copialettere'. Moreover the correspondence that is preserved, consisting of the original letters she addressed to the Marquis Federico and those that were written to advise the court in Mantua of her activities, are silent on the subject of her acquisitions. What documents exist come either from the correspondence written after the sack, at which time Isabella attempted to recover items that had been appropriated, or from the 'Libretto de Spese', which covers the period January–June 1527.[84] The account book records the purchase of no fewer than fifty-two medallions, in addition to a 'figure de metale di uno Herchule' and two *pietre dure* figurines from Maestro Raphaello. The latter were the subject of a protracted and inconclusive series of negotiations for the return of her money, since she believed the pieces to be modern.[85] The letters written between 7 October 1527 and 26 May 1528 concern negotiations for the return of those of her medallions and statuettes which had been appropriated by Cazadiavolo and others. These included 'uno nostro sardonio qual era intagliato cum figure' as well as a marble Hercules and Venus.[86] Several of the medallions and perhaps also the sardonyx were retrieved. Replacements for the other medallions were sought through Antonio Maria Pico della Mirandola, while she was compensated for the loss of her terracotta vases through a gift from Cardinal Palmieri in June of 1529.[87]

1530–38. Isabella received ten medallions and two 'metal' statuettes in 1530 from 'Zoan Napolitano', and 'alcuni medaglie' from Cardinal Ercole Gonzaga the following year.[88] In 1536 the latter sent her a cast from a recently discovered medallion portraying Aristotle.[89] Several years earlier, in 1533, Isabella agreed to accept four cameos in settlement of a debt owed her by the Marchesa of Caiazzo, and Isabella purchased an unspecified number of cameos for eighty ducats from a Venetian jeweller in 1538.[90] The correspondence concerning the antiques in Antonio Foscarini's collection is imperfectly preserved. If any purchases resulted from her enquiry to be 'melio informata della sorte et qualità di tutte le cose ch'ha lassato' they are not documented.[91]

Isabella d'Este's last will and testament was drawn up in 1535, four years before she died on 13 February 1539. Special provisions were made in it for the disposition of the 'antiquità, adornamenti, et gentileze quali essa Signora Testatrice ha nel loco chiamato 'La Grotta' posto in la città de Mantua'.[92] The collection Isabella bequeathed to her heirs represented the bulk of what she had acquired by gift and by purchase over a period of forty-one years. The importance of the documentary material available for her collection has long been acknowledged. The frequency with which it has been used stresses the need for the material to be published in a critical edition. The pilot volume of such an edition could well be devoted to the *raccolta d'antichità*, and might serve as a worthy, if belated, memorial to the 500th anniversary of Isabella d'Este's birth in Ferrara on 19 May 1474.

APPENDIX 18.1

1 *Onorato Agnelli to Isabella d'Este, Rome, 19 September 1501.* Busta 854.

alla venuta di Cappellecto prometto mandare a Vostra Illustrissima Signoria doi fauni, quasi de tucto rilevo, li quali fanno una musica sopra un sacrificio, in uno quadro de marmoro, vero è che ad uno mancha tucta la testa et a l'altro la mità, et credo et son certo che a quella piaceranno.

II *Giovanni Lucido Catanei to Isabella d'Este, Rome, 26 November 1499*. Busta 853.

Per Capelleto mando a Vostra Signoria certo broncino antiquo de mixtura, quale ritrovai in heredità de uno antiquissimo e valente dottore che me lassò herede d'alcune sue cose nè altro simile se ne trova et, benchè el non sia d'argento, pur ne ho tante volte retrovato certa summa de denari che ne farebe uno tutavia sempre l'ho servato a Vostra Signoria, dolendomi che 'l non sia anchora piú degno per Vostra Excellentia.

III *The Marchesa of Crotone to Isabella d'Este, Rome, 23 March 1503*. Busta 808.

Yo enbio a Vostra Ecelencia veinte medallas de plata todas que se an fallado acqui in una tiera mia. No se si son buenas peor[?] son antigas. Yo no cesaré de continuo de trovar cosas para la grota y muy presto l'enbiarè una ymagen de marmor, la mas perfeta cosa que nunca salió de Roma, que yo, que no m'entiendo conocco que no se puede dezir mas acabada cosa. Àmela dado el Principe de Rosa y tengo prometidas mil gentilezas quo non las puedo enbiar por la priesa grande que tengo. Dos medallas enbio a Vostra Señoria, en esta carta, que son de Cesaro sierto, sigun me dize quien las tenía caro como la vida.

IV *Cesare Bechadello Soldano to Isabella d'Este, Rome, 5 March 1508*. Busta 858.

Inverso la Pasqua, Vostra Signoria me scriva una sua et dica in dicta litera che io recorda al compare de Vostra Signoria che se ricorda de quella de qualche antiquaglie et basta. Già è trovato qualche cosa nova che marcharà benissimo in la camera de le antiquaglie de Vostra Excellentia: la litera serà una occasione de sollicitarlo con bon fondamento perché di qua è de molti domandatori de simil cosa et persone de conditione; ma me basta l'animo de farli spazare per litere de cambio et cetera.

V *Isabella d'Este to Cesare Bechadello Soldano, Mantua, 4 April 1508*. Busta 2994, Copia-lettere, Libro 20, cc. 98r–v.

Raccomandandone a Monsignore prefacto [Sigismondo Gonzaga] al qual non scrivemo piú di antiquità, perché sapemo che l'ha buona memoria et che l'è stato avisato da noi che la grotta nostra è finita, ma vui cum dextreza et importunità anchora fareti l'officio di buon procuratore.

VI *Cesare Bechadello Soldano to Isabella d'Este, Rome, 15 December 1508*. Busta 858.

Me venerebe. Quando Monsignore mio Reverendissimo venne a Mantoa per la volta de Roma, non poteti venere con quella per haverme mandato Sua Signoria in alchuni soi servitii. Desiderava molto de basare la mano a Vostra Excellentia: ricordo a quella che li sono vero servitore. A questi dí passati Monsignore mio Reverendissimo tene via et modo de havere una capra de marmora antiqua et hèbela et è tanto naturale quanto dire se possa al mondo. E'longa uno palmo et mezo et ha sotta alli piedi uno pezo de marmoro in tavola dove apogia tutto quattro li piedi et abasso li è uno certo vaso dove beve dicta capra: è una de le bella antiquaglie habia visto uno tempo fa. Essendo a rasonamento con Monsignore mio Reverendissimo disse: 'Se la Signora mia comare Marchesana de Mantoa havesse questa capra seria molto al proposito suo perché è cosa unica.' Li resposi quello me parve. Vostra Signoria non me faci auctore de cosa alchuna, scriva una litera a Sua Signoria Reverendissima con farli intendere che se ricorda de Vostra Excellentia, se li capita qualche cosa antiqua alle mane de marmore, et, quando quella scriva, facia che le litere li siano date in man propria et colui che le haverà a dare me avisi me du uno quarto d'hora inanti, perché farò bona opera.

VII *Cardinal Federico Sanseverino to Isabella d'Este, Viterbo, 4 August 1508.* Busta 858.

Per el presente nostro camarero mandiamo a la Signoria Vostra, per ornamento del suo camarino, una testa antiqua et un putino et una Capra. Et perché se propinqua el tempo de adoperare li livereri, li recordiamo a la Signoria Vostra che al presente nostro messo gli dei che sieno belli e boni, secondo quella ne ha promesso.

VIII *Giovanni Andrea de Caxal to Isabella d'Este, Viterbo, 6 August 1508.* Busta 858.

In lo presente mazo sono nove medaglie cioè cinque de arzento et quatro de metalla, qual credo ce ne sarà fra nove dui bone. In verità ano non s'è trovato niente di bono: se 'l si trovarà quest' altro ano, la Excellentia Sua pò essere certa non mancharò del officio di bon servitor. De le cose di marmor non ne parlo ma questo altro ano voglio poi parlarne. . . . Post Scripta: Mando alla Excellentia Sua dui altre medaglie in li scatolini che credo li piacerano et li ricordo la promessa ad observala como Sua Signoria è solita.

IX *Isabella d'Este to Giovanni Gonzaga, Mantua, 31 March 1515.* Busta 2996, Copialettere Libro 31, c. 82.

Ni è dogliuto molto de la morte del Signor Galeatio da Pesaro perché lo amavamo cordialmente, nondimeno bisogna che habbiamo pacientia considerando essere cosa commune et non se gli può remediare. Appresso sapemo che la bona memoria del Signor Gioanne da Pesaro, suo fratello, si delectava tenere antiquità et che ne havea parechie de belle quale devenero in mano dil Signor Galeacio, noviter defuncto, et, fra le altre cose belle, intendessimo che l'havea alcune teste di bronzo. Et perché ci persuademo che li heredi del prefacto Signor Galeatio non teneranno le dicte antiquità, ma piú presto non cavarano denari, ci è parso, per questa nostra, pregare Vostra Signoria, anchor che di ciò habbiamo scritto al Conte Lorenzo Strozo, che, volendo li heredi vendere ditte antiquità, sii contenta operare che non le diino ad alcuna persona peroché, essendoli cosa per nui, gli daremo li soi dinari sí come qualunque altra persona. Obtenendo questo Vostra Signoria la serà contenta darcene aviso, perché mandaremo uno nostro homo là per vedere se gli sarà cosa al proposito nostro et Vostra Signoria ni farà grandissimo piacere.

Sapemo che Vostra Signoria, considerando che nui novamente siamo venute da Roma dove è copia de antiquità, judicarà che ne siamo ritornate carriche in qua, ma essendo noi persona che quando vedemo alcuno havere qualche bella cosa et che gli sii cara mai ardiressimo non solum dimandargela ma pur fargline uno minimo cigno, siamo, per troppo nostro rispetto, venute in tutto prive da Roma. Potria dire Vostra Signoria che siamo redutte in mal loco a volere il suo favore in questo caso, per dilectarsine anchor Lei, ma, conoscendola non manco discreta di noi, ce persuademo che la farà piú per noi in questo caso che per se medema e cossí la pregamo offerendoni et raccomandandoni a Lei.

X *Giovanni Gonzaga to Isabella d'Este, Milan, 4 April 1515.* Busta 1641.

A quanto Vostra Excellentia mi scrive per questo ultimo cavallaro ch'io deba fare opera, essendo morto el Signor Galeacio da Pesaro, per quelle sue cose aciò che quella le possa havere, gli rispondo che ancora esso Signor Galeacio vive et benché el stia male, nondimeno la speranza de la liberatione sua non è al tutto perduta. Ben è vero che, mancando, farò l'opera che ricerca la mia servitù verso Lei et spero di farla rimanere satisfatta, perhoché queste cose, per testamento, doppoi la morte sua restano al prelibato Signor Duca, dal quale ne haveremo quella conditione che voremo noi. Bene mie duole che io gli havessi fatto sopra dissegno, pur, et in questo et in ogni altra cosa, son sempre per cedere voluntieri a la Excellentia Vostra et fargli conoscere el servitore che gli sono.

XI *Giovanni Gonzaga to Isabella d'Este, Milan, 5 April 1515.* Busta 1641.

Heri sera, trovandose meco a cena la Excellentia del Signor Duca ne la camera mia, entrò el cavallaro di Vostra Excellentia, quale è venuto per le cose del Signor Galeacio da Pesaro, et cosí Sua Signoria Illustrissima mi dimandò che era, a che risposi essere cavallaro di essa Vostra Excellentia et gli narai la causa per la quale Lei lo haveva mandato, cioè per havere quelle cose del prefacto Signore Galeacio mentre fosse mancato. Le qual parole udite da Sua Excellentia, cosí disse che ancora non era in tutto perduta la speraranza [sic] de la salute del prefacto Signore, ma che, se mancava, ne facea uno dono a Vostra Excellentia per essergli lassate ditte cose nel testamento; dil che per la observantia et servitù ch'io gli ho, mi è parso dargli adviso, sicomo quello fidele et optimo servitore che gli sono, subiungendogli che Sua Excellentia mi ha ditto volere essere lui il portatore de queste cose mentre che 'l manchi.

XII *Giovanni Gonzaga to Isabella d'Este, Milan, 8 April 1515.* Busta 1641.

Li giorni passati scripsi a la Excellentia Vostra de le parole che disse el Signor Duca, ne l'intrare in la mia camera del cavallaro di quella. Di novo gli replico, per questa mia che Sua Signoria mi disse che, mancando el Signor Galeacio, li donava quelle cose, che esso Signore Galeacio gli ha lassate per testamento et che Vostra Excellentia desidera d'havere, et che voleva essere el messo che gli le presentasse. Alhora mi parea che gli fosse qualche speranza de la vita sua et comminciasse a megliorare, ma, dopoi che 'l Signor Duca disse quelle parole, è sempre pegiorato di modo ch'io credo che la Excellentia Vostra haverà lo intento suo.

XIII *Isabella d'Este to Giovanni Gonzaga, Mantua, 8 April 1515.* Busta 2996, Copialettere, Libro 31, c. 84v.

Ni è piaciuto summamente intender che 'l Signor Galeazo da Pesaro non sii in quello termine che fu scritto e ditto perché il Conte Laurentio scrisse esser disperato di la salute sua, poi sopragionse fama de la morte la quale fu causa di farni scrivere alla Signoria Vostra quello che li scrivessimo. Ma, senza comparatione, maggior piacere haveremo che la Sua Signoria possi tener et godere longamente quelle antiquità cha, morendo, haverle noi, amandolo summamente et non mancho se ne fusse fratello; cosí pregamo Nostro Signor Dio gli doni sanitade et longa vita et pregamo anche Vostra Signoria a non lassare intendere al ditto Signor Galeazo quanto havemo scritto a Vostra Signoria et al Conte Lorenzo circa ciò, advertendoni esso Conte. Ringratiamo ben non mediocramente Vostra Signoria dil bono animo havea di servirni, offerendoni alli piaceri suoi sempre disposte.

XIV *Isabella d'Este to Giovanni Gonzaga, Mantua, 11 April 1515.* Busta 2996, Copialettere, Libro, 31, cc. 85v–86.

A noi è di molto magiore dispiacere lo aviso del pegioramento del Signor Galeazo da Pesaro, perché lo amavamo et amamo non mediocramente essendo anchor vivo, che non è il piacere de la speranza di havere quelle sue antiquità quale seressimo contente che potesse godere longamente. Ma non volemo già negare che non siamo per haverle care dal Illustrissimo Signor Duca, quando pur piacia a Nostro Signor Dio di chiamare a sè il Signor Galeazo, et tanto piú ni saranno senza altra comperatione accepte, essendone donate per mano de la Excellentia del prefacto Signor Duca de la cui presentia pigliaremo molto magiore piacer et contento che non faremo de la antiquità, però che di questa per la memoria de chi eranno, poteressimo sentirni tristitia, ma de la presentia del Signor Duca altro che letitia, satisfactionne et plena contenteza poteremo havere. Però pregamo Vostra Signoria vogli referirgli infinite gratie de l'una e l'altra offerta. . . . Post Scripta. Perché siamo in gran desiderio di havere queste antiquità, quando pur manchi il Signor Galeazo, constituimo Vostra Signoria nostro procuratore a pigliare cura di farle conservare accioché non fussero trafugate et ocultate, poiché lo Illustrissimo Signor Duca ce ha fatto cossí liberamente donatione; et appresso vi raccordamo che, quando la venuta del Signor Duca andassé a la longa, como soleno le cose de là, che la vogli operare che ni siano mandate perché, a dirli il vero, staremo col batticore finché non le havemo in casa.

xv *Giovanni Gonzaga to Isabella d'Este, Milan, 16 April 1515.* Busta 1641.

Per una di Vostra Excellentia de. XI. del presente, ho veduto quanto la mi scrive circa el caso del Signor Galeacio da Pesaro et de le antiquità sue; a che non occorre fare altra risposta se non che la serà advisata che sabato da matina circa le hore. XIIII., el prefacto Signor Galeacio rese el spirito al summo Creatore di tutte le cose et cosí esso Dio glorioso gli doni pace. De le antiquità serò bono procuratore suo apresso la Excellentia del Signor Duca, como la mi scrive, quale al presente se ritròva a Pavia, ma ben gli dico como la prelibata Vostra Excellentia haverà queste cose sopra conscientia perché posso veramente dire me ne habia privato. Et aciò la sapia queste antiquità essere di momento non mediocre, gli adviso essermi stato fatto intendere che le sonno di valuta de mille scuti, siché la può essere certa che siano belle cose, le quali perhò, quanto piú belle le seranno, per la servitù et observantia che a Lei ho, ne pigliarò tanto piú piacere che quella le habia et non mancarò de l'opera finché non la conduca a perfecto fine.

xvi *Isabella d'Este to Giovanni Gonzaga, Mantua, 21 April 1515.* Busta 2996, Copialettere, Libro 31, c. 89.

De la morte del Signor Galeatio ni dole sumamente, pur, non potendogegli remediare, bisogna havere bona pacientia et pregare Nostro Signor Dio che gli doni pace. Le antiquità di Sua Signoria pigliaremo volentieri sopra la consientia nostra, confessando ingenuamente haverne privato Vostra Signoria, la quale sapemo però che non restarà per questo di fare quella diligentia in questo caso che la faría se fussero sue proprie, et como speramo in Lei.

xvii *Isabella d'Este to Giovanni Maria Capilupi, Mantua, 11 May 1515.* Busta 2996, Copialettere, Libro 31, cc. 96r–v.

Il Conte Lorenzo Stroza fu qui heri per andar a Ferrara et ne dise che, ultra le antiquità quale havea lassate il Signor Galeazo da Pesaro a lo Illustrissimo Signor Duca de Milano erano de le altre in sua mano, quale se haveano a vendere per pagare alcuni servitori et legati del Signor Galeaz et per questo seria bene che tu expectasse il suo ritorno; però volemo che tu, in questo megio, tu procuri de haver quelle del Signor Duca con la instructione del Signor Zoanne (Gonzaga) et hauute quelle nanti il ritorno del Conte, volemo che ce le mandi per un veturale, accompagnate da questo o altro cavallaro, et poi tu, sotto scusa de havere da fare qualche altra cosa lí a Milano, expeti il Conte et faci poi quanto per lui te mandaremo a dire circa quelle antiquità che non sono del Duca, ma de quelle de Sua Excellentia procurarai et prima che 'l Conte ritorni et doppo, di haverle con quel modo che te haverà ordinato il Signor Zoanne.

xviii *Giovanni Maria Capilupi to Isabella d'Este, Milan, 13 May 1515.* Busta 1641.

Gionto qui giovedí, exposi al Signor Ducha quanto da Vostra Excellentia me fu comesso, dal qual hebbi assai grata audientia cum promissione de satisfare al desiderio de Vostra Signoria et promessa di Sua Excellentia. El dí sequente, vedendomi in Corte, da sè me disse che me expediría et che mandaría uno suo homo cum mecho: io restai quieto del volere di Sua Signoria. Heri sera me fece dire che tornasse a lui su la prima hora . . . et . . . me disse che dovesse dire a quella che volontiera gli faceva de tale cose dono, quale hora non gli mandava per me, per non essere tutte qui ne la terra, ma parte qui et parte a Cremona, ma che dovesse far certa Vostra Signoria che, fra sei giorni, ge li mandaria fino a Mantova per Messer Paulo Somenza.

xix *Isabella d'Este to Giovanni Maria Capilupi, Mantua, 16 May 1515.* Busta 2996, Copialettere, Libro 32, c. 1.

Restamo benissimo satisfatto de quanto ce hai scritto per la tua de XIII de questo et laudamo la diligentia tua. Poi che 'l Conte Lorenzo è gionto, potrai ritornare. Raccomandani al Signor Gianni, pregando Sua Signoria in nome nostro ad volere mò sollicitare che la Excellentia del Duca ce mandi quella antiquità, poi che la vole che Messer Paulo venghi ad presentarcele, et lo ringratiarai de l'opera facta fin qui.

xx *Isabella d'Este to Lorenzo Strozzi, Mantua, 29 May 1515.* Busta 2996, Copialettere, Libro 32, c. 5.

Non havemo resposto piú presto alla littera di la Magnificentia Vostra de. XVIII. de questo peroché la volevamo fare per il Signor Joanne, ma essendo partita tanto in fretta Sua Signoria, non havemo havuto tempo di fare scrivere. Ci è parso hora significarvi come havemo havuta essa vostra, insieme con le due capse con le antiquità ce haveti mandate, quale ni sono state molto care et grate. Ringratiamovi summamente de l'opera vostra et confessamo ingenuamente havere da voi la magior parte de epse, quale però haveti potuto tore sopra la conscientia vostra per esser capitate in bone mani. Nui vi absolvemo liberamente et, bisognando, vi faremo anche absolvere da altri, non potendosi chiamare questa vostra se non bona et sancta opera.

xxi *Ludovico Strozzi to Isabella d'Este, Milan, 10 August 1515.* Busta 1641.

Alla parte de le antigaie, forsi Vostra Excellentia se maraviglia che non le habia risposto. Io operai che'l Signor Galiazo le lasasi al Duca de Milan et fra le altre cose le è una testa de Adriano, che 'l Vescovo di Mantua ne volsi dare quatrocento duchati d'oro al Signor Joane et lui non la volse dar, et molte altre belle cose. Basta che navendone io parlato con el Duca, essendo lui nepote et figliolo di Vostra Signoria, non solo le farà parte de dite antigaie ma le darà el proprio core.

xxii *Alfonso Facino to Isabella d'Este, Rome, 29 January 1522.* Busta 866, c. 772.

Al presente si è ritrovato in un monastero. 4. pezi di antiquità dove gli è una Cibelle simile a quella che aveva Papa Lione ch'è tenuta cosa bellissima et una gamba gli è anchor ch'è cosa mirabil et credo che già ne adimandano quatrocento duchati. Se 'l Signore mio si ritrovasse meglio il modo non le lassaria per portarle a Vostra Signoria.

xxiii *Alfonso Facino to Isabella d'Este, Rome, 8 February 1552.* Busta 1902.

Diman sattisfaremo cum Sua Signoria Reverendissima [Ercole Gonzaga] dopoi che haveremo disnato in casa di Miser Angelo Maximo, qual ogi l'à invitato et li vuol mostrare certe belle cose che tiene in casa antique et li vuol far sentir musicha. Quella mi perdoni s'io son longo, perché mi pensso farli cosa gratta però piglio secureza di Lei, anchor che poco inporta quel ch'io scrivo. Non tacerò anchor che eri vedessimo un Socrate col suo Alcibiade apresso, cosa bellissima naturallissimo, come il discrive questi auctori, e molte altre antiquitate bellissime e un tripode d'Apollo el piede e le misure de antiqui e un Esculapio e molte cose notabille, e quella Cibelle ch'io scrissi a quella avria facto mercatto per averla per Vostra Signoria, ché so li piaceria, ma li manca il piú bello: la testa e le mani, che vano di bronzo, e però son restato. Il Signor mio gli duol assai non poter portar qualche bella cosa a Vostra Signoria come voria lui: quella aceptarà la bona voluntade, un' altra volta sattisfarà a l' intento suo.

XXIV *Isabella d'Este to Giovanni Battista Malatesta, Mantua, 4 May 1552.* Busta 2998, Copialettere, Libro 38, cc. 92v–93.

Havemo havuto il vaso di terra antico che ne hai mandato che n'e piaciuto sumamente et tenemolo per caro per respetto tuo et per essere bello.

XXV *Angelo Germanello to Federico Gonzaga, Rome, 22 July 1523.* Busta 867, c. 343.

Per altre mie scripsi el dono ha facto el Papa ad la Vostra Excellentia de la tabella marmorea de pese circa cinquecento libre: existimo la poterà portare uno mulo. E' antiquissima, dove è una parte de la fabula de Proserpina. Li sono sculpite queste figure: prima uno Plutone el quale è in sede in sua maiestate, et poi lì, subto de lui, uno Cerbero, con le tre teste, in forma de cane; li è anchora uno Mercurio con el caduceo, dereto al quale et sopra li va una quercu con uno serpente in giru, tra Mercurio et Plutone li è Proserpina che ha lo capu asconso in forma de la verecundia; dereto al Plutone li è una de le Furie infernale in forma de una donna la quale porrige et monstra uno poculo o taza. La interpretatione de dicte figure sta in quel verso de Vergilio in lo primo libro de la Ge[orgica] dum dicit: 'Nec repetita sequi curet Proserpina matrem'—213, havendo Cerere persa Pr[oserpina] diu la cercò et fo retrovata esser in lo inferno appresso de Plutone et con questa co[mmissione?]. li mando Mercurio ad redomandarla ad Plutone et fo declarato fosse restituita ad Sua Mat [re] [se] non havesse gustato alcuna cosa apud inferos, altramente non. Fo retrovato che haveva gustato alcuni grani de po[mo]granato, cioè che haveva persa la virginità et però sta in la tabella la imagine de Proser?[ina] in forma de la verecundia con el capo asconso in li sui panni medesimi et la Furia demons[tra] in lo poculo quello haveva Proserpina apud inferos gustato, facendo testimonio che, per la sentia de Jove, non doveva esser restituita ad Cerere sua matre. Et perché Mercurio è el datore de la vita, li è la quercu de retro et de sopra, attento che, prima Ceres trovasse seminar li frumenti, la quercu dava el victu ad li homini de la medulla de li quali nasce el serpente. Questa è la fabula la quale è sculta in la tavola de marmore predicta, salvo sempre el judicio de li piú periti et quisto è el judicio de Miser Fabio da Ravenna el qual me ha dicto haver inteso da lo Archiepiscopo de Cosensa esser uno romano che habita in Tristevere, el quale la decte ad Papa Leone che li domandava sopra dicta tavola cinquecento ducati allegendo haverli promissi Papa Leone de darlinne tanto. Veramente la tavola è bella e antiquissima. Vostra Excellentia se dignarà ordinare como se habia da mandare et per qual via, et la supplicaria volesse recognoscer in qualche cosa doi camerieri del Papa, li quali me la consegnarono de li quali una se domanda Miser Francesco et lo altro è el barbieri de la Sua Santità.

XXVI *Isabella d'Este to Alessandro Gablonetta, Mantua, 25 July 1523.* Busta 2998, Copialettere, Libro 42, c. 94.

La bella statua [*sic*] che la Santità di Nostro Signore ha donato allo Illustrissimo

Signore Marchese, nostro figliolo, Sua Signoria l'ha donata a noi et sicome la ni è gratissima per essere cosa, secundo ni è detto, molto antiqua et excellente, cossí desideramo di haverla presso noi. Però sapendo noi quanto Vostra Signoria sii solita essere diligente in tucte le cose nostre, la pregamo voglii pigliar cura di farla condure per via di mare a Pesaro, cum ordine che da lí na sii conducta poi a Mantua et, quanto piú presto, piú l'haverimo grato da Vostra Signoria.

xxvII *Alessandro Gablonetta to the 'Thesaurario di Madama Illustrissima', Rome, 29 October 1523.* Busta 867, c. 176.

Mando per dui gargioni del Furia la tavola marmorea, la qual donò Papa Adriano, et perché è stato necessario farla condure con dui muli, s'è fatto il mercato in .XIIII. ducati d'oro in oro larghi. Io gli ne ho datto delli mei sette de camera, li quali pregovi vogliate mandare subito a mia matre, per certo mio bisogno. Li altri sette et soldi trentacinque daretí alli prefati gargioni et presentare la detta tavola a Madama Illustrissima. De piú ho speso sei iulii in far fare la cassa della tavola, li quali similmente sareti contento mandare alla prefata mia matre.

xxvIII *Isabella d'Este to Alfonso Trotto, Mantua, 3 April 1524.* Busta 2999, Copialettere, Libro 44, c. 71v.

Da Roma ni è mandata una tabula marmorea in cassa et, secundo l'aviso che ni fo dato del dí che la fo inviata, ni maravigliamo che la non sii qua quatro giorni fanno, et perché el desiderio che havimo di haverla è grande, pregamo la Magnificentia Vostra voglii far vedere se per aventura la fossi sta' presentata in Gabella Ducale [in Ferrara] et, in caso che la vi fossi, gli piaccia fare opera che la ni sia mandata, che lo haverimo per troppo gran piacere da la Magnificentia Vostra.

xxIX *Alfonso Trotto to Isabella d'Este, Ferrara, 7 April 1524.* Busta 1248.

Ho visto quanto mi scrive la Excellentia Vostra de la tabula marmorea che cum tanto desiderio expecta e si maraveglia che non sia hormai giunta a prefacta Sua Excellentia havuto rispecto al dí che la fu inviata da Roma. Ho facto vedere qui in Gabella se la ge fusse, como mi commette Vostra Excellentia, et cosí de puncto ho trovato che de poco inante la vi era sta' portata, la quale per fare cosa che piacia a Vostra Signoria, per el presente nochiero, chiamato Marcoantonio Bagelo, ge la mando.

xxx *Isabella d'Este to Cardinal Palmieri, Mantua, 30 April 1529.* Busta 3000, Copialettere, Libro 49, c. 17v.

Tra le altre mie cose chare, ch'io persi alla partita mia da Roma, restai in perdita de li vasi di terra che Vostra Signoria Reverendissima me havea donati; et perché il desiderio mio saria de non restarni in tutto priva, la prego che, se ha il modo de potermi compiacere, mi ne voglia fare havere uno paro e farli consignare al Magnifico Messer Francesco Gonzago, oratore nostro lí, ché egli pigliarà la cura de mandarmeli per via sicura.

xxxI *Cardinal Palmieri to Isabella d'Este, Rome, 11 June 1529.* Busta 878.

Avemo a cquisti [sic] dí recevuta huna litere de Vostra Signoria Illustrissima in risposta di una nostra quale n'è stata al solito delettevole et circa el desiderio che Vostra Excellentia tiene de havere due delli vasi antiqui che ebbe da noi quando la fo in Roma per quilli haverelli persi et nui le scrissimo che meno noi 'ncenne trovavamo ma che averiamo mandato in el Rengno in lo locho dove se retrovano con istancia de quilli se potessero havere, ne fossero qui mandati et cossí è stato esequito et ogi me nne sonno venuti alcuni et benché per la distancia del camino et male strade siano venuti la mojor parte rocti, puro ò avuto sorte che 'ncenn' è stato un paro sani et belli quali mandamo a Vostra Excellentia per mano dello oratore del Signor Marchese, secondo Vostra Signoria ni comandò, dolendo non siano stati piú belli che tantto piú volintieri celli averiamo donati. Avemo bene rescrito se abbiano delli altri, avendo cosa degna per Vostra Excellentia selli mandarranno; resta solo che quella me tenga per suo et se degna comandarni che serrà piú servita che llei comandarà et de questo ne supplicamo Sua Signoria quantto possemo.

xxxii *Paolo Andreasi to Isabella d'Este, Mantua, 10 September 1530.* Busta 2514.

Per Simon di Monsignore Abate da Gonzaga, è stato portato di Roma a Vostra Excellentia medaglie numero dece de metallo et due figure di metallo, quale manda Messer Francesco Andreaso, de quelle che lui à aute da Zoan Napolitano, secundo ch'io li scrissi di commissione de Vostra Signoria Excellentissima, quali sono apreso di me.

xxxiii *Ercole Gonzaga to Isabella d'Este, Rome, 24 January 1531.* Busta 880.

Et se non mi trovavò hora occasione di mandar a Vostra Excellentia alcune medaglie che aposta ho cercate raccogliere insieme di qua et di là per Lei, sapendo quanto se ne intenda et diletti, dubito che di più qualche dí anchora sarebbono scorsi senza che a tanto debito havessi satisfatto. Quella, adunque, non guardando ad alcuna mia negligentia, si degnerà accettarle volentieri sicome molto mi sono laudate per bellissime.

xxxiv *Cardinal Ercole Gonzaga to Isabella d'Este, Rome, 19 February 1531.* Busta 880.

Li giorni passati mandai a Vostra Excellentia parecchie medaglie in una cassetta, le quali credo pure le saranno state fidelmente portate perché le feci consignare qua a Messer Galasso Ariosto, di che n'aspetto l'aviso dallei; ma perhò, fra tanto, essendomi capitate alle mani queste due che sono bellissime, non ho voluto restare di mandargliele medesimamente, persuadendomi le debbano essere grate.

xxxv *Isabella d'Este to Cardinal Ercole Gonzaga, Manuta, 28 February 1531.* Busta 3000, Copialettere, Libro 50, c. 53r.

Oltre le medaglie che mi mandò, molti giorni fanno, Vostra Signoria Reverendissima per la via di Messer Galasso Ariosto, ne ho novamente havute du altre et tutte mi sono summamente piaciute.

xxxvi *Isabella d'Este to Cardinal Ercole Gonzaga, Mantua, 15 August 1536.* Busta 2935 Copialettere, Libro 311, c. 156.

Non potrei dire a Vostra Signoria Reverendissima quant'io habbia havuta chara la medaglia ch'ella m'ha mandata imperoché oltre ch'io ho con mia satisfattione vista et considerata l'effigie d'Aristotile che prima non havevò veduta et pure era conveniente che fosse posto tra gli altri huomini eccellenti degni di memoria, m'è piacciuto di conoscere et per essa medaglia et per la littera di mano di Vostra Signoria Reverendissima ch'ella servi di me quella memoria che per ogni rispetto si conviene . . . promettendole di ripporre essa medaglia appresso l'altre piú chare nel loco ove ho riposto l'altre mie piú pregiate cose.

NOTES

All documents cited in this article, unless otherwise stated, come from the Archivio Gonzaga in the State archives, Mantua. In general archival and bibliographical references are as complete as possible; nonetheless it seems unnecessary to list more than one reference for documents which have already seen print, while no mention is made of duplicate archival material, such as second reminders. The notes would have become unwieldy if comments on misdatings, incorrect transcriptions and false interpretations in the published accounts had also been included. I am indebted to my collaborator in Mantua, Anna Maria Lorenzoni, for having checked the accuracy of the transcriptions of the documents which are published here. The original orthography of the documents has been rigorously respected. Modern punctuation and accent marks have been added, and all abbreviations have been expanded.

[1] (1) Isabella d'Este to Jacopo d'Atri, 29 March 1499, Busta 2993, Copialettere, Libro 10, cc. 9v–10; see A. Luzio, 'Isabella d'Este e i Borgia', *Archivio Storico Lombardo*, fourth series, XLI, 1914, p. 508. (2) Isabella d'Este to Cardinal Ippolito d'Este, 30 June 1502, Busta 2192; see A. Venturi, 'Il "Cupido" di Michelangelo', *Archivio Storico dell'Arte*, I, 1888, p. 4. (3) Isabella d'Este to Niccolò Frisio, 2 January 1507, Busta 2994, Copialettere, Libro 20, c. 8v. (4) Isabella d'Este to Cristoforo Chigi, 12 August 1508, Busta 2915, Copialettere, Libro 201, c. 20.

[2] G. Gerola, 'Transmigrazioni e vicende dei Camerini di Isabella d'Este', *Atti e Memorie dell'Accademia virgiliana*, new series, XXI, 1929, pp. 253–90.

[3] E. Verheyen, *The Paintings in the 'Studiolo' of Isabella d'Este*, New York, 1971.

[4] Specific citations will be given as they apply.

[5] J. Lauts, *Isabella d'Este, Fürstin der Renaissance*, Hamburg, 1952, pp. 188–208 (French edition, Paris, 1956). Andrew Martindale, 'The patronage of Isabella d'Este at Mantua', *Apollo*, LXXIX, 1964, pp. 183–91; R. Weiss, *The Renaissance Discovery of Classical Antiquity*, Oxford, 1969, pp. 197–9.

[6] Archivio Notarile, Estensione, K 10: Atti Notaio Odoardo Stivini. In addition to a version on parchment and the 'minute', both now in the Raccolta d'Autografi, three other copies are found in Busta 400; see A. Luzio, 'Isabella d'Este e il sacco di Roma,' *Archivio Storico Lombardo*, fourth series, XXXV, 1908, pp. 413–25. Stivini drew up a total of some forty-three separate inventories between October 1540 and December 1542. The order for this comprehensive survey of the holdings of the court was given, therefore, immediately after and as a direct consequence of Duke Federico's sudden and untimely death on 28 June 1540. Most of the inventories are limited to cataloguing *robbe*, i.e. household effects. The most notable exceptions are the lists of Isabella d'Este and Federico Gonzaga's books and the contents of their respective studies. It is unfortunate that the inventory of Federico's 'camerino nominato el Studio dalle Antiquità' has never been given the attention it deserves. A portion of it was, however, published by H. Hermann, 'Pier Jacopo Alari-Bonaccolsi gennant Antico', *Jahrbuch der Kunsthistorischen Sammlungen der Allerhöchsten Kaiserhauses*, XXVIII, 1910, pp. 414–18.

[7] The relief of the Two Satyrs (plate 18.4) is known to have been displayed in the Scalcheria, the large room adjacent to the Studiolo, see A. Levi, *Sculture greche e romane del Palazzo Ducale di Mantova*, Rome, 1931, pp. 52–3. According to R. Toscano *L'Edificatione di Mantova*, Padua, 1586, as cited in A. Luzio, *La Galleria dei Gonzaga venduta all'Inghilterra nel 1627–28*, Milan, 1913, pp. 35–6, the *giardino secreto* near the Grotta was decorated with antique statues. Andrea Arrivabeni speaks of the 'molti et eccellente anticaglia' he saw in the loggia outside the Appartamento della Grotta in 1561, see A. A[rrivabeni], *I Grande Apparati, Le Giostre, L'Imprese e i Trionfi fatti nella Città di Mantova nelle Nozze dell'Illustrissimo et Excellentissimo Signor Duca di Mantova, Marchese di Monferrato et cetera*, Mantua, 1561, unpaginated. It is not known if Toscano and Arrivabene saw what was Isabella's doing. The main decoration of the loggia,

the 'ritratti de tante famose città', certainly were commissioned by Isabella in the 1520s; see Gerola, 'Trasmigrazioni', p. 267.

[8] In at least one instance the relevant documentation can be found only in another archive. Giovanni Sforza of Pesaro's gift of several antique heads made in 1501 is known because Bishop Ludovico Gonzaga sought to have gesso casts made. The correspondence of Ludovico, of the Bozzolo branch of the Gonzaga family, is preserved in the Archivio di Stato, Parma; see U. Rossi, 'I medaglisti del Rinascimento alla corte di Mantova', *Rivista Italiana di Numismatica*, I, 1888, pp. 35–6, n. 3.

[9] A. Bertolotti, *L'Archivio di Stato in Mantova: cenni storici e descrittivi*, Mantua, 1892, pp. 1–61.

[10] Levi, *Sculture*, pp. 52–3 (Two Satyrs), 63–4 (Faustina), 89 (Proserpina); O. J. Neverov, *Antique Cameos in the Hermitage Collection*, Leningrad, 1971, pp. 57–9; G. Richter, *Engraved Gems of the Greeks and the Etruscans*, London, 1968, p. 155, No. 611; G. Bruns and A. Fink, 'Das mantuanische Onyxgefäss', *Kunsthefte des Herzog Anton Ulrich-Museums*, V, 1950, pp. 3–20; J. Schlosser, *Werke der Kleinplastik in der Sculpturensammlungen des allerhöchsten Kaiserhauses*, Vienna, two vols., 1910, I, p. 3. Addenda, p. 497.

[11] Hermann, 'Antico', p. 264.

[12] Anon (M. A. Michiel), *Notizia d'opere di disegno*, ed. G. Frizzoni, Bologna, 1884, p. 68. The classical prototype for the seated Jove was known to Michiel from the statuette in Pietro Bembo's collection; see [Michiel], *Notizia*, p. 53.

[13] Luzio, *Galleria*, pp. 137–67.

[14] Verheyen, *Paintings*, p. 30, n. 54; Luzio, *Galleria*, pp. 300–2.

[15] See n. 10 above, and also A. Berger, 'Inventar der Kunstsammlung des Erzherzogs Leopold Wilhelm von Österreich', *Jahrbuch der kunsthistorischen Sammlungen der Allerhöchsten Kaiserhauses*, I, 1883, CLXIX, No. 128.

[16] F. Zimmerman, 'Franz von Stamparts und Anton von Prenners; "Prodromus zum Theatrum Artis Pictoriae" ', *Jahrbuch der kunsthistorischen Sammlungen der Allerhöchsten Kaiserhauses*, VII, 1888, plate 30. The possibility that these statuettes might have come from Isabella's collection was first suggested by Hermann, 'Antico', p. 216, n. 3. The alabaster Leda (40.6 cm) is catalogued as a sixteenth-century piece by L. Planiscig and E. Kris, *Führer durch die kunsthistorisches Sammlungen in Wien. Katalog der Sammlung für Plastik und Kunstgewerbe*, Vienna, 1935, p. 60, No. 56. The date of these statues remains uncertain, although the Kunsthistorisches Museum now places them in the seventeenth century; I am indebted to Dr Leithe-Jasper for this information.

[17] Berger, 'Inventar', CLXIX, No. 126; Schlosser, *Kleinplastik*, p. 3.

[18] Hermann, 'Antico', pp. 255–7.

[19] As cited in F. Amadei, *Cronaca universale della città di Mantova*, Mantua, three vols., 1954–7, III, pp. 544–8.

[20] Bruns and Fink, 'Onyxgefäss', pp. 13–20.

[21] Neverov, *Cameos*, pp. 57–9.

[22] For the Gonzaga Triumphs see H. Toman, 'Mantuaner Schlachtenbilder aus dem 16. Jahrhundert auf Schloss Opočno in Böhemen', *Kunstchronik*, XXIII, 1888, pp. 237–9, 258–61; E. Marani and C. Perina, *Mantova—le arti*, Mantua, three vols., 1961–1965, II, p. 415, n. 125. Costa's 'Triumph of Federico' is discussed by E. Schaeffer, 'Der "Triumph des Federigo Gonzaga" von Lorenzo Costa', *Monatshefte für Kunstwissenschaft*, I, 1908, pp. 763–4. Addenda, p. 497.

[23] P. Norton, 'The lost Sleeping Cupid by Michelangelo', *Art Bulletin*, XXXIX, 1957, pp. 251–7; A. H. Scott-Elliot, 'The statues from Mantua in the collection of King Charles I', *Burlington Magazine*, CI, 1959, pp. 218–27. For the most recent attempt to identify the Michelangelo statue see A. Parronchi, *Il Cupido Dormente di Michelangelo*, Florence, 1971, pp. 2–41.

[24] N. Dacos and others, *Il tesoro di Lorenzo il Magnifico*, I, *Le Gemme*, Florence, 1973. 'For the fire', see S. B. Baxter, *William III*, London, 1966, pp. 363, 459. Addenda, p. 497.

[25] For a version in Vienna see J. von Schlosser, *Album ausgewählter gegenstände der*

kunstindustriellen Sammlungen des Allerhöchsten Kaiserhauses, Vienna, 1901, p. 13, plate XVIII; J. Leewenberg, *Beedouwkunst in het Rijksmuseum*, Amsterdam, 1973, pp. 376–7, No. 634. Another version is in the Museum of Fine Arts, Houston, Texas.

[26] The figure 449 was given by A. Magnaguti, 'Les piú illustre collezionista del Rinascimento', *Rivista Italiana di Numismatica*, XXVI, 1913, p. 388.

[27] The individual entries in the inventory were not numbered by Stivini, and Luzio did not provide them in his published transcription, 'Sacco', pp. 413–25.

[28] Hermann, 'Antico', pp. 236–8, 244–6, 259–60.

[29] L. Planiscig, 'Severo da Ravenna der "Meister des Drachens" ', *Jahrbuch der kunsthistorischen Sammlungen in Wien*, new series, IX, 1935, pp. 75–86. W. Bode, *Die italienischen Bronzestatuetten der Renaissance*, Berlin, three vols., 1906, I, p. 28, plates XLII–III. For a survey of the literature and the known versions see *The Frick Collection*, New York, four vols., 1968–70, III, by J. Pope Hennessy and T. W. Hodgkinson, pp. 80–7, 126–30.

[30] A survey of the documentary and visual evidence for early sixteenth-century copies of the Hellenistic group is found in A. Venturi, 'Il gruppo del Laocoonte e Raffaello', *Archivio Storico dell'Arte*, II, 1889, pp. 97–112.

[31] [Michiel], *Notizia*, p. 156, speaks of 'el piede marmoreo intiero sopra una baso fu de mano de Simon Bianco', in the Odoni collection in 1532. Several such 'fragments' are discussed by L. Planiscig, *Kunsthistorisches Museum in Wien. Die Bronzeplastiken*, Vienna, 1924, pp. 50–1, L. Goldschmidt; *Königliche Museen zu Berlin. Die italienische Bronzen der Renaissance und des Barock*, Berlin, 1914, p. 52, No. 252.

[32] W. Bode, *Die italienischen Bronzestatuetten der Renaissance*, Berlin, 1922, plate 80; Leevenberg, *Beedouwkunst*, pp. 395–6, No. 680.

[33] A. Michaelis, 'Geschichte des Statuenhofes im Vaticanischen Belvedere', *Jahrbuch des Kaiserlich Deutschen Archäeologischen Instituts*, V, 1890, pp. 5–72.

[34] Marani and Perina, *Mantova*, II, p. 540.

[35] On unicorn horns in general see G. Schönberger, 'Narwall-Einhorn. Studien über einem Seltenen Werkstoff', *Städel-Jahrbuch*, IX, 1935–36, pp. 167–247.

[36] For the *intarsia* panels in Urbino see P. Rotondi, 'Ancora sullo Studiolo di Federico da Montefeltro nel Palazzo Ducale di Urbino', *Restauri nelle Marche: testimonianze, acquisti e recuperi*, Urbino, 1973, pp. 561–613. For the panels from the Palace at Gubbio see C. H. Clough, 'Federico da Montefeltro's private study in his Ducal Palace of Gubbio', *Apollo*, LXXXVI, 1967, pp. 278–87, and the same writer's 'The Ducal Palace of Gubbio's and the decoration of its studiolo'; *Atti e Memorie della Dep. di Storia Patria per l' Umbria*, forthcoming. The *intarsia* panels in Isabella's Grotta are discussed briefly by Marani and Perina, *Mantova*, II, p. 580. For Lorenzo's *scrittorio* see E. Müntz, *Les Collections des Médicis au XVe siècle*, Paris, 1888, pp. 52–96. This text will be partially superseded when both volumes of the *Il tesoro di Lorenzo il Magnifico* have appeared in print; see n. 24 and addenda, p. 497.

[37] On 10 November 1514 the Marchesa advised Maddalena Taiapietra that 'circa la chiave di la Grotta, dicemo che quando ce sono qualche gentilhomini che la voliano vedere debiati pur dare la chiave a Zoan Jacomo castellano, facendovila poi restituire'. Busta 2996, Copialettere, Libro 31, c. 51. For Maddalena's letter, which raised the issue of a specific request from Zoan Jacomo to permit several visitors, including the English ambassador, to see the Grotta, see Busta 2489, letter dated 21 October 1514. The last reference I have thus far come across to a visit to the Grotta is found in Pietro Martire Cornacchia's letter of 29 July 1558: 'Il Signor Federico Illustrissimo fece vedere questa mattina a questi bolognesi il sangue di Christo et la Grotta, poi andato a desinare a Poggioreale, dice dimattina di venire a desinare a Marmiruolo, poi a cenare a DiPorto per fare vedere a questi forastieri tutti questi luoghi nanti che partino.' Busta 2565. Nine years earlier, on 21 May 1549, Francesco Tosabezzo spoke of sending to Mantua, from Sacchetta, 'la chiave della Grotta acciò che Vostra Signoria la possi fare vedere a que' duo scholari vicentini.' Busta 2545. Addenda, p. 497.

[38] G. Trissino, *La Sophonisba, Li Retratti, Epistola, Oratione al Serenissimo Princepe di Vineggia*, Venice, 1549, f. 47v.

[39] The letters which describe such discoveries, which are not otherwise discussed in this article, are as follows. *Laocoon*: Sabbadino degli Arienti to Isabella d'Este, 31 January 1506, Busta 1146, c. 171; see R. Renier, review of G. Sabadino degli Arienti, *Gynevera de la clare donne*, ed. C. Ricci and A. Bacchia della Lega, in *Giornale Storica della Letteratura Italiana*, XI, 1888, p. 205. *Hercules and Telephus*: Gregorio de Negroponte to Isabella d'Este, 19 May 1507; see n. 69. *Obelisk*: Stazio Gadio to Isabella d'Este, 19 October 1511, Raccolta Volto; see n. 75. *Installation of statues in the Belvedere*: Grossino to Isabella d'Este, 12 July 1511, 2 February 1512, Busta 859–60; see A. Luzio, 'Federico Gonzaga ostaggio alla corte di Giulio II', *Archivio della R. Società Romana di Storia Patria*, IX, 1886, pp. 524–5, 535–6, n. 1. *Tiber river god*: Grossino to Isabella d'Este, 24 January 1512, Busta 860; see Luzio, 'Ostaggio', pp. 532–5; Stazio Gadio to Isabella d'Este, 2 February 1512, Busta 860; see A. Bertolotti, 'Artisti in relazione coi Gonzaga Signori di Mantova', *Atti e Memorie delle Deputazioni di storia patria per le Provincie Modenesi e Parmensi*, third series, III, 1885, p. 68. *Cybele*: Alfonso Facino to Isabella d'Este, 29 January, 8 February 1522; see appendix 18.1, docs. XXII–XXIII. *Villa Madama, Jove*: Germanello to Federico Gonzaga, 7 April 1525, Busta 869; see Bertolotti, 'Artisti', p. 69; Francesco Gonzaga to Federico Gonzaga, 17 May 1525, Busta 870; see Luzio, 'Sacco', pp. 14–15. For the use made of several of these texts see J. Ackerman, *The Cortile del Belvedere*, Vatican, 1954, pp. 45, 48. See addenda, p. 497.

[40] See nn. 56, 60.

[41] A selection of the correspondence between Isabella d'Este and Giorgio Brognolo in Venice and Ludovico Agnelli and Floramente Borgnolo in Rome was published by A. Luzio, 'Il Lusso di Isabella d'Este Marchesa di Mantova', *Nuova Antologia*, fourth series, LXIII–LXV, 1896, LXIV, pp. 318–19, 322–3; see also A. Bertolotti, 'Le arti minori alla corte di Mantova nei secoli XV, XVI, XVII', *Archivio Storico Lombardo*, second series, XV, 1888, pp. 281–4. The correspondence relevant to these gems, many of which were set into rings is, too extensive to catalogue here. Two major and one minor commissions should, however, be noted: (1) Ludovico Agnello to Isabella d'Este, 21 May 1493, Busta 849, c. 389; 27 May 1494, Busta 850; the former was published by E. Müntz, *Les Antiquités de la Ville de Rome*, Paris, 1886, p. 56; (2–3) Luzio, 'Lusso', referred to a commission in February of 1491 for a stone inscribed 'Sequirò fin ch'io vivo', but overlooked the request of 18 December 1490 for one which read 'Fin ch'io viva doppo Morte', Busta 2904, Copialettere, Libro 136, cc. 71, 78v. Two groups of letters from 1496 deal with antiques other than semi-precious stones. On 20 December Ludovico Mantegna sent the Marchesa a medallion; see Raccolta d'Autografi, 7, c. 171, while Antonio Maria Pico della Mirandola wrote two letters about the *all'antica* Cupid by Michelangelo, see Busta 1331, cc. 207, 210; these two letters were published by A. Luzio, 'Isabella d'Este e Giulio II', *Rivista d'Italia*, XII, 1909, p. 854, n. 2.

[42] See nn. 52, 54.

[43] Verheyen, *Paintings*, pp. 14–15. His interpretation of the documents is occasionally highly individualistic. Addenda, p. 497.

[44] See appendix 18.1, doc. V.

[45] Niccolò da Correggio to Isabella d'Este, 9 May 1498, Busta 1313; see A. Luzio and R. Renier, 'Niccolò da Correggio', *Giornale Storico della Letteratura Italiana*, XXI–XXII, 1893, p. 253. Isabella d'Este to Francesco II Gonzaga, 9 March 1498, Busta 2112; see A. Luzio and R. Renier, 'Delle relazioni d'Isabella d'Este Gonzaga con Ludovico e Beatrice Sforza', *Archivio Storico Lombardo*, second series, VII, 1890, p. 654.

[46] The documentation for work undertaken in 1506–07 was published by Gerola, 'Trasmigrazioni', pp. 257–8. His interpretation of these and other documents may not prove reliable. Marchesa of Crotone to Isabella d'Este, 23 March 1503; see appendix 18.1, document III; Fra Serafino to Isabella d'Este, 7 February 1505; see n. 63.

Ludovico Canossa to Isabella d'Este, 7 March 1506, Busta 857; Luzio, 'Giulio II', p. 852, n. 2, and also C. H. Clough, 'L. Canossa', in *Dizionario biografico degli italiani,* XVIII, pp. 187–92.

⁴⁷ Isabella d'Este to Gian Cristoforo Romano, 5 August 1506, As in n. 50; Isabella's letter to Romano, 27 September 1505, Busta 2994, Copialettere, Libro 18, cc. 35*v*–36, where the reason given for rejecting a vase by Caradosso was that it was 'troppo grande da studio'; see A. Venturi, 'Gian Cristoforo Romano', *Archivio Storico dell'Arte,* I, 1888, pp. 116–17, n. 2.

⁴⁸ Luzio, *Galleria*, pp. 35–6. It is somewhat disconcerting to note that a distinction was drawn between 'quello beato camerino dal uscino caro [the Studiolo]' and the 'secreta grotta' in Margherita Cantelmo's unpublished letter of 14 June 1505, in Busta 1636.

⁴⁹ P. Hirschfeld, *Mäzene. Die Rolle des Auftraggebers in der Kunst*, Munich, 1968, pp. 122–3. Verheyen (*Paintings*, p. 2, n. 4) appears to err in his discussion of the relationship that existed between the terms *Studiolo* and *Grotta*, where he claims that 'During Isabella's time a strict distinction was made between the terms'. If this had been so it follows that visitors to Mantua were not shown the Studiolo, only the Grotta, since Pietro Soranzo in 1515, and subsequently Vincenzo di Preti in 1525, speak of visiting 'la Grotta' but not the other room; M. Sanudo, *I Diari*, Venice, fifty-eight vols., 1879–1902, XXI, cols. 281–3, provides the Sumario di una letera di Sier Piero Soranzo ... data in Chiara in brexano a dì 6 Novembre 1515; Vincenzo di Preti to Isabella d'Este, 17 February 1525, Busta 2506, c. 264. *Cf.* also in. 37 above for other references.

⁵⁰ Isabella d'Este to Gian Cristoforo Romano, 5 August 1506, Busta 2994, Libro 19, cc. 34–35*r*; Venturi, 'Romano', p. 151. The documents relevant to the agate vase are discussed by C. Brown, 'An art auction in Venice in 1506', *L'Arte*–XX, 1973, pp. 124–8, and those relevant to the Faustina bust by C. M. Brown, 'Comus Dieu des Fêtes, Allégorie de Mantegna et de Costa pour le Studiolo d'Isabella d'Este Gonzague', *La Revue du Louvre et des Musées de France*, XIX, 1969, p. 32, n. 8. Addenda, p. 497.

⁵¹ L. Alberti, *Descrittione di Tutta Italia*, Bologna, 1550, f. 353*v*; Luzio, *Galleria*, pp. 158, 165.

⁵² (1) Tolomeo Spagnolo to Isabella d'Este, 22 February 1497, Busta 852. (2–3) Ludovico Agnelli to Isabella d'Este, 5 February, 28 March 1498, Busta 852. (4–5) Isabella d'Este to Ludovico Agnelli, 11 March 1497, 7 March 1498, Busta 2992, Copialettere, Libro 8, cc. 58*r*–59, Libro 9, cc. 31*v*–32. (6–8) Onorato Agnelli to Isabella d'Este, 25 November 1499, 30 September, 17 November 1500, Busta 853, 854. (9) Isabella d'Este to Onorato Agnelli, 26 September 1500, Busta 2992, Copialettere, Libro 11, c. 94*v*. (10) Onorato Agnelli to Isabella d'Este, 19 September 1501; see appendix 18.1, doc. 1. Documents (1) and (4) were published by Rossi, 'Medaglisti', p. 169, n. 1; doc. III by A. Luzio, *I precettori di Isabella d'Este: appunti e documenti*, Ancona, 1887, p. 31, n. 2; doc. VI by G. L. Pélissier, 'Les relations de François de Gonzague, Marquis de Mantoue, avec Ludovico Sforza et Louis XII—notes additionelles et documents', *Annales de la Faculté des Lettres de Bordeaux*, 1894, pp. 76–7.

⁵³ *Mirandola*: (1) J. L. Cattanei to Isabella d'Este, 9 February 1499, Busta 853. (2–3) Antonio Maria Pico della Mirandola, 26 February, 3 May 1499, Busta 1331, cc. 286, 292. (4) Isabella d'Este to Jacopo d'Atri, 29 March 1499, Busta 2993, Copialettere, Libro 10, cc. 9*v*–10. (5–6) Isabella d'Este to J. L. Cattanei, 29 March, 8 August 1499, Busta 2993, Copialettettere, Libro 10, cc. 9*v*, 38. (7) Isabella d'Este to Antonio Maria Pico della Mirandola, 10 July 1499, Busta 2993, Copialettere, Libro 10, c. 31. Documents (2) and (4) were published by Luzio, 'Borgia', p. 508. The table is described in doc. 1 as 'molto galante, ... et è molto nobile de tante misture et varie diverse de serpentino, porfido et simile che non la saperia baptizare'. *Agnelli*: (1) Isabella d'Este to Jacopo d'Atri, 29 March 1499. Busta 2993, Copialettere, Libro 10, cc. 9*v*–10*r*. (2–5) Isabella d'Este to Onorato Agnelli, 24 December 1499, 26 September 1500, 5 August, 20 September 1501, Busta 2993, Copialettere, Libro 11, cc. 16*v*–17, 94*v*; Copialettere, Libro 12, c. 76*v*, 90. (6–9) Onorato Agnelli to Isabella

d'Este, 12 January, 29, 30 September 1500, 17 October 1501, Busta 854. (10) Cardinal Federico Sanseverino to Isabella d'Este, 28 September 1500, Busta 854. Documents (5) and (10) were cited by Luzio, 'Borgia', p. 677, n. 1, who assigned doc. (10) to the Cardinal of Santa Prassede (A. Pallavicino).

⁵⁴ Isabella d'Este to Benedetto Tosabezzi and Giorgio Brognolo, 13 November 1497, Busta 2992, Copialettere, Libro 9, c. 17v. (2) Isabella d'Este to Giovanni Andrea del Fiore, 14 November 1497, Busta 2992, Copialettere, Libro 9, cc. 17v–18. (3) Benedetto Tosabezzi and Giorgio Brognolo to Isabella d'Este, 22 November 1497, Busta 1437. (4) Giovanni Andrea del Fiore to Isabella d'Este, 29 March 1498, Busta 1438. (5) Isabella d'Este to Giovanni Andrea del Fiore, 4 April 1498, Busta 2992, Copialettere, Libro 9, c. 46. (6) Benedetto Tosabezzi to Isabella d'Este, 13 May 1498, Busta 1438, c. 64. (7) Tolomeo Spagnolo to Isabella d'Este, 13 October 1498, Busta 1438, cc. 351–2. Document (2) was mentioned by Luzio, *Precettori*, p. 31, n. 2, docs. (4) and (7) by Luzio, 'Lusso', pp. 320, 321. A transcription of the latter was published by Bertolotti, 'Arte minori', p. 280, where reference is also found to doc. (4).

⁵⁵ Isabella d'Este to Taddeo de Lardis, 8 March 1498. Busta 2992, Copialettere, Libro 9, c. 33v; Taddeo de Lardis to Isabella d'Este, 8 April 1498, Busta 1235, c. 478; Isabella d'Este to Cardinal Ippolito d'Este, 22 February 1502, Busta 2993, Copialettere, Libro 13, c. 47; see Venturi, 'Cupido', p. 4.

⁵⁶ *Antique vase*: G. L. Catanei to Isabella d'Este, 26 November 1499; see appendix 18.1, doc. II; Isabella d'Este to G. L. Cattanei, 24 December 1499, Busta 2993, Copialettere, Libro 11, c. 16v. *Beatrice d'Este's intaglio*: Isabella d'Este to Gualtiero da Basilicapietre, 29 May 1502, Busta 2993, Copialettere, Libro 13, c. 74; see Luzio, 'Lusso', p. 320; Gualtiero da Basilicapietre to Isabella d'Este, 6 June 1502, Busta 1635. *Medici vases*: the documents are transcribed in C. Brown, 'Little-known and unpublished documents', *L'Arte*, VII–VIII, 1969, pp. 194–206, except for two documents which remain unpublished: Francesco II Gonzaga to Francesco Malatesta, 27 March, 20 April 1502; Busta 2910, Copialettere, Libro 170, c. 96; Busta 2911, Copialettere, Libro 174, c. 20.

⁵⁷ (1–2) Isabella d'Este to Ludovico Bagno/to Ippolito d'Este, 30 June 1502, Busta 2192. (3) Ludovico Bagno to Isabella d'Este, 12 July 1502, Busta 855, c. 16. (4–5) Isabella d'Este to Francesco II Gonzaga, 15, 22 July 1502, Busta 2115, Raccolta Volta, Busta I. (6) G. F. Arsego to Ippolito d'Este, 28 July 1502, Modena, Archivio di Stato, Archivio Estense, Cancelleria Ducale. (7) Francesco II Gonzaga to Isabella d'Este, 29 July 1502, Busta 2115. (8) Ludovico Bagno to Isabella d'Este, 8 August 1502, Busta 855, c. 18. (9–10) Giovanni Lucido Cattanei to Isabella d'Este, 8 December 1503, Busta 855, cc. 425, 22 January 1504, Busta 856. (11) Isabella d'Este to Gian Lucido Cattanei, 29 December 1503, Busta 2994, Copialettere, Libro 16, cc. 88–89. Bibliographical references are found in P. Barocchi's ed. of G. Vasari, *La Vita di Michelangelo*, Milan, five vols., 1962, II, pp. 132–3, which fails to list Nos. (4) and (7); the former was published by A. Luzio and R. Renier, *Mantova e Urbino: Isabella d'Este ed Elisabetta Gonzaga nelle relazioni famigliari e nelle vicende politiche*, Turin, 1893, pp. 138–9, the latter by Luzio, 'Borgia', p. 679.

⁵⁸ The relevant documents number some forty items, of which sixteen are duplicate details. A selection was published by Luzio, 'Giulio II', pp. 856–8, but one of the letters Luzio overlooked is Floramente Brognolo's letter of 26 May 1496, Busta 851. The first published reference is to a letter of 12 August 1498, Busta 2908, Copialettere, Libro 159, cc. 61r–v. In 1496 the negotiations were between the Bonatto family and the Marquis Francesco, with Isabella's involvement dating from several years later. The letter of 2 October 1502 cited in the text was addressed to Francesco Troche, Busta 2993, Copialettere, Libro 14, cc. 26v–27; for Troche see C. H. Clough, 'N. Machiavelli . . . and the F. Troche episode,' *Medievalia et Humanistica*, XVII, 1966, pp. 127-49. The Marquis Francesco's involvement in the first round of negotiations with the Bonatto is contemporaneous with his second unsuccessful attempt to buy back Cardinal Francesco Gonzaga's collection of cameos. The correspondence rele-

vant to 'queste cussi cossi egregie, ornate del nome e de l'arme de la casa de Gonzaga' remain to be published. The archival citations are given at the end of this note. There is nothing to indicate that Francesco was interested in these objects because of their intrinsic worth, or that he desired to form a collection; see also n. 67. The archival citations for the cameos are as follows. Giovanni Arrivabeni to Francesco II Gonzaga, 2 January, 14 February, 5 March, 2 April 1486, Busta 847, cc. 484, 496–7, 507, 526; Francesco II Gonzaga to Giovanni Arrivabeni, 11 December 1485, Busta 2902, Copialettere, Libro 126, cc. 56*v*–57; the same to the same, 21 January 1486, Busta 2902, Libro 126, c. 71*r*–*v*; Francesco II Gonzaga to Zaccharia Saggio, 23 April 1486, Busta 2902, Libro 127, cc. 13*v*–14; Zaccharia Saggio to Francesco II Gonzaga, 28 April 1486, Busta 1629, c. 208; Floramonte Brognolo to Francesco II Gonzaga, 6 December 1497, Busta 852; Francesco II Gonzaga to Giorgio Brognolo, 22 August 1498, Busta 2908, Copialettere, Libro 160, cc. 67*r*–*v*. Francesco II Gonzaga 'al Thesaurerio', 25 November 1498, Busta 2908, Copialettere, Libro 160, c. 130; 'Nofri Tornaboni in Roma al Domino Donato Bonsi de Florentia', 1 December 1498, Busta 852. Addenda, p. 497.

[59] Marchesa of Crotone to Isabella d'Este, 20 November 1502, Busta 808; see A. Luzio and R. Renier, *La cultura e le relazioni letterarie d'Isabella d'Este*, Turin, 1903, p. 418, n. 1. Marchesa of Crotone to Isabella d'Este, 23 March 1503; see appendix 18.1, doc. III.

[60] *Medici Cameo*: Antonio Magistrello to Isabella d'Este, 25 April 1503, Busta 855, c. 497; see Luzio, 'Lusso', p. 321. *Rhodian bronze*: Lorenzo da Pavia to Isabella d'Este, 28 September 1503, Busta 1440, c. 296; see C. Brown, 'Giovanni Bellini and art collecting', *Burlington Magazine*, cxiv, 1972, p. 404. In a letter datable to September 1505 Fra Sabba compares a statue found at Lyndo to 'quello di metallo che è a Venetia in mano de Messer Andrea de Martinis, who owned it in 1503; see Busta 799 as in n. 68. Addenda, p. 497.

[61] Isabella d'Este to Lorenzo da Pavia, 9 September 1503, Busta 2994, Copialettere, Libro 16, cc. 28*r*–*v*; Lorenzo da Pavia to Isabella d'Este, 28 September 1503, Busta 1440, c. 296; see Luzio, 'Lusso', pp. 310–11; Francesco Malatesta to Isabella d'Este, 8 October 1503, Busta 1440, c. 299.

[62] Isabella d'Este to L'Antico, 26 March 1501, Busta 2993, Copialettere, Libro 12, c. 27*v*; Ludovico Gonzaga to Isabella d'Este, 27 January, 9 September 1503, Busta 1801; Isabella d'Este to Ludovico Gonzaga, 29 January 1503, Busta 2993, Copialettere, Libro 14, c. 96*v*; all published by Rossi, 'Medaglsiti', pp. 176–8.

[63] Fra Serafino to Isabella d'Este, 7 February 1505, Busta 1077, c. 76; see A. Luzio and R. Renier, *Mantova e Urbino*, p. 168; Giovanni Gonzaga to Isabella d'Este, 17 March 1505. Busta 1891, c. 45; Isabella d'Este to Giovanni Gonzaga, 28 March 1505, Busta 2994, Copialettere, Libro 17, c. 17; see Venturi, 'Romano', p. 108, n. 5.

[64] Isabella d'Este to Gian Cristoforo Romano, 30 October 1505, Busta 2994, Copialettere, Libro 18, cc. 46*r*–*v*; Gian Cristoforo Romano to Isabella d'Este, 1 December 1505, Busta 856; see Venturi, 'Romano', pp. 117, 148–9. The Ciampolini collection is discussed by R. Lanciani, 'La raccolta antiquaria di G. Ciampolini', *Bullettino della Commissione Archaeologica comunale di Roma*, xxvii, 1899, pp. 101–113.

[65] Isabella d'Este to Alessandro Bonatto, 6 February 1506, Busta 2994, Copialettere, Libro 18, c. 67*v*; Gerolamo Arsago to Isabella d'Este, 19 January 1506, Busta 857; see Luzio, 'Giulio II', p. 859; Isabella d'Este to the Marchesa of Crotone and another, to Gerolamo Arsago, 6 February 1506, Busta 2994, Copialettere, Libro 18, cc. 66*v*–67; L'Antico to Isabella d'Este, n.d. [1506], Busta 1813; Isabella d'Este to L'Antico, 18 May 1506, Busta 2994, Copialettere, Libro 18, c. 96. The two latter were published by Rossi, 'Medaglisti', pp. 186–7.

[66] Niccolò Frisio to Isabella d'Este, 27 November, 23 December 1506, Busta 1146, cc. 188, 189; both printed by C. D'Arco, *Delle arti e degli artefici di Mantova*, Mantua, two vols., 1857, II, p. 73; see also n. 1.

[67] Isabella d'Este to Gerolamo Arsago (with an enclosure for Tolommeo Folegno), 6 October 1506, Busta 2192; see Bertolotti, 'Artisti', pp. 67–8. The attribution of this letter to the Marquis Francesco was used by Weiss, *Renaissance Discovery*, p. 197, as proof of Francesco's interest in collecting, yet it is hard to believe that he could have dictated the phrase 'per le offerte che ne fece Vostra Signoria quando fu qua de essere nostro procuratore ad farni haver de le antiquità'. It was Isabella, and not her husband, who had had prior dealings with Arsago; see n. 65. The problem of attribution arises because the copy of the communication is found in the 'Minute della Cancelleria' rather than in Isabella's or Francesco's 'Libri dei Copialettere'. The Chancery copy is not signed, and no written response was apparently ever made. The internal evidence suggests that the letter might be assigned to Isabella. It is in any event asking too much to build a case for the Marquis on such equivocal evidence. Francesco had referred to her the offer he received to purchase several *pietre dure* vases from the Medici collection in 1502 because 'gli è cosi per Lei'. See n. 56. He had, furthermore, spoken disparagingly of her acquisition of the Montefeltro antiques: 'Et speremo a la ritornata nostra che nui seremo quello da li basi del putino et la Signoria Vostra de li basi de la figura de Cupido.' 29 July 1502, Busta 2115; see Luzio, 'Borgia', p. 679, n. 1; see also n. 58.

[68] With several exceptions the correspondence was published in its entirety by A. Luzio, 'Lettere inedite di Fra Sabba da Castiglione', *Archivio Storico Lombardo*, XIII, 1886, pp. 91–112; Fra Sabba's letters are in Busta 799.

[69] Gregorio de Negroponte to Isabella d'Este, 19 May 1507, Busta 857; see Luzio, 'Fra Sabba', pp. 93–4, n. 3; Ludovico Canossa to Isabella d'Este, 7 June 1505, Busta 856; see Luzio, 'Giulio II', p. 853, n. 1.

[70] Isabella d'Este to L'Antico, 15 November 1507, Busta 2994, Copialettere, Libro 20, c. 75v; see Rossi, 'Medaglisti', p. 188.

[71] See appendix 18.1, docs. IV–VI for the Sigismondo Gonzaga correspondence and VII for the Sanseverino letter.

[72] Cristoforo Chigi to Isabella d'Este, 7 July 1508, Busta 1106, c. 30; Isabella d'Este to Cristoforo, to Agostino Chigi, 12, 19 August 1508, Busta 2915, Copialettere, Libro 201, cc. 20, 23r. The first and the last letters were mentioned by Luzio, *Precettori*, p. 28, n. 1. Ludovico Brognolo to Isabella d'Este, 1 December 1509, Busta 858; see Venturi, 'Romano', p. 117.

[73] Emilia Pia to Isabella d'Este, n.d. [1508], Busta 1077; see Luzio, 'Fra Sabba', p. 94, n. 3.

[74] Giovanni Andrea de Casal to Isabella d'Este, 6 August 1508; see appendix 18.1, doc. VIII; Zuan Francesco Valier to Isabella d'Este, 5 June 1511, Busta 1894; see C. Brown, 'Unpublished negotiations between Isabella d'Este and Niccolò and Giovanni Bellini', *Art Bulletin*, LI, 1969, 374, n. 12.

[75] Stazio Gadio to Isabella d'Este, 19 October 1511, Raccolta Volta; Isabella d'Este to Stazio Gadio, 28 October 1511, Busta 2996, Copialettere, Libro 29, cc. 66r–v. The former was published by D'Arco, *Delle arti*, II, pp. 77–8, the latter by Luzio 'Ostaggio', p. 528, n. 2.

[76] The relevant correspondence was published by Brown, 'Unpublished negotiations', pp. 374–7.

[77] Giovanni Battista Catanei to Isabella d'Este, 20 June 1514, Busta 2489; see Rossi, 'Medaglisti', pp. 188–9, n. 4; Isabella d'Este to Niccolò Capilupi, to November 1514, Busta 2996, Copialettere, Libro 31, cc. 50r–v; see A. Luzio, 'Isabella d'Este nei primordi del papato di Leo X e il suo viaggio a Roma nel 1514–1515', *Archivio Storico Lombardo*, fourth series, XXXIII, 1906, p. 148.

[78] See appendix 18.1, docs. IX–XXI. Among the documents not transcribed is Isabella's letter to L'Antico of 26 May 1515 concerning the restoration of several objects from the Sforza collection, Busta 2996, Copialettere, Libro 32, c. 4; see Rossi, 'Medaglisti', p. 189, n. 3. Rossi suggested that the following letters also refer to additional restorations of Sforza antiques, although there is no proof of this: Isabella

d'Este to L'Antico, 13 November, 11 December 1515, 1 March 1516, Busta 2996, Copialettere, Libro 32, cc. 48v, 61v, 88.

[79] Isabella d'Este to L'Antico, 9 May 1515, Busta 2996, Copialettere, Libro 31, c. 88; see Rossi, 'Medaglisti', p. 189, n. 1.

[80] Niccolò Maffei to Isabella d'Este, 24 May 1517, Busta 2496, c. 265; see A. Bertolotti, *Figuli, fonditori e scultori in relazione con la corte di Mantova*, Milan, 1890, p. 82; Isabella d'Este to Giovanni Battista Malatesta, 4 May 1522; see appendix 18.1, doc. xxiv.

[81] L'Antico to Isabella d'Este, April 1519, Busta 2498; Isabella d'Este to L'Antico, 11 May 1519, Busta 2997, Copialettere, Libro 36, c. 56v; see Rossi, 'Medaglisti', pp. 190–1.

[82] See appendix 18.1, docs. xxii–xxiii.

[83] (1) Angelo Germanello to Federico Gonzaga, 22 July 1523; see appendix 18.1, doc. xxv. (2) Isabella d'Este to Alessandro Gablonetta, 25 July 1523; see appendix 18.1, doc. xxvi. (3) Alessandro Gablonetta to Isabella d'Este, 12 August 1523, Busta 867, c. 146; see D'Arco, *Delle arti*, p. 93. (4) Alessandro Gablonetta to Treasurer, 29 October 1523; see appendix 18.1, doc. xxvii. (5) Ercole Gonzaga to Federico Gonzaga, 20 February 1524, Busta 1150, c. 275; see D'Arco, *Delle arti*, p. 94. (6–7) Isabella d'Este to Alfonso Trotto, 3, 13 April 1524; see appendix 18.1, doc. xxviii for No. 6 and Busta 2999, Copialettere, Libro 44, c. 80v, for (7). (8) Alfonso Trotto to Isabella d'Este, 7 April 1524; see appendix 18.1, doc. xxix; see also D'Arco, *Delle arti*, p. 92, for Andrea Piperario's letter to Baldassare Castiglione, 29 July 1523.

[84] 'Libretto di spese diverse fatte in Roma et in altri luoghi per i Signori Gonzaga, con in fine nota degli argenti della credenza della Illustrissima Signora di Mantova', Busta 410B, fasc. 35; see Luzio, 'Sacco', p. 425.

[85] (1) Carlo Ghisi, 12 March 1529, Busta 878. (2–6) Isabella d'Este to Francesco Gonzaga, 31 May, 27 June, 12 August, 15 September, 29 September 1529, Busta 3000, Copialettere, Libro 49, cc. 24–25v, 33v–35, 44r–v, 51r–v, 54. (7–9) Francesco Gonzaga to Isabella d'Este, 14 June, 24 August, 4 September 1529, Busta 878. Several of these texts were cited by D'Arco, *Delle arti*, pp. 104–5, and a more complete survey of the material is available in Luzio and Renier, *Mantova e Urbino*, pp. 284–5.

[86] (1) Isabella d'Este to Marco Grimani, 12 May 1528, Busta 2999, Copialettere, Libro, 47, c. 71r–v. (2) Isabella d'Este to Felice della Rovere, 22 May 1528, Busta 2999, Copialettere, Libro 47, cc. 77r–v. (3) Isabella d'Este to Giovanni Battista Malatesta, 26 May 1528, Busta 2999, Copialettere, Libro 47, cc. 77v–78. (4) Isabella d'Este to Sinabaldo Fiesco, 19 May 1528, Busta 2999, Copialettere, Libro 47, cc. 73r–v. Except for (1) and (3) all were published by Luzio, 'Sacco', pp. 386–8.

[87] The correspondence with Pico is summarised by C. Brown, 'Documents on Renaissance artists', *Burlington Magazine*, cxv, 1973, p. 253; see appendix 18.1, docs. xxx–xxxi, for the letters to and from Cardinal Palmieri.

[88] Paolo Andreasi to Isabella d'Este, 10 September 1530; see appendix 18.1, doc. xxxii; Ercole Gonzaga's letters 24 January and 19 February 1531; see appendix 18.1, docs. xxxiii–xxxiv; Isabella's response; see appendix 18.1, doc. xxxv.

[89] Ercole Gonzaga to Isabella d'Este, 2 August 1536, Busta 886; see Bertolotti, 'Artisti', pp. 70–1; Isabella's response 15 August 1536; see appendix 18.1, doc. xxxvi.

[90] Isabella d'Este to the Contessa Caiazzo, 15, 24 April 1533, Busta 3000, Copialettere, Libro 51, cc. 99v, 100v. Both were published by Luzio, 'Lusso', p. 321. Giulio Romano to Federico Gonzaga, 16 July 1538, Raccolta d'Autografi, 7, c. 258; see C. D'Arco, *Istoria della vita e delle opere di Giulio Pippi Romano*, Mantua, 1842, pp. xxiii–xxiv, No. 20.

[91] Isabella d'Este to Alessandro Agnelli, 22 August 1538, Busta 3000, Copialettere, Libro 53, c. 11v; see Bertolotti, *Figuli*, p. 79.

[92] Dated 22 December, Busta 332, c. 11r.

Addenda: see p. 497.

WALTER H. KEMP   *Wilfrid Laurier University, Ontario*

19

SOME NOTES ON MUSIC
IN CASTIGLIONE'S
IL LIBRO DEL CORTEGIANO

'. . . anzi estimo per le ragioni che voi dite e per molte altre esser la musica non solamente ornamento, ma necessaria al cortegiano'.[1] The expository material on musical performance and aesthetics which excited Castiglione's affirmation through the mouth of Giuliano de' Medici that to the courtier music was 'not only an ornament but a necessity' has drawn just attention to *Il Libro del Cortegiano* as a source of paramount interest for a correct apprehension of the concept of music and musicianship as understood in the early Cinquecento court situation. As frequently cited by social as by musical historians are the same passages transplanted into Tudor England by Sir Thomas Hoby.[2] Clad either in his Italian or English garb, Castiglione's courtier, with his musicality, has become an indispensable personality in shaping the musicologist's view of the Renaissance.[3] However, certain ill defined renderings of the musical matter in the *Cortegiano* on the part of Castiglione's modern translators merit, especially for the non-specialist reader, the following summary comments upon the relevant portions of this famous guide to 'la forma di cortegiania'.

Castiglione seeks to demonstrate (I, xxxvii) that the stylistic individuality which one readily sees in a da Vinci or Mantegna may also be heard in the work of a musician.[4]

Vedete la musica, le armonie della quale or son gravi e tarde, or velocissime e di novi modi e vie; nientedimeno tutte dilettano, ma per diverse cause, come si comprende nella maniera del cantare di Bidon, la qual è tanto artificiosa, pronta, veemente, concitata e de così varie melodie, che i spirti di chi ode tutti si commoveno e s'infiammano e così sospesi par che si levino insino al cielo. Né men commove nel suo cantar il nostro Marchetto Cara, ma con più molle armonia; ché per una via placida e piena di flebile dolcezza intenerisce e penetra le anime, imprimendo in esse soavemente una dilettevole passione.

Bidon was a relatively esteemed singer who had passed from the Ferrara court to Mantua (1510–11), thereafter gaining rapturous acclaim while in the employ of Leo X.[5] He was credited, in an epitaph, with having no equal on earth 'in gorga et voce'.[6] His is the vocal delivery 'very fast and novel in mood and manner' ('velocissime e di novi modi e vie'),[7] with the effect calculated to excite listeners by bravura, by variety of successive turn and phrase sudden and surprising, and that primarily in chapel polyphony.[8] Contrasted to him is Marco Cara, a singer–instrumentalist–composer of much more lasting importance.[9] He was one of the leading composers in the 'Mantuan style' which had set the tone of the Italian secular lyric around the turn of the century: composers such as Josquin des Pres, Alexander Agricola and Bartolomeo Tromboncino, to name those who figure in Castiglione's life and writing.[10] Cara's is the art of gentle improvised song for solo voice and accompaniment, the 'soft' tuning of the string to accompany the dulcet air echoing the harmony of the universe: the 'touches of sweet harmony' which, enhanced by the 'soft stillness and the night . . . Creep in our ears.'[11] In the last decades of the Quattrocento improvisors at the courts of the Medici had cultivated this manner, and 'Simplex [canendi ratio] autem est ea / Quae languidius modificata cadit'.[12] In his comparison of the singing styles of Bidon and Cara Castiglione is restating the accepted Platonic–Aristotelian classification of the modes ('armonie') by their ethical qualities of relative excitation and mollification;[13] the key words are 'pronta, veemente, concitata e de così varie melodie', opposed to 'più molle armonia'.[14] In this restatement, however, the classic abstractions have become humanised through the force of their embodiment in two musical personalities well known to Castiglione's circle. Castiglione here records his keen sense of the subtleties of vocal expression which coloured the new art of his time. Himself a singer, his use of musical terminology can be trusted.[15]

In a slightly earlier section (I, xxviii),[16] he suggests how a vocalist may avoid affectation, and achieve a reputation for excellence and grace.

Un musico, se nel cantar pronunzia una sola voce terminata con suave accento in un groppetto duplicato, con tal facilità che paia che così gli venga fatto a caso, con quel punto solo fa conoscere che sa molto più di quello che fa.

Translators have had trouble with this sentence: 'a single note ending with a sweet tone in a little group of four notes' (Opdycke), 'a single word ending in a group of four notes with a sweet cadence' (Singleton), 'a single word ending in a group of notes with a sweet cadence' (Bull). Manfred Bukofzer corrected the misunderstanding about the meaning of 'groppetto': the courtier 'should always practise the fine art of understating his abilities. If, for instance, he was singing a difficult ornament like a "sweet double trill", he should only hint at the showy things that he could, but would not, do.'[17] The *groppetto* of sixteenth-century Italy was an ornament belonging to the trill class: the rapid alternation of two adjacent notes. The *groppetto duplicato* was a compound ornament, translated quite idiomatically by Hoby as 'double relise' (relish): a feature of sixteenth and seventeenth century instrumental music, embellishing with a trill each of two successive notes.[18] In solo vocal music—as is the intention here—the 'double relish' was the term used to translate *Gruppo*, the long trill of principal and upper adjacent note with final under-note turn, in the English version of Giulio Caccini's foreword to *Le nuove musiche* (1602), 'double' because tremolos on a single note were trills, or 'plain shakes': in trill and *gruppo* 'to begin with the first crotchet and to beat every note with the throat upon the vowel "a" unto the last breve. . . .'[19] The ornament to which Castiglione refers is at once a studied and a freely rendered gesture of the singer–improvisor, which by the end of the century would by necessity of multiple usage be crystallised and codified in print. It is one of the 'effects with that grace most sought after in good singing',[20] a decorative device in what would become 'una certa nobile sprezzatura di canto'.[21] Obviously Castiglione knew performance practice, and one can approach the more substantial passages on music in the *Cortegiano* with confidence in the author's expertise.

Commencing the first of two developed discussions on music (I, xlvii),[22] Count Ludovico da Canossa asserts that he would not be satisfied unless the courtier be a musician. The 'gran pelago di laude della musica' upon which the Count is tempted to launch, and does, is a rhetorical type. The 'ancients' are summoned as authority for his case, to validate his praise piece. There is not the mathematical, speculative or cosmological detail of a medieval treatise; the interconnections of *musica mundana*, *humana* and *instrumentalis* are exposed as accepted data in the opening sentence:

[reminding you] how it was the opinion of very wise philosophers that the world is made up of music, that the heavens in their motion make harmony, and that even the human soul was formed on the same principle, and is therefore awakened and has its virtues brought to life, as it were, through music.[23]

The classical allusions which comprise the body of the oration include only two myths, Orpheus with his taming lyre and Arion on the dolphin's back; the rest are drawn chiefly from history, and end with poetic pictures of music in rusticity and motherhood.[24] Each allusion features the ethical effect of *musica instrumentalis* and clearly points the moral lesson: music 'makes gentle the soul of man'.[25]

Such an oration is a product of Renaissance humanism as delineated by Kristeller. The dual concern for literary and scholarly elegance has classicism at its heart; the human values inherent in the subject under discussion are emphasised at the expense of specialised terminology, a terminology avoided in imitation of Cicero.[26] Castiglione's own knowledge of musical terms frequently reveals itself in the course of his book, but in the two longer set pieces on music we are given a gracefully phrased non-technical content restricted to the advocacy and merit of this particular discipline, carefully weighted as to its contribution to the committed 'cultural program and ideal', as Kristeller calls it.[27] Even the selection of sources is reflective of nascent humanist philological interests, in which are sought new illustrations of old truths; it has recently been pointed out that the complex of allusions to Themistocles, Epaminondas, Socrates and Alcibiades repeated in the Count's oration emerged as a Petrarchan tradition into the mainstream of musical treatises within the last quarter of the fifteenth century.[28]

It is in the conception of what music *is* that the new apologia for this art like the *Cortegiano* are separated from the treatises of the Middle Ages. Once functioning within the ecclesiastical and monastic singing schools for the preparation of the Divine Service (Disciple: 'What is music?' Master: 'The science of singing truly and the easy road to perfection in singing')[29] and forming the basis for conceptual rationalisation (Disciple: 'What is music?' Master: 'The rational discipline of agreement and discrepancy in sounds according to numbers in their relation to those things which are found in sounds'),[30] musical training is now the servant of a romantic aesthetic in which *musica instrumentalis*—despised by the 'ancients' and Church Fathers— must be undertaken in order to satisfy requirements of pride and love.

Do you not see that the cause of all gracious exercises that give us pleasure is to be assigned to women alone? Who learns to dance gracefully for any reason except to please women? Who devotes himself to the sweetness of music for any other reason? Who attempts to compose verses, at least in the vernacular, unless to express sentiments inspired by women?[31]

If music can penetrate to the depths of a woman's soul, who better suited than the courtier–musician himself to be the penetrator!

[Be a Musition] in Courtes, where . . . many things are taken in hand to please women withall, whose tender and soft breastes are soone pierced with melodie, and filled with sweetnesse.
  Therefore no marvell, that in olde times and now adayes they have alwaies beene inclined to Musitions, and counted this a most acceptable food of the minde.[32]

Renaissance court music was to be 'the food of love'; 'excess of it' was demanded.[33]

  And so Castiglione's Count declares in favour of the courtier's musician-ship:

e se, oltre intendere ed esser sicuro a libro, non sa di varii instrumenti . . .

The courtier must be trained thoroughly in the science of music: an education evidently accomplished by members of the company at Urbino, as witness the comments by Magnifico Guiliano on the consonance–dissonance factor in composition (I, xxviii).[34] He must be able to read his part securely (as a singer, implied), and play various instruments. This would satisfy the general criteria of what it was to be a musician, defined by Tinctoris (*c.* 1474–76): if music 'is that skill consisting of performance in singing and playing', then a musician 'is one who takes up the metier of singing, having observed its principles by means of study'.[35]

  Four types of music are recommended to the courtier in the course of Castiglione's second major statement on the subject (II, xiii).[36]

1 'Bella musica . . . parmi il cantar bene a libro sicuramente e con bella maniera'

Singleton missed the technical point here: 'In my opinion, the most beautiful music is in singing well and in reading at sight and in fine style.' Bull got it right: 'Truly beautiful music . . . consists, in my opinion, in fine singing, in reading accurately from the score and in an attractive personal style. . . .'[37] In effect, the injunction that the courtier be musically literate (I, xlvii) is

repeated. The beautiful in music lies (in part) in the fine quality ('maniera')
with which a printed work may be sung.

2 'ma ancor molto più il cantare alla viola'

Singleton's translation is the only current source in which the reader is
reminded that it is the *viola da mano* which is meant: not the bowed Renaissance viol, still less the viola of a later period.[38] Used to accompany solo song,
the *viola da mano* was a plucked instrument. It had a body shaped like a
guitar, its six strings in accordatura similar to the lute; at this time its name
was interchangeable with *viola*, *liuto* and even *lyra*; it was to have its great
vogue in sixteenth-century Spain as the *vihuela*.[39]

A plucked instrument is ideal to accompany a soloist, for its sounds are
conducive to focusing the listener's attention upon the vocal line, as Castiglione
affirms in this passage.[40] Song improvised to the sound of plucked strings had
been popular with the Medici: Lorenzo was charmed by a performer
'canendis ex tempore ad lyram', and Pietro patronised an individual skilled
in singing 'sulla lira all' improvviso'.[41] Marsilio Ficino sang to the lyre.[42]
Master of solo song in Castiglione's circle was Giacomo Sansecondo, in
whose presence, says our author, no one else should have the temerity to
perform: 'come soglio maravigliarmi dell' audacia di color che osano cantar
alla viola in presenzia del' nostro Iacomo Sansecondo" (II, xlv).[43]

Even the printed version of a frottola, the music here intended by
Castiglione, was itself a guide to improvisation.[44] The frottola texture was
best realised by voice and one instrument. The musical conception

is in general simultaneous, not successive; it is harmonic, not polyphonic. The starting
point is the freely invented upper voice provided with a text. Its counterpoise, the
bass, is also there from the first and this bass is a true instrumental supporting bass,
without the eloquent pauses of the soprano and without any immediate possibility
of an adaptation of the text. [The two textless inner parts] . . . are nothing but harmonic filling in the form of melodic movement . . . to serve as a guide to the singer's
accompanist. It was of course possible to perform the composition as written, with
one singer and three accompanying viols. . . . But a far more logical interpreter for a
serenade was the lute-player or, for chamber performances, the player of a keyboard
instrument; all he had to do was to condense the accompanying parts in one form or
another.[45]

That Cara and Tromboncino, chief of the Mantuan frottolists, were classified
in their own century as 'cantori al liuto', not 'cantori a libro',[46] demonstrates
that in the *Cortegiano* II, xiii Castiglione was purposely supporting two valid
but different skills: to sing written music in good style is beautiful, but to
render a frottola-like piece is even more lovely.

3 'Ma sopra tutto parmi gratissimo il cantare alla viola per recitare'

Increased emphasis upon the delivery of the word was a natural result of the
flourishing frottola repertoire, with its expressive vocal line and general
homophonic texture. Einstein exhibited a sonnet by Castiglione's 'nostro

Marchetto Cara' progressing in almost totally monodic declamation, through which are realised goals of the late Renaissance academies nearly a century in advance.[47] When highly prizing such text-oriented tiny premonitions of the writing of the Florentine Camerata, Castiglione is running in the main current of European musical thought.[48] He also is saluting a contribution to what Lowinsky has called the 'most radical innovation' in Renaissance composition: 'the transition from a successive to a simultaneous conception of parts . . . the newly acquired capacity to "think in harmonies" '.[49]

4 'Sono ancor armoniosi tutti gli instrumenti da tasti . . . E non meno diletta la musica delle quattro viole da arco'

Instrumental chamber music is listed last. It is true that one of the achievements of Renaissance culture lay in the fact that music 'became both more closely united with words and more independent of words'.[50] As yet, however, the corpus of compositions completely non-referential to any text or vocal ensemble was small, the bias weighted towards some sort of collaboration between voices and instruments. The keyboard is allowed certain advantages of full consonance ('perche hanno le consonanzie molto perfette'), yet this too suggests possibilities for accompaniment indicated by Einstein in the extract quoted above. In fact the human voice 'gives ornament and much grace to all these instruments. . . .'[51]

The consort of bowed viols is not too often confused any longer with the string quartet of two violins, viola and cello. Translators have managed to avoid the unhistorical statements of former years, such as 'String quartets and motets for different instruments were performed, especially those of Josquin de Près. . . .'[52] Wind instruments (i.e. those scorned by Alcibiades and Minerva) need not be the concern of the courtier. It is understood that these are unsuitable to collaborate with the singing voice in love song, hence their proscription in the text and their relegation to outdoor festival and indoor dance music.[53] Wind instruments should be the tools of the professional, the courtier at no time assuming a role other than that of a well practised, modest dilettante (II, xii).

Therefore, let the Courtier turn to music as a pastime, and as though forced, and not in the presence of persons of low birth or where there is a crowd. And although he may know and understand what he does, in this also I would have him dissimulate the care and effort that is required in doing anything well; and let him appear to esteem but little this accomplishment of his, yet by performing it excellently well, make others esteem it highly.[54]

This reticence in the display of technique, this disfavour shown to ungenteel virtuosity Castiglione commends equally to the lady (III, viii).[55] Her knowledge of letters, music, painting, dancing and entertaining should be accompanied 'con quella discreta modestia' (III, ix).[56] When she sings or plays the lady should not employ 'quelle diminuzioni forti e replicate, che mostrano più arte che dolcezza'. The 'vehement and repetitive diminutions which show more skill than ladylike grace' were a prominent element in

sixteenth- and seventeenth-century variations. The melody and the counter-
figures were broken up into progressively smaller note values to produce the
effect of accelerated movement, a virtuoso effect stimulating the admiration
of the audience.[57] Improvised diminution was a vocal skill.[58] It was certainly
not the rapid alteration of dynamic required in Bull's translation: 'nor,
when she is singing or playing a musical instrument, to use those abrupt and
frequent *diminuendos* that are ingenious but not beautiful'.[59]

In the *Cortegiano* Castiglione understands music as an art in which science,
craft and performance are held in easy balance, all three set in classical
perspective but realistically *au courant*.

A. The curatorial element, relatively brief, preserves the chosen selection
of exemplary illustrations from classical scholarship, in the recapitualation
of which are stressed their implicit moral. On the proof provided by these
citations drawn from the *studia humanitatis* of rhetoric, history, poetry and
moral philosophy, music is able to acquire a place in the 'humanistic'
cultural programme envisaged for the courtier.[60]

B. The social function of music espoused by Castiglione is involved with
what Alfred von Martin considered a renewed ideal of gallantry, in a court
where the lady, made intellectually independent by humanist education,
moulds its breeding 'in a new ideal of courtly manners and personal culture,
uniting humanist with chivalrous traits'; the *cortegiano* is 'the new kind of
knight: a man of the world and cultured in every resepct . . .'.[61] It must be
observed, however, that although the direction of the final form of Castiglione's
book may be 'a work with a serious intellectual purpose',[62] especially
considering the transcendental view of love in book iv, the role of music and
musicianship described in books i and ii convinces one of the view that 'the
ideas of love in the resolution have no specific relevance to the idea of the
courtier in his services as courtier.'[63] Indeed, the court atmosphere engendered by the sounds of the music he writes about and the texts of the new
compositions which fill that atmosphere 'dove, tra l'altre piacevoli feste e
musiche e danze che continuamente si usavano' (i, v) are almost 'exclusively
erotic'.[64] Style, content and sound embrace a sensuality which heralds a
fresh view of the meaning and use of theory, practice and aesthetic in
Western music: music celebrating the secular sphere of man's existence.

c. Castiglione promotes an appreciation of the new music—both its
loveliness and its power—and of the desirability of acquiring its secrets for
personal improvement. However, his book acts only as an encouragement to
seek out the teacher and the instrument; it is not a systematic compilation of
didactic particulars, neither a 'Musica practica', an 'Istituzioni armoniche',
nor 'A Plain and Easy Introduction to Practical Music'.[65] The manual is
truly cast in the philosophy of humanism. Its author rejects detailed content
in the manner of scholasticism and hence offers no technical training.[66] It
is a curriculum consisting of titles of disciplines and the defence of their
inclusion in that curriculum. The courtier, encouraged so far in music,
must go to the growing number of treatises on the mechanics of the art.

D. The legitimisation of vocal and digital dexterity (and, by assumption, of experimentation and perfection in the craft of instrument making) advocated within a system of education, the ends of which were to be socially and morally ennobling, participates in the 'intellectualisation of all mechanical professions'—a Renaissance stable synthesis of the liberal and mechanical arts, in which Erwin Panofsky includes

theoretical insight, which was supposed to be a matter of the pure intellect, and practical pursuits, including the representational arts, which were supposed to be a matter of mere sensory perception and manual skill.[67]

The passages reviewed are mirrors of such a synthesis forming in Cinquecento music. It is necessary to complete this study by observing some of them in their subsequent English translation, in order the better to estimate how much of Castiglione's message is representative of musical realities in the later English Renaissance.

It is an indication of Hoby's success in Anglicising Castiglione's text that the specific musical terminology is translated quite successfully. The twofold beauties of vocal music (II, xiii) are rendered into their equivalents in English practice. '. . . il cantar bene a libro sicuramente e con bella maniera' becomes 'pricksong [i.e. a written or printed work] is a faire musicke, so it be done upon the booke surely and after a good sorte'; 'cantare alla viola per recitare' becomes 'singing to the lute with the dittie': the freer, text-governed manner in which you 'dispose your music according to the nature of the words which you are therein to express, as whatsoever matter it be which you have in hand such a kind of music must you frame to it . . . for it will be a great absurdity to use a sad harmony to a merry matter or a merry harmony to a sad, lamentable, or tragical ditty.'[68] The 'diminuzioni' are 'divisions', the same technique in English as 'diminutions', but one customarily applied to instrumental music.

The 'sette [or chest] of Violes' is accurate, but Hoby substitutes 'all Instruments with freats' for those of keys ('tasti').[69] In the French editions of the *Cortegiano*, 1538 and 1585, 'tutti gli instrumenti da tasti' had been changed to 'Tous les aultres instrumens de bouche', for 'touche' (fret).[70] The technical terminology of book II, xiii, was weakened in the 1538 French version:[71]

Chanter sur le livre, respond messire Federigo, me semble une belle musicque pourveu que ce soit personne qui le faiche bien faire et en bonne mode, . . . mais sur tout chanter sur le lucz est pour récréer, se me semble, plus agréeable . . .

The slip, reading *ricreare* (Fr. *récréer*) for *recitare* was continued in the 1585 edition ('chanter pour plaisir sur la viole'). The initial material of the latter is closer to the original (notice that the literal 'viole' is back, for lute):[72]

Il me semble, respondit le seigneur Federic, que c'est une belle musique, scavoir chanter assuerement et d'une belle maniere sa partie, au livre, mais me semble encores plus beau scavoir chanter sur la viole, pource que toute la douceur consiste quasi en une seule chose. . . .

There are frequent passages in the French editions when the Italian original's distinctive meaning is lost in generalities: 'sonare la citara' (I, xlvii) is 'iouer des instrumens'; 'ballarono una roegarze con estrema grazia' (I, lvi) is 'se

mirent à danser plus gracement'.[73] Which returns us to Hoby, who also had
difficulty with the dance titles. Breaking his own definite theory of translation,
which never permitted textual freedom,[74] he put down 'they hand in hand
shewed them a daunce or two'.[75]

Hoby's avowed fidelity to Castiglione's text has raised queries as to the
wisdom of relying upon an Italian literary source in translation for ascertain-
ing data of English musical habits four decades removed from the original.
The 'sette of Violes' was common in professional playing at court and theatre,
'but their use as instruments for amateur recreation may be questioned';[76]
from available documents it may be gathered that the lute, virginals and
wire string instruments were more favoured for leisure and gentle upbringing.[77] Hoby was translating at a time when Italian professionalism was
a dominant influence in English musical life. Henry VIII had already
concentrated around his person foreign (especially Italian) musicians—at
least twenty played at his funeral; two-thirds of Elizabeth's professional
players were foreigners; in collections of solo lute music the repertoire of
fantasies was in the ratio 2 : 1 in favour of Continental composers, the
majority from Italy.[78] Printed Italian music was in demand for the instruction
of a courtier's children.[79] Lutes and virginals do strew the pages of the
account books, but almost invariably for the instruction of the daughter of
the house. A case in point is furnished in the Sydney family accounts:[80]

> 1571: For a lute for Mistress Marye Sydney, my lord's daughter
> 23 October 1595: Mistress Mary Sydney . . . is very forward in her learning, writing,
>   and other exercises she is put to, as dancing and the virginals, . . .

Apparently it was also desirable that personal servants should acquire a
certain amount of facility upon the 'soft' instruments. In the Rutland
accounts for 1537–42 is included mention of viols and lutes; subsequently,
however, while the Earl's children were tutored in dancing, fencing and
schooling, Weston the lutenist is paid (1558) for teaching 'Rycherd, my
lady['s] page, and my lord's page' to play upon the lute;[81] vagrant and
other musical servants continue to receive payments, but for the members of
the family itself there is little education in the art. Singled out in the accounts
are legal studies and sports as tutors' tasks for the budding English gentleman
citizen. For him 'Lord Julian' would have had to admit that music was an
ornament, but no longer a necessity.

English authors of educational manuals continued, however, to lift
passages from Castiglione/Hoby; their own social values remained Aristotelian
in the advocacy of musical performance purely for recreation and for the
pursuit of a quality life style.[82] In the dialogue on music in *Toxophilus* Roger
Ascham reproduced doctrine of *ethos* from both *Republic* and *Politics*; he
singled out plainsong and pricksong as fitting music, but this is copy, these
being the normal examples given to represent the accepted corpus of music—
oral and written respectively. There is little reflection of actual performance
practice in *Toxophilus*, nor in Ascham's *Scholasticus*, where the Hoby text
tradition is preserved by deeming that 'to sing, and playe of instrumentes
cunnyingly' is among the pastimes 'that be fitte for Courtlie Ientlemen'.[83]

Richard Mulcaster, in a weak derivation from the *Cortegiano* II, xiii, repeated that virginals and lutes are good for the young in that they offer a 'full sound'.[84] Sentences of Peacham's often quoted *The Complete Gentleman* read like translations of Castiglione or paraphrases of Hoby but designed so as to reconcile the *sprezzatura* of Urbino with the dutiful rectitude of London:[85]

I desire no more in you then to sing your part sure and at the first sight withall to play the same upon your viol or the exercise of the lute, privately to yourself.

I might run into an infinite sea of the praise and use of so excelent an art, but I only show it you with the finger because I desire not that any noble or gentleman should, save at his private recreation and leisurable hours, prove a master in the same or neglect his more weighty employments, though I avouch it a skill worthy the knowledge and exercise of the greatest prince.

It is customary to contrast Castiglione's admonition to the courtier–musician to find the right time and company for his performance (II, xii–xiii) in order to avoid 'bad form' with the disavowal of virtuoso expertise habitually made by English writers in order to escape distraction from public office and good government service.[86] Interestingly enough, Castiglione himself laid the ground for such a position in the fourth book. One is to keep a proper balance between the flowers and the real fruit, which is service of right judgement to one's prince (IV, v). In Hoby's words:

You may see that ignorance in musicke, in dancing, in riding, hurteth no man, yet he that is no musition is ashamed and afraide to sing in the presence of others, or to daunce, he that can not, or he that sitteth not well a horse to ride.

But of the unskillfulnesse to governe people arise so many evils, deathes, destructions, mischiefes, and confusions, that it may bee called the deadlyest plague upon the earth.[87]

Hoby's *The Book of the Courtier*, and its subsequent derivations, would continue to be for young gentlemen 'an encouraging to garnish their minds with morall vertues, and their bodies with comely exercises';[88] the emphases upon the contents and the attitudes guiding the selections and derivations would alter with the aspirations and necessities of public life.

Nevertheless the Englishman of any degree of leisure sought that sense of personality inherent in the doctrine of courtesy as introduced through Hoby's translated manual; the new conception of *virtù*, 'virtuosity in the art of life'.[89]

Courtier and citizen alike thanked the gods of learning for the Elizabethan equivalent of the works that make up the modern five-foot shelf containing books of general information.[90]

Within his own particular station the reader could acquire for his existence 'the assured consciousness of its own worthiness'.[91] The Renaissance scholar Gabriel Harvey could annotate his copy of Hoby, 'Both inside, & outside, must be a faire paterne of worthie, fine & Loouelie Vertu'.[92] And for the spirits to be in tune, man must at least care for music: 'e chi non la gusta si po tener per certo ch'abbia i spiriti discordanti l'un dall'altro'.[93]

In St Michael's Church, Cumnor, is an epitaph for Anthony Forster

(d. 1572), the lord of Cumnor Manor, which he acquired by purchase in 1561. In translation it reads:

Shrewd-minded, of high courage, active in body, melodious of voice, fluent in speech [*Eloquio dulcis, ore disertus erat*], upright in his actions, graceful in his conversation, grave of countenance, firm in faith was he. Well knew he to tune the clear lute's sounding strings, and to draw music from the lyre. The planting of wood and garden, the building of fair houses were his pleasure and his skill. Versed was he in forming varied phrase and ordered period, and many a sheet flowed from his learned pen.[94]

Renaissance man was incomplete without a measure of music about him, ideally within him:[95] 'not so much for the sake of that outward melody which is heard, but because of the power it has to induce a good new habit of mind and an inclination to virtue, rendering the soul more capable of happiness'.

non tanto per quella superficial melodia che si sente, ma per esser sufficiente ad indur in noi un novo abito bono ed un costume tendente all virtù, il qual fa l'animo più capace di felicità. . . .

NOTES

[1] Baldesar Castiglione, *Il Libro del Cortegiano*, I, xlviii; ed. Bruno Maier, Turin, U.T.E.T., second edition, 1964, p. 171; trans. Charles S. Singleton, New York, Doubleday Anchor Books, 1959, p. 77; trans. George Bull, Harmondsworth, Penguin Books, 1967, p. 96.

[2] *The Book of the Courtier* (1561); page references in this article are to the edition published by Dent in Everyman's Library.

[3] Although Castiglione's book is alluded to in virtually every secondary source dealing with music of this period, there are two articles in particular which should be consulted: Bianca Becherini, 'Il "Cortegiano" e la musica', *La Bibliofilia*, XLV, 1943, pp. 84–96, and Manfred Bukofzer, 'The Book of the Courtier on music', *Proceedings of the Music Teachers' National Association*, thirty-eighth series, 1944, pp. 230–5.

[4] Maier, pp. 147–8; Singleton, p. 60; Bull, p. 82.

[5] Alfonso d'Este of Ferrara had discharged the majority of his singers because of financial difficulties; most found their way to Mantua. Bidon was specifically requested from him by Francesco Gonzaga in March 1511; Cara was already in Mantuan service at the time. See Pierre M. Tagmann, *Archivalische Studien zur Musikpflege am Dom von Mantua (1500–1627)*, Bern and Stuttgart, 1967 (*Pub. der Schweizerischen Musikforschenden Gesellschaft*, second series, vol. XIV), pp. 11–13, 64. For Bidon at Rome see André Pirro, 'Leo X and music', *Musical Quarterly*, XXI, 1935, pp. 11, 14; Herman-Walther Frey, 'Regesten zur päpstlichen Kapelle unter Leo X. und zu seiner Privatkapell', *Die Musikforschung*, VIII, 1955, p. 62; IX, 1966, pp. 54–55, 148. Bidon's name is included in an encyclopaedic catalogue of singers and composers in canto XXI of Philippo da Bassano's *Monte Parnaso* (see H. Colin Slim, 'Musicians on Parnassus', *Studies in the Renaissance*, XII, 1965, p. 149); the poem may be dated *c.* 1519–22 (*ibid.*, p. 139).

[6] Hieronimo Casio, *Libro intitulato Cronica*, Bologna, 1528, f. 48v, cited in Pirro, *op. cit.*, p. 14.

[7] Singleton, p. 60.

[8] On style and figuration in improvised vocal polyphony (*contrappunto alla mente*) see, *inter alia*, two articles by Ernest T. Ferand: ' "Sodaine and Unexpected" music in the Renaissance', *Musical Quarterly*, XXXVII, 1951, pp. 10–27, and 'Improvised vocal counterpoint in the late Renaissance and early Baroque', *Annales Musicologiques*, IV, 1956, pp. 129–74.

[9] For biographical detail see Knud Jeppesen, 'Cara', in *Die Musik in Geschichte und Gegenwart*, ed. Friedrich Blume, II, pp. 823–30; for discussion on style see pertinent

references in Alfred Einstein, *The Italian Madrigal*, Princeton, N.J., 1949, 1, and Gustave Reese, *Music in the Renaissance*, New York, 1954.

[10] Josquin's fame was so proverbial as to occasion snobbish name-dropping, reported in the *Cortegiano*, II, xxxv. On Tromboncino and the Mantuan composers see Einstein, *op. cit.*, pp. 34 f.; Tromboncino set a canzone stanza or madrigal (*Queste lacrime mie*) by Castiglione, sung at the Urbino court in 1506 (*ibid.*, p. 109), and in 1517 Cara thanked him for his praise in the *Cortegiano* by setting Castiglione's sonnet *Cantai mentre nel cor lieto fioriva* (*ibid.*, pp. 112–13, *q.v.* pp. 109–11 for Cara's links with Bembo). In the second version of the *Cortegiano* (compiled 1518–20) Agricola's name appears where Bidon's was placed in the final version (copied May 1524 and published 1528); see Ghino Ghinassi, *La seconda redazione del 'Cortegiano' di Baldassarre Castiglione*, Florence, 1968, p. 50. Agricola died of the fever at Valladolid in 1506 while a member of the Burgundian court chapel in which he had served since 1500. He had achieved success under Galeazzo Maria Sforza at Milan (1471–74) and Lorenzo de' Medici (c. 1474–1476, 1491–92) as well as at the court of Charles VIII (see Martin Picker, 'A letter of Charles VIII of France concerning Alexander Agricola', in *Aspects of Medieval and Renaissance Music*, ed. Jan LaRue, New York, 1966, pp. 665–72). Since one of Castiglione's aims was to memorialise eminent personages of the first decade of the century, the recent death of the famous singer–composer would have warranted his inclusion in the initial drafts of the book. Bidon's reputation in the same vocal idiom would have been more fresh and vivid in Castiglione's immediate circle during the final copying period of the 1520s, and it is interesting to note that the year of the *Cortegiano*'s publication was the year of Bidon's epitaphs.

[11] *Merchant of Venice*, v, i.

[12] Pirro, *op. cit.*, p. 3.

[13] The relevant passages from the *Republic* and the *Politics* are printed with commentary in Oliver Strunk, *Source Readings in Music History*, New York, 1950, pp. 1–24.

[14] Bull's translation does not convey the sense of the musical philosophy: 'In music, for example, the strains are now solemn and slow, now very fast and different in mood and manner. . . . [Cara's] voice is so serene and so full of plaintive sweetness that he gently touches and penetrates our souls, and they respond with great delight and emotion.'

[15] Castiglione himself was a singer to the lute (*viola*); see Becherini, *op. cit.*, pp. 85–6, on his musical personality and on the musical spirit of the court at Urbino. In the prefatory letter to the *Cortegiano* he admits that 'I think that anyone who did not have some knowledge of the things that are spoken of in the book . . . could not well have written of them' (Singleton, p. 7); surely music is one of these subjects.

[16] Maier, p. 129; Singleton, p. 47; Bull, p. 70.

[17] Bukofzer, *op. cit.*, p. 232.

[18] 'Relish', Willi Apel, *Harvard Dictionary of Music*, Cambridge, Mass., second edition, 1969, p. 724.

[19] Anonymous seventeenth-century English translation in John Playford's *Introduction to the Skill of Music*, reprinted in Strunk, *op. cit.*, p. 384.

[20] Giulio Caccini, *Le Nouve Musiche*, ed. H. Wiley Hitchcock, Madison, Wis., 1970, p. 51.

[21] *Ibid.*, p. 44, n. 10; *q.v.* pp. 43–5 for Caccini's use of *grazia* and *sprezzatura*, Castiglione's concepts adopted in the moulding of the changing style of vocal art at the close of the Renaissance.

[22] Maier, pp. 168–71; Singleton, pp. 74–6; Bull, pp. 94–6.

[23] Singleton, p. 75. See Boethius, *De institutione musica*, I, 2, on 'the three kinds of music', reprinted in Strunk, *op. cit.*, pp. 84–5; on the creation of the world by musical scale in the *Timaeus* of Plato see Francis M. Cornford, *Plato's Cosmology*, New York, 1957, pp. 66–72.

[24] Sources are identified in the editions of Maier and Cian, Florence, third edition,

1929. Fifteenth-century authors of musical treatises had employed the same historical allusions from Cicero, Quintilian *et al.* as Castiglione (see *infra*, n. 28). Adam of Fulda, in his *Musica* (1490) (Martin Gerbert, *Scriptores ecclesiastici de Musica*, III, 339) draws on a *Carmen de laude musica* (*c.* 1424–26) by Jean Gerson (*Oeuvres complètes*, ed. Glorieux, Paris, 1962, IV, pp. 135–6), but omitting the last pair of lines of his source. By quoting Gerson's lines it may be shown that Castiglione, the classical humanist, already had a century of specifically Renaissance illustrative tradition from which to select his copy on musical *ethos* (*cf.* Maier, p. 170, and Cian, pp. 120–1).

> Quid numeremus aves humano quae capiuntur
> > Cantu nec cantum despicit ulla suum.
> Pisces et cervi mulcentur cantibus, aegris
> > Antidotum variis musica crebro fuit.
> Praebe fidem Graecis, delphinus Ariona vexit
> > Fluctus per medios dum lyra mulcet eum.
> Fistula pastoris pecudes armenta gregesque
> > Solatur, nec eas terret imago lupi
> Pascua tunc secura metunt minuitque magistro
> > Taedia pascendi rusticus iste sonus.
>
> . . .
>
> Femina dum texit dumve pueroque soporem
> > Ducens in cunis cantat inepta rudis.

[25] Singleton, p. 76.

[26] Paul Oskar Kristeller, 'The moral thought of Renaissance humanism', *Renaissance Thought*, II: *Papers on Humanism and the Arts*, New York, 1965 (originally published in *Chapters in Western Civilization*, New York, 1961), pp. 25–6, and 'Humanist learning in the Italian Renaissance', *ibid.* (originally published in *The Centennial Review*, IV, 1960), pp. 14–16.

[27] 'The moral thought of Renaissance humanism', p. 25.

[28] Conrad H. Rawski, 'Petrarch's dialogue on music,' *Speculum*, XLVI, 1971, 305, *q.v.* for a chart of the frequency in appearance of the named figures in a selected list of publications 1477–1690; textual parallels are well annotated, 313–14. Castiglione shares with Tinctoris and Wellendorffer the paired figures of Alcibiades and Minerva as despisers of the *tibia*; the contrast in musical prowess between Themistocles and Epaminondas does not vary among the references listed. Castiglione's employment of sources, similar to those of Adam of Fulda have been noted, *supra*, n. 24. It is instructive to observe that, whereas the 'Petrarchan fare' cites Socrates only as an example of a *senex* adopting musical techniques late in life (see Rawski, *op. cit.*, p. 313, n. 30), Tinctoris used the story to urge a youthful training: 'For, wherefore, I have discovered that Socrates himself, beginning to play so exceedingly late, although he was judged as the wisest of all . . ., has been named by not one writer as a divine musician . . .; so, in our time, I have known not even one man who has achieved eminent or noble rank among musicians, if he began to compose or sing *super librum* at or above his twentieth year of age.' Johannes Tinctoris, *The Art of Counterpoint* (*Liber de arte contrapuncti*, 1477), trans. Albert Seay, American Institute of Musicology, 1961, pp. 140–1; the implication that old Socrates may not have been a very skilful lyra player supports the argument in the *Cortegiano* (II, XIV) against allowing 'i poveri vecchi' to perform in public lest they be mocked—better 'in secreto e solamente per levarsi dell'animo . . . e per gustar quella divinità ch'io credo che nella musica sentivano Pitagora e Socrate' (Maier, p. 211). Further on the *senex amans* in Laurence V. Ryan, 'Book Four of Castiglione's *Courtier*: climax or afterthought?', *Studies in the Renaissance*, XIX, 1972, p. 172, n. 43.

[29] Odo of Cluny, *Enchiridion musices* (*c.* 935), reprinted in Strunk, *op. cit.*, p. 105.

[30] *Scholia enchiriadis* (*c.* 900), reprinted *ibid.*, p. 135.

[31] Singleton, pp. 257–8.

[32] Hoby, *The Book of the Courtier*, p. 75.

[33] *Twelfth Night*, I, i.

[34] Maier, pp. 127–8; Singleton, p. 45; Bull, p. 69.

[35] 'Musica est modulandi peritia cantu sonoque consistens.' 'Musicus est qui perpensa ratione beneficio speculationis canendi officium assumit.' (Johannes Tinctoris, *Dictionary of Musical Terms (Terminorum Musicae Diffinitorium)*, trans. Carl Parrish, New York, 1963, pp. 42–5.)

[36] Maier, pp. 208–10; Singleton, pp. 104–6; Bull, pp. 120–2.

[37] Opdycke's translation (London, 1902) also bears the right sense: 'I regard as beautiful music, to sing well by note, with ease and in beautiful style;' in most other instances this translation has been replaced by that of Singleton.

[38] *Cf.* Opdycke, pp. 88–9, 356; Bukofzer's discussion of national preferences for viol or lute (*op. cit.*, pp. 233–5) is based upon the same false identification of 'viola' with viol.

[39] See Isabel Pope Conant, 'Vicente Espinel as a musician', *Studies in the Renaissance*, v, 1958, pp. 135 ff; also Alfred Berner, 'Vihuela', *Die Musik in Geschichte und Gegenwart*, XIII, pp. 1621–23, Curt Sachs, *The History of Musical Instruments*, New York, 1940, p. 345, and Reese, *op. cit.*, pp. 619–20. The Spanish translation by Juan Boscan (1534) is 'cantar con una vihuela' (*Los quatros libros del Cortesanos*, ed. M. Menendez y Pelago, Madrid, 1942, p. 123). Tinctoris mentioned the 'leutum: quaslibet cantilenas (ut supra tetigimus) jocundissime concinant: ad violam tamen sine arculo in Italia et hispania frequentius'. (Karl Weinmann, *Johannes Tinctoris (1445–1511) und sein unbekannter Träktat 'Die inventione et usu musicae'*, Tutzing, 1961, p. 45.)

[40] Reese, *op. cit.*, p. 160.

[41] Pirro, *op. cit.*, p. 2.

[42] Kristeller, 'Music and learning in the early Italian Renaissance', in *Renaissance Thought*, II, pp. 157 ff (originally published in *Studies in Renaissance Thought and Letters*, Rome, 1956); on Ficino and music see also Kristeller, *The Philosophy of Marsilio Ficino*, New York, 1943, pp. 307–9, and Otto Kinkeldey, 'Franchino Gafori and Marsilio Ficino', *Harvard Library Bulletin*, I, 1947, pp. 379–82.

[43] Maier, p. 260; Singleton, p. 144; Bull, p. 154.

[44] Einstein, *op. cit.*, p. 61.

[45] *Ibid.*, p. 77, with example, p. 76.

[46] *Ibid.*, from Pietro Aron, *Lucidario* (1545).

[47] *Ibid.*, pp. 101–2.

[48] See Becherini, *op. cit.*, pp. 90–1.

[49] Edward E. Lowinsky, 'Music in the culture of the Renaissance', in Paul O. Kristeller and Philip P. Wiener, ed. *Renaissance Essays*, New York, 1968 (originally published in *Journal of the History of Ideas*, xv, 1954), p. 379.

[50] Donald Jay Grout, *A History of Western Music*, New York, 1960, p. 157.

[51] Singleton, p. 105.

[52] Julia Cartwright, *Baldassare Castiglione, the Perfect Courtier*, London, 1908, I, 100; erroneous interpretation in Cian, p. 157, n. 16, and Opdycke, p. 89. Each age has interpreted the source in terms of the musical practice with which it was familiar. Robert Samber, in his English translation of 1724 (p. 122) fashions the 'quattro viole da arco' into 'A Concert of Violins, with their Base', which is the baroque and pre-classical string orchestra concerto texture with its governing *basso continuo*. Certainly a less cerebral view of the idea of music, which was to be made more manifest in the coming decade of the century, is intimated in the 1727 translation by A. P. Castiglione of II, xlvii (p. 88), in which the moral philosophy of the original is quite superseded by a spirit of simple pleasure: 'It is not therefore to be wondered at, that now, as well as in former Times, they [ladies] have ever been addicted to Musick, and esteem'd it an agreeable Entertainment to the Mind.'

[53] The myth of Pallas/Minerva throwing away the *aulos* (Latin *tibia*) which she had invented because the act of storing the air supply in the mouth puffed up the player's

cheeks and contorted the face into ugly expressions was repeated as common humanist lore (see Rawski, *op. cit.*, p. 314, n. 32). Castiglione (II, xiii) merely cited it; Giovanni Della Casa retold the story in chapter xxx, *Il Galateo* (written in 1551–55, published in Venice, 1558). Della Casa substituted for *tibia* the Italian peasant's bagpipe, which in fact is a more developed version of the same performance principle (ed. G. Tini vella, Milan, 1954, p. 257). With Pallas 'si dilettò un tempo di sonare la cornamusa', the 'sconci atti del viso' became the more repugnant to a lady or gentleman because the instrument itself was rude and uncourtly. In Robert Peterson's translation (1576), which popularised Della Casa's book as 'A Treatise of the Maners and Behaviours', Pallas is made to play the cornett, a wind instrument very acceptable in professional consorts. To play it would force no unusual 'unseemely gestures of the countenance and face' (facsimile edition, New York, 1967, p. 120). The ban is a literary figure which by the Renaissance had lost some of its original justification, yet there remains from the classical tradition the bias against the professional class, that 'base condition and calling, that they must make it a gaine, and an art to live uppon it' (*ibid.*). Further literary references in F. W. Sternfeld, *Music in Shakespearean Tragedy*, London, 1967, pp. 226–35.

[54] Singleton, p. 104.

[55] Maier, pp. 347–8; Singleton, pp. 210–11; Bull, p. 215.

[56] Maier, p. 349; Singleton, p. 211; Bull, p. 216.

[57] A similar effect is communicated in an Indian *rāga*.

[58] See 'Ornamentation, I', *Harvard Dictionary of Music*, second edition, p. 629.

[59] For other dissatisfying moments in Bull's translation see the review in *The Times Literary Supplement*, 8 February 1968, p. 129.

[60] See Kristeller, 'Classical Antiquity and Renaissance humanism', in *The Renaissance Debate*, ed. Denys Hay, New York, 1965 (originally published in *The Classics and Renaissance Thought*, Cambridge, Mass., 1955), p. 109.

[61] Alfred von Martin, *Sociology of the Renaissance*, New York, 1963 (originally published 1944), pp. 73–4.

[62] Ryan, *op. cit.*, p. 158: 'it is intended as a guide to the fully realised human life, built upon the foundations of the Aristotelian ethico-political system and completed by Platonic metaphysical speculation about the nature of that happiness and perfection to which Aristotle says man is destined as an intellectual being.'

[63] Lawrence Lipking, 'The dialectic of *Il Cortegiano*', *PMLA*, LXXXI, 1966, p. 357.

[64] Hugo Leichtentritt, *Music, History and Ideas*, Cambridge, Mass., 1954, p. 82. Although there may have been the usual gulf between moral ideal and physical reality, it is not authentic to question the ideal itself nor the Courtier's appreciation of its philosophy, as does Wilhelm Schenk in his unhistorical, debunking essay 'The "Cortegiano" and the civilization of the Renaissance', *Scrutiny*, xv, 1949, p. 98.

[65] Bartolomé Ramos (Bologna, 1482), Gioseffi Zarlino (Venice, 1558), and Thomas Morley (London, 1597) respectively.

[66] See Wallace K. Ferguson, *Renaissance Studies*, London, Ont., 1963, pp. 105–6.

[67] Erwin Panofsky, 'Artist, scientist, genius: notes on the "Renaissance-Dämmerung" ', in *The Renaissance: Six Essays*, ed. W. K. Ferguson *et al.*, New York, 1962, pp. 131 and 140.

[68] Morley, *A Plain and Easy Introduction to Practical Music* (1597), 'Rules to be observed in dittying' (ed. R. Alec Harman, New York, [1952]), p. 290.

[69] *The Book of the Courtier*, p. 101; see Bukofzer, *op. cit.*, p. 235, but in the light of *supra*, n. 38.

[70] *Le Courtisan de messire Baltazar de Castillon, nouvellement reveu et corrige*, Paris, 1538, f. lxxix; *Le Parfait Courtisan du comte Baltasar Castillonois*, Paris, 1585, p. 181.

[71] Folios lxxviiiv–lxxix.

[72] Page 180.

[73] For further comparisons see Reinhard Klesczewski, *Die französischen Übersetzungen des Cortegiano von Baldassare Castiglione*, Heidelberg, 1966, pp. 77, 99.

[74] F. O. Matthiesen, *Translation: an Elizabethan Art*, Cambridge, Mass., 1931, pp. 28–31, *q.v.*, p. 44.

[75] *The Book of the Courtier*, p. 85; *cf.* Maier, p. 185; Singleton, p. 86; Bull, p. 104. On the dances see Bukofzer, *op. cit.*, p. 231.

[76] Warwick A. Edwards, 'The performance of ensemble music in Elizabethan England', *Proceedings of the Royal Musical Association*, XCVII, 1970–71, p. 121.

[77] Details in Walter L. Woodfill, *Musicians in English Society from Elizabeth to Charles I*, New York, 1969 (originally published 1953), pp. 252–79.

[78] David Lumsden, 'De quelques éléments étrangers dans la musique anglaise pour le luth', in *La Musique instrumentale de la Renaissance*, ed. Jean Jacquot, Paris, 1955, pp. 197–200; see Woodfill, *op. cit.*, chapter VIII.

[79] Accounts of the diplomat and poet Sir Thomas Chaloner (1521–1565), in Woodfill, *op. cit.*, p. 256: 'Jan. 1552: Paid for five sets of books of Italian music, 7s. Given to a Fleming musician who teaches my daughter for song books Italian in four parts, 10s.'

[80] *Ibid.*, pp. 272–3.

[81] *Ibid.*, p. 269.

[82] Discussed *ibid.*, chapter IX; Nan Cooke Carpenter, *Music in the Medieval and Renaissance Universities*, Norman, Okla., 1958, pp. 343–5.

[83] Roger Archam, *The Scholemaster*, ed. Edward Arber, London, 1870, p. 64.

[84] Cited in Woodfill, *op. cit.*, pp. 214–15.

[85] Peacham, *The Complete Gentleman* [1622], ed. Virgil B. Heltzel, Ithaca, N.Y., 1962, pp. 111–12.

[86] John M. Major, *Sir Thomas Elyot and Renaissance Humanism*, Lincoln, Neb., 1964, p. 63, *q.v.*, pp. 61–4.

[87] IV, viii; *The Book of the Courtier*, p. 264. Maier, p. 455; Singleton, p. 292; Bull, p. 287.

[88] Epistle to the Right Honourable the Lord Henry Hastings, *The Book of the Courtier*, p. 3.

[89] Sir Ernest Barker, *Traditions of Civility: Eight Essays*, Cambridge, 1948, pp. 144–5.

[90] Louis Wright, *Middle-class Culture in Elizabethan England*, Chapel Hill, N.C., 1935, p. 122.

[91] William Harrison Woodward, *Studies in Education during the Age of the Renaissance, 1400–1600*, Cambridge, 1906, p. 246, *q.v.*, chapter XII.

[92] Caroline Ruutz-Reese, 'Some notes of Gabriel Harvey's in Hoby's translation of Castiglione's *Courtier* (1561)', *PMLA*, XXV, 1910, p. 635: 'G.H. 1580'. Harvey (1550–1630/1) was interested in the etiquette and duty of a courtier, shown in his library titles, which included Castiglione in Italian, Latin and English; see Virginia F. Stern, 'The *Bibliotheca* of Gabriel Harvey', *Renaissance Quarterly*, XXV, 1972, pp. 12, 23–4.

[93] I, xlvii: Maier, p. 170; *cf. Merchant of Venice*, V, i, 83; see Sternfeld, *op. cit.*, pp. 200–202, 235–41.

[94] 'Argutae resonas citharae praetendere chordas/Novit, et aonia concrepuisse lyra'; the epitaph was probably composed after 1599.

[95] I, xlvii; Maier, p. 169; Singleton, p. 74; Bull, p. 95. *Virtù* and *felicità*, both encouraged in the soul by music: two most important qualities in the Neoplatonic system; see Erich Loos, *Baldassare Castigliones 'Libro de Cortegiano'. Studien zur Tugend-auffassung des Cinquecento*, Frankfurt, 1955, pp. 80–4.

20

WHOSE 'NEW COURTIER'?

Il nuovo cortegiano is a book which, to the best of my knowledge, was printed only once, in an edition bearing the name of no author or printer, no place of publication, and no date. Consequently it has often been wrongly catalogued, and indeed it has been taken to be an incunable by Hain and several other early authorities.[1] The bibliographical description of the book is as follows:

(woodcut border) IL NOVO / CORTEG / GIANO / DE VI- / TA CA / VTA / ET / MORALE. / CON GRATIA ET PRIVILEGIO. / Nessuno ardisca stampare il p̄sente uolume / sotto le pene che ne p̄uileggii si cōtēgono. [See plate 20.1.]

Quarto. Seventy leaves, the last two blank, signed A⁸B–P⁴Q⁶. Roman type. No foliation or pagination. Several woodcut initials in the text.

Max Sander[2] was not sure whether the book was printed at Florence or at Venice, but he remarks that the initial P on leaf 2r, showing a woodcut portrait of a monk, is in the Venetian style. In this detail he is right, for the British Museum, where the book was originally catalogued with the date [1510?], has subsequently identified the Venetian printer and dated the book much later: about 1530. A study of the types and the woodcut material in the book has enabled the cataloguers to attribute the printing with certainty to the press of Joannes Tacuinus de Tridino, who printed at Venice from 1492 to 1538. There is no longer any doubt that it came from his press about 1530. The two Cambridge datings of '*c.* 1510' and '*c.* 1535' seem to be the one a lot too early and the other a little too late.[3] The imprint 'Rome, Blado, 1540' in the old Bodleian catalogue at Oxford suggested a second edition, but this turned out to be a false piece of cataloguing: the Bodleian copy of *Il nuovo cortegiano* is the same as all the others, and is merely bound first before another book with the Blado imprint.[4] Most recently the work has been entered in the new American catalogue of sixteenth-century Italian books as though there were two different editions, printed in different towns and at an interval of thirty years, but really they are both the same.[5] It must be repeated that this mysterious book, after its first anonymous appearance in print at Venice about 1530, was never reprinted.

The copies which I have hitherto located are:

 1 British Museum. 715.c.8(2).
 2 British Museum. 231.i.1(1).
 3 Cambridge University Library. Acton d. sel. 68. (Adams N 365.)
 4 Oxford, Bodleian. 4°. C. 32. Art. (1.)
 5 Dublin, Trinity College.
 6 Vatican. Capponi IV, 463.
 7 Venice, B. N. Marciana. Misc. 2689.3.
 8 Florence, B. Riccardiana. N.A.I. 9 (bought in 1953).
 9 Siena, B. Com. XV. E. 39 (plate 20.1).
10 Modena, B. Estense.
11 Rome, B. Univ. Alessandrina. E.F. 23. f. 2ª.
12 Chicago, Newberry Library. Case Y 712. s 262.
13 Philadelphia, University of Pennsylvania Library.

Of these thirteen copies I have personally examined Nos. 1, 2, 3, 4, 8 and 11, and find them to be typographically identical.

CONTENTS

So much for the bibliography of the book. When we look into its contents we find that the authors most frequently quoted are Aristotle, Plato, Plutarch, Theophrastus, Marcus Varro, Cicero, Dante, Petrarch and Boccaccio. The Bible is rarely quoted. The chapter headings (roughly translated) are as follows:

 1 Praise of virtue, and persuading men to imitate it.
 2 On friendship.
 3 On love.
 4 On observation in love.
 5 On modesty.
 6 On providence against fortune.
 7 On patience against fortune.
 8 On honour.
 9 Of corrupt truth and faith.
10 On liberty.
11 On riches and avarice.
12 On the education of the young.
13 On the examination of other men's inner concepts.
14 On commiseration with the afflicted.
15 On divine providence.
16 On the immortality of the soul.
17 On diversion from evil.
18 On the militia.
19 Equity pertaining to judges.
20 Considerations befitting a minister in his own country.
21 Admonition to the Prince or 'Re novello'.
22 Persuasion to the religious man.
23 Memorial to the Pope.
24 Whether through corrupt prelates the Church becomes corrupt, and whether it is right for their subjects to correct these prelates.
25 Doubt whether the lord is more subject than the vassal, or the vassal than the lord.
26 Of the smallness of the world, and of the greatness of men's avarice.

27 What is real life, and what is the highest good on earth, and at the same time the
   way to achieve them.

We have here, then, a general treatise on the philosophy of life, touching
all its major aspects. Although the book is entitled *The New Courtier*, it is in no
sense a treatise on the behaviour of the ideal courtier as conceived by
Castiglione. It does not deal with Renaissance court life, yet by its very title
it seems to remind us in a vague way of Castiglione, and in its mention of the
Prince or 'Re Novello' of Machiavelli too. What can be said of its authorship?

For well over two centuries this strange book has been ascribed to no less an
author than Fra Girolamo Savonarola. The principal authorities who have
attributed it to his pen are:

1 *Catalogo della Libreria Capponi* (i.e. Marchese Alessandro Gregorio Capponi),
  Roma, 1747, p. 344.
2 J. N. C. M. Denis, *Annalium typographicorum V. Cl. Michaelis Maittaire
  supplementum*, Viennae, 1789, p. 659, No. 5852.
3 G. W. Panzer, *Annales typographici*, vol. 4, Norimbergae, 1796, p. 190,
  No. 1105.
4 L. Hain, *Repertorium bibliographicum*, vol. 2, pt. 2, Stuttgartiae et Lutetiae
  Parisiorum, 1838, No. 14472.
5 *Catalogo dei libri posseduti da Charles Fairfax Murray*, pt. 1, Londra, 1899, p.
  354, No. 2096. ('Attribuita a Savonarola', suggesting some doubt.)
6 Virgil B. Heltzel, *A Check List of Courtesy Books in the Newberry Library*,
  Chicago, 1942, p. 117, No. 1272. ('Florence? 1500?').
7 Max Sander, *Le Livre à figures italien depuis 1467 jusqu'à 1530*, III, Milan,
  1942, No. 6798 (entered under Savonarola with a query).

In addition the book was attributed to Savonarola by the author of the
Italian dictionary of anonymous works, Gaetano Melzi, and Sander remarks:

M. Melzi, vol. II, p. 259, attribue ce livre à Savonarole, peut-être parce qu'il contient
quelques mots de reproches adressés au pape et aux cardinaux. D'autre part le style
est bien loin de ressembler à celui de Fra Girolamo ou même à celui d'un moine
quelconque. L'auteur anonyme ne cite presque jamais un passage biblique, mais
bien des fois les sages et les héros de l'antiquité, puis Dante et Pétrarque, il parle de
la morale chrétienne comme d'une chose assez reccommandable . . .

This is quite true, and I agree with Sander; but one suspects that Melzi, who
was writing in 1852, entered the work under Savonarola's name not so much
because it contains words of reproach addressed to Pope and cardinals as
because he was merely copying previous authorities, especially Hain and
Panzer. Melzi had in all probability never read this book. But an attribution
of an anonymous book to a famous author dies hard, and to this day we find
the *Nuovo cortegiano* entered in the catalogue of printed books at the Vatican
not under the anonymous heading but directly under Savonarola and nowhere else.

It seems to me that few authors are less likely to have written *Il nuovo
cortegiano* than Fra Girolamo Savonarola. Not only are Sander's objections
quite valid, but we must remember the biographical facts. Savonarola was

burned at the stake in Florence in May 1498. He had never lived in Venice. Is it likely that an unknown work of his would have been found in manuscript and printed in Venice over thirty years after his death in Florence? Is it likely that Savonarola would have written a book on the subject of our *New Courtier*, and have made scarcely a reference to the Bible? Thirdly, I can find no mention of this book anywhere in the collected editions of Savonarola's writings, nor in the most reliable biographies or bibliographies of him. Even the Marquis Ridolfi never mentions it. Clearly no one among the many reputable authorities on the life and works of the Friar from Ferrara has ever considered the *Nuovo cortegiano*. There seems to be no means of knowing how or why the attribution to Savonarola ever arose in the first place—and I have traced it back at least as far as 1747.

Who, then, is the author of the *Nuovo cortegiano*? More than twelve years ago, when helping to work on the British Museum's *Short-title Catalogue of Italian Books, 1465–1600* (published in 1958), I saw that this book was stated to be 'by G. Savonarola'. I doubted it very much, and discussed the matter with more than one Professor of Italian. I was given the information that the book *might possibly* have been the work of Mario Equicola. This explains why I added the note[6] 'Not by Savonarola. Possibly by M. Equicola.'

It was Domenico Santoro, the future biographer of Equicola, who in 1888 first discovered a copy of the *Nuovo cortegiano* in the Biblioteca Comunale of Siena and reported it in a Sunday paper which I have been unable to consult.[7] On the title page of this copy was written in 'an old hand' (sixteenth-century?) the note 'di Mario Equicola', and below the subtitle, possibly in another hand, 'quello che ha fatto della Natura d'Amore'. Santoro accepted this attribution of authorship without question, so that when, two years later, in 1890, he published his 'Appunti su Mario Equicola'[8] he included the work among the genuine productions of Equicola and said no more about it. Two small observations should, however, be made here concerning Santoro's discovery. The first is that he believed the Siena copy to be unique; indeed, in his article of 1890 he writes, 'è unicamente nella comunale di Siena'. He had therefore not looked for it elsewhere; otherwise he would surely have traced at least one of the copies which we know to be in Venice, Modena and Rome. The second point is that Santoro was never aware that the book had been attributed to Savonarola, and he would now be disappointed if he knew that it has continued to be so attributed in the twentieth century, and that his own attribution to Equicola has gone virtually unheeded.

In 1906 Santoro published his definitive biography of Equicola, which has now become quite a rare book.[9] In it he devotes a short chapter to the *Nuovo cortegiano*, never considering the possibility that the book might *not* be by Equicola. He writes:

L'unico esemplare a me noto è privo di qualsiasi indicazione tipografica, e non reca a stampa il nome dell'autore: soltanto dopo le parole *Il Novo Cortegiano*, una mano non moderna ha aggiunto: 'di Mario Equicola', e, dopo il secondo titolo, a maggior chiarimento: 'quello che ha fatto della Natura d'Amore'.[10] [See plate 20.1.]

Commenting on the possible reason for the book's anonymous appearance, Santoro says:

Siamo quindi davanti a uno dei più acerbi frutti del suo ingegno, maturato forse prima della sua dimora a Ferrara [i.e. 1497]; del che potrebbe anche persuaderci l'insolita mancanza del nome e di qualsiasi lettera dedicatoria.[11]

In support of the manuscript note in the Siena copy Santoro observes that Equicola, in the first edition of his *Libro de natura de amore* (which was printed by Lorenzo Lorio de Portes at Venice on 23 June 1525, only one month before Equicola's death at Mantua), writes:

Altre uolte scrissi un piccolo uolume, ilqual si expose al grido del uulgo & maledicentia de inuidi, preponendo al paterno nido il publico: Iui disputamo quali habiano ad essere le parti di colui, ilqual di bon cortigiano po meritar il nome: Noi in quel nostro libretto concludemo la modestia, la mansuetudine, & urbanita essere le prime uirtu chel cortigiano ornano.[12]

Santoro concludes that the *Natura de amore* and the *Nuovo cortegiano* were both written in the same period, between 1490 and 1510. As we have seen, they were both printed for the first time considerably later, the one in 1525 and the other about 1530, both at Venice. If they were both the work of Equicola, then it is obvious that the *Nuovo cortegiano* is the earlier of the two in order of composition, possibly by as much as fifteen years. At first I thought that the *Nuovo cortegiano* was unlikely to have been written by Equicola, simply on account of its title: I believed that it was called *Nuovo* to distinguish it from the *Cortegiano* which was already in existence, that is to say, the work by Count Baldassare Castiglione, which was printed for the first time by the Aldine Press in April 1528, nearly three years after Equicola's death. It is true that Castiglione had composed his *Cortegiano* as early as about 1514 and that it had circulated in manuscript for some years before being published. It now seems that the *Nuovo cortegiano*, if indeed it is by Equicola, was written several years before Castiglione wrote his famous treatise; and in this case the word *Nuovo* in the title does not bear the same significance which I at first attached to it.

Contrasting the two works, Santoro remarks:

. . . il *Novo Cortegiano* è un grave trattato di filosofia practica; il Cortegiano invece è, come dicono, un libro vissuto: ha forma storico-dialogica, ed è avvivato di aneddoti, di descrizioni, di svariati particolari che ritraggono gli splendori della Corte di Urbino.[13]

It should be added that Vittorio Cian in one of his last books took it for granted that the *Nuovo cortegiano* was the work of Equicola. He did not even mention the fact that the work was anonymous.[14] Can we be sure, then, that the *Nuovo cortegiano* was written by Mario Equicola? We cannot: but he is the most likely candidate known to us, and no other candidate with a stronger claim to the authorship is ever likely to present himself. The positive evidence is the early manuscript note on the copy at Siena, and the passage in Equicola's own *Libro de natura de amore*, which seems (but only seems) to refer to the *Nuovo cortegiano*. But the crucial last sentence of this passage—'Noi in quel nostro libretto concludemo la modestia, la mansuetudine, & urbanita essere le prime uirtu chel cortegiano ornano'—is not exactly borne out in the *Nuovo cortegiano* itself, for in this book I do not find the exact words *mansuetudine* and *urbanita* used in the summing-up or concluding chapter, or even else-where. It is true that there is a chapter 'De modestia', but these three qualities are not directly ascribed to the ideal courtier. In fact, as we have seen, the book is not really about the ideal courtier at all, as Castiglione's book is. The *Nuovo cortegiano* remains an enigmatic, strange, mysterious composition; but we cannot do better than attribute it, with Santoro, to Mario Equicola, with some reserve.

If he wrote it about 1500 it was published posthumously some thirty years later. In that case the work which 'si expose al grido del uulgo & maledicentia de inuidi, preponendo al paterno nido il publico' was in manuscript only, just as Castiglione's work circulated in manuscript for some fourteen years before finding a printer. We must not forget, however, the possibility that those who decided to publish the *Nuovo cortegiano* after its author's death may have altered the text and may indeed have given it its present title. This we shall never know. It is to be hoped that one manuscript note on a copy of one book in Siena is the genuine solution to the problem of authorship of that curious enigma which is *Il nuovo cortegiano*.[15] If Equicola did not write it, then we are forced to conclude that he was the author of another book on the courtier which, whether published or in manuscript, has been irretrievably lost to us. A printed book on the subject would hardly be likely to have survived in no copies at all, since it belongs to neither of the two categories of early books which were often read and used out of existence —liturgical books and school grammars. If it remained in manuscript, at least two or three copies would almost certainly have survived in some university or ducal library. Therefore I believe that the *Nuovo cortegiano* as we have it is in truth the work of Mario Equicola.[16]

NOTES

[1] Since Hain had not seen a copy, he was presumably copying from Denis and Panzer. For the dates of these bibliographies see below.

[2] Max Sander, *Le Livre à figures italien depuis 1467 jusqu'à 1530*, Milan, six vols., 1942, III, No. 6798.

[3] '*Circa* 1510' in the general catalogue of Cambridge University Library, and '*c*. 1535' in H. M. Adams, *Catalogue of Books printed on the Continent of Europe, 1501–1600, in Cambridge Libraries*, Cambridge, two vols., 1967, II, No. N 365.

[4] This is the 'Angitia cortigiana, de natura del cortigiano' by Michel Angelo Biondo, completed by Antonio Blado on 16 October 1540.

[5] *Short-title Catalog of Books printed in Italy and of Books in Italian printed abroad, 1501–1600, held in selected North American Libraries*, ed. Robert G. Marshall, Boston, Mass., three vols., 1970, I, p. 469. Here the first entry, giving the imprint as [Florence? 1500?] is copied straight from Heltzel's Newberry catalogue of 1942, while the second, reporting the copy in Philadelphia, is obviously copied from the British Museum's short-title catalogue of Italian books. Seeing the two entries side by side, the editor might be expected to have guessed that they referred to one and the same edition, but he did not.

[6] British Museum, *Short-title Catalogue of Books printed in Italy ...*, London, 1958, last line on p. 753.

[7] *Fanfulla della Domenica*, XI, 1888, No. 19.

[8] *Giornale storico della letteratura italiana*, XV, 1890, pp. 402–13.

[9] D. Santoro, *Della vita e delle opere di Mario Equicola*, Chieti, 1906.

[10] *Op. cit.*, chapter XI, pp. 144–8.

[11] *Ibid.*, p. 146.

[12] Folio 166*v* (not, as Santoro says, 'p. 148*v*').

[13] *Op. cit.*, p. 147.

[14] V. Cian, *Un illustre nunzio pontifico del Rinascimento: Baldassar Castiglione*, Vatican City, 1951, Studi e testi, No. 165, p. 252. My thanks are due to Dr C. H. Clough for this reference.

[15] It is true that the copy in the Biblioteca Universitaria Alessandrina at Rome has the MS note 'Di Gir. Savonarola' written on a flyleaf, but this seems to belong to about the year 1800 and is not authoritative. It is clearly copied from one of the earliest bibliographies, which, as we have seen, are all wrong in their ascription; and in any case this note is perhaps 250 years later in date of writing than that in the copy at Siena.

Cf. Lathrop C. Harper, *Catalogue* 204, New York, 1971, p. 102, No. 175, where a copy of this book was offered for $285 with the note 'The ascription of this "Novo Cortegiano" to Savonarola is very doubtful and we don't know whether there exists a recent study on this subject. It contains references to Dante, Petrarch, Boccaccio, treats honor, modesty, love, education of the young, admonitions to princes, kings, popes, etc.' Here is yet another indication that the attribution to Mario Equicola has never gained the recognition which it deserves.

[16] L. Savino, 'Un precedente del "Cortegiano"', *Rassegna critica della letteratura italiana*, XV, 1910, pp. 102–12, suggests that the *Nuovo cortegiano* was later incorporated in the *Libro de natura de amore*, and takes for granted that Mario Equicola is the author.

C. P. BRAND   *University of Edinburgh*

21

ARIOSTO'S CONTINUATION
OF THE *ORLANDO INNAMORATO*

ARIOSTO'S DECISION to continue Boiardo's unfinished poem was, of course, influenced by the continuing popularity of Boiardo's poem and by an extensive contemporary curiosity about the outcome of the various adventures left incomplete in the *Innamorato*. That Ariosto should have adopted Boiardo's unfinished material as the basis of the *Furioso* must have seriously affected the composition of his poem; he takes over not merely Boiardo's characters but the particular situations and adventures in which they are individually engaged, and he completes these and fits them into his narrative. The full extent of Ariosto's relationship to Boiardo and the influence of the latter on the genesis of the *Furioso* have not, I think, been adequately examined, and I propose in this article to consider Ariosto's specific treatment of Boiardo's unfinished episodes and to investigate their effect on the structure of the *Furioso*.[1]

Ariosto does not, of course, begin exactly where Boiardo left off. The *Furioso* opens with the flight of Angelica following the defeat of the Christian army at Montalbano. This battle begins in the *Innamorato* (II, xxiii) where Carlomagno enlists the active support of both Orlando and Rinaldo by his pledge to each of them not to hand her over to the other. The battle is then left on one side while Boiardo pursues various other episodes and he does not return to it until III, iv, where the Christians are defeated and retreat to Paris. It is at this point that Ariosto begins the *Furioso*, with Angelica's flight from Duke Namo, in whose custody Carlomagno had placed her for the duration of the battle. Boiardo's narrative had, however, continued well past this point in time. In the final cantos of book III he pursues various other characters affected by the battle and carries the war on to a fierce conflict beneath the walls of Paris in which a sudden storm causes the pagans to withdraw. Ariosto does not reach this point in Boiardo's action until VIII, 69 of the *Furioso* where he reports the storm and the pagan retreat.

The reason for this, seemingly, is that although Boiardo has carried on the war to Paris he has not yet told us what has become of some of his leading characters after the Montalbano battle We know that Orlando and

Bradamante have gone on to Paris (III, viii, 18), that Ruggiero and Gradasso are being taken by a dwarf to avenge a 'fellonia' (III, vii, 38), and that Bradamante, having lost track of Ruggiero, has met Fiordispina (III, viii, 64). But we have had no further news of Angelica or of Rinaldo. If Ariosto chooses to begin this poem with Angelica, therefore, rather than, say, Orlando, or Ruggiero, or Bradamante, he has good reason for doing so in view of Boiardo's narrative situation. He goes back, as Boiardo presumably would have had to do eventually, to the characters who have been left behind. However, in choosing to open his narrative with the adventures of Angelica, Ariosto carries his readers back, not merely to the situation at the end of book III of the *Innamorato*, where she had been temporarily forgotten, but also to a parallel situation at the very beginning of the *Innamorato* where Angelica is fleeing from her various admirers, Christian and pagan:

> Or son tre gran campioni alla ventura:
> Lasciali andar, che bei fati farano;
> Rainaldo e Orlando, ch'è di tanta altura,
> E Feraguto, fior d'ogni pagano. [I, ii, 29]

Ferraù's presence in particular recalls the opening of the *Innamorato*. Feraguto had been left by Boiardo in II, xxxi, 14, trying to recover his helmet from where it had fallen into the water, an incident Boiardo clearly intended to relate (as Ariosto did subsequently) to his unfulfilled promise to the dying Argalia to return his helmet to the water where his body and the rest of his arms lie. However, Feraguto has a very small part in the *Innamorato* and there was no need for Ariosto to complete this episode so soon. That he did so was surely in conscious recollection of Boiardo's opening cantos. Ariosto also repeats, with variations, the discussion by the rival combatants, at the beginning of the *Innamorato* (I, iii, 79) as to the desirability of pursuing the escaping Angelica before continuing their fight for her. The effect, then, of Ariosto's opening canto for his contemporary readers must have been to recall the opening of the *Innamorato*, the pursuit of Angelica. It was, no doubt, a happy memory for them and a promising augury of coming enjoyment. But more than that, it brings the wheel of the beloved stories full circle—after all these adventures we are back where we started, with the eternal pursuit of beauty, eternally elusive.

Ariosto then turns to Bradamante. There was no compelling need to do so in respect of Boiardo's poem. On the contrary, we had news of Bradamante in the penultimate stanza of the *Innamorato*, where we found her in Fiordispina's company—and the outcome of this particular incident is not revealed until canto xxv of the *Furioso*. The reason for her early entry here is surely that Ariosto wished to emphasise her role as the leading lady of his poem, and her love for Ruggiero as the origin of that union which will lead to the long line of the Estensi. So the almost immediate resumption of the story of these two characters is significant. Ruggiero does not appear until book II of the *Innamorato*, where Agramante is advised to search him out as a potential battle winner, and eventually Ruggiero is got away from his guardian's custody and recruited for Agramante's army. His significance is explained in II, xxi: he is destined to become a Christian and meet his death as a result of the treachery of the house of Maganza. But his descendants will bring new glories to Italy, being the future Estensi, Boiardo's patrons— Bradamante, Rinaldo's sister, will become his wife. All this is forecast, but Boiardo never reaches this point. The pair meet and fall in love but are then separated. Ruggiero is last reported in the *Innamorato* as going off with Gradasso and a dwarf who had asked their intervention to avenge a wrong . . .

> Quel che Rugier facesse e il re Gradasso
> Vi fia poi racontato in altra parte. (III, vii, 56]

Ariosto's resumption of this incident is involved. Boiardo's introduction was so generic that it could have led anywhere: a dwarf asks them:

> Fati vendetta di una fellonia
> Maggior del mondo e più strana nequizia. [III, vii, 38]

Ariosto treats the 'fellonia' as Atlante's seizure of his ward, Ruggiero, for his own protection, and the capture of numerous other knights and ladies to keep him company. But the capture of Ruggiero is not related directly. Bradamante meets Pinabello, who witnessed the conflict of a knight on a hippogriph with Ruggiero and Gradasso, the outcome of which he failed to see. Bradamante is thus drawn to the unknown knight's castle in search of her lover and herself overcomes Atlante, who is forced to release Ruggiero. Ariosto's approach reveals a characteristic distinction between the two poets' narrative methods: Boiardo's normal narration in his own words, and Ariosto's use of direct speech. Much of the action of the *Furioso* occurs off-stage and is reported not by the author but by an eye-witness or a participant. The effect is to present action from a particular point of view, in this case in a sort of dual perspective: the duel between Ruggiero and the knight on the hippogriph is seen through Pinabello's eyes, but *his* narrative is in turn addressed to Bradamante, whose reactions we follow. So the reader's sympathy is enlisted for Bradamante in her quest for her lost lover, and our interest is aroused in Ruggiero, whom we shall meet later.

Boiardo promises at the beginning of book III that he will describe, Ruggiero's actions up to his death by treachery. This was not, of course, fulfilled by Ariosto, who gets no further than Ruggiero's marriage to Bradamante; it is interesting to speculate what sort of poem we might have had if Ariosto had in fact made Ruggiero's death the terminating point of his poem. This was in many ways Ariosto's most significant decision in his resumption of Boiardo's poem. The encomiastic note (the tribute to the Estensi) is, I think, highlighted by his concentration on the marriage rather than the full career of Ruggiero, and structurally the poem gains much by the balancing of Orlando's ill conceived and unsuccessful passion for Angelica with the virtuous and ultimately triumphant love of Ruggiero and Brada- mante. But his failure to carry through Boiardo's promise seems to have caused him considerable anxiety. The *Cinque Canti* may well have been motivated by the sense that the *Furioso* was incomplete in respect of the Ruggiero story, which is there carried on beyond the wedding with a purer, nobler, worthier Ruggiero, moving, one assumes, to a tragic death worthy of the Estensi. Ariosto's hesitations over the continuation of the 1521 edition were certainly closely connected with the role of Ruggiero.

The structure of Ariosto's opening cantos is therefore largely determined by his general decision to continue Boiardo's unfinished poem, and particularly by his acceptance of the three main strands outlined by Boiardo at the beginning of book III. So he begins with Angelica and then turns to Bradamante and Ruggiero. This still leaves two major characters of whom we have had no news since book II of the *Innamorato*—one is Rinaldo, left by Boiardo after the battle of Montalbano chasing his horse, Baiardo, with the hint of a happy encounter ahead (III, iv, 40)—which Ariosto gives us in his meeting with Angelica. So Rinaldo is introduced briefly in cantos I and II of the *Furioso*, following Angelica, but is then given a major role in cantos IV, V and VI, with his mission to Britain and the Ginevra episode. Then in canto VI Ariosto turns to Astolfo, who had been left by Boiardo departing on the whale's back for Alcina's island: 'Di lui poi molte cose avremo a dire' (II, xiv, 8)—a promise Boiardo never fulfils. So Ariosto gives Ruggiero the task of overcoming Alcina and freeing the captive Astolfo.

By canto VIII, therefore, Ariosto has brought all his major figures into the narrative up to the point in time at which Boiardo left the action of the *Innamorato*—that is, up to the siege of Paris—and in VII, 69–71, he refers to the storm that forced the pagans to withdraw, which Boiardo had reported in III, viii, 51–2. The war henceforth will occupy an important place in the narrative, parallel in effect to that of Orlando's madness and Ruggiero and Bradamante's courtship. Ariosto's explicit classification of his material in his opening stanzas is thus closely in line with Boiardo's *proemio* to canto i of book III:

> Le gran battaglie e il trïomfale onore
> Vi contaró di Carlo, re di Franza,
> E le prodezze fatte per amore
> Dal conte Orlando, e sua strema possanza;
> Come Rugier, che fu nel mondo un fiore,
> Fosse tradito. . . .   [III, i, 3]

What Boiardo promises optimistically and never completes Ariosto takes seriously and brings (almost) to a conclusion. Above all, he succeeds in binding his different strands into a coherent narrative—which Boiardo doesn't seem able, or to care, to do. Orlando has to be cured before the Christians can defeat their opponents, and the war must be won before Ruggiero can marry Bradamante. So in canto VIII of the *Furioso* the war is resumed and Orlando introduced—a late entry for the titular hero, motivated by the need to bring the other characters up to the point in time that Orlando had already reached in the *Innamorato* (III, viii).

The genesis of the first eight cantos is therefore largely determined by Boiardo's precedent. Thereafter Ariosto was free to follow his own inclinations. (It is interesting to note that the first of the 1532 additions, the Olimpia story, begins in canto IX, the earliest point at which Ariosto could conveniently make any insertion into his narrative.) Even at this point, however,

Ariosto had on his hands five further episodes left unfinished by Boiardo, all of which he is careful to complete. He clearly considers these less urgent and is prepared to insert them in his narrative as and when he finds it convenient. They occur in cantos XIV, XV, XVII and XXV respectively.

The first of these, concerning Mandricardo and Doralice, appears in canto XIV. Mandricardo was prominent in book III of the *Innamorato*, which opens with an account of his arrival in France to avenge the death of his father, Agricane, killed by Orlando; he also is pledged not to wear a sword until he has won Orlando's Durindana. He was left by Boiardo at the siege of Paris, fretting at being excluded by lot from an expedition to find Orlando (III, vii, 5; III, viii, 47). Ariosto takes him up at this point (XIV, 30) and follows through his pursuit of Orlando until his death at Ruggiero's hands in canto XXX. In this Mandricardo is true to his Boiardesque origins, but the interest of his appearance in canto XIV lies in his seizure of Doralice, the daughter of the king of Granada, who has been promised in marriage to Rodomonte. Doralice is only briefly introduced by Boiardo as 'da Rodomonte più che il core amata' (II, vii, 28; xxiii, 12), but in the *Furioso* she is developed as an amusing example of female flexibility, accepting and coming to love the violent Mandricardo in preference to her fiancé, the mighty Rodomonte. The story is inserted at this point almost certainly as a foil to the Isabella–Zerbino episode, begun in the previous canto. Isabella is faithful to her beloved Zerbino through all adversity, and when he is killed she contrives her own death. Doralice has no compunction about abandoning Rodomonte, and when Mandricardo is killed she casts longing eyes on Ruggiero.

> . . . per non si veder priva d'amore,
> avria potuto in Ruggier porre il core.
> Per lei buono era vivo Mandricardo:
> ma che ne volea far dopo la morte? [xxx, 72–3]

In canto XV Ariosto turns to another unfinished episode, concerning Orrilo, the enchanted knight whom Boiardo described as terrifying all who came near him with his crocodile and his grim trick of reuniting any severed portions of his body. Grifone and Aquilante had been left in the *Innamorato* in despairing conflict with Orrilo when a knight arrives with a giant he has on a chain (III, iii, 22). Ariosto takes up both these cues. He equates the giant with another such creature described by Boiardo (I, v, 80–2), who used a net to trap his victims, and the conquering knight with Astolfo. Astolfo then comes to the aid of Grifone and Aquilante, killing Orrilo by cutting the one fatal hair on his head. It is noteworthy here how Ariosto succinctly recapitulates the antecedents of his tale without referring directly to the *Innamorato*. We have no special introduction to Grifone and Aquilante.

> Questi erano i due figli d'Oliviero,
> Grifone il bianco et Aquilante il nero [xv, 67]

They are accompanied by two lady guardians:

> Ma non bisogna in ciò ch'io mi diffonda,
> ch'a tutto il mondo è l'istoria palese;
> ben che l'autor nel padre si confonda . . . [xv, 73]

—a covert allusion to *Ugger il Danese*, to whose account of the brothers' parentage Ariosto prefers Boiardo's. Characteristic also of Ariosto's method is his use here of classical sources to complete the medieval romance material.

The resumption of the Orrigille story in the same canto is determined by the presence of Grifone, just delivered by Astolfo from Orrilo. Grifone had met the treacherous Orrigille in II, iii, of the *Innamorato*; she had already tricked the infatuated Orlando and she does so again here in favour of Grifone. We last saw her, ill, in II, xx, 7, of the *Innamorato*, where Grifone takes leave of her to go off to a tourney. Ariosto now has Grifone go in search of Orrigille, who has taken a fresh lover, the cowardly Martano, who cuts such a poor figure at the tourney in Damascus. It was hardly necessary for Ariosto to continue this story; it was not in suspense—we could assume that Grifone had forgotten Orrigille. And Ariosto does not in fact really conclude the episode, as Orrigille is left to be punished according to Lucina's decision, and we never hear what this is or what happens subsequently—Grifone, clearly, is not cured of his infatuation (*cf.* XVIII, 92). Ariosto's motive for taking up this story was clearly that it interested him as an 'exemplum amoris'—the treacherous female infatuating the worthy male: apart from this fatal flaw Grifone is a model of chivalry.

The Lucina–Norandino adventures narrated in canto XVII of the *Furioso* are related to the rescue of Lucina by Gradasso and Mandricardo in the *Innamorato* (III, 3, 22 ff). Ariosto's episode is, however, not so much a continuation as an elaboration of Boiardo's story. In the *Innamorato* the two pagans find Lucina tied to a rock and hear from her a description of the terrible blind monster that tracks down its victims by their scent. She begs them to leave her to her fate, and to inform her lover of her death but not of her whereabouts, as he would risk his life to come and find her. The monster falls down a precipice, but pursues the ship in which the pagans escape with Lucina. They are saved, however, by a storm, which lands them on the French coast. The episode is thus apparently complete, except for the reuniting of Lucina and Norandino, but this is not what Ariosto sets out to tell us. It is the precedent that we are given in the *Furioso*, the circumstances in which Lucina was left chained on the seashore. Ariosto describes how Grifone, Martano and Orrigille, on their arrival in Damascus (XVII, 17) find festivities in progress which they are told are to celebrate the king, Norandino's receipt of the news of Lucina's safety. The knight who explains this was himself a witness of Lucina's misfortunes, having been shut up in the monster's cave along with Lucina, Norandino and the others of their suite. He then tells a variant of the *Odyssey* story. Norandino and the others escaped in goat skins, smeared with fat, but Lucina was caught by the monster and chained up as a punishment. The others fled, but Norandino continued to expose himself to danger, going in and out of the monster's cave daily so as to be as near his beloved Lucina. When she was rescued by Mandricardo, Norandino was shut up in the cave and so lost track of her, and then searched for her for three months before eventually learning of her whereabouts.

This is an interesting example of Ariosto's original use of a Boiardo story.

Ariosto grafts the classical legend, duly modified, on to Boiardo's original, which provides only the barest hint for this particular development (the blind monster itself). The two stories do not fit very well (a rare occurrence): in Boiardo's account Norandino is apparently ignorant of Lucina's treatment (Mandricardo and Gradasso are begged not to tell him), whereas in the *Furioso* he stays with her up to the time of her escape; indeed, in the *Innamorato* Norandino plays no part in this episode at all. And Boiardo's Lucina fears she will be devoured by the Orc, whereas it is known in the *Furioso* that the monster never eats women. Clearly Ariosto was attracted by the classical legend, which he saw he could use as an *exemplum* of loving constancy, and he inserted it at this point partially at least as a foil to the Orrigille–Martano–Grifone episode which follows immediately in the same canto. One lover's bravery is contrasted with the other's cowardice—and Lucina is subsequently deputed to decide Orrigille's punishment. Characteristically Ariosto shows no interest in describing Lucina's rescue, for which the reader of the *Furioso* is fairly agog after all the excitement of Norandino's attempt:

> ... a capitar venne a quel sasso
> il figlio d'Agricane e 'l re Gradasso.
>
> Dove con loro audacia tanto fenno,
> che liberaron la bella Lucina;
> ben che vi fu aventura più che senno. .... [xvii, 62–3]

—a tantalising allusion for most modern readers but transparent to Ariosto's contemporaries familiar with the *Innamorato*.

The last of Boiardo's unfinished stories to be completed by Ariosto is that concerning Bradamante and Fiordispina, begun by Boiardo at the end of his penultimate canto. Bradamante, with hair cut short because of a wound, is mistaken by Fiordispina for a man. Burning with desire, Fiordispina contrives to be alone with Bradamante, and we are left with the hint at the very end of the *Innamorato*:

> L'una de l'altra accesa è nel disio,
> Quel che li manca, ben sapre' dir io. [iii, ix, 25]

Ariosto completes the story in canto xxv, preparing the way in canto xxii, where Ruggiero and Bradamante hear of the imminent burning of a youth who has disguised himself as a woman in order to seduce a princess. They go off to save him but are separated and eventually it is Ruggiero who liberates the youth, whom he takes at first for Bradamante. It is in fact Bradamante's brother, Ricciardetto, who then tells Ruggiero his tale: how he heard from his sister of Fiordispina's passion for her, and so exploited his likeness to her, dressing in her clothes to gain access to Fiordispina's bed, thus satisfying a long-suppressed love he had conceived for her. It is an ingenious, wittily told, bawdy story, the only love story in the *Furioso* not clearly related to some moral lesson, and it is in this sense somewhat out of character. Indeed, it seems strange that the chaste Bradamante should so promptly judge this deceitful lover to be worthy of her intervention. Its inclusion is surely evidence of Ariosto's concern to complete all Boiardo's unfinished tales, and although one could argue that he might have contrived a different ending for it, this ending is, I think, not only consonant with Boiardo's hint in canto ix but very close in spirit to many of Boiardo's stories. But what is its function precisely at this point in the poem? It is really a self-sufficient episode, although loosely connected to the main action by the intervention of Bradamante and Ruggiero; but we hear no more of Fiordispina after this, and Ricciardetto apparently goes his own way, regardless of her feelings. It serves, I think, to lighten the tone of the poem, following the sad death of Zerbino in the previous canto; and it prepares the way, perhaps, for the only other bawdy tale, three cantos later, the Fiammetta story, which *is* closely related to a moral lesson.

Noteworthy, I think, in this survey of Ariosto's formal debt to Boiardo is the extraordinary thoroughness with which he continues the intricate web of Boiardo's action. Rarely is there any conflict between the two narratives: everyone is in his right place, going about his appointed business, and no one is forgotten. It seems remarkable that Ariosto should have picked up so many obscure clues and hints. Clearly he took the continuation of the *Innamorato* very seriously. Yet in spite of this careful integration of his narrative with that of his predecessor he at no point refers explicitly to the *Innamorato* or acknowledges his debt to his predecessor—not even in his *proemi*, where allusions to the Ferrarese court are so frequent. In taking up each unfinished tale Ariosto briefly resumes Boiardo's material, advertising it not as a summary of another poet's narrative but as his own account of the characters' situations: of Bradamante,

> La donna amata fu da un cavaliero
> che d'Africa passò col re Agramante. . . .   [II, 32,]

of the battle,

> Contrari ai voti poi furo i successi;
> ch'in fuga andò la gente battezzata.   [I, 9]

The *Furioso* is indeed, therefore, a continuation of another work, but it remains autonomous—in spite of the criticisms of neo-Aristotelian theorists who complained of its incomplete character. We have the illusion that we are witnesses in the *Furioso* to only a brief phase in the careers of knights and ladies who were alive and busy before we met them in this poem, and who will go on living after the poem ends. The *résumé* of Boiardo's material contributes to this illusion at one end; and at the other Ariosto himself does so. None of the paladins has retired and put away his armour: Orlando and Rinaldo are still in their prime, and Ruggiero, we know, is destined to a treacherous death. And many a minor character could be resuscitated if Ariosto or any of his fellow poets chose to do so—as, of course, they did. What happened to Angelica and Medoro in Cathay? What became of Fiordispina, or Orrigille? How did Gabrina and Odorico meet the ends that Ariosto only hints at? The *Furioso* is in fact open at both ends and reflects in this way the continuum of life. It does not rise to a grandiose finale, like the *Liberata*: there are various climaxes which succeed each other throughout the poem —the departure of Angelica and Medoro, the madness and cure of Orlando, the completion of the war, the marriage of Bradamante and Ruggiero, and even this is followed by another duel and the death of Rodomonte.

Interesting too is Ariosto's narrative technique in his continuation of these tales. As we have seen in the Bradamante–Atlante encounter, his use of direct speech gives a depth to stories which are little more than a chain of lively incidents in the *Innamorato*. This applies to the Fiordispina story, told by Ricciardetto from his own angle; to Astolfo's experiences with Alcina, described by Astolfo himself; and to the Norandino episode, narrated by one of the prisoners in the cave. The direct speech also helps to link the episodes with the main action in that it is addressed normally to one of the major characters, who is thus involved in the adventures of the subsidiary figures, sometimes intervening actively on their behalf, sometimes listening sympathetically and pondering on the relevance of these happenings to his own experience. So Ariosto tends to group a succession of separate incidents around one leading character: Angelica (cantos I–II), Bradamante (cantos II–IV), Rinaldo (cantos IV–VI), etc.

Characteristic too is Ariosto's relation of his borrowed material to a scheme of moral exemplification. All these unfinished tales, with the exception of that concerning Fiordispina, are fitted into a pattern of morally relevant relationships between men and women—Angelica–Rinaldo, Bradamante–Ruggiero, Astolfo–Alcina, Mandricardo–Doralice, etc. What Boiardo begins as a carefree entertainment Ariosto integrates into his vision of human nature. Boiardo's poem is relevant to him not merely as a mine of exploitable narrative action but as part of his subject itself, as a duplicate on an imaginative plane of human conduct in general, which the poet underlines by his skilful reinterpretation.

NOTE

[1] I have made frequent use of the commentary of L. Caretti in his edition of L. Ariosto, *Orlando Furioso* (*Letteratura Italiana, Storia e testi*), XIX, XX, Milan, 1963, and consulted other commentaries, notably that of P. Papini, Florence, 1903, and likewise P. Rajna's *Fonti dell' 'Orlando Furioso'*, Florence, 1900. Quotations of Boiardo are from the edition of his *Innamorato* by A. Scaglione, Turin, 1966. I know of no recent studies bearing directly on this article, although many critical works make interesting comparisons between the two poets, particularly in relation to language, style and narrative technique: among the most stimulating of these I have found R. Battaglia, 'L'Ariosto e la critica idealistica', *Rinascita*, VII, 1950, pp. 141–50; L. Caretti, 'Introduzione all'Ariosto', *Filologia e critica*, Naples, 1955, pp. 46–52, and his *Ariosto e Tasso*, Turin, 1961; E. Saccone, 'Note ariostesche', *Annali della Scuola Normale Superiore di Pisa*, second series, XXVIII, 1959, pp. 193–242; R. M. Durling, *The Figure of the Poet in the Renaissance Epic*, Cambridge, Mass., 1965.

JOHN SPARROW   *All Souls College, Oxford*

22

RENAISSANCE LATIN POETRY: SOME SIXTEENTH-CENTURY ITALIAN ANTHOLOGIES

THE PURPOSE OF this paper is to provide a survey, of necessity brief and summary, of a hitherto almost uncharted province in the domain of Renaissance literature:[1] the transmission and popularisation, through printed collections, of the Latin verse written by Italians. I limit my range to books published in the Cinquecento. Before that, manuscript collections of such verse were common enough, and they continued to be produced and circulated throughout the century; but they did not begin to emerge in print, side by side with books containing the Latin poetry of a single author, until its second and third quarters, when their frequency and popularity attested— and perhaps encouraged—the fecundity with which Latin verse was produced by the educated men of the time. The fashion for such printed collections persisted into the seventeenth century and spread over Europe, and I have extended my survey to cover one or two outstanding later examples.

To do full justice to this subject one would have to be both a historian and a bibliographer, with a thorough knowledge of the social and literary background; one might then provide a full catalogue of books of this kind, an account of their relation to their counterparts in the vernacular, and an assessment of their significance in the literature and life of the time. Limitations of space and knowledge compel me to confine myself to indicating the main features, as it were, of the landscape; to suggesting a rough classification of species within the genus; and to describing in some detail one or two of the more important examples in each class. This may at least encourage further research by bibliographers and literary historians.

From the wide range of anthologies, miscellanies, collections, *Flores* and the like that were published during the period I have singled out four types, which may be roughly classified as follows:

1 *Occasional collections,* i.e. collections consisting entirely, or in the main, of poems written for a special occasion or celebrating a particular event. Of these *Coryciana,* edited by Blosius Palladius and published by Ludovico degli Arrighi in 1524, may be taken as the prototype; the class also includes

the innumerable collections of nuptial and funerary verses produced throughout the sixteenth century and for at least a century and a half thereafter.

2 *Author collections*, i.e. books containing the Latin verse of a few authors. In most cases the publisher chooses, say, half a dozen authors who have not written a great deal of Latin verse, and prints what they have written in its entirety, or almost its entirety. The prototype in this class is *Carmina Quinque Illustrium Poetarum*, published in Venice in 1548 by Vincenzo Valgrisi. This collection was reprinted three times, and served as a model which was copied by publishers, not only in Italy, during the next 200 years.

3 *Author anthologies*. The books I would include in this category vary widely in size and scope, in the kinds of public they were intended for and in the principles on which their contents were selected. I call them 'anthologies' to indicate that they contain selections from, rather than collections of, the works of the authors represented, and I prefix the epithet 'author-' because usually the editor, though he does not attempt to give a representative selection from each of his authors, groups together the poems of each of them and evidently looks upon the book as an anthology of poets (so to speak) rather than an anthology of poems.

4 *National collections*. Most of the Latin verse anthologies published in Italy in the sixteenth century consisted entirely or almost entirely of poems by Italian authors, but none of them claimed to be comprehensive or to represent the achievement of the poets of Italy. No doubt there is a social, almost a political, explanation of this fact. While there was within Italy plenty of what some people today would call 'cultural exchange'—men of letters, clerics, diplomatists and mercenaries (whether scholars or soldiers) moved freely from one Italian town or court or university to another— there was, at least in the eyes of those who looked upon the scene from within, no national unity; and this may help us to understand why the first attempts to produce anthologies representative of the country as a whole should have been made by foreigners or Italians resident abroad. No 'national' collection worthy of the name appeared, so far as I know, in the first half of the century, and the first noteworthy effort to produce one—the *Carmina Illustrium Poetarum Italorum* (two volumes, 1576, 1577) of Giovanni Matteo Toscano—was made in Paris by an Italian expatriate.

Toscano's collection was made the basis of a more ambitious undertaking, which comprised some 200 poets 'huius superiorisque aevi', by Jan Gruter at the beginning of the seventeenth century; and, rather more than a hundred years later, the great Florentine Corpus (1719–26) carried the work down to the end of the Seicento and contained selections from the work of nearly 400 Italians.

I OCCASIONAL COLLECTIONS

In 1512 Johann Goritz, a native of Luxemburg, who served six successive Popes as a protonotary apostolic, placed in the Church of S. Agostino in Rome a marble group representing the Virgin, the infant Jesus and St Anne, which he had commissioned from Andrea Sansovino.[2] Soon after the installation of the statue a number of Goritz's acquaintances affixed to boards in front of it copies of Latin verses in honour of the Virgin, her child and her mother, and in praise of the sculptor's skill and the donor's piety.[3]

On St Anne's Day (27 July) 1512 Goritz, who was an enthusiastic patron of literature, gave a special party in his gardens above the Forum of Trajan at which his friends produced poems celebrating his presentation of the statue. This entertainment became an annual event, and Goritz kept the manuscripts of the poems contributed by his guests, resisting for a decade all pleas that he should publish them. In 1524 he was sent a poem of 192 elegiac couplets, written by Francesco Arsilli, one of his regular guests, entitled *De poetis urbanis* and giving brief characterisations of the poets who attended his parties; the sender, C. Silvius Germanicus,[4] urged Goritz to publish it together with the poems occasioned by the erection of the statues and by the anniversary celebrations of that event. Goritz eventually yielded, and the resulting volume came out in the summer of 1524 with the title *Coryciana*. The book was edited by Blossius Palladius, who in a dedication to Goritz describes how it came to be published.

Coryciana is divided into three books: book I (*Epigrammata*), which occupies more than half the volume, consists chiefly of poems in praise of Sansovino's work; book II (*Hymni*) chiefly of poems addressed to St Anne; book III (*Annales*) of poems occasioned by the annual celebrations; Arsilli's poem winds up the volume.[5]

Coryciana is notable in three respects: it was the first book to be printed in Arrighi's famous sloping cursive type; it provides a uniquely comprehensive survey of the Latin poets in the Rome of Leo X; and it is one of the finest and earliest examples of an anthology consisting of poems all of which were evoked by a single theme or event. There were more than 120 contributors to the collection, among them most of the leading Latin poets of the day— Bembo, Sadoleto, Vida, Castiglione, Paolo Giovio, Valeriano, L. G. Giraldi, Franchini, Angeriano, Beroaldo junior, Giano Vitale, M. A. Casanova, Ulrich von Hutten.[6]

Coryciana was the ancestor of an innumerable host of collections, produced not only in Italy but all over Europe, containing the contributions of authors recruited to celebrate in Latin verse some particular event—a birth, a death, a wedding, a jubilee, a victory or a disaster. As time went on, other languages challenged the monopoly of Latin in this field: such collections would include, or sometimes (especially, it would seem, in France) consist entirely of, poems in the vernacular. A slender collection of *Lacrimae* mourning M. A. Colonna, who died a soldier's death in 1522, published in that year by Mazzocchi, shows the beginnings of this polyglot tendency: after Latin elegies (or epitaphs) by Vida, Giano Vitale, Fabio Vigile, Lazzaro Buonamici, Valeriano, Arsilli, M. A. Casanova, Franchini and half a dozen others it concludes with a set of Greek elegiacs by one 'Q. Laelius Maximus' and a short piece in Hebrew, attributed to 'Leo Iudeus', which was probably the work of Leone Ebreo.[7]

Among the remote descendants of this family are the volumes of *Plausus, Luctus, Epithalamia* and *Gratulationes* (mainly in Latin, but increasingly polyglot as time went by) with which the members of Oxford and Cambridge Universities greeted the coronation or decease of a monarch, his marriage, or the birth of an heir, from the reign of Elizabeth I to that of George III.

In Italy it was the literary society, the *accademia*, rather than the university, that regularly came forward with such tributes. A typical mid-sixteenth-century example is the *Tempio* raised in Rome in honour of Joanna of Aragon by the Accademia dei Dubbiosi in 1554. This took the form of a collection of adulatory verses contributed by 'tutti i più gentili Spiriti, e in tutte le lingue principale del mondo', edited by Girolamo Ruscelli and printed in Venice by Pietrasanta. The first 388 pages of the *Tempio* contain poems by 220 authors in Italian, then come 118 pages of Latin poems by some seventy authors, followed by ten pages of poems in Greek and fifteen pages of poems in Spanish. Most of the Latin contributors are nonentities of the Dubbiosi, but they include a few familiar names, e.g. G. B. Pigna, Benedetto Varchi, Quintianus Stoa, Giovanni Carga, and Giano Vitale. The poems in Greek were contributed some of them by Greeks, others by Italians; the Spanish entirely by those to whom Spanish was their native tongue.

A good example of the collection celebrating not a personal occasion but an event of national importance is the *Poemata Varia*, 'Petri Gherardii Burgensis studio et diligentia conquisita, ac disposita', published in Venice by the brothers Guerra in 1572. The poems, all of them in Latin[8] and more than 300 in number, celebrate the victory over the Turks at Lepanto in October 1571; they were written by nearly a hundred named authors[9] and thirty-five 'incerti'. Gherardi, in a dedication dated from Rome 1 June 1572, declares that he has collected the contents 'voluptatis tantum causa' and published them at the insistence of his friends. One wonders how he managed to assemble so considerable a collection and prepare it for the press in little more than six months; a lengthy list of errata betrays the haste with which he executed his task.

2 AUTHOR COLLECTIONS

In 1548 Vincenzo Valgrisi published in Venice a well printed octavo of 280 pages entitled *Carmina Quinque Illustrium Poetarum* (fig. 22.1). The five *illustres poetae* were Bembo, Navagero, Castiglione, Cotta and Marcantonio Flaminio. Four of them were dead when the book came out: Bembo had died in 1547, Navagero and Castiglione in 1529, Cotta in 1510; Flaminio was still alive. The book contained no preface or dedication, and there is nothing in it to tell us what guided the publisher in his choice of authors, or whence he took his texts.

For Navagero the textual problem is soon solved: his *Lusus* (forty-four poems, mostly pastoral) had been published in an elegant folio by Tacuino in 1530, within a year of the poet's death, together with two of his *Orationes*: Valgrisi simply reprinted Tacuino's text.

With regard to Bembo and Castiglione the case is not so easy. Of Bembo,

Valgrisi printed eleven poems, most of them presumably from manuscript sources, since Bembo's collected poems, forty-one in number, were not published until 1552.[10] Three, however, of the poems included by Valgrisi had previously appeared in print: (1) *Benacus* had been published by Calvi in Rome in 1524, and was included in the 1527 Aldine edition of Sannazaro's *De partu Virginis*; (2) when this edition was reprinted in the following year there was appended to the text of Sannazaro a miscellany[11] that contained both *Benacus* and Bembo's *Hymnus ad D. Stephanum*; and (3) *Pro Goritio* had appeared in *Coryciana*.[12]

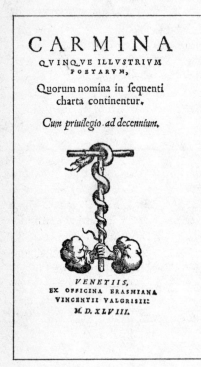

FIG. 22.1   Title page of Valgrisi's *Carmina Quinque Illustrium Poetarum*, Venice, 1548. B.M. 237 g 37

FIG. 22.2   Title page of the second edition (Florence, 1549) of Valgrisi's *Carmina Quinque Illustrium Poetarum*. B.M. G 9836

Of Castiglione, Valgrisi printed twelve poems, running to some 900 lines. No collection of Castiglione's poems had been published, and it seems that Valgrisi must have depended, as in the case of Bembo, mainly upon manuscript sources. In this case, too, he may have had recourse also to the Aldine miscellanies: *Ald. 1528 Misc.* contained Castiglione's elegy *Ad mare ne accedas*, and *Ald. 1533 Misc.* contained that elegy, two more elegies, his *Cleopatra*, and an epigram—all of which were printed by Valgrisi.[13] Valgrisi cannot have depended upon *Ald. 1533 Misc.* for his selection from Castiglione: he prints twice as many poems (indeed, he prints virtually all Castiglione's Latin verse: his eighteenth-century editors could add only half a dozen minor and doubtful pieces) and prints them in a definitely superior text.

Of the Latin poems of Giovanni Cotta barely a dozen have survived; eight of these (less than 250 lines of verse in all) were printed by Valgrisi. Here again it seems that he must have had recourse to the Aldine miscellany, or a comparable source in manuscript.[14] Six of the eight poems were included in *Ald. 1528 Misc.* and were printed by Bindoni in 1530;[15] in the meantime all eight of them had been printed, together with fifteen *carmina* of Flaminio, in an edition of Sannazaro's *Odae* brought out by an anonymous publisher in Venice in 1529; all eight (and a ninth) were included in *Ald. 1533 Misc.*

The four poets discussed above occupy ninety-six out of 280 pages in the first edition of Valgrisi; the remainder of the book is devoted to Marcantonio Flaminio. Flaminio had been a prolific Latin poet from his earliest youth, but it was difficult to persuade him to allow his poems to be printed. In 1515, when he was barely eighteen years old, a small collection of his verses was published by Soncino at Fano, together with the *Neniae* and *Epigrammata* of Marullo; a few more—fifteen—of his poems were printed together with the *Odae* of Sannazaro in Venice in 1529; and in 1546 he allowed Valgrisi to published his metrical version of thirty of the Psalms. Two years later, when he had returned to Rome after a year or so as one of the secretaries to Council of Trent—he was in poor health and had less than two more years to live, but he seems to have been more active than ever before in both writing and publishing—he authorised the publication by Gryphius at Lyons of a collection of *Carmina* in two books, and it must surely have been with his authorisation that, in the same year (1548), Valgrisi published, together with the poems of the other four 'illustres proetae', four books of his *Carmina* and reprinted his thirty verse paraphrases of the Psalms.

Valgrisi's collection was evidently popular: Torrentino, in Florence, published a second edition in 1549 (fig. 22.2) and a third in 1552; a fourth edition appeared, again in Venice, in 1558 from the press of Girolamo Giglio.[16]

In Torrentino's 1552 edition Valgrisi's text was revised, and the section devoted to Flaminio greatly enlarged by the addition of a fifth book of *Carmina* and a *Sacrorum Carminum Libellus*; the four other poets still occupy ninety-six pages, but Flaminio now runs to 290 (instead of 180) pages.

An interesting problem is presented by a collection entitled *Doctissimorum nostra aetate Italorum Epigrammata*, which was published in Paris (without date) by Nicolas Leriche ('Nicolaus Dives' in his imprint) at the instigation of his uncle, Jean Gaigny ('Joannes Gagnaeus'), Chancellor of the University of Paris. The title suggests an attempt at a 'national' collection, but the list of contents shows that, though his poets are all of them Italians, the compiler had no such grandiose aim in mind: the book comprises only 'M. Antonii Flaminii libri duo, Marii Molsae liber unus. Andreae Naugerii liber unus. Io. Cottae, Lampridii, Sadoleti et aliorum Miscellaneorum liber unus.' Plainly, this is more like an 'author collection'[17]—and, observing the names of the poets represented, one might suspect a connection with Valgrisi's

Carmina. The publisher's (undated) address to the reader, however, shows that Leriche's *Epigrammata* was independently produced. Gaigny, says Leriche, greatly admired the Latin poems of Flaminio, and had collected a number of his hymns and *epigrammata* with a view to publication, 'Cum ecce e Lugduno libri duo epigrammatum eius prodiere' (plainly a reference to Gryphius' 1548 edition of Flaminio's *Carminum libri duo*). Gaigny resolved to republish the *libri duo*, with the addition of 'epigrammata nondum edita' in his own possession. He procured also, with the help of friends, 'elegantia multa epigrammata', and now published the whole collection, together with the Lusus of Navagero (which he says—incorrectly—had not been separately published—'seorsim non editi'). It seems that Valgrisi's *Carmina* and Leriche's *Epigrammata* must both have come out in 1548—the date 1546 tentatively attributed to Leriche in the B.M. catalogue cannot be correct—and that each was quite independent of the other.

Carmina Quinque Illustrium Poetarum was an influential book; it provided the vulgate text of Cotta, Castiglione and Flaminio, and the 'quinque poetae' chosen by Valgrisi were, according to Gravina,[18] 'i cinque poeti illustri che per la più nelle stampe vanno congiunti'.

Valgrisi's first imitator was a rival; in 1562 Giunta brought out in Florence a collection, *Carmina Quinque Hetruscorum Poetarum*, in which a quintet of Tuscans—Vintha, Segnius, Berni, Accolti and Benedetto Varchi— were presented in competition, it would seem, with Valgrisi's northern poets.

The Giuntine collection, perhaps because of the manifest inferiority of its contents, was never reprinted; Valgrisi's remained a model for more than 200 years; even the title he chose for it died hard. In 1582, nearly a quarter of a century after the publication of the fourth edition of the book, a Parisian publisher, Denis Du Val, brought out a collection which in some ways resembled it. It was entitled *Tres poetae elegantissimi, emendati, & aucti*, the three poets being Marullo, Joannes Secundus and Angeriano.

In 1561 another Parisian firm, Wechel, had published pocket editions of the *Epigrammata* and *Hymni* of Marullo,[19] and of the poems of Joannes Secundus.[20] Du Val now reprinted both collections,[21] in the same small format, adding a reprint of the *Erotopaignion* of Angeriano and prefixing a general title page bearing the title quoted above. The sections containing Joannes Secundus' poems and the *Erotopaignion* collate separately and were separately paginated, no doubt in order that each of them might be issued on its own. In a general dedication the editor, 'Ludovicus Martellus Rotomageus', speaks of 'hos . . . poetas, a me intra paucos dies animi [? delectandi] causa perlectos, et a multis mendis, quae in prioribus editionibus contigerant, Duvallii nostri (qui nouam hanc adornabat) rogatu vindicatos'. It may be doubted whether Du Val had Valgrisi's collection in mind when he planned *Tres poetae elegantissimi* (or when he chose its name), but the book cannot be omitted from a survey of 'author collections' of the sixteenth century.[22]

In 1753 Pietro Lancelotti published in Bergamo a volume which he chose to call *Carmina Quinque Illustrium Poetarum*; the first three of his poets (like his

title) were the same as Valgrisi's (to whom, however, he made no acknowledgement). He had intended, he tells us in his preface, to publish an edition
of Bembo's Latin verse, but since that would not fill a volume he added
Navagero, Castiglione, Giovanni Casa and Poliziano (he prints practically
in full the poems of all four of them, including the Greek epigrams of
Poliziano), and included as a sort of appendix five eclogues of G. B. Amalteo,
the *Laocoon*, the *Curtius* and *Epistola ad Fregosos* of Sadoleto, and two or three
inedita of Lampridio and Flaminio.[23]

Meanwhile, in the seventeenth and early eighteenth centuries, Valgrisi's
lead had been more or less closely followed in the Low Countries and in
France. In 1662 Balthasar Moretus published in Antwerp, from the press of
Plantin, a collection consisting of *Septem Illustrium Virorum Poemata*, his seven
illustrious persons (he did well not to call them poets), being ecclesiastics of
the court of Alexander VII. And in 1738 the Abbé Joseph Olivet, author of a
history of the Académie Française, edited and published in Paris a collection
of Latin poems by six members of the academy of the time of Louis XV,
including himself;[24] the book was evidently popular: a second edition came
out at the Hague in 1740 and a third at Leiden in 1743. The first two editions
were entitled simply *Poetarum ex Academia Gallica . . . Carmina*; in the title to
the third edition Olivet supressed any reference to his own contribution,
calling the book *Recentiores Poetae Latini et Graeci Selecti Quinque*—the reduction
to five being perhaps due to personal modesty, perhaps to a reminiscence of
the model provided by Valgrisi 200 years before.

Perhaps the last, and certainly the boldest, appropriation of Valgrisi's title
was perpetrated by the anonymous publisher who brought out in Paris in
1791 *Quinque Illustrium Poetarum Lusus in Venerem*, a collection of erotic and
amatory poems by Panormita, Pacifico Massimo, Pontano, Joannes Secundus
and 'Ramusius', the last name covering a series of amoebean lyrics and
elegiac pieces exchanged between Hieronymus Donatus and a member of the
Ramusio family of Rimini, printed, apparently for the first time, from a
manuscript of the fifteenth century.

3 AUTHOR ANTHOLOGIES

This is a miscellaneous and not very clearly definable category, worth
distinguishing, however, if only to call attention to the fact that a large
proportion of the Latin verse collections as published during this period
were put together not so much in order to provide a collection of pleasing
poems, as to exhibit the proficiency of the contributors. Sometimes the poets
were drawn from a wide range, sometimes from a particular city; sometimes
the texts had all been published already, sometimes *edita* were mingled with
inedita; sometimes the poets belonged to past generations, sometimes all or
some of them were contemporaries. The choice of illustrative examples from
so diverse a field must be arbitrary, and one or two specimens must suffice.

One of the most remarkable of such collections is *Carmina Poetarum Nobilium*,
edited by Giovanni Paolo Ubaldini and published at Milan in 1563 (fig. 22.3).

It is dedicated to Consalvo, Duke of Suessa, a descendant of El gran Capitan, and among the 224 poems that it contains is a series of Horatian odes addressed to him; some of the forty contributors are contemporary non-entities, but distinguished poets, both contemporary and of earlier generations, are represented (e.g. Tebaldeo, Navagero, Aonio Paleario, Bonfadio, the brothers Amalteo, Giano Vitale and Niccolò d'Arco), and, though some of the contents may well have been taken from printed editions, Ubaldini declares that his texts were 'magna cura ac studio conquisitos', and he must have gone to manuscript sources for much of his material, e.g. the three odes of Giovanni Casa that he prints,[25] for his three poems of Niccolò d'Arco,[26] and for the ten important poems of Molza,[27] which alone are enough to give distinction to his anthology.

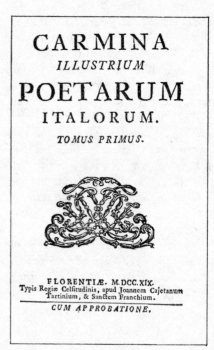

FIG. 22.3   Title page of Urbaldini's *Carmina Poetarum Nobilium*, Milan, 1563. B.M. G 9853
FIG. 22.4   Title page of vol. 1 of *Carmina Illustrium Poetarum Italorum*, eleven vols, Florence, 1719–26. B.M. 657 a 16–26

A couple of years later Giovanni Antonio Taglietti (who called himself Joannes Antonius Taygetus) brought out at Brescia, under the auspices of the Accademia degli Occulti, a not dissimilar collection, entitled *Carmina Praestantium Poetarum*. A good proportion of his fifty-one named contributors[28] were Brescians and themselves Occulti, and he took the opportunity of printing sixty-five of his own poems (no other contributor was allowed more than thirteen). Taglietti's collection is largely of local interest, and his claim (made on the title page) that the 194 poems it contained were 'Nusquam antea edita' cannot be sustained—Sadoleto's *Laocoon*, for instance, which is placed in the forefront of the collection, had been published by its author thirty years before—but it includes apparently unpublished pieces by such well known poets as Niccolò d'Arco, Castiglione and Molza.

The most comprehensive collection of this kind that had so far appeared was published in Paris by Guillaume Cavellat in two 16mo volumes, in 1555 and 1560; the compiler was a French scholar named Léger Duchesne ('Leodegarius à Quercu'), and he called his two volumes respectively *Flores Epigrammatum* (plate 22.1) and *Farrago Poematum* (deleo).[29] It is not very clear how Duchesne distinguished between 'Epigrammata' and 'Poemata': *Farrago Poematum* includes poems of almost every sort and length, whereas *Flores Epigrammatum*, though it consists mainly of short poems, mostly in elegiac couplets, admits also hexameter pieces running to as many as a couple of hundred lines. While *Flores* is described on its title page as 'Ex optimis quibusque authoribus excerpti', the poems in *Farrago* are said to be 'Ex optimis quibusque, et antiquioribus, et aetatis nostra poetis selecta'—though in fact *Flores* draws on the classics[30] and *Farrago* does not.

Duchesne made no claim to print hitherto unpublished poems. It is not clear on what principle he chose his poets, or how he distributed them between the two volumes: *Flores* comprises some forty named poets, *Farrago* nearly fifty; most of them are Italians, but other nations are represented: a fair amount of space is allotted to a few French poets in each volume;[31] More is given thirty-six pages in *Flores*, Buchanan thirty pages in *Farrago*; and a few poems are included in *Flores* from Erasmus, Joannes Secundus and Sabinus. Among Italians the lion's share in *Flores* is allotted to Pontano, Ercole Strozzi, Pittori and Alciati; in *Farrago*, to Flaminio (who, with 160 pages, gets three times as much space as any one else), G. F. Pico, Sfondrati, Navagero and Molza.[32]

Flores Epigrammatum was called 'Tomus Primus' on its title page; 'Tomus Secundus'—*Farrago Poematum*—did not follow it until five years later.[33] It seems that *Flores* was out of print when Cavellat brought out *Farrago* in 1560, for in that year another Paris publisher, Gilles Gorbin, issued an 'editio altera' of *Flores*, identical in *format* and typography with Cavellat's production, apparently in an effort to cash in on its success. Gorbin (impudently?) reprinted the six-year *privilegium* granted to Cavallet in 1554 (which, incidentally, Cavellat himself reproduced in *Farrago*), and reduced the bulk of *Flores* from 380 folios to 348 by (maliciously?) omitting (*inter alia*) the poems of the editor, Duchesne.

Despite its miscellaneous character and chaotic arrangement, Duchesne's collection remained for nearly twenty years the most comprehensive and representative anthology of Latin verse by modern Italian poets.

4 NATIONAL COLLECTIONS

Of the collections of Latin poetry written by Italians, the first that deserves to be called 'national' is Toscano's *Carmina Illustrium Poetarum Italorum*, which came out in two volumes in 1576 and 1577. Toscano's was not, however, the first attempt to produce a representative collection of the kind. Ten years earlier a young Fleming who called himself Aegidius Periander[34] had compiled three collections of love poetry (a *genus* to which he attributed a pretty wide extension), intended to represent the poetic production of Italy, Germany, and France respectively; he called them *Horti tres amoris*, allotting, with fanciful elaboration, to each of the authors he selected the name of a flower, bird or tree.

The first part of the *Horti*[35] was published by Feyerabend at Frankfort-on-Maine in 1567; it contained a large and fairly representative selection of Italian 'amatory' verse, covering nearly 700 pages and including thirty-five named authors.[36]

The second and third of the *Horti* followed in August of the same year; the former contains, in nearly 600 pages, a collection of *Elegiae*, *Epigrammata*, *Epithalamia* and *Encomia* by thirty-seven German poets, 'in quibus quid nostra possit Germania facile declaratur'; the latter, in just over 200 pages, presents ten poets (including Ausonius, and two Italians, Andrelini and Belmisseri, who had worked in Paris), intended to exemplify 'ingeniorum stylique suavitates Gallici'.

Periander's *Horti tres* was quite a notable achievement for a young man of twenty-two; but the Italian 'Hortus', judged as a representative selection, had its shortcomings: it was restricted to amatory verse, its editor's primary interest lay not in Italy but in Germany,[37] and it was hastily and carelessly put together.[38] Within ten years it was superseded by Giovanni Matteo Toscano's *Carmina Illustrium Poetarum Italorum*.

Toscano was a native of Milan, born about the turn of the century, who spent most of his life in France.[39] The first volume of his collection appeared in Paris in the closing months of 1576 from the press of Gilles Gorbin, the piratical republisher of Duchesne's *Flores*. In a preface addressed 'Lectoribus Poetices studiosis' Toscano explains why he brought out his book. Poetry, he says, is now held in low esteem. Why? *Because of the printing press*: 'Ars typographica . . . huic calamitati ansam praebuit.' Publishers are undiscriminating and seek easy profits; bad poets will print anything for cash ('famam praesentipecunia licitantur'); poor verse flows from the press and brings poetry into disrepute, so that good poets keep their poems to themselves and don't offer them to publishers. He himself has always (he says) been an avid reader of contemporary verse ('Siquis unquam novorum poetarum studio ab adulescentia flagravit, is ego sum'), and he now wishes to give others the benefit of his own reading. So he has made selections from the mass of poetry that he has read and has called in the aid of his friends, who 'ex multis Italiae urbibus undique petita bonorum autorum poemata abunde ad nos miserunt'. He has made a choice from what his friends have sent him, added poems that he himself collected in Rome, Milan and Bologna, and made them up into a volume; if it is well received, he says, he hopes to follow it up with a second.[40] A good part of the contents of his book (as its title page asserts) had not previously been published. He has deliberately (he says) restricted himself to Italian authors, in the hope that others better qualified than himself will do for France and Spain and other countries what he has done for Italy.

The first volume is a 16 mo of nearly 800 pages, divided into two separately foliated sections: the first section contains selections from thirty-six named poets, occupying nearly 600 pages; the second section consists of nearly 150 pages of Toscano's own poems, forty-four pages of poems that had been sent him from Italy without any author's name, and—an anomalous appendix—a batch of short pieces 'Ex vetustis lapidibus'.

Of the named poets, those to whom most space is allotted are Bembo, Navagero, Castiglione (virtually all their poems are given), Lampridio, Molza and Giovanni Casa; these occupy, between them, more than half the first 600 pages.

The second volume, which came out early in the following year, ran to some 720 pages and contained poems by fifty-six poets: the lion's share of space went to Fracastoro (110 pages) and Politian (154 pages), both represented almost in their entirety, and to Franchini and Lelio Capilupi.

Neither in his distribution of poets between the first and second volumes nor in the order in which he placed them in each volume did Toscano follow any discernible plan—save that it was his aim (apparently) to strengthen, as it were, the contents of each volume by including a few poets of the first rank; it may be that he excluded Pontano, Flaminio, Calcagnini and Sannazaro from the first two volumes because he was reserving them as *pièces de résistance* for the third.

In fact the third volume never appeared: a cryptic note on the verso of the title page of the second volume informs us

> Tertium Tomum iam editioni paratum, negotiis
> ita iubentibus, in aliud tempus distulimus,
> una cum Marulli poematis ab ipso autore
> recognitis et auctis.

What were the 'negotia', and what Toscano, or his publisher, meant by saying that the poems of Marullo that he proposed to publish were 'ab ipso autore recognitis et auctis'—these are unanswerable questions.[41]

Instead of the third volume of the *Carmina*, Toscano in 1578 brought out in Paris (but with a different publisher) *Peplus Italiae*, the book with which his name is perhaps most frequently associated. The *Peplus* consists of a series of short panegyrics in verse, each followed by a brief prose paragraph, composed by Toscano himself,[42] in honour of 200 Italian men of letters or of learning. This roll of honour is divided into four books, each containing fifty names; a roughly chronological order is preserved throughout, the first name being that of Dante. In his dedication (dated from Paris, 1 June 1578) Toscano refers to the *Carmina*, 'duplici volumine distincta'; he had published them, he says, 'superioribus annis'—it was in fact less than two years previously—not simply to do honour to his compatriots but to encourage people of other nations to do the same for their great men.

Toscano's *Carmina* seems to have held the field for the rest of the century.

Within two or three years of the expiry of its ten-year *privilegium* a Roman publisher, Giacomo Tornieri, paid it the sincerest of compliments—he stole from it on a large scale. Publishing a pocket edition of the Latin poetry of Sannazaro in 1590, Tornieri swelled the little volume to almost twice its size by adding to the 182 pages of Sannazaro another 170 pages of 'Carmina Selecta Illustrium Poetarum Italorum Ex primo tomo Io: Matthaei Toscani.'

Lack of the third volume and the consequent absence of several 'major' poets, and also the passage of years, made Toscano's *Carmina* inadequate and out of date. Early in the seventeenth century a collection was produced that more than doubled the number of poets contained in the *Carmina* and set in train the international competition that Toscano himself professed he wished to stimulate.

In 1608 Jan Gruter, librarian of the Palatine Library at Heidelberg, brought out at Frankfort two small fat volumes, containing respectively 1,399 and 1,481 pages of text, entitled *Delitiae CC. Italorum Poetarum, huius superiorisque aevi illustrium*; they were the first in what was to be a remarkable and famous series of *Delitiae*, all in the same small format, and all published in Frankfort during the following decade.[43] Gruter appeared on the title page under the anagrammatic pseudonym 'Ranutius Gherus' ('Collectore Ranvtio Ghero'), and he prefixed to the first volume a ten-page dedicatory epistle addressed to Gottlob a Berka, 'Baro de Duba et Lyppa, Dominus in Lauekowitz Weis, et Huuerwasser, &c'.

In his dedication Gruter explains that he had been approached by the printer, presumably Jonas Rosa,[44] who had it in mind to reprint 'tomum utrumque Io. Matthaei Toscani editum quidem ante annos triginta, ac saepe deinde frustra desideratum', and had asked Gruter whether any additions could be made to Toscano's collection. On Gruter's replying that Toscano's two volumes contained hardly a quarter 'vatum . . . quos fama etiamnum tota celebraret Italia', Rosa pressed him to make up the deficiency, which Gruter, 'pro meo erga rem literariam studio', proceeded to do. In the dedication of his second volume (to Albert Wenceslas Smirziz, 'L. B. a Smirziz, in Nachod, et Skworziz, &c'), Gruter justifies the additions he has made to Toscano's collection:

Nemo mihi vitio vertet, spero, quod telam a Toscano dudum inchoatam pertexuerim, atque Europaei orbis theatro repraesentarim delitias ducentorum pene,[45] nostra avorumque memoria[46] inter Italos poeseos laude clarorum.

The Florentine collection—*Carmina Illustrium Poetarum Italorum*—contains selections from just under 400 poets, ranged in alphabetical order, from Dante to the end of the seventeenth century. It came out in eleven volumes over the years 1719 to 1726 (fig. 22.4).[47] The publishers were Joannes Cajetanus Tartinius and Sanctes Franchius. There is no indication of the compiler's identity or explanation of his editorial procedures—how he chose his poets or whence he derived his texts—save an uninformative 'Ad Lectorem Praefactio' in the first volume, the anonymous author of which—was he perhaps Giovanni Tartini?—says that he prints some poems for the first time from MSS 'ex instructissimis ornatissimisque Bibliothecis . . . quarum praecipuae fuerunt Medicea Divi Laurentii, et Strozzia', adding 'his accesserunt Salvinii, Bargiacchiique quamplurima variorum Auctorum manuscripta carmina, mihi . . . libenter impertita'; he makes no reference to previous printed collections or anthologies.

CONCLUSIONS

Can any significant conclusions be drawn from the rough and far from exhaustive classification here suggested and the desultory examples adduced to illustrate it?

When I say that my suggested classification is far from exhaustive, I mean that there are many types of anthology and collection that I have left out of account. In drawing up my list of categories I might have included (for instance) categories defined by reference to subject matter or to literary genre, and so brought within the scope of my analysis collections of religious verse, pietistic or polemical (such as the anti-papal collections that made an appearance in Germany during the second quarter of the century), assemblages of bucolic or didactic or amatory verse (these last seem to have been especially popular in the seventeenth century, e.g. the *Veneres Blyenburgicae* of Damas van Blyenburgh, published at Dordrecht in 1600);[48] retrospective repositories of epithalamia, encomia or elegies, celebrating the marriages, the achievements or the deaths of the great (also very popular in the seventeenth century; *Deliciarum Gamicarum Aureolus* (Frankfurt, 1620), edited by A. Vigelius, and *Triumphus Poeticus Mortis* (Frankfurt, 1624), edited by M. Turnemain, are typical examples); and poetic manuals intended for schools and colleges, and literary 'aspirants', or *Florilegia* collecting together what the best poets have said on a variety of stock topics (like the *Viridarium* of Octavianus Mirandula, first published by Aldus in 1507 and reprinted many times all over Europe in the succeeding 150 years). I have left all such collections out of account, confining myself to compilations that were, at least professedly, literary in character—intended for readers of poetry and put together with (presumably) some sort of aesthetic considerations in mind. It is collections such as these that throw most light upon the literary tastes, or at any rate upon the literary fashions, prevailing at the time among the Latin-reading public.

The evidence afforded by these collections confirms what must, I suspect, be the first impression of anyone at all familiar with the Latin literature of the period—the inexhaustible fluency of the poets and the overwhelming profusion of the verse that they produced. They reveal also how smooth must have been the channels of communication between the editor of such a collection and his publisher on the one hand and his contributors on the other—witness the speed with which Gherardi was able to assemble and publish his Lepanto poems and the ease with which Toscano seems to have procured contributions for his *Carmina* from the length and breadth of Italy.

The format chosen for their publication suggests what kind of market it was that these books were intended for. None of them came out in folio or quarto; all were in octavo or a smaller size: they must surely have been meant—and no doubt their price bore this out—not for the shelves of libraries but for the ordinary reading public. The growth of that public during the course of the century must have created a demand for cheap pocket editions, and no doubt it was to satisfy this demand that Duchesne and Toscano, in the second half of the century, brought out in 16mo their *Flores*, *Farrago* and *Carmina*, and that Gruter and those who followed him as editors of the *Delitiae* in the early 1600s chose for that popular series the same miniature format.

What were the criteria that editors employed in making their choice of poets and poems for the collections I have called 'author anthologies'? Aesthetic considerations, or purely poetic quality, it must be said, seem to have been for them of only secondary importance. The adjectives to be found on their title pages, *illustres*, *nobiles*, *praestantes*—adjectives that qualify the poets, not the poems—give a key to the principles that guided the compilers. Their aim was to provide a representative selection of the Latin verse of persons who had achieved celebrity as poets, scholars or literary men. True, the identity of the writers was not the only thing the editors paid regard to, for they always, or almost always, included in their anthologies a number of anonymous poems or poems of uncertain authorship, and these can have been chosen only for their intrinsic quality. Still, almost all the contents of these collections were chosen as specimens of the work of pre-eminent, or at least well known, writers, and the arrangement of the contents accord with this design: the poems are grouped together not by reference to their *genre* or subject-matter, nor with a view to presenting them so that they will most effectively strike the reader, but simply by reference to their authorship; each poet's name is followed by the whole of his contribution: the plan adopted is that of *The Oxford Book of English Verse*, not that of *The Golden Treasury*.

If the editorial approach is not, on the one hand, that of the critic with aesthetic effect in mind, it is not, on the other, that of the historian or the scholar. The poets themselves are not presented chronologically, or indeed in any significant order; the arrangement seems in most cases to be quite arbitrary (in Gruter's *Delitiae* and the Florentine collection the order is alphabetical). Nor is the contribution of each author accompanied by biographical or critical matter, or even by a panegyric (as in Toscano's *Peplus*) from the pen of the editor or another. In their prefaces and dedications editors may single out a few names for praise (praise which usually involves a comparison with the Ancients), but scholarship (though Scaliger pointed the way in his *Poetice* in 1561) had not yet come to look upon the Latin poetry of the Renaissance as a chapter in the history of the development of literature: if another English analogy may be adduced, these anthologies are to be ranked with Dodsley's mid-eighteenth century *Collection* of contemporary and recent poets, not with the selection critically and historically presented in Ward's *English Poets* rather more than a hundred years later.

LIST OF ANTHOLOGIES MENTIONED

1 *Occasional collections*

(a) *Coryciana* (Arrighi, Rome, 1524): 8vo; 140 ff.; the title page bears the single word CORYCIANA; the colophon reads *Impressum Romae apud Ludovicum Vicentinum et Lautitium Perusinum. Mense Iulio MDXXIIII.* British Museum, London, G 10012 (*s.v.* Blosius Palladius).

(b) *Tempio a Giovanna d'Aragona* (Pietrasanta, Venice, 1554): 8vo; 576 pp.; title: *Del Tempio alla divina Signora Donna Giovanna d'Aragona, Fabricato da tutti i più gentili Spiriti, & in tutte le lingue principali del mondo, Prima Parte.* No 'Seconda Parte' appeared. B.M., 240 e 30 (*s.v.* Girolamo Ruscelli).

(c) *Gherardi* (Guerra, Venice, 1572): 8vo; 456 pp.; title: *In Foedus et Victoriam contra Turcas iuxta Sinum Corinthiacum Non. Octob. MDLXXI. partam Poemata uaria. Petri Gherardi Burgensis studio, & diligentia conquisita, ac disposita.* B.M., 11405 a 17.

2 *Author collections*

(a) *Carmina Quinque Illustrium Poetarum*

(i) *C.Q.I.P.* I (Valgrisi, Venice, 1548): 8vo; 280 pp.; title: *Carmina quinque illustrium poetarum*; pp. 7–21, Petri Bembi Carmina; pp. 23–58, Andreae Naugerii Patricii Lusus; pp. 59–95, Balthassaris Castilionei Carminum Liber; p. [97], second title page: *M. Antonii Flaminii Carminum Libri quattuor*; pp. 99–227, M. A. Flaminii Carmina; p. 229, third title page: *M. Antonii Flaminii Paraphrasis in triginta Psalmos*; pp. 233–75, Paraphrasis, and two additional poems. B.M., 237 g 37.

(ii) *C.Q.I.P.* II (Torrentino, Florence, 1549): 8vo; 318 pp.; title as in *C.Q.I.P.* I, adding *Secunda editio longe copiosior prima.* The additions consist of three poems by Cotta and thirty-three poems, most of them inserted in the first book of his *Carmina*, by Flaminio. B.M., G 9836.

(iii) *C.Q.I.P.* III (Torrentino, Florence, 1552): 8vo; 388 pp.; title as in *C.Q.I.P.* I, adding *Additis nonnullis M. Antonii Flaminii libellis nunquam antea impressis*; the 'additi libelli' are (1) a fifth book of *Carmina* (pp. 264–308) containing sixty-six poems, and (2) *Carminum Sacrorum Libellus* (pp. 363–86). B.M., 1070 d 17. An edition in 16mo came out simultaneously. B.M., G 9797.

(iv) *C.Q.I.P.* IV (Giglio, Venice, 1558): 8vo; 184 ff; title and contents as in *C.Q.I.P.* III. According to Mancurti (*M. A. Flaminii Carmina*, Padua, 1727), this edition is 'omnium pessima, et innumeris ingentibusque erroribus scatens'. B.M., G 9837.

(b) *Carmina Quinque Hetruscorum Poetarum* (Giunta, Florence, 1562): 8vo; 184 pp. pp. [1]–86, Francisci Vinthae Carmina; pp. 87–114, Fabii Segni Carmina; pp. 115–28, Francisci Berni Carmina; pp. 129–36, Benedicti Accolti Epigrammata; pp. 137–72, Benedicti Varchii Carmina. B.M., 238 m 27.

(c) *Poetae tres elegantissimi* (Du Val, Paris, 1582): 16mo; 220 ff; title: *Poetae tres elegantissimi, emendati, & aucti, Michael Marullus. Hieronymus Angerianus. Ioannes Secundus.* B.M., 238 i 32.

3 *Author anthologies*

(a) *Leriche* (Nicolas Leriche ('Nicolaus Dives'), Paris, [1548]: 8vo; 72 ff; title: *Doctissimorum nostra aetate Italorum Epigrammata*; ff. 2–30, *M. Antonii Flaminii Carmina* [two books]; ff. 31–40, *Marii Molsae Epigrammatum Liber unus*; ff. 40–58, *Andreae Naugerii . . . Epigrammatum Liber unus*; ff. 58–72, *Ioannis Cottae, Petri Bembi, Lampridii, Sadoleti, Honorati, et aliorum Miscellaneorum liber unus.* B.M., G 9842 (*s.v.* J. Gagnaeus).

(b) *Ubaldini* (Antoniani, Milan, 1563): 8vo; 107 ff; title: *Carmina Poetarum Nobilium Io. Pauli Ubaldini studio conquisita.* B.M., G 9853.

(c) *Taglietti* (Bozola, Brescia, 1565): 8vo; 140 ff; title: *Carmina Praestantium*

Poetarum, Io. Antonii Taygeti Academici Occulti ex quamplurimis selecta: nusquam antea in lucem edita. B.M., 11409 aaa 47(1).

(d) (i) *Duchesne Flores* (Cavellat, Paris, 1555): 16mo; 348 ff; title: *Flores Epigrammatum ex optimis quibusque authoribus excerpti per Leodegarium à Quercu ... Tomus Primus* ... imprint: *Lutetiae, Apud Gulielmum Cavellat, in pingui Gallina, ex ex adverso collegii Cameracensis,* 1555. B.M., 11403 a 29 (*s.v.* Leodegarius à Quercu).

(ii) *Duchesne Flores,* second edition (Gorbin, Paris, 1560): 16mo; 352 ff; title: as in *Duchesne, Flores*; imprint: *Parisiis, Apud Aegidium Gorbinum, sub insigne Spei, prope collegium Cameracense,* 1560. Bibliothèque Nationale, Paris, Rés. p Yc 1110–1111.

(iii) *Duchesne Farrago* (Cavellat, Paris, 1560): 16mo; 420 ff; title: *Farrago Poematum ex optimis quibusque, et antiquioribus, et aetatis nostrae poetis selecta, per Leodegarium à Quercu ... Tomus Secundus* ... imprint as in *Duchesne Flores,* but with date 1560. B.M., 11403 a 29.

4 National collections

(a) *Periander Hortus Italorum Poetarum* (Fabricius, Frankfurt, 1567): 8vo; 356 ff; title: *Horti tres Amoris amoenissimi, praestantissimorum poetarum nostri seculi, flosculis & plantulis odoriferis iam primum ab* AEGIDIO PERIANDRO *Bruxel. Brabant. consiti ... Pars Prima, Hortus Italorum Poetarum.* Bibl. Nat., Yc 7966.

(b) (i) *Toscano Carmina,* I (Gorbin, Paris, 1576): 16mo; 396 ff; title: *Carmina Illustrium Poetarum Italorum. Io. Matthaeus Toscanus conquisivit, recensuit, bonam partem nunc primum publicauit. Tomus Primus.* B.M., 686 a 15–17.

(ii) *Toscano Carmina,* II (Gorbin, Paris, 1577): 16mo; 266 ff; title: as in vol. I, with *Tomus Secundus* for *Tomus Primus.* B.M., 686 a 18–20.

(c) (i) *Gruter Delitiae,* I (Rosa, [Frankfurt], 1608): 16mo; 1,466 pp.; title: *Delitiae CC. Italorum Poetarum, huius superiorisque aevi illustrium, Collectore Ranutio Ghero.* B.M., G 9593.

(ii) *Gruter Delitiae,* II (Rosa, [Frankfurt], 1608): 16mo; 1,550 pp.; title: as in *Gruter Delitiae,* I, adding *Pars Altera* before *Collectore.* B.M., G 9594.

(d) *Florentine Collection* (Florence, 'Typis Regiae Celsitudinis, apud Joannem Cajetanum Tartinium, & Sanctem Franchium', 1719–26); 8vo; eleven volumes; title: *Carmina Illustrium Poetarum Italorum.* B.M., 657 a 16–26.

NOTES

[1] 'Almost uncharted': the qualification is rendered necessary by Lucia Gualdo Rosa's 'A proposito di una antologia dei poeti latini del Quattrocento' in *Latomus,* XXIII, fasc. 2, 1964, pp. 334–44. Professor Gualdo Rosa's valuable article is the fruit of her experience as joint editor of *Poeti Latini del Quattrocento* (Milan and Naples, 1964), itself a model of what an 'author collection' should be. Although Professor Gualdo Rosa writes with the poets of the Quattrocento chiefly in mind, her article throws light on the whole field of Renaissance Latin poetical anthologies.

[2] For an account of this group see J. Pope-Hennessy, *Italian High Renaissance and Baroque Sculpture,* London, 1963, III, iii, 50 (with a photograph, plate III, ii, 48).

[3] This practice was continued; Vasari says that he saw a book, kept in the church, in which the monks preserved the compositions of visitors.

[4] 'Forster oder Waldmann?' suggests Ellinger (*Italien und Deutsche Humanismus in der Neulateinischen Lyrik,* Berlin, 1929, p. 343).

[5] Tiraboschi, *Storia della letteratura italiana,* VII, Part IV (Modena, 1792), pp. 1653–72, reprints, from two manuscripts supplied to him by Francesco Cancellieri, a longer version of *De poetis urbanis,* which runs to 327 couplets and mentions more than ninety poets.

[6] For an account of the principal contributors, with particular reference to the Germans (who were Goritz's special *protégés*), see Ellinger, *op. cit.,* pp. 340–5.

[7] See C. Dionisotti, 'Appunti su Leone Ebreo', *Italia Medioevale e Umanistica*, II, 1959, pp. 409–28.

[8] Save for a Greek ode by G. B. Amalteo.

[9] Including the brothers Amalteo, Fabio Vigile, Ippolito Capilupi, Giovanni Carga, Gianantonio Taglietti and Trifone Benzi.

[10] I cite this book by reference to the date on the title page; the date in the colophon is 1553.

[11] I call this miscellany *Ald. 1528 Misc.* The rest of its contents consisted of an *epithalamion* by Altilius, six poems of Cotta, two of I. M. Aurelius, an elegy by Castiglione and four epigrams of M. A. Casanova. A much larger miscellany, which partially incorporated the contents of *Ald. 1528 Misc.*, omitting the two poems of Bembo, was appended to the 1533 Aldine edition of the *De partu*; I call this miscellany *Ald. 1533 Misc.*

Ald. 1528 Misc. was reproduced in part, with additions, in Francesco Bindoni's rare little edition of Sannazaro's poems, Venice, 1530.

[12] For *Pro Goritio* Valgrisi's editor evidently used not *Coryciana* but a revised text agreeing with that used by the editors of Bembo's *Carminum Libellus* in 1552; in *Benacus* Valgrisi agrees with Aldus 1527 whenever that text differs from 1552, except in l. 65, where each of the three goes its own way.

[13] Bindoni in 1530 had printed *Ad mare ne accedas*, *Cleopatra* and the epigram.

[14] For a full and scholarly account of the history of the transmission of Cotta's poems, with a text and apparatus, see V. Mistruzzi, *Giornale storico della letteratura italiana*, 1924, suppl. 22–3, pp. 1–131.

[15] They were also, according to Mistruzzi, included in two editions of the *De partu*, neither of which I have seen, published in Venice by de Sabio and by Stagnini in 1530 and 1531 respectively; both, apparently, were reprints of the Aldine edition of 1528.

[16] The dedication, signed by Flaminio's nephew Cesare, is dated October 1547; the title page bears the date 1548.

[17] The presence of the *Miscellaneorum liber*, which includes thirty-three pieces by sixteen named poets and twenty of uncertain authorship, removes it from this class into that of 'author anthologies'.

[18] *Della ragione poetica*, I, xi.

[19] The firm of Wechel had already published an edition of these poems in 1529. Some copies of the 1561 edition (and one at least of Duval's edition of 1582) bear the imprint of Jacques Dupuis (see A. Perosa, *Michaelis Marulli Carmina*, Zurich, 1951, pp. xl–xli).

[20] Said on the title page to be 'nunc secundum in lucem edita'; the editor was Georgius Cripius, a friend of the author; his text was based on (and much superior to) that of the edition of 1541 brought out by Joannes' brothers.

[21] Adding to the *Epigrammata* and *Hymni* of Marullo his *De principum institutione*, printed for the first time (at Basel) four years earlier.

[22] The title of *Ludovici Pascalis, Iulii Camilli, Molsae, et aliorum illustrium poetarum carmina* (Giolito, Venice, 1551) is misleading. This collection, edited by Lodovico Dolce, contains three books of poems by Pascale (who had submitted them to his friend the editor, it appears, some months before his death in 1557), which occupy (with the preliminary matter) fifty-two folios; then follow (1) *Theocrenus*, a hexameter epistle of Iulius Camillus addressed *Ad regem Franciscum* (ff. 53–4); (2) a ninety-two-line elegy of Molza ('Ecquid, sepositis dum te iuvat optime curis Hadriacis vitam ducere littoribus') (ff. 54–5); and (3) an elegy of Io. Ant. Vulpius, addressed to the editor ('Dulci, qui mulces aestus') (f. 56)—and nothing more.

[23] One suspects that he omitted Flaminio's *Carmina* because Mancurti's edition of Flaminio had recently been published, and substituted Poliziano because his Latin (and Greek) verse was not available except as part of his collected works.

[24] The others were P. D. Huet, Bishop of Avranches, C. F. Fraguier, Jean Boivin, Guillaume Massieu and Bernard Monet.

²⁵ The Giuntine edition of Casa's *Latina Monumenta*, which contained them, did not appear until the following year.

²⁶ Two of them are not to be found in *Nicolai Archii Numeri*, 1546; the other has significant textual variations.

²⁷ Only two of which had been printed by Leriche (*v. supr.*).

²⁸ There were also a dozen or so 'Incerti'.

²⁹ *Flores* consists of ff. [iv] + 380, *Farrago* of ff. [iv] + 416—in all some 1,600 pages of verse.

³⁰ It devotes thirty pages (ff. 269–84) to Catullus, twenty-six to Claudian, sixteen to poems from the *Appendix Virgiliana*, a dozen to Ausonius, and nearly a hundred to miscellaneous translations from Greek poets.

³¹ Beza, Claude Roselet and Dolet in *Flores*; de l'Hôpital, Turnèbe, Germain de Brie, Dorat, du Bellay and 'Chr. Aulaeus' (?de la Cour) in *Farrago*; Duchesne allots himself, in each volume, more space (fifty-two pages and seventy-five pages) than he allows to any other poet.

³² In *Flores*, Angeriano, Pigna, Dazzi, Politian and Marullo are among the Italians with a few poems or a few pages apiece; in *Farrago*, Cotta, Casanova, Franchini, Ippolito Capilupi, Sadoleto, Fascitelli, Lampridio, Benzi, Bembo, and T. V. Strozzi.

³³ I note a curious fact: at the head of the page in signatures E and F of *Farrago* (ff. 33–48) Cavellat's printer reproduced the running title *Flores Epigrammatum* instead of printing *Farrago Poematum*.

³⁴ Very little is known about him; his real name seems to have been Gilles Omma. He was born about 1545 and died before reaching the age of twenty-five. In 1567 (which must have been for him a busy year) he published, besides his *Horti amoris* and *Germania*, a translation of *Tyl Eulenspiegel* in Latin elegiacs.

³⁵ This is a rare book: there is no copy in the British Museum or in any Oxford library.

³⁶ Periander was generous in the space he alloted to the Strozzi and Pontano (who are the earliest poets included, with the strange exception of Claudian), Flaminio, Basilio Zanchi, Calcagnini, Dazzi, Castiglione, Bembo, Navagero, Franchini, Ariosto, Pigna, Molza and Sannazaro.

³⁷ In the same year he brought out (also with Feyerabend) *Germania*, a large and miscellaneous assembly of verse panegyrics (mostly by Periander himself) of distinguished German scholars and men of letters.

³⁸ Toscano, apologising at the end of his second volume (*v. infr.*) for the frequency of his printer's errors, says that he has himself corrected myriads of *errata* in the texts he used—'ut de una tantum editione loquar, Horti tres Amorum in Germania impressi sunt adeo depravati, ut liquido tibi adiurem, ipsos autores, si legant, vix sua poemata agnituros'.

³⁹ Very little is known about him: Ellinger must be wrong in saying (*op. cit.*, p. 306) that he died in 1576; Tiraboschi more prudently says that he probably died in France towards the end of the century.

⁴⁰ 'Quod si cupide legi ac probari a studiosis intellexero, brevi secundum tomum multo hoc etiam copiosius instructum publicabo.' In fact the work was from the outset planned to come out in three volumes: the *Privilegium*, granted before the first volume was published, describes it as consisting of 'Carmina. . . . in tres tomos distincta', and the second volume was printed off within a month or two of the first.

⁴¹ Marullo's poems were reprinted in Paris in 1582 (*v. supr.*), but not by Gorbin and with no assistance from Toscano—and, by an odd coincidence, Marullo's *De principum institutione* was printed for the first time in the very next year (1578), in Basel (see A. Perosa *M. Marulli Carmina*, Zurich, 1951, p. xli).

⁴² Some of these are repetitions, often with modifications, of verses which Toscano had prefixed to some of the selections contained in the *Carmina*.

⁴³ *Delitiae Poetarum Gallorum* (ed. Gruter, three vols., 1609); *Delitiae Poetarum Germanorum* (ed. A.F.H.G., six vols., 1612); *Delitiae Poetarum Belgorum* (ed. Gruter,

four vols., 1614); *Delitiae Poetarum Hungaricorum* (ed. J. P. Pareus, one vol., 1619). These were followed by Arthur Johnston's *Delitiae Poetarum Scotorum* (two vols., Amsterdam, 1637) and, *longo intervallo*, by Rostgaard's *Deliciae quorundam Poetrum Danorum* (two vols., Leiden, 1693).

[44] 'Prostant in officinâ Ionae Rosae' is the imprint on the title page.

[45] To be exact, the number of Gruter's poets is 198.

[46] This interprets the phrase 'huius superiorisque aevi' in the title, and explains the omission of (for example) Dante, Petrarch, and Boccaccio.

[47] Vols. I–IV, 1719; vols. V–VII, 1720; vol. VIII, 1721; vol. IX, 1722; vol. X, 1724; vol. XI, 1726. The order is alphabetical, save for some derangement, due to the printer's carelessness, in vols. I and IX. A few poets are awarded disproportionate space: Fracastoro (vol. V, pp. 1–114); Toscano (vol. IX, pp. 283–387); Vida (vol. XI, pp. 1–179); Montanus Vincentius (vol. XI, pp. 253–360). Several poets (e.g. Beccadelli and Aeneas Sylvius) are under-represented, by reason of the editor's policy, explained in his 'Praefactio', of omitting anything that tended to immorality. For a general criticism of Gruter and the Florentine collection see Professor Gualdo Rosa's article referred to in n. 1 above.

[48] Professor L. W. Forster gives an interesting analysis of this anthology in an article 'On Petrarchism in Latin and the role of the anthologies', in *Acta Conventus Neo-Latini Lovaniensis*, Leuven, 1973, pp. 235–44.

T. C. PRICE ZIMMERMANN   *Reed College, Portland, Oregon*

23

PAOLO GIOVIO AND THE EVOLUTION OF RENAISSANCE ART CRITICISM

IN HIS FUNDAMENTAL article on the history of aesthetics Professor Kristeller has clarified the history of thinking about the arts and the stages prior to the emergence of aesthetics as a systematic discipline.[1] As he makes clear, the Renaissance inherited from classical Antiquity comparatively little in the way of either formal aesthetic theory or practical criticism, and its own contributions to these areas were relatively modest. The problems of aesthetics as we now conceive them—that is to say, the problems of a separate discipline, art, to be understood and evaluated in the light of criteria peculiar to its distinctive nature—are the result of a tradition whose origins lie rather with the great philosopher–critics of the eighteenth century. They were not the creation of the Renaissance. In its failure to develop a body of criticism and theory commensurate with its achievements in art itself the Renaissance probably felt the lack of classical precedents such as provided the stimulus for achievement in other areas. Certainly Renaissance artists, working with the intuitive understanding which is the primary vehicle of artistic creation, had no difficulty in appropriating and learning from the legacy of classical art objects. It was criticism which lagged behind. Lacking a developed critical vocabulary and well articulated critical standards, Renaissance artists and critics were unable to give expression to concerns which evidently occupied the artist *qua* artist. For example in his descriptions of paintings, Vasari, the most advanced of Renaissance critics, rarely indicated the arrangement of the figures. Nor was this, Svetlana Alpers has persuasively argued, because Renaissance artists thought in terms of subject, not composition.

> The paintings are sufficient testimony against this view. Nor can we say that the composition was a natural product, a mystery which could not be verbalized. The problem is rather critical than artistic. There were no available terms with which to describe the composition of a work and what is more the relationship between composition and the expressive force of the subject.[2]

Vasari's concept of *disegno*, she argues, was not our modern notion of design but the creation of figures on natural models, where fidelity to nature—the chief critical standard of Antiquity—was taken as the primary goal of art. Vasari's method of description, it turns out, was the classical rhetorical mode, *ekphrasis*, or *descriptio*, which had been employed by ancient critics to provide verbal evocations of paintings. In these evocations the primary stress was on psychological and narrative details rather than on composition or form.

In the lack of a well developed *corpus* of ancient models for aesthetic theory and critical practice Renaissance theorists and critics, in order more systematically to comprehend the nature of the visual arts, began linking them to the sciences on the one hand or to literature on the other. André Chastel has in fact argued that in the absence of classical guides Renaissance criticism found its articulation 'only at the price' of using 'frameworks and borrowed notions'.[3] During the Quattrocento, when the exciting work was in progress of recovering and inventing the rules of perspective, optics and so forth, the view of painting as a science (in the sense of regularised, teachable knowledge) not unnaturally predominated, culminating in the extreme theoretical views of Leonardo, whose insistence upon the scientific nature of painting and its close relationship with mathematics would have caused it to be classified as a branch of natural science.[4] In the Cinquecento, once the problems had been solved of representing a three-dimensional world in a two-dimensional space, the emphasis of discussion tended to shift from the scientific relationships of painting to literary ones.[5]

The evolution of Renaissance art theory and criticism was thus the joint product of artists, humanists and literary critics.[6] This paper's primary concern will be the humanist contribution (taking 'humanist' according to Professor Kristeller's strict sense of one who has a professional interest in the subjects of *umanità*).[7] It was the humanists who mediated the legacy from the classics, however small, and who first helped draw the links to disciplines with more highly-developed theoretical bases. It was the humanists who, beginning in the Trecento, welcomed painting to the company of the liberal arts, overplaying the classical testimonies in its favour and endowing it with an intellectual stature superior to that which it had actually enjoyed in Antiquity.[8] The relationship between art and humanism in the Quattrocento has been fruitfully investigated, as has the manner in which later sixteenth-century humanists and critics adapted poetic theory to painting.[9] Less clear is the way in which humanists—or artists, for that matter—discussed their reactions to particular works and individual styles. We know that they had lively discussions regarding art works. Certain remarks of Petrarch's confirm this.[10] Likewise, Boccaccio's oft-cited remark that Giotto painted not for the multitude, as medieval painters had done, but to satisfy the intellect of the wise implied the existence of critical standards to which the wise in their intellects adhered.[11] Despite their interest in art, however, humanists—and some of the wise may have been among them—seldom wrote appreciations of individual works in which such standards were expressed. On the whole they were more apt to render judgements about works of art than to state the reasons for their judgements.[12] Yet reasons there must have been. E. H.

Gombrich, in one of his many stimulating articles on Renaissance art theory and criticism, has argued that although there was no corpus of Renaissance writings which confronted concrete problems of criticism, nonetheless Renaissance artists behaved as if they were aware of criticism, and that certain purposeful directions in Renaissance art suggest the existence of accepted standards by which works were judged.[13] Were these standards entirely intuitive or were they at least partly articulated? Were they the property of artists alone or were they shared with humanists, patrons and courtiers? The answers to these questions are difficult to give, and to the extent to which they can be given at all must rest largely on inference. By examining the remarks on art of the sixteenth-century humanist Paolo Giovio, however, the present study aims to afford at least a glimpse of the kinds of standards that were being used during the high Renaissance by humanists when judging works of art, and of the basis on which art was appreciated and evaluated.

Trained as a philosopher and physician in the schools of Padua and Pavia, Giovio migrated to Rome, where he obtained a readership in moral philosophy in the Roman Sapienza as restored by Leo X. After serving an apprenticeship in Latin style under the lights of the Roman Academy he turned to his life's ambition of writing history. As a professional teacher of *umanità* and a lifelong proponent of Latin, Giovio fits Professor Kristeller's strict definition of a humanist. Although he was not an academic philologist, his writings indicate extensive philological studies. In historiography he fell between the rhetorical–humanistic tradition of the Quattrocento and the more pragmatic and archivally oriented vernacular histories of the Cinquecento. Because of his strong humanistic preference for the ancients Giovio is a good indicator of the nature of reliance on classical models. His interests as historian, biographer and 'journalist' involved him deeply in the life of his own times, while his career as papal courtier placed him at its centre.

Art historians have long been interested in Giovio's famous museum of portraits at Como, his role in the genesis of Vasari's *Lives*, and his brief biographies of Leonardo, Michelangelo and Raphael—the earliest written of each.[14] More recently his writings have been exploited for clues to assist in reconstructing some of the standards which may have helped mould developments in Renaissance art.[15] Much of Giovio's life was indeed passed in tantalising proximity to some of the most consequential developments in sixteenth-century art. At Pavia, for example, his principal mentor in medicine was the young Veronese anatomist Marc'antonio della Torre, who at that moment was engaged in writing an anatomy text for which, according to Vasari, Leonardo was to supply illustrations.[16] While still a student, therefore, Giovio most probably witnessed at close hand that phase where art and science were partners in intellectual progress. In his life of Leonardo he expressed his admiration for the artist's going to dissect the bodies of criminals 'in the very schools of the physicians'.[17]

Giovio's arrival in Rome in 1512 coincided with the apogee of the high Renaissance. Michelangelo was just finishing the Sistine ceiling, and Raphael was at work on the *stanze*. The Stanza della Segnatura had already been completed and work on the Stanza del Heliodoro had begun. Under Bramante's direction the four great crossing piers of St Peter's had been erected and parts of the eastern porticoes completed in the Cortile del Belvedere. Attached by the new Pope, Leo X, to the retinue of his cousin, Cardinal Giulio, Giovio soon found himself in circles where the arts were a frequent topic of conversation. As a courtier of the Medici he would have had to learn at least to discuss them intelligently, but, as we shall see, his interest went deeper than the mere acquisition of those amateur graces recommended in *The Courtier* by his friend Count Baldassare Castiglione.[18]

Giovio's early years in the service of the Medici are somewhat obscure, but about 1520 he was apparently invited to design the programme for the banqueting hall at Poggio a Caiano, one of the great Florentine projects of the high Renaissance. He had gone to Florence in the train of Cardinal Giulio, who had been entrusted with the government of the city by Leo X following the untimely death of Lorenzo, Duke of Urbino.[19] Unfortunately Giovio's programme for the frescoes has not survived. Ingenious reconstructions have been put forth, particularly by Pontormo scholars seeking to account for the apparent discrepancy between the lunettes and the panels below. In regard to these latter there is no reason to discount Vasari's statement that they represent scenes from Roman history which prefigure the Medici.[20] Whatever the exact details of the programme, it is clear, as the iconographic disputes have emphasised, that like the Vatican *stanze* the ensemble was one in which art and history, image and letter, were inseparably linked. Beginning with the Quattrocento frescoes in the Sistine Chapel, which, beyond narrating the history of man *sub lege* and *sub gratia*, seem to have constituted an allegory of the rise and triumph of papal power, humanists and artists had collaborated at Rome in contriving historical–allegorical cycles.[21] Thus the *stanza* of Heliodorus not only narrated historical episodes in which the Church was delivered from persecutors but simultaneously prefigured the triumphs of Julius II in driving the barbarians from Italy. In like manner, but even more explicitly, Giovio's programme for Poggio a Caiano comprised episodes from Roman history with particular significance for the history of the Medici family. In fact, having been chosen predominantly for their prefigurative significance rather than their importance in Roman history, the scenes—with the possible exception of Cicero's return from exile—are difficult to decipher by themselves. In this respect the literary apparatus is predominant.

In the absence of the programme or any allusions of his to it, it is difficult to infer anything more of Giovio's views regarding the collaboration of brush and pen at Poggio a Caiano. Significantly, perhaps, in Giovio's subsequent collaborative project, the great hall of the palace of the Cancelleria at Rome, done with Vasari in 1546, descriptive Latin inscriptions accompany every panel.[22] Here, however, there is no erudite humanist scheme of historical prefiguration but actual scenes from the life and pontificate of Paul III. The narrative of the present is wholly dominant. In this regard it is interesting to note Von Schlosser's observation that the exaltation of narrative painting became increasingly characteristic of Vasari's own outlook and that it constituted a pronounced trend of sixteenth-century art in general.[23] As painting moved towards narrative the criticism of painting would find it increasingly natural to draw from literary criticism. Rensselaer Lee, in tracing the origin and development of the humanistic theory of painting, has drawn attention to the influence on sixteenth-century theorists of Aristotle's statement that human beings in action were the theme of painting.[24] By converting Aristotle's observation into a dictum later Renaissance theorists concluded that the accurate depiction of the bodily postures expressive of the passions of the soul was painting's chief goal. Such a view invited the interpretation of painting in literary terms, given that the task of literature had been similarly stated as to describe the movements of the soul by using words. By emphasising a task common to both arts this view prompted the development of an aesthetic in which the anomalies were gradually forgotten of transferring a criticism of the art of words succeeding one another in time (paraphrasing Lessing) to an art of figures coexistent in space.[25] To the extent, however, that literature may be more conformable to the goals of art than of science, this may have been a step nearer the evolution of distinctive criteria for the criticism of art.

Although he predated the theorists discussed by Lee, Giovio, as evidenced by the Poggio cycle, found it congenial to view art as narrative, and, as we shall see, he found it natural to draw from literary criticism when judging and describing it. He likewise endorsed the linking of painting to the liberal arts. At the very outset of his brief life of Leonardo, Giovio cited with approval the great master's assertion that painting could be rightly practised only by those who had applied themselves to 'the disciplines and noble arts, these being necessarily, as it were, the handmaidens of painting'.[26] Leonardo's pronouncement echoed Alberti's injunction to the painter to scan the poets and historians for subjects of universal interest and to cultivate learned men for ideas. As Lee points out, the tradition of the learned painter derived from the *doctus poeta* of antiquity. It also owed much to the tradition of the orator, who was similarly advised by Cicero, Quintilian and others to cultivate the historians and poets.[27] Neither Giovio's endorsement of the tradition of the learned painter, however, nor his involvement in projects of narrative painting seems to have blinded him to the intrinsic problems of painting. Certain phrases of his clearly suggest a developed awareness of artistic representation in its own right. Describing the Isola Viscontea at Pavia, for example, he characterised Filarete's castle as 'celebrated for its distinguished construction and pictorial charm'.[28] A century and a half earlier the fortress had been praised by Petrarch as 'the most august among all modern works'.[29] Giovio's phrase 'picturae iucunditate' seems to indicate an awareness of pictorial vision, presupposing elements of deliberate selection and composition.

In his dialogue *De viris illustribus*, composed at Ischia following the sack of Rome, Giovio gives evidence of his own connoisseurship, as well as of the tendency for criticism to link problems of literature and art in the *ut pictura poesis* tradition.[30] Giovio, the Marquis del Vasto and Giovanni Antonio Muscettola, a jurist who was one of Charles V's agents at Rome, are having a conversation about contemporary literature. As a short survey of literature the dialogue is reminiscent of the tenth book of Quintilian, although in form it is Ciceronian. While neither a poet himself nor a particularly profound or original critic, Giovio was a perceptive reader and abreast of the critical controversies of the day, particularly those regarding the merits of the vernacular and the role of imitation. One of the dialogue's principal themes is the relationship between art and nature, talent and training, imitation and creation, and it is in this context that the allusions to art occur. The first involves Perugino. Why is it, Muscettola queries, that precocious poets seldom endure? The answer, according to Giovio, is that when they lose the natural vitality of youth they are unable in maturity to compensate for it by breadth of culture and systematic discipline. Giovio himself cites the pathetic example of a musician who vainly strove as a mature man to master the new and more elegant forms coming into vogue. After laughing at Giovio's example Muscettola agrees and adduces the example of Perugino.

... This indeed seems to be most true, for we do discover certain boundaries of human talent in individual artists which are never easily surpassed, even with effort and skill. Did anyone who painted, for example, excel Perugino in his prime for celebrity or fame, who now as an octogenarian continues to paint consistently enough but without glory? Indeed, for a long time he was ostentatiously favoured by all the princes of Italy while he was creating in various places the most worthy—as it then appeared—monuments of art. For no one depicted more suavely and sweetly than he did the countenances and faces of divinities, especially angels, the chief witness to this being Pope Sixtus, who awarded him the palm of victory in the fruitful competition among the artists who were decorating the papal chapel. But after those celebrated lights of perfect art, Leonardo, Michelangelo and Raphael—risen suddenly from the shadows of that age—had obscured the fame and reputation of his works, it was in vain that Perugino tried by observing and imitating superior works to retain his stature; for owing to a sterility of talent he always came back to the pretty countenances which he had fixed upon as a youth, so that his spirit could scarcely bear the ignominy of comparison when those others depicted with stupendous variety the naked limbs of august images and the struggling powers of nature in multiple forms of everything.[31]

Here Giovio is within the classical tradition, illustrating points in a literary discussion with analogies from art which presuppose parallels in the creative process. It is interesting to see him applying the ancient rhetorical standard of *copia*, variety, to Michelangelo's advantage and Perugino's disadvantage.[32]

The dialogue's second allusion to art likewise concerns training and discipline. As preparation for the aspiring writer Giovio has been prescribing long years of reading Latin, with abstention from writing it until the age of twenty,

... just as in a separate, but not altogether dissimilar, art Leonardo da Vinci was accustomed to do with his favourite pupils, who in our age raised painting to the greatest dignity, skilfully uncovering the secrets of the ancients; for until the twentieth year, as we have said, he forbade them the use of brush and pigments, so that they might apply themselves to drawing with a lead stylus, diligently selecting and copying the best examples of older works and imitating in the simplest drawings the force of nature and the lineaments of bodies, which are revealed to our eyes beneath so great a variety of motions. He even wished them to dissect human cadavers. . . .[33]

This rule of Leonardo's Giovio strongly commends to the apprentice writer. For the mature author, however, he counsels daily practice, this time citing Donatello.

But subsequently the daily use of the pen is recommended without gainsay as the best and most direct guide to writing well, just as in other arts we plainly see the same to be true. It is related of the Florentine, Donatello, whose bronze equestrian statue of Gattemelata in the piazza of Padua displays the glory of distinguished art, that when anyone questioned him privately as to the best method of learning an art he was accustomed to respond, 'In art, to make often and remake is to progress.'[34]

While preceding analogies have been concerned with method, Giovio's concluding ones broach the question of style. Faced with the variety of great Latin models, what writer, exclaims Giovio, could hope to imitate them all? Rather, they are now to be admired who with ingenuity, labour and perseverance have attained a good and stable level and whose work can be readily recognised by stylistic individualities,

. . . just as by inspecting one of the better paintings we recognise at once the hand and brush of the artist; for in individuals, by the necessity of nature, the highest virtues are accompanied by particular and, indeed, inevitable marks. The figures of Michelangelo are notable for their profound shadows and admirable shading, so that the more brightly they are illuminated the more they stand out and protrude. In the human countenances which Sebastiano paints superbly we perceive soft and liquid strokes veiled in the most alluring colours; in the case of Titian praise is heaped upon the pleasing surface of things, set off by small dark strokes and exquisite oblique effects. Dosso is wonderfully delighted by images that are rough, vivacious, intertwined and shaded with smoky colours; and although in expressing, surely, the same nature and appearance of things the works of these painters are varied and dissimilar, nonetheless, as tastes and judgements have disposed, they have all received, each in its own way, the highest commendation for excellence. By this example I am readily persuaded to think that for unusually gifted students, burning with zeal to acquire eloquence, the reins should be loosened and slackened, so that even if they are unable to imitate the divine style of the ancients perfectly, nonetheless with each following his own inclination, according to his own nature, they will at least attain a tolerable and not ungraceful mode of writing.[35]

Several observations may be in order at this point. To begin with, Giovio stays within the classical tradition of *ut pictura poesis*. Examples from art are used to illustrate questions arising in a discussion of literature; literature is not being mined for rules of art. However, the understated phrase 'a not altogether dissimilar art' suggests that Giovio held the view of literature and painting as sister arts which was the condition of the eventual adaptation of literary theory to painting. His discussion of the relative importance of talent and training in developing a good Latin style is reminiscent of the discussions in Cicero's *De oratore*, in which one of the main themes is a running argument regarding the respective importance of these two factors.[36] While his discussion of literary style lacks the moral and philosophic overtones of the *De oratore*, with its confrontation of issues stemming from Plato's *Gorgias*, Giovio's dependency on Cicero is nonetheless obvious, and, considering his own penchants as a prose stylist and historian, hardly surprising. Here is another instance of the rhetorical legacy of humanism. For the sixteenth-century humanist critic the orator's training became, in a sense, the paradigm of training for all the arts.

But Giovio's dependence on the classics was by no means complete. In speaking realistically to the problems of mastering a foreign language Giovio could not rely wholly on Cicero or Quintilian, who were, after all, concerned with the acquisition of effective style by orators employing their native tongue. Whereas Quintilian recommends 'reading for a long time none save the best authors' he does not go as far as Giovio in recommending to the aspiring Latinist abstention from efforts at serious composition until at least the age of twenty.[37] Apparently Giovio thought it took this long for the mind to be thoroughly imbued with the cadences of the acquired language. To support his recommendation Giovio has introduced Leonardo's method of instructing his pupils, not so much as an illustration but as a substantial confirmation of his own theories. Like Latin, painting was also a new language, and Leonardo's methods were for Giovio a real precedent, perhaps even a source. Reliance on the arts for didactic method would have been quite in accord with the tendency of Quattrocento humanism to accept painting as a partner in intellectual developments.

With regard to the problem of imitation and style, which the third of Giovio's passages raises, it is evident that both the visual arts and the ancient orators could be brought to bear. In the *De oratore* Antonius suggests that as an orator Sulpicius, another of the interlocutors, has been formed both by nature, which endowed him with innate capacity, and by imitation of Licinius Crassus.[38] After cautioning the novice orator to study and imitate the excellences rather than the mannerisms of his model Antonius goes on to review the distinctive schools of oratory. In a similar passage Quintilian cautions the fledgling orator to imitate only the best authors, bewaring of the blemishes which even they reveal and always bearing in mind that imitation of stylistic characteristics will be vain if the student himself lacks that natural vigour of talent which is the fundamental source of the model's excellence.[39] That Giovio was in agreement with these strictures is suggested by his recommendation that imitation be not carried to the point of slavishness, but that after the basic elements of good Latin have been acquired the reins should be slackened and natural inclination given a chance to assert itself.

To illustrate his contention that individual style in oratory may differ within the bounds of the art in general, Crassus is made to argue in book III of the *De oratore*,

There is a single art and method of painting, and nevertheless there is an extreme dissimilarity between Zeuxis, Aglaophon and Apelles, while at the same time there is not one among them who can be thought to lack any factor in his art. And if this be surprising and nevertheless true in the case of what may be called the silent arts, how much more remarkable it is in oratory and in language![40]

More extensive is Quintilian's analogy between styles of oratory and the arts. In book XII when he resumes his discussion of style in oratory (*genere orationis*) he begins by arguing that since oratory is the product of both the art of rhetoric and the individual orator it will take many forms, just as in all instances involving an art and an artist.

> But they differ greatly from one another, and not merely in *species*, as statue differs from statue, picture from picture and speech from speech, but in *genus* as well, as, for example, Etruscan statues differ from Greek and Asiatic orators from Attic. But these different kinds of work, of which I speak, are not merely the product of different authors, but have each their own following of admirers. . . .[41]

There follows a *résumé* of painting and sculpture with regard to stylistic individualities. Giovio's debt to Quintilian in the passages from the *De viris illustribus* previously cited, down to the recognition of varying tastes of critics, need not be laboured.

The analyses of Cicero and Quintilian regarding style in oratory, including their concept of individual variation within different schools (Greek, Asiatic, Roman, etc), were more developed than Pliny's notions of style in art. Pliny (e.g. xxxv, 75) mentions the existence of schools of painting but does not attempt to expand on what distinguished them from each other. Neither of the Roman orators, however, carried over into his discussions of artists the same precision in classification that he displayed with respect to rhetoric. Where Giovio differs from his classical models is in his attempt to expand the potentialities of his art criticism by borrowing terms and expressions which they employed for literary criticism.

Basically Giovio's art vocabulary, in this dialogue and in the lives of Leonardo, Michelangelo and Raphael, derived from Pliny. From Pliny came expressions to describe light and shadow (*lumen atque umbras*, xxxv, 29), transition of colours (*colorum transitus, loc. cit.*), oblique effects (*obliquas imagines*, xxxv, 56) and symmetry (xxxv, 67). From Pliny derived expressions such as 'delicate line' (*lineam tenuitatis*, xxxv, 81) or 'convoluted' (*convolutum*, xix, 27), usages such as *imagines exprimere* (xxxv, 153) and adjectives such as *suavis* or *austerus* to describe colour or line (ix, 140; xxxv, 30). Of course these words were not exclusive to writers on art, but in Pliny, who had been one of his youthful preoccupations, Giovio found a certain number of usages ready-formed.[42]

Often, however, Giovio's language seems to have derived more from that intermediate zone where the same expressions describe effects both of painting and literature. Thus we find phrases such as in *eadem re . . . et specie*, *exquisita indole*, or *delicatae artis*. The phrase *suaves et liquidos tractus blandissimis coloribus convelatos* is more reminiscent of classical literary criticism than it is of Pliny's art criticism.[43] Sometimes Giovio will simply apply to painting expressions generally used in literary criticism: for example, *prudentius atque tranquillius* to modify *pinxisse*; or *luxuranti ac festiva* modifying *manu*.[44] A striking example of this tendency is Giovio's paraphrase of Cicero's strictures in *De oratore* regarding purple passages. The Ciceronian passage is as follows:

Sed habeat illa in dicendo admiratio ac summa laus umbram aliquam et recessum, quo magis, id quod erit illuminatum, exstare atque eminere videatur.[45]

Giovio's observations, cited above, regarding the figures of Michelangelo begin,

Habent Michaelis Angeli figurae profundiores umbras et recessus admirabiles, ut clarius illuminatae magis exstent et emineant.[46]

A passage from Pliny expresses the same concept:

Lumen et umbras custodiit atque ut eminerent e tabulis picturae maxime curavit.[47]

Yet it is clear that in usage Giovio is following Cicero rather than Pliny. Concepts and words may derive from Pliny but the context in which Giovio employs them is Ciceronian. In beginning thus to adapt the language of literary criticism to the description of art Giovio was contributing to the first stage in the evolution of Cinquecento art criticism.[48]

On the general questions of style, imitation and originality which Giovio's dialogue raises, literary criticism was considerably more advanced than art criticism and remained so for some decades. What effect discussions such as Giovio's concerning imitation versus originality may have had on artists in Roman circles is largely a matter of conjecture, although the problem of imitation was one which every major artist faced on a practical level when ending his apprenticeship. Vasari's tendency to see the course of Renaissance art as one of progressive fidelity to nature represented an attempt to organise variation from artist to artist in terms of an overriding principle, in this case the same principle which also appears to have formed the standard of Pliny's criticism, and one to which Giovio himself adhered.[49]

At roughly the same time as the dialogue *De viris illustribus* Giovio seems to have written his *vitae* of 'those celebrated lights of perfect art' Leonardo, Michelangelo and Raphael. As the earliest known lives of these artists, Giovio's brief biographies have been of continuing interest to art historians.[50] In format they correspond to the *elogia*, or 'inscriptions'—'short but penetrating biographies', as Giovio styled them—which he appended on parchment to the portraits of famous personages collected in his *musaeum* in Como.[51] It was Giovio's aspiration to publish both portraits and inscriptions in a fashion which Golzio has suggested would have imitated Varro's *De imaginibus*.[52]

Only two series of *elogia* were published during Giovio's lifetime, and without the portraits. A third series, never published at all, was to have comprised 'makers of great works of art', and for this series the biographies in question were no doubt destined. Like the dialogue *De viris illustribus*, they reveal a frequently astute connoisseurship and a predisposition to emphasise the links of art with humanism.

Brief as it is, Giovio's life of Leonardo is a remarkably balanced assessment of the philosopher–artist's character and contributions to art, stressing—not inappropriately—Leonardo's intellectual and philosophical bents. In the life of Michelangelo are found more judgements of an aesthetic nature, notably in regard to the Sistine ceiling.

Summoned by Julius II with a huge sum of money, Michelangelo, by completing an immense work in a comparatively short time, left in the Sistine chapel of the Vatican a testimony of absolute art. Painting supine, as necessary, he composed some of the figures in the recesses and bays in a soft, fleeting light, as with the dismembered body of Holofernes in the tent; in other places, however, as with Haman affixed to the cross, he so successfully produced the light itself, by means of expressive shadows, that with the real nature of bodies thus represented, even ingenious artisans marvelled at things that were flat as if they had been solid. Among the remarkable images of men there is to be seen in the centre of the vault the figure of an old man flying in the heavens, delineated with such symmetry that when seen from diverse areas of the chapel it seems to our deluded eyes always to revolve and change its posture.[53]

In thus describing Michelangelo's masterpiece Giovio clearly betrays the influence of Pliny. An interest in remuneration, size and speed are all characteristic of Pliny, as are pre-occupation with shadow, three-dimensionality and realism. Giovio's interest in the illusion created by the image of God separating light from darkness even recalls Pliny's description of the Minerva of Famulus.[54]

In view of Giovio's subsequent association with Vasari it is interesting to note that he speaks of Michelangelo's having been the next after Leonardo who 'approached the greatness of the ancients'. In Giovio we do not find the Vasarian notion of Quattrocento artists who equalled and Cinquecento artists who surpassed the greatness of the ancients, but only of those who approached it. With reference to Vasari it is likewise interesting to note Giovio's description of the Sistine ceiling as a proof of 'absolute art', indicating that, like Vasari, he believed the human nude was the supreme test of artistic achievement. Giovio's observations on Michelangelo's character obviously offended Karl Frey, who consequently set a low value on the author and the life.[55] Charles de Tolnay has more equitably observed that Giovio's biography 'reflects the reserve of the court of Leo X on the "unruly" nature of Michelangelo'.[56] Evidently Giovio set little store by the *furor divinus*. Here is the offending passage:

But while a man of so great genius, he was by nature so rough and untamed that, beyond the incredible scandals of his private life, he even begrudged posterity successors in his art; for even when implored by princes he could never be induced to instruct, or even to admit anyone at all to his workshop for the sake of observing.[57]

It is a comment in keeping with Giovio's avowedly Plutarchan propensities.[58]

Raphael Giovio ranked third, after Leonardo and Michelangelo, making some critically astute observations, most notably on the ill effect upon Raphael's art of his attempting to compete with Michelangelo in painting muscular nudes. 'In all his paintings of every sort a charm was never lacking, which is interpreted as grace, although he did go sometimes to excess in articulating the muscles of the limbs when he ambitiously strove to display a force of art beyond his nature.'[59] In speaking of Raphael's 'charm [*venustas*] which is interpreted as grace [*gratia*]' Giovio seems to be combining the descriptions given by Pliny and Quintilian of Apelles of Cos, who was renowned among ancient painters for these qualities. Pliny speaks of his *venustas*, Quintilian of his *gratia*.[60] Needless to say, the concept of grace (*grazia*) was a fundamental ingredient in the aesthetics of Vasari.

Being an intimate companion of the Pope—*commensalis perpetuus* he is styled in a bull of Clement VII—Giovio would have had a better opportunity than most to observe the frescoes of the *stanze*, which, being the Pope's private apartments, were not generally open to view. The order he gives for their completion, art historians have pointed out, is confirmed by contemporary documentation. With regard to the uses of the *stanze*, Redig de Campos was inclined to accept Giovio's statements as authoritative.[61] With Raphael's perspective Giovio at times found fault, but, like Ludovico Dolce, praised his use of colour above Michelangelo's.

He did not always accurately observe optical laws in dimensions and distances, but in drawing lines to terminate as if by boundaries what were to be contiguous areas of colour, and in mixing and mitigating the starkness of the more vivid pigments, he competed beyond all else with Buonarroti, whose one weakness was here, so that—a most pleasing artist—to pictures learnedly drawn he might add the lucid and imperishable ornament of colours mingled with oil.[62]

The phrase 'starkness of the more vivid pigments' suggests that Giovio may have had in mind Michelangelo's Doni Madonna, never a very popular work in its day. Of all Raphael's works the one Giovio seems to have admired the most was the Transfiguration. John Pope Hennessy suggests that at one point Giovio possessed the Alba Madonna, now in Washington, which he left to the Olivetan convent in his see of Nocera de' Pagani.[63] After his discussion of Raphael, Giovio praises his disciples, Giulio Romano and Gianfrancesco Penni, before going on to conclude with observations on Sebastiano del Piombo, Lorenzo Costa, Sodoma and Dosso Dossi, which should be of interest for the history of taste.

After Raphael's death several artists struggled with almost equal glory to succeed him, and of these his disciples Francesco and Giulio are distinguished in this one most exquisite talent of art, that they acutely and diligently emulate the hand of the master. Surpassing all others, however, Sebastian, a Venetian, paints portraits with incomparable felicity, who, with singular praise, learned to enliven pictures with wonderful fineness of line and then to shade them with pleasing transition of colours. In the precise works of Titian, likewise a Venetian, shine forth manifold virtues of refined art which are understood almost alone by artists, and not even the more pedestrian among them. The Mantuan Costa [actually a Ferrarese] paints in soft colours suave portraits of men with decent and composed bearing, such that it is judged that by no one could the images of armed and toga'd men be more pleasingly expressed. But expert critics desire of him not so much veiled as nude figures, as a greater proof of art, and these he is not easily able to furnish, since he has been unable to bring the more certain disciplines to bear on the use of painting, being content with less rigorous study. Sodoma of Vercelli, well known in Siena for a perverted and unstable judgement—to the point of insanity—when he recalls his mind to art, accomplishes admirable things, and with such an impetuous hand, and yet—the marvel is—no one gives the impression of painting more tranquilly and prudently than he does. The gentle manner of Dosso of Ferrara is esteemed in his proper works, but most of all in those which are called *parerga*. For devoting himself with relish to the pleasant diversions of painting he used to depict jagged rocks, green groves, the firm banks of traversing rivers, the flourishing work of the countryside, the gay and hard toil of the peasants, and also the far distant prospects of land and sea, fleets, fowling, hunting, and all that genre so pleasing to the eyes in a lavish and festive style.[64]

From these remarks it is clear that Giovio was aware that art, like literature, consisted of both tradition and innovation, and that it involved a study of both nature and convention. In accepting the nude as the standard of artistic achievement he followed Leonardo, at least to the extent of giving nature the predominant value.[65] Once a standard had been set it was natural to view the history of art, as did Vasari, as the perfection of means.[66] If his dialogue *De viris illustribus* is an accurate index the qualities Giovio particularly admired in literature were refinement, ease, flow and resourcefulness, and it is not surprising that he should have admired the same qualities in art.[67] Despite their brevity Giovio's remarks are, if anything, more descriptive of stylistic qualities of individual artists than are Vasari's descriptions. That Giovio was capable of *ekphrasis* is shown by his Pliniesque description of Dosso's landscapes, although the general tenor of his remarks suggests that he was more apt to speak of artistic qualities and style.

Professor Gombrich has called attention to the classical precedent for Giovio's description of Dosso's landscapes in Pliny's account of the Roman painter Studius

... who first introduced the most attractive fashion of painting walls with pictures of country houses and porticoes and landscape gardens, groves, woods, hills, fish-ponds, canals, rivers, coasts, and whatever anybody could desire, together with various sketches of people going for a stroll or sailing in a boat or on land going to country houses riding on asses or in carriages, and also people fishing and fowling or hunting or even gathering the vintage. His works include splendid villas approached by roads across marshes, men tottering and staggering along carrying women on their shoulders for a bargain, and a number of humorous drawings of that sort besides, extremely wittily designed.[68]

A comparison of the two passages in the original reveals how Giovio has amplified the type of description found in Pliny with more 'literary' phrases, *virentia nemora, praeruptas cautes, opacas perflentiam ripas*, etc.[69] Giovio's interest in landscape can be traced back to his earliest literary production, a letter describing his family's country villa at Lissago, near Como.[70] As model for this letter Giovio had taken the well known letters of Pliny the Younger describing his Tuscan, Laurentian and Como villas, together with their surrounding landscape. In the dialogue *De foeminis illustribus*, also composed during his Ischian sojourn of 1528, Giovio devoted considerable care to describing the setting, first the gardens of the *scopuli reginae* and then the grove by the fountain of Pontano.[71] Hence for describing landscape painting he was able to draw upon a long-standing interest in the classical genre of landscape description.

In conclusion, then, an examination of Paolo Giovio's principal statements on art (all of them, incidentally, pre-dating his relationship with Vasari) gives some idea of the standards used by an influential sixteenth-century humanist for judging art. They were largely the standards of ancient critics, presupposing fidelity to nature as the highest standard of art, regarding the human form as the supreme test, and admiring virtuosity, fertility and grace. But just as the ancients themselves were weak in descriptive statements about the qualities on which their stated judgements rested, so likewise Giovio was limited in giving expression to the basis for his critical judgements. His conception of art stressed its narrative aspects and its links with history and literature. Nonetheless in a seeming attempt to expand the scope of his observations in areas of intrinsic artistic concern, such as individual styles, Giovio not only exploited what critical vocabulary he had inherited from ancient commentators on art but enlarged it with borrowings both of words and concepts from the rhetoricians. In the evolution of Renaissance art criticism, accordingly, his place was with the reinterpreters of the classical *ut pictura poesis* tradition, but in borrowing from literary criticism to enhance the expressiveness of his judgements he indicated the way to greater borrowings which subsequently resulted in the *ut poesi pictura* tradition of the later sixteenth century. By attempting to understand the nature of art through linking it with literature Giovio typified the second tendency of Renaissance criticism (the first having been to link it with science). In failing to progress substantially beyond the level of ancient art criticism he illustrated the dependence of Renaissance humanists on the classics for basic modes of perception, and, given the limitations of classical criticism, the incomplete nature of the conceptual framework with which the Renaissance approached art.

NOTES

Materials for this study were gathered, and a first version presented, while I was the recipient of a fellowship from Villa I Tatti, and I should like to thank the director, Professor Myron P. Gilmore, for his encouragement and support. In its present form the study owes much to the criticism of my colleague at Reed in philosophy, Marvin Levich. For assistance I am also beholden to my colleagues in classics, Frederic Peachy and Richard Tron, and to Peter Parshall in art history. This seems an appropriate place, moreover, to acknowledge Professor Kristeller's generous assistance in my research on Giovio.

[1] P. O. Kristeller, 'The modern system of the arts: a study in the history of aesthetics', *Journal of the History of Ideas*, XII, 1951, pp. 496–527; XIII, 1952, pp. 17–45.

[2] Svetlana Alpers, '*Ekphrasis* and aesthetic attitudes in Vasari's *Lives*', *Journal of the Warburg and Courtauld Institutes*, XXIII, 1960, p. 193, n. 14.

[3] André Chastel, *Art et humanisme à Florence au temps de Laurent le Magnifique*, Paris, 1961, p. 8.

[4] Kristeller, p. 514. Leonardo's views, of course, must be separated from his practice. In the *Paragone* he called painting the highest form of science, but clearly his imagination was not inferior to his eye. Michelangelo stressed beauty over 'science'. For Vasari judgement was more important than measurement. According to Kristeller, only in the late seventeenth century did a clear distinction emerge between art and science. (*Ibid.*, p. 526.)

[5] Rensselaer W. Lee, '*Ut pictura poesis:* the humanistic theory of painting', *Art Bulletin*, XXII, 1940, pp. 200, 203.

[6] In the sixteenth century it began to be conceded that laymen could have useful opinions about art itself. (Anthony Blunt, *Artistic Theory in Italy, 1450–1600*, Oxford, 1940, p. 56.) Blunt speculates that Vasari's concept of grace may have derived from Castiglione.

[7] P. O. Kristeller, *Renaissance Thought: the Classic, Scholastic and Humanistic Strains*, New York, 1961, p. 10.

[8] Kristeller, *Journal of the History of Ideas*, XII, pp. 513–14.

[9] Beyond the article of Lee and the books of Chastel and Blunt cited above, see W. Guild Howard, '*Ut pictura poesis*', *Publications of the Modern Language Association of America*, XXIV, 1909, pp. 40–123. The recent work of M. Baxandall, *Giotto and the Orators*, Oxford, 1971, with its interesting arguments about the effect of Latin linguistic

structure on humanist perceptions of art, came into my hands too late for serious reflection and possible absorption into my principal argument.

[10] Theodor E. Mommsen, *Mediaeval and Renaissance Studies*, Ithaca, N.Y., 1959, p. 213. See also Prince d'Essling and Eugène Müntz, *Pétrarque: ses études d'art, son influence sur les artistes, etc.*, Paris, 1902.

[11] *Decameron*, VI, 5.

[12] Petrarch's judgements are almost exclusively 'quantitative', although he evidently had reasons for them. On the narrow range of commonplaces in which he expressed them see Baxandall, pp. 51–2.

[13] E. H. Gombrich, 'The leaven of criticism in Renaissance art', in *Art, Science and History in the Renaissance*, ed. Charles S. Singleton, Baltimore, 1967, p. 3.

[14] According to Tullia Franzi, their overriding value is as contemporary evidence. (*Résumés des communications présentées au XIIIe Congrès International d'Histoire de l'Art*, Stockholm, 1933, pp. 119–20.)

[15] E. H. Gombrich, *Norm and Form*, London, 1966, p. 113. The most recent study of Giovio's museum of portraits is by Paul Ortwin Rave, 'Das Museo Giovio zu Como', in *Miscellanea Bibliothecae Hertzianae*, Munich, 1961, pp. 275–84. For his role in the genesis of Vasari's lives see Vasari's account in his life of himself, and Wolfgang Kallab, *Vasaristudien*, Vienna and Leipzig, 1908, p. 143. For a sceptical view see Julius von Schlosser, *La letteratura artistica*, Florence, 1964, pp. 196, 291.

The biographies of Leonardo, Raphael and Michelangelo have recently been edited, along with fragments from Giovio's dialogue, *De viris illustribus*, by Paola Barocchi, *Scritti d'arte del Cinquecento*, I, Milan and Naples, 1971, pp. 7–18, 1098–101. I am in occasional disagreement with Barocchi's interpretation of Giovio's Latin.

[16] Life of Leonardo, *Le Vite*, ed. Milanesi, Florence, 1878–85, IV, pp. 34–5. See also J. Playfair McMurrich, *Leonardo da Vinci the Anatomist*, London, 1930, p. 62, and Kenneth Clark, *Leonardo da Vinci*, Cambridge, 1939, p. 161.

[17] Barocchi, p. 7.

[18] On Giovio's friendship with Castiglione see V. Cian, *Baldassare Castiglione*, Rome, 1951, p. 164. Although a philosopher by training, Giovio had a critical rather than a theoretical interest in art. He did not write works of a philosophical nature, like his contemporary Nifo's *De pulchro*.

[19] *Pauli Iovii opera*, Rome, 1956– , I, *Epistolarum pars prior*, ed. G. G. Ferrero, p. 86.

[20] Life of Franciabigio, *ed. cit.*, V, p. 195. Scholarly discussions of the banqueting hall include Kurt Forster, *Pontormo*, Munich, 1966; Janet Cox Rearick, *The Drawings of Pontormo*, Cambridge, Mass., 1964; Mattias Winner, 'Cosimo il Vecchio als Cicero', *Zeitschrift für Kunstgeschichte*, XXXIII, 1970, pp. 261–97; John Shearman, *Andrea del Sarto*, Oxford, 1965; André Chastel, *op. cit.*; Sidney Freedberg, *Andrea del Sarto*, Cambridge, Mass., 1963, and Philip Foster, 'Lorenzo de' Medici's Cascina at Poggio a Caiano', *Mitteilungen des Kunsthistorischen Instituts in Florenz*, XL, 1969, pp. 47–56.

[21] See L. D. Ettlinger, *The Sistine Chapel before Michelangelo*, Oxford, 1965.

[22] For a discussion of the cycle see Ernst Steinmann, 'Freskenzyklen der Späterenaissance in Rom. I. Die Sala Farnese in der Cancelleria', *Monatshefte für Kunstwissenschaft*, III, 1910, p. 46.

[23] *Op. cit.*, p. 331.

[24] *Op. cit.*

[25] *Ibid.*, p. 255. As Lee points out (p. 197), Cinquecento theorists reversed the Horatian dictum to read *ut poesi pictura*.

[26] Barocchi, p. 7.

[27] *Op. cit.*, p. 211. On the exaggeration in the sixteenth century of Alberti's strictures regarding the pre-eminence of historical subjects in painting see p. 236. A difference exists, however, between Alberti's Quattrocento stress on historical subjects and Cinquecento views of painting as narrative. The change comes with Leonardo's charge to the painter to paint the 'ideas in man's mind'. (Blunt, p. 34.) Pliny praises Aristides for depicting thought and emotions. (XXXV, 98.)

[28] *De vita Ferdinandi Davali, Illustrium virorum vitae*, Basel, 1578, p. 378.

[29] *Sen.* v, 1. Cited by John White, *Art and Architecture in Italy, 1250–1400*, Harmondsworth, 1966, p. 333. Petrarch's description of the castle (. . . *structurae mirabilis atque impensae . . . quo iuditio rerum es, cuncta inter modernorum opera, hoc augustissimum iudicasses . . .*) illustrates the humanist tendency to give quantitative rather than qualitative judgements about art and architecture.

[30] *De viris illustribus*, ed. G. Tiraboschi, *Storia della letteratura italiana*, Venice, 1795–1797, VII, part IV (vol. XIII), pp. 1594–1640. Where possible, citation will be from Barocchi's extracts (see n. 15).

[31] Hic arridens Musetius, hoc, inquit, Aedepol, verissimum esse videtur, nam certos quosdam humani captus terminos in singulis prope artificibus esse deprehendimus, qui nunquam vel laboriose et solerter enitendo facile superantur. Quis enim Perusino, qui nunc etiam octogenarius satis constanti manu, sed inglorius, pingit, quum aetate floreret, majore concursu vel claritate picturam exercuit? Favere siquidem illi aliquandiu et ambitiose quidem omnes Italiae principes, quum ille passim dignissima, ut tum videbantur, artis monumenta deponeret. Nemo enim illo divorum vultus et ora, praesertim angelorum, blandius et suavius exprimebat, vel testimonio Xisti Pontificis, qui ei palmam detulit, quum in pingendo domestico templo artifices questuosa contentione decertassent. At postquam illa perfectae artis praeclara lumina Vincius, Michael Angleus atque Raphaël, ab illis saeculi tenebris repente orta, illius famam et nomen admirandis operibus obruerunt, frustra Perusinus, meliora aemulando atque observando, partam dignitatem retinere conatus est, quod semper ad suos bellulos vultus, quibus iuvenis haeserat, sterilitate ingenii [rediret]. six ut prae pudore vix ignominiam animo sustineret, quando illi augustarum imaginum nudatos artus et connitentis naturae potestates in multiplici rerum omnium genere stupenda varietate figurarent. Tiraboschi, pp. 1604–05; Barocchi, pp. 19–20.) In regard to the issue of talent *v.* training it is interesting to recall Michelangelo's remark that 'Raphael had not his art by nature but acquired it by long study'. (Blunt, *op. cit.*, p. 76.) Despite its brevity, Giovio's passage is more descriptive of the artist's style than Vasari's life of Perugino. The quality in which Giovio thinks Perugino was surpassed by the other three seems to be imaginative power.

[32] On the significance of Giovio's remarks for the aesthetic distance between the Quattrocento and the Cinquecento see von Schlosser, p. 197. On *copia* in Vasari see Alpers, p. 206.

[33] . . . sicuti in dispari, sed non omnino dissimili facultate, carioribus discipulis praecipere erat solitus Leonardus Vincius, qui picturam aetate nostra, veterum eius artis arcana solertissime detergendo, ad amplissimam dignitatem provexit: illis namque intra vigesimum, ut diximus, aetatis annum penicillis et coloribus penitus interdicebat, quum iuberet, ut plumbeo graphio tantum vacarent, priscorum operum egregia monumenta diligenter excerpendo, et simplicissimis tractibus imitando naturae vim et corporum lineamenta, quae sub tanta motuum varietate oculis nostris efferuntur; quin etiam volebat, ut humana cadavera dissecarent. . . . (Barocchi, pp. 20–1.) The allusion to Leonardo has been discussed by Carlo Pedretti, 'A document on Leonardo da Vinci as a teacher of art', *Italian Quarterly*, VIII, 1964, pp. 3–9. Pedretti reasons that Giovio probably had his information from Leonardo himself. On the 'sister art' tradition see Baxandall, pp. 97–8. In Quintilian Giovio would have found support for his recommendations. 'For there can be no doubt that in art no small portion of our task lies in imitation. . . .' (x, ii, 1.)

[34] Caeterum postea quotidianus stili usus sine controversia rectissimus atque optimus bene scribendi magister existimatur, sicuti in aliis quoque artibus id verum esse liquido perspicimus. Ferunt Donatellum Florentinum, cuius est cum insignis artis gloria in Foro Patavino statua Gatamellatae aenea equestris, quum de summa discendae artis ratione ex arcano sententiam rogaret, respondere solitum: 'Facere saepius atque reficere in arte proficere est.' (Barocchi, pp. 21–2.) The phrase *gloria artis* is used by Pliny, e.g. *Naturalis Historia*, xxxv, 71. (All unspecified subsequent references to Pliny are to this work.)

[35] . . . sicuti inspecta nobiliore tabula penicillum et manum artificis statim agnoscimus: nam summas in singulis virtutes proprii et necessarii quidem naevi trahente natura comitantur. Habent Michaelis Angeli figurae profundiores umbras et recessus admirabiles, ut clarius illuminatae magis extent et emineant. In humanis vultibus, quos egregie Sebastianus exprimit, suaves et liquidos tractus blandissimis coloribus convelatos intuemur; in Titiano laetae rerum facies austeris distinctae lineolis et obliquitates exquisitae laudem ferunt. Doxium imagines rigidae, vivaces, convolutae, effumidis adumbratae coloribus mire delectant, quae tametsi in eadem re certius exprimenda et specie varia sint et dissimilia, summam tamen omnes aliam alio modo, uti genii iudiciaque tulerunt, excellentis industriae commendationem accipiunt. Quo exemplo facile adducor, ut habenas immittendas atque laxandas putem egregiis ingeniis eloquentiae studio flagrantibus, ut si divinum antiquorum stilum perfecte imitari nequeant, aliquam saltem tolerabilem nec invenustam dicendi formam proprio quodam delectu et suapte natura consequantur. (Tiraboschi, p. 1637; Barocchi, pp. 22–3.)

[36] *De Oratore*, I, ii, 5.

[37] Quintilian, *Institutio Oratoria*, x, i, 20.

[38] *De Oratore*, II, 88–9.

[39] Quintilian, *Institutio Oratoria*, x, ii, 14–17.

[40] *De Oratore*, III, 26. Loeb translation.

[41] *Institutio Oratoria*, XII, x, 1. Loeb translation.

[42] Giovio thus illustrates E. H. Gombrich's contention that 'It was to Pliny and his chapters on classical art that the educated Italian looked for terms and categories to discuss and conceive the art of his time'. (*Norm and Form*, p. 112.) According to Vasari, Giovio declared that his projected *elogia* of artists would have been 'a tract more similar to that of Pliny'. (Vasari, VII, p. 682). Both Giovio and his elder brother, Benedetto, took a keen interest in the disputed question of Pliny the Elder's *patria*. Benedetto's arguments against the theory that Pliny had been born in Verona, advanced by Petrarch and endorsed by Biondo and Valla, are incorporated in book II of his *Historia patriae* (ed. Francesco Fossati, Como, 1890, pp. 373–84). In his *elogium* of Ermolao Barbaro Paolo thanks the Venetian humanist for having by his erudition restored Pliny to Como. (The first edition of Barbaro's *Castigationes plinianae* was published in Rome in 1492.)

[43] See n. 35. Barocchi calls attention to the use of *convelare* in Aulus Gellius: *capite convelato* (*Noctes Atticae*, XIX, ix, 10); *argumentis convelat* (VI, iii, 44).

[44] See n. 64.

[45] *De Oratore*, III, 101.

[46] See n. 35.

[47] *Naturalis Historia*, XXXV, 131.

[48] At Como Giovio's brother, Benedetto, was engaged in an enterprise for expanding the scope of vernacular criticism, the translation and editing of Vitruvius, begun by Cesare Cesariano and published at Como in 1521. On the edition see W. Bell Dinsmoor, 'The literary remains of Sebastiano Serlio', *Art Bulletin*, XXIV, 1942, p. 60. For checking the colophon page to confirm Benedetto's collaboration I am indebted to Dr Fiametta Witt.

[49] See Alpers, p. 192. Pliny particularly admired lifelikeness. *E.g.* XXXV, 71.

[50] For a bibliography of works relating to these biographies see Barocchi, pp. 1098–1101. Unfortunately, the manuscript from which they derive is an early eighteenth-century copy of an original now lost, so that no possibility exists of determining the date of their composition from the manuscript tradition (see Dante Visconti, 'Nota su alcuni MSS gioviani', *Clio*, I, 1965, p. 104). Printed by Girolamo Tiraboschi in his *Storia della letteratura italiana* as an appendage to Giovio's dialogue *De viris illustribus*, known to have been set down at Ischia in 1528, the lives have more or less been assigned to that period. The lives of both Leonardo and Raphael are posthumous. The last definite event mentioned in the life of Michelangelo is the location o

Bandinelli's copy of the Laocoön in Florence, which according to Vasari took place in 1525. (*Le vite*, ed. Milanesi, VI, p. 146; John Pope-Hennessy, *Italian High Renaissance and Baroque Sculpture*, London, second edition, 1970, p. 362). A reference to the 'final' location of Julius's sepulchre in Florence may refer to the ill fated contract of the summer of 1526, arranged between the Pope's heirs and Michelangelo, who was then working in Florence, where most of the statutes for the project were to be found. The contract of 1532, on the other hand, definitely stipulated Rome as the site of the tomb, with Michaelangelo's being obliged to spend at least two months there each year until completion. (Martin Weinberger, *Michelangelo the Sculptor*, London and New York, 1967, I, pp. 227–33, 256–7.) Giovo would certainly have known of this contract, which necessitated a concession (revoked two years later) on the part of Clement VII. An allusion, moreover, to Michelangelo's 'having accepted many thousands of gold pieces' (*acceptisque multis millibus aureis*) would seem to recall more the atmosphere of 1525–26, with the sense of injury on the part of the della Rovere heirs and Michelangelo's proclamation of his willingness to make amends. Giovio's three lives, therefore, may be dated with certainty between 1525 and 1532 and with high probability to the period 1527–28.

[51] *Elogia virorum litteris illustrium*, Basel, 1577, p. 194.

[52] Vincenzo Golzio, *Raffaello nei documenti, nelle testimonianze dei contemporanei e nella letterature del suo secolo*, Franborough, revised edition, 1971, pp. 191–3.

[53] In Vaticano Xistini sacelli cameram a Iulio secundo ingenti pecunia accitus, immenso opere brevi perfecto, absolutae artis testimonium deposuit. Quum resupinus, uti necesse erat, pingeret, aliqua in abscessus et sinus refugiente sensim lumine condidit, ut Olophernis truncum in conopeo, in aliquibus autem, sicuti in Hamano cruci affixo, lucem ipsam exprimentibus umbris adeo feliciter protulit, ut repraesentata corporum veritate, ingeniosi etiam artifices, quae plana essent, veluti solida mirarentur. Videre est inter praecipuas virorum imagines media in testudine simulachrum volantis in coelum senis, tanta symmetria delineatum, ut si e diversis sacelli partibus spectetur, convolvi semper gestumque mutare deceptis oculis videatur. (Barocchi, pp. 10–11.) On the nude as gauge of absolute perfection see Alpers, p. 208. Michelangelo's remuneration was high for the time. Roberto Lopez, *Three Ages of the Italian Renaissance*, Charlottesville, 1970, p. 50.

[54] XXXV, 120.

[55] *Michelagniolo Buonarroti sein Leben und seine Werke*, I, *Michelagniolos Jugendjahre*, Berlin, 1907, pp. xxiii–xxv.

[56] 'Personalità storica ed artistica di Michelangelo', in *Michelangelo artista, pensatore, scrittore*, ed. Mario Salmi *et al.*, Novara, 1965, I, p. 48. See also Blunt, p. 44.

[57] Caeterum tanti ingenii vir natura adeo agrestis ac ferus extitit, ut supra incredibiles domesticae vitae sordes successores in arte posteris inviderit. Nam vel obsecratus a principibus numquam adduci potuit, ut quemquam doceret vel gratia spectandi saltem in officinam admitteret. (Barocchi, p. 12.)

[58] In the preface to his *Virorum illustrium vitae*, a collection of somewhat longer biographies, Giovio informs the reader that these have been written 'in a somewhat freer style in imitation of Plutarch, a philosopher of the greatest gravity'.

[59] Caeterum in toto picturae genere numquam eius operi venustas defuit, quam gratiam interpretantur; quamquam in educendis membrorum toris aliquando nimius fuerit, quum vim artis supra naturam ambitiosius ostendere conaretur. (Barocchi, p. 15.) For a critical discussion of this life see the article of Golzio already cited and his 'La fortuna critica' in *Raffaello, l'opera, le fonti, la fortuna*, ed. Mario Salmi *et al.*, Novara, 1968, II, pp. 609–10.

[60] XXXV, 79; XII, x, 6.

[61] Deoclecio Redig de Campos, *Raffaello nelle stanza*, Milan, 1965, p. 11; John Pope-Hennessy, *Raphael*, London, 1970, p. 288, n. 57.

[62] Optices quoque placitis in dimensionibus distantiisque non semper adamussim observans visus est; verum in ducendis lineis, quae commissuras colorum quasi

margines terminarent, et in mitiganda commiscendaque vividiorum pigmentorum austeritate iuncundissimus artifex ante alia id praestanter contendit, quod unum in Bonarota defuerat, scilicet ut picturis erudite delineatis etiam colorum oleo commistorum lucideus ac inviolabilis ornatus accederet. (Barocchi, p. 15.) For Dolce's remarks on Raphael's colour *v.* Barocchi, p. 787.

[63] *Op. cit.*, p. 288, n. 57.

[64] Eo defuncto plures pari prope gloria certantes artem exceperunt, et in his Franciscus et Iulius discipuli vel hac una exquisita artis indole isnignes, quod magistri manum perargute et diligenter aemulari videantur. Ante alios autem Sebastianus Venetus oris similitudines incomparabili felicitate repraesentat, qui et singulari cum laude picturas mira tenuitate linearum excitare ac amoeno subinde colorum transitu adumbrare didicit. In Titiani quoque Veneti exactis operibus multiplices delicatae artis virtutes elucent, quas soli prope, nec plebeii quidem artifices, intelligant. Mantuanus Costa suaves hominum effigies, decentes compositosque gestus blandis coloribus pingit, ita ut vestitae armataeque imagines a nemine iucundius exprimi posse iudicentur: verum periti censores non velata magis quam nuda, graviore artis periculo, ab eo desiderant, quod facile praestare non potest, quum certiores disciplinas ad picturae usum remissioribus studiis contentus conferre nequiverit. Sodomas Vercellensis praepostero instabilique iudicio usque ad insaniae affectationem Senarum urbe notissimus, quum impetuosum animum ad artem revocat, admiranda perficit, et adeo concitata manu, ut nihilo secius, quod mirum est, neminem eo prudentius atque tranquillius pinxisse appareat. Doxi autem Ferrariensis urbanum probatur ingenium cum in iustis operibus, tum maxime in illis, quae parerga vocantur. Amoena namque picturae diverticula voluptuario labore consectatus, praeruptas cautes, virentia nemora, opacas perfluentium ripas, florentes rei rusticae apparatus, agricolarum laetos fervidosque labores, praeterea longissimos terrarum marisque prospectus, classes, aucupia, venationes, et cuncta id genus spectatu oculis iucunda, luxurianti ac festiva manu exprimere consuevit. (Barocchi, pp. 16–18.) The two sentences on Dosso are E. H. Gombrich's translation. (*Norm and Form*, p. 113.)

[65] It is interesting to note, in this regard, that as a physician Giovio reposed more confidence in nature than in the 'art' of the doctor. See his *Lettera di Paolo Giovio Vescovo di Nocera sul vitto umano a Felice Trofino Vescovo di Chieti*, ed. Giambattista Giovio, Como, 1808.

[66] Alpers, p. 192.

[67] *E.g.* his admiration for Navagero's 'in toto orationis fluxu mira lenitas', or his description of Paolo Emilio, 'stili ubertate fecundissimum senem'. (Tiraboschi, pp. 1619–20.) *Cf. De oratore*, III, 28.

[68] ... qui primus instituit amoenissimam parietum picturam, villas et porticus ac topiaria opera, lucos, nemora, colles, piscinas, euripos, amnes, litora, qualia quis optaret, varias ibi obambulantium species aut navigantium terraque villas adeuntium asellis aut vehiculis, iam piscantes, aucupantes aut venantes aut etiam vindemiantes. Sunt in eius exemplaribus nobiles palustri accessu villae, succollatis sponsione mulieribus labantes trepidis quae feruntur, plurimae praeterea tales argutiae facetissimi salis. (XXXV, 116–17; Loeb translation.)

[69] *Opaca ripa*, Cicero, *De legibus*, I, v, 15; *praerupta cauta*, Ovid, *Metamorphoses*, I, 719; *procera nemora*, Pliny the Younger, *Letters*, v, vi.

[70] Ms of the Società Storica Comense. See Dante Visconti, 'Nota su alcuni manoscritti gioviani', *Clio*, I, 1965, p. 104.

[71] Como, Biblioteca Comunale, MS 1. 6. 16.

ROGER JACOB *University of Aberdeen*

24

DOMINIQUE PHINOT, A FRANCO-NETHERLANDER COMPOSER OF THE MID-SIXTEENTH CENTURY

I

Pero no os admireys si yo hablo desta manera, porque, quando la felice memoria del señor Domingo Phinot componia una obra, ponia todo su estudio y usava toda su industria: pensava muy bien, estudiava muy de proposito, y escudrinava muy por menudo lo que avia compuesto, antes que le diera fin, y que la mandara a luz. Y assi, no por otra causa que por estas, fue y es tenido de los primeros y mejores compositores de su tiempo. . . .[1]

UNTIL COMPARATIVELY RECENTLY there have been serious obstacles in the way of the student who wished to acquire a true and balanced picture of music in the sixteenth century. To begin with, a considerable proportion of music composed during this period was unavailable in modern transcription. Secondly, much of what had been transcribed was misleading not only in the interpretation of technical devices but, more important, because editors had concentrated almost exclusively on composers such as Palestrina, Victoria and Byrd who had become canonised, so to speak, by historians during the last century. There was a time, therefore, when the composer to be discussed here was but a shadowy textbook name even to the most informed musicologist.

Recent researches, however, have done much to redress the balance. Thanks to numerous anthologies and complete editions published over the past few decades, we have a clearer idea of musical developments during, in particular, the period between the death of Josquin des Prez (1521) and the 1560s when far-reaching changes took place, sometimes almost imperceptibly, in the principles of musical composition; and the work of the foremost composers of this period such as Gombert, Clemens non Papa and Verdelot is no longer *terra incognita*.

Kristeller[2] has reminded us that 'the modern cult of genius has tended to isolate the composer from his social environment and from the learning of his time', and adds that the study of the history of music has suffered a similar fate. With regard to the Renaissance, however, the situation is now being remedied, for many new and penetrating studies have provided as never before compelling evidence of both the profound interaction between the arts and the special relationship of music to society at this time.

The picture is, alas, by no means complete. A disconcertingly large amount of archival material, notably in Italy, still awaits patient exploration; and it is an inescapable fact, too, that certain areas of knowledge relating to the first half of the sixteenth century can never be fully implemented, the devastation of two world wars having caused irreparable losses of source material. From records, inventories, chronicles and payrolls that have survived we can nevertheless do much to reconstruct the careers of many musicians who, unlike their more widely known superiors, lived in almost total obscurity.

Until the present century the few lexicographers who mentioned Dominique Phinot offered scant or ill founded biographical data about him. Fétis[3] and Eitner[4] believed that he was French and that he was born in Lyons, but neither contention has been proved. The only clue to his origins is in fact provided in a passage from an essay by his contemporary, the eccentric mathematician and writer Girolamo Cardano,[5] who refers to 'Dominicus . . . Tinotus [sic] Gallus, insignis musicus'. Assuming the initial T in the surname to be an error and that this 'insignis musicus' is indeed our composer, the term 'Gallus'[6] enables us at any rate to categorise him as a Franco-Netherlander; and this appears to be supported by the fact that his works usually appear in sixteenth-century anthologies in which Franco-Netherlander composers predominate.

If, as is likely, Phinot was in his late twenties by the time his first published work appeared in 1538,[7] then we can place his date of birth around 1510 or even slightly earlier. His music was printed and reprinted with significant frequency between 1538 and about 1565; and, as his earliest works appeared most frequently in northern Italy (and particularly in Venice) it is likely that his career began in that area. In 1547–48 he made a sudden and spectacular debut with the Lyonnais printers G. and M. Beringen in the form of four volumes of *chansons*[8] and motets,[9] certain aspects of which imply that Lyons was his centre of activity at that time: two volumes are dedicated to persons with Lyonnais connections, for instance, while several of his *chanson* texts are by the Lyons-based poets Maurice Scève and Charles Fontaine, and two others deal with subjects relating to the locality.

Phinot's importance in his own day as a composer is reflected not only in the volume of works published during his lifetime but also in the opinions of several contemporary writers who praise him without reservation as in the case of Cerone, who is quoted at the outset of this essay. Cerone[10] even goes so far as to say that Phinot was a formative influence on Palestrina's style, a claim which, however sceptical we may feel about its validity, has not yet been investigated.

Researches over the past forty years or so have established that Phinot was employed, possibly for a considerable part of his career, by Guidobaldo II, Duke of Urbino from 1538 to 1574. L. Werner[11] has drawn attention to a work, now housed in Szombathely, Hungary, on a page of which appear the

handwritten words 'Pesaurj cum Dominico Phinotto'. A more convincing
piece of evidence connecting Phinot with Pesaro, at that time the administrative centre of the duchy of Urbino, is provided by his *Liber secundus
mutetarum*[12] of 1554, which was not only published in Pesaro by Bartolomeo
Cesano[13] but was inscribed, moreover, to Guidobaldo II.

During the years 1967–68[14] the present writer located two memoranda
which indicate that Phinot was in the service of Duke Guidobaldo II. The
first,[15] dated 26 March 1545, is a request to the Duke of Ferrara by his
treasurer for reimbursement of

Scudi quattro doro in oro per tant[i] che io ho datti a Messer Finotto musico del
Duca d'Urbino che le dona quell[i] per haverli a presentare certe operete di musica.

The second memorandum[16] records payment in Pesaro on 20 November
1555, together with the provision of clothes and equipment, to, among others,
'Finotto musico'. There can be little doubt, therefore, that Phinot held an
official position in the court, probably as a performer or as a composer-in-
residence; and the dates of these documents suggest that he was attached to
Urbino (apart from temporary secondment to a centre such as Lyons) for
longer than ten years.

The unique contribution which the court of Urbino made to the Renaissance is well known and need not be recounted here; it is sufficient to
mention the names of literary figures, artists and theorists such as Castiglione,
Bembo, Titian, Baroccio, Commandino and Paciotti to remind the reader of
the astonishing vitality and range of human endeavour which Urbino
witnessed over a period of some eighty years. C. H. Clough[17] has suggested
that the wealth which engendered such cultural activity was derived mainly
from the military commitments of Frederigo da Montefeltro, and that these
conditions were for various local and national reasons not maintained under
his successors Guidobaldo I and Francesco Maria I della Rovere. The
resultant loss of wealth, together with the turbulence of political life in
Urbino during the reign of the last-named, may therefore account in some
measure for what seems to be a partial decline in the court's cultural life from
1520 onwards. It would nevertheless be wrong to suppose that Urbino had
ceased to be a cultural centre by the middle of the sixteenth century, for
there is abundant evidence that many great minds remained in close contact
with the court and exerted a strong influence on its life.

Music had been cultivated at a high level in Urbino since the time of
Frederigo da Montefeltro, although the court never achieved the reputation
of being a centre of *avant-garde* music-making as did Mantua and Ferrara.
A well documented, if slightly over-eulogistic, article by Saviotti[18] paints a
beguiling picture, however, of a community where, it seems, everyone
played an instrument or sang to his heart's content (if not always to the
comfort of his friends and neighbours). The court's musical heyday in all
probability coincided with the reign of Francesco Maria I della Rovere
(1508–38), whose wife, Eleonora Gonzaga, was a gifted musician who
generated, among members of her family as well as among the courtiers, a
pride in musical accomplishment.

Eleonora's son, Guidobaldo II, who evidently commanded considerable respect as a patron, did much to preserve Urbino's musical traditions. On the one hand, the ducal chapel undoubtedly enjoyed a high standard of music under the direction of Paolo Animuccia,[19] and with the services of Franco–Netherlander musicians such as Olivier Brassart,[20] Jachet Bontemps[21] and, at a later stage, Leonard Meldert.[22] The secular life of the court, on the other hand, was enhanced by staged performances and theatrical diversions, for which the duke had a predilection, and in which virtuoso instrumentalists of the calibre of Stefano, a celebrated lute player, participated.

Such was the environment in which Phinot may have spent what was the most productive period of his composing career. In view of his eminence in the field of sacred music he almost certainly held a post in an ecclesiastical establishment—probably the cathedral at Pesaro or the ducal chapel in Urbino[23]—for which many of his motets may have been written. Nor is it too fanciful to speculate that in the intellectual atmosphere of the court were nurtured those humanistic sympathies which, as will be seen later, found expression in his secular compositions.

The fecundity and dynamism which characterised the intellectual life of Lyons[24] in the sixteenth century was due in considerable measure to the town's convenient geographical position. It was far enough away from Paris to be relatively independent of the latter's academic, social and political pressures, and yet was accessible to Italy, Switzerland and Germany. The four annual fairs which were held in Lyons until the middle of the century attracted merchants, therefore, from the major European centres, and the town's prosperity was further increased through the presence of Italian and German bankers who set up businesses there. In such a cosmopolitan community many shades of intellectual opinion were to be found, and, predictably, the powerful influence of the town's Italian colony[25] is reflected in much of the humanistic literature which was produced in Lyons at that time.

In the case of two of Phinot's Lyonnais publications the dedicatees are persons of Italian origin. Luca de Grimaldi,[26] to whom the first book of motets is inscribed, belonged to an aristocratic Genoese family a branch of which ruled the princedom of Monaco. The second book of *chansons* is dedicated to César Gros, a native of Riva near Chieri in Piedmont who took French nationality in 1541 and who, having become established as a merchant in Lyons, attained a position of eminence in the town's public life. He also appears to have been well known as a patron in the town's literary circles, as is testified, for instance, by the dedication to him of Gabriel Chappuys' *Cinq Discours . . . de Mʳ Loys Arioste*.[27]

Hansen[28] considers that the dedicatory 'Au Seigneur Cesar Gros son singulier amy D. Phinot' implies that the composer's social status was at this time better than that of the average sixteenth-century musician; and it may at any rate be assumed that the two men met frequently and in the company of a mutual friend, Nicolas Bave,[29] the dedicatee of Phinot's first book of *chansons*. It may have been as a member of the Gros entourage, therefore, that Phinot sampled the artistic life of Lyons, meeting, no doubt, many of the town's literary figures, such as Scève, Labé and Fontaine, and acquainting himself with many aspects of what Montfalcon[30] described as 'la plus belle époque de la civilisation Lyonnaise'.

Near the beginning of *Il Cortegiano*, that remarkable commentary on the style and tenor of courtly life in the sixteenth century, Castiglione coins the word *sprezzatura* to describe what John Shearman[31] interprets as 'the courtly grace revealed in the effortless resolution of all difficulties . . . that kind of well bred negligence born of complete self-possession'. Shearman also observes that the word was later taken up by Lodovico Dolce in connection with works of art.

Such a term could well be applied to the Franco–Netherlander school of composition with which Phinot seems to have the closest affinities. After about 1520, when music had become reorientated as the result of new harmonic and linear concepts, the members of this school, most of whom came from either north-eastern France or the Low Countries, had evolved a musical language which was noteworthy for, in particular, the fluency and suppleness of its textures. Even if a certain intellectual severity characterises the work of major figures such as Gombert and Crecquillon, and even if various facile elements occasionally result in conventionality, it is nevertheless important to recognise the assurance with which they build their musical edifices; their gifts of organic, rhythmic and melodic growth, and their feeling for musical sonority are revealed with a self-effacing mastery which could be considered as the musical manifestation of Castiglione's Renaissance attitude.

In view of the absence of information about Phinot's musical upbringing any supposition concerning the origins and development of his style can be made only when all volumes of the current edition[32] of his works have been published; sufficient material is already available, however, to justify an assessment in the following pages of some of the basic elements in his musical personality.

Whatever lacunae may now exist in the body of sixteenth-century music, the student of the period has a major advantage in so far as he is dealing with an epoch which, in its preoccupation with its own culture and aspirations, produced a quantity of theoretical works on a multitude of subjects, among which music loomed large. Allowing for the extravagance and subjectivity which tend to colour these writings, they are nevertheless of prime importance to the musicologist in his appraisal of the taste and tendencies of the period.

Among several writers who mention Phinot, two are of particular interest at this point in that they seem to place him deliberately beside Gombert. The first is the German theorist Hermann Finck, who, in his important treatise *Practica Musica*,[33] makes the following evaluation:

Nostro vero tempore novi sunt inventores, in quibus est Nicolaus Gombert, Josquini piae memoriae discipulus, qui omnibus musicis ostendit viam, immo semitam ad quaerendas fugas, ac subtilitatem, ac est author Musices plane diversae a superiori. Is enim vitat pausas et illius compositio est plena cum concordantiarum tum fugarum. Huic adjungendi sunt Thomas Crecquillon, Jacobus Clemens non Papa, Dominicus Phinot, qui praestantissimi, excellentissimi, subtilissimique et pro meo iudicio existimantur imitandi.

The first sentence, which is well known, makes an important and probably justifiable claim for Gombert as an innovator in the field of thematic imitation at this particular moment in musical history. Whether or not this statement should be accepted at its face value, it is unlikely that a writer of Finck's sound judgement would draw an arbitrary parallel between Gombert and the three other composers on a fundamental issue of this nature, and the significance of the paragraph, therefore, should be fully understood.

A further reference to Phinot occurs in Pietro Ponzio's *Dialogo della musica* (Parma, 1595), during a discussion of what constitutes good and bad composition. After denouncing 'dead composition', i.e. music in which there is insufficient rhythmic independence of part writing, Ponzio continues as follows:

Si permette pero alle volte ne' Motetti, & altre compositioni per un tempo di Semibreue, ouer di Breve al piu, che le parti si possino fermar'insieme; ma, fatto questo, le Parti poi cominciano a far movimento, seruando l'ordine, e lo stile delle Compositioni de' periti Musici, come cio ben scoprono i Motetti di Adriano, Gomberto, Finotto, & altri simili, i quali per non dilongarmi tacero.'

[It is permissible at times in motets and other pieces, for the space of a semibreve, or breve at most, that the parts should close together; but, this being done, they should once more begin to move, in the manner and style of the compositions of expert musicians, as in the motets of Willaert, Gombert, Phinot and others too numerous to mention.[34]]

This time Phinot is ranked not only with Gombert but with Willaert, who, by virtue of his unique and long-standing service in St Mark's, Venice, exerted as great an influence as any member of this Franco–Netherlander school on music in Italy prior to 1560. The importance of these statements by Finck and Ponzio, however, derives from the fact that each is related to a specific point of style and can therefore hardly be dismissed as a whim on the part of its author; and independent observations such as these leave us in no doubt that Phinot's *oeuvre* should be considered primarily in relation to the Franco–Netherlander tradition.

Phinot's known compositions consist of two parody masses, ninety-eight motets, fifteen vesper psalms, two magnificats, sixty-three French *chansons* (with an appendix of three canons[35]) and two Italian madrigals. Although no specifically instrumental music by Phinot has been traced, some of his motets are to be found in keyboard tablature versions.[36] Phinot's secular music seems to have made less of an impact in his day than did his sacred works, and the only *chansons* to be reprinted outside Lyons[37] were the three eight-part pieces *Vivons, m'amye, Qu'est-ce qu'amour?* and *Par un trait d'or* which appeared in the Parisian Le Roy et Ballard's *Livre de meslanges* of 1560 and its subsequent re-edition of 1572 as *Mellange de chansons*. The opening measures of the Superius of his chanson *Plorez, mes yeulx* are quoted in C. de Blockland's

Instruction fort facile pour apprendre la musique practique (Lyons, 1573), which suggests that the composer's reputation was quite strong at a fairly late date in the century. A brief consideration of his reprinted works, however, leaves us in no doubt that it was his motets which attracted the greatest attention in the sixteenth century. Their wide dissemination and frequent reappearance in some of the most distinguished collections[38] of the time testify to Phinot's importance not only as a polychoralist (an aspect to be discussed below) but as a composer of responsorial motets and vesper psalms.

Much of the foregoing information may lead the reader to anticipate an assimilation of both old and new ingredients in Phinot's music, written as it was during a crucial period of transition. Hansen[39] has demonstrated in some detail that this is so in many of the motets. The picture which emerges from his commentary is that of a composer who at his best has an impressive command over his resources and who shows versatility in setting sacred texts. Phinot's maturer approach to motet composition is characterised by an integrity and purity of melodic line (which was conceivably one of the reasons governing Cerone's claim that Phinot influenced Palestrina); while from the harmonic point of view he frequently seems to be preoccupied with the establishment of a clear tonal centre by emphasising what today would be called the tonic, dominant and subdominant chords. Example 24.1, which is the opening of his five-part setting of *Non turbetur cor vestrum*,[40] demonstrates such progressive tendencies, and at the same time underlines Phinot's indebtedness to the Gombert school in that the passage is unified by no fewer than twelve imitations of the opening motive (Tenor II).

Hansen has found that a consistent line of development in the composer's motet style can be traced from the earliest printed examples, beginning in 1538, to the publications of Beringen in Lyons in 1547–48 and those of the 1550s such as the Pesaro collection mentioned above. The early motets contain certain features which are reminiscent of the period of Josquin: in some of these (e.g. the second part of *Pater peccavi*[41]) considerable proportions of both homophonic and contrapuntal writing are found side by side, and there are instances of final chords consisting of octaves and fifths but no thirds. The later works, many of which are five-voiced, following the fashion of that time, achieve a more homogeneous outcome through the greater use of imitation and the avoidance of disruptive contrasting elements.

From a formal point of view, too, some of the later motets show an awareness of the advantages of unifying a movement by means of musical recapitulation. *Quae est ista*,[42] for example, is, in common with many motets of the period, divided into two separate sections (*partes*), both of which end with the same words and music, thereby creating an overall structure which can be formulated as ABCB, a pattern frequently to be met with in the second half of the sixteenth century. In *Apparens Christus*[43] formal unity is achieved by the interpolation three times in the text of an *alleluja* refrain, which, as Hansen observes, becomes more extended each time and thereby produces an impressive climax.

If there is one single aspect of his work which earns for Phinot a place in musical history it is surely his polychoral motets. Our knowledge of the origins and growth of polychoral music is still incomplete, but during the present century several salient facts have been uncovered which correct some serious misconceptions about this important form of composition, and which also put Phinot into clearer historical perspective. To begin with, Willaert can no longer be credited with having invented polychoral writing (also known by the Italian equivalent *coro spezzato*). The generally accepted theory that he did so has been disproved by G. Benvenuti,[44] whose argument is strengthened by Casimiri's[45] discovery of an eight-part *coro spezzato* mass which he identifies as the work of Fra Ruffino Bartolucci of Assisi, dating it from the period 1510–20 when Fra Ruffino was *maestro di capella* at Padua Cathedral; and Bukofzer[46] has shown that polychoral singing was known even as early as the fifteenth century.

EX. 24.1

In a recent and most valuable study by J. Höfler[47] of *coro spezzato* developments in the mid-sixteenth century it is suggested that Willaert's celebrated vesper psalms of 1550,[48] of which only eight show even minimal portions of simultaneous polychoral writing, are really no more than written realisations of what was an established performing practice in northern Italy; that they fulfil certain liturgical demands and do not mark a new departure in polychoral composition. If this is so, Höfler argues, then we can no longer consider Willaert as even an important link in the development of *coro spezzato* composition during the 1540s and 1550s; and it therefore follows that we must instead take Phinot's double-choir motets of 1548 as the proper forerunners of the Venetian polychoral works of the late Renaissance.

A comparison (to be only briefly summarised here) of the polychoral techniques of these two composers, therefore, at once reveals essential differences. In some respects Phinot is understandably less forward-looking than Willaert. His tonality, for instance, relies more on modal patterns than Willaert's does, and in matters of declamation and in his general response to text setting Phinot is rarely the equal of the Venetian master. From the point of view of textural organisation it is abundantly clear that, as Höfler implies, Phinot allows his imagination to be catalysed by the potentialities of *coro spezzato*, whereas Willaert is committed, probably for liturgical or declamatory reasons, to a rather rigid antiphonal usage of his two choirs, introducing true eight-part writing only in the *Gloria Patri* sections and occasionally in overlapping between the end of one choir's phrase and the beginning of the next. Phinot's most sustained passages of simultaneous eight-part writing, moreover, are more contrapuntally animated than those of Willaert, which are predominantly homophonic. Of the two composers Phinot is unquestionably the more versatile in handling the polychoral medium, and he succeeds in achieving even a degree of dramatic tension on more than one occasion by varying the length of time in the alternation of the choirs.

In the last eight bars of the eight-part motet *Tanto tempore vobiscum sum*[49] (ex. 24.2), Phinot uses a simple harmonic pattern not only to stabilise the tonality but to enable the melodic lines to develop in the most resonant vocal registers, thereby intensifying the sonority.

The present assessment of Phinot's compositional style must inevitably raise the question as to whether the composer at any time shows an allegiance to a school other than that of Gombert. It has already been stated that the early motets contain some archaic, if relatively minor, features which could be taken as the vestiges of a youthful admiration for an earlier composer's work. In at least one of the masses and in a handful of *chansons*, however, there are considerable grounds for speculating that Phinot was more than superficially acquainted with the work of the Parisian composers of the 1520s and 1530s, and in particular with that of their leader, Claudin de Sermisy.

It is a commonplace that Cinquecento composers (apart from those of the great Roman school) seldom bring to their mass settings the level of inspiration which characterises their best motet composition, and it is therefore inadvisable to attach undue importance to their stylistic content, especially when, as often happens, they derive liberally from pre-existent models and from *chansons* in particular. A recent transcription by the writer of several

movements of Phinot's mass *Si bona suscepimus*[50] shows that the model, a
motet by Sermisy, is frequently used and is instantly recognisable, particularly in the earlier movements. But Sermisy's influence is not confined to
quotations of or allusions to the motet. The emphasis throughout seems to be
on polished, elegant paragraphing rather than on formalised imitative
points, and there is a noticeable proportion of homophonic or partially
contrapuntal writing; the structure of the melodic lines and cadential
mannerisms are likewise more Parisian than Netherlander in character.

EX. 24.2

Parisian traits are even more in evidence in a few *chansons* whose freshness
and naïve gaiety provide a striking contrast with the more learned, closely
woven textures to be found elsewhere. If a piece such as *Catin, ma gentille
brunette* (ex. 24.3) does not quite achieve that lightness of touch which
typifies the best of Sermisy, its kinship with the latter is evident in the
terseness of its expression, its rhythmic patterns and harmonic clichés.

Without counting the polychoral examples, Phinot's *chanson* output in
general represents a cross-section of the main types of *chanson* writing to be
met with in the mid-sixteenth century, and in view of their fluency and
variety of musical invention it is difficult to see why many of them were not

better known at that time. The answer to this may partly be found in Phinot's
choice of unusual texts, many of which appear not to have attracted the
attention of other composers.[51] Saulnier[52] remarks that both Phinot and
Lupi, the Lyons-based composer of the third volume in this Beringen series,
draw frequently on recently composed texts, and observes that at least two
dozen are from anthologies dating from the period 1544–48, a fact which in
Phinot's case may strengthen the possibility of his being in closer contact with
France at this point in his career. As stated above, several of Phinot's
chansons employ texts which were either written by poets connected with
Lyons or whose subjects are to do with the town. Another notable group of
texts are those containing strong humanistic elements which would obviously
have increased their chances of success in a centre such as Lyons. Three of
these, *En feu ardant*, *Quand je pense au martire* and *L'eau qui distille*, all from the
second book, are settings of verses from Jean Martin's translation[53] of
Bembo's *Gli Asolani* (1505), while *Vivons, m'amye*[54] is clearly derived from
Catullus' *Vivamus, mea Lesbia*. Phinot's preference for poetry of a relatively
serious nature is underlined by the comparative lack of erotic texts present in
these volumes, most of the love poems belonging to the platonic category.

EX. 24.3

Phinot's *chanson* settings embrace a wide range of musical expression, and
in nearly every case a remarkable equilibrium is maintained between form
and thematic content. In company with engaging trifles such as the piece
already quoted we find more extended works whose momentum is sustained
by energetic points of imitation, as in, for example, *Si j'en dy bien*. The forms
of several *chansons* in the first book correspond to those in vogue in the 1520s
and 1530s, some recapitulating the music of the opening couplets at the

close of the piece, as in the case of *Si le mien cœur*, a practice which is invariably governed by musical rather than textual demands.

The reader will already have surmised that Phinot's creative response to word setting is comparable to that of many composers of his generation: namely that, although no serious faults of declamation are detectable, his music in general attempts neither to convey the emotional tone of a text nor to create musical imagery or symbolism. In his second book of *chansons* there is a higher incidence of through-composed settings than in the first, and it is in these that we occasionally find the seeds of what was for Phinot a new *rapport* between music and text, proof, it would seem, of his acquaintance with current tendencies in Italy. *En chascun lieu* (ex. 24.4), a poem of homage to a loved one by Michel d'Amboise, shows from the outset little affinity with the conventions of ex. 24.3: the composer instead pinpoints the text by a more insistent use than usual of suspended dissonance and well organised motives. In bar 36 the mood of the music is abruptly changed by a chordal setting of the words 'Tu es mon bien, ma mort',[55] with a striking E flat major chord on 'mort', after which the counterpoint is revived appropriately at the words 'ma vie entière'.

EX. 24.4

The four polychoral *chansons* are on a par with Phinot's finest achievements in *coro spezzato* composition and will be dealt with elsewhere in a special study.[56] Here, as in his sacred polychoral works, the composer makes full use of his forces, balancing antiphonal passages with *tuttis* of considerable brilliance. Generally speaking, each choir sings the entire text of the poem, but even in the antiphonal sections Phinot varies the musical texture sufficiently to compensate for the necessity of phrase repetition. The form of these settings is in essence that of the Italian *dialogo* or dialogue-madrigal, which was then in its infancy and to which Phinot contributed his 'Simile a questi smisurati monti'.[57] Much of the writing in these pieces is homophonically conceived (more so than in the double-choir motets), so that declamation is often syllabic. *A dieu, Loyse* is, however, an eight-in-four canon throughout, but even here Phinot does not allow technical expertise to obscure or to detract from the text. This chanson can in fact be regarded as the epitome of Phinot's art, both sacred and secular: eschewing theatricalism and novelty for its own sake, it seeks to extend the boundaries of musical expression by developing existing idioms and practices.

NOTES

[1] 'But don't be surprised at this way of expressing myself, because when the felicitous brain of Sr Domingo Phinot composed a work he put his entire mind and industry into it; he thought it but thoroughly, studied and scrutinised in great detail all aspects of what he had written before it was completed and published. It's for this reason and no other that he was, and is still considered to be, among the foremost composers of his period.' (D. P. Cerone, *El Melopeo y Maestro*, Naples, 1613.)

[2] P. O. Kristeller, *Studies in Renaissance Thought and Letters*, Rome, 1956, p. 451.

[3] F. J. Fétis, *Biographie universelle des musiciens* . . . , second edition, Paris, 1860–65, VII, p. 41.

[4] R. Eitner, *Biographisch-Bibliographisches Quellenlexikon der Musiker und Musikgelehrten* . . . , Leipzig, 1899–1904, VII, pp. 426–7.

[5] This passage, which occurs in Cardano's *Opera Omnia*, Lyons, 1663, II, p. 354, implies that Phinot was executed for homosexuality. Commenting on this information in 'Jerome Cardan on Gombert, Phinot and Carpentras', *The Musical Quarterly*, LVIII, No. 3, 1972, pp. 412–19, C. A. Miller points out that, as the author claims to have written the work in 1561, Phinot must have died between 1557 and 1560. The present writer is indebted to Dr J. Höfler, who first drew his attention to Cardano's statement and who has also kindly assisted in the preparation of material for this essay.

[6] The term *Gallus* in the sixteenth century was sometimes applied to those whose cultural background was French but whose origins were Flemish or Dutch.

[7] Four motets in *Primus liber cum quinque vocibus. Motetti del frutto*, Venice, A. Gardane.

[8] *Premier livre contenant trente et sept chansons*, 1548; *Second livre contenant vingt et six chansons*, 1548.

[9] *Liber primus mutetarum quinque vocum*, 1547; *Liber secundus mutetarum sex, septem, et octo vocum*, 1548.

[10] *Op. cit.*

[11] L. Werner, 'Una rarità musicale della biblioteca vescovile di Szombathely', *Note d'archivio per la storia musicale*, VII, 1931, p. 91.

[12] See P. S. Hansen, 'The life and works of Dominico Phinot', unpublished Ph.D. dissertation, University of North Carolina, Chapel Hill, N.C., 1939, p. 14.

[13] Cesano also published a book of madrigals by Vincenzo Ruffo in 1555; comparatively little music, however, appears to have been published in Pesaro in the sixteenth century.

[14] The writer wishes to acknowledge his indebtedness to the University of Aberdeen for the award of a travelling fellowship during the academic year 1966–67 to enable him to undertake a research project on aspects of Phinot's life and work, and for further financial assistance since that date to continue his researches.

[15] Now preserved in the Archivio di Stato, Modena, A.S.E., Archivio per Materie, Musica e Musicisti, b. 1.

[16] 'Registro di lettere e memorie del Governo del Duca Guid'Ubaldo II dal 1551 al 1565', MS Classe I, Div. G., Filza 105, No. 6, Archivio di Urbino, in the Archivio di Stato, Florence. This document is cited in A. Saviotti, 'La musica alla corte dei Duchi di Urbino', *La Cronaca Musicale*, XXX, Pesaro, January 1909, p. 119.

[17] C. H. Clough, 'Sources for the history of the court and city of Urbino in the early sixteenth century', *Manuscripta*, VII, 1963, p. 67.

[18] *Op. cit.*

[19] Paolo, the brother of Giovanni Animuccia (*maestro di capella* at the Vatican from

1555 to 1571), was *maestro di capella* at the Lateran from 1550 to 1552 and was known as a composer of motets and madrigals.

[20] According to Saviotti (*op. cit.*), Brassart was a protégé of the Cardinal of Urbino at that time, the music-loving Giulio della Rovere, to whom he dedicated a book of madrigals (Rome, A. Barré, 1564).

[21] Saviotti deduces, from unspecified documents he examined in Pesaro, that Bontemps is the real name of 'Giachetto organista', who is mentioned several times in the *Diario* (written from 1555 onwards) of the musically minded court jester, Monaldo da Cagli.

[22] Meldert, *maestro di capella* in Urbino from 1582 to 1590, was known primarily as a composer of madrigals; his setting of *Cresci bel verde Alloro*, for instance, appeared in the celebrated collection *Il lauro verde, madrigali a sei voci*, (Ferrara, V. Baldini, 1538).

[23] For a fully documented account of music at the cathedral in Urbino during this period see B. Ligi, 'La Capella Musicale del Duomo di Urbino', *Note d'archivio per la storia musicale*, II, 1925, pp. 3–87; further background reading is provided by V. Rossi, 'Appunti per la storia della musica alla corte di Francesco Maria I e di Guidobaldo Della Rovere', *Rassegna emiliana di storia e letteratura ed arte*, I, Modena, 1888, pp. 453–69.

[24] See S. F. Pogue, *Jacques Moderne, Lyons Music Printer of the Sixteenth Century*, Geneva, 1969, both for concise summaries of information and an extensive bibliography on Lyons at this time. The musical, literary and general cultural situation is dealt with in F. Dobbins, 'The chanson at Lyons in the sixteenth century', unpublished D.Phil. dissertation, Oxford, 1971.

[25] In connection with the Italian influence in sixteenth-century Lyons see E. Picot, *Les Italiens en France au XVIe siècle*, Bordeaux, 1901, and H. A. S. Charpin-Feugerolles, *Les Florentins à Lyon*, Lyons, 1889.

[26] Grimaldi was the dedicatee also of a book of madrigals by Vincenzo Ruffo (Venice, G. Scotto, 1554).

[27] Lyons, 1582; information from J. Tricou, *Recherches sur les Gros de Saint-Joyre*, Lyons, 1934, pp. 11–15.

[28] *Op. cit.*, p. 9.

[29] Bave was probably from the Savoy/Piedmont area, according to V. L. Saulnier, 'Dominique Phinot et Didier Lupi, musiciens de Clément Marot et des marotiques', *Revue de Musicologie*, XLIII, July 1959, p. 64, n. 1.

[30] J. B. Montfalcon, *Histoire monumentale de la ville de Lyon*, Lyons, nine vols., 1866.

[31] J. Shearman, *Mannerism*, London, 1967, p. 21.

[32] *Dominique Phinot, Opera Omnia*, ed. J. Höfler, in *Corpus Mensurabilis Musicae*, LIX, Rome, 1972– , I– .

[33] Wittenberg, 1556.

[34] Both the original passage and this translation appear in L. Lockwood, *The Counter-reformation and the Masses of Vincenzo Ruffo*, Venice, 1967, pp. 200–1.

[35] The canon *Hault le boys, m'amye Margot* is for twelve equal voices, with an optional second canon forming a two-voice pedal point.

[36] The library of Uppsala University, for example, contains transcriptions, probably dating from the late sixteenth century, of the eight-part motets *O sacrum convivium* and *Jam non dicam vos servos* (*Vok. mus. i. hs.* 89), both originally published in the Beringen collections of 1548; and the six-part *Cerne meos esse gemitus* was printed in *Tabulaturbuch, Auff Orgeln und Instrument . . . Durch Johannem Ruhling*, Leipzig, J. Beyer, 1583.

[37] F. J. Fétis, *Biographie universelle, loc. cit.*, and C. F. Becker, *Die Tonwerke des XVI. und XVII. Jahrhunderts*, Leipzig, 1855, p. 220, both mention, without giving details, editions of Phinot's *chansons* by Beringen in 1549 and 1550. The *Catalogue de la bibliothèque de F. J. Fétis*, Brussels, 1877, p. 293, records that a chanson by Phinot was included in the *Unzieme livre*, no longer traceable, of Moderne's *Parangon des chansons*, Lyons, 1543.

[38] Phinot's motets appear both in Italian collections (principally those of Gardano in Venice) and in other publications such as *Thesaurus Musicus*, I–III, published by Berg and Neuber in Nuremberg (1564) and the *Libri Modulorum* of Du Bosc and Guéroult in Geneva (1555–56).

[39] *Op. cit.*, pp. 23–79; see also the same author's '*Liber Secundus Mutetarum* by Dominico Phinot: a modern transcription with an introduction', unpublished Master's thesis, Eastman School of Music, Rochester, N.Y., 1935.

[40] *Liber primus mutetarum*, Lyons, 1547. Phinot's first five-part setting of this text appeared in *Mutetarum divinitatis liber primus*, Milan, A. Castiglione, 1543.

[41] *Primus liber cum quinque vocibus. Motetti del frutto*, Venice, A. Gardane, 1538.

[42] *Liber secundus mutetarum*, Lyons, 1548.

[43] *Liber primus mutetarum*, Lyons, 1547.

[44] G. Benvenuti, 'Andrea e Giovanni Gabrieli e la musica strumentale in San Marco', *Istituzioni e monumenti dell'arte musicale Italiana*, I, Milan, 1931, pp. xxxiv–xxxv.

[45] R. Casimiri, 'Il coro "Battente" e "Spezzato" fu una novita di Adriano Willaert?', *Bollettino Ceciliano*, XXXVIII, Rome, 1943. See also G. d'Alessi's study 'Precursors of Adriano Willaert in the practice of "Coro Spezzato"', *Journal of the American Musicological Society*, V, 1952, pp. 187–210.

[46] M. Bukofzer, 'The beginnings of polyphonic choral music', *Papers of the American Musicological Society*, Cleveland, Ohio, 1940, pp. 23–4.

[47] J. Höfler, 'Dominique Phinot and the beginnings of Renaissance polychoral music (1548–1568)', *ZVUK. Jugoslovenska muzička revija*, No. 100, Sarajevo, 1969, pp. 497–515.

[48] *Di Adriano et di Jachet. I salmi appertinenti alli vesperi per tutte le feste dell'anno, parte a versi, et parte spezzadi* [*sic*] . . . , Venice, A. Gardane, 1550.

[49] *Liber secundus mutetarum*, Lyons, 1548. In this extract the last four bars, which have been transcribed from the original without editorial accidentals, may be performed with B naturals and C sharps if the Picardy third is preferred in the final chord.

[50] *Sex misse. Liber primus missarum sex, cum quatuor vocibus*, Venice, A. Gardane, 1544. The other masses in this volume are by Berchem, Hesdin, Lupus and Verdelot.

[51] Phinot's indebtedness to pre-existent material is seen clearly in two works whose texts were set by other composers. *Quand je pense au martire*, which, as already stated, is a translation of a text by Bembo, is thematically derived from Arcadelt's madrigal setting, first published in *Il primo libro di madrigali d'Archadelt a quatro* (Venice, A. Gardane, 1539), of Bembo's *Quand'io pens' al martire*; and the opening of the canon *Hault le boys, m'amye Margot* is based on the main motive of Godard's setting which appears in *Tresiesme livre contenant xix chansons nouvelles* (Paris, P. Attaingnant and H. Jullet, 1543).

[52] *Op. cit.*, pp. 67–8.

[53] Paris, 1545.

[54] See A. Einstein, *The Italian Madrigal*, Princeton, N.J., 1949, I, pp. 310–11, in which the text is identified as being a combination of Catullus V and VII. Einstein points out the interesting resemblance between Phinot's text, which is anonymous, and that of a strambotto, *Baciami, vita mia*, set by Domenico Ferabosco, who in 1542 dedicated a book of madrigals to Duke Guidobaldo II of Urbino.

[55] The harmony at this point recalls a similar musical response to the words 'et io piangendo' in the opening measures of Arcadelt's celebrated madrigal *Il bianco e dolce cigno*, first published in *Il primo libro di madrigali d'Archadelt* (Venice, 1539).

[56] The writer's doctoral dissertation, now in progress, on Phinot's secular works.

[57] This work is discussed at some length in J. Höfler, 'Some early examples of the Italian *dialogo*: a contribution to the problems of Renaissance polychoral music', *Muzikološki Zbornik*, VIII, Ljubljana, 1972, pp. 40–56.

J. R. Hale   *University College, London*

25

THE MILITARY EDUCATION
OF THE OFFICER CLASS
IN EARLY MODERN EUROPE

INTRODUCTION

THE CREATION OF institutions for the formal military education of potential and serving army officers is rightly associated with the period 1650–1750, with large native standing armies and with the widening influence of scientific and technological ideas.[1] The nature of these institutions (and of the conservatism they had to overcome) was, however, prepared for by earlier suggestions, detailed projects and actual experiments which, taken together, form both an introduction to the later period and an extension of the research carried out by historians of Renaissance humanism and of its implications for educational theory and practice.[2] The process whereby the notion of institutionalised military education began to erode that of the well born individual's right to command on the basis of birth and a familiarity with horse and sword has not yet been charted. This essay provides a preliminary survey of the subject, followed by a narrative check list of proposals and institutions which may act as a guide to a fuller and more satisfactory account.

TRADITION AND REFORM

In 1497 Giovanni Sabadino reminded his patron, Ercole I d'Este, how he had been prepared as a warrior: 'venuto in la adolescente estate cominciasti scrimire e cavalcare armato sopra legiadri e potenti cavalli, correndo con la lanza con altri nobilissimi toi equalli in la augusta corte de Alphonso de Aragonia.'[3] At the age of eighty-five Giulio Savorgnan, reviewing in 1595 a lifetime devoted to the military service of Venice, described himself as a pupil of the *condottiere* Duke of Urbino, and his nephew Germanico as 'degno scolare della militar disciplina del Signor Duca di Parma'.[4]

Swordplay and riding, skills learned at home if adequate masters were available, otherwise in a household or court distinguished for its martial tone; then experience in the field under a commander of fame: the late medieval syllabus for a military career survived radical changes in the qualities and skills required in army officers with remarkable consistency. Lacking adequate masters, proposals to train young Venetian patricians for military commands in 1515 envisaged sending them at once into the field under the supervision of the republic's captain general, Bartolomeo d'Alviano.[5] Having them available in Florence, the Grand Duke Francesco turned them on to his young bastard brother, Giovanni, and then, when he was nineteen, sent him off to put his skills into practice in Flanders—skills and practice which were to make Giovanni in his turn captain general of the Venetian forces during the 1615–17 war of Gradisca. In a century that inherited and widely developed a belief in the value of education, Pietro Aretino, friend of the great soldier Giovanni delle Bande Nere and himself a professional man of letters, wrote to a young nobleman in 1549 with advice of unflinching conservatism. 'I consider it of little importance or none that Your Excellency has set yourself to studying treatises and compendiums upon the art of war. A man of your talent and your valour should rather have some great captain for his instructor. . . . You should study and consider things military in actual warfare and not in the classroom.'[6]

At about this time, however, increasing concern was coming to be expressed for the adequate preparation of army officers for their combat duties. For the reformers with whom this essay will be concerned it was no longer enough simply to be brave and a gentleman, to know how to ride and to use a lance and a sword. Weapons were changing and so, in their wake, tactics. 'The art of war is now such that men be fain to learn it anew at every two years' end,' as Granvelle pointed out to Sir Thomas Chaloner in 1559.[7] And the pace of change increased after the mid-century. There are 'evrie day newe inventions, strategems of warres, change of weapons, munition, and all sorts of engins newlie invented and corrected dailie', Sir Roger Williams warned in 1590.[8] Well before the radical tactical innovations associated with Maurice of Orange and widely discussed early in the seventeenth century, the untrained captain, however courageous, was seen as a source of confusion and of potential risk to the lives of others; do not make men captains, Blaise de Monluc pleaded with Henry IV, simply on account of their birth or 'à l'appetit d'un monsieur ou d'une madame'.[9] And the need for officers who could use their heads as well as their hands was still further emphasised by changes in the nature of fortifications and the consequential shift from open battle to campaigns of siege and skirmish. The potential officer needed to know more about a more complex and a more disciplined craft of war than had his late medieval predecessor.

The recognition of this need was supported by the wider concern with the condition of the traditional officer class, a concern expressed in three ways: a desire to moderate its lawlessness; an urge to protect its status as the natural leader of society; and—allied to this—worry about its decreasing militancy. The worry here was not that men who a century before would have been warriors were turning to the law or civilian court service but that those who did not bring themselves forward in these ways were becoming drones, guzzling and hawking themselves to the very margins of social usefulness.[10]

Not all military commands went to nobles, aristocrats and gentlemen. Men from other backgrounds became ensigns, lieutenants and captains, if the senior ranks were largely closed to them. But a concern for the methodical education of potential officers was linked to a concern for sobering and instructing the whole class which formed the traditional reservoir of military leaders, and the proposals for reform discussed here related only to them, either as an adjunct to a general education or as a specialised way of finishing it. These proposals were strengthened by the growing conviction that a country's army should be nationally officered, independent of the expertise of foreign mercenaries. And although they anticipated the lines along which the formal military education of the future was to develop, and to a significant effect conditioned that development, they had little practical impact; they remained on paper or affected small numbers. But before turning to the traditional ways of becoming prepared for a military career let us look at three attempts to canalise them into a formal curriculum, one English, one Italian and one German.

The first is well known, though its military scope has never, I think, been sufficiently emphasised: Sir Humphrey Gilbert's proposal of 1570 for 'the erection of an academy in London for education of her maiestes wardes and others the youth of nobility and gentlemen'.[11] It was to cater for boys from twelve years old, but its facilities were also to be open to 'gentlemen of the Inns of Cowrte which shall not apply themselves to the study of the lawes' and to 'cowrtiers and other gentlemen . . . all which now for the moste parte loose their times'. Its purpose was fourfold: to deliver boys from *ad hoc* and often careless private tuition; to break down clannish antipathies by bringing up young aristocrats together—putting age group before family loyalties; thirdly, in contrast to the universities, to provide youth with an education suited 'for the service of their countrie'; finally, its non-academic subjects were to constitute a finishing school 'in qualities meet for a gentleman'.

The syllabus was to include Greek, Latin and Hebrew; divinity; civil and common law; natural philosophy and medicine; cosmography and astronomy. There were to be teachers of French, Italian, Spanish and High Dutch. The military relevance was to be provided by a mathematician or engineer who

shall one day reade arithmetick, and the other day geometry, which shall be only employed to imbattelinges, fortifications, and matters of warre, with the practiz of artillery, and use of all manner of instrumentes belonging to the same. And [he] shall once every month practize canonrie (shewing the manner of underminings), and train his awditorie to draw in paper, make in modell, and stake owt all kindes of fortificac[i]ons, as well to prevent the mine and sappe as the canon, with all sorts of encampinges.

A teacher of logic and rhetoric was chiefly to teach through 'orations made in English, both politique and militare, taking occasions out of discourses of histories . . . with the examples and stratagemmes both antick and moderne'. A reader in moral philosophy was to devide his readinges by the day into two sortes, the one concerning civill pollicie, the other concerning martiall pollicy ... Touching warres he shall also particulerly declare what manner of forces they [all monarchies and best known common wealths] had and have, and what were and are the distinct discipline and kindes of arminge, training and maintaining of their soldiers in every particuler kind of service.

On the less academic side there was to be instruction in music, dancing and gymnastics ('vawlting'). Also 'there shalbe one who shall teache to draw mappes, sea chartes, &c., and to take by view of eye the platte of any thinge, and shall reade the growndes and rules of proportion and necessarie per-pective and mensuration belonging to the same'. There was to be a master of defence to teach the handling of weapons: rapier and dagger; sword and target; the use of dagger, battle-axe and pike. In addition there was to be a

perfect trained sowldiour who shall teach them to handle the harqubuz, and to practize in the same achademie all kindes of skirmishinges, imbattelinges, and sondry kindes of marchinges, appointinge amonge them some one tyme, and some another, to suply the rooms of captaines and other officers, which they may very well exercize without armes and with light staves in steade of pikes and holbeardes.

And finally

there shalbe entertained into the said achademy one good horsman to teache noble men and gentlemen to ride, make and handle a ready horse, exercising them to runne at the ringe, tilte, towrney, and course of the field, if they shalbe armed. And also to skirmish on horsbacke with pistolles.[12]

The combination of the trilingualism of northern humanism with the Castiglionesque range of polite accomplishments plus mathematics and applied science is remarkable in itself. Even more remarkable is the width of the programme's relevance to the military needs of the day. It keeps the three gentlemanly career options—law, war, politics—open, while offering both a general understanding of warfare and an up-to-date practical knowledge that would stand any officer in excellent stead when he saw action for the first time. But its implementation would have been expensive, it poached on jealously guarded educational monopolies all the way from the universities and the Inns of Court to the private riding and fencing masters of London, and the queen at no time showed any interest in professionalising the leaders of her army. Her academy remained a paper one.

Between 1608 and 1610, on the other hand, four academies were actually set up in Padua, Verona, Udine and Treviso. Subsidised through judicial fines, their purpose was to provide an outlet for the violence of the young nobles of the Venetian *terraferma* and a pool of trained recruits for the republic's permanent force of heavy cavalry. Each had a riding and a fencing master. In addition each had a mathematics lecturer, whose duties, as set out by Piero Duodo, the moving spirit behind the Paduan Academia Delia, were as follows: to teach the theory and design of fortifications and armed camps, the elements of ballistics and rangefinding, and the use of square roots for planning troop formations.[13] This addition of mathematics was not surprising in Padua, where Galileo was already lecturing on forti-fication in the university and giving private tuition in his home on the military applications of arithmetic and geometry. That similar instruction should be offered to the still largely feudalised young bloods of Udine is more revealing evidence of the extent to which mathematics were taken for granted as a desirable element in a potential officer's education.

The third example is a full-fledged professional military college, the first of its kind in Europe: John of Nassau's *schola militaris* at Siegen in Westphalia. Opened in 1617, it drew students between the ages of seventeen and twenty-five from as far afield as Holland and Bohemia. It was socially exclusive. Its descriptive brochure invited applications only from 'Fürsten, Grafen, Adeliche and Patriziersöhn'. But while it provided opportunities for riding and fencing, its chief emphasis was on turning out technically competent infantry officers. More time was spent on the parade ground than in the classroom; the only frills promised were Latin, Italian and French, and probably only the last was actually taught.

Tirelessly propagandist for the reforms of Maurice of Orange, John either wrote or directed the writing of a play about the college's activities. His spokesman lists six, all severely practical: the handling of weapons, including the pike; drill 'auf niederländsch manier'; marching and battle formations; their variation under combat conditions, including the use of reserves; the defence and siege of fortifications, including the use of artillery. The play then introduces an old soldier, Octeranus, who has learned his craft the hard way by fighting in Poland, Sweden and Hungary. He regards this school in Germany with heavy scorn:

> Daß ich dennoch in so viel Jahrn
> Von Kriegssachen fast wenig erfahn,
> Solt man denn in so kurzer Zeit
> Erlangen solch geschicklichkeit
> In dieser Schule?—Das Glaub ich nicht.

Nor is he convinced when the training programme is explained to him.

> Ha, ha, ha! Das wüßt ich gern,
> Wie man ohn Krieg kriegführen lern!

But after watching their weapon training and drill on the parade ground, followed indoors by war games with cards, each representing a tactical unit, which they combine into various formations, he is converted. He is forced to admit that

> auch ein junger Knab
> Von Kriegssachen mehr Wissen hab
> Als mancher der viel Jahr und Tag
> Die Krieg gebraucht selbst haben mag.

And John has made this defeat of a representative of the conservative majority all the more significant because Octerarus, when quizzed by the students, is unable to justify his own military practice. He defends, for instance, the old massive formations of pike. But most of the men are just passengers within them, the students point out. The aim should be to enable every man to bring effective pressure to bear on the enemy. This means using many small formations, thoroughly drilled to work effectively in mutual support. Hence the need for many well trained officers and for training establishments to prepare them.[14]

The Siegen *schola militaris* apparently ran into administrative difficulties and closed even before John of Nassau's death in 1623. It was a logical adjunct to the advanced military practice of the time, but Octeranus had been routed only on paper. For most soldiers combat experience was the only worthwhile tutor. 'A campe continuallie maintained in action,' as Sir Roger Williams put it, 'is like an universitie continuallie in exercises.'[15] Writing of Maurice's reforms a year before Siegen opened, John Bingham paid tribute both to him—'a prince born and bred up in arms'—and to the United Provinces, 'which countries at this day are the scoole of war, whither the martiall spirits of Europe resort to lay down the apprentiship of their service in armes'.[16]

The vast majority of well born recruits first saw action—some as gentlemen rankers but many already with the rank of captain and with responsibility for a hundred or more men—with little or no formal preparation for war. Apart from those who had first joined the permanent establishment of princely guards and garrison forces which all countries maintained, the nearest approach to handling a body of men they could have gained was at musters of the local militia, and here more time was commonly spent checking names and equipment than performing drill and evolutions. Only the Spaniards, from the middle of the sixteenth century, systematically sent recruits to train in garrison before sending them into action,[17] at the same time encouraging the enlistment of gentlemen rankers in the infantry by allowing them special baggage and transport privileges. Nor did the page system, the apprenticeship served by young aristocrats in a military household, guarantee more than a prior acquaintance with horses, weapons and stories of past campaigns.

In order to estimate the degree of preparedness a young officer brought with him to siege or battlefield, therefore, we must concentrate on his *in*formal military education, a matter of family tradition and class expectation, private tuition and reading, and of such paramilitary activities as riding and swordsmanship.

To the extent that the tuition given a youth had a humanistic flavour, it would almost certainly have stressed military matters.

Arms and methods of warfare change from age to age . . . But whatever the method or the weapon of the time, let there be ample practice for our youth, with as great variety of exercises as can be devised, so that they may be ready for combat hand to hand or in troop, in the headlong charge or in the skirmish. We cannot forestall the reality of war, its sudden emergencies, or its vivid terrors, but by training and practice we can at least provide such preparation as the case admits.[18]

Thus Vergerio, in his pioneering treatise on education of about 1392. And whether written by a Palmieri for a republic or by an Aeneas Sylvius Piccolomini for a prince, the sword was prominently displayed alongside the pen by Vergerio's Quattrocento successors.[19] The extent to which a young noble should learn every aspect of warfare, from swimming and riding to the casting of artillery, was set out in prose and woodcut in Maximilian I's *Weißkunig* and elaborated in Rabelais's account of Gargantua's education.[20] And to the humanistic strain and the technologically conscious chivalric strain in educational thought was added the balanced range of accomplishments attributed by Castiglione to his *Courtier*. When in 1615 Sir George Buc was justifying his calling London the third university in England, he pointed out that it was possible to study not only the traditional liberal arts there but also the more up-to-date ones. And

in the choice of the arts of this kind I will not be mine owne carver but will receive them of the recommendation and warrant of that most learned and iudicious noble gentleman the Count Baldesser Castilio, who, recounting the qualities and arts necessary and properly appertaining to a gentleman (and so consequently to be esteemed liberall and ingenuous) giveth to the arts gladiatorie, or of defence, and of ryding, and of paynting and of pourtraying, and of dauncing, place amongst them.[21]

Blending the Castiglionesque canon with the Maximilian one, Sir George also described where instruction in swimming and the firing of artillery was to be found. It was not only in Spain, where the aristocratic ideal remained ostentatiously militaristic, and where the Jesuit Juan de Mariana advocated mock battles to prepare young nobles for cavalry and infantry combat,[22] that educational theory took the military potential of the aristocracy for granted. Renaissance theory required more learning, and allowed for a greater variety of careers, without eroding the medieval connection between high birth and arms. If anything, it played up the theme of military responsibility in order to increase the socially distancing image of the Second Estate, to help to distinguish its members from the thriving urban bourgeoisie and the wealthy farmers who had risen from peasant stock. And this educational theory, with its emphasis on an 'all round' self-development—increasingly within a group—became more and more widely accepted during an age which saw the progressive breakdown of the page system of early entry to a military career.

The age at which boys went to serve as pages in the late fifteenth and during the first half of the sixteenth centuries varied. Bayard, the future 'chevalier sans peur et sans reproche', was sent as page to the Duke of Savoy at thirteen; Dürer's friend Willibald Pirckheimer was sixteen when he became a page at the chivalrous court of the Bishop of Eichstätt; Peter Ernest of Mansfeld was only eleven when he became a page. In return for serving at his lord's table a boy could expect to learn horsemanship and the management of weapons from the *escuyer* into whose charge he was placed, to compete in wrestling, jumping and running with the other pages, and to learn to dance. In theory the *escuyer* should encourage his charges to read 'une ou deux heures du jour . . . en quelque beau livre'; when this did happen the book was commonly a chivalrous romance or chronicle of wars.

After two or three years the page would be promoted 'hors de page' and given a junior command or sent to a garrison for further training. If fighting were going on during his pageship a boy would accompany his lord. At the age of fifteen I set off, recalled Jean de Mergey, 'sur un petit cheval barbe, mais fort viste, ayant en ma teste mon morion à banniere avec un beau panache, et un javelot de Brezil, le fer doré bien tranchant, avec belle houppe d'or et de soye, ma casaque de page, belle et bien estoffé de broderie, de sorte que je pensois estre quelque petit dieu Mars'. Normally the young page was not expected actually to fight. On one occasion, however, de Mergey's company was surprised and was forced to charge as a whole. He himself ran one of the enemy through and then found that he could not pull the lance out of the man's stomach before he was forced to retreat. The reaction of this little Mars was not pride but fear: fear that he would be whipped for losing his weapon.[23]

The gallantry and personal initiative fostered by the page system was taken for granted. But as the century wore on, doubts were increasingly expressed about its effect on character and its suitability as a preparation for wars where there was less and less need for the individual daring of a cavalryman. The system was also collapsing from within. The military training in great households was becoming more perfunctory; pages were being exploited as servants; their morals were ignored, their education skimped; their irresponsibility when given a command was deplored. From 1530 the emphasis was on later entry to a military career after a broader education.[24]

The part that reading could play within that broader education is revealingly described by that tough and conservative old soldier Sir John Smythe, who was born in 1531.

I even from my very tender years have delighted to hear histories read that did treat of actions and deeds of arms, and since I came to years of some discretion and that by my father's rank I was brought up to school and brought with time to understand the Latin tongue somewhat indifferently, I did always delight and procure my tutors as much as I could to read unto me the commentaries of Julius Caesar and Sallust and other such books. And after that I came from school and went to the university ... I gave myself to the reading of many other histories and books treating of matters of war and sciences tending to the same.[24]

The relevance of classical to contemporary warfare was sometimes queried but never denied. Paradoxically gunpowder, by reducing the role of heavy cavalry and encouraging the introduction of less bulky, less vulnerable infantry formations, had led sixteenth-century tactics actually to resemble those of ancient Greece and Rome more closely than those of the Middle Ages; the Ancients' stress on morale and training was also directly relevant to the contemporary situation. Towards the end of our period John of Nassau, founder of Siegen and contemporary of Galileo, listed among the books which, if read *ex fundamento* 'einen rechtschaffenen Capitein machet', works by the following authors: Livy, Polybius, Appian, Dio, Josephus, the emperor Leo, Xenophon, Thucydides, Vegetius, Tacitus and Aelian.[26] And because, as the Italian translator of Frontinus put it in 1574, 'Latin is not widely understood today, especially by the majority of those who make a career of arms',[27] there was a steady flow of translations of classical military texts, most of them dedicated to princes and prominent soldiers.

The demand for Smythe's 'other histories' was catered to by printed accounts of contemporary campaigns. An author in 1546, commenting on his fellow countrymen's thirst for news, wrote that 'we will not sticke to spend a quarte of wyne or two of a caryer or serving man that commyth out of the northe partyes to heare tel what skyrmishes hath been betwixt us and the Scottes',[28] and two years later, by spending a few pence, they could read a full and lively account of the Pinkie campaign by Sir William Patten, illustrated with battle plans.[29] The demand for newsletters describing battles had become so great that the author of an account of the actions round Noyen in 1591 was forced to protest that it 'is not forged or fained . . . neither is it fetched from flying and fabulous letters, ordinarie reports on the Exchange, or published uppon rash warrant as some, I know, will not stick to utter'.[30] In more considered vein, a translation of a Spanish narrative of the Flanders wars from 1567 to 1577 advertised itself as 'convenable à ceux qui suyvent le train de la guerre, font profession des armes & manient les affaires d'Estat'.[31]

As for the third category of books mentioned by Smythe—'books treating of matters of war and sciences tending to the same'—there is need to do little more than note in passing the flood of books dealing with the conduct and technology of war that steadily mounted in volume through the sixteenth and early seventeenth centuries.[32] The problem is to know who read them, at what age, and with what effect. It is from the last quarter of the sixteenth century that authors stress and cater for the need to keep informed and up to date through books during the lulls between wars,[33] and that there is an increase in the number of books not only aimed at the inexperienced would-be officer but likely to be actually comprehensible to him;[34] and by now the use of that valuable explanatory aid, the diagram, had become habitual. All the same, writing in 1607, John Cleland takes a somewhat moderate view of the young nobleman's appetite for book learning: 'for military affaires yee maie read the Lord of Noue, who is somewhat difficil for some men, & also the commentaries of the L. Monluc which are good both for the younge soldier and an old captaine'.[35] Autobiographical evidence is scanty. All, perhaps, that can be concluded is that the enduring controversy between these who stressed the need for preliminary study before reaching the battlefield and those who relied wholly on combat experience suggests—as do the economics of the book trade and the number of reissues of military works—a body of readers some of whom, at least, must have been young men who had not yet gone to the wars.[36]

With increasing regularity sixteenth-century travellers had paid attention to fortifications, armouries and musters of troops, as well as to antiquities, religious relics, feather beds and pretty women. And as a hortatory literature of travel developed towards the end of the century one of the reasons suggested as compensating for the moral and physical dangers of foreign travel was that it enlarged the military education of the potential as well as of the serving officer. 'What captain of warre is to be appointed over an army,' asked Hermann Kirchner, 'if not he that hath searched the manners of other people, & hath scene their skirmishes and exercises in military affaires?'[37] Cleland's advice is specific almost to the point of positive hazard.

When you are in Hungarie, mark the forts; and if the Christian army be in the field, observe their order and fashion of martial exploits. . . . Come to Flanders . . . you shall not spare to salute the Arch-Duke and to see his forces, aquainting yourselfe with his Spanish captaines, ever to learne some good observation in martial affaires. . . . This [he goes on] is the place where you maie learne to be perfect in militarie discipline; there you shal be moved by example & encouragement to be valiant: yet I wish you not too rash in endangering your life and reputation, where neither your death nor wounds can be either honourable or profitable.[38]

The commonest form of preparation for war arose, however, from the nature of the physical pastimes of the class from which officers were drawn. The relevance of hunting was taken for granted throughout the period. 'Hunting is a military exercise,' as Lodowick Lloyd put it; 'the like strategems are often invented and executed in warres against soldiers as the hunter doeth against divers kindes of beasts.'[39] There were complaints that men were so besotted with the music of hounds that they stopped their ears to the trumpets of war,[40] and that hunting took up time which could have been spent reading about war or studying mathematics,[41] but no one queried its relevance to the physical fitness, the eye for terrain or the bloodthirsty *brio* needed in war.

The tournament, which at times—as at the court of Henry II of France— became *the* obsessive aristocratic pastime,[42] was increasingly looked on less as a preparation for the shock of encounter in battle than as an occasion for the display of physical strength and skill. This paralleled the decline of the heavy lancer in war, and as the tilt came to be overtaken by running at the ring, and still more when the pistol quintain took the place of the ring, the relevance of this form of entertainment to the actual practice of light cavalry remained close. However, it was not quite true to say, with an Italian enthusiast in 1600, that 'every form of mounted game of skill [*giostra*] and combat has real combat as its end and purpose',[43] because a number of these 'combats' were horse ballets pure and simple, designed to show off the riders' exquisite management of specially schooled horses.

The breeding of horses for looks, strength and intelligence, while not new, took on a special significance from the mid-century. Horses became a cult— that is, the Great Horse of the *manège*. Instead of talk about the merits of different strains, the names of individual outstanding beasts were breathed with reverence. And with the cult of the horse came the cult of the riding master and the riding school. 'The professors of this art,' wrote one of them, 'truly deserve higher praise than those who teach any other art in the world.'[44] Sir Philip Sydney was hardly exaggerating when he said of his Italian riding master in Vienna that 'to so unbeleeved a point hee proceeded as that no earthly thing bred such wonder to a prince as to be a good horseman. Skill of government was but a pedanteria in comparison.'[45] Throughout the later sixteenth century Italians were considered the supreme masters, and though they set up establishments as far afield as Vienna and London, Italy itself remained the Mecca of the aspirant horseman. Within the peninsula state competed with state both to attract free-spending foreigners and to prevent their own young bloods from seeking instruction elsewhere.[46] The Neapolitan master Pignatelli, who died in 1596, was cited as a familiar symbol of the teacher of a physical skill as late as 1668.[47] But even his fame was eclipsed when his pupil, Antoine de Pluvinel, established his school in Paris early in the seventeenth century, and while status-conscious painters could point to the emperor Charles V picking up Titian's brush for him, future generations of riding masters could henceforward fondle the pages of de Pluvinel's books, where in one sumptuous engraving after another Louis XIII is shown in close conversation with the author, or touching his arm with eager and deferential attention.[48]

Even before 1600 the riding masters were having to counter complaints that their caracoles and standing jumps were irrelevant to war.[49] 'The principall use of horsses,' wrote Thomas Bedingfield in the most moderate of the answers to this charge, 'is to travell by the waie, & serve in the war: whatsoever your horse learneth more is rather for pompe or pleasure, than honor or use.' He merely maintained that riding the great horse should be continued for motives of delight, prestige and horse-breeding.[50] Few men, however noble, could in fact afford to master the art, let alone buy its instrument, but at least it raised the reputation of horsemanship in general and probably encouraged the recruitment of men and mounts to the cavalry, that branch of military science which was still essential even if it did not in fact 'surpasse de beaucoup toutes les sciences du monde (excepté la Theologie).'[51]

It was again from the mid-sixteenth century, and once more under Italian influence, that fencing joined riding as an accomplishment to be expected of a young man of good birth. Fencing guilds, with their degrees of membership corresponding to the student, Bachelor and Master of the universities, were flourishing earlier in the sixteenth century: the *arte palestrinae* of Spanish Perpignon, the *Marxbrüder* of Frankfort, the *Federfechter* of Prague, the Masters of Defence of London.[52] And instruction was not available only in large cities. 'For of fence in everie towne,' wrote Roger Ascham in 1545, 'there is . . . maisters to teach it.'[53] Nor was this surprising at a time when much of the execution in war, by horse and foot, was accomplished by the sword, when roads and forests were haunted by footpads and outlaws, and when one of the privileges of gentility (and of gentlemen's servants) was licence to carry a sword.

It was the mid-century honour code that promoted swordsmanship from a necessity to an art, from habit to fashion, the honour code with its dubiously glamourous companion, the duel. The result was that the fencing master acquired the title 'professor', which he has retained ever since, and a spate of books in which one new method trod with a nice sense of malice and superiority on the heels of the last. These books may have warned their readers against the duel, but they knew the social tide was with them. Arms, cautioned one Italian author, may be used only 'in defence of the faith, one's country, one's person, and in the last resort one's honour', but he also invited the reader to consider that 'this science is chiefly practised in royal courts, in those of every prince, and is studied in the most famous cities by barons, counts, *cavalieri* and persons of outstanding distinction'.[54] And this was not unjustified. James I, in spite of his dislike of the duel, recommended fencing in his *Basilikon Doron*, and Louis XIII allowed himself to head the illustrious list of sponsors of Girard Thibault's *Academie de l'espée*, a work dedicated to 'Empereur, Roys, Princes, Ducs, Comtes et toutes autres seigneurs et nobles fauteurs & amateurs de la tresnoble science de manier les armes'.[55]

For the gentleman, fencing as a social accomplishment became increasingly identified with the rapier, or at least with rapier and dagger; in any case, with the use of the point rather than of the edge. And it was for this reason that a science which, according to the fencing master George Silver, was 'noble, and in mine opinion to be preferred next to divinitie'[56] came under attack for no longer being relevant to war, even though the authority of Vegetius favoured the point.[57] By this time, however, deaths in combat were increasingly caused by guns, pistols, pikes, halberds and lances rather than by swords. In any case, edged weapons were not neglected by the schools of fence, though they were given less prominence than the foil-like employment of the rapier. Moreover under the influence of the fencing schools wrestling, which was declining in repute as an exercise for gentlemen, was modified into a respectable and useful form of judo, with special emphasis on the unarmed man's defence against an armed assailant.[58] And any sort of fencing helped promote the sort of physical strength and dexterity—with, in the case of one author,[59] the help of setting-up exercises—that the military life called for.

In 1596, at the age of seventeen, François de Bassompierre and his brother travelled to Italy to round out the bookish education they had had at school and from tutors. At Naples they attended Pignatelli's riding school. Then they moved to Florence, 'ou nous demeurasmes à apprendre nos exercises, moy sous Rustier Picardini à monter à cheval, mon frère sous Terenant. Pour les autres exercises, nous eusmes mesmes maistres, comme Maistre Agostino pour dancer, Mr Marquino pour tirer des armes, Julio Panigy pour les fortifications.'[60]

Ten years later he might well have stayed in Paris. De Pluvinel's accomplishment was to bring together at the Louvre the sort of teaching talent that de Bassompiere described as scattered through Florence or Sir George Buc through London. De Pluvinel's academy became the best-known martial finishing school in Europe.[61] There a man could learn to ride with the controlled nonchalence that had become the hallmark of gentlemanly accomplishments,[62] as well as fence, do gymnastics, dance and learn mathematics and military drawing.[63] For however far the great horse and rapier were removed from remount and pistol, the pursuit of these activities was associated with the possibility of a future military career, and it was accepted that for such a career mathematics was needed as a background to fortification, gunnery and the marshalling of troops (and, it might be added, for fighting according to certain schools of fence[64]), and also enough drawing to design a fort and map a plan of campaign.[65] The idea of the many-sided officer recruit arose within the conservative fostering of 'politeness' as well as among the more progressive spokesmen for a professionalised army. And both schools of thought moved in the direction of institutionalisation.

A NARRATIVE CHECK LIST, c. 1530–c. 1630

This, then, is the background against which we can pass in brief review a mixed bag of suggestions, projects and experiments bearing on the military education of the potential officer class. They are numbered (in square brackets) in chronological order.

Sir Humphrey Gilbert's proposals of 1570 were not without precedent in England. [1] In the mid-1530s Thomas Starkey had deplored the irresponsibility of an aristocracy amongst whom 'every man privately in his own house hath his master to instruct his children in letters'. These children should be brought up together in 'the discipline of the common weal'. Where? Well, there are 'over-many' monasteries and abbeys, so 'to this use turn both Westminster and St Albans, and many other. . . . Here they should be instruct not only in virtue and learning but also in all feats of war pertaining to such as should be hereafter, in time of war, captains and governors of the common sort.'[66]

[2] A few years later Sir Nicholas Bacon, Thomas Denton and Robert Cary submitted a memorandum relating to Henry VIII's proposal to erect a college in London 'whereby your grace hereafter might be the better served of your grace's own students of the law, as well as in forein countries as within this your grace's realm'. While agreeing that the main emphasis should be on law, Latin and French, they urged that the students should also acquire 'some knowledge and practice in martial feats, whereby they may be able to doo the king's grace and the realm service both in time of peace and war'. They also suggested the erection of an archive of military science. Whenever war broke out between princes on the continent a number of suitable students were to 'repair into those parts not only to view themselves the order and fashion of their camps, and assaulting and defending, but also to set forth in writing all the whole order of the battel, and this to be registered in their house, and to remain there for ever'.[67]

[3] In 1561 Bacon wrote on his own account to Sir William Cecil a proposal for 'the bringing up in vertue and lerning of the queenes maiesties wardes'. There were to be five schoolmasters, one for Latin and Greek, one for 'frenche and other languages', one for music, one to teach the boys 'to ryde, to vawlte, to handle weapons and such other things as thereto belongeth'. And 'every Tewsdaie and sattersdaye all the wardes that be XVI years of age and upwards shall spende the daie as he that teacheth to ryde and to handle weapons shall appoint'. The fifth was 'to read a lecture of the temporall or cyvill lawe' each other working day between eight and nine in the morning and 'a lecture de disciplina militari' every afternoon between four and five—again, for boys of sixteen and over.[68]

[4] In 1563 Giovanni Maria Memmo pleaded that his fellow countrymen should not confine their military role only to naval warfare but that Venetian citizens should be trained to take the place of the mercenaries used on land. His proposals do not include the setting up of a formal academy, but the regular use of an open space where physical training and weapon handling can be carried on in the manner described by Vegetius—even to the use of dummies on which to practice swordplay, and vaulting horses to prepare for the agile mounting of real horses—with the addition of training in the handling of the arquebus. To this classical curriculum à la Campus Martis he adds drills and manoeuvres as practised by the contemporary militia of the Venetian Terraferma, and a knowledge of arithmetic and geometry to aid in the brigading of troops and the construction and siege of fortifications. Though as a project for military education his ideas are blurred by an aspiration to create religious and virtuous citizens as well as trained soldiers, and though no notice was taken of them in Venice itself, Memmo's ideas form part of the body of opinion that was to lead to the setting up of formal academies on the Terraferma.[69]

[5] In Paris in 1570 (for Gilbert's proposal of the same date [6] see above, pp. 442–3) Jean Antoin de Baïf's academy was founded as 'an institution in which all subjects were studied, natural philosophy no less than poetry, mathematics as well as music, painting in addition to languages, even military discipline and gymnastics'.[70] [7] In his *Discours politiques et militaires*, written between 1580 and 1585, Francois de la Noue proposed the setting up of academies first in four cities—Paris, Lyons, Bordeaux and Angers—and in four little-used royal *châteaux*—Fontainebleau, Moulins, Plessis le Tour and Cognac, and then in the chief town of each province. Here, from the age of fifteen, young members of the *noblesse* would follow a syllabus comprising the following subjects: riding and running at the ring, both with and without armour; the handling of weapons; gymnastics, swimming and wrestling; music and painting; possibly dancing. There would be lectures, all in French, on the writers of Antiquity 'qui traitent des vertus morales, de la police & de la guerre', and on ancient and modern history. Each academy would have from eight to ten teachers, paid well and in proportion to the importance of their subject, 'car chacun sçait qu'un qui monstreroit à manier chevaux meriteroit plus qu'un peintre'. He reckoned the cost at 3,000 écus per academy.[71] [8] In the late 1580s Scipio Ammirato, fired by Pope Sixtus V's grandiose crusading plans, suggested that a number of Italian orphanages should be turned into military academies.[72]

These schemes all remained on paper. [9] However, from 1589 the Collegium Illustre of Tübingen was combining riding and fencing with a syllabus heavily biased towards law, history and modern languages, while [10] with Maurice of Hesse's foundation of the Collegium Mauritianum in Kassel in 1599 Gilbert's plan appeared to come to life in Germany. It offered a secondary education to young aristocrats 'in allen Ritterlichen Thugenden und Übungen'. Four masters taught theology, moral philosophy, medicine (*Physices*) and dialectic and rhetoric. Four others taught languages:

two for Latin, one for Greek, one for French, Italian and Spanish. One of the eight had also to teach the military applications of mathmatics, with special reference to fortification and siegecraft and to the planning of troop formations. Another of the eight also taught history. There were instructors in dancing, music and drawing, riding, the handling of weapons for horse and foot, and the principles of military evolutions.[73]

[11] At about the same time Henry IV of France attempted to rationalise the education of the young nobles at his court by establishing what his panegyrist, Jean-Baptiste Legrain, calls an 'Academie pour la noblesse & autre ieunesse. . . . Ayant ordonné une compagnie de maistres, les uns pour les lettres, les autres pour les armes, autres pour monter à cheval, autres pour l'escriture, autres pour la musique, les instrumens, & la dance, bref, pour tout honeste exercice.' First mooted in 1594, the academy was designed to provide a training in skills that had hitherto been sought abroad, especially in Italy, and was seen by mathematical practitioners as a natural market for their wares, 'qui ne proffitent pas seullement durant la paix, mais produisent leurs plus beaux effects en temps de guerre.' By 1598 the king's chief riding master gave lessons every day, and from the fees paid him by the academicians he engaged masters of fence, dancing, music and mathematics; moreover the example of Paris had been followed in Rouen and Toulouse.[74]

[12] Far more hazy is the evidence suggesting that at this court at Nonsuch Palace the king's namesake, Henry, Prince of Wales, was being brought up in a similar atmosphere. In 1607 Sir Thomas Chaloner, the prince's tutor, an ex-soldier and something of a scientist, described Henry's household as 'a courtly college, or a collegiate court',[75] and in the same year Cleland wrote 'without offence to either of the famous universities here, or our colleges in Scotland, for all sorts of learning, I recommend in particular the academie of our noble prince, where young nobles may learne the first elements to be a privie counseller, a generall of an armie, to rule in peace, & to commande in warre'.[76] (The Venetian academies [13] of 1608–10 are described above, pp. 443–4.) Finally, at some time before his death in 1612, when still only eighteen, Prince Henry was associated with proposing yet another scheme for the education of royal wards: [14] an 'academy for the learning of the mathematiques and language, and for all kinds of noble exercises, as well of arms as other'. Its expenses were to be defrayed from an increase in the fines imposed in Star Chamber[77]—a suggestion paralleling the method of subvention used to support the contemporary riding academies in the Veneto.

Cleland's picture of a milieu that can produce instant privy councillors and instant generals is at least evidence of a growing faith in institutionalised education for young gentlemen. It was echoed across the Channel by Jean de Tavannes. [15] The educational whims of fathers and tutors could no longer be trusted, he wrote. The page system had degenerated into producing mere 'valets et macqueraux'. Travel to seek the riding and fencing masters of Italy led to youths returning 'plus chargez de vices que de vertus'. What was needed was 'colleges de noblesse' where 2,000 young gentlemen could be educated at the expense of the king or the Church: 'seroit-ce une grande gloire de voir sortir à vingt ans des generaux d'armées de ces escolles'.[78] And if courts like those of the two Henries were reflecting—or were being interpreted as reflecting—academic theories about the relevance of education to responsible public life, learned academies themselves were affected by the pastimes and interests of courtiers. [16] In 1612 David de Flurance Rivault, tutor to the young Louis XIII, set up a short-lived academy which not only allowed 'the methods of warfare of different peoples' to be discussed on an equal footing with questions of theology and literature, but was to provide for the teaching of 'military exercises and the art of war'.[79]

[17] It was quite in keeping with this atmosphere that Jean Chesnel, Seigneur of Chappronnoye, should, with the young Louis's encouragement, found in 1614 a new military order. Named after the Magdalen, it had three purposes: to maintain the Catholic faith, to suppress irresponsible duelling and to train a military *corps d'élite*. Its members were to fall into two categories: knights (those with three generations of noble blood) and 'brethren servants' ('from the most honorable families in townes and cities, next to the nobility'). The headquarters was to be in Paris, where 500 knights could be accommodated during the two-year period of probation before they were admitted to vows of charity, obedience and conjugal chastity; and those who so chose could stay on longer. They swore loyalty to the king and to avoid duels unless they were forced on them. Between eighty and 100 were to wait upon the king daily as a sort of special guard, and the motherhouse was to employ 'esquires, maisters in actions of arms, learned mathematicians, and some numbers of well experimented souldiours to enstruct military agilities and exercises fit for horse and foot'. Moreover there was to be a fund to help 'poore gentlemen'—not members of the order—'to the exercises that have no means for their learning'.[80] The project was never realised, though as proof his sincerity Chesnel spent the rest of his life as a rather prestigious hermit.

[18] In that same year, 1614, the English Privy Council allowed an increase in the membership of the London Artillery Garden to 500. With its armoury and practice fields, this institution was to be referred to as a 'nursery of military discipline' and a 'shoole' which taught 'martiall policy or discipline'. Its members were proud to reflect that, like the Greeks and Romans 'we [have] our academies and military schooles; witnesse our Artillery Garden . . . wherein the choice and best-affected citizens (and gentry) are practised and taught the rudiments of our militia'.[81] Its members had weapon training in the use of halberds, pikes and muskets, drilled and practised evolutions and possibly carried out mock sieges. They also tried out new weapons, like William Neade's combination pike and gun. There were training periods each fortnight (sometimes once a week), and at least once a year these future officers could expand their evolutions with the whole of the local trained bands. They kept abreast of Continental tactical changes and followed the postures and written directions of the drill books seriously enough to stir the

mockery of Jonson and his fellow dramatists. Translations of ancient writers on the art of war were dedicated to them. Clearly there were far more citizens than gentry among their members, and though Prince Charles and various sheriffs and deputy lieutenants attended some of their meetings neither the Artillery Garden nor the other training establishments modelled on it had either the aristocratic enrolment or the polished and learned emphasis required to justify the term 'academy' save in partisan eyes.[82]

The Siegen academy ([19], see above, pp. 444–5) closed with the death of its founder, John of Nassau, in 1623. [20] In 1624 came another French proposal, this time from the man who had for many years run the nearest approach to a school for officers which France had produced, de Pluvinel. He was, he represents himself as saying in a dialogue with Louis XIII, dismayed at the extent to which the aristocracy had slid into idleness and vice. Let the king, therefore, found academies in Paris, Bordeaux, Lyons and in Tours or Poitiers. Those who could afford to pay, would; but the sons of impoverished aristocrats should be subsidised. The syllabus reads like a more serious version of the courses available at his own establishment. In the mornings, tuition in riding and practice in running at the ring. On Monday, Wednesday, Friday and Saturday afternoons, lessons in weapon management, dancing, gymnastics and mathematics. On Monday and Thursday afternoons, lessons in moral philosophy, drawn from ancient and modern history, and in politics tailored to the needs of future army officers, governors of towns and provinces and ambassadors. Once a month, moreover, there should be something more like modern field exercises,

pour leur apprendre la maniere d'aller au combat, le moyen d'attaquer une escarmouche, la forme de se retirer. Bref, tout l'ordre de la guerre, & faire ces combats tantost à cheval tantost à pied, en faisant faire des forts de terre, & les faire attaquer et deffendre à ceste ieunesse (selon leur force) pour leur enseigner à bien attaquer une place & à la bien deffendre; donner les commandemens alternativement aux uns & aux autres, afin de les rendre tous dignes de bien commander & bien obeyr.

Such academies, he guaranteed, would create a loyal and law-abiding aristocracy 'capables de servir leur prince soit en paix, soit en guerre'. At this point the king breaks silence to ask how much it would cost. Thirty thousand livres a year, Pluvinel replies, and the dialogue closes with the king making non-committal noises of approval.[83]

[21] From 1628 the Friedländische Akademie provided the sort of education for aristocratic boys between nine and seventeen that was to be continued by the numerous German *Pagenakademien* or *Ritterakademien* of the second half of the seventeenth century: religion, mathematics and other 'nützlichen Studien', riding, the handling of weapons, dancing. But it died with its founder, Waldstein, in 1634.[84]

[22] Similarly short-lived was my last example, Louis XIII's establishment in 1629—at Richelieu's instance—of an Académie des exercises militaires. How large its enrolment was is not clear, but Richelieu added scholarships for twenty sons of poor gentlemen aged fourteen or fifteen. These awards were for two years, and as well as following the standard courses given at the

academy in riding, gymnastics, mathematics and fortification, and so forth (for the syllabus seems close to that of Pluvinel's private school), they were to learn the elements of logic, physics and metaphysics and moral philosophy— all taught in French. They were also to learn some geography and the out-lines of universal history 'comme aussi de l'histoire des principautés modernes, singulièrement de l'Europe, dont les intérêts nous touchent de plus prés pour leur voisinage'. At the end of their two years the scholarship youths were to spend two years in the king's service, 'dans le régiment de ses gardes, en ses vaisseaux, ou autrement'.[85] This school also died with its founder, but, as with the other proposals listed here, the momentum of its intention helped to support the institutions that were later to endure.

NOTES

[1] See Frederick B. Artz, *The Development of Technical Education in France, 1500–1850*, London, 1966, and the papers by David Bien, John Shy, Thomas Hughes and Gunther Rothenberg in *Science, Technology and Warfare: Proceedings of the third Military History Symposium*, U.S.A.F. Academy, Washington, D.C. [1970], pp. 51–84.

[2] This essay owes its origin to the encouragement I received at one of Professor Kristeller's seminars at Columbia University.

[3] *Art and Life at the Court of Ercole I d'Este: the 'De triumphis religionis' of Giovanni Sabadino degli Arienti*, ed. Werner L. Gundersheimer, Geneva, 1972, pp. 39–40.

[4] Archivio di Stato, Venice, Materie miste notabili, 18, f. 66v.

[5] Marin Sanuto, *Diarii*, Venice, 1879–1903, xx, cols. 116, 149, 151, 185–8; xi, 147–9.

[6] T. C. Chubb, 'The Letters of Pietro Aretino', n.p., 1967, 280.

[7] J. A. Froude, *History of England . . .*, London, twelve vols., 1870, vi, p. 286.

[8] *A Briefe Discourse of Warre*, ed. John X. Evans, in *The Works of Sir Roger Williams*, Oxford, 1972, p. 27.

[9] *Commentaires*, ed. P. Courteault, Paris, three vols., 1925, iii, p. 389. He accepts that higher commands—generals of cavalry and colonels of infantry—will still go to men of noble blood, experienced or not; but the risks are reduced if they rely on well trained marshals and junior officers.

[10] One complaint can stand for many. 'A great sort of our gentlemen . . . doo take more comfort to be called good faulkners or expert woodmen than either skilful souldiers or learned scollers.' (Sir William Segar, *The Booke of Honor and Armes*, London, 1590, p. 72). His point is that gentlemen should exert themselves in either arms or learning or both.

[11] *Queen Elizabeth's Academy*, ed. F. J. Furnivall, E.E.T.S., extra series, viii.

[12] The academy was also to have the first copyright library in Europe, for 'all printers in England shall for ever be charged to deliver into the library of the acha-demy, at their own charges, one copy well bownde, of every booke, proclamacion, or pamflette, that they shall printe'. And it was to inaugurate the policy of 'publish or perish'; every six years each teacher was to produce one work of his own and two translations of foreign works.

[13] A. Favaro, *Galileo e lo studio di Padova*, Florence, two vols., 1883, ii, p. 331. Galileo was one of three candidates voted on for the position of mathematics lecturer to the Delia; he received the fewest votes. (Archivio di Stato, Padua, P.V., 2610, libro secondo ff. 12r f.) And see J. R. Hale, 'Military academies on the Venetian Terra ferma in the early seventeenth century', *Studi Veneziani*, 1973.

[14] Extract from the 'Festspiel' are quoted in Max Jähns, *Geschichte der Kriegswissen-schaften*, Munich, three vols., 1889, ii, pp. 1026–9, and in W. Hahlweg, *Die Heeresreform der Oranier und die Antike*, Berlin, 1941, p. 148.

[15] *Op. cit.*, n. 8, p. 27.

[16] *The Tacticks of Aelian*, London, 1616, sig. A 2*v*. Sarpi, too, wrote of the Netherlands as 'the learnedest schoole for that kind of discipline, that at this time is in all Europe, yea in the whole world'. (Tr. Bishop William Bedell as *The Free Schoole of Warre*, London, 1625, sig. B iiii*v*. When Thomas Head was appointed in the Armada year to give lectures in London on 'mathematicall science, a knowledge most convenient for militarie men', he anticipated the reaction of the conservatives. 'But heer some men per happes will say, what needeth this cost? what? those famous captaines of ours now in the Low Countries, or those of ancient time before ... were they trained up in this kind of learning?' (Sig. A iiii*r–v*.) Only his first lecture, in fact, had a military bias; as the war scare eased, he devoted himself increasingly to the mathematics of navigation. The lecture is reprinted in F. R. Johnson, 'Thomas Hood's inaugural address ...', *Journal of the History of Ideas*, III, 1942, pp. 94–106.

[17] Geoffrey Parker, *The Army of Flanders and the Spanish Road*, Cambridge, 1972, pp. 32–3, and see also 40–1, 118–19.

[18] Translated in W. H. Woodward, *Vittorino da Feltre and other Humanist Educators*, Cambridge, 1897, p. 115.

[19] W. H. Woodward, *Studies in Education during the Age of the Renaissance*, Cambridge 1924, p. 71; *De liberorum educatione*, ed. J. S. Nelson, Washington, D.C., 1940, pp. 105–7.

[20] The *Weißkunig*, though composed between 1505 and 1516, was not published until 1775. Gargantua's education is described in book 1, chapters 23 and 24. There are, however, some remarkable similarities between their descriptions of their heroes' military education.

[21] Appendix to John Stowe, *Annales ...*, London, 1631, p. 1087. First printed in the edition of 1615. 'Paynting and ... pourtraying' was, as in Castiglione, for military purposes; see *Il Cortegiano*, trans. G. Bull, London, 1967, p. 97. By 1615 dancing had become accepted as giving a bodily grace that helped in the handling of weapons. The Academy at Treviso employed a 'ballarino'. (Archivio di Stato, Venice, Senato, Dispacci Rettori, Treviso, 28 March 1610.) Aristocratic foreigners presented their coats of arms to record their visits to the chief dancing school in Padua. (L. Pearsall Smith, *Sir Henry Wotton*, London, two vols., 1907, I, p. 458.)

[22] *De Rege*, trans. G. A. Moore, Washington, D.C., 1948, p. 113.

[23] *Mémoires*, in M. Petitot, *Collection complete des mémoires relatifs a l'histoire de France*, Paris, 1832, p. 18.

[24] For a retrospective glance at the system see Salomon de la Broue, *Le Cavalerice françois*, Paris, 1602, pp. 2 and 18–22. For the unreliability and thoughtlessness of young officers see Agrippa d'Aubigné, *La Vie*, in *Oeuvres*, ed. H. Weber *at al.*, Paris, 1969, p. 393, and Jean de Tavannes, *Mémoires* (of Gaspard by Jean, but containing much comment by Jean) in Petitot, *Coll.*, *cit.*, Paris, three vols., 1822, I, p. 319. The latter sets out a preferable programme, under the charge of private tutors, on pp. 157–8 and 168–73.

[25] Quoted in *Certain Discourses Military*, ed. J. R. Hale, Ithaca, N.Y., 1964, p. xv.

[26] Hahlweg, *op. cit.*, p. 128.

[27] *Stratagemi militari*, trans. M. A. Gandino, Venice, 1574, sig. a 2*v*.

[28] Paolo Giovio, *A Shorte Treatise upon the Turkes Chronicles*, trans. P. Ashton, London, 1546, f. iv*r*, preface.

[29] *The Expedition into Scotlande* [no place, no date].

[30] Anon., *A True Declaration of ... the Winning of Noyan, August 1591*, London, n.d., epilogue.

[31] Title page of Bernadin de Mendoce, *Commentaires memorables ...*, Paris, 1591.

[32] See generally M. J. Cockle, *A Bibliography of English and Foreign Military Books up to 1642*, London, 1900; repr. 1957. For England, Henry J. Webb, *Elizabethan Military Science: the Books and the Practice*, London, 1965.

[33] E.g. Sancho de Londoño, *Discurso sobre la forma de reduci la disciplina militar ...*, Brussels, 1589, epistle dedicatory.

[34] A generation later, titles begin to stress the 'do it yourself' approach, e.g.

J. Jacobi von Wallhausen, *Alphabetum . . . der Soldaten zu Fuess ihr A.B.C.*, Frankfurt, 1613, and J. T., *The A.B.C. of Armes . . .*, London, 1616; C. Köber, *Tyrocinium militare . . .*, Danzig, 1616; Anon., *Scola militaris exercitationis. Das ist ein schul darinnen die angehende Soldaten zu Fuß . . . auff die newe und jetzundt ubliche Weiß gemunstert . . . gelehret und underricht werden . . .*, Cöllen, 1619.

³⁵ *The Institution of a Young Noble Man*, Oxford, 1607, p. 153. The works he refers to are *The Politicke and Militarie Discourses of the Lord de la Nove* (François de la Noue), trans. E. A., London, 1587. *Cf.* Roger Williams on la Noue: 'the little experience I got was from him, and from such others as himself' (*op. cit.*, p. 33). And Blaise de Monluc, *Commentaires . . .*, Bordeaux, two vols., 1592; no English translation until 1674.

³⁶ The debate, as far as England was concerned, was opened in 1562 by John Shute: 'I desyre of god that this [military] discipline maye be better knowen in oure countrie than it is, so shall we not have so many as we have that shall saye, give me the untrayned souldiour and take the trayned that lyste'. *Two very Notable Commentaries*, London, 1562, sig. iiv. See also Anthony Esler, *The Aspiring Mind of the Elizabethan Younger Generation*, Durham, N.C., 1966, *passim* but especially p. 109; F. de la Noue, ed. F. E. Sutcliffe, Geneva, 1967, pp. 161–2, 175.

³⁷ Trans. in Thomas Coryat, *Coryat's Crudities . . .* [1611], Glasgow, two vols., 1905, I, p. 191.

³⁸ *Op. cit.*, pp. 267–8.

³⁹ *The Practice of Policy*, London, 1604, pp. 10–11.

⁴⁰ Thomas and Dudley Digges, *Foure Paradoxes, or Politique Discourses*, London, 1604 (written before 1595), p. 79.

⁴¹ Tavannes, *op. cit.*, p. 291.

⁴² See E. Bourciez, *Les Moeurs polies et la littérature de cour sous Henri II*, Paris, 1886, pp. 18 ff.

⁴³ A. Massari Malatesta, *Compendio dell'heroica arte di cavalleria . . .*, Venice, 1600, f. 51*v*.

⁴⁴ Claudio Corte, *Il cavallerizzo*, Venice, 1573, sig. b 2*v*.

⁴⁵ Quoted in Clare Howard, *English Travellers of the Renaissance*, London, 1914, p. 127.

⁴⁶ Thus the Grand Duke Francesco set up a riding school under Rustico Piccardini in 1585, 'quod nobilissimorum adolescentium qui equestri splendore se ornari cupiunt in primisque Joannis fratris'. G. Sommi Picenardi, 'Don Giovanni de' Medici', *Nuovo Archivio Veneto*, new series, XIII, p. 115.

⁴⁷ Chevalier de Méré, *Les Conversations* [1668], ed. C. H. Boudhors, Paris, 1930, p. 69.

⁴⁸ *Le Maneige royal*, Paris, 1624, extended in *L'Instruction du roy . . .*, Paris, 1625.

⁴⁹ Malatesta, *op. cit.*, attempts an answer, f. 20*r*.

⁵⁰ *The Art of Riding* (trans. Giulio Corte, cited in n. 37 above), London, 1584, sig. A *iiv*.

⁵¹ J. Jacobi von Wallhausen, *L'Art militaire pour l'infanterie*, Paris, 1615, sig. 3*r*. From the letter to the reader in which he describes his other books.

⁵² Egerton Castle, *Schools and Masters of Fence*, London, 1892, pp. 41–5; J. D. Aylward, *The English Masters of Fence*, London, 1956, ch. 2.

⁵³ *Toxophilus*, quoted in Alyward, *op. cit.*, p. 18.

⁵⁴ Almoro Lombardo's preface to Nicoletto Giganti, *Scola ... e modi di parare et di ferire di spada . . .*, Venice, 1606, sig. b 3*r*.

⁵⁵ Paris, 1628.

⁵⁶ *Paradoxes of Defence*, London, 1599, quoted in Ruth Kelso, *The Doctrine of the English Gentleman in the Sixteenth Century*, Urbana, Ill., 1929, pp. 151–2.

⁵⁷ Achille Marozzo, *Onera nova . . .*, Venice [?1517], could claim ('Proemio') that of G. A. de Lucha's *scuola* 'si puo ben dire che sieno piu guerrieri usciti che dal Troiano cavallo', but later writers are forced to plead the military relevance of fencing, e.g. G. dall'Agocchie, *Dell'arte di scrimia . . .*, Venice, 1572, sig. A iiir and f. 5*r*.

Some books have illustrations (in the Thurber 'Touché!' vein) to show what bloody damage can be done with the point: e.g. N. Giganti, *Scola overo teatro* . . ., Venice, 1606. Montaigne thought that the 'turnings, windings, and nimble-quicke motions, wherein youth is instructed and trained in this new schoole, are not onely unprofitable, but rather contrary and damageable for the use of militarie combate.' (trans. Florio, lib. II, ch. 27.)

[58] See illustrations in A. Marozzo, *Arte dell'Armi*, Venice, 1568, and J. Jacobi von Wallhausen, *Art de Chevalrie*, Frankfurt, 1616.

[59] Giacomo di Grassi, *Ragione di adoprar sicuramente l'arme* . . ., Venice, 1570, trans. I.G., ed. T. Churchyard, as *Giacomo di Grassi his true Arte of Defence*, London, 1594, sig. Ee, ir f.

[60] *Mémoires*, Cologne, two vols., 1665, I, pp. 38–9.

[61] Howard, *op. cit.*, 121–2; John Walter Stoye, *English Travellers Abroad, 1604–1667*, London, 1952, pp. 56 f.

[62] The influence of Castiglione's notion of *sprezzatura* is very strong in the riding literature, e.g. riding 'deve adoprare arte & industria, ma in termine che dimostri esser fatta senza fatica e sforzo, quasi dotato natural gratia, coprendo l'arte con l'istessa arte'. (A. Massario Malatesta, *Compendio* . . ., Venice, 1600, f. 6v.) In his *Il cavallerizzo* (Venice, 1573) he says he is going to describe the perfect riding master 'per essere il modello, l'esemplare, & il bersaglio' on the lines of Plato, Xenophon and Castiglione. See especially ff. 128v f.

[63] Pluvinel employed Crispin de Pas the younger, who later produced the magnificent folio *La prima parte della luce del dipingere et desegnare*, Amsterdam, 1643, a teaching manual in Italian, Dutch, French and German, concerned with the correct drawing— by relating real to geometrical forms—of human figures, animals, birds and insects. In the preface he explains how he taught de Pluvinel's students how 'ils peussent facilement ordonner les bataillons & fortifier des places regulierement.' (Sig. A 4r.)

[64] It was works by authors like C. Agrippa, *Trattato di scientia d'arme* . . ., Rome, 1553, and Thibault, *op. cit.*, that prompted these lines in a prefatory poem to 'A.G.' in *Pallas Armata*, London, 1639: 'Thankes, mathematic fencer, that dost tye/The sword to th' booke and fight in geometry.'

[65] An idea urged previously, e.g. D. Mora, *Il soldato*, Venice, 1569, pp. 219–26.

[66] Thomas Starkey, *A Dialogue between Reginald Pole and Thomas Lupset*, 1553–56, ed. K. M. Burton, London, 1948, pp. 169–70.

[67] Edward Waterhous, *Fortescutus illustratus*, London, 1663, pp. 539 and 542. The memorandum is here acribed to 1539–42.

[68] J. Conway Davis, 'Elizabethan plans for education', *Durham Research Review*, 1954, p. 2. The proposal is described by J. P. Collier in *Archaeologia*, 1855–56, pp. 343–344.

[69] *Dialogo nel quale* . . . *si forma un perfetto principe ed un perfetto republica, e parimente un senatore, un cittadino, un soldato e un mercatante*, Venice, 1563, pp. 132–7, 182. For the academies, see above, pp. 473–4.

[70] F. A. Yates, *French Academies of the Sixteenth Century*, London, 1947, p. 25.

[71] *Ed. cit.*, pp. 152–5.

[72] Eric Cochrane, *Florence in the Forgotten Centuries*, Chicago, 1972, p. 127.

[73] F. Paulsen, *Geschichte des gelehrten Unterrichts auf den deutschen Schulen und Universitäten*, Leipzig, second edition, two vols., 1896, I, pp. 503–6.

[74] *Decade contenant la vie et gestes de Henri le Grand* . . ., Paris, 1614, p. 428; J. Errard, *La Géometrie* . . ., Paris, second edition, 1602, dedication; E. Albèri, *Relazioni degli ambasciatori veneti al Senato*, Florence, 1839–63, xv, appendix, p. 103.

[75] T. Birch, *Life of Henry, Prince of Wales*, London, 1760, p. 97. The household accounts (*ibid.*, pp. 449 f.) only mention, as relevant to this description, a music teacher, a librarian (the mathematician Edward Wright), a master of the horse and the 'keeper of the riding-house at St James's', George Blastone.

[76] *Op. cit.*, p. 35.

77 *Collecteanea Curiosa*, ed. J. Gutch, two vols., Oxford, 1718, 1, pp. 213–14.

78 *Op. cit.*, p. 175.

79 Yates, *op. cit.*, pp. 277–8.

80 Andrew Favyn (= André Favine), *The Theatre of Honor and Knight-hood*, London, two vols., 1623, trans. from Paris edition of 1620, 1, pp. 55–65.

81 Henry Petow (1622), quoted in G. Goold Walker, *The Honourable Artillery Company, 1537–1926*, London, 1926, p. 30; Edward Cooke, *The Character of Warre*, London, 1626, sig. A 3v; William Bariffe, *Mars his Triumph*, London, 1638, sig. aa 2v.

82 In 1636 Sir Francis Kynaston announced the setting up (with royal assent) of his Musaeum Minervae. It offered instruction from teachers of philosophy and medicine, astronomy, geometry (including fortification), music, languages, weapons, instruction, dancing, painting and riding. He justified it by saying that 'hitherto no such places for the education and trayning up of our own young nobilitie and gentrie in the practise of arms and arts have been instituted here in England'. (*Constitutions of the Musaeum Minervae*, London, 1636, sig. C 2r–4r.) The work was published to reply to criticism of his scheme. He stresses the fact that he intends no competition with the universities or the Inns of Court.

83 Antoine de Pluvinel, *L'Instruction* . . ., Paris, 1625, pp. 191–204. The work is posthumous. Apart from this dialogue, it reproduces *Le Maneige* . . .

84 Max Jähns, *op. cit.*, II, p. 1030.

85 F. Funck-Brentano, 'L'Éducation des officiers dans l'ancienne France', *Réforme Sociale*, 1918, pp. 21–2. The Assembly of Notables had proposed a military school for young nobles in 1626. (Frederick B. Artz, *op. cit.*, p. 43.)

26

MANUSCRIPTS OF ITALIAN PROVENANCE IN THE HARLEIAN COLLECTION IN THE BRITISH MUSEUM:
their sources, associations and channels of acquisition

INTRODUCTORY

WE ARE FORTUNATE in possessing for the history of the Harleian collection of manuscripts, which was brought together in the first four decades of the eighteenth century by Robert Harley, first Earl of Oxford (1661–1724), and his son, Edward, the second Earl (1689–1741), a considerable amount of documentation. This is due almost entirely to the fact that the Harleys employed as their librarian a man of quite outstanding ability and initiative, Humfrey Wanley, well known even today as the author of the first comprehensive catalogue of Anglo-Saxon manuscripts, which was published in 1705 and which as a work of scholarship has held its own until the present day, being superseded only in 1957 with the publication of Dr Neil Ker's similar work. Wanley was actively employed by the Harleys from 1705 until his death in 1726. The material to which we owe our knowledge about the formation of the collection comprises correspondence between Wanley and Edward Harley running from 1711[1] to December 1724, letters from various correspondents to Wanley, miscellaneous notes and memoranda (including lists of collections offered for sale), book bills, and finally, and most important of all, Wanley's own diary, a sort of 'official' journal kept by him from 2 March 1714–15 to 23 June 1726 (with, unfortunately, a gap between 1716 and 1720) in which he recorded his day-by-day activities as librarian.[2] These included meetings with dealers or booksellers, examining and listing books offered by them for purchase and negotiating for their acquisition, putting together material for binding and checking the items on return from the binders, discussing future plans, receiving visitors and scholars and showing the former the more spectacular books, and so on. For the purpose of this study we shall rely almost entirely on the diary, since it is through the pages of this that we shall meet those from whom the manuscripts of Italian provenance were acquired, such as John Gibson and Andrew Hay, *marchands amateurs*; John Wright, Lord Kinnoull's librarian; and Conyers Middleton, chief librarian (*Protobibliothecarius*) of the University of Cambridge; and Nathaniel Noel, the bookseller and dealer.[3]

JOHN GIBSON

The person from whom Edward Harley was to obtain most of the manuscripts of Italian provenance was John Gibson. Of him we know nothing except what Wanley himself tells, namely that he was a 'Scots Gent[leman] buyer of Books' and was to be found at Mr Wright's house at 'the upper end of Scrope's Court in Low Holbourne' (presumably by Scrope Inn, opposite St Andrew's Church): we are introduced to Gibson in the diary on 20 January 1719–20, when Wanley writes, 'Mr John Gibson came, & said that he ha's a small parcel of MSS. lately come from Italy, as also a parcel of fine printed books'; the MSS were twenty-four in number, of which twenty-three were sent in at once by Gibson. On the following day Wanley went to Gibson, saw the printed books and brought away the remaining MS, a Lucius Florus, now Harley 2557. The Lucius Florus had been in the possession of Lorenzo Buoninsegni of Siena (see f. 139*v* and initials L.B. on verso of front flyleaf). It is worth looking at the list of this first recorded Gibson parcel:[4] it contained no fewer than seven dated MSS—a copy written by Bartolomeo Fiatto, a notary of Padua (1423–69), in 1438 (Harley 4769: see colophon, f. 263*v*, and Fiatto arms on f. 1), of a work by Sicco Polenton of Padua, the pupil of Giovanni di Ravenna (whose *ex libris* occurs, f. 145*v*, as the owner of a MS of Boccaccio's 'De Casibus Virorum Illustrium' also in this list, Harley 3565); a copy of Boccaccio's Eclogues written in Florence in 1408 (Harley 5421: see f. 57*v*); a Dante of 1469 (Harley 3460: see f. 86), 'cum rudioribus picturis';[5] a Sallust, also of 1469 (Harley 2541: see f. 100), which contains also Aurispa's translation of Hippocrates' alleged Epistles; a Macer herbal of 1448 (Harley 2651: see f. 44); a Juvenal of 1410 'eleganter et scriptus & illuminatus' (Harley 2648: see f. 77*v*);[6] and a Virgil of 1454 written at Palermo (Harley 3518: see f. 201*v*).[7] In addition to the dated MSS, always accessions of immense interest, this parcel contained a Servius on Virgil (Harley 2680) and a commentary on eight comedies of Plautus (Harley 2454), both of which were among the MSS given by Pietro Montagnana of Padua to the Augustinian house of San Giovanni in Verdara in 1478 (see inscriptions on ff. 192 and 85*v* respectively); to the same monastery and to the same parcel belonged a Lucan (Harley 2507) and a miscellaneous volume containing Ovid's Ex Ponto (Harley 3234), both of which had been given to San Giovanni in Verdara by Giovanni Marcanova (*c.* 1418–67), who had been Professor of Philosophy at Bologna from 1452 until his death; Harley 3234 had been obtained by him in Padua in 1440 (see inscription, f. 1).[8] Thus in addition to the dated MSS we have four MSS of great interest by reason of their having been once in the possession of two well known humanists, Montagnana and Marcanova, and of a famous monastic house. Marcanova has an added interest for us, too, since he was one of the *testes* of William Grey (subsequently, 1454, Bishop of Ely and a central figure in humanism in England, who studied under

Guarino of Verona at Ferrara) for his degree of Doctor of Divinity at Padua in 1445. These four MSS are important evidence too for the dispersal of the San Giovanni in Verdara library which was going on in the early years of the eighteenth century, one of those most responsible being Thomas Coke, who had made a heavy purchase from the library in 1717.[9] One of Coke's San Giovanni in Verdara/Montagnana MSS, the famous Greek–Latin psalter executed in the Friuli *c.* 1200 (Holkham MS 22) has also reached the British Museum collections and is now Additional MS 47674. One of the dated MSS in this parcel, a Juvenal, Harley 2648, already referred to above (p. 463), and the Horace, Harley 2642, in the same parcel came from the Discalced Carmelites of Florence, and are two of several from this house that were to come from Gibson; the others are Harley 2527, a Terence written in 1471, Harley 2554, a Lucretius, and Harley 2758, Ovid's Epistles (acquired 1 June 1720, [9 November 1721] and 13 February 1723–24 respectively). All bear the book stamp of the Carmelite convent and also that of the Barone Pandolfo di Ricasoli of Florence.[10] Other classical authors represented in this purchase are a Persius (Harley 2588) which belonged at one time to Alessandro Acciaiuoli (see *ex libris*, f. 1*), and a Juvenal (Harley 3896) with some unidentified names on f. 97; the list concludes with a MS of Manuel Chrysoloras' famous Erotemata, Harley 5569.

Less than a month later, 18 February 1719–20, we find Gibson reporting to Wanley that he 'ha's 3 very fine MSS. lately come from Italy', and on 23 April 1720 a group of ten MSS, including the three referred to, was brought:[11] one of these Wanley records under his preliminary inspection of them (18 March 1719–20), Harley 2986, a breviary, was 'lately bought in the monastery of San Pietro d'Arena in Genoa' (a report that Wanley recorded in the memorandum which he has inscribed on f. 1 of the MS, any original flyleaves that may have contained the corroborative evidence being now wanting); in this group of ten was only one dated MS, that, written in 1465, of Virgil, Harley 2502 (see f. 46), and in addition to the Genoa MS, only one other came from an identified monastic house, Harley 2469, Cicero's De Amicitia, etc, which came (according to the *ex libris* inscriptions on ff. 80, 81*v*) from the Augustinian Hermits of Santa Maria Incoronata in Milan.

We hear nothing more of MSS from Gibson until 20 March 1720–21, when he told Wanley that he had about sixteen good MSS coming from Italy, and these were bought on 17 June 1721, when Wanley went to Gibson and 'found him sitting upon the Books he had newly received from Italy'; they proved to be only fifteen in number.[12] They included two dated MSS, a Pliny's Epistles, Harley 2780, written at Siena by a Venetian, 'Iacobus Macarius', in 1463 (see f. 177*v*) and a Justin's Historia, Harley 2740, written in 1451 (see f. 84), and also two MSS that had belonged formerly to Lodovico Petroni, of Siena, the humanist, who was ambassador to King Alfonso in 1454 and Sienese orator in Florence in 1458, and a senator of Rome, this last distinction perhaps accounting for the SPQR in chief in his coats of arms which appear in the two MSS in question in this list, namely Harley 2658, a Scriptores Historiae Augustae, and Harley 4883, Leonardo Aretino's version of two works of Aristotle (at f. 1 in each MS); the transcript of the latter was begun by Petroni late in 1451 and finished by him in July of 1452. Other Harley MSS at one time in his possession and bearing his arms also came from Gibson at subsequent (and widely separated) dates, namely Harley 2768, an Aulus Gellius MS, on 5 May 1722 (which Wanley says was alleged to have belonged to Pope Pius II, the Piccolomini Pope—'olim ut dicitur peculium Pij II. Pont. max. . . .' (see *The Diary of Humfrey Wanley*, I, p. 143), an attribution based presumably on a misinterpretation of the Petroni painted coat of arms on f. 1); Harley 3109, St Jerome's Epistles, on 27 January 1723–24; and Harley 3276 (a MS of Leonardo Aretino's De Bello Italico, etc) on 22 February 1724–25.[13] Meanwhile, on 28 March 1721, Gibson had told Wanley that 'a Correspondent of his in Italy ha's lately procured some choice MSS. for him' and one of these, a Pliny's Natural History, subsequently Harley 2676, we learn on 3 July 1721 'is Shipped of[f] from Leghorn' (it was actually in the library, with seven other MSS, on 7 November 1721) (see below p. 465), and concurrently, on 3 June 1721, Gibson reported that 'his Correspondent in Italy ha's found out an antient Copie of Homer in Greek, written in two folios of Velum'; a month later, 3 July, he told Wanley that 'his Florentine Monk raise's up the Price of his Velum-MS. of Homer in Greek yet higher; & care's not to part with it'. Nevertheless, the two volumes were acquired on 10 September 1722 and became Harley 5600 and 6325; they proved, however, to be not 'antient' but an Iliad and Odyssey in Greek written by the famous scribe John Rhosos of Crete in Florence in 1466, enthusiastically described as 'una raccolta veramente Reale' by Gibson's agent. This was not all that Gibson had to report on 3 July 1721; he told Wanley of an 'Italian Abbat . . . willing to sell a most curious MS. of the Hebrew Bible in several large Volumes in fol. (which the Undertakers of our Polyglott Bible formerly offered largely for, but were refused:) but that the price will be great'. This was never bought, since the price was revealed at not less than 1,000 Roman ducats and Wanley would not bite, 'still holding-off as I have long done with relation to this Book' (23 October 1722). The 'Italian Abbat' was also reported on 23 October 1722 by Gibson as keeping 'a Copie of the Four Gospels in Greek, in a fine Case; fancying it to be very old & very Valuable, and ha's hitherto refused to part with it'.

To revert to the eight MSS 'lately arrived from Italy' agreed for on 7 November 1721, it is of interest to note that contrary to his usual practice Wanley did not enter on the flyleaf of these MSS the date of purchase, giving as his reason for not doing so 'lest any inquisitive person coming in, should thereby perceive how lately they were bought'. Only a few of these are of interest from the point of view of provenance: the splendid MS of Pliny's Natural History, Harley 2676 (referred to above, p. 465), which has, as Wanley correctly noted, the arms of the Medici (on f. 19, a painted coat of *or* eight roundels *gu*, an example of the less usual arrangement of eight roundels instead of the more familiar six roundels arranged orlewise), and a Cicero, Harley 3925, written in 1433, which belonged to a member of the Guicciardini family of Florence, Luigi Piero Guicciardini (see ff. 94, 188*v*;

see also p. 466 n. 18).[14] Harley 2554 has already been referred to among the MSS that derived from the Discalced Carmelites of Florence (see p. 464 above). Also 'lately come from Florence' according to Gibson was the parcel of eleven MSS brought into the library on 5 May 1722; among them was the Petroni MS, Harley 2768 (referred to above, p. 465), which was alleged in Wanley's list to have belonged to Pius II—'olim ut dicitur peculium Pij II. Pont. Max.', who was also claimed in the same terms as the owner of another MS in this list, Harley 3976, a copy of his own Cosmographia. The next group of MSS (twenty-five in number) from Italy, however, contained several more important MSS, as was recognised by Wanley himself, who described them, when he examined them in July 1722, 'as to the Main . . . very curious, 11 of them being in Greek': these, received on 5 September 1722 and listed by Wanley under 10 September in his diary, included the important fifteenth-century MS of Livy's Third Decade, Harley 2684, and also the two volumes of the copy of Homer, Harley 5600 and 6325, made by John Rhosos of Crete (referred to above, p. 465): the second volume bears on f. 1 the arms of the Tornabuoni family of Florence. Two early MSS in this group require specific mention: a psalter arranged in triple columns of Greek, Latin and Arabic, Harley 5786, written in 1153 (according to the partially obliterated description, f. 173v),[15] and a Greek psalter, Harley 5535, written in 1284. Also to be noticed is the autograph MS of Giovanni Mario Filelfo's poem on Lorenzo de' Medici, Harley 2522,[16] written in 1474 (see f. 245v) (see also p. 474 below). For provenance the most important MS is Harley 5696, Proclus' commentary on Plato's Alcibiades, which belonged to the Augustinian house of San Spirito in Florence (see sixteenth- or seventeenth-century book stamp on f. 2).[17]

It was about this time (October 1722), following these extensive purchases from Gibson, that Wanley had a general discussion with Gibson about 'the present State of the Trade of buying old Books and Manuscripts in Tuscany; many of which, by the means of Him [Gibson] & others are happily reposed in this Library', and it was six months later that we find Wanley remarking, after the receipt of a parcel of MSS which were alleged to come out of a 'Monastical Library Founded or Endowed by the Guicciardini', that 'they seem to shew, what I hear from others, that the Italian Monasteries do now begin to be pretty much drained of their old Printed books & MSS.'. The MSS from the Guicciardini 'Monastical Library', with another parcel from Gibson, were listed *together* by Wanley, so that although a number of the items in that list (4 April 1723) have definite evidence of Guicciardini ownership we do not know how many others may have come from this source, nor has it been possible to identify the monastic house referred to.[18]

The first item of the list of 4 April 1723 is a Pliny's Natural History (reported by Wanley under 11 February 1722–23 as 'being an older Copie than that which he [Gibson] sold to my Lord' [i.e. Harley 2676 on 9 November 1721]), namely Harley 2677, which belonged to Aeneas Sylvius Piccolomini, presumably before his elevation to the papacy in 1458, since the Piccolomini arms on f. 1 are surmounted by a cardinal's hat,[19] as also did Harley 2731 in the same list, which bears (f. 1) his arms as Pope. Several mss in this list derived from identifiable monastic houses, only two of which were Florentine: Harley 2758, from the Discalced Carmelites (a house already referred to, p. 464) and 2615, from the canons of San Salvadore attached to the church of San Donato de 'Scopeti' (the convent of Silva Lacus).[20] For the rest, two, Harley 3107 and 3141, were gifts to the Carmelites of San Pietro Cigoli at Lucca by its bishop (1477–99), Niccolò Sandonino, in 1491 (see ff. 1*v, 1v respectively), and Harley 2614 was bequeathed to San Francesco della Vigna in Venice by Johannes Franciscus Vaca, apparently late in the sixteenth century (see f. 1). One was a dated ms, namely 3379, a copy of Leonardo Aretino's Latin translation of Aristotle's Ethics, made in November 1448 (see colophon, f. 118v).

The next parcel listed from Gibson did not come in until early 1723–24. In the list under 10 February occurs another and earlier ms of Aretino's translation of Aristotle's Ethics, Harley 3305, a splendid vellum ms bearing in the lower margin of f. 5v (and in the initials on ff. 22, 70v, 84) the painted coat of arms of Iñigo Davalos, commander of the Spanish troops in Naples, who died in 1484, to whom the ms was presented by the ducal chamberlain, Jacobus de Ardicijs, on 27 April 1440, according to Davalos's own memorandum on f. 121v.[21] In addition to one dated ms, a Eusebius, Harley 3477, written in 1460 by Ioannes Meruelt, a Westphalian (see f. 210v), there may be noted two early mss, namely a tenth/eleventh-century copy of Gregory's Homilies, Harley 3048, and an eleventh-century St Augustine, Harley 3051. Two mss associated with Florentine families are Harley 2734, which has, on f. 1, the arms of the Del Pugliese family, and 2617, an Ovid, which about 1507 belonged to a Pazzi, 'Frater Johannes Franciscus de Passis de Florentia' (see ex libris, f. 80), while a copy of Cicero's De Amicitia, Harley 2630, had been in the possession of the Dominican convent of San Marco (its pressmark being 'L.I'), having been bequeathed to it by Hieronymus Panzanus, 'ciuis florentinus uir indubitato et doctus et probus' (thus the inscription on f. 69v).[22]

The items in the next parcel (sent in 28 August 1724) were characterised by Wanley as 'in the main but mean', and this is not an unfair generalisation. Most were fifteenth-century manuscripts of classical authors (many in poor condition), with some theological texts and a few in Italian itself, the last category containing a Petrarch, Harley 3264,[23] and a Dante, 3459.[24] Included were three dated mss, Harley 2595, written in 1471 (see f. 69v); Harley 3174, written in 1454 (see f. 3v); and Harley 3551, a Latin translation of Plato's Phaedo, which was written by Niccolò da Camulio, notary and chancellor of Genoa, in 1416 at Caffa, one of the Genoese colonies in the Levant (see colophon, f. 33v), and was given by his son Prospero to Count Alberto Scotto on 10 February 1457 (see inscriptions, ff. 1, 1v; the Scotto coat of arms [az a bend arg. between two mullets or, the shield being set between the initials A C S] is on f. 2).[25] No fewer than three mss are associated with Piacenza—Harley 3678, 3682 and 4285; of these, 3678 contains a chronicle of Italian affairs compiled in 1290 which was of sufficient historical importance to be discussed and printed (in part) in the Monumenta Germaniae Historica.[26]

The next parcel of MSS to be sent in by Gibson was on 22 February 1724–25 and was listed by Wanley in his diary under 23 February, but they were not settled for until 22 June 1726, and the MSS have this last date entered in them by Wanley. Of the items in this purchase the most interesting are the nineteen MSS that had belonged to Zomino (Sozomenes, Σωζομενος) (d. 1458), of Pistoia, one of the Poggio group of humanists at Florence, who bequeathed his collection to Pistoia.[27] Most of these were copies of classical texts, several in Zomino's autograph or bearing annotations by him and his library press marks, and many contain notarial inscriptions entered after his death; two (Harley 6324, 6332) were bought by him from the Florentine bookseller (*cartolaio*) Piero Bettuci in 1431 and 1428 respectively, according to memoranda written by Zomino in the MSS. Nine other MSS which can be identified as Zomino's but bear no date of acquisition by Wanley may yet have come in through Gibson later (see p. 468 below). One other Zomino MS had been received nearly two years before these in the 23 February 1724–1725 list at present under discussion and is Harley 2748 (a Cicero's Rhetorica) which had belonged also to Jacopo Guicciardini (on the Guicciardini MSS see p. 466 above, and n. 18). In addition to the Zomino MSS may be noted one Petroni MS, Harley 3276 (see p. 465 above), and two MSS, Harley 3268 and 6500, which had belonged to a 'Frater Euangelista de Cortona', both containing compositions of a Cortona priest; both bear press marks, 10.k and 9.j respectively. Of the Greek MSS, one (Harley 6875) bears the date 1468 and contains grammatical works of Constantine Lascaris (1434–1501), whose bequest of MSS to Messina, transferred in 1679 to Palermo, had been yet again transferred to the newly founded National Library at Madrid only twelve years before the period we are dealing with.

Just over a year later, 23 March 1725–26, Gibson told Wanley about a parcel he expected to receive soon from Italy 'wherein are 5 Greek MSS.; one of which contain's part of Plato's Works; & another, the Orations of Aristides'. These did not come into the library until 23 June 1726, just before Wanley's death; Wanley's last entry in his diary says of this collection that it consisted of about twenty-five MSS 'whereof 4 are in Greek'. Wanley's death intervened before he was able to list these, but a Zomino MS, Harley 5547, of Plato and Aristides has an inscription on the flyleaf by Edward Harley himself 'Feb: 17: 1726/7'. And it may be that the *other* nine Zomino MSS alluded to above came into the library in this unlisted 23 June group; they are Harley 3956, 4804, 4822, 4829, 4869, 5204, 5285, 5587, 5660. Of these, Harley 5204 bears autograph annotations by Petrarch, and is thus one of the three MSS in the Harleian Library associated with Petrarch (the other two being Harley 2493, 4927; on both see below, p. 478), and Harley 4829 may be a copy of the Quintilian MS discovered by Poggio at St Gall in 1416.

ANDREW HAY

Andrew Hay is an elusive person. He appears frequently in the annals of connoisseurship in the first half of the eighteenth century, primarily as dealer in pictures and marble busts and bronzes, and travelled widely in France and Italy, returning to Scotland in 1745, having, wrote George Vertue, 'in thirty years from small beginnings in painting set out for a Dealer, gained some thousands and retired home' (see Vertue's *Note Books*, III, p. 125). The 'small beginnings in painting' may allude to his having studied under Sir John Baptist Medina, who practised in Scotland from 1688 until his death in 1710. Vertue's statement that he 'retired home' may provide some support for equating him with the Andrew Hay who, according to Musgrave's *Obituary* (III, p. 176), died at 'Carrubers', presumably Carruthers, in Dumfriesshire, on 24 October 1754 and was described in the *Scots Magazine* of that month as 'a noted antiquary'. So far as his activities as an art dealer were concerned he certainly sold pictures to Edward Harley in 1716 and 1723, but his greatest coup was his purchase in Paris in September 1720 of the MSS formerly belonging to Pierre Séguier (1588–1672), the French chancellor;[28] these were the first fruits of the commission which Wanley drew up for him, on Harley's orders, under the date 26 April 1720, which was delivered to Hay on 3 May, he intending to set out for France on the 11th of that month.[29] The commission covered Italy as well, and Hay had already told Wanley in the January that he was setting forward for Italy by way of France 'next spring'. Actually very little in the way of MSS resulted from Hay's Italian tour, so that we find Wanley writing to him in Rome on 28 April 1721 reminding him of Harley's commission to buy 'MSS. in France, Savoy, Italy & Sicily; & desiring him to putt it in Execution'; in fact his activities yielded so little that on 17 April 1722 Wanley wrote again to him desiring him to return the commission for buying MSS abroad, 'he having done nothing therein', and Hay returned the commission on the 20th of the same month 'together with a Civil Letter'. Wanley's 'nothing' was, however, somewhat exaggerated. On 22 December 1720 George Hay had given Wanley a list of books and MSS his brother had lately bought in Italy, and subsequent to Andrew Hay's return we find Wanley, on 9 February 1722–23, taking a short catalogue of 'a little Parcel of MSS. lately brought out of Italy by Mr. Andrew Hay'; Hay sent in the MSS on 18 March. On 7 June Wanley went again to Hay's and saw sixteen MSS, which were sent in to the library the next day. On 13 July 1723 Wanley 'told-over' the MSS from both parcels and made them thirty-seven in all, 'which by Virtue of our late Agreement, my Lord is to have for as many Pounds or Guineas. This I see is a cheap Bargain, the Things being much more worth.' This was certainly so of the most important MS in the list, namely Harley 3281, perhaps the original volume of drawings executed for, and dedicated to, Federigo da Montefeltro (d. 1482), Duke of Urbino from 1474, by the Sienese architect and sculptor Francesco di Giorgio.[30] Another, Harley 2912, a liturgical MS, has painted on f. 1 the arms of Cardinal Guglielmo Sirleto (1514–85), Bishop of San Marco in Calabria in 1566 and of Squillace in 1568. There were several dated MSS (Harley 2701, a copy of Virgil's works, written in 1447; [31] 2883, a Book of Hours, written in 1471; and 4342, written in 1456 at Ferrara), and two eleventh-century MSS—a Priscian (Harley 2763) and a Gospels (Harley 2831).

In April 1724 Hay sent in four MSS; they were dated 31 December 1724 and were Harley 3289, 3266, 3377 (the last being a catalogue of the coins of Queen Christina of Sweden) and one other unidentified.

Early in their relationship Andrew Hay had called on Wanley, 21 January 1719–20, and had been shown the library, 'to his great Satisfaction'; it was on the occasion of that visit that Andrew Hay told Wanley that 'Mr. Cook of Norfolk might be induced to part with his MSS. to my Lord, in Excha[n]ge for other things'. This was Thomas Coke of Holkham (1697–1759), who had succeeded his father in 1707 and had made extensive tours on the Continent, especially in Italy, during the period 1712–18, under the guidance of Dr Thomas Hobart and his tutor, Domenico Ferrari (himself a bibliophile who left his library to Coke). We have already had occasion to mention Coke in connection with his purchases of MSS from the monastery of San Giovanni in Verdara at Padua (see p. 464 above). Coke's purchases of MSS were extensive, and Wanley himself had the opportunity of visiting Coke on 17 May 1721 and was shown by Coke himself 'part of his MSS. with much humanity for above 3 hours together': Coke told him that he had bought all the MSS of the family of Giustiniani at Venice, including their Greek MSS,[32] and 'ha's assurance of 300 MSS. more, to be sent to him soon'.[33] Coke was therefore one of Harley's strongest rivals in this field, and Coke's purchases show what could be acquired on the spot by a wealthy man travelling in Italy in the early decades of the eighteenth century.

CONYERS MIDDLETON

Dr Conyers Middleton (1683–1750), head librarian (*Protobibliothecarius*) of the University Library at Cambridge (1721–50), was another traveller in Italy in the 1720s who took the opportunity of acquiring small parcels of MSS. He was one of the distinguished visitors on whom Wanley had spent a lot of time; we learn from the diary, for example, that on 11 July 1723 Middleton was shown 'Rare & Valuable Manuscripts to his great Surprise & Satisfaction', and five days later he spent two hours in the library 'talking about Library-affairs' and on this occasion renewed 'his Offers to serve my Lord in his Travels'.[34] These offers indeed materialised. On 11 December 1724 Harley sent up to London from Wimpole, his country seat in Cambridgeshire, eighteen MSS and '2 Books printed upon Velum' which he had received from Conyers Middleton for Wanley to give his opinion on them. On 13 February 1724–25 Middleton was again in the library and said that he had 'another parcel of MSS. (besides those he hath already offered to sell my Lord) now coming for England'. We hear no more of these, but the MSS actually bought from Conyers Middleton were listed by Wanley under 20 and 25 February 1724–25. At his visit on 13 February there was obviously much talk about Middleton's travels, and he told Wanley that 'a Bookseller at Pisa hath a good Parcel of MSS.' and that 'Monsignor Passionei at Rome, hath several very choice Manuscripts'; this was Domenico Passionei (1682–1761), whose MSS and printed books were to find a home in the Biblioteca Angelica at Rome.

The MSS acquired from Middleton were miscellaneous in character and origin, but several are interesting and one at least is a very beautiful MS; this is Harley 3229, a richly illuminated copy of the life of St Francis by St Bonaventura, which was written in the Hospital of San Paolo at Florence in 1504 by Alessandro di Bologna, an Augustinian, and bears on f. 26 the painted coat of arms of Giovanni Francesco di Malatesta-Tramontana, probably Podestà of Lucca.[35] Among the interesting items is Harley 2692, Cicero's De Officiis, the work of the famous Bartolomeo Sanvito (1435–1518 or later), canon of the Collegiate Church of Santa Giustina at Monselice, Padua, and the friend of Bernardo Bembo, father of the more famous Pietro, written by Sanvito at Rome in 1498 (see colophon, f. 155v for date, accompanied by the initials B.S.).[36] Two other MSS in the Harleian Library associated with Sanvito are Harley 3510 (Horace's Odes) and 3567 (Petrarch's poems) both of which have marginalia and corrections in his hand;[37] these, however, came into the library from the dealer Nathaniel Noel, and will be dealt with below (see p. 474). Among the Middleton MSS one, Harley 5760, belonged to Cardinal Niccolò Ridolfi (d. 1550), the nephew of Pope Leo X, and contains his library press mark (namely 'No 79 tertiae, No. 24 /|°') and, according to a sixteenth-century Italian inscription (f. 1v), was brought from Greece for Lorenzo de' Medici (1448–92), 'Il Magnifico', by Janus Lascaris, who assisted Ridolfi in the formation of his library; another, Harley 3561, bears on its binding the arms (as cardinal, created 1633) of Cardinal Stefano Durazzo, Archbishop of Genoa, 1635–64, a volume containing documents of 1631 relating to the State of Urbino; and a third, Harley 2993, part of which (ff. 2–86v), a martyrology, was written at Venice in 1437 by Stephano de Nouaria, a Crutched Friar of the same place (see colophon, f. 86v), was bequeathed to the Augustinians of Messina by their Master General, Julianus à Salem (see inscription, f. 1). Apart from one or two dated MSS (a Seneca, Harley 2461, written in 1416–17; a miscellaneous volume, Harley 3530, the greater part of which was written in 1463), two Greek MSS were written by the famous scribe John Rhosos of Crete (see pp. 465 above and 474 below for other MSS written by him), Harley 5669 and 5658, the latter (Homer's Odyssey) by him in 1479. Bibliographically most interesting is the group of four MSS (Harley 2353, 2810, 3368, 5128) all bearing the enigmatic press mark

$$\overset{S}{\underset{A}{\bigcirc}}\overset{M}{\underset{V}{}}$$

One other MS in the Library bears this press mark, Harley 5367, for which the source of acquisition is unknown.[38] Of these, one, Harley 2810, belonged also to an unidentified Professor of Theology, Petrus de Castile, and the first manuscript, Harley 2353, a Bible, has an inscription on f. 430v recording the gift of it to a Friar Minor by the Vicar General of the Minorite province of Milan. Another Middleton MS, Harley 3436, had associations with Milan, having belonged to Leonardo Spinola (c. 1525–98) of the Milanese family of that name, the names of other members of the family being scribbled in the volume. Although Conyers Middleton made several later visits to the library, there is no evidence that any other Italian MSS came from him, and although he remained a personal friend of Edward Harley for many years relations between them were subsequently broken off because of Middleton's latitudinarianism, which was unacceptable to Harley.

JOHN WRIGHT

Like John Gibson, John Wright was described by Wanley on his first recorded visit to the library (8 February 1722–23) as 'a Scots Gent' and of him we know nothing more except that he is said, again by Wanley, to have been 'my Lord Kinnouls Library keeper'. This was George Henry Hay, seventh Earl of Kinnoull, who had succeeded to the title in 1719 and was married to Robert Harley's youngest daughter, Abigail. On his first visit Wright brought a small group of MSS and old printed books to sell; subsequent entries show that the printed books were rejected and that the prices he asked for his MSS were considered too high; only on his abatement of these prices did Harley buy them. Thirteen in number, they are listed by Wanley under 24 June 1723 in the addenda to the second volume of his diary.[39] Of the MSS acquired at this date from John Wright the most interesting are five (Harley 3046, 3481, 3482, 3485, 3699) that derived from the Aragonese library at Naples of Ferdinand I (d. 1494), king of Naples from 1458; he had also been the owner of Harley 4965 (which was written for him in 1482) but of this MS we have no information about its acquisition for the library.[40] All five, plus the last-mentioned, also bear the late sixteenth-century book stamp of Sant' Andrea [? della Valle], presumably to be identified with the mother church of the Theatines at Rome, which had been founded in 1524, as does Harley 3746, also a MS in the Wright purchase. These present a problem; it is impossible to know from what source Wright obtained them or the seven other MSS in his parcel, whether in this country or on travels of his own in Italy. But it is significant that on 25 January 1725–26 he brought in six MSS 'lately come from Italy': these are not listed in the diary. The date of execution of two of the Aragon books is recorded in their colophons; Harley 3699, a Josephus, was written at Florence in 1478 (see colophon, f. 388*b*)[41] and bears (on f. 1) the arms and motto of Ferdinand, and 3485 (also bearing his arms) in 1470 (see colophon, f. 428). Of the other MSS acquired from John Wright, Harley 3154, a Lactantius, was written by Johannes de Hollandia for Antonius De Lauro, a Friar Minor, in 1433; Harley 3216, a copy of à Kempis's De Imitatione Christi, and other works, was formerly in the possession of Johannes Pastritius (fl. *c.* 1700), a Dalmatian, author of liturgical works and Reader in Theology in the Collegium de Propaganda Fide at Rome (the MS has inserted in it miniatures removed from other MSS); and Harley 3308, a MS illuminated in Florentine style,[42] has on f. 5 the painted coat of arms of Cardinal Jorge da Costa (d. 1508), owned by him after his elevation to the cardinalate in 1476. Most of Wright's MSS are large, handsome MSS finely illuminated.

.   .   .

NATHANIEL NOEL AND GEORGE SUTTIE

The dealer upon whom the Harleys relied most heavily for the purchases of printed books and MSS for their library was the London dealer Nathaniel Noel (fl. 1681–*c.* 1753), bookseller first in Duck Lane and later in Paternoster Row, who is one of the most frequently mentioned people in Wanley's diary.[43] It was through him that most of the MSS from abroad were obtained, and for these Noel was indebted to the activities of his foreign agent, George Suttie, who had been travelling on the Continent visiting monastic and other libraries from as far back as 1707, when he was seen by Zacharias von Uffenbach, the famous German bibliophile. His first appearance in the library was 21 June 1715, when he is recorded by Wanley (under the description 'the man, Mr. Suttie') as having been with Robert Harley. Most of Suttie's journeyings were in France, the Low Countries, the Rhineland and south Germany. His movements can be traced to a limited extent over a few years, from extracts from his reports to Noel that were made and annotated by Wanley and are now preserved in Welbeck Wanleyana. Thus we can follow him in the period 1717 to 1720 at such places as Trier, Coblentz, Cologne, Worms, Mainz, Nuremberg, Wurzburg and Ingolstadt; in 1720 against information that Suttie was going from Châlons to Lyons and Grenoble Wanley has noted that 'he is going for the Danube'. But we do know that he also went to Italy. On 28 February 1720–21 the diary reports Noel as having received two letters and catalogues from Suttie 'now in Italy' and again we learn from Wanley's extracts in Welbeck Wanleyana of a letter written by Suttie from Piacenza dated 21 September 1722. The fruits of these Italian journeys were included in two big block purchases from Noel, those on 20 January 1721–22 and 18 January 1723–24, but these had unfortunately been merged with the very large accumulation of MSS purchased by him on his journeys in the Rhineland and other parts of Germany. These seem to have been collected at Coblentz before being shipped down the Rhine to Rotterdam.[44] It is difficult to distinguish always between those MSS of Italian origin which Suttie had purchased while in Italy and those which he had acquired from German collections, such as those of the Peutingers at Augsburg and of Cardinal Nicholas Cusanus derived from his foundation at Cues on the Mosel. The MSS in the two parcels referred to that have evidence of former Italian ownership and may most probably be conjectured as having been obtained by Suttie during his stay in Italy include many interesting items. Surely from Mantua must have come the block of MSS from the Capilupi library (Harley 2556, 2570, 2579, 2707, 2730, 2744, 5656) since we know that the Capilupi library was still in existence at Mantua when Juan Andrés compiled his catalogue of the MSS in it in 1797. Among them Harley 2556 and 2707 belonged to Benedetto Capilupi, Secretary of State to the Marchese Francesco Gonzaga, who died in 1519; both have in them also the name of his son, the Italian poet Lelio Capilupi (1497–1563), who also owned Harley 2570, 2730 and 2744. Harley 5656 belonged possibly to

Camillo Capilupi (the inscription (f. 1*) is actually 'Camilli Lupi'), who is most likely to be Camillo I, son of Benedetto, who was born in 1504. Also associated with Mantua and the Gonzaga and probably from the ducal archives are Harley 3312, 3313, 3494, being registers of State letters addressed to the Duke of Mantua by Count Alessandro Strigi of Mantua while Minister at Madrid in 1626–31; Strigi also owned the beautiful little Horace, Harley 3510, which was in the library of Bartolomeo Sanvito and has in it the latter's marginalia:[45] of another Sanvito MS we shall speak below. Two other MSS with Gonzaga associations may be noted: first, Harley 3567, a Petrarch, written by Matteo Contugi of Volterra ('the gossiping, Pepysian, indolent Matteo Contugi', as Wardrop characterised him),[46] bears on f. 9 the painted coat of arms of the Gonzaga[47] and has the further interest (like Harley 3510) of containing marginalia and corrections by Bartolomeo Sanvito.[48] The second, Harley 5790, an illuminated MS of the Gospels in Greek, was written at Rome in 1478 for Cardinal Francesco Gonzaga (d. 1483), Bishop of Mantua from 1466 to 1483, by John Rhosos of Crete (who had also written for him the Vatican Homer in 1477 [Vat. Gr. 1626]), and was later in the possession of the cardinal's secretary, Giovanni Pietro Arrivabene (d. 1504), a native of Mantua, a pupil of Francesco Filelfo, and subsequently Bishop of Urbino from 1491 to the year of his death.[49] Francesco Filelfo's books were acquired by Lorenzo de' Medici but an autograph MS of Francesco's son, Giovanni Mario Filelfo (1426–80), who was at Mantua during Pope Pius II's congress convened there to secure help against the Turks, is Harley 2605; it contains Filelfo's poems and was written by him at Turin in 1458 (see colophon, f. 63).[50] Two MSS that have an interest in the story of Italian humanism and came through Noel are Harley 2655 and 2485. The former, a twelfth-century MS of Ovid, had been purchased from the Florentine bookseller Maffio di Figline in 1357, as we learn from the inscription in the manuscript (f. 50), by Lino Coluccio Salutati (1331–1406), the son of Piero Salutati of Stignano and chancellor of Florence, a noted figure in the history of humanism. The MS was one of those sold after his death by his sons to Niccolò Niccoli (1363–1437), the protégé of Salutati and friend of Poggio. Most of Niccoli's MSS were presented in 1441 by Cosimo de' Medici, one of his executors, to the newly founded Florentine convent of San Marco, built for Cosimo by Michelozzo.[51] The MS has Salutati's press mark (f. 1), '52. Carte lij' (a similar press mark, '63. Carte lxxiiij', occurs in another British Museum Salutati MS, Egerton 818).[52] The second MS referred to, Harley 2485, a volume of Seneca's Tragedies, is of special interest for the way in which it illustrates the contacts between the Italian humanists and England; the MS was written for himself in 1460 by John Gunthorpe (d. 1498), subsequently Dean of Wells, while a student at Ferrara attending Guarino da Verona's lectures on Seneca there (see inscription, f. 197).[53] Two other MSS illustrative of the history of humanism in England, Harley 2471 and 2639, the first associated with Robert Sherborne and the second with John Tiptoft, Earl of Worcester, came from another source and will be dealt with below (p. 476).

Another MS associated with Ferrara, a fifteenth-century Tacitus, Harley

2764, has at the foot of f. 1 the painted coat of arms and motto of the Sacrati family, one of whose members was the famous sixteenth-century lawyer Laomedonte Sacrati, professor at the University of Ferrara. Three other MSS from Noel connected with identifiable Italian families are Harley 3442, a fifteenth-century Petrarch, bearing (f. 1) the arms of the Priuli family of Venice; Harley 2593, an illuminated MS of Manetti's De Dignitate Hominis, written in 1454–55 by Gherardus Johannes Cerasius (Gherardo del Ciriagio or Ciliagio), a notary of Florence (see colophon, f. 106),[54] belonged to the Strozzi family of Florence, whose arms are on f. 1; and an illuminated Book of Hours, Harley 2448, also from Florence, in which on facing pages (ff. 13v, 14) are painted the arms of the Morelli and Lottini families.[55] Manuscripts associated with two well known individuals are Harley 5609, a Greek MS of the works of St Basil and others, which belonged to Filippo Caimo, the lawyer, of Udine, in the Friuli (ex libris on f. 1v), another member of whose family—Jacopo—gave his collections to Padua,[56] and Harley 5552, St Paul's Epistles in Greek, which belonged to Paolo Emilio Cadamosto, of Vicenza, the editor of the 1626 edition of Alciati's Emblemata, published at Padua. In passing it is worth noting that one MS, Harley 5697, if we may believe the inscription in it (f. 1), 'βιβλ . . . βησσαριωνος καρδηναλ . . . του τ . . . Τουσκλων', was owned by the famous Cardinal Bessarion (d. 1472), whose library was bequeathed to the republic of Venice and forms the nucleus of the Marciana. From monastic houses came Harley 2673, a MS of Ovid's Metamorphoses once in the possession of the Augustinian canons of the Lateran of St Epiphanius at Pavia (if the ex libris [f. 1, of c. 1600], 'Iste liber est Monasterij Sancti Epiphanij', is correctly interpreted)[57] and Harley 5474 and 5475, two Arabic MSS, which had been in the library of the Augustinian priory of Santa Agnese and SS Quaranta at Treviso, having been bequeathed (see inscriptions on ff. 1v, 1* respectively) to the priory by Antonius De Fantis (fl. c. 1515–30), 'artium et medicinae doctoris celeberrimi' of Treviso, author of a commentary on Duns Scotus.

These are perhaps the most interesting items in the material Suttie accumulated on his Italian journeys. Thereafter we hear of him only in France, where he was said, to quote Wanley's diary, 22 January 1724–25, to be living 'a vagrant & idle Life in Paris, without doing any business at all, for above a year last past'. As a result, and since no letters had arrived from Suttie, Noel himself decided to set out for France to see if he could find him, and proposed to 'go to Boby-Abbey near Naples, and thence having visited the Back-Skirts of Italy, to pass into Sicily; & see what may be picked up at all these places'.[58] Noel did indeed get as far as Calais, arriving there on 30 August 1725, and arranged with Suttie that the latter would travel again according to his order. And finally, Noel told Wanley, 5 January 1725–26, that he was himself going to Italy and Sicily the next spring with Suttie. Letters were again received in April and May 1726 from Suttie reporting purchases, but the abrupt ending of the diary in June, followed by Wanley's death in July, makes it impossible for us to know whether the projected tour was ever carried out.

ITALIAN MSS ACQUIRED BY HARLEY FROM ENGLISH COLLECTORS

Other MSS of Italian provenance either came to Harley directly by gift or purchase from other English collectors or were acquired at the dispersal of their collections by auction or privately in London. Thus in the large gift of MSS (Harley 1585–1747, with Harley 1811 and 1812) made to Robert Harley at some indeterminable date, but certainly before 13 December 1712, when Wanley began to catalogue it, by Colonel Henry Worsley (d. 1747), son of Sir Robert Worsley, third Baronet of Apuldurcombe, and envoy to Portugal 1714, and later (1721) Governor of Barbados, is to be found the MS (Harley 1705) of the Latin translation of Plato's Republic written by Piero Candido Decembrio (1392–1477) and presented by him to Humphrey, Duke of Gloucester (d. 1447):[59] the importance of both men in the history of humanism in Italy and England needs no amplification.[60] Two MSS that had belonged to the great collector Cardinal Domenico Grimani (1461–1523) of Venice, Patriarch of Aquileia,[61] are to be found in the library; the first, Harley 497, came with the library of the antiquary Sir Simonds D'Ewes, which Robert Harley bought from his grandson in 1705, and the second, Harley 2766, with the collection of MSS belonging to Robert Bourscough (1651–1709), Archdeacon of Barnstaple (1703), purchased after his death from his widow in 1715; both MSS bear (on ff. 1*v, 1, respectively) the inscription 'Liber D. Grimani Car: lis S. Marci'. More important are the two MSS (Harley 2471, 2639) that belonged to Ambrose Bonwicke (1652–1722), headmaster of the Merchant Taylors' School (1686–91), both of which were acquired by him at the sale of 21 November 1687 (where they appeared in the sale catalogue under p. 83, lot 62, and p. 86, lot 108, respectively). They were bought by Edward Harley, 11 September 1725, from William Bowyer the younger, a pupil of Bonwicke. Of these the more interesting is Harley 2639, which was written for John Tiptoft, Earl of Worcester (d. 1470), and must have been sent to him after his return from Italy to England in September 1461, the MS having a scribal note on f. 43v dated 1462, with Tiptoft's painted coat of arms on f. 2;[62] it contains Tacitus' Dialogus de Oratoribus and Suetonius' De Grammaticis et Rhetoricis, 'being probably the first manuscripts of them to reach England' (Weiss). The second, Harley 2471, is a beautiful MS of Pliny the Younger, written in a humanist hand in 1385, which belonged to Robert Sherborne (1440?–1536), Fellow of New College, Oxford, 1474, self-appointed Bishop of St David's, 1505, and later (1508) Bishop of Chichester; Sherborne's interest in neo-classicism may have been stimulated by the gift of Duke Humphrey's MSS to Oxford University.[63] The MS had previously belonged to Thomas Wynterburn (d. 1478), Fellow of All Souls College 1437, and subsequently came into the hands of William Warham (1450?–1532), Archbishop of Canterbury 1504, to whom it was presented by Sherborne (see f. 2v).[64] One of the most important classical MSS in the Harleian Library is the ninth/tenth-century MS of Lucian's Dialogues, Harley 5694,[65] which had belonged to John Chalceopylus of

Constantinople, according to an inscription (f. 1*) in a fifteenth-century Italian hand—'libro de ⨍ chalceopylus: / Constantinopolitanus ℮ '.[66] The manuscript had also belonged to 'Henricus Casolla', presumably of the Casola family of Naples, a member of which, Simone Casola, was treasurer to Ferdinand I of Aragon c. 1492; Henricus gave it to Antonio Seripandi (d. 1539)—'Antonij Seripandi ex Henrici Casolle / amici opt. munere'. And by Antonio's brother, Cardinal Girolamo Seripandi (1493–1563), General of the Order of Augustinians (whose name, '⨍. Hieronymi Seripandi', occurs on f. 244v), it was bequeathed with his library to the Augustinian monastery of San Giovanni di Carbonara at Naples. When Montfaucon visited the library in 1702 he noted that part of it had been removed 'a Batavo':[67] this was Jan de Witt, and it was presumably from Holland following the dispersal of Jan de Witt's library at Dordrecht in 1701 that it eventually came to England, Harley obtaining it at the sale of the library of John Bridges (1666–1724), the Northamptonshire historian and antiquary, in March 1726 (sale catalogue, lot 4313). This was not the only MS in the Harleian Library, however, that had belonged to Antonio Seripandi; he had also been the owner of a Sallust, Harley 2675; an Odyssey, Harley 5674, and an Iliad, Harley 5693. Of these the second, Harley 5674, is endorsed by Edward Harley 'Feb: 2: 1726/7', and the third similarly. Harley 5674 was an important thirteenth-century minuscule Odyssey with *scholia*, while Harley 5693, in addition to the Seripandi *ex libris*, bears an inscription (f. 1v) in capitals: 'HOMERI · ILIAS · RES · GASPARIS · VOLATERRANI · APOSTOLICAE · SEDIS · PROTONOTARII · '.

Another MS from Italy that was acquired by Harley as a single item at an auction sale was Harley 5571, a twelfth-century Greek psalter that had belonged to Santa Maria in Organo at Verona, according to an inscription on f. 1*; it had been obtained by Thomas Grey, second Earl of Stamford, in 1693 and was bought by Harley at the Ballard auction of Stamford's books on 16 January 1720–21 following the earl's death in 1720.

Besides Thomas Coke of Norfolk, one other collector, Edward Harley's keenest rival as a book collector, was active in obtaining books from Italy: this was Charles Spencer (d. 1722), third Earl of Sunderland, who developed the library at Althorp and who was reputed to have bought manuscripts from Joseph Smith of Venice while he was actually in treaty with Harley for them.[68] On 6 February 1722–23 Wanley went to the Earl of Sunderland's to look into the MSS that Sunderland had bought from Joseph Smith of Venice. But quite apart from this Smith–Sunderland transaction, however, we find as long before as 6 September 1719 Edward Harley writing to Wanley, 'pray put an S. in ever[y] MS. that came from Ld. Sun. and put them in a box by themselves'. There is no recorded sale of Sunderland's books in 1719, and the allusion must be to some private transaction conducted through Noel, who was involved in buying books for Sunderland. This may offer an explanation of the mysterious entry 'SUND' in Wanley's hand in nine Harley MSS, viz. 2561, 2589, 2632, 2660, 2690, 2694, 2712, 3922 and 4144. Several of these are of Italian provenance and two, Harley 3922 and 4144, bear (ff. 1 [3922], 1v, 2 [4144]) the book stamp of the Servite convent of the Santissima Annunziata of Florence. Sunderland was prepared to pay almost any price for the books he desired, and this led Wanley to remark acidly on receiving the news of Sunderland's death that as a result 'this Commodity may Fall in the Market; and any Gentleman be permitted to buy an uncommon old Book for less than fourty or fifty Pounds'.[69] One of the nine, Harley 2690, a Cicero's De Amicitia, appears to have belonged to an unidentified Englishman, J. Astley, while sojourning in Naples in the late seventeenth century (see *ex libris*, f. 2*). According to another *ex libris* on f. 65 the manuscript belonged in 1692 to 'Pesinus Vincentius'. On f. 1 in the illuminated border is a painted coat of arms now mutilated; a cardinal's hat can still be distinguished above it. Two other MSS in this parcel may be noted. Harley 2694 is a Lucretius, De Natura Rerum, written in a humanist hand of late fifteenth-century date and possibly emanating from Naples (see J. J. G. Alexander and A. de la Mare, *op. cit.*, pp. 84–5, for discussion on Abbey MS 31. J.A. 3183, to which Harley 2694 is related in script and decoration); it has on f. 1 in the illuminated border an unidentified coat of arms (checky *or* and *gu*). And Harley 2632 belonged in 1630 (or 1650?) to 'Mattheus Mirax' of Florence (see f. 2, with a painted coat of arms on the same folio, paly *arg* and *gu* with a fess of the latter).

ITALIAN MSS ACQUIRED BY HARLEY THROUGH UNIDENTIFIED CHANNELS

At some unidentified date there came into the library a large block of no fewer than seventy MSS[70] that had belonged to the Jesuit college at Agen in southern France founded in 1591 and not suppressed until 1762. The *ex libris* inscriptions in these MSS are of seventeenth-century date and at one stage the fortunes of the college were at a low ebb financially.[71] It may have been at such a time that the college yielded up some of its contents. Almost all the MSS are of classical texts, mostly in fifteenth-century Italian hands, with a few of twelfth-century date. Much the most important is that of Livy originally written about 1200, Harley 2493, which belonged to Petrarch (1304–74) and Lorenzo Valla (1406–57); it contains not only annotations but substantial portions of the text in Petrarch's own hand, the latter added by him about 1325–27, and notable emendations by Lorenzo Valla,[72] whose abbreviated name or initials appear on ff. 113, 143, 167, 172. Among the Agen books was yet another MS owned by Petrarch, Harley 4927, a twelfth-century copy of Cicero's Orations, which has Petrarch's annotations throughout.[73] Harley 5342, another Agen MS, a Suetonius, came from the famous library of Andrea Matteo III Acquaviva (1458–1529), of Naples, Duke of Atri, his coat of arms being painted on f. 1, and belonged subsequently, in 1556, to Bernardinus Scardeonius, Canon of Padua, author of the *De Antiquitate Urbis Patavii*, published at Basel in 1560.[74] Also worth noting among the Agen dated Italian MSS are Harley 5248 and 4842. Harley 5248 comprises three tracts; the first (ff. 1–121v) bears on f. 121v a colophon recording the writing of the MS by

Giovanni Aretino at Venice in 1423; the second tract (ff. 122–127v) is also signed by him. (The third tract, ff. 127v–133, is in a later hand.) Harley 4842 was written at Rome by Franciscus Caballus Montefortinas, according to the colophon on f. 87. In the Agen library was incorporated also part of the library of the unfortunate Pedro Galés (Petrus Galesius) (c. 1537–c. 1595), a native of Tarragona, who, after travels in Italy and a professorship at Orange, 1588–91, was arrested by the Inquisition as a Huguenot and had his collection of books confiscated: some found their way to Agen, and the Galesius MSS in the Harleian Library were three in number, Harley 4858, 5252 and 5288, all of Italian origin. Harley 4858 has a painted coat of arms at the foot of ff. 10, 137 (or a bend engrailed az between two sixfoils gu), and Harley 5288 has, f. 1*v, an inscription recording the purchase of the MS at Siena in 1574 by Josephus Stephanus Valentinus. Of other MSS whose source of acquisition for the library has not been identified, two may be mentioned in conclusion.[75] One, Harley 3346, was presented to George Neville, the younger brother of Richard Neville the Kingmaker, Archbishop of York 1465–76, by George Hermonymus of Sparta during his visit to England in 1475–76; it is an illuminated copy of one of his Latin translations of gnomic sayings ascribed to the Greek philosophers. Neville played an important part in the diffusion of humanism in England.[76] The second, Harley 5271, is a volume of his letters compiled between 1471 and 1475 at Bologna and Verona by Felice Filiciano (c. 1432–80), 'Felix Antiquarius', a friend of Mantegna and Giovanni Marcanova (referred to above, p. 463), and a great collector of ancient inscriptions.[77] The MS includes at the beginning three vellum leaves, the first two stained green, the third purple, with lettering in silver and gold. It bears on f. 1 in Edward Harley's hand 'Janu: 9: 1728/9'.

NOTES

[1] From this date the business of the Library seems to have been in the hands of Edward Harley, Robert Harley being presumably preoccupied with public affairs.

[2] In the period before the gap, i.e. 2 March 1714/15–18 July 1716, Wanley always refers to himself as 'The Secretary': in the period following the resumption of the journal 'by my Lord Harley's Order' on 11 January 1719–20 Wanley speaks throughout in the first person.

[3] Wanley's diary is to be found in B.M. Lansdowne MSS 771, 772; the text was published in two volumes by the Bibliographical Society in 1966, *The Diary of Humfrey Wanley, 1715–1726*, edited by C. E. Wright and Ruth C. Wright, in the Introduction to which will be found a description of the material referred to above and its present location (pp. xi–xiii), besides a history of the library from 1705 until the death of the second Earl in 1741. (References to the diary in this paper will be throughout to this printed edition under the short title, *The Diary of Humfrey Wanley*.) For Humfrey Wanley himself see also C. E. Wright, 'Humfrey Wanley: Saxonist and library-keeper' (Sir Israel Gollancz Memorial Lecture, British Academy, 1960), *Proc. of the British Academy*, XLVI, pp. 99–129, and for Edward Harley the same author's 'Edward Harley, second Earl of Oxford, 1689–1741' (Portrait of a Bibliophile, VIII), *The Book Collector*, XI, summer 1962, pp. 158–74, and A. S. Turbeville, *A History of Welbeck Abbey and its Owners*, I (1539–1755), 1938, chapters XIII–XV.

[4] The list is printed in *The Diary of Humfrey Wanley*, I, pp. 194–5.

[5] On this Dante MS see E. Moore, *Contributions to the Textual Criticism of the Divina Commedia*, 1889, p. 596; L. Volkmann, *Iconografia Dantesca*, 1897, p. 51.

[6] The script of this early humanist MS is described by B. L. Ullman, *The Origin and Development of Humanistic Script*, Rome, 1960, p. 82.

[7] One manuscript in this parcel, Harley 3293, a copy of Niccolò Perotti's Latin translation of Polybius, dedicated to Pope Nicholas V (1447–55), is interesting for the portrait in an illuminated medallion on f. 2 of the Byzantine emperor John VIII Palaeologus, which is based on Pisanello's famous portrait (see Roberto Weiss, *Pisanello's Medallion of the Emperor John VIII Palaeologus*, London, 1966, p. 26, plate xv, 4). The manuscript has at the foot of f. 2 an unidentified painted coat of arms (*az* on a bend *or* three mullets *az* between two fleurs-de-lys *or*).

[8] For reproduction of the inscriptions in Harley 2507, 3234 see C. E. Wright, *Fontes Harleiani*, 1972, plate viii (*a*) and (*b*).

[9] See Seymour de Ricci, *A Handlist of Manuscripts in the Library of the Earl of Leicester at Holkham Hall*, Bibliographical Society, 1932, pp. ix–x. On Coke see also below, p. 470.

[10] A catalogue of the Ricasoli library is in Florence, Bibliotheca Marucelliana MS A.cxcvii. misc. (see P. O. Kristeller, *Iter Italicum*, i, 1963, p. 107).

[11] For list of these see *The Diary of Humfrey Wanley*, i, pp. 196–7.

[12] For list see *The Diary of Humfrey Wanley*, i, pp. 113–14.

[13] This manuscript (Harley 3276) was written after Aretino's death; at the end of Aretino's dedication to King Alfonso the date 1442 has been added in a contemporary hand (f. 1), and Poggio's elegy on Aretino occupies ff. 72–4*b*, while on f. 74*b* is written also Maffeus Veggius's epigram on Aretino.

[14] The *ex libris* on f. 94 is as follows: 'Ex libris Loysii Petri Domini Loysii de Gvicciardinis. de Florentia. sub annis Nostri Salvatoris. xx xi.TPR.PP. Eugenij. iiij'; that on f. 188*b* appears in the following form: 'Li. Lo. Pe. De.G.'.

[15] See *Palaeographical Society*, first series, plate 132.

[16] See L. Agostinelli and G. Benadduci, *Biografia e Bibliografia di Giovan Mario Filelfo*, Tolentino, 1899, p. 55.

[17] It is worth observing that another MS in this acquisition has associations with Florence, viz. Harley 4150, in which, on f. 193, is a note by the Inquisitor of Florence dated 1539 (?).

[18] The MSS in which the names of specific members of the Guicciardini family appear, either by themselves or in inscriptions, are as follows: Harley 3387 (Dimona Camilla de Guicciardini), 3458 (Gualtro Guicciardini), 2748 (Jacopo Guicciardini); 3714 was written for 'Magnifico Equiti Domino L. de Guicciardinis' according to the colophon on f. 156. In addition, of course, is the Guicciardini MS, Harley 3925, referred to above, p. 465, which is not in the list at present under discussion.

[19] It is, I think, more likely that the owner is to be identified with Pius II than with his nephew Francesco Todeschino Piccolomini (1439–1503), created cardinal in 1460 and afterwards (1503) becoming for only twenty-six days Pope Pius III, who bore the same coat of arms as his uncle (*arg*, five crescents *or* on a cross *az*) (see D. L. Galbreath, *Papal Heraldry*, second edition, revised G. Briggs, 1972, pp. 85, 87–8). The Pius II MS, Harley 2683, also came through Gibson but not until 27 January 1723–4 (listed 10 February 1723–4.) For two *alleged* Pius II MSS, Harley 2768 and 3976, see above, p. 466.

[20] Harley 3651 was a gift by Jacobus Nicholas Chocchi in 1475 to 'Sancti Salvatoris Librarie' (see f. 1*). Is this to be identified with the same house? It came from Gibson in January 1723–24.

[21] Davalos also owned B.M. Additional 15246 (arms on ff. 28*v*, 29: see *B.M. Reproductions from illuminated MSS*, third series, plates xxxix, xl), a MS believed by Dr Albinia de la Mare to be in the hand of the Florentine scribe Piero Strozzi (*c.* 1416–*c.* 1492) (see her paper 'Messer Piero Strozzi, a Florentine priest and scribe', in *Calligraphy and Palaeography: Essays presented to Alfred Fairbank ...*, London, 1965, pp. 55–68:

Add. 15246 is No. 19 in her list on p. 66. For a note on Iñigo Davalos see *op. cit.*, p. 62, n. 34).

[22] For three other MSS in this parcel, namely the Piccolomini MS, Harley 2683, see above, n. 19, the Petroni, Harley 3109, see above, p. 465, and the 'Sancti Salvatoris Librarie' MS, Harley 3651, see n. 20). For another Harley San Marco MS (2655) see below, p. 474.

[23] A late manuscript of mid-sixteenth-century date probably written by a scribe connected with Bembo's group; it may be the manuscript given by Bembo to Marcello Cervini (later Pope Marcellus II), from whose library it passed in 1583 to Fulvio Orsini, who bequeathed it to Cardinal Odoardo Farnes—thus the pedigree suggested by Roberto Weiss in *Times Literary Supplement*, 11 December 1948, and in his *Un inedito Petrarchesco*, Rome, 1950.

[24] On which see E. Moore, *Contributions to the Textual Criticism of the Divina Commedia*, Cambridge, 1889, p. 599. The manuscript bears on f. 1v a note dated 1487.

[25] Alexander and de la Mare, *The Italian Manuscripts in the Library of Major J. R. Abbey*, London, 1969, pp. xxiv, 28, n. 1; note that Abbey MS 7.J.A.4233 was written by the same Camulio. On f. 35 of the manuscript is written in capitals Franciscus Scotus Comes, with a pen-and-ink sketch of the arms above, and on f. 34v is scribbled with the date 1516, 'Iste liber est meus philipus de gnacys qui est bonus discipolus'. Other scribblings are on the same page.

[26] See *M.G.H. Scriptores* XVIII, pp. 405–9, 457–581, and XXIV, pp. 119, 122–36.

[27] For these and other Zomino MSS in the Harleian collection see my *Fontes Harleiani*, pp. 368–9 and plate XVII, and bibliographical references there cited. The nineteen MSS are 3440, 3989, 4838; 5267 A, ff. 1–40; 6313; 6324, 6328–32, 6502, 6506, 6510, 6512; 6855, ff. 52–113; 6874; 7400, 7642.

[28] On Andrew Hay and his relations with Edward Harley and Wanley and also on his brother George Hay see *The Diary of Humfrey Wanley*, II, p. 451, and references there cited.

[29] On this and similar commissions drawn up by Wanley see C. E. Wright, 'Humfrey Wanley: Saxonist and library-keeper', *Proceedings of the British Academy*, XLVI, 1961, p. 111, n. 5. The original of the Hay commission then in the possession of Mrs Alston-Roberts-West of Alscot Park was sold at Sotheby's, 29 October 1962, as part of lot 185. It was printed first, imperfectly, in the 1759 *Catalogue of the Harleian MSS* and again in *A Catalogue of the Harleian MSS in the British Museum*, I, 1808, pp. 6–7.

[30] On the MS see A. E. Popham, *Italian Drawings in the Department of Prints and Drawings . . .*; *The Fourteenth and Fifteenth Centuries*, 1950, pp. 32–8.

[31] Harley 2701 was apparently acquired by Andrew Hay in Venice (on a slip of paper pasted on to f. 1b is the note 'Andréa Haij. Venetia 1722'). Wanley thought, or had been told, that the MS had belonged to Aldus Manutius (see note by Wanley on f. 1b, 'Hic Codex olim fuit Aldi Manutij'. On f. 1 is the signature, in a seventeenth-century hand, 'G. Baruffald[i]'. (See my *Fontes Harleiani*, pp. 65 (for Baruffaldi), 182–4 (for Hay), and 233 (for Manutius)).

[32] It is interesting to note that a year before (18 January 1719–20) it had been reported to Wanley that Joseph Smith, subsequently consul at Venice, had said that the Giustiniani would not part with their Greek MSS (see *The Diary of Humfrey Wanley* under 18 January 1719–20).

[33] See *The Diary of Humfrey Wanley* under 18 May 1721 (I, p. 107, and nn. 2 and 3).

[34] See *The Diary of Humfrey Wanley* under 11 and 16 July 1723; and for other references to Middleton, *op. cit.*, II, p. 456; see also my *Fontes Harleiani*, p. 239.

[35] See *B.M. Reproductions from Illuminated Manuscripts*, third series, third edition, 1925, plate XLVIII. The illumination is to be related to that in Abbey MS 58.J.A.6991 (for reproduction of the Abbey MS see colour plate LXXV in J. J. G. Alexander and A. de la Mare, *op. cit.*).

[36] For list of Sanvito MSS see James Wardrop, *The Script of Humanism*, Oxford, 1963, pp. 50–3 (the MS cited on p. 51 as Harley 6051 should be Additional 6051); for a

later list see J. J. G. Alexander and A. C. de la Mare, *op. cit.*, pp. 105–10. For other Harley MSS associated with Sanvito see also my *Fontes Harleiani*, p. 297.

[37] On these two MSS see Wardrop, *op. cit.*, p. 32, and for reproductions from the MSS plates 33 (Harley 3510) and 32 (Harley 3567).

[38] This book stamp appears also in Sir John Soane's Museum MS 10 (*cf.* N. R. Ker, *Mediaeval MSS in British Libraries*, I, London, Oxford, 1969, p. 294). It has been suggested that this was the book stamp of the convent of Franciscan Annunciates at Varese; see A. G. Watson, 'A Varese library stamp identified', *The Library*, fifth series, XXVIII, 1973, pp. 147–8.

[39] See *The Diary of Humfrey Wanley*, II, pp. 416–18.

[40] For details see my *Fontes Harleiani*, p. 150, and the bibliography there quoted.

[41] See James Wardrop, *The Script of Humanism*, p. 10, and plate 7 (reproducing colophon and scribal motto, f. 388*v*). On the illumination see J. J. G. Alexander and A. de la Mare, *op. cit.*, pp. 104–10 in relation to Abbey MS 39.J.A. 7368 (Harley 3699 is cited on p. 108).

[42] On the MS see Paolo d'Ancona, *La miniatura fiorentina*, II, 1914, p. 427.

[43] On Nathaniel Noel see *The Diary of Humfrey Wanley*, II, p. 457, and references there cited; also my *Fontes Harleiani*, pp. 253–7.

[44] On the Suttie journeys see *The Diary of Humfrey Wanley*, I, pp. xlviii–l.

[45] See page reproduced in Wardrop, *The Script of Humanism*, plate 33.

[46] James Wardrop, *The Script of Humanism*, pp. 9–10; and for reproduction from the MS see *ibid.*, plate 32. See also letter from James Wardrop in *Times Literary Supplement*, 27 May 1949, p. 347.

[47] The coat of arms is surmounted by a cardinal's hat, and the volume may have belonged to Cardinal Sigismondo Gonzaga (1469–1525), Bishop of Mantua from 1511 to 1520, as I suggested in my *Fontes Harleiani*, but I think on further reflection that it is perhaps more probable that its possessor was Cardinal *Francesco* Gonzaga, for whom Harley 5790 (see above, p. 474) was written.

[48] For another Sanvito MS in the library, Harley 2692, see p. 471 above.

[49] In his *Illuminated Manuscripts* (1911) J. A. Herbert noted (p. 65) that the 'single figures and small groups painted on some of the margins' were copied from Byzantine models, but see the comments on the MS and its decoration in J. J. G. Alexander and A. de la Mare, *op. cit.*, pp. 107, 109.

[50] Another Harley MS written by Giovanni Mario Filelfi is 2522, a copy of his Laurenziad written by him in 1474 (see colophon, f. 245*v*); this was purchased for the library from John Gibson (see p. 466 above and n. 16). For the history of the Gonzaga library at Mantua see C. H. Clough, 'The library of the Gonzaga of Mantua', *Librarium*, XV, No. 1, 1972, pp. 50–63.

[51] On the MS and its owners see H. I. Bell, in *Speculum*, IV, 1929, p. 453. The inscription recording its gift to San Marco by Niccoli's executors is on f. 50. See also on Coluccio and this MS B. L. Ullman, *The Origin and Development of Humanistic Script*, Rome, 1960, p. 19 and n. 24.

[52] Another MS in the library associated with San Marco is Harley 2630, which was obtained not from Noel but from John Gibson, 13 February 1723–24, and is referred to above, p. 467.

[53] On Gunthorpe see my *Fontes Harleiani*, p. 174, and bibliographical references there cited, and on the part played by him in English humanism see especially Roberto Weiss, *Humanism in England*, 1941 edition, pp. 122–7; the MS is discussed p. 123, n. 6. This MS presents a problem, since in 1617 it was in the possession of 'Suicard ab Holdingen' and bears also the *ex libris* of St Peter's, Salzburg, and may therefore have been picked up by Suttie on his way to or from Italy and not in Italy itself, especially since another MS, Harley 3849 (a fourteenth-century medical work) also bearing the *ex libris* of St Peter's, Salzburg, in a sixteenth-century hand was included in this same parcel of 18 January 1723–24 from Suttie.

[54] Cerasius (d. 1472), the son of a Florentine silk dyer, called himself notary from

1447; he was notary of the Signoria of Florence in 1457 and 1464 (see B. L. Ullman, *The Origin and Development of Humanistic Script*, Rome, 1960, pp. 111–13, 117). A page of this MS is reproduced in Alfred Fairbank, *A Book of Scripts*, London, 1949, plate 13.

⁵⁵ Other MSS in these parcels formerly belonging to members of identifiable families are: Harley 4090 (arms of Rizzoni of Verona on f. 3) and 2599 (arms of Calderari of Verona on f. 84v).

⁵⁶ On this see G. F. Tomasini, *Bibliothecae Patavinae Manuscriptae publicae et privatae* . . ., Udine, 1639.

⁵⁷ From the more famous Certosa of Pavia came Harley 2470, Cicero's Ad Familiares, not a Noel purchase but acquired 6 August 1724 through Zamboni from the library of the classical scholar, J. G. Graevius (see my *Fontes Harleiani*).

⁵⁸ For this and the confusion in Noel's (or Wanley's) mind about Bobbio and Naples see *The Diary of Humfrey Wanley*, II, p. 372 and n. 1.

⁵⁹ See Roberto Weiss, *Humanism in England*, Oxford, 1941, pp. 56–8; for a reproduction of Decembrio's dedicatory inscription (f. 5) and Duke Humphrey's *ex libris* (f. 96v) see my *Fontes Harleiani*, plate v (a) and (b).

⁶⁰ Two other Harley MSS, 5608 and 5641, were owned by Decembrio; 5608, a Missal of Dominican Use, contains Decembrio's partially erased name on f. 1, and Harley 5641, a grammatical work in Greek, bears on f. 2 the inscription '~. Monasterij Angelorum Petrus Candidus'. We have no information as to the date on which or the source through which these two manuscripts were acquired by Harley.

⁶¹ On Grimani see Roberto Weiss, *The Renaissance Discovery of Classical Antiquity*, Oxford, 1969, pp. 169, 193–4, 200 and references there cited.

⁶² On Tiptoft and his place in the history of English humanism see Roberto Weiss, *Humanism in England*, 1941 edition, pp. 112–22; Tiptoft was the subject of one of Vespasiano da Bisticci's *Vite di uomini illustri del Secolo XV* (see Waters's translation, pp. 335–8).

⁶³ Sherborne has been suggested as the scribe of Bodl. Lib. MS Lat. misc. d.34 (SC.36217). See R. Weiss, *Humanism in England*, p. 168, n. 1.

⁶⁴ For reproduction of f. 3 of Harley 2471 showing the signatures of Cecil and Bonwicke see my *Fontes Harleiani*, plate x.

⁶⁵ See *B.M. Catalogue of Ancient MSS, Greek*, p. 15, plate 18.

⁶⁶ A similar inscription is in B.M. Sloane MS 745, f. 1v.

⁶⁷ Bernard Montfaucon, *Diarium Italicum*, 1702, p. 308.

⁶⁸ See *The Diary of Humfrey Wanley* under 17 December 1720. On Sunderland see S. de Ricci, *English Collectors of Books and Manuscripts (1530–1930)*, Cambridge, 1930, pp. 38–9.

⁶⁹ See *The Diary of Humfrey Wanley* under 19 April 1722. In 1719–20 Noel told Wanley that Alexander Cunningham had offered him (Noel) 200 guineas to let the Earl of Sunderland have the preference before all others as to the buying of his old books (*cf. The Diary of Humfrey Wanley*, I, p. 22).

⁷⁰ For complete list of the Agen MSS see my *Fontes Harleiani*.

⁷¹ See Philippe Lauzun, *Notice sur le Collège d'Agen, 1581–1888*, Agen, 1888.

⁷² See L. D. Reynolds and N. G. Wilson, *Scribes and Scholars; a guide to the Transmission of Greek and Latin Literature*, Oxford, 1968, pp. 106–7, 109, 118, 184, plate xv.

⁷³ A third Petrarch MS in the Harleian Library is Harley 5204, which belonged to the humanist Zomino da Pistoia, upon whose MSS see above, p. 468.

⁷⁴ On the library of Acquaviva see Hermann Julius Hermann, *Miniaturhandschriften aus der Bibliothek des Herzogs Andrea Matteo III Aquaviva (Jahrbuch der kunsthistorichen Sammlungen des allerhöchsten Kaiserhaus*, XIX, pp. 147–216), Vienna, 1898.

⁷⁵ It would be interesting to know the channel through which Harley acquired the beautiful little manuscript of Petrarch's Triumphs and Sonnets, Harley 5761, which belonged to the Medici; it has the Medici arms on f. 11 and the Medici device of a diamond ring on f. 10v. Folio 24 is reproduced in *B.M. Reproductions from Illuminated MSS*, second series, plate 48; the MS is allied in decoration to Abbey MS 20.J.A.3217 and

Holkham MS 41, the illumination of which has been attributed to Ser Benedetto di Silvestro, who worked with Francesco d'Antonio (*c.* 1469) (see J. J. G. Alexander and A. de la Mare, *op. cit.,* p. 60.

[76] On Neville see Roberto Weiss, *Humanism in England,* chapter IX, especially p. 146 on this MS.

[77] On him see James Wardrop, *The Script of Humanism,* 1963, pp. 16–18, and on the MS Victor Scholderer in *Gutenberg-Jahrbuch,* 1933, pp. 34–5. A page from the MS is reproduced in Wardrop, *op. cit.,* plate 10; in the index this plate reference is incorrectly cited as Harley 3271. The letter in Harley 5271 by his brother describing Feliciano's character is quoted, Wardrop, *op. cit.,* pp. 16–17. See also C. Mitchell, 'Archaeology and romance in Renaissance Italy', in *Italian Renaissance Studies,* ed. E. F. Jacob, London, 1960, pp. 474–8, 480–1.

27

MANUSCRIPTS
CAPTURED
AT VITORIA[1]

BY THE LATE afternoon of 21 June 1813 it was clear to the civilians and other non-combatants waiting behind Vitoria that the French army under Joseph Bonaparte and Marshal Jourdan had suffered a disastrous deafeat. The Anglo-Portuguese and Spanish army commanded by Lord Wellington,[2] advancing rapidly from the west, had cut the direct road to France. The waggons with the regimental and divisional baggage, the ammunition train and commissariat, and the generals' carriages carrying the possessions accumulated during five years in the peninsula—not always by legitimate means, to say no worse—as well as those of the unfortunate Spanish civilian collaborators, the *Afrancesados*, had caused a chaotic traffic jam on the minor road leading to Salvatierra. King Joseph and Jourdan had stationed themselves on a low hill half a mile east of the city to direct the evacuation.

At this moment the British cavalry broke through from the north and, seeing in front of them—a cavalryman's dream—the confused *mêlée* of retreating troops and vehicles, charged towards the king and the marshal. Among the French their approach caused an instant panic. 'En peu d'instants,' according to an eye-witness,[3] 'le désordre fut porté au comble.'

Of what followed accounts differ. A British version[4] relates that Captain Henry Wyndham of the 14th Light Dragoons and Lieutenant the Marquess of Worcester of the 10th Hussars caught up with Joseph's travelling carriage and fired their pistols through the nearside window. The king threw himself out of the far side on to a horse that was conveniently waiting for him, and made good his escape, covered by the Lancers of the Guard. The imperial proved to contain 220 paintings, cut from their frames and rolled up, State papers and private correspondence,[5] drawings and prints, a Sèvres breakfast service[6] and the thirty-two volumes listed below, all of which, having become by the laws of war the property of the opposing general, were delivered to Wellington the following day. Count Miot de Mélito, on the other hand, a member of Joseph's staff throughout the battle, makes no mention of the escape from the imperial. However this may be, it is clear that the king's possessions were transported in a number of other carriages as well, all of which were captured and picked over long before there was any question of handing them to the commander-in-chief. The British army, 'occupé à recueillir les fruits de sa victoire', Miot de Mélito drily observed, 'ne mit pas une grande activité à nous poursuivre'. Wellington himself described events more bluntly. 'The baggage of King Joseph after the battle of Vitoria fell into my hands,' he wrote to his brother, Sir Henry Wellesley, 'after having been plundered by the soldiers.' Major Leith Hay, visiting the battlefield early the next morning, found it 'strewed with manuscripts, broken trunks, or shattered carriages'. A conspicuous trophy was Joseph's silver *pot de chambre*, carried off by Lord Worcester's regiment, honourably promoted to hold champagne, and still in use to drink toasts from on guest nights.[7]

Wellington was not a man to waste time during a campaign on random booty. The pictures, books and other objects were sent home after only a cursory inspection, and it was not until February 1814 that his brother wrote from London to let him know that the consignment included many valuable works by Titian and other masters. 'The books,' added the Hon. William Wellesley-Pole, whose interest in literary matters was evidently less easily aroused than in artistic ones, 'are a few Splendid Classics by French Printers, and some illuminated Missals that are curious'—a description only too typical of a period when English connoisseurs automatically assumed that any manuscript in a gothic script with illumination must be a missal. Wellington guessed correctly that many of the pictures had been stolen from the royal palace in Madrid, and wrote on 14 March from his headquarters at Aire in the Landes to ask for a Spanish representative to be sent to identify and reclaim the king of Spain's property. There was no answer to this request, and the correspondence dragged on until 1816, conducted partly through the duke's brother, Sir Henry Wellesley, British ambassador in Madrid, partly through the Spanish ambassador in London, Count Fernán Núñez, Duke of Montellano. At last an official reply was received and forwarded to the duke on 29 November 1816. Ferdinand VII desired Wellington to keep everything that had been captured at Vitoria. 'His Majesty,' Fernán Núñez explained in a covering letter, 'touched by your delicacy, does not wish to deprive you of that which has come into your possession by means as just as they are honourable.'[8]

Eight years later the duke, browsing through the manuscripts,[9] came on Martin de Murúa's *Historia general del Perú*, the letters concerning Francis I's challenge to Charles V and the register of the latter's decrees (Nos. 7, 16 and 17), and wrote to inform Sir Walter Scott of his discovery, remarking how useful they would have been to Charles V's biographer, Professor Robertson.[10] The three volumes were dispatched to Edinburgh for the novelist's inspection, accompanied by a plea from Mrs Arbuthnot: 'I . . . intreat you to suggest to the Author of Waverley that he could not have a better subject or a fairer field for his unrivalled descriptions than the one which these manuscripts relate to and illustrate.'[11] Nothing came of this interesting suggestion, and no other record of the manuscripts has survived until 1945, when they were rediscovered at Apsley House by the seventh Duke of Wellington. The same three manuscripts that failed to persuade Sir Walter Scott to set one of his novels in sixteenth-century Spain have since been studied by Spanish scholars. The Martin de Murúa has been published in full, and accounts have appeared of the other two, after they had been lent in 1950 for examination by the Real Academia de la Historia in Madrid.

Where had these manuscripts come from? To answer this question the history of the royal library in Madrid must be briefly considered.

When Philip V ascended the Spanish throne he presented the library collected by the Hapsburg kings (which seems to have included the two Leonardo notebooks recently rediscovered) to the Spanish nation as the Real Biblioteca Pública, the ancestor of the modern Biblioteca Nacional. For sixty years the Palacio de Oriente contained no private library belonging to the royal family until Charles III formed a collection of about 3,000 volumes—very much a statesman's library, with law, government, economics and warfare as the chief subjects.

Charles IV, who succeeded to the throne in 1788, was a keen bibliophile, and in the next thirteen years the palace library was expanded to 20,000 volumes. Between 1799 and 1801 José Angel Alvárez Navarro, the sub-librarian and an accomplished calligrapher, compiled a catalogue of the collection in an elegant italic hand. About 1800 Charles IV appears to have decided to assemble a central archive of documents relating to Spanish history, and in the next eight years a large number of manuscripts were acquired, both singly and in groups. Part of the library of two Valencian savants, the brothers Gregorio and Juan Antonio Mayans y Siscar, was purchased, probably after the latter's death in 1801.[12] Charles III had caused the famous *Colegios Mayores* in the universities of Salamanca, Valladolid and Alcalá de Henares to become extinct by allowing vacancies to remain unfilled. In 1798 a superintendent was appointed to take charge of their property, and in late 1802 or early the following year the manuscripts from the Colegios Mayores of San Bartolomé and of Cuenca, both of Salamanca, were transferred to the royal palace. The transfer was probably supervised, and an index of the manuscripts drawn up, by D. Antonio Tavira y Almazán, the bibliophile Bishop of Salamanca (1737-1807).[13]

In 1807 Charles IV gave orders for numerous manuscripts in public ownership to be sent to the royal palace, among them being a valuable collection on America from the Secretariat of Grace and Justice of the Indies. Documents belonging to private owners were pursued with the same thoroughness. The correspondence concerning one such transaction has been published.[14] The replies to Charles V's circular letter enquiring whether he should accept Francis I's challenge to single combat, now in the Duke of Wellington's collection (list No. 17), belonged to D. José Ignacio de Arriola, of Elgoibar in the Basque province of Guipúzcoa, who declared that they had been preserved by his family for three centuries. On being notified in 1803 by the Minister of State, D. Pedro Ceballos, that the king would be pleased to receive them as a gift, D. José patriotically replied that as a loyal subject he regarded not only his entire property but his life too as being at his royal master's disposal. The letters were handed to an intermediary and reached the royal palace in February 1804. Many of the manuscripts acquired in these years were bound or rebound in uniform mottled calf with red morocco title labels on the spines.[15]

When the books captured at Vitoria are viewed in the light of this history it is clear that the majority came from Charles IV's library in the Palacio de Oriente—though several were very recent arrivals on the royal shelves. Ten manuscripts had come to the palace from the Colegio Mayor de Cuenca (Nos. 2–11), and one from the Colegio Mayor de San Bartolomé (No. 1). One had belonged to Mayans (No. 18). The documents describing the acquisition of the papers concerning Francis I's challenge (No. 17) have already been mentioned. Ghezzi's caricatures (No. 22) can be identified with reasonable certainty in the library catalogue of 1799–1801. Two other volumes bear Charles IV's crowned cipher (Nos. 20–1); a third (No. 12) is bound in the characteristic mottled calf of the royal library. Others (Nos. 24 and 15) are bound by Gabriel de Sancha, who worked for the royal collection—binding, for example, the six volumes of José Angel Alvárez Navarro's catalogue—or Pascual Carsí y Vidal, who seems to have succeeded him as the king's favourite binder. (It is fair to add that he had no objection to working also for Joseph Bonaparte.[16])

Of the printed books, one copy of the Ibarra *Sallust* of 1772 (No. 27)—a work of special interest to the royal family, as the Spanish translation was by Charles IV's brother, the Infante Don Gabriel—can be identified as the king's from the royal library press mark and the inscription 'Rey N[uestro] S[eñor]', while the collection of engravings published as *Estampas de la Sagrada Historia* (No. 30) is the dedication copy to the king's other brother, the Infante D. Antonio Pascual. D. Antonio's library seems to have been kept in the Palacio de Oriente, but shelved separately from the royal collection. It was dispersed following his death in 1817, part being still in the palace library, while another part was sold at auction on the evening of 8 April 1823 by M. & S. Thomas of Philadelphia—a notable instance of the gigantic upheaval of book ownership caused by the Napoleonic wars.[17] Although there is no direct evidence on the subject, it is probable that the man responsible for shipping D. Antonio's books across the Atlantic was Obadiah Rich, an American diplomat turned book dealer in Madrid.[18] José Angel Alvárez Navarro's catalogue of the Infante's collection, lot 71 of the sale, is now the property of the Library Company of Philadelphia.

In fairness to Joseph Bonaparte, however, it must be said that there is no reason to suspect him of acquiring two of the printed books—the Didot *Virgil* of 1798 and the second copy of the Ibarra *Sallust*, both bound by Pascual Carsí y Vidal—by other than legitimate means. We cannot look so tolerantly on his ownership of the other seven manuscripts. All are of Spanish origin or had belonged to Spanish collectors; all are of the type that had flowed into the royal palace between 1801 and Charles IV's abdication; and although Joseph Bonaparte seems to have had a conventional taste for contemporary fine printing[19] and was interested enough in one of the volumes

(No. 16) to have his collector's mark[20] stamped on it, it strains credibility to imagine him searching out and buying such odds and ends. It is more natural to assume that they belonged to the palace library and were snatched up more or less at random with the pictures and the more obviously desirable manuscripts of classical authors when he transferred his headquarters to Valladolid in March 1813.

It may be noted in passing that these were not the palace library's only losses during the French occupation—the one known copy in Spain of the first edition of Cervantes's *Novelas ejemplares* (Madrid: Cuesta, 1613) vanished at the same time, to reappear in a catalogue of the Parisian bookseller Rodriguez in 1816[21]—just as it is probable that Joseph Bonaparte set off from Madrid with more books than are now preserved in the Duke of Wellington's library, the British troops' looting of the French baggage being the cause of the remainder's disappearance.

Five Italian manuscripts of classical authors were recovered from the battlefield. All had come from Salamanca, a Virgil from the Colegio Mayor de San Bartolomé, the others from the Colegio Mayor de Cuenca. I have not been able to discover how and when the latter reached Spain, though it was presumably after the death in 1499—allegedly by poison—of Ludovico Agnelli, the owner of Bartolomeo Sanvito's *Suetonius* (No. 2), and perhaps not long after the college's foundation in 1500. The college owned manuscripts that had belonged to Lorenzo Ramírez de Prado,[22] but none of those in question can be traced in his sale catalogue.[23]

The early history of the Virgil, however, presents a more promising field for conjecture. The manuscript has both a Latin and a Greek colophon (f. 184v):

> Virgilius Biblos dedit hos dulcore refertus
> december calamo descriptos prebet Ubertus.

> Ἐγράφη ἐν Μεδιολάνῳ τῆς λιγουρίασ. καὶ εθε ἐτελειωθῆ ἐτα ἀπὸ τῆς χ[ριστο]υ γεννίσεως χιλιοστῷ τετρακοσιαστῷ δεκαεπτα. μηνος ιουλίου εικοστὴ. ὄντος του ιγεμονος του Μεδιολανου φιλιππου τῆς Μαρῆας τριτου.
> ¶ θ[ε]ῷ τας χαριτας. αμιν.

The scribe Uberto Decembrio, father of Pier Candido Decembrio, the humanist mentor of Humphrey, Duke of Gloucester, learned his Greek shown off in this colophon and, if not faultless, impressive for its time and place, from Emmanuel Chrysoloras during the latter's residence in Lombardy in 1400–03. Uberto, born in Vigevano about 1370, was employed as secretary by Petros Philarges, the Cretan bishop successively of Piacenza, Vicenza and Novara, subsequently Archbishop of Milan and Anti-Pope with the title of Alexander V. In 1405, when Philarges was summoned to Rome, or soon afterwards, he entered the service of the Visconti, but through unwisely involving himself in the power struggle between the duke, Giovanni Maria, and his brother, Filippo Maria, was arrested early in 1411. His imprisonment lasted about sixteen months. Lean years of unemployment seem to have followed, and the family's fortunes did not revive until Pier Candido was appointed one of the ducal secretaries in 1419.[24] It is only too likely that during this period of need he earned a living, or at least supplemented his income, by working as a professional scribe. Supporting evidence for the view that the manuscript was copied by sale is provided by what seems to be a contemporary bookseller's inscription on the end flyleaf.[25]

If this hypothesis is correct, an interesting possibility can be considered. The manuscript, as we have seen, was completed by the scribe in Milan on 20 July 1417. Illumination (which includes seventeen historiated initials of excellent quality) must have followed transcription, and the volume could have been completed, bound and ready to be sold by the early months of 1418.

D. Diego de Anaya Maldonado (1357–1437), bishop successively of Tuy, Orense, Salamanca and Cuenca, and finally Archbishop of Salamanca, and founder (in 1401) of the Colegio Mayor de San Bartolomé, had been chosen in 1416 to lead the Castilian delegation to the Council of Constance. The delegation set off in November, reaching its destination the following March. When the council dispersed after the final session on 22 April 1418 D. Diego, according to his biographer,[26] 'wished to see some cities of Lombardy'. Bologna—not a Lombard city—is the only place visited that is specifically mentioned, but it seems unlikely, to say the least, that his tour of Lombardy would have omitted Milan, the capital, especially as one of his objects was evidently to buy books. His purchases, presumably on this occasion, included other Italian illuminated manuscripts,[27] and he presented some classical texts to his college—Seneca's *Letters to Lucilius* and *Tragedies* (the latter with Nicholas Trivet's gloss), Valerius Maximus, Vegetius and Galen—as well as four by Italian authors: a glossed Dante, Petrarch's *De fortuna* (presumably the *De remediis utriusque fortunae*) and *De vita solitaria*, and a work also attributed to Petrarch and titled 'Flores philosophiae' in the inventory.[28]

D. Diego could therefore have bought the Virgil in Milan in 1418 and the purchase would have been quite consistent with the programme of acquisition he seems to have set himself. Whether he did buy it or not must, however, remain an open question, as the manuscript does not figure in the list of books which he gave or bequeathed to the college.[29] It is easy to find an explanation for this—he may have given it away in his lifetime, or the Fellows may have considered it for some reason unsuitable for the chained library which had been established by his direction.[30] In any event the volume was in Spain before the end of the century, as a fifteenth-century Spanish hand has noted the contents on the end flyleaf, 'todas las obras del V[ir]gilio'. It appears under the brief title 'Virgilius MS' in an inventory of the college's library compiled in 1550 by a certain Cristobal Salazar Grysalba, now known only from a copy by the eighteenth-century librarian of the Real Biblioteca Pública, Juan de Iriarte;[31] and again in Roxas's list of 1770.[32]

It only remains to notice that some other manuscripts of the *colegios mayores*, after a century and a half in Madrid, were returned to Salamanca in 1954 and are now in the University Library.

BOOKS CAPTURED AT VITORIA[33]

MANUSCRIPTS

(a) *From the Colegio Mayor de San Bartolomé, Salamanca*

1. Virgil. *Bucolica, Georgica et Aeneis.* Milan: copied by Uberto Decembrio, 20 July 1417.

Vellum. 184 leaves. 335 × 225 mm. Gothic text hand. Seventeen historiated initials. Royal Library binding of mottled calf, *c.* 1800. 'JB' stamp on flyleaf. Ownership inscription on f. 1, 'Ex lib. Collegii Divi Bartholomei Salmantini'.

Madrid B.N., MS 18037, San Bartolomé No. 194, 'Virgilii Maronis Opera = Codex membranaceus optimae notae. f⁰. 1. v.'

(b) *From the Colegio Mayor de Cuenca, Salamanca*

2. Suetonius. *Vitae duodecim Caesarum.* [Padua: copied by Bartolomeo Sanvito, last quarter of the fifteenth century.][34]

Vellum. 282 × 175 mm. Humanistic cursive hand. Finely illuminated. Arms of Lodovico Agnelli, Archbishop of Cosenza. Modern morocco binding. 'JB' stamp on flyleaf.

Madrid B.N., MS 2952 f. 43, 'Suetonio iluminado . . .'; *ibid.*, MS 18037, Cuenca No. 81, 'C. Suetonii tranquilli de duodecim Caesaribus = Codex membran[aceu]s magni pretii. f⁰. 1. v.' No ownership inscription but the inventory number, 81, is written on a flyleaf.

3. Juvenal and Persius. *Satyrae.* [Italy, *c.* 1460.]

Vellum. Eighty-nine leaves. 225 × 140 mm. Litera fere humanistica. Royal Library binding of mottled calf, *c.* 1800. 'JB' stamp on flyleaf. Ownership inscription, 'De la Bibliotheca del Col[egi]o M[ay]or de Cuenca'.

Madrid B.N., MS 2952, f. 25.

4. Tibullus, Maximianus and Propertius. *Opera.* [Florence ?, *c.* 1470.]

Vellum. 143 leaves. 193 × 115 mm. Humanistic cursive hand. Royal Library binding of mottled calf. red morocco title label, *c.* 1800. Ownership inscription, 'De la Bibliotheca del Col[egi]o M[ay]or de Cuenca'.

Madrid B.N., MS 18037, Cuenca No. 217.

5. Horace. *Carmina.* [Venice, *c.* 1480.]

Paper. Eighty-six leaves. 203 × 135 mm. Humanistic cursive hand. Fine historiated initials somewhat in the style of Franco dei Rossi (*cf. The Book Collector*, XXI, 3, autumn 1972, p. 347). Royal Library binding of mottled calf, red morocco title label, *c.* 1800. Ownership inscription, 'Es de la Libreria del Collo. M[ay]or de Cuenca'.

Madrid B.N., MS 2952, f. 40; MS 18037, Cuenca No. 49.

6. Latin Bible. [France, thirteenth century.]

Vellum. 150 × 92 mm. Minute gothic text hand. Royal Library binding of mottled calf, *c.* 1800. 'JB' stamp on flyleaf. Ownership inscription, 'del Collo. M[ay]or de Cuenca'.

Madrid B.N., MS 18037, Cuenca No. 214.

7. Fray Martin de Murúa. *Historia general del Perú, origen y descendencia de los Incas.* 1613.

Paper. 289 × 193 mm. Many full-page illustrations. Modern red morocco binding. Ownership inscription of the Colegio Mayor de Cuenca.

Madrid B.N., MS 2952, f. 32.

Published from this manuscript in 1962 (Fray Martin de Murúa, *Historia general del Perú, origen y descendencia de los Incas*, ed. Manuel Ballesteros-Gaibrois, with an introduction by the Duke of Wellington. Two volumes. Madrid, 1962).

8. Francesillo de Zuñiga. *Corónica del Emperador Carlos V* [a burlesque chronicle by Charles V's jester].

Paper. Small 4to. Royal Library binding of mottled calf, *c.* 1800. Ownership inscription, 'De la Bibliotheca del Col[egi]o M[ay]or de Cuenca'.

Madrid B.N., MS 18037, Cuenca No. 33, 'Es obra toda burlesca y desvariada como de un loco'.

9. Pedro López de Ayala. *Corónica del Rey don Enrique tercero de este nombre*. [Sixteenth century.]

Paper. Folio. Royal Library binding of mottled calf, *c.* 1800. Ownership inscription on flyleaf, 'De la Bibliotheca del Collo. M[ay]or de Cuenca'.

Madrid B.N., MS 2952, f. 37v; MS 18037, Cuenca No. 317.

10. *Relación sumaria de la historia verdadera del Rey Don Pedro de Castilla*, and other pieces, mostly heraldic or genealogical. [Seventeenth century.]

Paper. Folio. Various hands. Royal Library binding of mottled calf, *c.* 1800. Ownership inscription on f. 1, 'De la Bibliotheca del Col[egi]o M[ay]or de Cuenca'.

Madrid B.N., MS 18037, Cuenca No. 4.

11. Guido Fabricius Boderianus (Guy Lefèvre de la Boderie). *Grammatica Chaldaea*. [Seventeenth century.]

Paper. Small 4to. Royal Library binding of mottled calf, *c.* 1800. Ownership inscription, 'De la Bibliotheca del Col[egi]o M[ay]or de Cuenca'.

Madrid B.N., MS 2952, f. 21; MS 18037, Cuenca No. 139.

(c) *From other sources*

12. Latin Bible. [France, thirteenth century.]

Vellum. 155 × 104 mm. Minute gothic text hand. Royal Library binding of mottled calf, red morocco title label, *c.* 1800. 'JB' stamp. Belonged to the Dominicans of Lyons.

13. Latin Bible. [North-eastern Spain?, thirteenth century.]

Vellum. 217 × 172 mm. Gothic text hand. Madrid eighteenth-century binding, blue morocco, dentelle borders, small red morocco central onlay, red morocco title labels on spine lettered 'Biblia Sacra' and 'Mano Escrito en Bitela'. Ownership inscription of the Capuchins of Vich, Catalonia.

14. Horae B.V.M. [Flanders, fifteenth century.]

Vellum. 163 × 110 mm. Gothic liturgical hand. With miniatures. Royal Library binding of mottled calf, red morocco label, *c.* 1800. Inscribed on a flyleaf, 'Son estas horas de Nicolas Domingo Esteban Villalba de Sebastian Gutierez Ramayo y Castro que Dios guarde muchos años de edad 17 años versante en el Colegio de Predicadores el año 1755'.

15. Alfonso X of Castille, 'el Sabio'. *Historia general del mundo*. Part 2 only. [Spain], 1381.

Vellum. 205 leaves. 345 × 250 mm. Spanish gothic text hand. Straight-grained red morocco gilt, *c.* 1800, by Pascual Carsí y Vidal, with his ticket. An illuminated border on f. 1 contains a coat of arms in the lower margin. Ownership inscription on the same page of the Licenciado Diego de Colmenares.[35]

16. Register from Charles V's chancery, with copies of royal decrees from 20 June 1516 to 15 July 1526.

Paper. Folio. Calf. 'JB' stamp.

Cf. Mercedes Gaibrois Riaño de Ballesteros, 'Dos manuscritos de la biblioteca del Duque de Wellington y Ciudad Rodrigo', *Boletín de la Real Academia de la Historia*, cxxvii, 1950, pp. 357–442.

17. Collection of forty-two letters from Spanish grandees, prelates and cities in answer to Charles V's request for advice how to reply to François I's challenge to a duel. The challenge had reached Charles V at the Cortes of Monzón in early June 1528.

Bound in a volume. Folio. Calf.

These letters were preserved in the private archives of D. José Ignacio de Arriola at Elgoibar (Guipúzcoa) until 1803, when, at Charles IV's request, the owner presented them to the king and they were transferred to the royal palace in Madrid. The letters concerning this transaction are printed by Doña Mercedes Gaibrois Riaño de Ballesteros, 'Dos Manuscritos', pp. 436–42.

18. Collection of forty-six letters to the Duke of Alcalá, Viceroy of Naples, from Philip II (thirty-eight), the Infante Don Carlos (three), Elizabeth de Valois (one), the emperor Maximilian II (two), and Archdukes Rudolf and Ernest (one each), and one letter from Alcalá to Philip II, 1564–69.

Bound in a volume. Folio. Calf, with the usual Royal Library red morocco title label. Ownership stamp of D. Gregorio Mayans y Siscar.

19. *Cartas del Rey don Phelipe 2º. para Rodrigo Vásquez tocantes a la sucesion en Portugal y otras de otros ministros.* A collection of letters about Portugal, 1579–80.

Bound in a volume. Folio. Wrappers.

20. François de Lorraine, duc de Guise. *Mémoires*, in an anonymous Italian translation. [Eighteenth century.]

Paper. Quarto. Spanish eighteenth-century calf, spine gilt with the crowned cipher of Charles IV.

21. Notebook containing excerpts from Machiavelli's *Istorie fiorentine*, in Italian, and from the *Consejos del Emperador Carlos V a su hijo Felipe II*, in Spanish, with a short passage from a work in English beginning, 'It is to be noted in scripture the great respecte which is hadde to primogenitura . . .' [Eighteenth century.]

Paper. Small 8vo. Written in an untidy cursive hand. Spanish eighteenth-century calf, spine gilt with the crowned cipher of Charles IV. Press mark on flyleaf: 'Sal.3a. En.16.Ca.2'.

22. Pierleone Ghezzi. Collection of his caricatures. Title page dated Rome, 1780.

Three volumes. Folio. English half-calf bindings of *c.* 1820. Probably to be identified with an entry in Angel Navarro's catalogue of the Royal Library: 'GHEZZI Pittore Romano (Cavaliere Pier Leone) Disegni originali rappresentanti alcuni Ritratti in caricatura. fol. mag.III . . . N . . . 1'. (One volume now rebound in three?)

23. Miscellany comprising
   (i) *Discurso hecho por Fray Augustín Salucio . . . acerca de la Justicia y buen govierno de España en los estatutos de limpieza de sangre.* [Seventeenth century.] Forty-four leaves.
   (ii) *Manifiesto del Reino de Portugal en el qual se declara el derecho, las causas y el modo que tuvo para eximirse de la obedencia del Rey de Castilla, y tomar la voz del serenissimo don Juan quarto de nombre.* [Seventeenth century.] Twenty-four leaves.

(iii) Giovanni Battista Naccher. *Specchio del prencipe in materia di stato*. With a dedication to D. Pedro Fernández de Castro, Conde de Lemos, d'Andrada y de Villalba, dated 1611. Ninety-three leaves.

(iv) Mattheo Rencí. *Tratado de paciencia*. With a dedication to D. Gaspar de Guzmán, Conde-Duque de Sanlúcar, dated 1629.[36] Seventy-five leaves.

Four tracts in different hands bound in one volume. Paper. Small 4to. Eighteenth-century calf. Provided with a title, 'Papeles manuscritos tomo 7mo.', and index.

24. Miguel Antonio de la Gandara. *Apuntes para formar un discurso sobre el bien y el mal de España*. [Eighteenth century.]
Paper. Folio. Eighteenth-century calf by Gabriel de Sancha, signed with monogram on the spine.[37]

25. *Informe de la Real Sociedad Econo[mica] de Amigos del Pais de Madrid*. [c. 1770.]
Paper. Folio. Contemporary red morocco.

26. *Descripción geográfica y topográfica de la provincias pertenecientes al Reyno de Perú*. [Eighteenth century.]
Paper. Folio. Vellum binding.

PRINTED BOOKS

27. Sallust. *La conjuración de Catilina y las guerra de Jugurta*. Madrid: Ibarra, 1772.
Folio. Contemporary Spanish red morocco gilt. With a note, 'Rey N[uestro] S[eñor]', indicating that this was one of the king's copies, and the press mark of the Royal Library, I.N.2.

28. Another copy, with the 'JB' stamp on a flyleaf. Bound in red morocco, *c.* 1810. by Pascual Carsí y Vidal, signed at the foot of the spine 'Pasqual Carsi lo enquadernó',

29. Virgil. *Bucolica, Georgica et Aeneis*. Paris: Pierre Didot, 1798.
Folio. Bound in red morocco by Pascual Carsí y Vidal, with his ticket. 'JB' stamp.
Sold by the sixth Duke of Wellington in 1941: J. W. Hely Hutchinson, sale Sotheby's, 14 March 1956, lot 621; Messrs Martin Breslauer catalogue 84, 1956, No. 480. Now in the Bibliothèque Nationale, Paris.

30. *Estampas que representan los principales sucesos de la Historia Sagrada. Para uso de S.A. el Sermo. Sr. Infante Dn. Antonio Pasqual*. Madrid, 1795–1800.
Three vols. Folio. The dedication copy on vellum paper ('papel vitela') to the Infante Don Antonio, with his ownership stamp (the letters S.D.S.Y.D.A.—'Soy del Serenísimo Ynfante Don Antonio'—inside a coronetted wreath) and library press-mark, 'E.XIV.T.VIa.'. Contemporary red morocco, with onlays, by Pascual Carsí y Vidal, with his ticket.

NOTES

[1] I am extremely grateful to the late Duke of Wellington for showing me these manuscripts, and to his grace the present Duke for allowing me to inspect them again.

[2] Arthur Wellesley, Earl of Wellington, created first Duke of Wellington in May 1814.

[3] Comte Miot de Mélito, *Mémoires*, Paris, second edition, three vols., 1873–4, III, pp. 316 ff.

[4] Sir Archibald Alison, *History of Europe from 1789 to 1815*, Edinburgh, ninth edition, thirteen vols., 1855, X, p. 244; Evelyn, Duchess of Wellington, *A Descriptive and Historical Catalogue of the Collection of Pictures and Sculpture at Apsley House*, London, 1901, I, Introduction. *Cf.* the seventh Duke of Wellington's introduction to Fray Martin de Murúa, *Historia general del Perú*, ed. Manuel Ballesteros-Gaibrois, Madrid, 1962.

[5] The seventh Duke returned the letters from Joseph's wife and children to France (Elizabeth Longford, *Wellington: the Years of the Sword*, London, 1969, p. 316 n.).

[6] Now in the Wellington Museum, Apsley House, London.

[7] Wellington, *Dispatches*, ed. Gurwood, 1852, VI, p. 22; Major Leith Hay, *A Narrative of the Peninsula War*, 1831, II, p. 69; Elizabeth Longford, *op. cit.*, p. 315. The chamber pot now belongs to the 14th/20th King's Hussars, who also preserve a fine linen tablecloth captured in the same action, as Lieut.-Col. R. V. L. ffrench-Blake, D.S.O., kindly informs me.

[8] Evelyn, Duchess of Wellington, *ut cit.* She prints part only of William Wellesley-Pole's letter of 9 February 1814. The quotation given here is from the original.

[9] See the list on pp. 491–4.

[10] William Robertson's *History of Charles V* was first printed in 1769 and his *History of America* in 1771.

[11] Sir Walter Scott, *Letters*, ed. H. J. C. Grierson, VIII, 1935, pp. 452–3. I owe this reference to the kindness of the late Mr Francis Needham. *Cf.* Lockhart, *Memoirs of the Life of Sir Walter Scott*, 1837, V, p. 402; Philip Henry, Earl Stanhope, *Conversations with the Duke of Wellington*, 1888, p. 100.

[12] Another part was bought by the bookseller Vincente Salvá. Manuscripts from the Mayans brothers' collection were included in a sale in London by Wheatley & Adlard on 10 March 1829. *Cf.* Nigel Glendinning, 'Spanish books in England, 1800–1850', *Transactions of the Cambridge Bibliographical Society*, III, 1, 1959, pp. 70–92.

[13] The index is extant in several copies. I have used Madrid, Biblioteca Nacional MS 18037. Ms 2952 is a list of manuscripts in the Colegio Mayor de Cuenca compiled by Dr D. Andrés Navarro, a Fellow of the college, in 1782. The books from the two *colegios mayores* outside Salamanca (Santa Cruz at Valladolid and San Ildefonso at Alcalá de Henares) never reached the royal palace. The whole process is described by Guy Beaujouan, 'Manuscrits scientifiques médiévaux de l'Université de Salamanque et de ses "Colegios Mayores" ', *Bibliothèque de l'École des Hautes Études Hispaniques*, fasc. XXXII, Bordeaux, 1962.

[14] Mercedes Gaibrois de Ballesteros, 'Dos manuscritos españoles de la biblioteca del Duque de Wellington y Ciudad Rodrigo', *Boletín de la Real Academia de la Historia*, CXXVII, 1950, pp. 436–42.

[15] I have called this style 'Royal Library binding' in the list.

[16] Carsí y Vidal returned to Madrid in 1797 with an English wife, Mary Clark, after serving his apprenticeship as a binder in England. Matilde López Serrano, 'La encuadernación madrileña en la época de Carlos IV', *Archivo español de arte*, XC, 1950, pp. 122–5.

[17] I am most grateful to Mr Edwin Wolf II for informing me of the existence of this sale and for sending me copies of the relevant pages in the catalogue.

[18] Glendinning, 'Spanish books in England, 1800–50', pp. 79–80, gives an account of Rich's career.

[19] His copy of the Chevalier de Querelles' *Héro et Léandre*, Didot l'aîné, 1801, with plates by P. L. Debucourt, bound by Bozérian, is mentioned by Cohen–De Ricci 833. The binding is illustrated by Messrs Lathrop C. Harper, New York, catalogue 26.

[20] 'JB Grand Electeur' (i.e. heir apparent to his brother, a title granted by Napoleon) in red. Reproduced in the Hely Hutchinson sale catalogue, Sotheby's, 14 March 1956, lot 621.

[21] Salvá, quoted by Glendinning, 'Spanish books in England, 1800–50', p. 75.

[22] 'Historia de los tres Reyes Magos', which before Ramírez de Prado had been in the possession of Cristobal de Salazar Mardones (Madrid, B.N., MS 18037 Cuenca No. 272), and his MS library catalogue (*ibid.*, MS 2952, f. 23).

[23] Joaquín de Entrambasaguas, *La Biblioteca de Ramírez de Prado*, Madrid, 'Colección Bibliográfica', 1943, two vols.

[24] Argellati, *Bibliotheca scriptorum Mediolanensium*, II, 2, cols. 2106–8; Mario Borsa, 'Un umanista vigevanasco del sec. XIV', *Giornale ligustico*, XX, 1893, pp. 81–111,

199–215; Giuseppe Cammelli, *Manuele Crisolora*, Florence, 1941, pp. 122–7. A *Terence* in the Bodleian Library, Rawl. G135, was copied by Uberto Decembrio at Pavia in 1400. The manuscript of his works in the Biblioteca Ambrosiana, B 123 sup, does not appear to be autograph.

[25] Folio 185: 'quat[er]ni xxviij duc̄ xxiij ann et [duo] auro. ad muifi [munificentiam?]'. Can this be a calculation of the payment due to the copyist? Its interpretation is complicated by the fact that the manuscript has 184 leaves, which cannot easily be made to correspond to twenty-eight quaternions.

[26] Francisco Ruiz de Vergara, *Vida del illustrissimo Señor Don Diego de Anaya Maldonado*, Madrid: Diego Díaz de la Carrera, 1661, pp. 32–3. *Cf.* J. G. Gaztambide, 'Los españoles en el Concilio de Constanza', *Hispania Sacra*, XVIII, 1965, pp. 145–61, and L. Sala Balust, 'Las primeras constituciones del Colegio de San Bartolomé de Salamanca, copia de los primeros estatutos del Colegio de San Clemente de Bolonia', *Estudios eclesiásticos*, XXXV, 1960, pp. 253–63.

[27] E.g. Joannes Andreae, *Super decretales*, with Bolognese miniatures: J. Domínguez Bordona, *Manuscritos con pinturas*, Madrid, 1933, I, pp. 443–4.

[28] The register of his gifts to the college is in the Bibliothèque Nationale, Paris, ms. esp. 524. The works mentioned are noted on ff. 5*v*, 14*v*, 16*v*, 33 and 35*v*.

[29] The arms at the foot of f. 1 of the manuscript have been defaced, but they seem to have been painted over an earlier coat, now also indecipherable.

[30] For the chained library, see Joseph de Roxas y Contreras, marqués de Alventos, *Historia del colegio viejo de San Bartholomé, Mayor de la celebre Universidad de Salamanca*, Madrid, 1770, III, p. 25. D. Diego's will (*ibid.*, p. 241) provided that the Fellows were to make a choice of his books to be placed in the library.

[31] 'Index voluminum quae in Bibliotheca Collegii D. Bartolomaei continentur, digestus per ordinem Alphabeti. Scripsit et hunc et titulos omnes Bibliothecae Christophorus Salazarius Grysalba. Anno 1550. Index hic et Tituli omnes Bibliothecae scripti sunt Rectore Bartulo Sanctio.' Copied by Juan de Iriarte and completed on 1 March 1748, from a manuscript—presumably the original—lent him by P. Salgado, O.S.A., of the Convent of San Felipe el Real, Madrid. Phillipps MS 10772, sold as part of a large collection of Iriarte's papers (Bibilotheca Phillippica, new series, VI, 15–16 June 1970, lot 1286), now in a Spanish private collection.

[32] Roxas y Contreras, *Historia*, p. 340.

[33] For a note on Madrid B.N., MSS 18037 and 2952; see n. 13 above.

[34] *Cf.* James Wardrop, *The Script of Humanism*, Oxford, 1963, p. 53.

[35] Diego de Colmenares was the historian of Segovia and priest of the parish of San Juan in that city. The manuscript is not mentioned either by D. Mariano Quintanilla, 'La biblioteca de Colmenares', or by P. Teófilo Ayuso Marazuela, 'Algunos libros de la biblioteca de Colmenares', in *Estudios Segovianos*, III (Segovia, Instituto Diego de Colmenares). For the dispersal of Colmenares's library *cf.* A. R. A. Hobson, 'A sale by candle in 1608', *Transactions of the Bibliographical Society*, fifth series, XXVI, 3, September 1971, p. 230.

[36] Professor J. H. Elliott has pointed out to me that another treatise by Rencí, dedicated, like this one, to Olivares, *Tratado del privado perfecto*, 1622, is in the British Museum, MS Egerton 2053, ff. 48–78*v*.

[37] *Cf.* Matilde López Serrano, 'La encuadernacion madrileña en la epoca de Carlos IV', plate Xc5.

Addenda, chapter 18

I wish to give my warmest thanks to the editor of this volume for helpful stylistic and bibliographic suggestions, and also to underline my indebtedness to my collaborator, Anna Maria Lorenzoni of Mantua.

Page 345, n. 10. An important reference to the Gonzaga cameo in Leningrad is in E. Vico, *Discorsi sopra le medaglie de gli antichi*, Venice, 1555, book II, p. 92: 'Peggiormente quella di Livia Drusilla moglie del Divo Augusto, perché ella si vede naturale insieme con quella del suo marito e col suo nome in lettere scritto, fra le cose rare e preciose della Grotta dell'eccellentissimo Signor Duca di Mantova, scolpita in uno bellissimo e gran cameo di inestimabile pregio alla cui similitudine ne ha una in corgniuola intagliata Monsignore [Torquato] Bembo'. The Gonzaga cameo is that which Rubens later mentioned, see P. P. Rubens, *Letters*, ed. R. S. Magurn, Cambridge, 1955, pp. 200–1.

Page 346, n. 22. The Triumphs are discussed by C. T. Perina, 'Considerazioni su alcuni aspetti della cultura figurative del cinquecento a Mantova', *Antichità Viva*, XIII, 1974, pp. 26–7.

Pages 346–7, nn. 24, 36. The *pietre dure* vases are discussed in *Il Tesoro di Lorenzo il Magnifico*, II (exhibition catalogue), ed. D. Heikamp and A. Grote, Florence, 1975.

Page 347, n. 37. See also Sabino Calandra's letter of 9 September 1547 (Busta 2541).

Page 348, n. 39. Under *Installations of statues* ... note that Grossino's letter of 2 February 1512 is actually dated 1511, but the contents make it clear that it was written in 1512. Grossino's letter to Isabella d'Este of 16 August 1511 (Busta 859) also relates to the installations of statues.

Page 348, n. 43. My reasons for mistrusting Verheyen's treatment of the studiolo documents are given in my forthcoming review of his book for *Art Quarterly*; see also S. Beguin and others, *Le Studiolo d'Isabella d'Este: les dossiers du Départment des Peintures* . . ., Paris, 1975.

Page 349, n. 50. For the identification of Faustina's busta in the Palazzo Ducale, Mantua, as in Mantegna's collection originally, see my forthcoming letter to the editor of *Art Bulletin*.

Pages 350–1, n. 58. The recently discovered inventory of Cardinal Francesco Gonzaga's collection is to be published by Giuseppe Frasso in a forthcoming issue of *Italia Medioevalia et Umanistica*.

Page 351, n. 60. The *Rhodian bronze* has been identified and discussed by M. Perry, 'A Greek bronze in Renaissance Venice', *Burlington Magazine*, CXVIII, 1975, pp. 204–11, and see my supplementary information in a 'Letter to the editor', shortly to be published.

INDEX OF MANUSCRIPTS

MARGARET ANNE CLOUGH

FLORENCE, BIBL. MED. LAURENZIANA
Plut.—contd.

46, 6	165, 166, 167, 168, 169, 171, 176 Ap. 9.2 (618), Ap. 9.3 A (ii), (iv), (vi); 180 (No. 27), 194 n. 39, 195 n. 45, 196 nn. 61, 65–6, 76–8, 81; 197 n. 81
47, 4	167, 172 Ap. 9.1 (21); 175 Ap. 9.2 (555); 176 Ap. 9.3 A (i), (iv); 180 (No. 28), 196 nn. 61, 66; 199 n. 123, 200 Ad.
47, 25	165, 168, 169, 174 Ap. 9.2 (537); 180 (No. 29), 181, 188, 195 n. 47, 196 n. 72, 197 n. 83, 199 n. 110
47, 35	165, 166, 167, 168, 169, 175 Ap. 9.2 (548); 176 Ap. 9.3 A (ii); 180 (No. 30), 194 n. 39, 195 n. 45, 196 nn. 55, 65, 74, 77–8, 81; 197 n. 81
49, 2	163, 165, 168, 169, 170, 172 Ap. 9.1 (8?); 176 Ap. 9.3 A (vi); 181 (No. 31), 195 n. 50, 196 nn. 71, 73, 78; 198 n. 98, 199 n. 116. Plate 9.3
49, 22	164, 167, 168, 176 Ap. 9.2 (615), 9.3 A (ii), (v), (vi); 181 (No. 32), 196 nn. 65, 73
50, 36	164, 167, 175 Ap. 9.2 (558); 176 Ap. 9.3 A (ii), (v); 181 (No. 33), 196 n. 65
50, 42	164, 167, 168, 175 Ap. 9.2 (562); 176 Ap. 9.3 A (ii), (v), (vi); 181 (No. 34), 196 nn. 65, 73
53, 5	165, 168, 169, 176 Ap. 9.2 (616); 180, 181 (No. 35), 188, 195 n. 46, 196 n. 72, 197 n. 83
53, 21	164, 194 n. 36
54, 17	164, 167, 175 Ap. 9.2 (575); 176 Ap. 9.3 A (iv); 181 (No. 36), 182, 184, 195 n. 48, 196 nn. 61, 66; 199 n. 110
63, 7	165, 168, 175 Ap. 9.2 (547); 181 (No. 37), 182, 195 n. 48, 196 n. 81
63, 8	165, 168, 176 Ap. 9.2 (602); 181 (No. 38), 182, 195 n. 48, 196 n. 81
63, 9	165, 168, 176 Ap. 9.2 (601); 181 (No. 39), 195 n. 48, 196 nn. 71, 81
63, 32	165, 168, 169, 176 Ap. 9.2 (603), 9.3 A (vi); 182 (No. 40), 184, 195 n. 46, 196 nn. 72, 76; 197 n. 83
64, 30	165, 168, 169, 174 Ap. 9.2 (533); 182 (No. 41), 195 n. 46, 196 nn. 72, 77, 81. Plate 9.2
65, 8	165, 167–8, 169, 175 Ap. 9.2 (597); 176 Ap. 9.3 A (iii), (vi); 181, 182 (No. 42), 184, 195 n. 48, 196 nn. 71, 73, 79, 83
65, 10	173 Ap. 9.1 (28?); 176 Ap. 9.2 (641?); 182, 188 (No. 76), 199 nn. 129–30
65, 11	167, 173 Ap. 9.1 (29?); 175 Ap. 9.2 (544) or (561); 176 Ap. 9.3 A (i), (iv); 182 (No. 43), 188, 196 nn. 61, 66; 199 n. 130
65, 16	165, 167, 175 Ap. 9.2 (544) or (561); 176 Ap. 9.3 A (i), (iv); 182 (No. 44), 195 n. 43, 196 nn. 61, 66; 199 n. 130
65, 19	165, 167, 175 Ap. 9.2 (583); 176 Ap. 9.3 A (i), (iv); 182 (No. 45), 196 nn. 61, 66
65, 52	166, 171, 175 Ap. 9.2 (579?); 186, 188 (No. 77), 196 n. 57
66, 7	165, 166, 168, 169, 175 Ap. 9.2 (541); 182 (No. 46), 195 n. 45, 196 nn. 54, 72, 77, 79; 197 n. 85

GENERAL INDEX

ALISON QUINN

THE PLATES

2.1

2.2

4.1

9.1

9.2

9.3

9.4

18.1

18.2

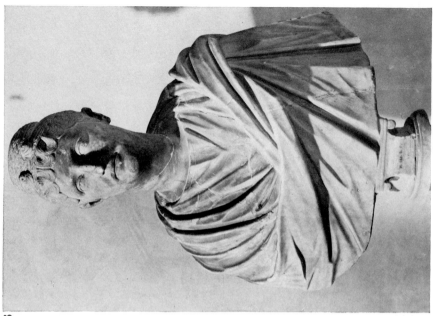

18.3

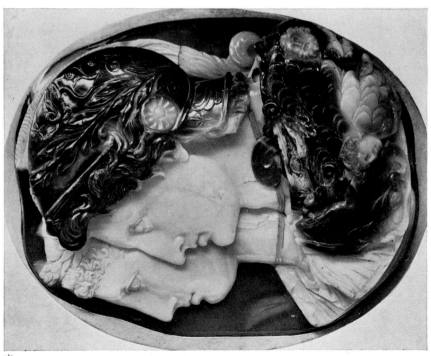

18.4

18.5

18.6

18.7

18.8

18.9

18.10

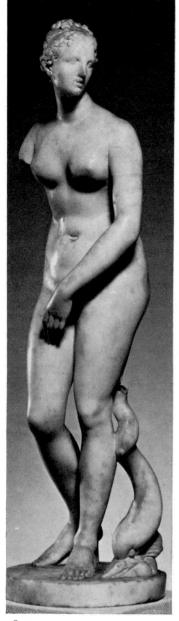

18.11   18.12

18.13

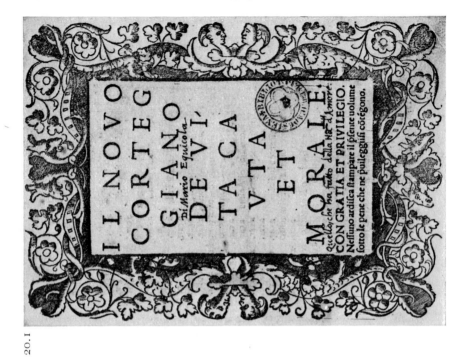

20.1

22.1